# WHAT IF?

## Eminent Historians
## Imagining What Might Have Been

Essays By

•Caleb Carr •John Lukas •John Keegen
•James Bradley •Stephen E. Ambrose •And Others

Edited By

# Robert Cowley

Includes the complete text of What If? and What If? 2

WHAT IF? is a trademark of American Historical Publications, Inc.

The sidebar articles were previously published in the spring 1998 issue of *MHQ: The Quarterly Journal of Military History*. They are reprinted by permission of the authors.

G. P. Putnam's Sons
*Publishers Since 1838*
a member of
Penguin Group (USA) Inc.
375 Hudson Street
New York, NY 10014

Special Markets ISBN: 978-0-399-15696-0
This edition created exclusively for Barnes & Noble Inc., under ISBN: 978-1-4351-1825-6.

Library of Congress Cataloging-in-Publication Data available upon request.

Printed in the United States of America

3   5   7   9   10   8   6   4   2

Book design by Carla Bolte and Michelle McMillian
Map and picture research by Sabine Russ
Maps © 2001 Jeffrey L. Ward
Title and Chapter Opener Art: Foto Marburg/Art Resource, NY
Endpapers: Detail of Bayeux Tapestry, Musée de la Tapisserie, Bayeux, France.
Copyright Erich Lessing/Art Resource, NY.

# CONTENTS

# LIST OF MAPS

## LIST OF ILLUSTRATIONS

# INTRODUCTION

I t has been said that "what if?" (or the counterfactual, to use the vogue word in academic circles) is the historian's favorite secret question. What ifs have a genuine value that goes beyond the "idle parlor game" (the historian E. H. Carr's phrase). They can be a tool to enhance the understanding of history, to make it come alive. They can reveal, in startling detail, the essential stakes of a confrontation, as well as its potentially abiding consequences. What if the Persians had beaten the rowers of Athens at Salamis in 480 B.C.—perhaps the single most important day in the history of the West—or if the Spanish Armada had won and the Duke of Parma's army had occupied London? On the night of August 7–8, 1588, a chance of wind is all it might have taken to reverse the result of another of history's most famous naval confrontations. Or what if the Germans had beaten back the D Day landings? What if the storm that raged over Europe on June 5, 1944—the day before the Normandy invasion was scheduled—had not unexpectedly let up? Once again, weather made all the difference. Stephen E. Ambrose examines some of the consequences of a D Day failure, none of them pleasant— including the atom bombing of Germany.

History is properly the literature of what did happen; but that should not diminish the importance of the counterfactual. What ifs can lead us to question long-held assumptions. What ifs can define true turning points. They can show that small accidents or split-second decisions are as likely to have major repercussions as large ones (the so-called "first-order" counterfactual). Consider the sudden fog on the East River that allowed George Washington and his badly beaten army to escape to Manhattan after the Battle of Long Island in the summer of 1776. Without that fog, as David McCullough points out, Washington might have been trapped on Brooklyn Heights and forced to surrender. Would there have been a United States if that had happened? You can also cite the British captain's decision not to pull the trigger when he had Washington in his gunsights at the Battle of Brandywine a year later. That might have had the same result. Few events have been more dependent on what ifs than the American Revolution. We are the product of a future that might not have been.

What ifs have a further important function: They can eliminate what has been called "hindsight bias." After the Battle of Britain failed, was there any way that Hitler could have won the Second World War? For the past fifty-odd years, historians have viewed the summer of 1940 as his high-water mark. But one of our foremost military historians, John Keegan, points out in these pages that if Hitler had decided not to invade Russia, history could have turned out much differently. If, after his victory in Greece in the spring of 1941, he had decided to invade Turkey or the Near East, he could have seized the oil he so desperately needed—and taken on the Soviet Union later, with a better chance of victory. Much as we like to think otherwise, outcomes are no more certain in history than they are in our own lives. If nothing else, the diverging tracks in the undergrowth of history celebrate the infinity of human options. The road not taken belongs on the map.

This is a book about the key events of military history seen in a new light: as they might have been if certain outcomes had been different. In the tenth anniversary issue of *MHQ: The Quarterly Journal of Military History*, we asked historians this question: What do you consider the most important might-have-beens of military history? The answers we got were by turns surprising, entertaining, and occasionally frightening— but at all times plausible. (You will find some of those original scenarios reprinted here.) Frivolous counterfactuals have given the question a bad name, and we avoided speculations such as what would have happened if Hannibal had possessed an H-bomb or Napoleon, stealth bombers— problems actually posed in one of our war colleges. Plausible, then, is the key word.

As George Will wrote, "The salutary effect of *MHQ's* 'What if' exercises is a keener appreciation of the huge difference that choices and fortuities make in the destiny of nations."

This volume, with its twenty chapters, is an expansion of the original concept. The authors of these chapters are some of the same historians who wrote for that feature: Stephen E. Ambrose, William H. McNeill, Theodore K. Rabb, Alistair Horne, Geoffrey Parker, John Keegan, Victor Davis Hanson, Stephen W. Sears, Lewis H. Lapham, Thomas Fleming, David McCullough, and James M. McPherson, to name a few. The book is organized chronologically, and ranges over 2,700 years of the human record. Nothing is more suited to what if speculation than military history, where chance and accident, human failings or strengths, can make all the difference.

What if a mysterious plague had not smitten the Assyrian besiegers of Jerusalem in 701 B.C.? Would there have been a Jewish religion? Or Christianity? Talk about split-second outcomes: What if the upswing of a battle-ax had not been interrupted and a twenty-one-year-old Alexander had been killed before he became "the Great"? Or if Cortés had been captured (as he nearly was) at the siege of Tenochtitlán, today's Mexico City? It's very likely that a young United States would have had to deal with a major Native American empire on its southern borders. Consider, too, the role of accident: If, in our Civil War, the famous "Lost Order" hadn't been lost, the chances are, as James M. McPherson writes, that the Confederate states would have remained independent. But, in fact, a similar Lost Order affected the outcome of the Battle of the Marne in September 1914—and hence of World War I itself.

For historians, as the maxim goes, the dominos fall backward. In *What If?* we will attempt to make them fall forward.

—*Robert Cowley*

# WILLIAM H. McNEILL

# INFECTIOUS ALTERNATIVES

*The Plague That Saved Jerusalem, 701 B.C.*

Military events, even seemingly insignificant episodes, can have unforeseen consequences, ones that may not become apparent at the time they happen and occasionally not even for centuries. It seems appropriate to begin this book with such a moment in history, the Assyrian siege of Jerusalem, then the seat of the tiny kingdom of Judah, in 701 B.C. That siege, by Sennacherib, king of Assyria, was lifted after a large part of his army succumbed to a mysteriously lethal contagion. The Assyrians simply moved on: For the largest empire of its time, the reduction of yet another walled city was not cost effective. For those holed up inside, however, deliverance came as a heavenly sign (though its causes were probably environmental), and one that, needless to say, would have far-reaching implications. But what if disease had not intervened? What if the walls had fallen, and the usual pillage, rape, murder, and forced exile of the population had been Jerusalem's lot? What would our lives, our spiritual underpinnings be like 2,700 years later?

1

*Whatever the pestilence was, it became the leveler at Jerusalem. Disease has to be counted as one of the wild cards of history, an unforeseen factor that can, in a matter of days or weeks, undo the deterministic sure thing or humble the conquering momentum. History is full of examples. There was the plague that ravaged Athens for more than a year and led to its capture and the dismantling of its empire in 404 B.C. An outbreak of dysentery weakened the Prussian force invading France in 1792 and helped to convince their leaders to turn back after losing the Battle of Valmy, thus saving the French Revolution. The ravages of typhus and dysentery are the hidden story of Napoleon's calamity in Russia. The war-vectored influenza epidemic of 1918 may not have changed immediate outcomes, but how many potential reputations did we lose to it—people who might have made a difference to their generation? Bacteria and viruses may thus redirect vast impersonal forces in human societies, and they can also become forces in their own right.*

✦ *William H. McNeill, professor emeritus at the University of Chicago, won the National Book Award for his RISE OF THE WEST. Among his twenty-six other books are a survey of military history, THE PURSUIT OF POWER, PLAGUES AND PEOPLES, and, most recently, KEEPING TOGETHER IN TIME: AN ESSAY ON DANCE AND DRILL IN HUMAN HISTORY. In 1997, he received one of the most prestigious international prizes for a lifetime of distinguished scholarship, the Erasmus Award.*

W hat if Sennacherib, king of Assyria, had conquered Jerusalem in 701 B.C. when he led his imperial army against a coalition of Egyptian, Phoenician, Philistine, and Jewish enemies, and handily defeated them all? This, it seems to me, is the greatest might-have-been of all military history. This may be an odd thing to say about an engagement that never took place; yet Jerusalem's preservation from attack by Sennacherib's army shaped the subsequent history of the world far more profoundly than any other military action I know of.

From Sennacherib's point of view the decision not to press the siege of Jerusalem to a conclusion did not matter very much. The kingdom of Judah was only a marginal player in the Near Eastern balance of power, being poorer and weaker than Sennacherib's other foes. And the king of Judah had been well and truly punished for having dared to revolt against him. For as Sennacherib declared in an inscription on the walls of his palace at Nineveh that recorded the victories of the entire campaign, his army had occupied no fewer than forty-six walled places in the kingdom of Judah and compelled Hezekiah, king of Judah, to shut himself up in Jerusalem "like a bird in a cage."

But, unlike other rebellious rulers in the area, Hezekiah did retain his throne, and the worship of Jahweh in the Temple of Solomon continued uninterrupted. Sennacherib's victory over the kingdom of Judah was therefore incomplete, a fact whose consequences were far greater than he or anyone else at the time could possibly imagine.

Hezekiah (ruled ca. 715–687 B.C.) began his reign in a time of acute uncertainty. Seven years before he ascended the throne and became Jerusalem's thirteenth ruler of the house of David, the neighboring kingdom of Israel, comprising the larger and richer part of David's kingdom, met irretrievable disaster when an Assyrian army, commanded by Sargon II, captured the capital, Samaria, and carried off thousands of survivors to distant Mesopotamia. Strangers came at Assyrian command to cultivate the emptied fields, but they left the city of Samaria a shattered ruin.

Did this mean that the God of Moses and of David, the selfsame God still worshipped in the temple that Solomon had built for him in Jerusalem, was no longer able to defend his people? Or had God punished the Israelites and their rulers for disobedience to his will as made known in sacred scriptures, continually refreshed and brought up to date by the inspired words of his prophets?

The question was urgent, and all the more portentous because, if one took the second view, the God of Moses and of David had used the mightiest ruler of the age as an instrument for punishing his people, even though the Assyrians worshipped other gods and did not even pretend to honor God's commandments. This ran counter to common sense, which held that the gods worshipped by different peoples protected their worshippers as best they could. Victory and defeat therefore registered the power of rival deities as well as the strength of merely human armies. It followed that when the Assyrians began their imperial expansion, each new victory unsettled older religious loyalties and ideas among the peoples they conquered, creating a religious vacuum in the ancient Near East that was eventually filled by the unique response that occurred among the people of Judah.

That response began to take shape when King Hezekiah embraced the view of a party of religious reformers who set out to purify the worship of Jahweh by concentrating it in the temple. Destroying "high places" in the countryside where other rituals prevailed was part of the program. So was respectful consultation with inspired prophets, among whom Isaiah, son of Amoz, was then the most prominent.

But King Hezekiah did not rely entirely on supernatural help. He also strengthened Jerusalem's walls and expanded his borders modestly before joining the alliance against Sennacherib. And when the invading Assyrians defeated the Egyptians, he hurried to come to terms with the

4

victors and had to pay dearly for the privilege of remaining on his throne, handing over various precious materials, including three hundred talents of silver and thirty of gold, some (perhaps most) of which came from the temple in Jerusalem. But he did retain his throne; and his heirs and successors maintained the little kingdom of Judah for another century and more by paying tribute to Assyria and carefully refraining from rebellion. Nevertheless, balancing precariously between rival great powers based in Egypt and Mesopotamia did not last forever. Instead, in 586 B.C., the kingdom's autonomy collapsed when Nebuchadnezzar, king of Babylon, did what Sennacherib had threatened to do, capturing Jerusalem after a long siege and bringing the dynasty of David to an end, destroying the temple, and carrying most of the surviving inhabitants off to an exile in Babylon.

As we all know, this was not the end of Jewish history, for the exiled people of Judah did not pine away. Instead they flourished by the waters of Babylon, and reorganized their scriptures to create an unambiguously monotheistic, congregational religion, independent of place and emancipated from the rites of Solomon's destroyed temple in Jerusalem. Moreover, the revised Jewish faith, tempered in exile, subsequently gave birth to Christianity and Islam, the two most powerful religions of our age, and of course also retains its own, distinctive following around the world and especially in the contemporary state of Israel.

None of this could have come to pass if the kingdom of Judah had disappeared in 701 B.C. as the kingdom of Israel had done a mere twenty-one years earlier in 722 B.C. On that occasion, the exiles from Israel soon lost their separate identity. By accepting commonsense views about the limits of divine power, they abandoned the worship of Jahweh, who had failed to protect them, and became the "Ten Lost Tribes" of biblical history. In all probability, the people of Judah would have met the same fate if the Assyrian army had attacked and captured Jerusalem in 701 B.C. and treated its inhabitants as they had treated those of Samaria and other conquered places before. If so, Judaism would have disappeared from the face of the earth and the two daughter religions of Christianity and Islam could not possibly have come into existence. In short, our world would be profoundly different in ways we cannot really imagine.

But figuring out what actually happened before the walls of Jerusalem so long ago is quite impossible. Sennacherib's boastful inscription carved onto the walls of his palace of Nineveh is a piece of imperial propaganda rather than sober history; and the three biblical narratives that tell the story of how the Assyrians failed to take the holy city were shaped by ideas about God's miraculous intervention in public affairs that few historians accept today.

Nonetheless, the biblical stories, inaccurate or exaggerated though they may be, were what really mattered. In all subsequent generations, they shaped Jewish memories of what had happened before the walls of the city, and this memory made it plausible to believe that the God of Moses and of David was in fact omnipotent, protecting his worshippers from the mightiest monarch of the day. This episode, as interpreted by the pious party in Jerusalem, made monotheism credible as never before; and emphatic uncompromising monotheism was what fitted the Jewish religion to survive and flourish in the cosmopolitan age that the Assyrian conquests had inaugurated. After all, mere local gods were hard to believe in when every part of the ancient Near East came to depend on what distant rulers, alien armies, and other groups of strangers did, and failed to do. Only God's universal power could explain public events satisfactorily. Consequently, Jewish monotheism prospered and was able to exercise an ever-widening influence, especially through its two daughter religions, down to our own time.

Religious ceremonies tied to a single, sacred place did not suffice in such a world. But abandoning local, ancestral religion and accepting the gods of alien, imperial rulers, whose superior power had been demonstrated by success in war, was a craven, unsatisfactory response. Uniquely, the inhabitants of the small, weak, and dependent kingdom of Judah had the temerity to believe that their God, Jahweh, was the only true God,

**THE ASSYRIAN JUGGERNAUT**

*A relief from the Assyrian captial of Ninevah shows the final assault by battering rams, left, on Lachis, in Israel's twin kingdom of Judah, 701 B.C. Captives are marched away, lower right. Sacked and burned, the city ceased to exist. It was a fate that seemed to await nearby Jerusalem and the nascent Jewish faith—without which Christianity and Islam are inconceivable.*

(Photograph by Erich Lessing/Art Resource, NY)

whose power extended over all the earth so that everything that happened was in accordance with his will. The circumstances of the Assyrian withdrawal from the walls of Jerusalem in 701 B.C. confirmed this implausible belief, proving God's universal power to pious and eager believers more clearly and far more convincingly than ever before. This makes it the most fateful might-have-been of all recorded history.

The biblical version of the campaign appears three times over, in II

Kings 18–19; II Chronicles 32; and the Book of Isaiah 36–37. The three accounts agree in all the essentials and in some instances even employ the same words and phrases. Let me quote from Isaiah, according to the King James version:

> Then Rabshakeh [commander of the Assyrian army sent against Jerusalem] stood and cried in a loud voice in the Jews' language, and said, Hear ye the words of the great king, the king of Assyria, . . . Beware lest Hezekiah persuade you, saying: the Lord will deliver us. Hath any of the gods of the nations delivered his land out of the hand of the king of Assyria? Where are the gods of Hamath and Arphad? . . . have they delivered Samaria out of my hand?
>
> [Isaiah 36:13, 18–19]

Hezekiah responded to this direct challenge to God's power by praying:

> O Lord of hosts, God of Israel, that dwelleth between the cherubims, thou art the God, even thou alone, of all the kingdoms of the earth; thou hast made heaven and earth. Incline thine ear, O Lord, . . . and hear all the words of Sennacherib, which hath sent reproach to the living God . . . Now therefore, O Lord our God, save us from his hand, that all kingdoms of the earth may know that thou art the Lord, even thou only.
>
> Then Isaiah, son of Amoz, sent unto Hezekiah, saying . . . thus saith the Lord concerning the king of Assyria, He shall not come into this city, nor shoot an arrow there, nor come before it with shields, nor cast a bank against it . . . For I will defend this city to save it for mine own sake, and for my servant David's sake.
>
> Then the angel of the Lord went forth and smote in the camp of the Assyrians a hundred and fourscore and five thousand; and when they arose early in the morning, behold, they were all dead corpses. So Sennacherib, king of Assyria, departed and went and returned and dwelt in Nineveh. And it came to pass . . . that his sons smote him with the sword . . . and Esarhaddon his son reigned in his stead."
>
> [Isaiah 37:16–17, 20–21, 33, 35–38]

Thus, according to the Bible, God saved his people and destroyed the impious Assyrians by spreading lethal pestilence among them. Such a miraculous deliverance showed that both King Hezekiah and the prophet Isaiah were right to rely on God's power and protection. More than that: It proved God's power over the mightiest ruler of the age. Who then could doubt that the prophets and priests of Judah, who so boldly proclaimed God's universal power, were telling the truth? Who indeed?

Yet doubters remained, as the biblical account of the reign of Hezekiah's son and successor, Manasseh (ruled ca. 686–642 B.C.), makes clear. King Manasseh remained tributary to the Assyrians throughout his reign and thought it prudent to come to terms with alien gods as well, setting up "a carved image, the idol he had made, in the house of God," and allowing other heathen forms of worship that, according to the Book of the Chronicles, were "evil in the sight of the Lord." [II, 33: 2, 7]

Moreover, for those of us who are disinclined to believe in miracles, the biblical account of how Hezekiah prepared for the Assyrian attack on Jerusalem contain some tantalizing hints that suggest entirely mundane factors that may have provoked epidemic among the besieging Assyrians. It is also easy to imagine other pressing reasons why Sennacherib may have decided to refrain from besieging the strongly fortified city of Jerusalem, quite apart from epidemic losses his army may have suffered outside the walls. (Incidentally, the figure of 185,000 disease deaths must be vastly exaggerated; no ancient army came close to such a size, much less one operating in the barren environs of Jerusalem.)

What really happened therefore remains entirely unsure. But wondering about how the course of world history was affected by subsequent interpretation of the actual course of events remains enticing. For example: Did King Hezekiah save his throne by foreseeing that the Assyrian army would have difficulty finding enough water for a lengthy siege of Jerusalem? The Books of the Chronicles tells us that "when Hezekiah saw that Sennacherib was come, and that he purposed to fight against Jerusalem, he took counsel with his princes and his mighty men to stop the waters of the fountains which were without the city; and they did help him. So there was gathered much people together who stopped all the fountains and the brook that ran through the midst of the land, saying, Why should the kings of Assyria come and find much water?" [II Chronicles, 32: 2–4]

Some modern archaeologists believe that Hezekiah ordered the construction of a 600-foot tunnel that still carries water from the spring of Gihon to the pool of Siloam, just outside Jerusalem's ancient walls. Such a difficult project must have taken a long time and can scarcely be equated with the emergency effort to deny the Assyrian adequate access to water described in Chronicles. But the tunnel may well have been part of a general effort to improve the city's defenses undertaken before or after the confrontation of 701.

In any case, one may wonder whether Hezekiah's effort to "stop the fountains" around Jerusalem compelled Assyrian soldiers to drink contaminated water and thus expose themselves to widespread infections. If so, the fact that Hezekiah and his princes and mighty men foresaw how difficult it would be to find enough drinking water in Jerusalem's dry environs may have had more to do with the Assyrian retreat than the miracle recorded in the Bible

Until the reign of King Josiah (ruled 640–612 B.C.), the pious interpretation of how God had saved Jerusalem and miraculously compelled Sennacherib to withdraw competed with the commonsense view, illustrated by King Manasseh's policy of introducing heathen worship into Jerusalem as a way of supplementing Jahweh's limited jurisdiction by appealing to other, more powerful gods as well.

For centuries, Hebrew prophets had denounced such policies, declaring that Jahweh was a jealous God who demanded exclusive devotion and obedience to his will, as revealed through their inspired utterances. As literacy spread, the words of God, delivered through his prophets, and instructing the faithful what to do in public and private matters, were (at least sometimes) written down. Hence the biblical books of prophecy began to accumulate, beginning about 750 B.C. Priests of Solomon's temple, likewise, defended the exclusive rights of the God they worshipped, and priestly editors and compilers were presumably responsible for collecting and preserving the sacred texts from which the rest of the Jewish scripture was eventually compiled. Priests and prophets did not always agree, but both championed the exclusive worship of Jahweh and rejected the commonsense religious view that recognized multiple, local gods who struggled against one another just as humans did.

Decisive triumph for the champions of Jahweh came early in King Josiah's reign, when the Assyrian empire began to collapse, and the pious party persuaded Josiah, while still a boy, to repudiate all the alien cults his father Manasseh had admitted to Jerusalem. Then, while refurbishing the temple, the high priest "found a book of the law of the Lord, given to Moses." [II Chronicles, 34:14] This, the Book of Deuteronomy, became the basis for a strenuous effort to reform religious practices and bring them into conformity to God's will as newly recovered.

Thirty-six years later, when the principal successor to the Assyrian empire, King Nebuchadnezzar, destroyed the kingdom of Judah, razed the temple, and carried the Jews away to his capital at Babylon, the pious party of Jahweh had to figure out why God had allowed such a disaster to take place. But by then the idea that God did in fact govern all the world was so firmly established that abandoning Jahweh, as the Israelites had done after 722 B.C., was inconceivable. Instead, long-standing prophetic denunciations of the sins of the Jewish people made it obvious that the Babylonian exile was God's punishment for the failure of Judah's rulers and people to observe his commandments to the full. For no matter how strenuous their effort at religious reform had been, even the most pious still fell short of obeying all of God's prescriptions.

Further effort to amend their ways, discovering God's will by careful study of the sacred scripture, was the only appropriate response. Accordingly, when weekly meetings for reading and meditating upon the meaning of the sacred scriptures became customary among the exiles, Judaism assumed its enduring form. The Jewish religion ceased to be local and became an effective guide to everyday life in cosmopolitan, urban settings, fit to survive and flourish across succeeding centuries into the indefinite future.

It may seem paradoxical to argue that the vindication of Isaiah's prophecy and of Hezekiah's religious policy by Sennacherib's withdrawal was critical for the emergence of unambiguous monotheism in the little Kingdom of Judah, whereas Nebuchadnezzar's success in carrying through what Sennacharib had merely threatened, instead of discrediting that faith, had the effect of confirming Jewish monotheism, and permitted the daughter religions of Christianity and Islam to arise in later centuries. But so it was, or so it seems to me, although most historians are so much shaped by the world's subsequent religious history as to be unable or unwilling to recognize how fateful the Assyrian withdrawal in 701 B.C. turned out to be.

But, at least for me, pondering how a small company of prophets and priests in Jerusalem interpreted what happened outside the city walls in 701 B.C. and reflecting on how their views came to prevail so widely in later times are a sobering exercise of historical imagination. Never before or since has so much depended on so few, believing so wholly in their one true god, and in such bold defiance of common sense.

✦ BARBARA N. PORTER ✦

# A GOOD NIGHT'S SLEEP
# CAN DO WONDERS

What if King Gyges of Lydia had stayed up late worrying about the approaching Cimmerian hordes, had entirely missed the famous dream in which the god of Assyria advised him to become an Assyrian vassal, and in the morning, tired and dispirited, had failed to trounce the Cimmerians and had died at their hands on the field of battle then, instead of several years later?

If all this had happened, modern Western culture might look a little different. Lacking his dream—and dead moreover—Gyges would never have sent his ambassadors to far-off Assyria, armed with two captured Cimmerian chiefs as a friendly present, to establish the first alliance between the two nations, in about 652 B.C. Without this initial friendly contact, Gyges's surviving sons might not have succeeded later in persuading the Assyrians to prod their allies in Asia Minor to help Gyges's heirs hold on to the throne of Lydia—whence they eventually succeeded in driving the Cimmerians out of Asia Minor altogether. And they would never have founded the Lydian empire of Asia Minor, renowned for its gold and commerce, music and art.

Since most people have never heard of the Lydian empire, this might not seem to be much of a loss, but there is worse to come. With the Lydians defeated, there would have been no one to stop the Cimmerians from continuing their ferocious march toward the sea and seizing the Greek colonial cities on the coast. With the ships of those cities in their hands, the Cimmerians could easily have gone on to attack the cities of mainland Greece, which were only a short distance to the west and which were then edging toward the great cultural flowering that was to make fifth century B.C. Greece the birthplace of Western culture as we know it. Instead, mainland Greece would have become the home of the Cimmerian horse nomads, Herodotus might have written treatises on horse training instead of inventing Western historical writing, and people like Euripides might have spent their days herding horses instead of writing plays.

The moral of Gyges's story would appeal to one's mother: Go to bed early and get a good night's sleep; the fate of Western civilization may depend on it.

✦ *Barbara N. Porter is an authority on the political and cultural history of the Neo-Assyrian empire.*

## VICTOR DAVIS HANSON

# NO GLORY THAT
# WAS GREECE

*The Persians Win at Salamis, 480 B.C.*

*There are few moments in history when so much was decided in so little time as the naval encounter between the Greeks and Persians at Salamis in 480 B.C. (Hiroshima may also qualify, but barring our nuclear extinction, the epochal returns on it are still out.) Salamis was more than just a battle. It was the supreme confrontation between East and West, in which all manner of futures were either set in motion or denied. The Persians may have taken the lead in an attempt to check the spread of Greek individualism, but the other centralized despotic powers of the eastern Mediterranean basin apparently cheered them on. The Greek words "freedom" and "citizen," Victor Davis Hanson points out, did not exist in the vocabulary of other Mediterranean cultures.*

*As military operations go, the one mounted by the Persian emperor Xerxes has to be ranked in terms of size, lengthy preparation, and sophisticated planning with the Spanish Armada and the D Day invasion. That operation, which culminated at Salamis, turned out to be a last chance to stamp out the irrepressible culture of the West. "Had Fortune favored numbers, we would have won the day," a messenger tells*

15

the mother of Xerxes in Aeschylus's The Persians. *(The Athenian playwright had himself supposedly fought at Salamis.)* "The result shows with what partial hands the gods weighed down the scale against us, and destroyed us all." But what if that scale had been weighted at the opposite end? What if the Persians had won? It nearly happened. It should have happened. If the rowers commanded by the Athenian states-man-general Themistocles had not prevailed, would there be, some 2,500 years later, a Western civilization in the form we know it? Or would Themistocles, had he survived Salamis, have resettled the Athenian people in Italy, thus giving the ideals of freedom and citizenship a chance for a second flowering?

✦ *Victor Davis Hanson has published nine books, including* THE WESTERN WAY OF WAR, THE OTHER GREEKS, *and* WHO KILLED HOMER? *(with John Heath). His book on the death of the family farm,* FIELDS WITHOUT DREAMS, *was voted the best nonfiction title of 1995 by the San Francisco Book Reviewers Association. Hanson teaches classics at California State University in Fresno.*

The interest of the world's history hung trembling in the balance. Oriental despotism, a world united under one lord and sovereign, on the one side, and separate states, insignificant in extent and resources, but animated by free individuality, on the other side, stood front to front in array of battle. Never in history has the superiority of spiritual power over material bulk, and that of no contemptible amount, been made so gloriously manifest.

So wrote the often apocalyptic German historian and philosopher Georg Hegel of the aftermath of Salamis. The Greeks of the time agreed. Aeschylus's play *The Persians* is the only extant Greek tragedy based on a historical event, that of the singular victory at "Divine Salamis," where the gods punished the arrogance of the Medes and rewarded the courage of a free Greece. Epigrams after the battle recorded that Hellenic sailors had "saved holy Greece" and "prevented it from seeing the day of slavery." Legend had it that on the day of the majestic Athenian-led victory, Aeschylus fought, Sophocles danced at the victory festival, and Euripides was born. For the last 2,500 years, Western civilization has celebrated the miracle of Salamis as both the very salvation of its culture and the catalyst for a subsequent literary, artistic, and philosophical explosion under the aegis of a triumphant and confident Athenian democracy. The temples on the Acropolis, Athenian tragedy and comedy, Socratic philosophy, and the genre of history itself followed the Persian Wars: Thus, not only did the victory at Salamis save Hellenism, but the spiritual exhilaration and material bounty from the Athenians' astonishing victory made these cultural breakthroughs possible.

Before Salamis most of the Greek city-states were agrarian, parochial, and isolated, intimidated by 70 million subjects of the Persian Empire to the east, and overshadowed by millions more in the Near East and Egypt. After Salamis, the ancient Greeks would never again fear any other foreign power until they met the Romans. Indeed, no Persian king would ever again set foot in Greece, and for the next 2,000 years no easterner would claim Greece as his own until the Ottoman conquest of the Balkans in the fifteenth century—an event that proved that an unchecked Eastern power most certainly would and could occupy a weakened Greece for centuries.

Before Salamis, Athens was a rather eccentric city-state whose experiment with radical democracy was in its twenty-seven-year-old infancy, and the verdict on its success still out. After the battle arose an imperial democratic culture that ruled the Aegean and gave us Aeschylus, Sophocles, the Parthenon, Pericles, and Thucydides. Before the naval fight, there was neither the consensus nor confidence that Greek arms would protect and enhance Greek interests abroad. After Salamis, for the next three and a half centuries murderous Greek-speaking armies, possessed of superior technology and bankrolled by shrewd financiers, would run wild from southern Italy to the Indus River.

If the Persian Wars marked a great divide in world history, then Salamis served as the turning point in the Persian War. And if Salamis represented a dramatic breakthrough in the fortunes of the Greek resistance to Persia, then the role of Themistocles and a few thousand Athenians explains the remarkable Hellenic victory against all odds. Hence, it really is true that what a few men did in late September 480 in the waters off the Athenian coast explains much of what we take for granted in the West today.

First, we should remember that the decade-long Persian Wars—comprising the battles of Marathon (490), Thermopylae and Artemesium (480), Salamis (480), Plataea (479) and Mycale (479)—offered the East the last real chance to check Western culture in its embryonic state, before the Greeks' radically dynamic menu of constitutional government, private property, broad-based militias, civilian control of military forces, free scientific inquiry, rationalism, and separation between political and religious authority would spread to Italy, and thus via the Roman Empire to most of northern Europe and the western Mediterranean. Indeed, the words freedom and citizen did not exist in the vocabulary of any other Mediterranean culture, which were either tribal monarchies, or theocracies. We should keep in mind in this present age of multiculturalism that Greece was a Mediterranean country in climate and agriculture only, but one entirely *anti*-Mediterranean in spirit and values compared to its surrounding neighbors.

Hegel knew, as we may have forgotten, that had Greece become the westernmost province of Persia, in time Greek family farms would have become estates for the Great King. The public buildings of the agora would have been transformed into covered shops of the bazaar, and yeomen hoplites paid shock troops alongside Xerxes' Immortals. In place of Hellenic philosophy and science, there would have been only the subsidized arts of divination and astrology, which were the appendages of imperial or religious bureaucracies and not governed by unfettered rational inquiry. In a Persian Greece, local councils would be mere puppet bodies to facilitate royal requisitions of men and money, history the official diaries and edicts of the Great King, and appointed local officials mouthpieces for the satrap ("the protector of power") and the magi.

The Greeks might later fine or exile their general, Themistocles; had the Persians dared the same with Xerxes, they would have ended up disemboweled—like the eldest son of Pythias the Lydian, who was cut in half, his torso and legs put on each side on the road for the royal army to march between. Such was the price Pythias paid when he dared request from Xerxes military exemption for one of his five sons. Despite the arguments of recent scholarship, the cities of the Persian empire were not in any fashion city-states. We would live under a much different tradition today—one where writers are under death sentences, women secluded and veiled, free speech curtailed, government in the hands of the autocrat's extended family, universities mere centers of religious zealotry, and the thought police in our living rooms and bedrooms—had Themistocles and his sailors failed.

The thousand or so Greek *poleis* that arose sometime in the eighth

**SAVIOR OF THE WEST**

*The statesman-admiral Themistocles (shown here in this idealized bust) led the Athenian navy at Salamis. Had he lost, would he have transported citizens of Athens en masse and Aeneas-like to Italy, there to found a new democratic city-state?*

century B.C. immediately faced an undeniable paradox: The very conditions of their success also raised the possibility of their own ruin. The
isolated valleys of Greece, the general neglect from the rest of the
Mediterranean world, the extreme chauvinism of highly individualistic
and autonomous small Greek communities—all that had allowed the
creation and growth of a free landowning citizenry like none other. Yet,
there germinated no accompanying principle of national federalism or
even a notion of common defense—all such encompassing ideas of government and centralized power were antithetical to the Greeks' near fanatical embrace of political independence and individuality; for crusty
yeomen citizens, the very thought of federal taxes was an anathema. Today's supporters of the United Nations would find themselves without
friends in ancient Greece. Indeed, even the most radical proponent of
states' rights might seem too timid to the early Greeks. In terms of the
Greek legacy of regional autonomy, John C. Calhoun, not Abraham Lincoln or Woodrow Wilson, was the true Greek.

By the sixth century B.C., the economic energy, political flexibility,
and military audacity of these insular Greeks had nevertheless allowed
them to colonize the coast of Asia Minor, the Black Sea region, southern
Italy, Sicily, and parts of North Africa. In other words, a million Greeks
and their unique idea of a free polis had gained influence well beyond either their natural resources or available manpower. Again, there was no
accompanying imperial or even federated notion that might organize or
unify such expansionary efforts; instead, roughly 1,000 bustling city-
states—as Herodotus said, unified only by their values, language, and religion—pursued their own widely diverse agendas.

Other far older and more centralized powers—whether theocracies
in North Africa or political autocracies in Asia—took notice. In broad
strategic terms, by the early fifth century Persians, Egyptians, Phoenicians,
and Carthaginians had seen enough of these intrusive and ubiquitous
Greeks as shippers, traders, mercenaries, and colonists. Could not this
quarreling and fractious people be overwhelmed by the sheer manpower
and wealth of imperial armies *before* its insidious culture spread well be-

21

yond the Hellenic mainland and made the eastern Mediterranean a lake of their own?

Darius I and later his son Xerxes took up that challenge in the first two decades of the fifth century. After their respective defeats, there never again was a question in the ancient world about the primacy of the Western paradigm. In the decades following Salamis, relatively small numbers of Greeks—whether Athenians in Egypt, Panhellenic mercenaries hired by Persian nobles, or Alexander's Macedonian thugs—fought in Asia and North Africa for conquest and loot; never again were Hellenic armies pressed on Greek soil to battle for their freedom. After the defeat of Xerxes, when Greeks abroad faltered, either due to manpower shortages or to the sheer hubris of their undertaking, no Eastern power dared to invade their homeland. And when the Greeks succeeded overseas, which was far more often, they habitually wrecked their adversaries' culture, planted military colonies abroad, and then sent home slaves and money. Salamis established the principle that Greeks would advance, others recede, both in a material and cultural sense.

Much has been written about Rome's later great showdown with Carthage. But despite three murderous wars (264–146 B.C.), and a nightmarish sixteen-year sojourn of a megalomaniac Hannibal on Italian soil, the ultimate decision was never in doubt. By the third century B.C., the Roman manner of raising, equipping, and leading armies, the flexibility and resilience of republican government, and the growing success of Italian agriculturists, financiers, traders, and builders—all beneficiaries of past Hellenic practice ensured by the Greeks' successful emergence from the Persian Wars—made the ultimate verdict of the Punic Wars more or less foreordained. Given the size of the Roman army, the unity of republican Italy, and the relative weakness of Punic culture, the wonder is not that Carthage lost, but that it was able to fight so savagely and for so long.

In contrast to the later Romans, at Salamis the quarreling Greeks were faced with a navy three to four times larger. The Persian army on the mainland enjoyed still greater numerical superiority and was anywhere from five to ten times more numerous than the aggregate number of Greek hoplites. Persia itself could draw on manpower reserves seventy times greater than present in Greek-speaking lands and possessed coin money and bullion in its imperial vaults that would make Greek temples' treasuries seem impoverished in contrast.

Indeed, without an imperial structure, the Greek city-states were quarreling over the defense of the mainland right up to the first signs of the Persian assault. After Xerxes' descent through northern Greece in late summer 480, ostensibly more Greek *poleis* were neutral or in service to the Persians than to the Hellenic cause. And unlike Rome during the Hannibalic invasion, Athens by September 480 was not merely threatened, but already destroyed and occupied—and the population of Attica evacuated and dispersed. The situation was far worse than that which prevailed in Western Europe in mid-1940 after the Nazi victories over the European democracies.

Imagine a defeated and overrun France—without allies, Paris already destroyed, the Arc de Triomphe and Eiffel Tower in ruins, the country-side abandoned, its remaining free population in transit in small boats toward England and its North African colonies—choosing to stake its entire recovery on an outnumbered but patriotic French fleet in the harbor of Toulon. And then conceive that the French patriots and their outnumbered ships had won!—wrecking half the Nazi vessels, sending Hitler in shame to Berlin, and in a few months fashioning a heroic resistance on the occupied French mainland where its infantry went on to destroy a Nazi army many times larger and to send it back in shambles across the Rhine.

But granted that the Persian Wars marked the last chance of the other to end the nascent, though irrepressible, culture of the West, was Salamis itself the real landmark event in the Greeks' decade-long resistance to Darius and Xerxes? We can easily dispense with the first engagement at Marathon, the heroic Athenian victory fought a decade earlier. The Athenian victory there was magnificent and it prevented for the time being the burning of Athens. But Darius' invasion force of 490 on the small Attic plain northeast of Athens was not large—perhaps not much over 30,000 in all—and it had previously occupied only a few Greek islands. Darius in this probe had neither the resources nor the will to enslave Greece. At most, a Persian victory would have served as retribution for Athens's recent unsuccessful intervention on behalf of the rebelling Ionian Greeks on the coast of Asia Minor. An Athenian defeat at Marathon would have also led to a renewed indigenous tyranny under the offspring of the former tyrant Pisistratus, more sympathetic to Persia. Thus due to limited objectives and the avoidance of war with most of the other Greek city-states, a Persian victory at Marathon by itself would have sidetracked, but not ended, the Greek ascendancy.

Darius died in 486, and the task of avenging the shame of Marathon now fell to his son Xerxes. The latter was intent not on another punitive raid, but envisioned a mass invasion, one larger than any the eastern Mediterranean had yet seen. After four years of preparation, Xerxes had his troops mobilized in 480. He bridged the Hellespont into Europe and descended through northern Greece, absorbing all the city-states in his wake, unfortunate Hellenic communities that had little choice other than destruction or surrender. Whereas there is no credibility in ancient accounts that the Persian army numbered more than a million men, we should imagine that even a force of a quarter- to a half-million infantry and seamen was the largest invasion that Europe would witness until the Allied armada at D Day, June 1944. We need not agree either with ancient accounts that the Persian cavalry numbered over 80,000 horses. But it may well have been half that size, still nearly five times larger than the mounted forces Alexander would use to conquer Asia more than a century and a half later. And there were probably well over 1,200 Phoenician, Greek, and Persian ships in the Great King's naval armada.

The Greeks agreed to try to stop the onslaught at the narrow defile of Thermopylae, the last pass in Greece above the Isthmus of Corinth, where terrain offered a credible defense for outnumbered troops. At that

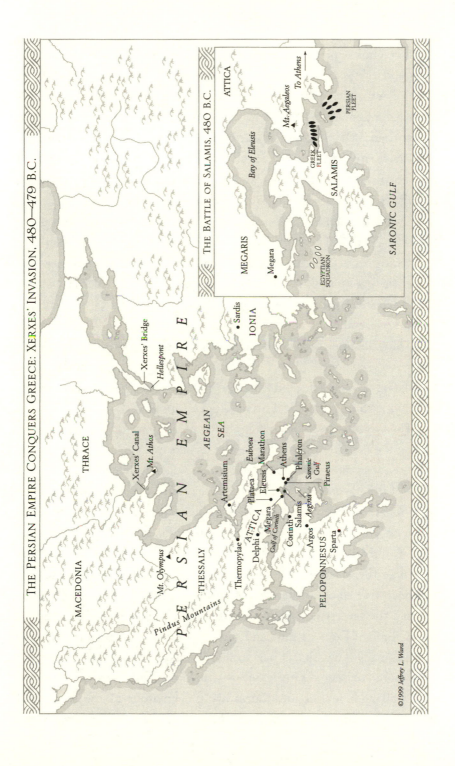

THE PERSIAN EMPIRE CONQUERS GREECE: XERXES' INVASION, 480—479 B.C.

MACEDONIA

THRACE

Mt. Olympus

THESSALY

Pindus Mountains

Thermopylae

Delphi

ATTICA

Plataea

Megara

Gulf of Corinth

Corinth

Argos

Salamis

Aegina

Sparta

PELOPONNESUS

Euboea

Marathon

Athens

Eleusis

Phaleron

Saronic Gulf

Piraeus

Artemisium

Xerxes' Canal
Mt. Athos

AEGEAN SEA

Xerxes' Bridge

Hellespont

Sardis

IONIA

P E R S I A N   E M P I R E

©1999 Jeffrey L. Ward

THE BATTLE OF SALAMIS, 480 B.C.

MEGARIS

Megara

EGYPTIAN SQUADRON

ATTICA

Bay of Eleusis

Mt. Aegaleos

To Athens

GREEK FLEET

PERSIAN FLEET

SALAMIS

SARONIC GULF

northern choke point there was less than fifty feet of passage between the cliffs and the sea. Accordingly, in August 480 the city-states sent the Greek fleet under Athenian leadership up the nearby coast to Artemisium. King Leonidas of Sparta followed by land with a token allied force of less than 7,000 hoplites. If the Persian fleet could be stalled, and the massive enemy army bottled up, all the city-states to the south might yet rally northward, join Leonidas, and so thwart the advance without much damage to the prosperous interior of central and southern Greece.

That bold Greek strategy quickly collapsed, and despite the courage of the Spartans at Thermopylae and the loss of much of the Persian fleet due to storms at Artemesium, both land and sea battles comprised together the greatest military defeat in the history of the Greek city-states. A Spartan king was now dead and his body mutilated, over 4,000 crack hoplites were killed, a large percentage of the Greek fleet was damaged, and everything north of the Isthmus at Corinth lay naked before the invader. An abandoned Athens was to be burned, and then perhaps rehabited as a regional capital of the Persian empire—a Greek Sardis, Babylon, or Susa—to collect money for Persepolis.

Thus the battle of Salamis loomed as the next—and last—occasion to stop the Persian onslaught. Had the Greeks not fought at Salamis—or had they lost there—the consequences are easy to imagine. The Greek fleet—if it had survived or if its fractious remnants could still have been kept together—would have sailed south to the Isthmus at Corinth, where in conjunction with the remaining infantry of the Peloponnese, they would have once more tried to fashion a last-ditch defense effort similar to the failed land-sea attempt at Thermopylae and Artemisium. But now with all of northern and central Greece conquered, the Athenians and the largest Greek naval contingent eliminated, and the Persian forces jubilant from a spring and summer of constant conquest, there is no reason to doubt that a half million Persians—aided by troops from even more conquered Greek states—would not have breached the isthmus wall and poured into Corinthia and environs to the south and west. The infantry invaders would have been aided, of course, by the massive Persian fleet, which could land supplies and men where needed to the rear of the Greek defenders in Argolis and on the northern coast of the Peloponnese. In later Greek history, garrisoning the isthmus had never kept any invading force out of the Peloponnese—Epaminondas, even without naval support, proved that four times during the 360s B.C. alone.

The great battle of Plataea, fought in the spring after the Greeks' victory at Salamis, resulted in the destruction of the remaining Persian infantry in the field and marks the final expulsion of Xerxes' forces from Greece. But that landmark battle is understood only in the context of the tactical, strategic, and spiritual triumph of Salamis the September before. The Persians at Plataea fought without their king—Xerxes and some of his best Persian infantry had withdrawn to Persia after the naval defeat. There was to be no supporting Persian fleet off the coast of eastern Boeotia. And while the Greeks had bickered and fought up to the very moments before the battle at Salamis, at Plataea they were unified and confident by reason of their past naval success. Indeed, there may have been more Greeks at Plataea—70,000 hoplites and as many light-armed troops—than would ever marshal again in Greek history. Thus the Persians fought as a recently defeated force, without the numerical superiority they enjoyed at Salamis, and without their king and his enormous fleet. They could not be reinforced by sea. The Greeks, in contrast, poured en masse into the small plain of Plataea, convinced that their Persian enemies were retreating from Attica, demoralized from their defeat at Salamis, and abandoned by their political and military leadership.

The victories at Marathon and Plataea—and of course the unsuccessful Hellenic resistance at Thermopylae and Artemesium—were not in themselves the deciding battles of the decade-long Persian-Greek conflict. If Marathon delayed the hope of Persian conquest, and Plataea finished it, Salamis made it impossible. When the Persians retreated from Salamis, it was as a weakened army without its king, its fleet, and a great many of its soldiers.

Yet if Salamis was the key to the Greek victory in the Persian Wars, what accounts for the Greeks' remarkable victory there? From the fifth-century accounts in Herodotus and Aeschylus's *Persians*, together with much later second- and third-hand sources—the historian Diodorus and the biographer Plutarch being the most prominent—and topographical reconnaissance around Salamis itself, scholars can more or less reconstruct the battle with some certainty. After a tumultuous meeting of the admirals of the Panhellenic fleet, the Greeks agreed to accede to the Athenian Themistocles' plan to pit their much smaller fleet—a little over 350 ships against somewhere between 600 and 1,000 Persian vessels—in the narrow straits between the island of Salamis and the Greek mainland west of Athens. The Persians had occupied all of nearby Attica and patrolled as far south as Megara, a few hundred yards opposite the northwest tip of Salamis. In contrast, the Athenian populace was dispersed, with men of military age at Salamis, the elderly, women, and children sent to the more distant island of Aegina and the coast of Argolis to the southwest.

Besides the need to reclaim his homeland, Themistocles' more critical plan was to precipitate an immediate fight while the Greeks still had some remnant notion of Panhellenic defense and his own country was in enemy hands for only a few weeks. Themistocles argued that within the confined space of the Salamis narrows, the Persians both would lack room to maneuver and could not employ the full extent of their fleet—allowing the outnumbered though heavier Greek ships to nullify their enemy's vast numerical superiority. In such confined waters, the less-experienced Greek sailors had little worry about being outflanked and surrounded by skilled crews in sleek triremes, and so could sail out to battle, ship to ship, in massed order, seeking to ram their own stouter vessels against the first ranks of the lighter Persian, Ionian, and Phoenician fleet. Any Persians or their allies who survived could be speared by Greek hoplites posted on nearby small islands, while the disabled Greek ships and their crews could find refuge on Salamis proper.

The sea battle was fought all day—most likely sometime between

September 20 and 30, 480 B.C.—and by nightfall the Persians had lost half their ships and the fleet was scattered. The key to the Greek success was to nullify Persian numbers and superior seamanship; this was done brilliantly both before and during the battle. Misled into thinking the Greeks were withdrawing to the northwest through the channel between Megara and Salamis, the Persians committed what would turn out to be two blunders: First, they detached a large portion of their armada to safeguard the exit, thus drawing off valuable ships from the scene of the battle itself. Second, Xerxes ordered his forces, while it was still night, to sail up the channel between Salamis and the Attic mainland—ensuring that his crews received no sleep or food, while nullifying their numerical superiority in the confined waters. Our ancient accounts are in conflict over the details of the fighting, but it seems most likely that about 350 Greek triremes set out in two lines, each ranging about two miles long across the channel, intent on ramming the three opposing lines of Persian ships, which were in disorder and at this point perhaps only enjoyed a two-to-one numerical advantage. Herodotus, Aeschylus, and later sources say little about the actual collision, but the Greeks, desperate to ensure the safety of their families on Salamis and to the west in the Peloponnese, used their heavier ships to repeatedly ram Xerxes' fleet, until his various national contingents began to break off and flee the melee. Although they still outnumbered the Greek fleet, the Persians' morale was shattered and within a few days, Xerxes sailed home to the Hellespont, accompanied by an infantry guard of 60,000, leaving behind his surrogate Mardonius with a large army to continue the struggle on land the next spring. Such are the barest outlines of the battle of Salamis.

On at least two critical occasions, the leadership of Themistocles ensured that the battle was fought at Salamis and that it was won there. Quite literally, had he not been present or had he advised different measures, the Greeks either would not have engaged the Persians or they would have been defeated. Very shortly afterward the Persian Wars would have been lost, and the culture of the West would have died in its infancy after little more than two centuries. Other than Themistocles, there was no other Greek leader able or willing to marshal the Hellenic forces by sea in defense of Athens.

First, the decision to fight the Persians at sea seems to have been Themistocles' own. Earlier he had convinced his countrymen that the Delphic oracle's prophecy of salvation through the "wooden wall" meant the new Athenian fleet off the coast, especially the mention of "Divine Salamis" in Apollo's last two lines of the hexameter verse. Thus the Athenians had evacuated Attica and their capital at Athens, and fled by sea on Themistocles' initiative—a wise move since die-hard conservative hoplite infantrymen would have preferred to commit to a glorious last stand in the Athenian plain. And we should remember that the Athenian fleet of some 250 ships was recently constructed and in excellent shape—and entirely due to the persistence of Themistocles' statesmanship two years earlier. In a heated and polarizing debate, he had previously convinced the Athenian assembly not to dole out the returns from their newly opened Attic silver mines at Laurium to individual citizens, but rather to use that income to build ships and train seamen to protect the new democracy from either Greek or Persian attack. His prescient efforts in 482 had ensured that the Athenians now had a newly constructed armada right off its shores.

After the battered Greek flotilla limped down the coast from Artemesium, Herodotus relates that Eurybiades, the Spartan commander of the reconstituted Greek combined fleet, put the decision of where to fight to a council of Greek admirals. We should believe Herodotus' account that the non-Athenian Greeks quickly urged a withdrawal to bases to the south in Argolis, where they could fashion a defense at the nearby Isthmus of Corinth: "Since Attica was already lost, the majority of the views that were given came to the same conclusion, that is to sail to the isthmus and fight for the Peloponnese." That way, the Greeks felt, if defeated, they might still find refuge in their own harbors.

At that point in his narrative, Herodotus makes the Athenian Mnesiphilus despair of such a decision: "Then everyone will go back to their own city, and neither Eurybiades nor any other will be able to hold them together, but the fleet will be scattered abroad and Greece shall perish through its own stupidity." Like the failed Ionian revolt a decade earlier, the mainland Greeks, Mnesiphilus knew, would also disperse after a crushing defeat, all boasting of further resistance as they privately sought accommodation with the Persians.

But once rebuffed, Themistocles immediately called a second meeting and convinced Eurybiades to marshal the Greeks at Salamis and fight where the narrow channels between the mainland would favor the defenders, where victory meant the salvation of the displaced Athenian people, and where the Peloponnesians could defend their homeland while the enemy was still distant. Themistocles added that the Greeks could ill afford to give up any more Greek territory—the islands in the Saronic Gulf and the Megarid were now defenseless. Indeed, the Persians were building a mole to Salamis itself, over which they planned to march in order to capture the exiled Athenians holed up on the island.

It would be utter insanity, Themistocles added, to fight in the open seas off Corinth where the Greeks' slower ships and smaller numbers ensured that they would be enveloped and outmaneuvered. Finally, now in open council, he threatened to take the Athenian fleet out of battle altogether and transport his people en masse over to Italy to refound the city, should the Greeks sail away and abandon Salamis. To this last-ditch effort and threats, the Greek admirals reluctantly gave in. The decision in mid-September was made to stay put and wait for the enemy. But would the Persian ships come into the narrow straits, or simply wait off the occupied Attic coast for the nearby moored Greek ships to feud and disband?

Themistocles' second great feat was to lure the invaders' vessels into the narrows. Herodotus reports the story that Themistocles sent his slave Sicinnus across the channel at night to the Persian camp with a planted story: Themistocles and his Athenians wished a Persian victory, Sicinnus reported to the enemy. He added that the Greeks were squabbling and about to flee from Salamis for the isthmus. Xerxes' last chance to trap them would be to sail immediately in the morning between Attica and Salamis and catch the Greek ships unprepared and unorganized. Indeed, the Athenians and others might switch sides and join the Persians once they entered the straits.

Classical scholars still argue over the authenticity of Herodotus's story of a Themistoclean ruse. While the tale appears melodramatic and puts the decision to deploy over a 1,000 ships on the rumor of a single slave, there is no reason to doubt either Themistocles' guile or the Persians' gullibility. After all, the Persians a few weeks earlier had won at Thermopylae solely through the betrayal of Ephialtes, a Greek traitor, who showed them a route around the pass. Very early the next morning, after the successful nocturnal mission of Sicinnus, the Persians were convinced by the ruse and began rowing into the narrows and the Greek trap. From the descriptions of Herodotus and Aeschylus, the Persians ships were stacked and confused in the narrow bay off Salamis and were unable to use either their numbers or swiftness to penetrate or outflank the Greeks, who methodically rammed them with their heavier vessels. Themistocles fought bravely in his own clearly marked ship, while Xerxes watched the debacle in safety from his throne atop nearby Mount Aegaleus.

By any fair measure, Themistocles seems mostly responsible for the Greek victory. The existence of a large Athenian fleet was critical to the Greek cause and its creation was his legacy. Other than at Salamis, there were no other naval theaters between Athens and the southern Peloponnese that so favored the smaller and slower Greek fleet. Once invaded, Themistocles persuaded his countrymen to put their faith in ships, not hoplites, had them evacuate Attica, and then convinced the Greek admiralty to risk an all-out engagement in Athenian waters, which alone offered the chance for victory. Whatever the actual circumstances of the Persians' costly decision to fight according to Greek wishes, contemporaries at least believed that Themistocles had fooled Xerxes into committing his forces immediately into the narrows. And finally, at the key moment of the engagement Themistocles led the Athenian contingent, aided by favorable tides, to cut into the enemy flank and rout the Persian fleet. In short, the key to the salvation of the West was the Persian defeat by the Greeks, which required a victory at Salamis, which in turn could not have occurred without the repeated efforts—all against opposition—of a single Athenian statesman. Had he wavered, had he been killed, or had he lacked the moral and intellectual force to press home his arguments, it is likely that Greece would have become a satrapy of Persia.

There is a postscript to Salamis that is too often forgotten. The Greek victory may have saved the West by ensuring that Hellenism would not be extinguished after a mere two centuries of polis culture. But just as importantly, the victory was a catalyst for the entire Athenian democratic renaissance. As Aristotle saw more than a century and a half later in his *Politics*, what had been a rather ordinary Greek polis, in the midst of a recent experiment of allowing the native-born poor to vote, would now suddenly inherit the cultural leadership of Greece.

Because Salamis was a victory of "the naval crowd," in the next century the influence of Athenian landless oarsmen would only increase, as they demanded greater political representation commensurate with their prowess on the all-important seas. The newly empowered Athenian citizenry refashioned Athenian democracy, which would soon build the Parthenon, subsidize the tragedians, send its triremes throughout the Aegean, exterminate the Melians, and execute Socrates. Marathon had created the myth of Athenian infantry; Salamis, the far greater victory, had just superseded it. Imperialists like Pericles, Cleon, and Alcibiades, not the descendants of the veterans of Marathon, were the key players on the horizon.

No wonder crotchety Plato in his *Laws* argued that while Marathon had started the string of Greek successes and Plataea had finished it, Salamis "made the Greeks worse as people." More than a century after the battle, Plato saw Salamis as a critical juncture in the entire evolution of early Western culture. Before Salamis, Greek city-states embraced an entire array of quite necessary hierarchies—property qualifications to vote, wars fought exclusively by those landowners meeting the infantry census, and a general absence of taxes, navies, and imperialism. Those protocols defined freedom and equality in terms of a minority of the population who had ample capital, education, and land. Before Salamis, the essence of the polis was not equality for all, but the search for moral virtue for all, guided by a consensus of properly qualified and gifted men.

Plato, Aristotle, and most other Greek thinkers from Thucydides to Xenophon were not mere elitists. Rather, they saw the inherent dangers in the license and affluence that accrued from radically democratic government, state entitlement, free expression, and market capitalism. Without innate checks and balances, in this more restrictive view, the polis would turn out a highly individualistic, but self-absorbed citizen with no interest in communal sacrifices or moral virtue. Better, the conservatives felt, that government should hinge on the majority votes of only those educated and informed citizens with some financial solvency. War—like Marathon and Plataea—should be for the defense of real property, on land, and require martial courage, not mere technology or numerical superiority. Citizens should own their own farms, provide their own weapons, and be responsible for their own economic security—not seek wage labor, public employment, or government entitlement. The oarsmen of Salamis changed all that in an afternoon.

With the Aegean wide open after the retreat of the Persian fleet at Salamis, and Athens now at the vanguard of the Greek resistance, radical democracy and its refutation of the old polis were at hand. The philosophers may have hated Salamis, but Salamis had saved Greece, and so the poor under the leadership of Themistocles had not ruined, but reinvented, Greece.

A new, more dynamic, exciting, and in some sense reckless West would emerge under the leadership of the boisterous Athenian *demos*. What later philosophers such as Hegel, Nietzsche, and Spengler would deplore about Western culture—its rampant equality, uniform sameness, and interest in crass material bounty—in some sense started at Salamis, an unfortunate "accident," Aristotle said, but one that nevertheless shifted forever the emphasis of Western civilization toward more egalitarian democracy and a more capitalistic economy. Whatever we may think of the great strengths of, or dangers, in present-day Western culture—consumer democracy increasingly set free, rights ever more expanded, the responsibilities of the citizenry further excused—that mobile and dynamic tradition is also due to Themistocles' September victory off Salamis.

In late September 480, Themistocles and his poor Athenians not only saved Greece and embryonic Western civilization from the Persians, but also redefined the West as something more egalitarian, restless—and volatile—that would evolve into a society that we more or less recognize today.

JOSIAH OBER

# CONQUEST DENIED

*The Premature Death of Alexander the Great*

The historian Arnold Toynbee once put forward a counterfactual speculation that has gained a certain fame. What would have happened if, instead of dying at thirty-two, Alexander the Great had made it to old age? Toynbee saw Alexander conquering China and dispatching naval expeditions that would circumnavigate Africa. Aramaic or Greek would become our lingua franca and Buddhism our universal religion. An extra quarter century of life would have given Alexander the chance to achieve his dream of One World, becoming in the process a kind of benevolent advance man for a United Nations, ancient style.

Josiah Ober, the chairman of the Department of Classics at Princeton, has come up with an alternative scenario for Alexander the Great, and one darker than Toynbee's: What if Alexander had died at the beginning of his career, before he had the opportunity of adding "the Great" to his name? That nearly happened at the Battle of the Granicus River in 334 B.C., and Alexander's literal brush with death reminds us how often the interval of a millisecond or a heartbeat can alter the course of history. The conquests of the young Macedonian king would never have been realized, the Per-

*sian Empire would have survived unchallenged, and the brilliant Hellenistic period, that cultural seedbed of the West, would have been stillborn. Suppose, however, that Alexander had outlasted his bout with an unnamed fever in 323 B.C.? Given his appetite for conquest and for terror as a political weapon, Ober feels, he might only have filled another two decades of life with fresh occasions for "opportunistic predation." The culture of the known world, and Hellenism in particular, might have been the worse for Alexander's reprieve.*

✦ *Ober is the author of* THE ANATOMY OF ERROR: ANCIENT MILITARY DISASTERS AND THEIR LESSONS FOR MODERN STRATEGISTS *(with Barry S. Strauss) and, most recently,* THE ATHENIAN REVOLUTION *and* POLITICAL DISSENT IN DEMOCRATIC ATHENS.

At the Battle of the Granicus River in northwestern Anatolia, during the first major military engagement of Alexander the Great's invasion of the Persian Empire, young King Alexander came very close to death. At the Granicus, the Macedonians and their Greek allies encountered local Anatolian cavalry and Greek mercenary infantry under the joint command of Persian regional governors (satraps). The enemy was massed in a defensive formation on the opposite bank of the river. The river was fordable, but the banks were steep and Alexander's senior lieutenants counseled caution. After all, the king was barely twenty-two years old and presumably still had much to learn. A serious setback early in the campaign could end the invasion before it had properly begun. Ignoring their sensible advice, Alexander mounted his great charger, Bucephalus ("Oxhead"). Highly conspicuous in a white-plumed helmet, the king led his Macedonian shock cavalry in an audacious charge across the river and up the opposite bank. The Persian-led forces fell back before the Macedonian's charge, and he penetrated deep into their ranks. This was probably exactly what the Persian tacticians had planned for from the beginning. Due to the startling success of his charge, Alexander, accompanied only by a small advance force, was momentarily cut off from the main body of the Macedonian army.

At this critical moment in the battle, young Alexander was surrounded by enemies, including one Spithridates, an ax-wielding Persian noble who managed to deal the Macedonian king a heavy blow to the head. Alexander's helmet was severely damaged. The king was disoriented, unable to defend himself. A second strike would certainly kill him. And with the young king would die the hopes of the entire expedition and Macedonian imperial aspirations. In the next few seconds the future

## ALEXANDER THE GREAT

*A helmetless Alexander the Great, riding Bucephalus, ancient history's most famous horse, leads a charge on fleeing Persians. How different would our world be if he had died in battle—as he nearly did? This mosaic, uncovered in Pompeii, was based on a Greek painting, probably completed in Alexander's lifetime.*

(Alinari/Art Resouce, NY)

of the Persian empire and the entire course of Western history would be decided. Did Alexander's life flash before him as he awaited imminent extinction? How had he come to arrive at this place, at this untoward fate? How could so much have come to depend on a single blow?

❖   ❖   ❖

Alexander was born in Macedon (the northeastern region of modern Greece) in 356 B.C., the first and only son of King Philip II of Macedon and Olympias of Epirus (modern Albania). Philip had seized control of

Macedon just three years prior to his son's birth, following the death in battle of his royal brother, Amyntas III. Prior to Philip's accession, Macedon had been a relative backwater—a semi-Hellenized border zone pressured on the north and west by aggressive Danubian tribes and to the east by imperial Persia. When not confronting system-level tribal or imperial threats, Macedon's rulers were consistently outmaneuvered diplomatically by the highly civilized Greek city-states to the south. Internally, Macedon was dominated by semi-independent warlords who followed the lead of the weak central government only when it pleased them. Yet by instituting a dramatic reorganization of the Macedonian armed forces, technological innovations (for example, the extra-long thrusting spear known as the *sarissa* and hair-spring powered catapult artillery), economic restructuring, and astute diplomacy, Philip had changed all that—seemingly overnight. By the time Alexander was ten years old, Macedon was the most powerful state on the Greek peninsula. The Danubian tribes had been first bought off, then humbled militarily. Some of the Greek city-states bordering Macedon had been destroyed: The sack of Olynthus in 348 had shocked the rest of the Greek world. Many other Greek cities were forced into unequal alliances. Even proud and powerful Athens had eventually seen the wisdom of making a peace treaty, after suffering a series of humiliating military and diplomatic setbacks at Philip's hands.

Meanwhile, Alexander was being groomed to help govern the kingdom and, eventually, assume the throne. He was well trained: His tutor in intellectual and cultural matters was the philosopher Aristotle; his mentor in military and diplomatic affairs was his own father, probably the best military mind of his generation. And in the corridors of the royal palace at Pella, Alexander learned the murkier arts of intrigue. The Macedonian court was beset by rumor and factions. The counterpoint was the hard-drinking parties favored by the Macedonian elite, all-night events that featured blunt speech and, sometimes, sudden violence. Alexander and his father had come close to blows on at least one of these drunken occasions.

41

In Alexander's twentieth year, Philip II was cut down by an assassin. The killer, a Macedonian named Pausanias, was in turn butchered by Philip's bodyguards as he ran for his horse. Although Pausanias may well have held a personal grudge against his king, there was suspicion that he had not acted alone. One obvious candidate for the mastermind behind the killing was Darius III, the Great King of Persia—in the mid-fourth century a mighty empire that stretched from the Aegean coast of Turkey, to Egypt in the south, and east as far as modern Pakistan. In the years before the assassination, Philip had been making open preparations for a Persian expedition; a few months prior to his death his lieutenants had established a beachhead on Persian-held territory in northwestern Anatolia. "Cutting the head from the dangerous snake" was a well-known Persian modus operandi and (at least according to later historians) Alexander himself publicly blamed Darius for Philip's death. But Darius was not the only suspect; other fingers pointed at a jealous wife— Olympias—and even at the ambitious young prince himself.

In any event, Alexander's first order of business after his father's death was the establishment of himself as undisputed king: The Macedonian rules for succession were vague and untidy, in fact any member of the royal family who could command a strong following had a chance at gaining the throne; Alexander proceeded to establish his claim with characteristic dispatch and equally characteristic ruthlessness. Potential internal rivals were eliminated, the restive Danubians crushed in a massive raid deep into their home territory. Immediately thereafter a hastily pulled together anti-Macedonian coalition of Greek city-states was smashed by Alexander's lightning march south. In the aftermath of Alexander's victory, the great and ancient Greek city of Thebes was destroyed as an example to others who might doubt the new king's resolve.

Alexander had proved himself his father's son and worthy of the throne, but his treasury was seriously depleted. He had no choice but to follow through with the planned invasion of the western provinces of the Persian empire. The prospect of war booty fired the imagination of his

Macedonian troops. The restive southern Greeks were brought on board by the prospect of revenge for long-past, but never-forgotten, Persian atrocities during the Greco-Persian wars of the early fifth century B.C. Crossing at the Hellespont, Alexander had sacrificed at Troy to the shades of Homeric Greek heroes, and then proceeded south, toward the Granicus, where he met his first significant opposition. Now, with Spithridates's ax arcing down toward Alexander's shattered helmet for the second time, it appeared as if the glorious expedition would end before it had begun.

Yet the deadly blow never landed. Just as Spithridates prepared to finish off his opponent, one of Alexander's personal bodyguard "companions," Cleitus (nicknamed "the Black"), appeared at his king's side and speared the Persian axman dead. Alexander quickly rallied, and the wild charge that might have ended in disaster spurred on his troops. Most of the Persian forces crumbled; a stubborn body of Greek mercenaries was eventually cut down. Alexander was spectacularly victorious at the Granicus—losing only 34 men and reportedly killing over 20,000 of the enemy. Spoils from the battle were sent back to Greece to be displayed in places of honor. Alexander was now on his way, and it seemed nothing could stop him. In the course of the next decade, Alexander and his Macedonians repeatedly demonstrated their capacity to overcome tremendous obstacles. They went on to conquer the entire Persian empire, and more. Alexander's conquest of the Persian empire is among the most remarkable—and most terrifyingly sanguinary and efficient—military campaigns of all time. By 324 B.C. Alexander had laid the foundations for a successor empire that might have included both the entirety of the old Persian holdings, penisular Greece, and various outlying areas as well. He established an imperial capital at Mesopotamian Babylon and began to lay plans for internal administration—and further military expeditions. Yet Alexander did not long outlive his great campaign of conquest. He died of disease (perhaps malaria) complicated by the effects of hard living (multiple serious wounds, heavy drinking) in June of 323 B.C. at the age of thirty-two, ten years after the Granicus.

The would-be unified empire never came about; in the course of two generations of savage warfare Alexander's generals and their lieutenants and sons divided amongst themselves the vast territories they had helped to conquer. Some distant northern and eastern provinces fell away from Macedonian rule—control of northwestern India was formally ceded to the aspiring native dynast Chandragupta Maurya (founder of the great Mauryan empire) in exchange for 300 war elephants. But vast regions remained: Within a generation of Alexander's death, Egypt, most of Anatolia, Syria-Palestine, and much of western Asia (as well as the Macedonian homeland and contiguous regions in Europe) were being ruled by relatively stable Macedonian dynasties. And because the Macedonian elite eagerly adopted Greek culture, this extensive region was incorporated into a Greek sphere of political and cultural influence. Dozens of major and minor Greek cities were established by Alexander and his successors: Egyptian Alexandria, Macedonian Thessaloníka, Anatolian Pergamum, and Syrian Antioch are only a few of the most famous. The Greek language quickly became the common vernacular for a large part of the civilized world—and the dominant language of trade, diplomacy, and literary culture.

The brilliant Hellenistic civilization that arose in the generations following the death of Alexander not only enlarged exponentially the geographic range of Greek culture, it provided a historical bridge between the classical Greek culture of the sixth to fourth centuries B.C. and the coming age of imperial Rome. Hellenistic scholars at the famous library in Egyptian Alexandria preserved and codified the best of earlier Greek literature, while Hellenistic historians did the same for the memory of Greek accomplishments in the political and miltiary spheres. Philosophical speculation—especially the relatively individual-centered Stoicism and Epicureanism flourished among the educated elites. Local experiments in religious practice and thought were granted the possibility of a vast audience, due to the prevalence of a common language and a general attitude of religious tolerance among the ruling elites.

There were remarkable demographic shifts as people gravitated toward new opportunities: Greeks and Macedonians—in high demand as soldiers and administrators—to be sure, but also Jews, Phoenicians, and other peoples of the Near East who established enclaves in the new and burgeoning Greek cities; meanwhile older cities (including Jerusalem) were made over in a new cosmopolitan and increasingly Hellenic image. This Hellenistic (or "Greek-oriented") world was similar to the classical era in its political focus on semi-independent city-states and its highly developed urban culture. It was different from the classical era in that "Greekness" was now defined as much by cultural affinity as by ethnic heritage—individual Syrians, Egyptians, Bactrians in central Asia, along with people from many other ethnic backgrounds living in regions controlled by descendants of Alexander's generals became increasingly Greek in their language, education, literary, and athletic tastes—even while remaining quite un-Greek in their religious practices. The Hellenistic world was the milieu in which Judaism came to the attention of the Greeks and achieved some of its distinctive "modern" forms. It was the context in which Jesus of Nazareth preached his new message and in which Christianity grew up as a religion. It was, in short, Hellenistic Greek culture that was inherited by the Romans, and subsequently preserved for rediscovery in the European Renaissance and Enlightenment. And so, it is not too much to say that to the extent that modern Western culture is defined by a "Greco-Roman-Judaic-Christian" inheritance, it is a product of the world that grew up in the wake of Alexander's conquests.

✦ ✦ ✦

Alexander's seemingly premature death at the age of thirty-two stimulated one of the best known historians of the twentieth century, Arnold Toynbee, to develop an elaborate and romantic "counterfactual history," which has become a classic of the genre. Postulating a sudden recovery from his debilitating fever, Toynbee imagined a long productive life for Alexander in which conquest and exploration were nicely balanced by thoughtful administrative arrangements and a generous social policy that saw all residents of the great empire as worthy of basic human dignity. In Toynbee's optimistic counterfactual scenario, Alexander and his unbroken line of successors promoted both culture and technology, leading to the early discovery of (for example) steam power. Consequently, the great empire was invincible; Rome never became a serious threat. With the discovery of the Western Hemisphere by Alexandrian explorers, the empire eventually becomes a genuine world-state. It is ruled by a benevolent monarchy; in Toynbee's counterfactual present, Alexander's direct lineal descendent still sits secure on his throne, his subjects enjoy peace and prosperity, and all really is right with the world.

Toynbee's counterfactual was heavily influenced by the cheerful portrait painted by his contemporary, W. W. Tarn, an eloquent and domineering historian who had depicted the historical Alexander as a cosmopolitan, thoughtful, and far-sighted proto-Stoic. Tarn's Alexander engaged in warfare only as a means to a higher end—Tarn envisioned that end as a broad-based "brotherhood of man" (centered on a policy of intermarriage between Greek- and Persian-speaking groups) that would flourish beneath the benevolent imperial aegis. Yet more recent commentators (notably E. Badian and A. B. Bosworth) have emphasized a much darker side of Alexander's character. They focus on the brutality of the means by which Alexander's tenure of power and the Macedonian conquest of Persia were effected, and they assert that there was no grand vision of a higher or humanitarian end. Under this revisionist theory, Alexander cared much for slaughter and little for imperial management. Under his direct leadership the Macedonians proved to be remarkably good at wholesale butchery of less militarily competent peoples—but they contributed little in the way of culture. This alternative view of Alexander allows the development of a grim alternative to Toynbee's "Alexander survives" counterfactual. We might posit that if Alexander really had lived for another thirty years, there would have been much more widespread destruction of existing Asian cultures and disastrous impoverishment in the process of the sapping of local resources to finance a never-ending cycle of opportunistic predation that offered little but misery in its wake. And so we might posit that the Hellenistic world (and its modern legacy) might never have come about if its progenitor had lived much longer.

Yet, realistically speaking, Alexander did not die young. People in antiquity could not expect to live nearly as long as do modern people in developed countries: Disease and risks of battle tended to end their lives much earlier than we would regard as "normal life expectancy." So it is hardly remarkable that Alexander expired before turning gray—a man who repeatedly exposed himself to extraordinary physical risks on the battlefield and suffered several appalling wounds, who had many personal enemies, who indulged in frequent bouts of binge drinking, and who spent most of his life outdoors, traveling thousands of miles in an era before the development of modern sanitation or medicine in areas with diverse and unfamiliar disease pools. Rather the wonder is that Alexander lived to the "ripe old age" of thirty-two. The explanation for his relative longevity in the face of the many risks he took and the stresses he inflicted on his body can be put down to some combination of remarkable personal vigor and equally remarkable luck. And so, in terms of really plausible counterfactual history, it seems more sensible to ask ourselves, not, "What if Alexander had lived to be sixty-five?" but, "What if Alexander had died in his early twenties?" To make it more specific: What if Alexander had been just a bit less lucky at the Battle of the Granicus? What if Cleitus had been a heartbeat too late with his spear?

There is good reason to suppose that, although Alexander was very lucky indeed to ride away from the Granicus with his head intact, it was not just luck that placed Spithridates just an ax-length from the Macedonian commander early in the battle. The Persians certainly knew just where Alexander was riding among the Macedonian cavalry. The king's white-plumed helmet was a clear marker, as indeed it was intended to be, for the Macedonians. And the Persian commanders had ample reason to suppose that Alexander would lead the charge personally. The place of an ancient Greek general was typically at the front of the line, rather than in the rear echelons. Moreover, young Alexander, at the outset of an audacious expedition against a mighty opponent, had a special need to cement a reputation for personal bravery and charismatic leadership. When the Macedonian charge came, Alexander could be expected to be at its head.

If the Persian generals took any account of recent history, they had very good reason to fear well-led Greek invaders—and equally good reason to supppose that if its commander were killed, the Macedonian expedition as a whole would quickly founder. Two generations past, in 401 B.C., Cyrus II, a highly talented and consequently overambitious younger brother of the reigning Persian king, had led an army of some 13,000 Greek mercenaries against his royal elder sibling. At the battle of Cunaxa, near Babylon (in modern Iraq), the disciplined Greek hoplites trounced their opponents. But at a moment at which his victory seemed quite possible, Cyrus had led a spirited cavalry charge that smashed deep into the opposing ranks. Much too deep, as it turned out. Lacking Alexander's fortune, Cyrus was cut down as soon as he became isolated from his main force. With the military commander and pretender to the throne dead, the expedition immediately lost its purpose and its impetus. About 10,000 Greek surivors managed to fight their way out of the heart of the Empire in an epic retreat immortalized in Xenophon's autobiographical *Anabasis* ("The March Up-Country"). The success of the hoplite force at Cunaxa and the subsequent march of the 10,000 clearly demonstrated, to Greeks and Persians alike, the military potential of Greek soldiers when led against Asian forces: Persian kings of the fourth century B.C. took the point and regularly hired Greek mercenaries. But the political threat to the Persian empire had died with Cyrus II, and that lesson was not lost on his countrymen, either. Whether Cyrus's unhappy fate was due to his opponents' tactical planning or his own rashness, it provided a model for how to deal with a young, ambitious would-be conqueror at the head of a genuinely dangerous army: Lure him out and away from his main force and then cut him down at leisure. With its head amputated (given Spithridates' weapon of choice, the metaphor is particulary apt), the serpent would necessarily die. And so, what if the simple and sensible

Persian plan of "isolate and eliminate the commander" had worked at the Granicus—as it so nearly did? If Alexander had died at age twenty-two, instead of ten years later after having conquered the Persian empire, human history would have been very different indeed.

✦ ✦ ✦

With the second blow of the ax, Alexander's skull was cleaved; he died instantly. Cleitus arrived in time to dispatch his foe, and a fierce battle over the body of the fallen king ensued. The Macedonians eventually prevailed and drove back the enemy forces, but they took many casualties and the main body of the Persian forces withdrew largely intact. Moreover, King Darius III, the young, energetic, and battle-proven Persian monarch, was even now raising a huge force: Madeconian victories against Darius's local governors would be meaningless as soon as the royal army arrived in western Anatolia. Meanwhile, Darius's admirals were preparing to carry the conflict back into Greece. With no great success to report, and with the news of Alexander's death impossible to contain for long, the Macedonian expeditionary force was faced with the prospect of a major Greek uprising. With the Macedonian throne vacant; the Greeks would play the familiar game of supporting this pretender or that—and the future of every member of the Macedonian elite was bound up in the outcome of the ensuing struggle. The Macedonian war council following Granicus was brief and to the point: There was no sense in continuing the campaign, every reason to beat a quick retreat, taking whatever plunder could be grabbed up quickly on the way home. As Macedon devolved into civil war, the brief Macedonian golden age sparked by Philip's organizational genius came to an end: The next several generations closely recapitulated earlier Macedonian history, a series of weak kings in thrall variously to Greeks, Danubians, Persians, and their own strong-willed nobles.

Persia, on the other hand, entered a long period of relative peace and prosperity. Darius proved diplomatically adept and allowed the semi-Hellenized western satraps to deal with the Greeks on their own terms.

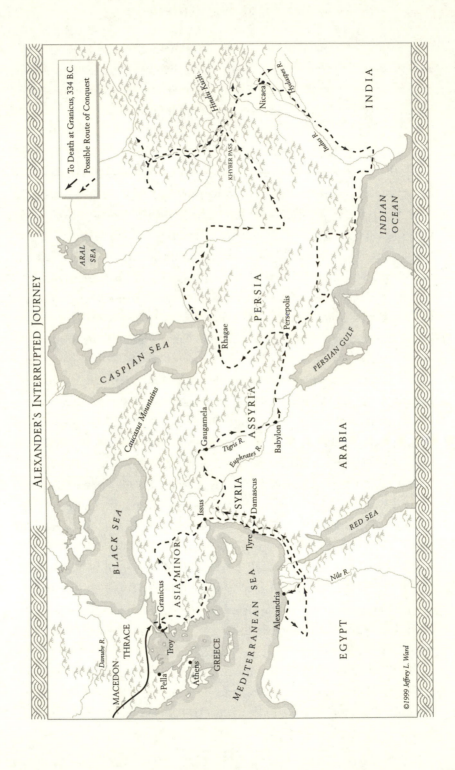

ALEXANDER'S INTERRUPTED JOURNEY

To Death at Granicus, 334 B.C.

Possible Route of Conquest

INDIA

Hindu Kush

Nicaea

Hydaspes R.

KHYBER PASS

Indus R.

ARAL SEA

INDIAN OCEAN

PERSIA

Rhagae

Persepolis

PERSIAN GULF

CASPIAN SEA

Caucasus Mountains

Gaugamela

ASSYRIA

Babylon

Tigris R.

Euphrates R.

ARABIA

Issus

SYRIA

Damascus

BLACK SEA

ASIA MINOR

Granicus

Troy

Tyre

MEDITERRANEAN SEA

RED SEA

Nile R.

Alexandria

MACEDON

THRACE

Danube R.

Pella

Athens

GREECE

EGYPT

©1999 Jeffrey L. Ward

The general modus vivendi that had pertained earlier in the fourth century was expanded: Trade between Greece, Anatolia, the Near East, and even the further reaches of the empire expanded; there was less and less reason for anyone in Greece to imagine that the Greek cities of the western Anatolian littoral would welcome "liberation" from the Persian master, and the Persians had long ago lost interest in military adventurism among the bronze-clad warriors to their west. Although the Persian kings stuck by the old and successful Persian policy of religious toleration (which helped to avoid costly uprisings among the pockets of the Empire's population that were especially touchy about matters of religious purity), the worship of the God of Light and the Truth, Ahuru-Mazda, and a cosmology based on his eternal struggle with darkness and the forces of the Lie continued to spread among the multiethnic elites of the Empire, providing some level of cultural continuity that helped to undergird Persia's conservative military policy and efficient system of taxation.

Meanwhile, in mainland Greece, the big winner was the city-state of Athens. Athens's two traditional rivals, Sparta and Thebes, were both out of the picture: Thebes had been eliminated by Alexander and Sparta never recovered from a crushing defeat at the hands of the Thebans in 371 B.C. and the subsequent liberation of Sparta's serf population in nearby Messenia. With Macedon in a state of near collapse, Athens was once again the dominant military power on mainland Greece: The Athenian navy was now larger than it had been at the height of the Periclean "golden age" in the mid-fifth century. But the Athenians saw little advantage to imperialistic adventurism on the mainland or toward the east. The democratic city had proved capable of flourishing economically without an empire, focusing on its role as an international port and trading center. With Athenian warships patrolling the Aegean, piracy was kept to a minimum. Given the generally good relations Athens was able to maintain with the western satraps of Persia, the conditions were ideal for an expansion of peaceful trade in both luxury items and bulk commodities. As Athenian trading interests expanded, so too did the ten-

51

dency for the expansive tendency of Athenian democracy to include non-natives and it became increasingly common for successful resident foreigners in Athens to be granted citizenship. Always a cultural mecca, Athens now became the unquestioned center of Greek intellectual and cultural life—there were relatively few Greek philosophers, poets, scientists, or artists who willingly lived elsewhere. As the citizen body and state revenues from harbor taxes grew in tandem, so too did the capacity for Athens to extend its influence into new zones.

The western Mediterranean beckoned: Italy, Sicily, southern Gaul, Spain, and North Africa were all quite well known to the mainland Greeks, and the Athenians had attempted the conquest of Sicily back in the late fifth century. But there was a real problem: The imperial Phoenician city-state of Carthage (located on the North African coast near modern Tunis) had long regarded overseas trade in the western Mediterranean as an exclusive Carthaginian monopoly, and the Carthaginians had backed up this policy with a strong naval presence. Tension between Carthaginian and Athenian traders eventually flared into open conflict between the two great sea powers. In the long and debilitating war that followed, neither side managed to gain a clear advantage. Both sides had large citizen populations from which to recruit rowers and marines; both had large war chests and so each side was able to augment its citizen levies with mercenary forces. Tens of thousands of men were lost in massive sea battles, and even more drowned when sudden Mediterranean storms caught fleets of oared warships too far from protective harbors.

The theater of war expanded: Other mainland Greek states, and especially the Greek cities of Sicily and southern Italy, were inevitably drawn into the fray, on one side or the other. As Athens and Carthage poured more and more of their resources into the bitter and futile war, other non-Greek states moved in to pick up the trade: Phoenicians in the east, and eventually Latin speakers from central Italy in the west. As the conflict droned on, new traders took over the routes and new trade goods from inner Asia, Egypt, and Europe came available; the popularity of

Hellenic cultural icons, for example, in architecture, decorated vases, and literature, tended to fade in the western provinces of the Persian empire. And Greek culture had never really caught on in most of the West.

With Carthage and the western Greek cities weakened by warfare, the big winner in the western Mediterranean was Rome. Only a mid-range regional power at the time of Alexander's death on the Granicus, Rome grew in strength by creating a coherent central-Italian defensive league; the influence of the league spread rapidly and Rome eventually entered the Atheno-Carthage conflict, ostensibly on the Carthaginian side. The result was the rapid absorption of all of Italy, then Sicily, and eventually a much-reduced Carthage into a rapidly growing Roman confederation that had by now become a genuine empire. A temporary truce with Athens and the mainland Greeks proved ephemeral: The Romans soon found an excuse to launch an invasion of Greece. With Athens weakened by two generations of unceasing conflict, the Roman victory was assured. But Athenian stubbornness in refusing to surrender after a lengthy siege tried Roman patience. When the walls of the city were finally breached, the Roman soldiers ran amok. The massacre was general and the city burned. Along with the extermination of Athens was lost the bulk of Greece's intellectual and cultural treasures: Only tattered remnants of Greek tragedy, comedy, philosophy, and science survived the sack. The Greek world never regained its cultural or economic vibrance; the surviving city-states were strictly controlled by the vigilant Romans. Most Romans had developed no taste for Greek culture and despised what little they knew. "Greek studies" eventually became a very minor area of the larger world of Roman antiquarian research, of interest to a few scholars with especially arcane and esoteric tastes.

The conquest of Greece brought the Romans into direct confrontation with the Persians. Yet a generation of skirmishes between the two great empires proved indecisive: Although Rome took over Egypt and so completed its conquest of North Africa, the Romans found that they did not have the manpower simultaneously to pacify their vast holdings in the west and at the same time to engage in a really effective large-scale war with Persia. For their part, the Persians had long ago given up thoughts of westward expansion; holding onto central Asia was enough of a challenge. Moreover, in the course of protracted diplomatic exchanges, the ruling elites of two great powers found that Persian and Roman aristocrats had much in common. Both cultures had immense respect for tradition and authority. Both were highly patriarchal, oriented toward duty and ancestors. The Romans found Ahuru-Mazda worship much to their liking—the starkly dualistic vision of a cosmos divided between forces of good and evil fit their worldview and they found it quite easy to integrate Ahuru-Mazda into the religious mishmash they had interited from the Etruscans. The Persians, for their part, found that adopting some aspects of Roman military organization helped them consolidate their hold on their eastern provinces. There was a fair amount of intermarriage between Roman and Persian noble families; and in time the two cultures became harder and harder to tell apart.

This is the world as we might have known it, divided into the relatively stable bipolar structure that has, from time to time, seemed self-evidently the appropriate and indeed inevitable fate of mankind. Under this international regime, the peoples of the world, almost infinitely diverse in their cultures and their beliefs, simply remained so—there was (for better or for worse) no hegemonic "master culture" or "central canon" to unite them. This means that there would have been no Renaissance, no Enlightenment, no "modernity." The very concept of "the Western World" as exemplifying a set of more or less clearly articulated (if always contested and imperfectly realized) cultural, political, and ethical ideals would never have arisen.

There would perhaps have been occasional outbreaks of religious enthusiasm, but these would have remained local matters, never to transcend the provincial level. For indeed by what means could they become generalized? While Latin in the West and Aramaic in the East would prove workable adminstrative languages, they were not hospitable linguistic environments for transcultural exchanges. Traders inevitably would have learned a few languages, but most people would continue to speak their own local language and nothing but, live by local laws, worship their local deities, tell their local stories, and think their local ideas. Their contact with whichever of the great empires they happened to inhabit would be limited to paying taxes and occasional military service. The peculiarities of diverse cultures might be of interest to the state-supported scholars who would make it their business to collect and categorize knowledge about the world; but these would remain few and would be supported by the governments of the two empires only because abstruse knowledge sometimes comes in handy in dealing with problems of tax collection or keeping order.

✦ ✦ ✦

And so, if Cleitus had stumbled as he hastened to save his king, we would inhabit a world very different from our own in terms of geopolitics, religion, and culture. I have suggested that it would be a world in which the values characteristic of the Greek city-states were lost in favor of a fusion of Roman and Persian ideals. The stark dualism of Ahuru-Mazda worship became the dominant religious tradition. A profound reverence for ritual, tradition, ancestors, and social hierarchy—rather than Greek reverence for freedom, political equality, and the dignity of the person— defined the ethical values of a small "cosmopolitan" elite that would rule over a diverse mosaic of cultures. And this could take place because there was no long and brilliant "Hellenistic Period"—and so no integration of a wider world into a Greek cultural/linguistic sphere.

Without the challenge of strong Greek cultural influence and subsequent Roman mismanagement in Judea, Judaism would have remained a localized phenomenon. The Persians were quite sensitive to local religious concerns; under continued Persian rule there would have been no great Maccabee uprising, no Greek Septuagint, no violent Roman destruction of the Second Temple, no great Jewish diaspora. Likewise, Jesus of Nazareth (had he not chosen to stick to carpentry) would remain a local religious figure. The New Testament (whatever form it took) would never have been composed in "universal" Greek and so would not have found a broad audience. Without the wide diffusion of Jewish and Christian texts, the cultural domain in which Mohammed grew up would have been radically altered; if a new religion emerged within the Arabian peninsula it would take a form quite different from that of classical Islam and it seems highly unlikely that it would have generated the remarkable cultural and military energies we associate with the great Jihad. Indeed, the very concept of "culture" would have a very different meaning; culture would remain overwhelmingly local rather than developing viable aspirations to universality.

Ironically, the values of our own world, which I have suggested is a result of Alexander's good luck at the Granicus, would not have pleased Cleitus the Black. As a staunch Macedonian conservative who despised innovation, Cleitus would be more likely to approve of the counterfactual Romano-Persian regime described above. But Cleitus did not live to see the world his spear thrust made: Seven years after saving his king at Granicus, he was speared to death by Alexander in a drunken quarrel over the cultural future of the nascent empire. Their quarrel, even more ironically, was (as it turned out) over contrasting counterfactual scenarios: Cleitus believed that Macedonians should stick by their traditions and should have nothing to do with the customs of the people they conquered; he dreamed of a world in which the victorious Macedonians would be culturally unaffected by their military success. Alexander, seeking to unify his empire and to gain the manpower needed for future conquests, was eager to adopt Persian court ritual and to train Persian soldiers to fight side by side with his Macedonian veterans. But neither Cleitus's Macedonia-first conservatism nor Alexander's hope for a unitary empire and unending imperial expansionism had much to do with the real new world that came into being upon Alexander's very timely death in Babylon, at age thirty-two, in June of 323 B.C.

LEWIS H. LAPHAM

# FUROR TEUTONICUS: THE TEUTOBURG FOREST, A.D. 9

T*he first century* A.D. *saw the Roman Empire near its height. Its capital, Rome, was not just the center, but the envy, of the known world. In the words of the classicist Edith Hamilton, the Emperor Augustus (63* B.C.–A.D. *14) had "found Rome a city of bricks and left her a city of marble." The newest target for imperial expansion was the wilderness region beyond the Rhine known as Germany. Then in* A.D. *9, twenty-two years into pacifying, civilizing, and homogenizing— its traditional modus operandi for barbarian lands—Rome suffered a reverse there from which it never recovered. In the Teutoburg Forest, tribesmen led by a chieftain named Arminius surprised and annihilated three Roman legions—15,000 men plus camp followers. Arminius had the heads of his victims nailed to trees: It provided a telling psychological message that was not lost on Rome. Violence became its own reward. The empire retreated behind the Rhine and, except for occasional forays, left Germany alone.*

*Almost two millennia later, we have to wonder what kind of imprint a Romanized Germany would have left on history. What if Germany had not remained for cen-*

turies a frontier, one of Europe's last—with a frontier mentality, in its darker manifestations especially, that the descendants of Arminius—or Hermann, as he was later called—have never completely surrendered? What if Arminius had not become a kind of Shanelike figure but just another co-opted local prince? What if the Roman Empire, with its temples, amphitheaters, and system of law, had extended to the Vistula? Would we have ever considered the dire prospect of a "German Question"?

✦   Lewis H. Lapham deals with some of those possibilities in the following essay. Lapham is the editor of Harper's magazine and the winner of the National Magazine Award for his essays, which have been likened to those of H. L. Mencken and Montaigne. He is the author of eight books, including two just published, THE AGONY OF MAMMON and LAPHAM'S RULES OF INFLUENCE. He is a well-known lecturer and television host.

> You may not be interested in war, but war is interested in you.
>
> *—Leon Trotsky*

During the first decade of the era not yet revealed as Christian, the Emperor Caesar Augustus was more concerned with military dispatches from Mainz than with reports of miracles at Bethlehem. He had ruled as princeps for nearly thirty years, dictating an end both to the Roman republic and a century of civil war, and at all points of the imperial compass his augurs observed auspicious omens— tranquility in Egypt, peace in Africa and Spain, the Parthians quiescent, vineyards in Aquitaine, gymnasia in Cyzicus and no cloud of rebellion anywhere on the blue horizon of the Mediterranean world.

Except, of course, in Germany. Augustus wasn't familiar with the song of Seigfried or the insignia of the thousand-year Reich, but as an army commander in the wilderness east of the Rhine he had come up against the Germanic tribes known to his legions as the Furor Teutonicus, a horde of superstitious barbarians, invariably hostile and usually drunk, worshippers of horses and moonlight, keeping their primitive calendar by counting nights instead of days, roaming like wolves through fog and snow.

Augustus assumed that eventually it would occur to one of their chieftains to turn the wagons south, and he had it in mind to prevent that accident by extending the frontier of the empire as far north as the Elbe River, possibly as far east as the Vistula and the Baltic Sea, the force of arms followed by a show of aqueducts and apple trees and the Goths reduced, as Julius Caesar had reduced the Gauls west and south of the

Rhine, to a harmless rabble of submissive colonies, "well supplied with luxuries and accustomed to defeat."

The policy was optimistic but not implausible. The Roman power in the first Century A.D. brooked neither rival nor contradiction, and its magistrates were in the habit of issuing writs of omnipotence in the name of a monarchy comprehending, in Edward Gibbon's phrase, "the fairest part of the earth and the most civilized portion of mankind," the obedient provinces, "united by laws and adorned by arts," the roads running in straight lines from the Atlantic Ocean to the Euphrates, the frontiers defended by "the spirit of a people incapable of fear and impatient of repose." If Augustus had managed to accomplish his German project, giving it the weight of milestones as well as colors on a map, the course of European history over the next 2,000 years might have taken a very different set of turns—the Roman empire preserved from ruin, Christ dying intestate on an unremembered cross, the nonappearance of the English language, neither the need nor the occasion for a Protestant reformation, Frederick the Great a circus dwarf, and Kaiser Wilhelm seized by an infatuation with stamps or water beetles instead of a passion for cavalry boots.

The Romans began the work of German pacification in 13 B.C., the year that Tiberius, the emperor's heir and stepson, brought his legions across the Alps into Austria, lower Wirtemberg, and the Tyrol. A temple to Jupiter appeared at Cologne, and soon afterward the construction of naval fortifications at the mouths of the rivers opening the German wilderness to an approach from the North Sea. The more prominent barbarians received the favor of Roman citizenship, their intransigence tempered by the music of flutes, their suspicions relieved by gifts of silk and gold. Their sons acquired an acquaintance with the Latin language, learning to fasten their cloaks with jewels instead of thorns, and for twenty years the lines of Roman settlement edged eastward into the Westphalian forest.

But in A.D. 6, the barbarians in the province Illyricum, the modern-day Balkans, rose in murderous revolt, and Tiberius was sent from Trier to punish their presumption. The brutal lesson in civility lasted three years, and while it was in progress Augustus assigned the continuing education of the Germanic tribes to Publius Quinctilius Varus. The plan was sound, but Augustus entrusted it to the wrong Roman. A soft and complacent man, Varus at the age of fifty-five owed the favor of his promotion to his marriage with the emperor's grandniece. He had served as proconsul in Africa and legate in Syria, but his knowledge of military strategy derived from the gossip of his subordinates, and his character was that of a palace functionary—dissembling, avaricious, indolent, and vain.

As "Governor of Germany across the Rhine," Varus assumed command of the empire's three most formidable legions, and he arrived from Italy with the opinion that his army was invincible and the barbarians broken to the harness of Roman law. Neither supposition proved correct, but Varus, of whom it was later said, "Fate blindfolded the eyes of his mind," didn't take much interest in facts he found disagreeable or inconvenient. He conceived his task as administrative and relied on his belief that Augustus, his wife's fond and careful uncle, wouldn't have sent him to Germany unless the work was easy. Choosing to regard Germanic tribes as easily acquired slaves rather than as laboriously recruited allies, he forced upon them a heavy burden of taxation in the belief that they would come to love him as a wise father.

Among the barbarians serving as officers on his staff, Varus bestowed the greater part of his trust and affection on Arminius, a prince of the Cherusci who had campaigned with Tiberius in Illyricum and appreciated the poetry of Horace. The contemporary historian Velleius describes Arminius as a fiercely handsome man in his late twenties, "brave in action and alert in mind, possessing an intelligence quite beyond the ordinary barbarian." He also possessed a talent for duplicity well beyond the intelligence of Varus, who thought of him as his most devoted flatterer. Arminius took the trouble to profess his admiration for all things Roman, meanwhile making the preliminary arrangements for a literal-minded performance (no orchestra, no costumes, nothing operatic) of Götterdämmerung.

The chance presented itself in the autumn of A.D. 9. Several days before Varus moved his three legions—15,000 infantry in company with 10,000 women, children, auxiliaries, slaves, and pack animals—for their summer encampment near Minden to winter quarters further west, apparently somewhere near the modern town of Haltern. Arminius disclosed the line of march to those of the Cherusci, who shared his resentment of the empire. The malcontents recruited like-minded allies among the Chatti and Bructeri, and halfway between the two military strong points, in the thickly wooded ravines of the Teutoburg Forest, a mob of screaming barbarians fell upon the Roman column.

The historians still argue about the exact whereabouts of the ensuing massacre, and over the last several hundred years they have deployed the meager literary and archeological remains—old manuscripts, gold and silver coins found buried in peat moss, shards of Roman armor, the local place names of Knochenbahn (Bone Lane) and Mordkessel (The Kettle of Death)—to suggest as many as 700 theories about the likely point of attack. Some historians place Varus's column among the upper tributaries of the Ems River, others place it nearer the rivers Lippe or Weser, but all the authorities agree that the Romans died like penned cattle. The difficulty of the terrain (a narrow causeway between steep embankments, the wet ground "treacherous and slippery around the roots and logs," overturned wagons, bewildered children, horses dying in the mud) prevented the legions from bringing to bear their superior weapons and tactics. Trained to fight in the open field, they carried heavy javelins and the short Spanish sword with which they were accustomed to cutting down their enemies in the manner of farmers reaping wheat. But in the German forest they were caught in a tangle of trees, encumbered by a baggage train strung out over a distance of nine miles, unable to form their cohorts into disciplined lines. The barbarians began the attack at dusk, hurling their spears from the rock outcroppings higher up on the hillsides, and during three days and three nights of leisurely slaughter in a cold and steady rain, they annihilated the entire Roman army. Varus committed suicide. So did every other officer who knew that it was the practice of the Cherusci to nail their vanquished but still living enemies to the trunks of sacred oak trees.

Arminius sent Varus's head to Maroboduus, a barbarian king in Bohemia on whom he wished to make a favorable impression, and Maroboduus, for diplomatic reasons of his own, forwarded the head to Rome. Dio Cassius reports the effect as memorable, Augustus so shocked by the utter destruction of so fine an army that he "rent his garments and was in great affliction," and Gibbon remarks on the emperor's consternation with his familiar irony, ". . . Augustus did not receive the melancholy news with all the temper and firmness that might have been expected from his character."

The fear of barbarian invasion drifted through the city with rumors of strange and terrifying portent—the summit of the Alps was said to have fallen into a lake of fire, the temple of Mars struck by a thunderbolt, many comets and blazing meteors seen in the northern sky, the statue of Victory, which had been placed at a crossroads pointing the way toward Germany, inexplicably turned in the opposite direction, pointing the way into Italy. Suetonious speaks of the emperor dedicating extravagant games to Jupiter Best and Greatest on condition that the Germans failed to appear on the Palatine and Capitoline Hills. Augustus declared the day of Varus's death a day of national mourning; for many months he refused to cut his hair or trim his beard, and from time to time until the end of his life, at the age of seventy-seven in A.D. 14, he was to be seen wandering through the rooms of his palace, beating his head against a wall and crying out, in a voice the historians describe as thin and old, "Quinctilius Varus, give me back my legions."

Mocked by the defeat in the Teutoburg Forest, Augustus abandoned the project of civilizing the German wilderness, and in the will that he left to his successor, Tiberius, he bequeathed the virtue of prudence—"Be satisfied with the status quo and suppress completely any desire to increase the empire to greater size." By and large, Tiberius heeded the advice, but in A.D. 15 he allowed his nephew, Germanicus, to undertake a revengeful campaign against the Cherusci. Germanicus burned crops and pagan temples, murdered large numbers of barbarians (many of them women and children, quite a few of them in their sleep) and in a dark wood between the Lippe and Ems Rivers, his army came across the remnants of their former companions-in-arms, a scene that Tacitus describes in the *Annals* as one "that lived up to its horrible associations . . . whitening bones, scattered where men had fled, heaped up where they had stood and fought back. Fragments of spears and of horses' limbs lay there, also human heads, fastened to tree trunks." Germanicus's army recovered two of the three golden eagles lost with the legions of Varus, but it didn't manage to defeat Arminius in a decisive battle, and on its recall to Rome in A.D. 16, Tiberius adopted the policy of settling the empire's northern boundary along the angle formed by the Danube and the upper Rhine.

✦ ✦ ✦

The Roman withdrawal left the Furor Teutonicus unmolested by amphitheaters and well-supplied with spears and drinking songs. The barbarian clans knew Arminius by the name of Hermann, and they proclaimed him first a hero and then a legend. Their enthusiasm was approved by Tacitus, who refers to Arminius as "unmistakably the liberator of Germany. Challenger of Rome—not in its infancy, like kings and commanders before him, but at the height of its power . . . to this day the tribes sing of him." It didn't matter that Arminius failed in his attempt to unite the northern tribes in the cause of German independence; nor did it matter that in A.D. 21, at the age of thirty-eight, he was assassinated by his own clansmen, who objected to his proclaiming himself a king. His mistakes were forgiven because he had defied the majesty and cynicism of Rome, not only in the Teutoburg Forest but also in pitched battles against legions under the command of both Germanicus and Tiberius, and the memory of him was consecrated in the blood of his enemies.

Tacitus wrote his histories during the reign of Trajan, and his disappointment in the character of the emperors subsequent to Augustus inclined him to present the imagined virtues of the noble savage (loyal, freedom-loving, chaste) as moral counterpoint to the certain viciousness of Caligula and the proven decadence of Nero and Domitian—"No one in Germany finds vice amusing, or calls it 'up-to-date' to seduce and be seduced." Elaborating the theme in the *Germania*, Tacitus praises the Saxon tribes for their self-sufficiency, for having attained "that hardest-of-results, the not needing so much as a wish," and in recognition of their strength and courage he gives voice to the hope that they "ever retain, if not love for us, at least hatred for each other; for while the destinies of empire hurry us on, fortune can give no greater boon than discord among our foes."

The German inheritors of the tale adorned it through successive generations with the heavy ornament of Teutonic myth. During the third and fourth centuries A.D. the name and triumph of Arminius served as a metaphor for the valor of the barbarians crowding south upon the decay of Rome. The eighth century associated the old story with the glory of Charlemagne, the twelfth century with the conquests of Frederick Barbarossa; the chroniclers of the high Middle Ages extended the compliment of comparison to the dynasties of Hapsburg, Wittelsbach, and Holenzollern. By the end of the eighteenth century, Hermann was at one with Seigfried in the halls of Valhalla, and when the fury of early nineteenth century German romanticism descended upon the town of Detmold, the citizens voted to erect a colossal statue of Hermann on the summit of the highest mountain in the Teutoburger Wald. Nobody knew exactly where Varus had kept his appointment with doom, but Detmold was certainly somewhere in the vicinity, and the town council imagined the great hero triumphant with uplifted sword, the statue mounted on gothic columns hewn from living oak, the whole of the edifice rising to a height of nearly 2,000 feet and visible at a distance of sixty miles.

The enterprise failed for lack of funds, but what couldn't be rendered in bronze found expression in scholarship, in the work of the late nineteenth-century historians (in Britain and France as well as in Germany) advancing the several flags of European nationalism. Leopold von Ranke discovered in the prowess of Hermann an early proof of Aryan supremacy—stalwart blond people, blue-eyed and fair-skinned, resisting the advance of the mongrel races enlisted under the imperial eagles of Roman luxury and greed. Several French intellectuals traced the wonders of Newtonian science to the ancient freedoms of the German forest, and Sir Edward Creasy, prominent in Victorian England as both historian and lecturer, thought Arminius worthy of a statue in Trafalgar Square. "Had Arminius been supine or unsuccessful," said Sir Edward, in *Fifteen Decisive Battles of the World*, "this island never would have borne the name England." The book appeared to favorable reviews in 1852, and the next two generations of British and American historians (among them Teddy Roosevelt) endorsed Creasy's theory of the Roman Empire as a corruption of "debased Italians" deserving of defeat at the hands of purebred Anglo-Saxons notable for "their bravery, their fidelity to their word, their manly independence of spirit, their love of their natural free institutions, and their loathing of every pollution and meanness." Richard Wagner set the words to music, and the American pioneers carried them west against the Sioux, and the rulers of Nazi Germany fitted them to the design of Auschwitz.

✦　✦　✦

Begin the sequence of historical event with a different set of circumstances in a German forest in the autumn of A.D. 9 (dry weather, Varus a competent general, the rage of Arminius modified by a second reading of Virgil's *Georgics*), and Adolf Hitler might not have danced his victorious jig in a French forest in the spring of 1940. Augustus wouldn't have known how to read Luther's Bible or the flashes of Gestapo uniform (the Furor Teutonicus not having yet acquired the art of letters) but if a few words in a Gothic script appeared one afternoon on the column of a Roman peristyle, the emperor could have guessed well enough at their probable meaning. Germany-across-the-Rhine he regarded as the antithesis of civilization, a wilderness "thankless to till and dismal to behold," and although he was by no means given to a republican practice or democratic sentiment, he understood the uses of poets, the fictions of government, the glory of bees. "Wheresoever a Roman conquers," said

## A ROMAN GERMANY

*Mare Germanicum*

BRITANNIA

SCANDIA

*Mare Suevicum*

*F. Albis*

*F. Vistula*

*F. Rhenus*

*F. Viadua (Oder)*

G E R M A N I A

Germania Inferior

BELGICA

Germania Superior

RHAETIA

*F. Danubius*

NORICUM

PANNONIA

LUGDUNENSIS

GAUL

AQUITANIA

NARBONENSIS

I T A L I A

*Mare Adriaticum*

*F. Danubius*

ILLYRICUM

*Mare Tyrrhenum*

• Roma

©1999 Jeffrey L. Ward

## BATTLE OF THE TEUTOBURG FOREST, A.D. 9

North Sea

Baltic Sea

■ Hamburg

*Elbe R.*

• Bremen

G E R M A N I A

*Werre R.*

*Weser R.*

Kalkriese
Osnabrück

*Ijssel R.*

*Ems R.*

• Minden

*Rhine R.*

■ *Lippe R.*

Paderborn

| | |
|---|---|
| ▲ | Imperial Camps |
| ■ | Imperial Fortifications and Depots |
| ✗ | Possible Battle Sites |
| → | Possible Routes of Varus's Legions |
| 🌲 | Teutoburg Forest |

©1999 Jeffrey L. Ward

Seneca, "he inhabits," and if Augustus had fostered the planting of orchards as far north as Berlin, the empire thus strengthened and enlarged might have denied passage to the Mongols, admitted Moscow to the freedom of Rome, found in the aureus an early equivalent of the euro.

Nine centuries after the collapse of the Roman power, Western Europe constructed the premise of the Renaissance on the rediscovered blueprints of Latin literature—Cicero's politics, Virgil's verse forms, the histories of Tacitus and Livy, Ovid's metaphysics, Martial's epigrams. The first translations emerge in those countries that retained a memory of the empire (in Italy, England, and France, not in Germany, and nowhere east of the Vistula), but it was another 300 years before the models of classic antiquity began to be handed around among the advisors to the courts at Brandenburg and Dresden. The delay possibly accounts for the German confusion about imperialism (its nature and purpose, the distinction between diplomacy and *blitzkrieg*) that provided the twentieth century with the *causus belli* for two world wars.

Assume as antecedent that Roman conquest of Germany in the first and second centuries A.D. and the improvisation of derivative narratives no doubt could entertain a faculty of historians for the whole of a college semester. The professors might choose to set up their propositions in the manner of a board game, playing Bismark and the *ubermensch* against the drawings of Albrecht Dürer and the cantatas of Johann Sebastian Bach. No doubt they would quibble over the relative value of Schiller's lyrics and Hindenburg's artillery shells, but I suspect that the general tone of conversation would tend to prefer the solemn calm of empires to the crowd noises of the unruly provinces.

Gibbon published his history of Rome's decline and fall in 1776, the same year in which the American colonies declared themselves independent of the British crown; the tide of the Enlightenment was turning to the ebb, and within the next fifty years it was followed by a surge of revolutionary romance—in Mexico and Brazil as well as France and Germany. New definitions of freedom gave rise to the belief that even the smallest quorum of nationalist identity deserves the status of a sovereign state. The Treaty of Versailles returned the administration of Illyricum to the incompetence of the Balkan tribes, and I can imagine both Gibbon and Augustus comparing the foolishness of Woodrow Wilson to the stupidity of Publius Quinctilius Varus. A similar prejudice informs the writing of the contemporary diplomats and foreign policy analysts who mourn the absence of "transnational institutions" capable of managing the world's affairs with the sang-froid of the old Roman empire. Confronted with the chaos of unregulated capital markets—also with rogue states and renegade ideologies, with war in Africa, civil unrest in Judea, tyrants in Parthia and Leptis Minor, too much cocaine crossing the frontier near Chalcedon, too many poisons in the Mediterranean Sea—the would-be makers of a postmodern peace dream of Gibbon's "supreme magistrate, who by the progress of knowledge and flattery was gradually invested with the sublime perfections of an Eternal Parent and an Omnipotent Monarch." Augustus would have been pleased to grant them an audience.

BARRY S. STRAUSS

# THE DARK AGES
# MADE LIGHTER

*The Consequences of*
*Two Defeats*

This chapter is the story of two battles and what might have happened if their
results had been reversed—as well they might have been. Both involved
powers on the cusp of advance or retreat. In the first, Adrianople (A.D.
378), the Roman Empire suffered a disaster even worse than that of the Teutoburg
Forest, and one that went far to send it reeling into its final decline. In the second,
Poitiers (probably 732), a Frankish army turned back Muslim invaders near the
Loire River at the moment when they seemed ready to spread across Europe—"The
Great Land," as they called it.

Did the Roman Empire—or at least the part of it that dominated Western Europe—have to die and so give birth to the Dark Ages? Did the Dark Ages themselves
(which may not have been all that dark) have to happen? As Barry S. Strauss tells us,
much of the blame may fall less on Spenglerian fatigue than on the poor judgment of
one man, the emperor Valens, who squandered an army in a battle that he should
have avoided or delayed fighting. (Adrianople—the present Turkish city of Edirne—
has the distinction of being the most fought-over city in the world, Valens's fatal re-

71

verse being one of fifteen major battles or sieges that have taken place there in just short of 1,700 years.) The Visogoths who slaughtered Valens's troops, and who also killed him, would eventually move west to capture and sack the city of Rome itself. By that time the empire was all but beyond rescue. It did not have to be that way, Strauss argues. What would a world that Rome continued to lead have been like?

The dynamism that had once belonged to the Roman Empire would pass to a new locus of power: Arabia. Less than a century after the death of the prophet Mohammed in 632, the armies of Islam had established rule as far west as Spain—the kingdom they called Al-Andalus. How important was Poitiers? Strauss comes down on the side of those historians who see it as a turning point. It certainly brought us the foremost dynasty of early medieval Europe, the Carolingians: Charlemagne was the grandson of the victor, Charles Martel. But if the battle had gone differently, so might history. As an anonymous Muslim chronicler put it: "On the plain of Tours [as the battle is sometimes called] the Arabs lost the empire of the world when almost in their grasp." It would have been an empire full of luster: These Arabs were the foremost broadcasters of enlightenment in their time.

Both Adrianople and Poitiers are cases of what might be called first-order counterfactual theory—that is, a major rewriting of history stemming from small changes. How different would our lives have been if only Valens had been more patient. If only Abd Al-Rahman, the Muslim commander at Poitiers, had survived to rally his forces.

♦ Barry S. Strauss is professor of history and classics and the director of the peace studies program at Cornell University. His books include FATHERS AND SONS IN ATHENS, THE ANATOMY OF ERROR: ANCIENT MILITARY DISASTERS AND THEIR LESSONS FOR MODERN STRATEGISTS (with Josiah Ober), and ROWING AGAINST THE CURRENT: ON LEARNING TO SCULL AT FORTY.

In the European early Middle Ages two events took place—the fall of the Roman Empire in the West and the Muslim tidal wave of conquest—that might have changed everything had they turned out differently. Had imperial Rome maintained control of Europe or had imperial Islam restored a single, central authority there, Europe would have been spared the chaos of the Dark Ages (ca. A.D. 500–1000). To be sure, even chaos can yield dividends in the long run: Some would say that the Dark Ages sowed the seeds of later Western freedom; others deny that there was anything dark about them. Yet dark or bright, they undeniably lacked the order and stability that an empire brings. The fate of an empire, be it Roman or Muslim, may have hinged on battles—battles whose results could have gone either way.

True, the rise and fall of an empire is a long process, but the heaviest doors pivot on small hinges, and at the battles of Adrianople (August 9, 378) and Poitiers (October 732) the hinges turned. At Adrianople, a Germanic people, the Visigoths, destroyed a Roman army and killed the emperor, thereby setting in motion a century of defeats that would finally bring down the empire in the West. Yet it was a near-run thing. A little patience on the part of the commander, a little rest for the men, a change in the weather—any of these might have changed the outcome at Adrianople and ultimately saved the Roman Empire. At Poitiers, a Frankish force defeated a Muslim army. It was a smaller engagement than Adrianople but it proved a psychological and political turning point, because it blunted the triumphant Arab advance northward and because it propelled the efforts of the Frankish general Charles Martel to establish a dynasty. Under his grandson Charlemagne (r. 768–814), that dynasty governed a far-flung state that laid the foundations for much of what would follow in Europe—from kingdoms like France and Germany to local government by royal vassals to the Christian culture of cathedral schools and decorated manuscripts. Yet had the Frankish army not killed the Muslim commander that day at Poitiers, they might have lost the battle; Europe would have lost the family that built a great Frankish state; and what might have emerged, instead, was a Muslim France or even a Muslim Europe.

Historians no longer think of early medieval Europe outside of Spain as the time and place of the Dark Ages but rather as the seedtime of European greatness. Where historians once saw a sharp break between Rome and its Germanic conquerors, they now find continuities in the "Romano-German" kingdoms; where once they perceived poverty and misery, they now see prosperous trading networks and free farm laborers; where once they saw cultural decline, they now find creativity—in Celtic manuscripts, for example, or the poetry of *Beowulf,* or the monasticism of the Benedictines. In short, many scholars no longer ask whether the Dark Ages could have been avoided because they don't believe they should have been avoided.

Yet not even the most sunny interpretation of the fifth to tenth centuries A.D. can dodge gloom altogether, not in Western Europe. Around A.D. 350, a single empire—Rome—governed much of the Near East and North Africa, as well as what is now England, France, Belgium, the Netherlands, Spain, Italy, Switzerland, and western Germany. Then violent invasions began to tear that empire apart. In the east, the Roman Empire survived as the Byzantine state for a thousand years, until the Turkish conquest of Constantinople in 1453. In the West, the last Roman emperor was dethroned in 476, a generation after the Western empire had become little more than a legal fiction. The Western empire had been tottering for years. Roman land was plundered, Roman cities were attacked—Rome itself was sacked in 410 and 455—Roman men were killed and Roman women were dragged off as war booty to marry Germanic chiefs. The central government could not stop foreigners from settling en masse on Roman lands and from eventually carving out separate kingdoms in the Roman state. The population declined enough for Pope

Gelasius (r. 492–496) to write of "Emilia, Tuscany, and the other provinces [of Italy] in which nearly not a single human existed." An exaggeration, but what really happened can be seen in the fate of the city of Rome, which may have contained one million people in the time of Christ, but by the ninth century A.D. had a population of about 25,000. By contrast, in the tenth century A.D. Córdoba, the capital of Muslim Spain, had a population of about 100,000, and Seville perhaps 60,000. In short, a single Roman Empire was replaced by smaller states, and in the process, society became more violent and less urbanized.

Europe would have been spared violence, anarchy, and misery if the Roman Empire could have survived or, once having fallen, it could have been pieced back together again. Which is why the battles of Adrianople and Poitiers are so important and so tantalizing. Each could have had a different result, if just a few changes are imagined. Let us examine each in turn.

✦ ✦ ✦

Throughout its long history, the Roman state had to face continual military challenges from the warlike peoples on its frontiers. A double threat confronted Rome in the fourth century A.D., with Persia on the rise in the east and various Germanic peoples pushing from the north. In response to frequent emergencies, the empire was divided in two, with one emperor in Constantinople and another at Rome—or rather, at Milan, the de facto Western capital because it was closer to the battle zone.

In the early fourth century A.D. the Visigoths, a Germanic people, had settled north of the Danube in Dacia (modern Romania), formerly a Roman province. About fifty years later they were invaded by other Germanic tribes, who were in turn fleeing from the Huns, a ferocious people who had ridden out of central Asia. Pushed to the point of famine, in A.D. 376, the Visigoths asked the government in Constantinople for permission to cross the Danube to seek refuge—and a permanent home—in Roman Thrace, all 200,000 or so of them, including women and children (to follow a reasonable modern estimate of numbers). It would be mass emigration of a people who gave the Romans the shivers. Yet the Eastern emperor, Valens (r. 364–378) agreed to their request.

He was no humanitarian. Valens knew that the Visigoths were dangerous warriors but he planned to co-opt them and add them to his armies, which already had a Visigothic contingent. He needed more soldiers to fight Persia. He also knew that Visigothic refugees would bring wealth with them, which his officials could skim off if not plunder outright—corruption being a depressing reality of Late Roman administration. In return, he insisted that the Visigoths lay down their arms when they crossed the Danube. The Visigoths agreed, but Valens should have known better.

No sooner did the Visigoths cross the Danube then they came into conflict with Roman officials, who outdid themselves in coming up with creative ways to fleece the refugees. The trouble was, the Visigoths fought back. In early 377 they began a revolt that defeated a Roman army and spread among other aggrieved groups such as miners and slaves. Eventually, with the help of a large cavalry contingent from their allies, they forced a Roman retreat. "The barbarians," writes the Roman historian Ammianus Marcellinus, "poured over the wide extent of Thrace like wild animals escaping from their cage."

In spring 378, the Emperor Valens prepared to counterattack with an army estimated at thirty to forty thousand men. Meanwhile, the Western emperor, Valens's nephew Gratian (r. 367–383), marched to his aid from Raetia (roughly Switzerland) where, the winter before, he had defeated other Germanic invaders. Unfortunately, Valens "rose to the level of his mediocrity," as we might say today. He had the opportunity to crush a cornered, but by no means defeated enemy; he turned it instead into disaster. Instead of waiting for Gratian's reinforcements, Valens insisted on fighting—according to critics, he did not want to share the glory of victory. In his overconfidence he gave credence to intelligence reports that the Visigoths had only 10,000 men (we don't know how many men they did have but it was far more than that). The battle would take place on

**ISLAM CHECKED AT THE BATTLE OF POITIERS**

*Charles Martel, flourishing a battle ax, center, inspires his Christian Frankish troops to defeat the Muslim Moors at Poitiers. Had the Arabs won the battle in 732, would Islam have continued to spread across Europe?*

(Carl von Steuben, 1788–1856, Battle of Poitiers. Giraudon/Art Resource, NY)

the plains near the city of Adrianople (modern Edirne, in Turkey) and it would take place immediately. It was August 9, 378.

Barbarians the Visigoths might have been, but their leader, Fritigern, had a sure instinct for the enemy's weak points, none more important than Valens himself. The emperor sent his men into battle in the broiling heat of an August afternoon in the Balkans (summer temperatures of 100 degrees Fahrenheit are common in the region) with no rest or food after an eight-mile march over rough country. The Visigoths, encamped behind a circle of wagons, were surprised by the Romans, but their men were rested and they used their opportunity well. First, they deftly sent their cavalry to turn the Roman lines and trap the legionnaires between the wagons and the Visigothic infantry. Ammianus Marcellinus describes that fateful ride: "The Gothic cavalry . . . shot forward like a bolt from on high and routed with great slaughter all that they could come to grips with in their wild career."

Then, having attacked the Romans with their cavalry first on one side and then the other, the Visigoths hit them head on with their infantry. They slaughtered the closely packed enemy troops.

It is estimated that as many as two-thirds of the Romans in the battle were killed, including thirty-five high-ranking officers. The greatest casualty was Valens himself. The catastrophe is made all the more poignant by the knowledge that it could have been avoided. Had the emperor waited for reinforcements or, failing that, had he attacked with fed and rested men the next morning, the outcome would probably have been different. Nor can we underestimate the role of accident. The Visigothic cavalry only arrived on the battlefield at the last minute; had they been detained further, there would have been no Visigothic victory. Keenly aware of their importance, Fritigern played for time by sending various negotiators to the Romans until the eleventh hour. The Roman high command might even have accepted his offer to parley, but the troops took matters into their own hands. Roman archers and cavalry disobeyed orders and began to attack the Visigoths, thereby forcing battle. So perhaps the fate of the Roman Empire lay in the hands of a nervous skirmisher.

Flush with victory, the Visigoths were now free to roam the Balkans. The loss of perhaps 20,000 to 25,000 men was big enough to imperil Rome's manpower needs. It was, said St. Ambrose of Milan on hearing the news of the battle, "The end of all humanity, the end of the world." It was, at any rate, the end of the old Roman ability to bounce back from defeat, so prominent a feature of the empire's previous history. Far from closing in for the kill, Rome allowed the enemy to settle within the boundaries of the empire, south of the Danube, in the area of modern

Bulgaria. Worse still, Rome allowed the Visigoths to keep their arms. They were, in theory, allies of Rome, but in practice they were a rival state. In the 390s, for example, the Visigoths looted Greece and the Balkans, and then, after 400, they did the same to Italy. The height of disaster came in 410, when the Visigoths, led by the wily and aggressive Alaric, took the city of Rome and sacked it for three days. It was a sign of things to come for the tottering empire.

Why did the Romans tolerate Visigothic settlement within the empire? For one thing, they needed the Visigoths as soldiers, and the Romans believed they could co-opt and tame them. Second, as Roger Collins argues, defeatism may have been at work. For many Romans, the lesson of Adrianople seems to have been that Rome could not prevail in battle against the enemy. At least, that may explain why four times between 395 and 405, in Italy and the Balkans, Roman armies fought and beat the Visigoths under Alaric, but each time they allowed them—and him—to escape and fight again. It is hard not to wonder whether Adrianople had done to Rome what the Battle of Verdun (1916) did to France—not in its military outcome, for France won at Verdun, but in its psychological outcome. The bloody battle devastated French morale for a generation and weakened military manpower badly.

Thirty years after Adrianople, Alaric and the Visigoths were in Italy. After sacking Rome, they eventually settled in Gaul and Spain. In the meantime, to save Italy, the Roman government had to withdraw troops from Britain and Gaul, which gave other Germanic tribes the opportunity to invade the empire. Britain was lost to Rome after 407, and within a generation large parts of Gaul, Spain, and North Africa were effectively independent. Now largely dependent on barbarian mercenaries to defend it, Rome had traveled far down the road to 476, when the Germans in Italy deposed the last Western Roman emperor, Romulus Augustus (r. 475–476), whose "empire" was mere fiction.

What could have been done? Arther Ferrill maintains that Rome's best hope would have been to reverse the outcome of Adrianople; that is, to win the battle, kill the Visigoths' commander, Fritigern, and two-thirds of his men. That would not have ended the security threat, because there was no shortage of barbarians ready to probe the empire's defenses and attack it, but it would have bought Rome time to regroup. It might, moreover, have generated the confidence and political will to ram through the political and military reforms needed to man the Roman army. Without such reforms, the empire would have remained weak in the long term. With Rome victorious, though, Adrianople might have proved not a Roman Verdun but a Roman defeat of the Spanish Armada, turning back the invader and inspiring assurance and reform.

What if the Roman Empire had survived? What if it had bounced back from the crisis of the years 376–476 the way it had earlier recovered from the crisis of the years 188–284? Like the Chinese Empire, the Roman state would have remained a great power dominating a huge area. With the resources of the Western empire to help it, the East Roman, or Byzantine, Empire might have defeated the Muslims in the seventh century and kept the Mediterranean a Christian lake. Beyond the Rhine and Danube, Germanic and Slavic rivals to Rome would have developed, or perhaps Rome would eventually have conquered them too. There would, of course, have been periods of disorder, inevitable invasions such as China suffered from time to time. But the empire would always have bounced back. It might have even expanded, stretching at its greatest extent from Mesopotamia to Morocco and from Britain to the Elbe, the Vistula or even—who knows?—the Dnieper.

Latin-speaking Europe, governed from a capital in Italy, would have become a more orderly and stable society than the boisterous and freedom-loving Germanic kingdoms that replaced imperial Rome. The emperor, whose office had been around seemingly forever, would have been endowed with a charisma no less potent than the "mandate of heaven" that the rulers of China enjoyed. There would have been no feudalism, no knights, no chivalry, but no Magna Carta either, no doctrine of the right of rebellion, and no parliaments.

The Roman world would have been Christian, but Christianity might not resemble what we know today. It would be Roman, of course, and Catholic—that is, universal—but the pope, if the bishop of Rome had so grand a title, would be strictly subordinate to the Defender of the Faith, that is, the emperor, just as in Eastern Orthodoxy the patriarch stayed under the Byzantine emperor's thumb. No pope could have made a Roman emperor kneel in the snow outside his door, as Pope Gregory VII did the German monarch Henry IV at Canossa in 1078. There would have been no conflict of church and state, no papal monarchy, and no Protestant Reformation. If Martin Luther ever penned his Ninety-Five Theses, he would have done so in his native Latin. They would have been delivered in executive session at a church council, and if the emperor was not amused, he would have sent Luther straight to the lions. The Romans never had much patience for dissent.

There would, of course, have been no Renaissance since, without the death of classical culture in the early Middle Ages, there would have been no need for it to be reborn. Whether Columbus would have sailed across the Atlantic from Hispania without the scientific and commercial spirit of the Renaissance to inspire him is a good question, but one thing is certain: A new Roman Empire in the Americas would have been far less dedicated to individual liberty than the English colonies turned out to be. Governed by a proconsul resident in the city of Nova Roma (New Rome, perhaps today's New Orleans), the United Provinces of America would stand as a model of the ideal proclaimed by Cicero: *otium cum dignitate:* that is, "peace with respect for rank." Merciless with their enemies but not racists, the Romans might have treated the Indians much as the Spanish did, with a mixture of brutality, missionary zeal, and a surprising willingness to intermarry.

Like the Roman Empire, the U.P.A. would be an oligarchy rather than a democracy. Truth to tell, the American founders had great respect for Rome and thought pure democracy dangerous; to some degree they modeled our government on Rome's. Yet they admired the Roman Republic and its political ferment, not the Roman Empire and its centralized monarchy. Our constitution contains a Bill of Rights; our culture is founded on a revolution in the name of liberty; our society prizes equality, although it often fails to achieve it. Were America a New Rome, it would have the same inequality of the United States today without a movement to change it; it would have a judicial system without such rights as *habeas corpus* or the guarantee against self-incrimination; it would have no reason to have abolished the profitable slave systems that grew up in the New World. New Rome would have bread and circuses but no citizens' assembly in the forum.

✦  ✦  ✦

All of this assumes that Rome could have survived the great military challenge that ripped through the Old World in the early Middle Ages—the challenge of Islam. As it turned out, the Muslim armies wreaked havoc on the surviving East Roman or Byzantine state, driving the Byzantines out of the Levant and back to their base in Anatolia and the southern Balkans. There the Byzantines were able to regroup and in places even drive back the enemy. Perhaps this is not surprising, because the Byzantines were, after all, Romans. They had inherited a thousand years of military and political skill to call on in a pinch. Had it survived, the Western Roman empire could have come to Byzantium's help, and together the two of them might have pushed Islam eastward, leaving the Mediterranean and Europe to Rome. What did happen, of course, is very different.

It was one of military history's most lightninglike accomplishments. Within a generation of the death of the prophet Muhammad in 632, the armies of Islam had conquered most of the Near East, threatening the Byzantine capital of Constantinople itself. In 711, after conquering Egypt and North Africa, Muslim armies crossed the straits of Gibraltar and attacked the Christian kingdom of Spain, which had been established by descendants of the Visigoths who beat Rome at Adrianople. The Muslims crushed the Visigoths' army and killed their king, Roderic. In less than a decade, the Muslims conquered most of the Iberian Peninsula. They called their kingdom Al-Andalus. Then, in 720, they crossed the Pyrenees Mountains to attack the region known as Septimania. Today part of

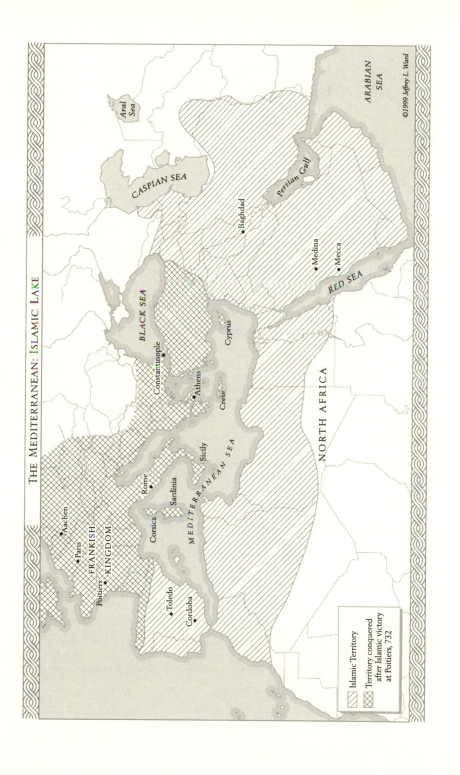

THE MEDITERRANEAN: ISLAMIC LAKE

©1999 Jeffrey L. Ward

ARABIAN SEA

Aral Sea

CASPIAN SEA

Persian Gulf

Baghdad

Medina
Mecca

RED SEA

BLACK SEA

Constantinople

Cyprus

Athens

Crete

NORTH AFRICA

Sicily

Rome

Sardinia

MEDITERRANEAN SEA

Corsica

FRANKISH
KINGDOM

Aachen

Paris

Poitiers

Toledo

Cordoba

Islamic Territory

Territory conquered
after Islamic victory
at Poitiers, 732

France (Languedoc), at the time it had been a Visigothic province in Gaul. Furthermore, it was the doorway into what Arab authors referred to as "the Great Land," a vague term not just for Gaul but for all of Europe. Some even envisioned their armies marching all the way to Constantinople, attacking the capital of the Eastern Roman empire by the back door, as it were.

The Muslims quickly took the city of Narbonne, an old Roman colony and an excellent strategic base. They were defeated outside Toulouse in 721, where their commander, As-Sanh ibn Malik, governor of Al-Andalus, was killed. The presence of a seasoned and disciplined officer, Abd Al-Rahman, prevented the setback from turning into a rout: He led an orderly retreat to Narbonne. Shortly afterward, the Arabs returned to the offensive, slowly expanding eastward into the Rhône valley and attacking cities from Bordeaux to Lyon. By the mid-730s, all of the major cities of the French Mediterranean coast between the Pyrenees and the Rhône were in Muslim hands. Around 730, the governorship fell to the man who had saved the day at Toulouse, Abd Al-Rahman. He was popular with the men for his largesse as well as his cool on the battlefield, but he would have his hands full with threats on both sides of the Pyrenees.

Strong central government was the exception and not the rule in the early Middle Ages. Across the Pyrenees, the "kingdom" of the Franks was more like a collection of quarreling princes. In Al-Andalus, a fault line ran between the Arab elite and the Berber tribesmen of North Africa, recent converts to Islam. The Berbers had formed the bulk of the conquering Muslim army in 711 and later years, but they complained that the Arabs took the best land and booty for themselves. By 732, the Berber leader, Munuza, had carved out a splinter kingdom in the strategic eastern Spanish high plain bordering Gaul. According to one source, Munuza made an alliance with his neighbor Duke Odo of Aquitaine. Although a Christian, Odo was a thorn in the side of his nominal overlord, the Frankish king; like Munuza, Odo aimed at his own independence. In 732, Abd Al-Rahman turned on both men. He led an expedition that captured and killed Munuza, and then he crossed the mountains and marched through Gascony and Aquitaine. We do not know the size of his army, but it was large enough to crush Odo's forces near Bordeaux, to burn and loot Christian strongholds, and to capture a large number of civilians. An estimate of 15,000 Muslim soldiers in this army, which some historians have suggested, is probably not far off the mark.

Abd Al-Rahman's men drove all the way north to Poitiers, just short of the great sanctuary of St. Martin of Tours, a kind of national shrine of the Franks, famous for its Christian piety and wealth. Tours is only a little over 200 miles from Paris.

They would go no further. Somewhere between the cities of Poitiers and Tours, perhaps at Moussais on the old Roman road, they met the army of the leader of the Franks, Charles the Pippinid. In theory only "Mayor of the Palace" (r. 714–741), a kind of prime minister, he was the *de facto* king of the Frankish kingdom, which straddled northern France and western Germany. Although he had made war on the Franks before, a desperate Odo had now sought Charles's aid.

True, the Franks were not the power they had once been under their first great king, Clovis (r. 481–511), but under the Pippinids they were on an upward trajectory. A bastard son who had to fight for power after the death of his father, Pepin II (d.714), Charles fought well—and often. Charles was a seasoned and popular warrior at the head of a victorious army when he came to Poitiers, but so was Abd Al-Rahman. It ought to have proved a dramatic showdown.

So it did, but we know frustratingly few of the details. Contemporary evidence insists that the battle took place on a Saturday in the month of October and in the year that most would date to 732, although some scholars opt for 733. The preliminaries lasted seven days, each side observing the other and, in skirmishing, looking for some advantage of terrain or timing. This would suggest that the two forces were relatively evenly matched; that is, each side had roughly 15,000 men, to make an educated guess. Although they had some cavalry, the heart of the Frankish army was the infantry, who fought closely massed and wore heavy armor, carried large wooden shields, and fought with swords, spears, and axes. The Muslims were renowned for their cavalry. Their infantry had adopted the European style of heavy armor but perhaps with mixed emotions; after all, a Bedouin curse recalled the Arabs' origins as light-armed fighers: "May you be cursed like the Frank who puts on armor because he fears death."

Finally, the great clash came. The near-contemporary continuator of the *Chronicle of Isidore* implies that the Muslims attacked: At least he emphasizes the point that the Franks held their ground—"like a wall . . . and like a firm glacial mass"—unlike other Christian armies of the day with a reputation for fleeing the battlefield. By contrast, the continuator of the *Chronicle of Fredegar* has Charles charge aggressively, "scattering them [the Muslims] like stubble before the fury of his onslaught. . . ." Fortunately, both sources agree on one point: Frankish warriors killed Abd Al-Rahman. There is reason to think that this proved decisive. True, the continuator of *Fredegar* has the Frankish victory turn into a rout, but the author worked under the patronage of Charles's brother Childebrand, so he could hardly make the Franks look less than glorious. The continuator of *Isidore* tells a more complex story: The battle continued until nightfall. The next day, the Franks approached the Muslims' tents in battle order, expecting a fight, but the enemy had withdrawn at night beneath their noses. If this account is true, then the Franks had not inflicted an obvious, crushing defeat on the Muslims. They expected that the enemy could still fight—and perhaps he could have, were he not leaderless. The Muslim army withdrew. Tours was saved.

News of the victory at Poitiers (or Tours, as the battle is sometimes called) reached as far as northern England, where the Anglo-Saxon scholar the Venerable Bede heard of it. Later generations gave Charles the surname "Martel" or "Hammer" because of his success against the Muslims. As for the Muslims, never again would their armies reach so far north in Western Europe. To the great historian Edward Gibbon, Poitiers was "an encounter which would change the history of the whole world."

In his magisterial *Decline and Fall of the Roman Empire*, Gibbon envisioned the possible consequences of Arab victory at Poitiers:

> A victorious line of march had been prolonged above a thousand miles from the rock of Gibraltar to the banks of the Loire; the repetition of an equal space would have carried the Saracens to the confines of Poland and the Highlands of Scotland: the Rhine is not more impassable than the Nile or Euphrates, and the Arabian fleet might have sailed without a naval combat into the mouth of the Thames. Perhaps the interpretation of the Koran would now be taught in the schools of Oxford, and her pulpits might demonstrate to a circumcised people the sanctity and truth of the revelation of Mahomet.

More recent scholars tend to be less sure that Poitiers made a difference. Even had Abd Al-Rahman and his men carried the day, they argue, they could not have done much more damage, since they were only a raiding party, not an occupying army. Nor could they have made the most of victory, not given the revolts about to burst forth in Spain in the 730s and 740s, revolts both on the part of Berbers and Arabs.

But if it is possible to build too much on the events of that day in 733, it is also possible to build too little. Like the Battle of Britain in 1940, Poitiers had not cut a deep crack in the invader's armor, but it had deterred him from further advance. The Muslims made Abd Al-Rahman into a martyr, but they smarted from the shame of having left booty behind for the enemy. The raid had failed: safer to stay in the fortified bases in southern Gaul. But what if the Muslims had defeated the Franks on the eighth day at Poitiers? What if the general of the Franks, Charles Martel, lay dead with many of his men? A Muslim victory might have rendered Poitiers a fishing expedition that showed that the water was well stocked and unguarded.

Even if the Muslim expedition of 732 was far from an all-out attack, it is hard to imagine it simply stopping and going home after having faced a challenge from the war leader of the Franks and having killed him. After all, the attack on Spain in 711 also began as a raid; victory whetted the appetite for conquest. No, the victorious warriors of Al-Rahman would have sacked Tours as they had sacked Poitiers, and they would have been tempted by the road to Orléans and Paris.

Meanwhile, the sons of Charles—no longer surnamed Martel—would have quarreled over the succession. No doubt one of them would have prevailed eventually, and the new leader, either Carloman or Pepin the Short, would have had to do what his father, Charles, in fact did after his victory at Poitiers: fight far-flung battles against Frisians, Burgundians, Provençals, and Muslims. That is, if he had the energy to achieve what his father would: expanding the Frankish state to the Mediterranean Sea and the Jura Mountains. But it would have been difficult, because the new leader would not be commanding men made united and confident by their victory at Poitiers, nor facing, in the Muslims, an enemy that feared the Franks: after all, the Muslims had found them wanting at Poitiers. Charles's successor accordingly might not have retaken Avignon, as Charles did in 737, nor defeated the Muslims in battle again, as Charles did, in the marshes of the river Berre in Corbières in 738. Without these victories to build on, that commander might not have driven the Muslims out of Septimania and back over the Pyrenees, as Pepin did between 752 and 759. And faced with a continued major Arab presence in southern Gaul, Pepin's successor, Charlemagne, would have lacked a free hand for his campaigns in Italy and the East—that is, if the militarily unsuccessful Pippinids had stayed in power long enough for there even to be a Charlemagne.

As for the Muslims, had they maintained their hold on their province across the Pyrenees, sooner or later they would have given in to the temptation to expand it. After all, even with the expulsion from Septimania in 759, even with Charlemagne's and his generals' campaigns across the Pyrenees in 778 and 801, the Muslims continued to raid southern France until 915. With cities like Narbonne and Avignon as bases, there would have been no need to be content with mere raids. The Muslims might have returned to the practice of sending governors of Spain to command their armies, as had been the rule before Charles's victory at

Poitiers. Berbers and Arabs might have put aside their differences in order to win booty and glory in the Great Land. Undeterred by the weakened Frankish monarchy, the conquerors might have gone from strength to strength until they crossed the English channel and planted the crescent, as Gibbon imagined, in Oxford. It would then have been emirs and imams, not dukes and bishops, who faced the challenge of invasion by Vikings in the ninth and tenth centuries. Had they been successful, the empire that had once governed Western Europe from Rome might have reemerged—as the caliphate.

What would a Muslim Western Europe—an Al-Andalus stretching from Gibraltar to Scandinavia, from Ireland to the Vistula or even beyond—have been like? Christianity would have survived, but as a protected and ever-shrinking enclave, not as the ruling faith. While continuing to practice their religion, many Christians would have become all but Arabs in their language and customs, just as happened in Muslim Spain. Many would have gone all the way and converted to Islam, as many Christians did in Spain, and more would have, if not for the steady advance of the Christian *reconquista*. No doubt the vast majority of Europeans would have become Muslims, as the vast majority of North Africans and Middle Easterners eventually did.

Nor would Christianity have expanded across the globe. If Western Europeans had crossed the Atlantic in 1492 they would have done so under the banner not of the cross but the crescent. A great naval power in the Mediterranean under the Umayyad Dynasty (A.D. 632–750), a great trading power in the Indian Ocean until the advent of the Portugese, Islam is likely to have taken to the Atlantic with gusto. In the Americas they would have turned the natives into proper Europeans—that is, Muslims. Today there would only be one world religion: Islam.

In Europe, meanwhile, the Muslim elite would have made the most of its new provinces conquered after Abd Al-Rahman's victory at Poitiers. The Muslims built in Spain arguably the most civilized Western European society since the Roman Empire's heyday. In Al-Andalus, as the Arabs called their kingdom in the Iberian Peninsula, the tenth century witnessed a world of abundant agriculture and booming towns, of palaces and poetry, of art and enlightenment. Its cities put northern Europe's to shame, its traders covered wider ground, its philosophers dwarfed Westerners in their knowledge of the classical Greek heritage.

Europe would have gained much had Al-Andalus spread north of the Pyrenees. In Spain, North Africa, the Near East, indeed, wherever they went, the Muslims had the Midas touch. They encouraged prosperity through trade, agriculture, irrigation works, and city building. To be sure, not all had equal shares in prosperity. Muslim society was thoroughly hierarchical and slavery was a standard feature. In the tenth century, for example, Islamic Spanish armies and even government bureaucracies were staffed with captives from northern Spain, Germany, and above all, from the Slavic countries—our word "slave" comes from "Slav." The city of Verdun, in northern France, was Europe's greatest slave market. No doubt that market would have moved further east had the Arabs conquered Western Europe—to some outpost east of the River Elbe, maybe even to the future Berlin. In any case, Western Europe, too, would have become a slave society, and perhaps, in time, the slaves would have become the masters, coming to power in Europe as they eventually did in the Middle East.

Servile much of Islamic Europe might have been, but it would never have been coarse. When the first Arab conquerors had encountered the refinements of Persia and Byzantium it was love at first sight; no matter how far their travels took them in later years, the victorious Arabs insisted on bringing along the comforts of home. So Islamic England, France, and Germany would have been filled not just with mosques and military camps but with palaces, baths, gardens, and fountains. Tenth-century Paris might have become a second Córdoba, teeming with prosperous workshops and merchants' quarters in which every language of the Old World could have been heard; gleaming with gold-roofed, marble-columned palaces; adorned with the colors of dyes imported from India, instead of what it was—a glorified small town. Had Aachen been the seat of a caliph rather than Charlemagne's capital, it might have been adorned with light and airy mosques instead of heavy proto-romanesque churches. Nor would the improvements have been merely physical. Patrons par excellence of poetry and philosophy, the Arabs would have turned Europe into an intellectual powerhouse. Works of Plato and Aristotle would have been known by the leading minds north of the Pyrenees in the tenth instead of the twelfth century. Poets would have composed the sort of refined verses that might have pleased a courtier in Baghdad instead of the rough-hewn rhythms of *Beowulf*. No wonder that Anatole France bemoaned the outcome of Poitiers: "It was," he said, "a setback for civilization in the face of barbarism."

Yes, one is tempted to reply, but only in the short term. Islam represented the cultivated heritage of the great empires of the ancient Near East and Mediterranean, not the raw, new, and semibarbaric mores of Western Europe, under whose Germanic conquerors Roman civilization had been diluted. But in the long run the new society of the West proved more productive economically and stronger militarily than the ancient culture of Islam. Historians have no easy time explaining this paradox: why rude, Christian Europe rose to world power, beginning the Scientific and Industrial Revolutions and inventing capitalism along the way, while civilized Islam lay quiescent economically and fell to Western arms. There are no easy answers, but the most promising line of explanation may have to do with Western pluralism.

Precisely because Western Europe was barbaric it proved ungovernable; no one centralizing authority emerged. Feudal government—if that isn't a contradiction in terms—never succeeded in reining in individual knights; over the centuries, individualism became democratized and a highly prized Western value. Barons never succeeded in conquering the towns, whose merchant oligarchs pursued profit with the same aggressiveness that medieval knights made war. The Christian church never succeeded in taming the princes. As often as not, church and state were at loggerheads. Eventually, during the Reformation era, individual states opted for independence from the church. The culture that developed in Europe was, compared to Islam, decentralized, secularized, individualistic, profit-driven. It had little respect for the older civilization to the south. No wonder that it was Europe that witnessed the Renaissance, the Reformations, the origins of modern science and industrialism; no wonder that it was Europe that, for centuries, ruled the world.

The irony is that it might never have happened if not for the Dark Ages. A European caliphate after 732, like a revived Western Roman Empire after 476, might have guaranteed stability and cultural resplendence, but it would have nipped modernity in the bud. Neither caliphate nor empire would have permitted the freedom and restlessness out of which the European takeoff eventually emerged. For Europe, the Dark Ages were like a terrible medicine that almost killed the patient but ultimately rendered her stronger.

On top of all this, Europe was lucky. The years 476 and 732 would only be footnotes today if things had turned out differently in 1242. In that year, the most powerful invaders the continent had ever seen withdrew after a lightning conquest of Eastern Europe the year before. If not for the death of their king, the conquerors would have begun an unstoppable ride to the Atlantic. It is doubtful that a revived Roman Empire could have defeated them; it is all but certain that an Arab Europe could not have, given the Arab collapse before the victorious invaders in the Middle East a decade later (the capital city of Baghdad was destroyed in 1258). Those victors may have been, quite simply, the greatest set of warriors the world would ever know. They were the Mongols.

CECELIA HOLLAND

# THE DEATH THAT SAVED EUROPE

*The Mongols Turn Back, 1242*

The Dark Ages were pure light compared to what could have happened to Europe if, in the thirteenth century, it had been overrun by the Mongols. In 1242, Mongol conquerors had reached Eastern Europe. They had destroyed one Christian army in Poland and another in Hungary; their vanguards had reached Vienna and the Adriatic, and they were in the process of establishing the largest connected land empire in the history of the world. These horse warriors out of the central steppes of Asia, with composite bows that were far superior to European crossbows, formed the most disciplined and quick-moving fighting forces of their time. They looked, Cecelia Holland writes, "strikingly like a modern army set down in a medieval world." No one was able to stand up to them. Despisers of city dwellers, culture, and elites of any kind, they were the Khmer Rouge of their day. But if the Khmer Rouge laid waste to an entire country—Cambodia—the Mongols rampaged through an entire continent and were about to swallow another, leaving a killing-field detritus behind them. Never, probably, was the West, and the historical phenomenon it represented, in so much danger. At the last moment, blind luck spared Europe. History may be a matter of momentum, but we can never forget that the life—or death—of a single individual can still matter.

✦ Cecelia Holland is one of our most acclaimed and respected historical novelists, the author of more than twenty books.

In the summer of 1241, an observer on the walls of Vienna might have caught a glimpse of strange horsemen drifting over the plains east of the city. Had the observer been well-informed, he would have known that these odd and ominous riders on their little horses were Mongols, scouts from the vast army at that moment camped only a few hundred miles away down the Danube, and the sight of them on the outskirts of his city would have frozen his blood.

Against these marauders, Vienna was almost defenseless. The Mongols had already disposed of the two most formidable armies in Eastern Europe. The decisive battles occurred within a day of each other, although widely separated in distance.

On April 9, 1241, a sizeable army of Germans, Poles, Templars, and Teutonic knights marched out of Liegnitz to attack a slightly smaller force of Mongols advancing steadily westward across northern Poland. The two armies met on the flat field of Wahlstadt. The initial charges of the heavily armored Christian knights seemed to break the Mongols, who fled. Duke Henry's men pursued, in growing disorder, straight into a perfectly laid Mongol ambush. Duke Henry's army died almost to the last man.

The Mongol army that delivered this defeat was only a diversionary force. While they were driving through Poland, the great general Sabotai and the main body of his troops forced the snowy passes of the Carpathians and descended onto the Hungarian plain. A third and smaller Mongol force circled south of the mountains through Moldavia and Transylvania to screen their flank.

Thus Sabotai was coordinating his forces across two mountain ranges and several hundred miles. One of Genghis Khan's "four hounds," or favorite generals, Sabotai was an old man in 1241, one of history's unsung military geniuses. His long and brilliant career ranged from northern China to this current campaign in Europe. His operation in Europe, in a difficult, and for him, unusual terrain, was flawless.

He and his army descended into Hungary after marching 270 miles in three days, through the snow. As the Mongols approached across the plain the Hungarian king Béla advanced from his capital, Buda, to oppose them. Sabotai backed slowly away, until he reached the bridge over the Sajo River. There the Mongols made their stand.

On April 10, one day after Liegnitz, Béla attacked this bridge and drove the Mongols back. Fortifying his camp with heavy wagons lashed together, he swiftly built a makeshift fort securing both sides of the bridge. When night fell he seemed in a commanding position.

But Sabotai's scouts had meanwhile discovered a ford downstream. During the night, the great general himself led half his army downriver and across. At dawn, Batu Khan and the rest of his army mounted a concentrated frontal assault on the Hungarians' position. Béla swung to meet this pressure, and Sabotai attacked him from behind.

Swiftly Béla's battered troops were driven back into the wagon fort. The Mongols surrounded it, and for most of the rest of the day assaulted the Hungarians with arrows, catapults of rocks, burning tar, and even Chinese firecrackers, keeping up a constant barrage, until the embattled Christians were at the breaking point. Then suddenly a gap opened in the wall of Mongols surrounding the Hungarians. Some of Béla's exhausted and disheartened men made a dash for it. When the first few seemed to escape, the rest followed, panicking, in a wholesale rout. Attacking from either side, Sabotai and his men at their leisure destroyed the confused and demoralized mob that Béla's army had become. Only a few escaped back to Buda. One was King Béla, who did not stop running until he reached an island out in the middle of the Adriatic Sea.

With Hungary under their control and spring turning the wide plains green, the Mongols stopped. They put their herds to graze and raised their yurts on the broad flat grasslands, so much like their native steppes.

Through the summer, they rested and collected themselves for the next assault.

Western Europe awaited them, stunned and almost helpless. The Christian community was at a moment of critical weakness. The two most powerful rulers in Europe were locked in a bitter struggle for supremacy. On one side was the Holy Roman Emperor, the brilliant and brutal Frederick II, and on the other a succession of popes, determined to bring him to heel.

Preoccupied with Italy, Frederick had abandoned his German inheritance to the local nobility. Constantly at each other's throats, these lordlings showed no inclination to unite to meet the threat posed by the huge army out there on the plains of Hungary. Young King Louis IX of France, vigorous and idealistic, was gathering an army of his chivalry, but he had at best a few thousand knights. No Christian army so far had stopped the Mongols, or even slowed them down. The well-informed Viennese observer had every right to tremble for his people. The scourge of God was upon them.

✦ ✦ ✦

The impact of the Mongol conquests can hardly be overestimated, although the swift arc of their ascendancy spanned only a hundred years. Until the rise of Temujin, the remarkable man who became Genghis Khan, the name Mongol denoted only one of a number of nomadic peoples who hunted, herded, and warred over the central steppes of Asia and the Gobi Desert. Temujin changed that. He stoked up the central Mongol belief that they were born to rule the world and led his people off on a conquest that ultimately stretched from the East China Sea to the Mediterranean. His chief targets were the Chinese empires to the east of Mongolia, the Islamic states to the west and south, and the Russian cities beyond the Volga. What he did to them changed the world forever.

The wonderful chronicle *The Secret History of the Mongols* reports this conquest from the inside out, steeped in the ethos of the nomad warrior, the basis of Ghengis Khan's success. His armies were bound together by ties of sworn brotherhood and obligation, and by the powerful personality of the great khan himself. The soldiers who gathered under his standard—who took the name Mongol because that was his tribe—did so because Temujin projected such an aura of invincible will, courage, and commitment that to defy him was to defy fate. He seemed divinely ordained to rule the world. At the same time, he gave endlessly to his people. *The History* abounds with evidence of his love for them. He was the embodiment of their spirit, the living soul of the whole nation.

Toward those who were not Mongol he turned another face.

"They came, they sapped, they burnt, they slew, they plundered, and they left." In 1209, Genghis Khan and his armies attacked northern China, there learned how to storm cities, and began the long process of grinding down the world's oldest and most populous civilization. Every city fell and was destroyed. For a while the great khan contemplated depopulating the whole of northern China and converting it to pasture for his horses; he was deterred from this when an adviser pointed out that living Chinese would pay more taxes than dead ones.

In the West, steady Mongol expansion against the Turkomani peoples of central Asia brought them into contact with the flourishing states of Islam, especially Khwarezm, a land of fertile fields and fabled, thriving cities: Samarkand, Bukhara, Harat, Nishapur. In 1218, Genghis Khan invaded Khwarezm and devastated it.

Part of Genghis Khan's strategy was calculated massacre: if a city resisted his armies, once it fell to him—and they always fell—he had all the inhabitants slaughtered. The chroniclers' reports of the numbers of dead are staggering; 1,600,000 at Harat, in 1220. Rumor reached the Mongol prince Tuli that some had survived there by hiding among the piled corpses, and when he took Nishapur, some time later, he ordered the heads cut off all the bodies. At Nishapur, according to contemporaries, 1,747,000 died.

The figures are ghastly, unbelievable. What they convey is the con-

98

temporary sense of utter destruction. Even when a city surrendered, it was looted and destroyed. After Bukhara yielded, the people were ordered out of the city so that it could be sacked, the young men and women and children were carried off into slavery, the site was leveled "like a plain."

Only a few years later, the attack on Russia began. The first campaigns along the Volga won the Mongols a foothold, but the project was put on hold when Temujin died. According to Mongol custom, the great khan's eldest son received the largest portion of territory, the farthest from the center of the empire. Since by the time of Temujin's death, his eldest son, Jochi, was already dead, the inheritance fell to his grandson, Batu Khan, the founder of the Golden Horde.

In 1237, with Sabotai masterminding the campaign, Batu's Mongols attacked Russia and systematically reduced the cities there to rubble. The loss of life again was shocking; hundreds of thousands died. Then, in 1241, after a summer's fattening on the great plains of southern Russia, the Mongols turned to Eastern Europe.

✦ ✦ ✦

Why were they so unstoppable? In fact the Mongol army looks strikingly like a modern army, set down in a medieval world. Their strengths were speed and maneuverability, firepower, discipline, and an excellent officer corps.

The armies of the great Khan were organized by tens, hundreds, thousands, and tens of thousands, each segment with its officers, who were chosen not according to favor or birth but proven ability. In the Russian campaigns, although the army and the conquest belonged to Batu Khan, and a number of other members of the royal family fought in the war, everybody obeyed Sabotai, a man of relatively low birth.

This same emphasis on merit influenced the succession. Even before the great khan died, his two elder sons, Jochi and Chatagai, were enemies; if one was elected over the other, they themselves acknowledged, there would be civil war. "But Ogadai (the third brother) is a prudent man," Chatagai said; "let us elect Ogadai!" They did, and the succession passed smoothly from Genghis Khan to his third son—whom the other brothers served loyally.

Mongol life emphasized such discipline. The Mongol horseman was born into a life of war. When he wasn't fighting, he was hunting, which exercised his fighting skills. From babyhood he rode; he could travel scores of miles in a day, stop, and camp on the ground and eat a handful of meat he had brought with him and get up at dawn and go another forty miles, day after day, in snow and desert heat and wind and rain, fighting all the way. He drove three or four extra horses along with him as he rode, and could change mounts without breaking out of a gallop.

Enemy armies consistently overestimated the numbers of the Mongol forces, because for every man, there were four or five additional horses. Occasionally, the Mongols helped them along in this mistake by tying dummies onto the extra horses.

The Mongol soldier carried a double recurve bow of laminated horn, with a pull of 160 pounds, which dispatched arrows accurately up to a distance of 300 meters as fast as he could pull them out of his quiver. He wore no heavy clumsy armor, but padded leather to skid aside arrows, and silk underwear to keep wounds clean. He seldom closed with an enemy hand to hand; he died at a much lower rate than the opposition.

Above all, he obeyed orders. The battles of medieval Europe were mostly confused melees studded with individual combats; a good general was somebody who managed to get the bulk of his available forces to the battlefield before the fighting was over. Sabotai coordinated the movements of tens of thousands of men, across mountain ranges and in unknown territory, as precisely as movements on a chessboard. In battle, through a signaling system of colored banners, he could advance thousands of men at a time, send them back, turn them, and direct their charges—and when he gave orders, his men did instantly what they were told. Not for centuries would there be another army as efficient and efficacious at the gruesome business of leveling other people's societies.

Level them they did. China's population declined by more than 30 percent during the years of the Mongol conquest. Khwarezm and Persia were crisscrossed with an elaborate underground irrigation system that since antiquity had sustained a thriving culture; the Mongols destroyed them. Arabic scholars contend that the region's economy has yet to recover fully from this devastation.

The wars of the khans in Iraq and Syria went on for sixty years and reduced a vigorous civilization almost to ruins. The caliph of Baghdad, Islam's supreme authority, defied the khan, which meant he had to die. The Mongol general had the caliph tied into a leather sack and trampled to paste by horses—a sign of respect, actually, since, symbolically anyway, it avoided the shedding of his blood. The caliphate has never been restored.

The psychological impact of the invasion was incalculable. Before the Mongols swept through, the Islamic world that centered on Baghdad was intellectually vigorous, bold, adventuresome, full of poetry and science and art. They had, after all, defeated the Christians and won the long wars of the Crusades. After the invasion, the dour conservatism of the fundamentalists darkens it all.

So too with Russia. The cities were fat on their river trade, great Novgorod, Ryazan, Kiev with its golden gate, until the terrible winters of the 1230s; a dozen years later, travelers found Kiev a village of a hundred souls, huddled in a blackened boneyard. The famous Russian xenophobia is often attributed to their experiences at the hands of the Mongols.

In every conquered territory, the Mongols set up a governor and a tax collector, to continue to plunder the remaining inhabitants. Almost four hundred years later, the natives of Siberia were still paying tribute in furs that they called the *yasak*, after the *Yassa*, the Mongol law code. Once the Mongols had ridden through, no country was ever the same again.

Some intuition of this might have gone through the mind of the well-informed observer on the walls of Vienna, as he watched the Mongol horsemen in the distance and pondered the fate of Europe. The Mongols launched their campaigns in the dead of winter, so that their horses were fat and strong on summer grass. In January or February they would advance. Surely they would fall first on Vienna, just up the Danube from Hungary.

Vienna could buy some mercy by submitting at once, but that mercy was generally of a strained quality: If they suffered the same fate of Bukhara, the inhabitants would be allowed to leave the city, so that it could be plundered and destroyed, and then many of the children, women, and young men would be taken away into slavery. The rest would be scattered into the countryside, because the Mongols hated cities, and Vienna would be leveled.

By this time, the princes of Europe would be sufficiently aroused to send out another army. The well-informed observer had no reason to suspect this army would have any more success than Henry of Silesia's, or Béla of Hungary's. When that army was destroyed, Europe would lie defenseless.

The Mongols' reconnaissance was always expert and efficient. Therefore they would surely strike first for the riches of the Low Countries, overrunning Antwerp, Ghent, Bruges. Seeking pasture for their horses, they would swerve south, toward the broad meadows of middle France. On the way they would destroy Paris.

Possibly a detachment would force the passes of the Alps and descend to northern Italy, where on the plains of the Po they would again find grass to feed their horses, and cities to plunder. Some of the Italian cities might surrender, saving thereby some of their people. Cities that chose to fight would be annihilated. The Mongols would carry off everything they could lift, and burn the rest. What people remained would be in a condition of abject poverty, huddled in tiny villages. The Mongols would install governors and tax collectors, winter over on the grasslands of northern Italy and Champagne, and then, by the grace of God, they would leave.

What would remain?

Wiping out the cities of the Low Countries would erase the nascent financial center of Europe. In the thirteenth century, the vigorous wool

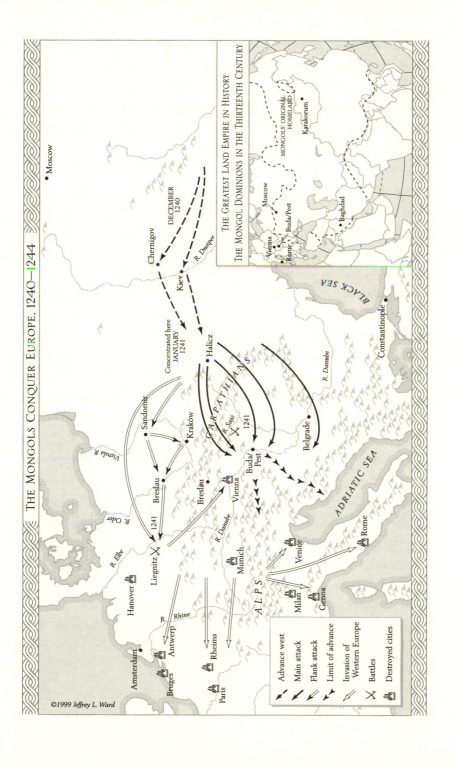

# THE MONGOLS CONQUER EUROPE, 1240–1244

Moscow

Chernigov

DECEMBER
1240

Kiev

R. Dnieper

Concentrated here
JANUARY 1241

Halicz

C A R P A T H I A N S

R. Danube

Constantinople

BLACK SEA

Sandomir

Vistula R.

Krakow

R. Sajó

1241

Belgrade

Breslau

Breslau

Buda

Pest

Vienna

R. Oder

1241

R. Elbe

Liegnitz

R. Danube

Munich

A L P S

ADRIATIC SEA

Rome

Venice

Genoa

Milan

Hanover

R. Rhine

Antwerp

Rheims

Amsterdam

Bruges

Paris

©1999 Jeffrey L. Ward

**Legend:**
- Advance west
- Main attack
- Flank attack
- Limit of advance
- Invasion of Western Europe
- ✕ Battles
- Destroyed cities

## THE GREATEST LAND EMPIRE IN HISTORY
### THE MONGOL DOMINIONS IN THE THIRTEENTH CENTURY

MONGOLS' ORIGINAL HOMELAND

Karakorum

Moscow

Buda/Pest

Vienna

Rome

Baghdad

trade centering on Antwerp and Ghent was fueling steady economic growth throughout Western Europe that would continue for three centuries; the first stock market originated somewhat later in Antwerp. The Mongol assault would pull up this developing society by the roots. Depopulated, the whole area would regress rapidly to wilderness. No one would be left to tend the windmills and dikes; the sea would come in again across Holland. The great delta of the Rhine-Meuse-Scheldt would revert to swamp. There would be no rise of capitalism or the middle class. No printing press, no humanism. No Dutch Revolt, the seedbed of the great democratic revolutions from England to America to France. No Industrial Revolution.

The destruction of Paris would be even more disastrous. Paris was the intellectual center of the High Middle Ages; at the university, the intense study of Aristotelian logic was laying the groundwork for a fundamentally new world view. The Nominalists were already insisting on the irreducible reality of the material world. A rector of the University of Paris would, a hundred years after the Mongols, develop the first theory of inertia. On these ideas would stand the great theories of Galileo, Kepler, Newton. The coming of the Mongols would leave nobody to thank them.

If the Mongols penetrated Italy, and there was nothing really to stop them, what would become of the pope? Would the Mongols tie him, too, into a sack and trample him, out of reverence for his exalted blood? The caliphate, the central authority of Islam, died with the coming of the Mongols. The papacy, surely, was in some ways more flexible, since the pope did not have to be a descendant of Saint Peter. Nonetheless, if the papacy failed, then Christendom itself would begin at once to change. Without a central authority to proclaim and enforce orthodoxy, however imperfectly, the faith would collapse into dozens of divergent sects. Without a central authority to focus opposition against, there would have been no Reformation, with its powerful new ideas about human nature.

Destroying Rome, the Mongols would destroy European society's strongest link to its antique past. Without the examples of classicism to inspire them, could there be a Dante, a Michelangelo, a Leonardo? Even if their ancestors survived the massacres, the desolation of their cities and countrysides would have reduced these people to a bleak struggle for survival with little room for poetry and art. The Mongols, in any case, would have made short shrift of Dante, with his outspoken political opinions. Leonardo, one imagines, they would have found a use for.

The well-informed observer on the walls of Vienna in 1241 could have known nothing of Leonardo, of course. He knew only that out there on the plains of Hungary waited such a terror as would level his world, steal its energies and resources, and crush its aspirations. So he watched from the walls, and girded himself, and waited for the blow to fall.

It never came. Early in 1242, the Mongol army suddenly withdrew. Thousands of miles from Vienna, a single death had saved Christendom from disaster. A single death, and the very ethos that drove the Mongol army.

The death was Ogadai's. The brilliant, humane, and drunken third son of Genghis Khan had not only kept his father's empire together but had directed its expansion. Still, the political organization of the khanate did not match its military sophistication. The Mongols remained nomad tribesmen, bound by a personal loyalty to their chiefs. When the khan died, their law required them to go in person back to their heartland to elect a new khan. On the brink of the assault on Europe, great Sabotai let the job go, and went home again.

The Mongols never returned. Their focus thereafter was on China, and in the West on Persia and the Arab states. In 1284, a Mameluke army from Egypt met a Mongol army at Ayn Jalut, in the Holy Land, and defeated them there. It was the beginning of the end. The Japanese and the Vietnamese repulsed Mongol invasions in the distant east. The tide was ebbing. The terrible ordeal was over.

In Poland, they still celebrate April 9 as a day of victory—reasoning that, however awful the defeat of Liegnitz, somehow it sapped the invaders' strength and will to continue on. Thus they cling to the illusion that the terrible sacrifice was meaningful—that they deserved to triumph. But the valor of the defenders had nothing at all to do with it. In fact it was the Mongol worldview—that same force that propelled them so furiously outward—that sucked them back home again, and so saved Europe. That, and a stroke of blind luck.

THEODORE  K.  RABB

# IF ONLY IT HAD NOT BEEN
# SUCH A WET SUMMER

## The Critical Decade of the 1520s

M any events conspired to make the 1520s so important. What happened during those ten years, both in Europe and the rest of the world, would permanently affect the way we now live our lives. Not for the first time in history and, as we shall see, not for the last, weather would be a major historical player. What would have happened if, in the summer of 1529, unusually heavy and persistent rains had not delayed the progress of the huge army of the Ottoman Sultan Suleyman the Magnificent in its progress toward Vienna, the main eastern outpost of Europe's dominant Habsburg dynasty? What if Suleyman's siege had not begun so late in the year? Or if he had not been forced to leave behind his mired heavy artillery, without which he could not batter down the city walls? And what would have happened if he had actually taken Vienna? An Ottoman Europe probably would not have been the result: Christian opposition ultimately would have been too powerful. More important, though, far-reaching deals would inevitably have been struck, and those who opposed the Habsburg ascendancy in the continent would have been emboldened to challenge it. One certain loser would have been Martin Luther and his burgeoning but still fragile Protestant heresy. Henry VIII of England might have received papal blessing for his divorce from his Habsburg queen, and there would have been no Anglican Church—and no lost Catholic country for the Spanish to try to reconquer half a century later.

✦ Theodore K. Rabb is professor of history at Princeton University, and the author or editor of such notable works as THE NEW HISTORY, THE STRUGGLE FOR STABILITY IN EARLY MODERN EUROPE, CLIMATE AND HISTORY, RENAISSANCE LIVES, and JACOBEAN GENTLEMAN. He was the principal historical advisor for the acclaimed and Emmy-nominated PBS television series, RENAISSANCE.

Few decades of Western history have been as fraught with consequences as the 1520s. They began with the first recorded passage of the Straits of Magellan, under the leadership of the captain who gave the Straits their name; and, in the same year, a revolt in Spain and a Danish bloodbath in Stockholm that helped shape the political future of both Iberia and Scandinavia. Just a few months later, in April 1521, Luther defied the Habsburg Holy Roman Emperor Charles V at the Diet of Worms, setting the stage for a permanent split in the Roman church. And before the decade ended, eight years later, a peasant uprising in Germany had unleashed new levels of virulent social repression; Sweden had become an independent kingdom; Cortés had conquered Mexico; the Turks had overrun Hungary and reached the walls of Vienna; Henry VIII had intensified his quest for a divorce, which was to transform English politics and society; and Charles V's troops had stormed through Italy in a campaign that climaxed in one of the most devastating cultural catastrophes of European history, the sack of Rome.

Depending on their interests and viewpoints, therefore, historians have at various times settled on this decade as the moment of crucial transformation in the emergence of modern times: the beginning of the Reformation; the first major conquest in Europe's overseas expansion; the start of a new intensity in the struggle between Islam and the West; a turning point in the consolidation of the secular state; the end of the Italian Renaissance. And in most cases, these decisive shifts could easily have taken different forms or moved in different directions, if only one or two contingencies had changed.

Luther's fragile revolt, for example, was little more than three years old when he came to Worms. His early ideas had been put forward in three short tracts published the previous year, but without his leadership and further writings, the fragmentary eruptions of support that had appeared by 1521 might well have petered out. There were German princes, it was true, who were genuinely moved by Luther's message, and others who had political or economic reasons to resist the will of their overlord, the Emperor Charles V, who sought to suppress the heresy following the confrontation at Worms. But when Luther vanished from sight just a few days after his appearance before Charles, it was widely assumed that he had been removed from the scene, not by his friends (as was the case) but by his enemies.

The artist Albrecht Dürer, though he was never to leave the Roman church, reacted to Luther's disappearance with a lament that echoed the fears of many:

> Is he still alive, or have they murdered him? If we have lost this man, who has written more clearly than anyone else, send us another who will show us how to live a Christian life. O God, if Luther is dead, who will explain the Gospel to us?

If Dürer's foreboding had come true, there is a good chance the Reformation would have been snuffed out, as had Jan Hus's similar protest in Bohemia a century before. For within three years, a peasant revolt claiming inspiration from Luther swept through southern and western Germany. Had the reformer not survived to condemn the peasants and reassure the princes that religious change was not an excuse for social upheaval, there is little doubt that Germany's rulers would have taken fright, rushed to reconcile with the emperor, and removed the critical support that enabled Luther to succeed.

That Cortés's vastly outnumbered incursion into Mexico, or Magellan's perilous expedition around Cape Horn, could also have come easily to grief scarcely needs arguing. Spain would probably have persisted in seeking an American empire, but one can question whether it would have been conquered so quickly and so cheaply. And it is worth remembering that, if progress had been slower overseas, it might have been overtaken in the 1530s by Charles V's mounting determination to overcome his Muslim foes in the Mediterranean. As he revised Spain's priorities, he would have regarded Algeria as a more important target of expansionist aims and resources than the wilds of a new continent. It could well have been in North Africa rather than Peru, therefore, that Pizarro and other adventurers would have sought their fame.

And that other major event of the decade, the sack of Rome, was equally beset by happenstance. As Charles V's troops, having defeated their main enemy, France, moved across a seemingly helpless Italy, none of their commanders had any designs on Rome. Indeed, the emperor was to be furious when he heard of the assault on the holy city. Charles's magisterial biographer, Karl Brandi, noted over half a century ago how much that terrible event owed to sheer ill fortune:

> Now and again in history long-forgotten decisions and long-suppressed emotions, under the direction of some invisible impulse, generate elemental forces which, like gigantic and slowly rolling dice, work out their horrible and destructive course, guided by chance alone.

Thus it was with the sack of Rome, which was inflicted on the city by an army out of control, driven by a frenzy of hunger, lack of pay, and a generalized hatred of the papacy and all its works. The result was a destruction of life, art, and treasure of awesome proportions, not to mention a flight of talent that affected Roman culture for a generation (while at the same time giving Venice, a safe refuge, an unprecedented infusion of new ideas and creativity). Yet all of this, too, could have been avoided, not only by better supply and firmer command in the imperial army, but also if either of two accidents had turned out differently the previous year.

Charles V's army had crossed the Alps under the command of Georg Frundsberg in 1526. Essential to their advance was a good supply of heavy artillery, which they had been unable to carry over the mountains, and for which their best source in Italy was Ercole d'Este, Duke of Ferrara. The Estes were a perpetual thorn in the papacy's side, particularly now, when a Medici from the rival city of Florence, Clement VII, sat on the papal throne. To forestall any deal between Ferrara and the emperor,

Clement decided to send a bribe to Ercole, but he moved too slowly and his offer arrived after the transaction had been completed. Had the pope's payment not been delayed, the artillery might never have been delivered.

The second accident occurred in November 1526, when the one really effective soldier in the Medici family, a young man named Giovanni della Bande Nere—who bore an uncanny resemblance to the later conqueror of Italy, Napoleon—was accidentally wounded by a cannon-ball from one of the Ferrarese guns in a small skirmish with Frundberg's troops. He died soon thereafter, thus removing the last military commander who stood between the imperial army and Rome.

Nor did this succession of misfortunes have serious consequences merely for the holy city and its medieval and Renaissance wonders. For in the very month of the sack, May 1527, nearly a thousand miles away, the queen of England, Catherine of Aragon, was being told by her husband, Henry VIII, that he wanted a divorce. Thus began "the king's great matter"—his quest for a new wife who could provide him with a male heir, a demand that at first seemed straightforward. After all, Henry had married his brother's widow; there were good biblical grounds for annulling such a marriage; and popes usually obliged the crowned heads of Europe. But this pope was now under the control of Catherine's nephew, Charles V, and so the permission was not forthcoming. Within a few quick years Henry solved the problem by having himself proclaimed head of an independent Anglican church; the Reformation gained a crucial and redoubtable ally; and English society and institutions were transformed beyond recall.

Of all the near misses and "what ifs" of the 1520s, however, none is as pregnant with possibilities as the aftermath of the Battle of Mohács in Hungary in 1526. For here we can speculate on consequences that encompass not merely one but a number of the great changes of the time: not only the Italian Renaissance and the Lutheran and Anglican Reformations, but also the clash between Christendom and Islam, and the heritage in Germany and Spain of the greatest political figure of the age, Charles V.

The victory won by the Ottoman Sultan Suleyman the Magnificent at Mohács on August 29, 1526, was unquestionably one of the decisive military engagements of world history. It was nearly three-quarters of a century since the conquest of Constantinople, but now the Turks were on the move again. Sweeping through the Balkans, Suleyman had captured the powerful citadel at Belgrade in 1521, and five years later, after turning aside to conquer the hostile island of Rhodes from the crusading order of the Knights Hospitaler of St. John, he was ready to advance further into Europe. At Mohács he encountered and destroyed the flower of the kingdom of Hungary, the last Christian power capable of resisting the Muslims in the Balkans. The slaughter that followed was ghastly. Not only did the king, two archbishops, five bishops, and the bulk of the aristocratic leadership of Hungary perish, but some 30,000 troops on the losing side either died on the field or were killed by a victor who took no prisoners. Suleyman's exultation on behalf of his faith as well as his regime leaps from the pages of his announcement of victory:

Thanks to the Most High! The banners of Islam have been victorious, and the enemies of the doctrine of the Lord of Mankind have been driven from their country and overwhelmed. Thus God's grace has granted my glorious armies a triumph, such as was never equaled by any illustrious Sultan, all-powerful Khan, or even by the companions of the Prophet. What was left of the nation of impious men has been extirpated. Praise be to God, the Master of the World!

The Turks were masters of the Balkans. But the question remained: What next?

Suleyman's answer in 1526, as it had been in 1521 after the capture of Belgrade, was to take his crack troops, the Janissaries, back to Constantinople to regroup. Not for three years did he venture forth again, to probe further up the Danube into Austria, and to besiege Vienna. By then Charles V's brother Ferdinand (already the dominant figure in the Habsburgs' Austrian and Bohemian domains) had established his claim to what remained of the crown of Hungary against his rival, John Zapolya of Transylvania, and Zapolya in response had turned to Suleyman for help. Aware that the Habsburgs were his chief antagonists in central Europe, the sultan agreed to help the Transylvanian gain the crown on the condition that he pay tribute and owe allegiance to the Ottomans. With that agreed, Suleyman at long last marched from Constantinople on May 10, 1529, at the head of an enormous army of perhaps 75,000 men.

It was now that contingency intervened. The summer of 1529 happened to be one of the wettest of the decade. In the laconic judgment of Suleyman's biographer, Roger Bigelow Merriman, the rains "were this year so continuous and torrential that they seriously affected the outcome of the campaign." If we change "seriously affected" to "determined" we will come closer to the truth. Because of the rains, Suleyman was forced to abandon, on the way, his hard-to-move heavy artillery, which had been a crucial asset in earlier sieges. Moreover, the adverse conditions prevented his troops from marching at their normal speed; they covered ground so slowly that nearly five months passed before they reached the gates of their target, Vienna. Not until September 30 (virtually the end of the campaigning season) was Suleyman ready to send his bedraggled and weary troops into the attack, and by then he also had to contend with another consequence of the delay: the Viennese had had the time to reinforce their position. Over the summer they had been able nearly to double the size of the defending garrison, which now held some 23,000 men, 8,000 of whom had reached the city only three days before the Turks arrived. The sultan's assaults proved futile, and by mid-October he had decided to withdraw—only, so he later claimed, because Ferdinand had run away, and there would be no glory in capturing the city without his adversary.

But let us suppose it had not been such a terribly wet summer—or, to rely on human rather than meteorological happenstance, suppose that Suleyman had pressed ahead more promptly, in the much drier summer of 1527 that followed the battle of Mohács. In 1532 he showed that he was fully capable of overrunning the Habsburg territory when, despite another very wet summer, he laid waste to the Austrian province of Styria—though he did avoid Vienna, which by now was massively defended by what Merriman calls "possibly the very largest [army] that Western Europe had ever been able to collect." What might the outcomes have been if the incursion had begun in 1527 (rather than 1529 or 1532), when the conditions were right and the Habsburgs were far less prepared?

One has to assume, first, that Suleyman would almost certainly have captured Vienna. And, secondly, that he would soon have found allies in the West. As titular rulers of all Germany, and effective rulers not only of Austria, Bohemia, and the Netherlands, but also of large stretches of Italy and all of Spain, the Habsburgs were feared and resented by almost every other leader in Europe. They might now stand on the front line against the Muslims, but that did not mean their fellow Christians stood with them, for their power often seemed far more threatening than Islam. Indeed, in the very year of Mohács, the papacy, France, and many of the Italian states formed the League of Cognac to try to sweep the Habsburgs out of Italy. The campaign that led to the sack of Rome was to be Charles V's reply, but he could never have mounted that campaign if Suleyman had threatened his flank from Vienna. Indeed, there is a good chance that the participants in the League of Cognac, emboldened by the emperor's troubles, would have made a pact with Suleyman and thus have been able to end, almost before it began, a Habsburg ascendancy in Italy that was to last nearly a century and a half. After all, the Venetians had already signed a commercial treaty with the sultan in 1521, and the French were to ally with him in the 1530s. Although the pope would have had to stay aloof, the other Italian princes would have had no more compunction about joining with the infidel against the hated Habsburg in 1527 than did the Venetians or the French in these years.

With Charles distracted by Suleyman in the north, those Italian states that were his allies would soon have succumbed to the League of

Cognac. And the consequences for European culture would have been enormous, for not only the treasures of Rome but the city's entire artistic culture would have been spared the sack of 1527. Investigating the effects of that terrible event over a decade later, the art historian and painter Giorgio Vasari recounted in painful detail the grim experience of the distinguished artists whose lives had been shattered. Some had been killed; many had been assaulted, ruined, or forced into menial occupations; others had fled; and all had in one way or another been deeply affected. "One need only understand," wrote Vasari, "that violence makes delicate souls lose sight of their primary objective and regress." Indeed, one of the victims, Sebastiano del Piombo, wrote: "I don't seem to be the same Sebastiano I was before the sack; I can never again return to that frame of mind."

Even a heartwarming story recounted by Vasari—and there were not many of them—had no happy ending. As he tells it, the great Mannerist painter Parmigianino was unable to complete his *St. Jerome*

> because of the catastrophic sack of Rome in 1527. This not only caused a halt in the arts, but for many artists the loss of their lives as well. It would have taken little for Francesco [Parmigianino] to lose his too, for when the sack began, he was so immersed in his work that despite the eruption of soldiers into the houses, and Germans already inside his own, with all the noise they made, he continued to work. Bursting in on him, and seeing him at work, they were so amazed by the painting that, evidently men of breeding, they let him go on . . . But when these soldiers left, Francesco was a hair's breadth from disaster.

Eventually, Parmigianino escaped and returned to his native Parma. Whether or not Vasari was echoing a similar story from antiquity—of an artist, interrupted during a siege of Rhodes, who told the soldiers he assumed they had come to make war on Rhodes, not on art—the message was unmistakable.

Nor was this merely the exaggeration of contemporaries. The chief modern historian of the sack, André Chastel, has described Roman art as

116

traumatized for a generation, though he acknowledged that those who fled could enrich the culture of other cities, notably Venice, the prime refuge for the persecuted. And it is also worth noting that there would have been one other momentous result had Charles's troops been kept out of Italy. The emperor would not have controlled the papacy; Clement would doubtless have granted Henry VIII his divorce; and England might well have remained a Catholic nation indefinitely.

That likelihood would surely have been strengthened by the effect on Germany of Suleyman's presence in Vienna. A quick look at the map will suggest the implications of the capture of the Austrian capital for the future of Central Europe, especially if one imagines the sultan continuing westward along the Danube to the rich cities of Passau, Regensburg, and Augsburg, ravaging the terrified dukedom of Bavaria, and so forth. Either some of the princes in his path would have made deals with him—keeping their positions if they paid tribute and allegiance to Constantinople, as Zapolya had done in Hungary—or they would finally have been forced to rally around Charles V. Not that the second option would have seemed inevitable, even in the face of invasion. There had been civil warfare in western Germany in the early 1520s and a huge peasant uprising in the mid-1520s, and the emperor's pleas for unity and help against the Turk had little effect. Typical was the behavior of one gathering of princes, summoned to discuss the Turkish advance through the Balkans. Before agreeing to provide support, they decided they needed a fact-finding mission; delaying even this action, they did not finally vote to dispatch a delegation to Hungary until the day before the battle of Mohács.

Whether making deals with Suleyman or joining together to protect their lands, however, the princes of Germany would almost certainly have realized by the late 1520s that they could no longer afford the divisive presence of religious dissent. To link up with the devout Charles V they would probably have agreed to end their support for Luther, and most would have realized anyway that a united front required the suppression of the animosities caused by the Reformation. Bereft of essential protectors, and with Charles seeking to placate the papacy, Luther would

117

have been isolated and his following would have dwindled, though the reformer himself might have found a protector in the north, far from the Danube. New movements to reform the church would undoubtedly have arisen, and Luther's impact might have been postponed rather than eradicated; but the religious complexion of Europe at midcentury would have been radically altered, with immense consequences for all her states.

One in particular catches the eye. If both England and the Netherlands had remained Catholic, and the Habsburgs had given up their Italian ambitions to concentrate on their German and Spanish territories, the struggles of the second half of the sixteenth century would have taken very different forms. With religious antagonisms subdued, Spain would not have aroused such enmity elsewhere in Christian Europe, and she would have been able to develop her empire in the New World largely free of the hatreds that eventually propelled her challengers. Today, as a result, all Americans, both North and South, would have spoken Spanish. If only it had not been such a wet summer . . .

◆ PETER PIERSON ◆

# IF THE HOLY LEAGUE HADN'T DITHERED

What if twenty-year-old King Charles IX of France had followed his heart and answered the summons of Pope Pius V to join the Holy League against the Turks in 1570? Instead he accepted the cautions of Queen-Mother Catherine de' Medici, and listened to Admiral Coligny's urging that he take advantage of Spain's distraction to make gains for France—and, as Coligny hoped, the Protestant cause. Following the league's great victory at Lepanto on October 7, 1571, in which its armada crushed the Turkish fleet, Philip II of Spain fretted about French designs and kept his half brother Don John of Austria, the league's commander, in port well into 1572. The Turks rebuilt their fleet and crushed Christian rebellions in Greece. Coligny's Huguenots invaded Philip II's Netherlands, to commence the costly two-front war that would compel Philip to downgrade the Mediterranean. By the time Don John mobilized the Holy League's entire force, the 1572 campaigning season was nearly over, and he achieved nothing. Though Coligny perished in the St. Bartholomew's Day Massacre on August 24, France persisted in a foreign policy hostile to Philip. That is what did happen.

Had the league struck early in 1572, as Don John planned, with its ranks enlarged by the chivalry of France, then Greece and the Balkans may have been restored to the rest of European civilization. Instead, the Balkans would remain largely under Ottoman Turkish rule well into the nineteenth century. Frequent revolts by Balkan Christians led to ever crueler repression by the Turks and local people who converted to Islam. The resultant divisions and animosities in Balkan society still plague the world.

◆   *Peter Pierson is professor of history at Santa Clara University.*

ROSS HASSIG

# THE IMMOLATION OF HERNÁN CORTÉS

*Tenochtitlán, June 30, 1521*

One of the central episodes of the 1520s was, of course, the taking of the Aztec capital of Tenochtitlán—today's Mexico City—by the Spanish conquistador Hernan Cortés. The question most asked is how so few men could topple an entire kingdom. One answer is that the Spanish force, perhaps 900 men in all, was joined by nearly 100,000 Indian allies, all eager to destroy their hated Aztec oppressors. Disease has never been a respecter of historical odds. Smallpox, which the Spanish brought with them, killed off 40 percent of the population of Mexico in a year, including one Aztec king. But Cortés, who was undoubtedly a remarkable soldier and a born opportunist, was also extraordinarily lucky. As Ross Hassig points out, "There are no shortage of plausible turning points for the Conquest." Several times the Spanish could have been stopped or annihilated in battle. Like Alexander the Great, Cortés himself missed death only because of the intervention of one of his men—who was killed as he managed to save his leader. Had Cortés been captured, he would have been sacrificed soon after, and the conquest

121

would have crumbled. Once again we are reminded of the heavy-handed role of time and chance.

The question that is almost never asked is: What would have happened if Cortés had been killed or if his expedition had failed? Would the Spanish, as Theodore K. Rabb suggested in the previous chapter, have turned their acquisitive instincts elsewhere—North Africa, for instance? Would another attempt at conquest have been more successful? Would Christianity have been able to make inroads, even if the soldiers of Spain could not? What about the practice of human sacrifice? What sort of nation would have evolved from the Aztec Kingdom? And down the road, what effect would a large and totally Native American nation have had on the growth of the United States?

✦ Ross Hassig is professor of anthropology at the University of Oklahoma and one of the foremost authorities on the Aztecs. Among his many books are MEXICO AND THE SPANISH CONQUEST, WAR AND SOCIETY IN ANCIENT MESOAMERICA, and AZTEC WARFARE: IMPERIAL EXPANSION AND POLITICAL CONTROL.

Cortés and his men leapt across the breach in the causeway to pursue the fleeing Aztecs, only to see them turn and attack. Drawn into the trap, Cortés and sixty-eight other Spaniards were captured and dragged off, leaving scores of others dead on the road. Ten captives were killed immediately and their severed heads were thrown back over the front lines, sowing consternation among the disheartened Spaniards. The remaining fifty-eight were taken to the towering Great Temple, which could plainly be seen from the Spaniards' camps, made to dance before the statue of the Aztec god of war, Huitzilopochtli, and then, one by one, they were sacrificed. Their hearts were torn out and their faces and hands flayed so they could be tanned and sent among the wavering towns as a warning. Cortés escaped this fate only through the intervention of Cristóbal de Olea, who sprang to his defense, killed the four Aztecs who were dragging him off, and freed his leader at the cost of his own life. The very conquest of Mexico hung on this single act.

The final military event in the conquest of Mexico was the Aztec surrender on August 13, 1521, after the Spaniards broke through the last defenses and fought their way into the Aztec capital of Tenochtitlán. The city lay in ruins and, for four days, the Spaniards' Indian allies continued to attack the defeated Aztecs, looting the houses and killing thousands. But the events of the Spanish conquest did not have to unfold as they did. There were many points when decisive actions by various individuals, misadventure, or poor decisions could have drastically altered the outcome of the conquest as we know it.

Mesoamerica was discovered by Francisco Hernández de Córdoba, who landed in Yucatan in 1517, where he clashed with the Maya and was ultimately repulsed with devastating losses. This expedition was followed by a second in 1518, under Juan de Grijalva, who also clashed with the Maya but who sailed beyond Yucatan and up the gulf coast to central Veracruz, where he encountered the Aztecs. Even before Grijalva's return, Governor Velázquez of Cuba authorized a third expedition under Hernán Cortés, but when he later tried to relieve him, Cortés abruptly set sail and reached Yucatan in early 1519 with as many as 450 men. If Governor Velázquez had succeeded in removing Cortés from command before the expedition's departure, the conquest would have been still-born.

But having slipped out of Velázquez's grasp, Cortés followed the route of the first two expeditions until he reached Grijalva's anchorage on the central Veracruz coast. There, Cortés was greeted by Aztec officials bearing food and gifts, but when the Spaniards refused to accede to Aztec requests to move their camp, the emissaries left. Had the Aztecs met the Spaniards with massive force, again the conquest would have been aborted or forestalled. But they did not, and once they abandoned the Spaniards on the coast, the local tribe, called the Totonacs, established contact and eventually allied with them. The Totonac king could do this because the Aztec empire relied on conquest or intimidation to subdue opponents, and left the local rulers in place. No imperial offices or officeholders were imposed to hold the system together, so this system was also vulnerable to shifts in the local power balance that could quickly and easily alter allegiances. The Spanish arrival was such a change and the Totonacs seized on it.

Having achieved the goals of exploration, contact, and trade, as authorized by Governor Velázquez, many of Cortés's men wanted to return to Cuba. Had they left, Cortés would have had too few men to continue and, once again, the conquest would have failed. However, Cortés founded the town of Villa Rica de la Vera Cruz a few miles north of present-day Veracruz, appointed a city council under the claimed authority of King Charles V of Spain, which then declared that Velázquez's authority had lapsed, and elected Cortés as captain directly under the king; he was now free from the governor's constraints. To gain royal support,

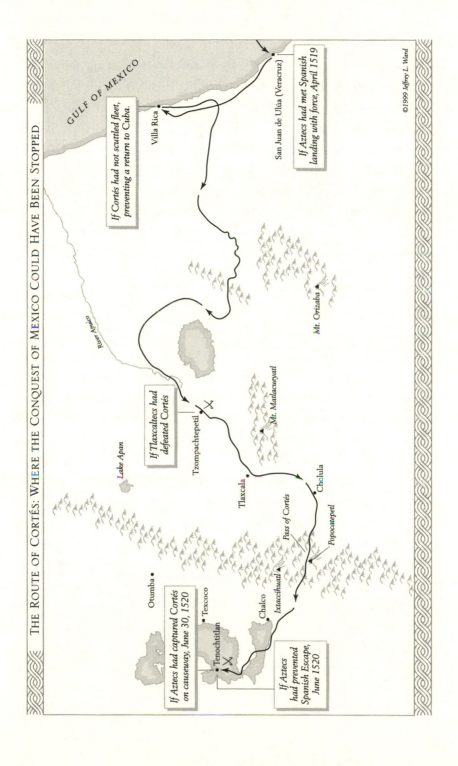

# THE ROUTE OF CORTÉS: WHERE THE CONQUEST OF MEXICO COULD HAVE BEEN STOPPED

GULF OF MEXICO

Villa Rica

San Juan de Ulúa (Veracruz)

If Cortés had not scuttled fleet, preventing a return to Cuba.

If Aztecs had met Spanish landing with force, April 1519

Mt. Orizaba

River Apulco

Lake Apan

Tzompachtepetl

If Tlaxcaltecs had defeated Cortés

Mt. Matlacueyatl

Tlaxcala

Pass of Cortés

Cholula

Popocatepetl

Ixtacchuatl

Otumba

Texcoco

Chalco

Tenochtitlan

If Aztecs had captured Cortés on causeway, June 30, 1520

If Aztecs had prevented Spanish Escape, June 1520

©1999 Jeffrey L. Ward

Cortés dispatched a ship to Spain with all the gold they had gathered thus far as a gift to the king. To keep his men from deserting, he scuttled the ten remaining ships, giving his men little option but to follow him. Leaving 60 to 150 men in the fort at Vera Cruz, Cortés marched inland with 300 Spanish soldiers, 40 to 50 Totonacs, and 200 porters.

En route to Tenochtitlán, the Spaniards neared the province of Tlaxcallan (Tlaxcala), where they advanced to capture a small party of armed Indians. But they were drawn into an ambush and were saved only by their superior firepower. Attacked repeatedly in the days that followed, the Spaniards suffered many wounded; their supplies were running low. Recognizing that he faced an overwhelming hostile force, Cortés sent repeated peace entreaties to the Tlaxcaltecs. The two sides eventually forged an alliance. The Tlaxcaltecs could have defeated the Spaniards, and had they continued the battle, as their commander wanted, Cortés's adventure would have ended. But the Tlaxcaltecs had their own reasons for allying with the Spaniards. They had been engaged in a long-term war with the Aztecs and, completely encircled and cut off, their defeat was only a matter of time. The coming of the Spanish offered them an unforeseen way to win. A major tactic in Mesoamerican battles was to breach the opposing lines and turn the enemies' flanks, which was very difficult to do. But Spanish cannons, the matchlock muskets called harquebuses, crossbows, and horsemen could disrupt enemy lines and, though the Spaniards were too few to exploit these breaches, the Tlaxcaltecs were not. Spanish arms greatly multiplied the effectiveness of the Tlaxcaltec army.

The Spaniards stayed in Tlaxcallan for seventeen days before marching to the province of Cholollan (Cholula). Though welcomed by the Chololtecs, Cortés claimed he learned of a plot to attack him with Aztec help: He assembled the nobles in the main courtyard and massacred them. His reason does not ring true. Cholollan had recently switched their allegiance from Tlaxcallan to the Aztecs, so a Spanish attack was a way to resolve a political problem. A new king was chosen and Cholollan re-allied with Tlaxcallan. Two weeks later, Cortés marched into the Valley of Mexico and reached Tenochtitlán on November 8. He was greeted by Moteuczoma (Montezuma) and housed in the palace of his deceased father, Axayacatl, who had been the king from 1468 to 1481.

An enormous island-city of at least 200,000, Tenochtitlán was connected to the mainland by three major causeways that could be quickly severed. Recognizing the precariousness of his position, Cortés seized Moteuczoma within a week of his arrival, held him captive, and ruled through him for the next eight months.

When Governor Velázquez learned of Cortés's perfidy, he dispatched Pánfilo de Narváez with a fleet of nineteen ships and over eight hundred soldiers to Vera Cruz to capture him. But on learning of his arrival, Cortés marched to the coast with 266 men in late May and, aided by duplicity and judicious bribery, defeated Narváez.

Meanwhile, Pedro de Alvarado, who had been left in Tenochtitlán with eighty soldiers, claimed he had learned of an Aztec plot to attack them, placed artillery at the four entrances of the walled courtyard of the Great Temple, and then massacred an estimated eight to ten thousand unarmed Aztec nobles trapped inside. Word of the massacre spread throughout the city, the populace attacked, killed seven Spaniards, wounded many others, and besieged them in their quarters. When Cortés learned of the uprising, he began the return march with a force now numbering over 1,300 Spaniards and 2,000 Tlaxcaltecs, and reached Tenochtitlán on June 24.

Once he was inside the city, the Aztecs raised the causeway bridges and the Spaniards were apparently trapped. With their supplies dwindling and unable to fight or negotiate their way out, Cortés took Moteuczoma onto the roof to order his people to stop the attack, but to no avail, and the king was ultimately killed, either by stones thrown from the Indian throng or by his Spanish captors.

Cortés ordered portable wooden spans built to bridge the gaps in the causeways and, during a heavy rainstorm just before midnight on June 30, the Spaniards began their escape. They were quickly discovered, and only a third of the force got away. Cortés reached Tlaxcallan, but not until he had lost over 865 Spaniards and more than a thousand Tlaxcaltecs. Had the Aztecs assailed the fleeing Spaniards immediately and continuously, few if any would have survived. The 440 surviving Spaniards rested for three weeks and then, in early August, marched again and conquered nearby Aztec tributary cities.

The Indians now faced a new, nonmilitary threat. Smallpox arrived with Narváez's expedition and swept though central Mexico, killing some 40 percent of the population of Mexico in a year, including Moteuczoma's successor, King Cuitlahua, who ruled for only eighty days. Because the epidemic devastated both the Aztecs and their Indian opponents, depopulation does not, of itself, account for the conquest. But it did produce political disruption: The death of Cuitlahua meant that with the accession of his successor, Cuauhtemoc, the Aztecs had three kings in less than six months.

The first time Cortés entered Tenochtitlán, he had been trapped inside; now he sought to reverse that situation and ordered the construction of thirteen brigantines in Tlaxcallan, using the rigging salvaged from the ships he sank at Vera Cruz. There was an intermittent influx of arrivals from the coast throughout the conquest, and Cortés's forces had grown to 40 horsemen and 550 Spanish foot soldiers. Accompanied by 10,000 Tlaxcaltec soldiers, Cortés began his return march to the Valley of Mexico.

But Cortés's first major victory there was political. Since 1515, Tetzcoco, the second most important city of the empire, had been politically divided over who should succeed to the throne. Cacama took the throne with strong Aztec support, but another contender, Ixtlilxochitl, fought a civil war, conquered the area north of Tetzcoco, which he then ruled in an uneasy accommodation with Tenochtitlán. When Cortés entered the valley, Ixtlilxochitl seized the opportunity to ally with him, and the reigning king of Tetzcoco fled. Ixtlilxochitl's support gave the Spaniards a strong foothold for their attack and provided a secure logistical base. Cortés won the allegiance of disaffected cities in the valley and fought a series of battles with the Aztecs. But since Tenochtitlán was supplied by

guzmā.   mich̄u aca.

**CORTÉS VS. THE AZTECS: CONQUEST IN THE BALANCE**

*The Spanish conquistador Hernán Cortés (in dark clothes, left) and Indian allies meet, and best, Aztec warriors. Had his attempt to conquer Mexico failed, an enduring Native American kingdom might one day have collided with an expanding United States.*
(Corbis/Bettman)

canoe, Cortés had to control the lake. When the timbers being cut in Tlaxcallan reached Tetzcoco around the first of February, the Spaniards began assembling the brigantines. On April 28, 1521, Cortés launched his ships—each over forty feet long, with twelve oarsmen, twelve crossbowmen or harquebusiers, a captain, and an artilleryman for its bow-mounted cannon. Supported by thousands of Indian canoes, they barricaded Tenochtitlán and cut off its flow of food and water.

The Spaniards now numbered just over 900, and those not on the brigantines were divided into three armies of fewer than 200 Spaniards each and "supported" by 20,000 to 30,000 Indian troops each. On May 22, Pedro de Alvarado led one army to Tlacopan, while Cristóbal de Olid marched to Coyohuacan, and Gonzalo de Sandoval went to Ixtlapalapan. Cutting off three of the major routes into Tenochtitlán, the Spaniards attacked along the causeways, whose narrowness allowed them to concentrate their firepower. The Aztecs responded by building barricades and assaulting the Spaniards on both sides from canoes. But Cortés then breached the causeways, sailed his ships through, and drove off the enemy canoes. In response, the Aztecs limited the ships' movements by planting sharpened stakes in the lake floor to impale them.

There is no shortage of plausible turning points for the conquest and the examples are far from exhausted by those already suggested. But the likeliest such point, involving the fewest alterations in historical events, took place on June 30, 1521. The Spaniards and their Indian allies had been assaulting the causeways that linked Tenochtitlán to the shore for more than a month. The battles were back-and-forth struggles during which the Aztecs built barricades, removed bridge spans, and destroyed portions of the causeway, both to delay the Spanish advance and as tactical ploys. When the Spaniards crossed these breaches, the Aztecs often redoubled their efforts and trapped them when they could neither easily retreat nor be reinforced. To avoid this, Cortés ordered that no breaches were to be crossed until they had been filled. But, on June 30, when the Aztec defenses seemed to crumble in the heat of battle, the Spaniards crossed an unfilled breech on the Tlacopan causeway. Their ploy having succeeded, the Aztecs turned, trapped the attackers against the breach, took sixty-eight Spaniards captive and killed many more. The captives were all sacrificed and, fearing a shift in the tide of war, most of Cortés's allies left. Though the Spaniards ultimately survived this reversal and their allies eventually returned, it could easily have been otherwise.

Had Cristóbal de Olea not sacrificed his own life to save Cortés, he too would have been taken and sacrificed, and the defection of his Indian allies would likely have been permanent. The Spanish leader had three lieutenants but there was no clear second in command. Moreover, the Spaniards were never completely united, even behind Cortés. Repeatedly, he threatened and cajoled them and twice ordered Spaniards hanged for plotting to desert. And now with Cortés gone, Spanish unity would have disintegrated. The conquest would have been lost. What, then, would the Spaniards have done?

Exposed on the western shore of the lake without allies, the Spaniards alone could not long hold out against the Aztec assaults. And the factionalism that seethed just below the surface could not have been suppressed without Cortés since there was no single leader of equal determination and ruthlessness. Without overwhelming Indian support, there was no hope for the Spaniards and they faced three plausible choices. They could have continued the battle, but that offered only annihilation. They could have surrendered en masse but that meant death for most, if not all, of them, though isolated individuals might have slipped away with their erstwhile allies, perhaps to be hidden until the Aztecs spent their fury. Or they could have attempted an orderly withdrawal. But to where? They had been allowed to slip away during the flight from Tenochtitlán a year earlier and the Aztecs were unlikely to permit a repeat of that mistake. Moreover, then they had an ally in Tlaxcallan—who would now have abandoned them. So their only recourse was to abandon their heavy equipment and begin a 200-mile withdrawal to the gulf coast through hostile territory, a journey most were unlikely to complete. But given their fragmented loyalties and divided command, the Spaniards would probably have fallen apart and, the weakened remainder would have been vulnerable to the inevitable Aztec counterattack. The only question was how many Spaniards would have survived. Some may have reached the gulf coast and then sailed to Cuba, but most would have died in battles en route—though a lucky few may have survived capture or have been sheltered by former allies. The conquest would be over.

What would have been the probable Spanish response to this defeat?

131

What the surviving Spaniards in Mexico thought is not of concern here, but the opinions of the Spaniards in the Indies and Spain is. Given the seasonal pattern of transatlantic sailings, word of Cortés's defeat would probably not have reached Spain until late summer or fall of 1522 at the earliest, with any response arriving in the Indies no sooner than the following summer. New World conquests and colonization were backed by the Crown, but it was not a governmental enterprise underwritten by a national army, so a concerted military response was unlikely. Cortés's death and the disaster that beset his men, however, would have made the repudiation of his expedition politically easy. Since Cortés had violated Governor Velázquez's orders and authorization, he had also effectively gone against the king and, in light of his failure, royal support would now be solidly behind the governor.

Awareness of Mexican civilizations, lands, and wealth was too widespread in both Spain and the Indies to be ignored. But in light of the Crown's support for Velázquez, its most likely response would be to adopt the governor's original plan for trade rather than colonization. To justify his original plans and current political position, Velázquez would probably have tried to enforce his approach rigorously and with royal backing. Some degree of quarantine would be likely, with the probable emergence of a single trading center on the coast, much as Macao served Portuguese trade interests in China and Japan in the sixteenth century. It is doubtful that the Spaniards could long be held to commerce alone and the continuation of such a trading relationship may not have survived Velázquez's death in 1524 unless some other strong patron managed to secure the Crown's approval for a monopoly. But if there was to be another attempt to conquer Mexico, it would probably be some years off: Exploration elsewhere in the Caribbean was absorbing all available men and material. And the surviving Spanish adult male population of the Indies would require time to recover from the loss of some 2,000 men in Cortés's ill-fated scheme. Moreover, the increased Spanish migration that actually followed the conquest of Mexico would probably not have materialized without increased opportunities in the New World. Thus, the

Spaniards of the Indies were distracted, politically constrained, and militarily weakened. Perhaps their energies would have been absorbed by the conquest of the Incas that began in the late 1520s, where the way had been smoothed by an Inca civil war and by the devastating spread of smallpox into the Andes from Spanish settlements in Panama. Instead of Mexico, a conquered Peru would have drawn Spanish migrants, but the riches thus seized would doubtless have tempted the Spaniards to make another bid for the wealth of Mexico.

A Spanish reconquest was probably delayed rather than deterred, but the issue of the Aztec response to their victory over the Spaniards would have remained. Would they have simply lapsed back to the status quo? Not likely. Even with an Aztec victory, Mexico would have been profoundly changed by the Spanish presence. The smallpox epidemic of 1519 to 1520 had been devastating, but the deadly typhus epidemics of 1545 to 1548 and 1576 to 1581 would not have occurred without a major Spanish presence, or at least not that soon. The Aztec political landscape was significantly altered, not in the offices themselves, but in the personalities of those who replaced leaders lost to war or disease. The political infrastructure of neighboring cities and of the empire would have continued intact, but the way many rulers had switched sides during the conquest would certainly have led to retribution.

The political future of rulers in various cities who had taken their thrones with Spanish/Tlaxcaltec support was bleak and some would now be displaced as Aztec loyalists or political opportunists took advantage of the shift in power. Cities allied with Tlaxcallan would likely have defected to the Aztec side. Meanwhile, Tlaxcaltec factionalism would probably have led to the pro-Spanish ruler being deposed; his replacement would have allied with the Aztecs in an effort to forestall their own conquest. Thereafter, other defectors would have been dealt with easily, swiftly, and terminally. The Aztecs were smaller in population and weaker than before, but politically, they were stronger, having replaced rulers of dubious loyalties.

What would this have meant for a new Spanish invasion? During the first one, Cortés exploited the poorly integrated nature of the Aztec empire and the presence of a major enemy—Tlaxcallan—to secure allies. With Tlaxcallan no longer hostile, could the Aztecs cement their alliances to eliminate the rivalries Cortés had exploited? The Aztec empire was only loosely bound together. Roads and a system of porters were better developed within it than elsewhere, both basic and exotic goods flowed among its many markets, but no rigidly enforced political hierarchy bound it together. Instead, local rulers were left in power, which meant that as soon as the Aztecs showed weakness or incompetence, they might defect. Moreover, while general Mexican cultural practices were widely shared, there was no unifying religion or ideology. Intermarriage among rulers created some cross-cutting loyalties, but these took many years to form and, in the absence of an alternative way to integrate the empire more tightly, the Aztecs could not create a solid front that would be impenetrable to the returning Spaniards.

If they could not reorganize their empire, the Aztecs nevertheless had two major options open to them—they could take the offensive or they could adopt new military weapons and tactics. Since the Spaniards had built and sailed ships in the Valley of Mexico and may well have abandoned some at Vera Cruz in their flight, it is possible that the Aztecs could have launched a counteroffensive into the Indies. Though used on the Pacific coast of South America, sails were unknown in Mexico, and the Aztecs were generally ignorant of the existence or location of the Indies. So as appealing as the image is of Aztec soldiers storming Havana, it is improbable. Alternative routes for a return attack by the Spaniards were blocked from the south by other native states that were too small and too far away to materially assist them and from the north by an inhospitable desert that offered few allies, little food, and great dangers. So an Aztec offensive stance, at best, would have meant patrolling the gulf coast and waiting for a Spanish return before trying to push them back into the sea, though this costly effort would probably have flagged as the years passed uneventfully.

But Cortés's attempt to conquer them unquestionably would have affected Aztec tactics. The primary Spanish technological introductions were horses (and mounted lancers), cannons, harquebuses, and cross-bows. As they had done during their first flight from Tenochtitlán, the Spaniards probably abandoned their cannons, but this time the Aztecs might not have destroyed them as they did earlier. Some of the other weapons likely to have fallen into Aztec hands included swords, armor, crossbows, perhaps harquebuses, and maybe even horses. But what would any of this have meant to the Aztecs? They had used captured swords—some attached to poles as scythes against horses—and a cross-bow against Cortés, so even though the Aztecs did not work iron and so could neither repair nor replicate these arms, those they recovered could easily be integrated into their own forces. After all, the Aztecs already had their own broadswords, spears, bows, and armor. Indeed, since the Indians who had allied with Cortés had been taught to make excellent copper-headed bolts, there was a potentially inexhaustible supply of am-munition for the crossbows. Cannons and harquebuses required gun-powder, and while all of the ingredients were locally available, its concoction was unknown to the Aztecs, but horses might be mastered, offering the tantalizing possibility of Aztec cavalry such as Americans later encountered on the Great Plains. And if the Spaniards actually es-tablished a trade center at Vera Cruz, bladed weapons and perhaps even firearms would have flowed into Aztec hands, whether officially sanc-tioned or not. To make the most of these arms, however, actual instruc-tion would be needed and, for that, there were probably surviving Spaniards.

Changing sides was not unprecedented. Gonzalo Guerrero, who had been shipwrecked off Yucatan in 1511, had risen to the rank of military leader among the Maya, led one of their attacks on Córdoba, and refused to rejoin the Spaniards despite Cortés's entreaty. Moreover, Spain was a newly emerging entity whose king, Charles V, though the son of the rulers of Castile and Aragon, was raised in the Netherlands and was ef-fectively a foreigner. Many Spaniards owed whatever loyalties they had to their cities or provinces rather than to "Spain" and some who participated in the conquest were Portuguese or Italian, so shifting loyalties from Cortés to Cuauhtemoc was imaginable, probable, and, in fact, indispensable if they did not wish to be sacrificed to the Aztec gods. But what could the Spaniards teach the Aztecs that they had not already learned in combat? Weapons use, certainly. For instance, Spanish swords were made of steel with both cutting edge and point and so could thrust as well as slash, whereas the Aztecs' were oak broadswords edged with obsidian blades and could be used only to slash. And perhaps the Aztecs could even make gunpowder, since the three necessary ingredients were available in the Valley of Mexico, though whether they could use explosives is questionable. But new weapons aside, battle strategies and combat practices could certainly be improved as the Aztecs learned the full capabilities and limitations of the Spanish weapons and tactics.

Most of what the captured Spaniards could teach the Aztecs was refinement. They already understood the basics. And what was important was less how it affected their battlefield tactics than the political environment. The Tlaxcaltecs initially allied with the Spaniards because they recognized that those few soldiers could serve as shock troops to punch through and disrupt opposing formations in a way their own weapons and tactics could not. It had not been the presence of the Spaniards per se that had been important, but the decisive advantage they conveyed on the Tlaxcaltec army. With the surviving Spanish arms, however, this advantage was now also held by the Aztecs.

If and when the second conquest came, the various Aztec tributaries and allies would probably have been only marginally more tightly bound to the empire than before; yet even with cannons and harquebuses, the Spaniards were no longer offered the golden opportunity they had the first time. Yes, they could still perform a shock function, but any Indian group that might consider allying with them could not fully exploit it because the Aztecs, even with a limited number of Spanish arms, could also now employ shock tactics and disrupt their formations, and coupled with vastly larger armies, an Aztec victory was ultimately assured.

So, by the time the Spaniards subjugated the peoples of the Andes, leaving them crippled with deadly disease and exploitation, and they finally turned their attention back to Mexico, in the mid to late 1530s, their opportunity had passed. The allies of a returning Spanish force would have been few, their victories ephemeral, and the lucky ones would have been pushed back into the sea—the heads of the rest would have adorned the skullracks of Tenochtitlán. Any reconquest would have to await far larger numbers, more artillery, and more horses than were available in the Indies.

Time changed the situation on both sides. While there was no pan-Mexican ideology to unify the various groups, word of the inhabitants' fate in the Indies and South America slowly made its way to Tenochtitlán and a sense of Indianness that had heretofore been absent emerged in opposition to the Spaniards and expressed itself militarily as well as politically.

Limited as the Spaniards were to more passive exploitation by trade and conversion, gold and silver still flowed into Spanish coffers made wealthy by the pillage of Peru, but Spanish innovations in tools and animals were rapidly adopted by the Aztec elite, and percolated down into the commoner ranks, establishing indigenous livestock and craft industries. Instead of becoming the center of Spanish industry, with lesser benefits falling to the Indians, these innovations were adopted by the natives, even if the nobility dominated, if not monopolized, major herding activities, but with benefits that flowed throughout their society. For instance, wool would have been quickly adopted by their thriving weaving industry, just as bronze and iron would have been added to the range of goods produced and repaired by native metalworkers. Moreover, the development of the native economy made possible by these innovations strengthened indigenous rulers and filled the vacuum into which Spanish colonists would otherwise have flowed.

Spanish intrusions would have been blunted, though not eliminated, and religious orders, obeying their missionizing imperative, would have gradually infiltrated the country ahead of potential settlers. But now, confronting a vigorous indigenous priesthood that enjoyed state support and a flourishing school system, conversion was far slower. The Spanish priests also brought literacy with the Latin alphabet to Mexico and if this spread to all classes, social turmoil would likely follow, so the indigenous elite would doubtless monopolize this knowledge to increase their political and administrative hold. But a more Christianized indigenous tradition would likely have emerged. Without the sword to force conversion, persuasion and example alone were available, resulting in some Christianization and, most likely, a cessation of human sacrifice. But continued personal religious bloodletting may have been reconceived, if not toward a monotheistic end, then toward one that blended the Christian God with one or more of the more important native gods in an elevated, if not exclusive, position above the native ones.

With the gradual emergence of a far stronger indigenous economy and the development of at least a tolerable approximation of Christianity, Mexico would have been far more difficult to conquer. Mexico could have continued as a regional power and survived the expansion of the European colonies in Central and North America, if their more limited exposure to Europeans dispersed the demographic shock of introduced diseases and they prevented Europeans from exploiting it. The nation that emerged may have been much like the Mexico of today, though perhaps limited to central Mexico, organized on strong indigenous lines, yet having undergone modern development from empire to constitutional monarchy. Had this been so, American expansion toward the West may have been halted far earlier than it was—perhaps at the Mississippi, for France, which sold the United States its rights, would have had no claim on the land to the West, and Mexico, whether freely or as the better of limited options, may have left the United States of today far smaller and bordering a nation of truly indigenous Americans.

## GEOFFREY PARKER

# THE REPULSE OF THE ENGLISH FIRESHIPS

### *The Spanish Armada Triumphs, August 8, 1588*

The defeat of the Spanish Armada in 1588 has come down through history as a tale of missed connections, a devastating fireship attack that broke the armada's order, a sea battle that forced the Spanish ships into the North Sea, followed by a storm-plagued passage around the British Isles. A third of the fleet and half of the men aboard would never return to Spain.

We forget how close the Spanish king, Philip II, came to success. The man who controlled the world's first empire on which "the sun never set" was determined to get rid of England's Protestant queen, Elizabeth, and make her nation once again safe for Catholicism. He wanted to end English meddling in the Netherlands, which he ruled, and keep Elizabeth from gaining a foothold in the New World. To those ends, he sent a great armada of 130 ships, which was to rendezvous with the Duke of Parma's army, veterans of the Netherlands rebellion, and escort it to a landing in Kent. But, off Calais, an English fleet intercepted the armada first—and here the what ifs begin. What if on the night of August 7–8, 1588, the winds had blown in a different direction, keeping the English fireships and battleships away from the Armada? What if the Spanish had been able to hang on until Parma and his troopships arrived? Or if they had known that the English shot lockers were practically empty? What if Parma's army had actually made its landing in Kent? The evidence suggests that Parma's seasoned troops could have marched to London, opposed only by terrified conscripts and poorly equipped militia. Philip II might have easily achieved his objective. But as Geoffrey Parker observes, he could be his own worst problem.

✦ Geoffrey Parker is professor of history at the Ohio State University and the author of such works as THE DUTCH REVOLT, PHILIP II, THE MILITARY REVOLUTION, THE SPANISH ARMADA (with Colin Martin), and, most recently, THE GRAND STRATEGY OF PHILIP II. He is (with Robert Cowley) the editor of THE READER'S COMPANION TO MILITARY HISTORY.

If some British historians had their way, August 8 would be declared a national holiday, because on that day, in the year 1588, Elizabeth Tudor's navy decisively repulsed Philip II's attempt to conquer England. The failure of the Spanish Armada laid the American continent open to invasion and colonization by northern Europeans, and thus made possible the creation of the United States.

Philip II already ruled Spain and Portugal, half of Italy, and most of the Netherlands, and the Iberian colonies around the globe—from Mexico, through Manila, Macao and Malacca, to Goa, Mozambique, and Angola—creating an empire upon which, as his apologists boasted, "the sun never set." In addition, his cousin Rudolf II of Habsburg, who had grown up at the Court of Spain, ruled Germany and Austria, while his ally the Duke of Guise, leader of the French Catholics, pledged unconditional support for Philip's plans. Only the northwest Netherlands caused problems. Rebellion against the king's authority broke out in 1572, and the provinces of Holland and Zealand had defied him ever since, despite the expenditure of vast sums of money and the efforts of his best generals and his finest troops. Their sustained ability to resist infuriated Philip and the commander of his forces in the Netherlands, his nephew Alexander Farnese, duke of Parma. Gradually they convinced themselves that only English support sustained the Dutch Revolt, and in fall 1585 Philip resolved to switch his resources from the recapture of Holland and Zealand to the conquest of England. He sought and received aid from other Catholic rulers for his plan to depose Queen Elizabeth and replace her with a sound Catholic. Tuscany provided a galleon and a grant; Mantua supplied an interest-free loan; the pope promised a huge subsidy and a plenary Indulgence for all who took part.

Meanwhile the king's National Security advisers searched for a suitable invasion plan. In the summer of 1586, Philip received an annotated map that evaluated different invasion strategies. Its author, Bernardino de Escalante, dismissed as too risky a naval assault either on northwest England (by sailing north to Scotland and then into the Irish Sea) or on Wales, and instead envisaged a joint expedition by a large fleet sailing from Lisbon, which would carry an expeditionary force to southern Ireland, while the duke of Parma led a surprise attack on Kent by veterans from the Spanish Netherlands. They would cross the channel aboard a fleet of small transports as the English navy sailed away to defend Ireland. Philip II made only one—as it transpired, fatal—change. He decreed that the fleet from Lisbon must sail to the Netherlands, rather than to Ireland, and provide an escort for Parma's veterans as they crossed to England. He felt confident that his armada would prove invincible: If Elizabeth's ships tried to prevent its journey up the channel, they would fail. Parma had only to await the fleet's arrival in order to succeed.

Philip issued precise orders on how to proceed after the troops came ashore. They must march through Kent, take London by storm (preferably with Elizabeth and her ministers still in it), and hope that the queen's enemies on the periphery of the kingdom and in Ireland would rise in rebellion to aid the invaders. If no Catholic rising took place, however, or if London held out, Parma must use his presence on English soil to force Elizabeth to make three concessions: toleration of Roman Catholic worship, an end to all English voyages to American waters, and the surrender to Spain of all Dutch towns held by English troops.

In many ways, the first phase of the operation went according to plan. On July 21, 1588, a fleet of 130 ships, the largest ever seen in north European waters, sailed under the command of the duke of Medina Sidonia to effect its rendezvous with Parma's 27,000 veterans, and their 300 troop transports assembled in the harbors of Dunkirk and Nieuwpoort. On July 29, the armada entered the channel and on August 6, with its order intact despite repeated attacks by the Royal Navy, it dropped anchor off Calais, only twenty-five miles from Dunkirk. News of the fleet's approach only reached Parma that same day, however, and although he began embarking his troops on August 7, it proved too late. That night, the English launched a fireship attack that finally disrupted the armada's formation. In a ferocious battle on August 8, Elizabeth's powerful galleons managed both to inflict severe damage on individual ships and to drive the entire enemy fleet northward, away from the rendezvous.

No sooner had the armada entered the North Sea than arguments began over where the enterprise had gone wrong. "There is nobody aboard this fleet," wrote Don Francisco de Bobadilla (senior military adviser to the duke of Medina Sidonia), "who is not now saying, 'I told you so' or 'I knew this would happen.' But it's just like trying to lock the stable door after the horse has bolted." Bobadilla therefore propounded his own explanation of the debacle. On the one hand, he admitted, "We found that many of the enemy's ships held great advantages over us in combat, both in their design and in their guns, gunners and crews, . . . so that they could do with us as they wished." On the other hand, most Spanish ships experienced an acute shortage of ammunition. "But in spite of all this," he continued, "the duke [of Medina Sidonia] managed to bring his fleet to anchor in Calais roads, just seven leagues from Dunkirk, and if, on the day that we arrived there, Parma had come out [with his forces], we should have carried out the invasion."

The first English historian who seriously considered these questions, Sir Walter Raleigh, in his *History of the World* of 1614, entirely agreed. The English, he wrote, were "of no such force as to encounter an Armie like unto that, wherewith it was intended that the prince of Parma should have landed in England." The Army of Flanders, which had been fighting the Dutch with scarcely a break since 1572, had indeed been molded into a superb fighting force. Some veterans had been on active duty for thirty years and they served under experienced and resourceful officers who had risen through the ranks. During the previous decade they had conquered the rebellious provinces of Flanders and Brabant, culminating in the capture of the port of Sluis in August 1587 in the teeth of a spirited defense by the best troops and most experienced com-

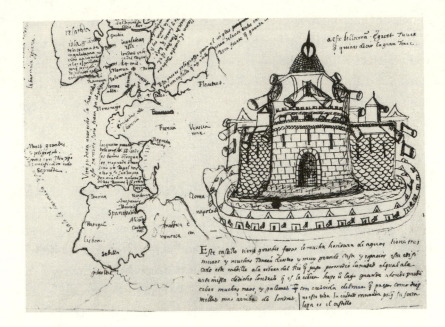

## PLANNING THE CONQUEST

*In July 1586, Bernardino de Escalante, a soldier-turned-priest, sat down to explain to Philip II the various ways to invade England. He had resided there thirty years before—and remembered the Tower of London ("E greet tuure," on the right) as the only important stronghold. His map therefore assessed the options of sending a fleet from Spain to sail either around Scotland and attack northeast England, or into the Irish Sea and land in Wales. Either operation seemed less dangerous than a direct assault up the channel, where, as Escalante noted, the armada would encounter "el enemigo." Events would prove him right.*

(Biblioteca Nacional, Madrid, manuscript 5785/168)

manders of the Dutch and their English allies. Over the next year Parma prepared a meticulous embarkation schedule, including the precise itinerary and sequence for each unit's march from their billets to the designated ports, and even supervised two rehearsals. The fact that, when the armada arrived, almost all the 27,000 men detailed for the invasion managed to embark within thirty-six hours—no mean feat for an army in any age!—testifies to the military effectiveness of both the troops and their commanders.

Parma's panoply lacked only sufficient warships to protect his troops from assault by their Dutch and English enemies as they crossed the channel and a train of siege artillery. Philip II had anticipated both problems. To remedy the first deficiency, the armada included four heavily armed *galeasses*, huge oar-powered warships of shallow draft capable of driving off the Dutch ships blockading the Flemish ports. To meet the second need, the Spanish fleet carried twelve forty-pounder siege guns, together with all their accoutrements. Parma's army would thus have enjoyed full artillery support.

Very few towns and castles in southeast England could have resisted a battery from such weapons. Only solid-angled bastions, projecting beyond the main walls and protected by wide moats, could withstand heavy bombardment; and in southeast England only Upnor Castle on the River Medway, built to defend the naval dockyard at Chatham, possessed those. The larger towns of Kent (Canterbury and Rochester) still relied on their antiquated medieval walls. No defense works at all seem to have existed between Margate, the projected beachhead, and the Medway; while Upnor alone could scarcely stop the Duke of Parma and his army. Philip II had deftly selected his adversary's weakest point.

With so few physical obstacles in his path, Parma would have moved fast. When he invaded Normandy in 1592, with 22,000 men, the duke covered sixty-five miles in six days, despite tenacious opposition from a numerically superior enemy. Four years earlier, the invaders might therefore have covered the eighty miles from Margate to London in a week. Even London represented a soft target because the capital still relied on its medieval walls. They had scarcely changed since 1554, when Sir Thomas Wyatt raised a rebel army in protest against the marriage of Mary Tudor, Elizabeth's half-sister and predecessor, to Philip II. The insurgents marched through Kent, crossed the Thames at Kingston (west of the capital), advanced with impunity through Westminster, and surged down Fleet Street until they reached the city walls, where Wyatt, lacking artillery, finally lost his nerve.

Parma well knew, however, that the state of a town's physical de-

The Spanish Invasion of England, 1588

fenses did not always prove decisive. Several Netherland towns with poor, outdated fortifications had escaped capture thanks to the determination of the besieged population; conversely, a few strongholds boasting modern defensive systems had fallen to the Spaniards before their time because their citizens, their garrison, or their commander succumbed to bribes. As an English officer with the Dutch army wrote on hearing of the premature surrender of yet another town to Parma: "Everybody knows that the king of Spain's golden salvoes made a bigger breach in the heart of the traitor in command than did the siege artillery." Elizabeth's troops in the Netherlands had a distinctly uninspiring record in this respect. In

1584 the English garrison of Aalst sold their town to Parma for £10,000 and in 1587 Sir William Stanley and Roland Yorke, together with over 700 English and Irish soldiers under their command, betrayed to Parma the places entrusted to their care (Deventer and a fort overlooking Zutphen), and for the most part subsequently fought for Spain against their former comrades.

Elizabeth and her advisers nevertheless set great store by the comrades of these traitors, recalling 4,000 men of the English expeditionary force in Holland to form the nucleus of the army intended to repulse the invaders. Its quartermaster general was the brother of Roland Yorke; its third-in-command, Sir Roger Williams, had fought for Philip II in the Netherlands in the 1570s. One cannot exclude the possibility that some of these men might have been prepared to sell strongholds to Parma, as their fellows had done in the Low Countries.

Elizabeth, however, had little choice. She depended on the veterans from Holland because she could call upon very few other experienced troops. The London "trained bands," who had been drilling twice weekly since March, might have put up a good fight (although some doubted it) but little could be expected from the rest of the English county militias. Few men possessed firearms, and some of those received only enough powder for three or four rounds; the militias of the southern shires proved so disorderly that their commanders feared they "will sooner kill one another than annoye the enemye"; while the queen felt obliged to maintain 6,000 soldiers along the Scottish border in case King James VI, whose mother (Mary Stuart) Elizabeth had executed the previous year, should decide to throw in his hand with the Spaniards.

All English preparations fell dangerously behind. The queen only issued orders for the southern militias to muster on July 27—as the armada approached the channel—and even then she ordered them to move toward Tilbury in Essex, separated by seventy miles and the Thames from the beachhead chosen by Philip II. A boom across the river designed to keep out enemy shipping broke at the first high tide and was never repaired; a bridge of boats designed to link the queen's forces in

Kent and Essex remained incomplete. Even at Tilbury, the linchpin of England's defenses, work only began on the fortifications on August 3, the day the armada passed the Isle of Wight. Three days later, as the fleet dropped anchor off Calais, the troops in Kent began to desert in considerable numbers. In any case, they numbered only 4000 men, a ludicrously inadequate force to throw in the path of the seasoned Spaniards, and they lacked a clear strategy. The local commander, Sir Thomas Scott, argued that his forces should spread out along the coast and "answer" the enemy "at the sea side," while the general officer commanding in the southeast, Sir John Norris, more prudently wished to withdraw all but a skeleton force inland in order to make a stand at Canterbury and there "staye the enemye from speedy passage to London or the harte of the realme."

Much of this unpreparedness and confusion stemmed from poverty and isolation. Elizabeth could raise no loans either at home (because hostilities with Spain had caused a trade recession) or abroad (because most continental bankers thought Spain would win), forcing her to delay every stage of her counterinvasion plans until the last possible moment in order to save money. On July 29, 1588, her treasurer complained that outstanding bills totaling £40,000 lay on his desk "with no probability how to get money" to pay them. "A man might wish," he concluded dourly, that "if peace cannot be had, that the enemy would not longer delay, but prove, as I trust, his evil fortune." Apart from the Dutch, England stood entirely alone.

By contrast, although on one occasion Philip II had to pawn his family jewels to raise money, he managed to provide huge sums for the Enterprise of England. The French Catholic League received 1,500,000 ducats from Spain between 1587 and 1590, and over the same period the Army of Flanders received some 21,000,000 more. The king himself claimed that he had spent 10,000,000 on the armada itself. Since about four ducats equaled one pound sterling, his total outlay on the project thus exceeded £7,000,000, at a time when Elizabeth's annual revenues hovered around £200,000. At the same time, Philip's diplomats managed either to win over or neutralize every other state in Europe. In July 1588, as the armada entered the channel, an admiring ambassador at the Court of Spain noted:

> At the moment, the Catholic King [Philip II] is safe: France cannot threaten him, and the Turks can do little; neither can the king of Scots, who is offended at Queen Elizabeth on account of the death of his mother [Mary Stuart]. The one [monarch] who could have opposed him was the king of Denmark, who has just died, and his son is young and so has other things to deal with . . . At the same time, Spain can rest assured that the Swiss cantons will not move against him; nor will they allow others to do so, since they are now his allies.

In short, he concluded, no foreign power could prevent the execution of the king's Grand Strategy for the conquest of England and the hegemony of Europe.

✦ ✦ ✦

Were these optimistic contemporary analysts correct? In *Pavane*, a novel published in 1968, Keith Roberts graphically suggested the enormous advantages that might have accrued from a complete Spanish victory.

> On a warm July evening of the year 1588, in the royal palace of Greenwich, London, a woman lay dying, an assassin's bullets lodged in abdomen and chest. Her face was lined, her teeth blackened, and death lent her no dignity; but her last breath started echoes that ran out to shake a hemisphere. For the Faery Queen, Elizabeth the First, paramount ruler of England, was no more.
>
> The rage of the English knew no bounds . . . The English Catholics, bled white by fines, still mourning the Queen of Scots, still remembering the gory Rising of the North, were faced with a fresh pogrom. Unwillingly, in self-defense, they took up arms against their countrymen as the flame lit by the Walsingham massacres ran across the land, mingling with the light of warning beacons from the sullen glare of the auto-da-fe.
>
> The news spread; to Paris, to Rome, to . . . the great ships of the ar-

mada, threshing up past the Lizard to link with Parma's army of invasion on the Flemish coast . . . The turmoil that ensued saw Philip ensconced as ruler of England; in France the followers of Guise, heartened by the victories across the channel, finally deposed the weakened House of Valois. The War of the Three Henrys ended with the Holy League triumphant, and the Church restored once more to her ancient power.

To the victor, the spoils. With the authority of the Catholic Church assured, the rising nation of Great Britain deployed her forces in the service of the popes, smashing the Protestants of the Netherlands, destroying the power of the German city-states in the long-drawn Lutheran Wars. The New Worlders of the North American continent remained under the rule of Spain; Cook planted in Australasia the cobalt flag of the [papal] throne.

✦ ✦ ✦

At first sight, this "best-case outcome" for Spain of the armada campaign does not seem too fanciful. Assassination, the constant nightmare of the childless Elizabeth's ministers, had become commonplace in early modern Europe. In France, Catholic extremists murdered not only the Protestant faction leaders Anthony of Navarre (1563) and Gaspard de Coligny (1572), but also King Henry III (1589) and his successor, Henry IV (1610.) Elizabeth survived at least twenty assassination plots: the success of any of them would have extinguished the Tudor dynasty and left a council of Regency both to direct resistance against the advance of the relentless invaders, and to find a successor.

Even without the removal of Elizabeth, whether by assassination or by capture, a Spanish occupation of Kent alone might have produced important results. Parma could have exploited his advantage to wrest concessions from a Tudor government terrified of rebellions in the north and in Ireland. Persecution of English Catholics would have ceased, allowing their numbers and confidence to increase. The overseas exploits of Sir Francis Drake and the other "seadogs" would also have ceased, leaving North America securely in Spain's sphere of influence (missionaries had already begun to advance from Florida into Virginia.) Finally, English forces would have withdrawn from the Netherlands, abandoning the Dutch to make the best settlement they could.

The Republic already contained a vociferous peace party. Although most political leaders in Holland and Zealand firmly opposed talks with Spain, some towns dissented, while the adjacent provinces that bore the brunt of the war against Spain argued strongly in favor of a settlement. According to one of Elizabeth's envoys to the Dutch: "The Common Wealth of these Provinces consisting of diverse Parts and Professions as, namely, Protestants, Puritans, Anabaptists and Spanish Hearts, which are no small number; it is most certain that dividing these in five parts, the Protestants and the Puritans do hardly contain even one part of five." And, the envoy continued, only the "Protestants and Puritans" favored a continuation of the war. Had the Enterprise of England succeeded, leaving the young republic to withstand Philip's power alone, internal pressure for a compromise would probably have become irresistible.

Without the need to maintain a costly army in the Netherlands, Spain would have been free, just as Keith Roberts fantasized, to intervene decisively elsewhere. The expulsion of the Protestants from France and the recovery for the Roman Church of many Lutheran areas of Germany, both of which occurred in the seventeenth century, would no doubt have taken place several decades earlier. The newly confident Counter-Reformation church, assisted by the power of the Habsburgs, would have virtually extirpated Protestantism from Europe. Overseas, the Spanish and Portuguese empires would have continued their expansion and steadily increased their mutual contacts, creating a unified Iberian empire whose resources would have extended the authority of Philip II and his successors all around the globe.

✦ ✦ ✦

Or would it? Counterfactual experiments in history should always include two limitations: the "minimal rewrite rule" (only small and plausible changes should be made to the actual sequence of events) and "second order counterfactuals" (after a certain time, the previous pattern may reassert itself.) In the case of Philip II, it seems reasonable to speculate that the fireships released by the Royal Navy on the night of August 7, 1588, might somehow have failed to destroy the armada's battle order—as it was, the Spaniards managed to intercept two of them and tow them out of harm's way. Medina Sidonia could then have waited for Parma and his troops, who completed their embarkation by August 8, to set forth and join him. They would then have crossed the Narrow Seas in irresistible force. Beyond that, however, the "rewrite" becomes more than "minimal."

We cannot assume that Philip II would have exploited his victory prudently. Having ruled and resided there during the 1550s (as husband of Mary Tudor), he regarded himself as both omniscient and divinely inspired where England was concerned. "I can give better information and advice on that kingdom and on its affairs and people than anyone else," he once informed the pope. This supreme confidence helps to explain why he sought to micromanage every aspect of the armada campaign, starting with the creation of a master plan that imprudently involved the junction of a fleet from Spain with an army from Flanders, separated by a thousand miles of sea, as the ineluctable preliminary to invasion. He refused to allow anyone—whether councilor, general, or admiral—to challenge the wisdom of his Grand Strategy. Instead, he urged them to "believe me as one who has complete information on the present state of affairs in all areas." Whenever obstacles threatened the venture, Philip insisted that God would provide a miracle. When, for example, a freak storm in June 1588 drove the armada back to port soon after it had set forth, and Medina Sidonia suggested that this might be a warning from the Almighty that the enterprise should be abandoned, Philip responded with naked spiritual blackmail. "If this were an unjust war," he scolded the duke, "one could indeed take this storm as a sign from Our Lord to cease offending Him. But being as just as it is, one cannot believe that He will disband it, but rather will grant it more favor than we could hope . . .

I have dedicated this enterprise to God," the king concluded briskly. "Pull yourself together, and do your part!"

Philip also rashly insisted that the armada should advance to Calais as fast as possible, without waiting for confirmation that the Army of Flanders was ready. It never seems to have occurred to him that the numerous English and Dutch warships in the channel might prevent Medina Sidonia's from sending reports of his progress, his problems, and his estimated time of arrival from reaching Parma. Instead, stinging royal rebukes awaited those aboard the fleet who counseled caution and delay.

There seems no reason to suppose that a successful Spanish invasion of southeast England would have reduced Philip's desire to meddle. Rather, he would have tried to retain total control of events, demanding that all major decisions be referred to him—a two- to three-weeks' journey away in Spain—for resolution. He would also probably have insisted that Parma should strive for total victory instead of seeking a compromise, just as he had refused to discuss a compromise settlement after every major success in the struggle against the Dutch, thus creating a stalemate that drained his resources. This, too, would have affected the continuing continental struggles. With the invasion of England bogged down, Dutch resistance would have continued and the position of the French Catholics deteriorated, straining Spain's resources yet further and pushing it toward bankruptcy. As it was, the royal treasury had to suspend all payments in 1596.

When Philip II died in 1598, at the age of seventy-one, his empire passed to his only surviving son, the nineteen-year-old Philip III. The absence of an older, more accomplished successor arose from the peculiar genetic heritage of the Spanish Habsburgs. For generation after generation, they married close relatives. Philip II's oldest son Don Carlos, arrested and imprisoned because of his dangerously unstable behavior, could boast only four grandparents instead of eight, and only six great-grand parents instead of sixteen. The gene pool inherited by his half-brother Philip (III) was scarcely better: his mother, Anna of Austria, was

Philip II's niece and cousin as well as his wife. This endogamy—or as Spain's enemies termed it, incest—arose from the desire to join territories together. Don Carlos descended from three generations of intermarriage between the ruling dynasties of Portugal and Spain. This policy, although technically successful (the kingdoms were united in 1580), literally carried within itself the seeds of its own destruction. No wonder the Spanish Habsburgs died out after only two more generations of endogamy! The conquest of England would have done nothing to improve the Habsburg gene pool; it would merely have served to create more for Philip III and his successors to lose. Second order counterfactuals suggest that, even had the armada succeeded, Spanish hegemony would not have lasted for long.

At least, however, Philip's victory in 1588 would have gone down in history as an exemplary "combined operation." Historians would have praised the selection of an ideal invasion area, the formidable planning, the immense resources, the successful diplomacy that neutralized all opposition, and the operational brilliance that (against all the odds) joined an irresistible fleet from Spain with an invincible army from the Netherlands. If, despite all its deficiencies, the duke of Parma and his veteran troops had begun their march on London on Monday August 8, 1588, then—whatever the ultimate outcome—everyone today could regard the invincible armada as Philip II's masterpiece, all Americans would now speak Spanish, and the whole world might celebrate August 8 as a national holiday.

# THOMAS FLEMING

# UNLIKELY VICTORY

*Thirteen Ways the Americans Could Have*
*Lost the Revolution*

The American Revolution is practically a laboratory of counterfactual history. There is hardly an opportunity for an alternative scenario that doesn't exist in those eight years (1775–1783). At times, as Thomas Fleming demonstrates, the unexpected seems the only real certainty. Sometimes sheer luck intervenes. A British marksman has Washington in his sights and doesn't pull the trigger. Commanders display too much or too little caution. The British make a picture-perfect landing on Manhattan Island, and then pause to wait for reinforcements while George Washington and his Continentals slip the noose. At the Battle of the Cowpens, Banastre Tarleton, like the emperor Valens at Adrianople, is too impetuous, and the Americans hold on in the South. (There are times when a short rest and a good breakfast could have changed history.) Gambles work. Washington attacks Trenton in a Christmas night snowstorm and reinvigorates the patriot cause. Good or bad choices are made under stress. Benedict Arnold disobeys orders at Saratoga, and the result is an American victory. Would the French have joined the war on our side otherwise? Animosities influence events. In a turf struggle, the British commander in chief, Sir Henry Clinton, tells his Southern commander, Charles, Lord Cornwallis, to retreat to an obscure Virginia tobacco port called Yorktown, fortify it, and ship much of his army back north. The vagaries of weather are a given, of course, as they always have been in military operations. Take the two violent storms that sealed the fate of the British troops trapped at Yorktown in October 1781: The first prevented a rescue fleet from sailing from New York harbor and the second, a break-out attempt across the York River a few days later. How different would the outcome of the Revolution have been if the British had escaped?

By any reasonable stretch of the imagination, Fleming reminds us, the United States should have expired at birth. We were hardly inevitable.

✦ Thomas Fleming is the author of such historical studies as 1776: YEAR OF ILLU-SIONS, biographies of Thomas Jefferson and Benjamin Franklin, THE MAN FROM MONTICELLO and THE MAN WHO DARED THE LIGHTNING, LIBERTY: THE AMERICAN REVOLUTION, and, most recently, DUEL: ALEXANDER HAMILTON, AARON BURR AND THE FUTURE OF AMERICA. He has also written numerous historical novels, including two set during the Revolutionary War, LIBERTY TAVERN and DREAMS OF GLORY. Fleming has served as chairman of the American Revolution Round Table and is the former president of the American Center of P.E.N., the international writer's or-ganization.

When a historian ponders the what ifs of the American Revolution, chills run up and down and around the cerebellum. There were almost too many moments when the patriot cause teetered on the brink of disaster, to be retrieved by the most unlikely accidents or coincidences or choices made by harried men in the heat of conflict. Seldom if ever was there a war with more potential for changing the course of history. Imagine the last two hundred years—or at the very least, the last hundred—without a United States of America! Picture a world in which the British Empire bestrode not only the subcontinent of India, but the entire continent of North America.

Almost as tantalizing is the society that might have arisen, with a different outcome. If the Americans had lost the war early in the struggle, they might have been permitted a modicum of self rule; there would have been few, if any hangings or confiscations. If victory had come later, when the British government and people were exasperated by long years of resistance, Americans might well have become a subject race, savagely repressed by a standing army, and ruled by an arrogant local aristocracy. The impact on Great Britain would have been almost as dire. The hardliners in the aristocracy, backed by a king who was equally narrow-minded, would have created a state that was relentlessly intolerant of democracy.

Within these extremes are other outcomes. One of the most intriguing appeared even before the war began. The child—independence—could easily have been strangled in its cradle, if some of its parents had not realized that they were performing on a stage far larger than the provincial seaport of Boston.

*What if Samuel Adams had gotten his way after the Boston Massacre?*

Sam Adams deserves his niche as the master agitator on the torturous path to independence. But he had a tendency to brinkmanship, demonstrated by his less than brilliant staging of the Boston Massacre. With the town occupied by two regiments of British troops, Sam thought his well-armed bullyboys from the North End of Boston could terrify the royal army into a humiliating evacuation. On the night of March 5, 1770, a well-armed 400-man mob pelted the seven-man British detachment guarding the customs house with chunks of ice and pieces of lumber. Screaming insults, they surged to within a few feet of the soldiers' guns. Sam had assured the rioters that the redcoats would never pull their triggers without a magistrate first reading the riot act, officially branding the mob as violators of the king's peace and warning them to disperse. This was something no judge in Boston dared to do, lest he get his house torn down around his ears.

Someone in the crowd struck a soldier with a club, knocking him to the ground. The man sprang to his feet and was struck by another club, thrown from a distance. He leveled his musket and pulled the trigger. Seconds later, the other members of the guard imitated him. The mob fled. As the gunsmoke cleared, five men lay dead or dying. Six more men were wounded.

Although he professed to abhor the bloodshed, Sam Adams was secretly delighted. He foresaw a trial for murder in which the soldiers would be found guilty. Rather than let them hang, the British would intervene, declaring their indifference to the verdicts of American juries. Meanwhile, Sam's propaganda machine would be denouncing the royal murderers and their London backers. It never occurred to Sam that moderates in other colonies and in England would see this denouement as proof that Boston was in the hands of an anarchistic mob, and the British might be excused for resorting to draconian measures to restore law and order.

Fortunately, one man in Boston saw this clearly—Sam's cousin, John

Adams. Although he had been active in Sam's movement, John was shocked when friends of the soldiers informed him that not a lawyer in Boston was willing to defend them, for fear of getting his windows and possibly his face smashed by Sam's sluggers. John announced he would take the soldiers' case. With masterful skill, he managed a plea of self-defense without quite revealing Sam and his friends as the perpetrators of the riot. The soldiers were acquitted and for the rest of his long life, John Adams maintained that his "disinterested action" in defending the redcoats was "one of the best pieces of service I ever rendered my country." He was unquestionably right. Moderate men in England and New York and Virginia were able to tell each other that the Bostonians were worthy of their support.

If Sam had triggered a draconian response, there might never have been a Boston Tea Party. In a town patrolled by six or seven regiments, no further riots would have been tolerated, and Sam and his lieutenants might well have been taken into custody during the peaceful three years between the Massacre and the dumping of the tea into the harbor. Instead, outsiders viewed the confrontation over a piddling but highly symbolic tax on imported tea as British arrogance and stupidity in action. The tea party was greeted with tut-tuts by the moderates but no one saw it as another demonstration of endemic Yankee lawlessness—and the moderates quickly agreed that the British government's reaction to it—closing the port of Boston and remodeling the government of Massachusetts to extract the democratic elements—was egregious overkill and a step toward tyranny. Soon Sam and John Adams were on their way to the First Continental Congress in Philadelphia.

Back in Massachusetts in early 1775, with the British 4,500-man army in Boston under a state of semisiege, confronted by swarms of well-armed minutemen whenever detachments marched into the country, Sam showed he had learned nothing from the Massacre fiasco. He proposed bringing matters to a head by launching an all-out attack on the regulars. Cooler heads prevailed, arguing that the rest of America would never support such a move—and the British would welcome it as proof that there really was a rebellion in Massachusetts, no different from the ones they had suppressed with ruthless efficiency in Ireland and Scotland.

Again, there is no doubt that the cooler men were right. When an impatient ministry pushed the British commander in Boston, Major General Thomas Gage, into action, he sent 700 men on a night march to Concord, hoping to seize the rebels' gunpowder and other war material and effectively disarm them. On Lexington Green, the marchers encountered the town's militia company. Gunfire broke out, leaving dead men on the grass. It was followed by more gunfire and bloodshed at Concord and by a running battle between the British and swarming minutemen on the road back to Boston. Sam Adams had the incident he needed to unite the Americans—and give moderate men in England grounds for attacking the government in Parliament and in the newspapers.

### What if the British plan had worked at Bunker Hill?

Two months later the embryo war could have gone either way at Bunker Hill. The mythical version of this battle has the British marching stupidly up the hill to get blasted by American marksmen. In fact, the British had a sophisticated battle plan that could have ended the war if they had been able to execute it.

The field commander, Major General William Howe, intended to outflank the exposed fort on Breed's (not Bunker's) Hill by sending a column of crack light infantrymen up the beach on the shore of the Mystic River and sealing off the narrow neck of the Charlestown Peninsula, trapping the Americans like insects in a bottle. Simultaneously, the other half of the British army was to assault the weakened American lines around Cambridge, where the rebels had most of their powder and ammunition. If all went well, the Americans would be a fleeing mob by the end of the day.

Fortunately for the future of the yet unborn United States, Colonel John Stark, commander of a New Hampshire regiment and a veteran of the French and Indian War, spotted the deserted beach as a potentially fa-

BOSTON

CHARLES TOWN

View of *The* ATTACK *on* BUNKER'S HILL, *with the* Burning *of* CHARLES TOWN, *June* 17, 1775.

*Drawn by Mr. Millar.* *Engraved by Lodge.*

## BUNKER HILL: REVOLUTION'S PREMATURE END?

*An early nineteenth-century engraving shows the Battle of Bunker (Breed's) Hill and a burning Charlestown, Massachusetts, on June 17, 1775. Had even one of the naval vessels in the harbor came to the aid of the British troops trying to take the hill from the other side—out of view, here—the Revolution might have been throttled that afternoon.*

(Anne S. K. Brown Military Collection, Brown University Library)

tal flaw in the American position. He ordered 200 of his best men there and took personal command of them. When Howe saw this checkmate, he asked the British admiral on the Boston station to send a sloop up the Mystic River to scatter Stark's men with a few rounds of grapeshot. The admiral demurred, saying he had no charts of the river.

Howe sent his light infantrymen forward anyway, gambling that the American amateurs could not get off more than a round before the professionals were on top of them with their bayonets. It did not work that way. Stark's New Hampshire sharpshooters littered the beach with British dead and Howe was reduced to a desperate frontal assault, which cost him almost half his little army before he carried the Breed's Hill fort.

If that British admiral had the energy or the brains to chart the Mystic River, or if John Stark had failed to spot the importance of that beach, Bunker Hill would have been a very different story. Except for some sputters of resistance in Virginia and a few other colonies, the American Revolution might well have ended on June 17, 1775. Instead, the Americans were enormously emboldened by their ability to inflict crippling casualties on their foes—and the British were forced onto a humiliating defensive in a Boston ringed by hostile Yankees.

## What if Washington had attacked the British army in Boston in early 1776?

A fascinating possibility preoccupied George Washington after he took command of the American army outside Boston in July of 1775. For nine months a stalemate ensued, largely caused by Washington's shortage of artillery and his inability to prevent most of his Yankee army from going home on January 1, 1776, when their enlistments expired. In March of 1776, his spies reported that numerous British ships in the harbor were taking on water and provisions, preparing to withdraw from Boston. Their destination was presumed to be New York.

By this time, Washington had acquired plenty of artillery from captured Fort Ticonderoga and his army was again a respectable size. The American commander decided to abort this enemy plan to seize New York, where they would be far more dangerous to the Revolution than they were on a cramped defensive in Boston.

Washington concocted a daring, even a hair-raising plan. First he would seize Dorchester Heights, south of the city, and emplace cannon on it. When the British attacked the position, he would send 4,000 men in forty-five bateaux, supported by 12-pound cannon on rafts, to assault Boston from the Charles River. While half the force seized Beacon Hill and similar high ground in the city, the other half would attack British fortifications on Boston Neck, opening the way for reinforcements waiting to rush overland from Roxbury. Washington was convinced that the destruction of Howe's army would cripple the British war effort and lead to an immediate peace.

At first, everything went according to plan. On the night of March 4, Washington seized Dorchester Heights and mounted cannon in a series of forts that the British would have to attack or abandon Boston. General Howe readied his army for an assault on March 5. Still an ambitious gambler, Howe planned to attack Washington's Roxbury lines with 4,000 men as the rest of his troops—about 2,200 men—advanced on Dorchester. That left only 400 redcoats guarding the side of Boston at which Washington was aiming his amphibious assault.

The stage was set for a titanic showdown. But as darkness fell on March 5, a cold, biting wind began to blow, mixing snow and hail. Soon it was a "hurrycane," in the words of one of Washington's junior officers. Howe called off his attack and Washington's plan also went into the circular files. Would it have worked? When the British evacuated Boston thirteen days later, Washington had a chance to study, at close range, the fortifications he was hoping to assault. He was awed by their strength. "The town of Boston," he admitted, "was almost impregnable." In a letter to his brother Jack, Washington called the storm a "remarkable interposition of providence."

A Washington defeat at that point in the war, while it would not necessarily have ended the conflict, would have been calamitous for his reputation. Critics in the Continental Congress and in the army were already sniping at him, fretting over his supposed timidity and indecisiveness. Would a Washington victory have ended the war, as he hoped? Probably not. The British government was in the process of shipping to America an army four times the size of the one in Boston.

*What if the British had trapped Washington's army on Long Island or Manhattan?*

George Washington had urged the Continental Congress to give him an army of 40,000 men, enlisted for the duration of the war. Congress believed the fantasy Sam Adams exported from Boston after Lexington and Concord: Yeoman farmers had sprung to arms to defeat British regulars. In reality, Massachusetts had an embryo army of minutemen who had been training for nine months and were five times the size of the British garrison in Boston. Washington was told to limit his army to 20,000 men, enlisted for a single year, and rely on militia—part-time soldiers who, unlike the minutemen, had little or no training. Then Congress nibbled away at Washington's army, demanding that detachments be shipped to bolster the losing war the Americans were fighting in Canada.

As a result, Washington showed up in New York with little more than 10,000 regulars—Continentals, as they were called—and summoned a horde of militia from New England, New York, New Jersey, and Pennsylvania to bolster his force. He confronted a royal army that numbered almost 30,000 men, including about 12,000 German mercenaries. At the battle of Long Island on August 27, the British, once more commanded by William Howe, devised a flanking strategy that worked. The calamitous day ended with most of Washington's army trapped in forts in Brooklyn Heights.

Two nights later, with the help of a favorable wind and a fortuitous fog, Washington stealthily withdrew his army to Manhattan. There he had two more narrow escapes. On September 15, the British landed at Kips Bay (present-day Thirty-fourth Street), routing thousands of Connecticut militia. Only excessive caution prevented the British from trapping a third of the Continental Army in lower Manhattan.

On October 18, the British landed at Pell's Point in Westchester. A fighting retreat by a 750-man Massachusetts brigade gave Washington time to get his army off Manhattan Island. By this time Washington had no illusions about the militia; most of them had gone home. While many American leaders despaired, Washington kept his head and took charge of the war. He told Congress the American army would no longer seek to end the struggle in one titanic battle. "We will *never* seek a general action," he informed the president of Congress, John Hancock. Instead, "We will protract the war." This seemingly simple change in strategy transformed the conflict into a war of attrition—precisely the kind of war the British were least prepared to fight.

If Washington and his army had been trapped in Brooklyn Heights or Manhattan, the war would have ended quickly. The stupidity of Congress's reliance on militia had become apparent to everyone. It would have been very difficult for Americans to raise another army, after the routs on Long Island and at Kips Bay. Worse, the alternative general action strategy called for replicating the Battle of Bunker Hill, an idea that obsessed most American generals. The British would never have repeated that mistake. Without Washington's new strategy, despair would have seeped through the revolutionists' ranks.

### What if Washington had decided not to attack Trenton and Princeton or failed in either attempt?

Retreating across New Jersey, Washington watched the the British begin pacifying this crucial state. They circulated a proclamation, urging the civilians to swear "peaceable allegiance" to George III and receive a "protection," a guarantee that their lives and property would not be forfeited. Thousands took advantage of the offer to bail out of the apparently lost cause. The New Jersey militia, 17,000 strong on paper, evaporated. Barely 1,000 men turned out. It was a preview of how the British hoped to end the war in other colonies.

To protect the loyalists, the British stationed garrisons in various towns across the state. Washington noted they were "a good deal dispersed"—making them ripe targets for a defeat by a concentration of superior force. On Christmas night, 1776, Washington slashed across the Delaware in a driving snowstorm to capture three German regiments at Trenton. New Jersey and the rest of the almost stillborn nation became, in the words of one dismayed Briton, "liberty mad" again.

Ten days later, Washington took an even more nerve-racking gamble. He had returned to the New Jersey side of the Delaware to rally the state—and found himself confronting some 7,000 well-armed redcoats commanded by Charles, Lord Cornwallis. Wheeling around the enemy flank in a night march that was a neat riposte to Howe's maneuver on Long Island, Washington chewed up the British garrison at Princeton and retreated with booty and prisoners to high ground in Morristown. The befuddled British, fearful that he was planning to strike their main base at New Brunswick, relapsed to a timid defensive around that town, abandoning most of New Jersey to the rebels.

If Washington had hesitated to launch these two daring attacks with his ragged, barefoot army, or had failed in either attempt, the middle colonies—New York, New Jersey, Pennsylvania, Maryland, and Delaware—would have surrendered almost immediately. The South, or at least haughty Virginia, might have taken longer to subdue and the stubborn New Englanders even longer. But King George's men, skillfully appealing to moderates with the assurance that "British liberty" was a central part of the conciliation package, would have inevitably prevailed. Within a year or two at most, Americans would have been on their way to becoming replicas of the Canadians, tame, humble colonials in the triumphant British empire, without an iota of the independent spirit that has been the heart of the nation's identity.

*What if General Benedict Arnold had not turned himself into Admiral Arnold on Lake Champlain?*

A similar outcome could have resulted if things had gone differently in another part of the war in the fall of 1776. If Brigadier General Benedict Arnold had lacked the nautical know-how—and incredible nerve—to launch an American fleet on Lake Champlain in the late summer of 1776, the British would have wintered in Albany and been ready to launch a war of annihilation against New England in the spring of 1777.

Routed from Canada by massive British reinforcements, Arnold and the remnants of the so-called Northern Army had retreated to Fort Ticonderoga, at the foot of Lake Champlain. A more unpromising situation was hard to imagine. The British commander, Guy Carleton, was

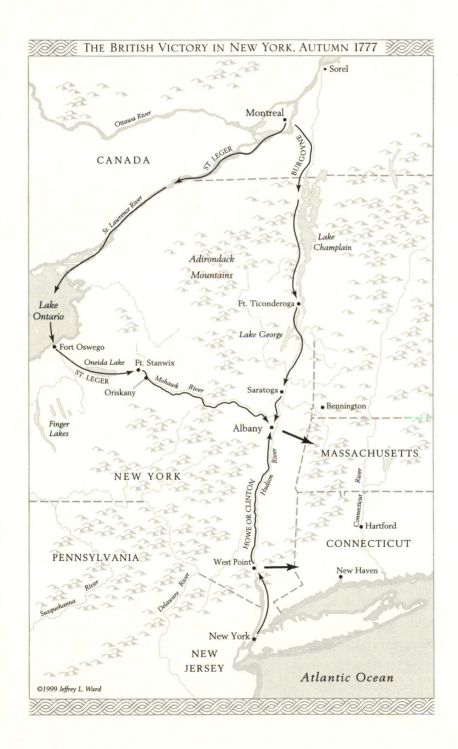

Sorel

Montreal

Ottawa River

CANADA

ST. LEGER

BURGOYNE

St. Lawrence River

Lake
Champlain

Adirondack
Mountains

Lake
Ontario

Ft. Ticonderoga

Fort Oswego

Lake George

Oneida Lake      Ft. Stanwix

ST. LEGER          Mohawk       River

Oriskany

Saratoga

Bennington

Finger
Lakes

Albany

MASSACHUSETTS

NEW YORK

Connecticut River

Hudson River

HOWE OR CLINTON

Hartford

CONNECTICUT

PENNSYLVANIA

River

West Point

New Haven

Susquehanna River

Delaware River

New York

NEW
JERSEY

Atlantic Ocean

©1999 Jeffrey L. Ward

planning to assault the so-called "Gibraltar of America" with perhaps 16,000 men and numerous Indians. To oppose him, the Americans had barely 3,500 broken, dispirited men, ravaged by smallpox and defeat.

Marching down Lake Champlain's forested 135-mile shore was out of the question. Carleton planned to come by water, backed by a fleet. Arnold decided to turn himself into an admiral and create a fleet of his own. He had made many voyages to the West Indies and Canada as a merchant and knew his way around a ship. Procuring carpenters virtually by legerdemain, he knocked together thirteen clumsy row galleys and gondolas made of green wood and crewed them with soldiers who had never been on a ship in their lives. With an insouciance that bordered on insanity, Arnold sailed this makeshift squadron up the lake and dared the British to come out and fight.

Almost too late, the impromptu admiral learned that Carleton was building a full-rigged 180-ton man-of-war, HMS *Inflexible*, which had enough firepower to annihilate his matchbox fleet all by herself. Arnold retreated down the lake to Valcour Island, where he took up a defensive position. In the British camp, numerous officers urged Carleton to advance without *Inflexible*. It was already September. In another month, snow might begin to fall. They had twenty-four gunboats, two well-armed schooners, and a huge artillery raft called the *Thunderer* afloat. But the cautious Carleton, impressed by Arnold's bravado, demurred and his army sat at the head of the lake for another four weeks while *Inflexible* was rigged and armed.

Not until October 11th, 1776, did Carleton's armada approach Arnold's fleet, anchored across the mouth of Valcour Bay. In a wild six-hour melee, the Americans took a terrific beating but held their battle line until nightfall. In the darkness, Arnold led a runaway retreat but the British caught up to him over the following three days and destroyed all but five of his ships. Ticonderoga was Carleton's for the taking. He had a five-to-one advantage in men and guns.

The American garrison pretended to be eager to fight, hurling cannon balls and curses at British scouting parties. Carleton, remembering

Bunker Hill, ruled out a frontal assault and decided it was too late in the year to begin a siege. As the British retreated to Canada for the winter, one of Carleton's officers groaned: "If we could have begun our expedition four weeks earlier." It had taken exactly four weeks for Carleton to launch *Inflexible*. Admiral Arnold and his green fleet had broken the momentum of the British counterattack from the North.

If Carleton had captured Ticonderoga in the fall of 1776 and routed or captured the Northern Army, there would have been nothing to prevent him from seizing Albany before the snow fell. In the ensuing spring he would have been able to smash into New England wherever he chose, much as Sherman ravaged the South from its exposed western flank in the Civil War. Even before he marched, Carleton would have converted Albany into a center of loyalist resistance to the Continental Congress. The Canadian commander was a far more astute conciliator than the Howes. He paroled all the prisoners he had captured in Canada and sent them home well fed and forgiven. Loyalism was strong in Northern New York, as the five-year-long bloody battles of the so-called "border warfare" would soon attest.

## What if Benedict Arnold had obeyed orders at Saratoga?

A year later, it did not look as if General/Admiral Arnold's Valcour Bay heroics meant much. General John Burgoyne had replaced Carleton as the British northern commander and in early July he sailed unopposed down Lake Champlain and captured Ticonderoga with stunning ease. The disorganized Americans had largely wasted the precious months Arnold had bought them with his driving energy and combative spirit.

To oppose Burgoyne's 9,000-man army, Congress chose Major General Horatio Gates, a former British staff officer with no battle experience worth mentioning. To bolster him on the fighting side, Washington sent him Arnold, now a major general, and huge pugnacious Colonel Daniel Morgan of Virginia with his corps of riflemen. Constructing elaborate fortifications on Bemis Heights, some twenty-eight miles north of Albany, Gates hunkered down to await Burgoyne's attack. He seemed to think he could reenact Bunker Hill in the forest.

Burgoyne had no intention of cooperating with him. He had gone to immense trouble to drag some forty-two heavy guns through the woods from Ticonderoga. His plan of attack called for a flanking movement that would enable him to position these guns on high ground and hammer Gates's fortifications—and army—to pieces. Arnold saw the danger and after a ferocious argument convinced the timid Gates to let him fight the British in the woods. The result was a tremendous battle in and around cleared ground known as Freeman's Farm, in which Arnold and his men inflicted heavy casualties on the British and forced them to retreat.

Three weeks later, on October 7, Burgoyne attacked again. Now his motive was desperation. His men were on half rations; sickness and defeatism were multiplying. In a move that combined jealousy and stupidity, General Howe had abandoned him. Instead of fighting Washington in New Jersey, from which forced marches could have brought him to Burgoyne's aid, Howe had sailed south from New York to attack Philadelphia from the head of the Chesapeake. Capturing the American capital seemed to Howe a far better way to end the war than Burgoyne's plan to subdue New York and split the New England states from the rest of the American confederacy. As the British commander in chief, with an army three times the size of Burgoyne's, Howe also had no enthusiasm for letting Gentleman Johnny become the man who won the war. This otherwise incomprehensible decision is a good example of how often history turns on grudges and antagonisms between men in power.

On the American side, the sneaky Gates had infuriated Arnold by giving him no credit for his exploits in the first battle of Freeman's Farm. After an exchange of insults, Gates had relieved Arnold of command and confined him to his tent. But when the second battle began, Arnold disobeyed orders and rode to the sound of the guns. Once more his presence on the battlefield was electrifying. At the climax of the struggle, he led a frontal assault that captured a key British redoubt as a bullet shattered his leg. Gates finally emerged from his tent and ordered the redoubt held "at all hazards." Its cannon commanded the British camp.

The following night, the British tried to retreat. But swarming militia cut them off and Burgoyne surrendered his army to Gates on October 17, 1777, an event of earthshaking importance in both the military and diplomatic history of the Revolution. In France, Louis XVI's advisors decided the Americans could win the war and began backing them with desperately needed money and guns. England declared war on their ancient enemy and the conflict spread to the West Indies, Africa, and India.

If Arnold had gone along with Gates at the first battle of Saratoga, Burgoyne, a far more aggressive general than Carleton, would almost certainly have destroyed Gates's army and seized control of the Hudson River Valley. If Howe had stayed in New York and then advanced up the Hudson to meet Burgoyne, Gates's destruction would have been guaranteed with or without Arnold's heroics. A halfhearted last-minute attempt to rescue Burgoyne by a 4,000-man detachment from the New York garrison threw the Americans into near panic, even though it came to nothing.

Without Benedict Arnold at Valcour Bay and Saratoga, the war might well have ended in 1777. Without the feud between Burgoyne and Howe, it might have ended no later than 1778. By this time, the denouement would not have been so conciliatory. Many British and loyalists were calling 1777 "the year of the hangman." America's future as a dominion of England was veering from the benign fate of loyal Canada to the tragedy of rebellious Ireland. This trend would acquire ever-more vengeful momentum as the war dragged on.

*What if Captain Ferguson had pulled the trigger?*

Meanwhile, George Washington was fighting and losing the battles of Brandywine and Germantown in defense of the American capital, Philadelphia. As the first of these clashes developed there was a moment when the twitch of a finger on the trigger of a rifle might have changed American history forever. Washington was reconnoitering the countryside, trying to decide where to position his army to stop Howe's advance from the head of the Chesapeake. As he rode through a patch of woods near Brandywine Creek, he encountered Captain Patrick Ferguson of the British Army.

Ferguson was the inventor of the first breech-loading rifle, and he had one of those deadly weapons in his hands. It could spew out six bullets a minute and was far more accurate than the musket that was the standard gun in both armies. With no idea he had come face to face with Washington, Ferguson called on the horseman and his escort, a brightly uniformed hussar officer, to surrender. The officer shouted a warning and Washington wheeled his horse and galloped away. Ferguson took aim, then lowered his gun. He could not bring himself to shoot an unarmed enemy in the back. He was also more than a little impressed by the man's cool indifference to sudden death.

If Washington had been killed in the fall of 1777, the American war effort would have been more than a little demoralized. By now it was becoming apparent to many people that the tall Virginian was the linchpin of the struggle, the man who combined an ability to inspire loyalty in the Continental Army with a steadfast commitment to the ideals of the Revolution. On the eve of Trenton, Congress had given Washington dictatorial powers to deal with the situation—and he had humbly returned this Cromwellian authority to the politicians six months later. The probability of finding another Washington was more than remote—it was almost certainly impossible.

*What if Gates had replaced Washington as commander in chief?*

A few months after Washington's narrow escape from Captain Ferguson, the American commander confronted a conspiracy inside the army and Congress to depose him in favor of Major General Horatio Gates, the victor at Saratoga. If the plot had succeeded, the results would have been, if anything, more disastrous than an outcome wreaked by Ferguson's bullet.

Horatio Gates was a cunning egotist who allowed aides and friends to puff him into a competitor for the top command. After all, Washington had lost two crucial battles and the British had captured Philadelphia. The American army was now starving at Valley Forge. It was at least superficially plausible to call for new leadership.

One of the pointmen in the conspiracy was an Irish-born volunteer from the French Army, General Thomas Conway, whose name has become affixed to the plot. In fact, the "Conway Cabal" was a New England conspiracy, run from Congress by Sam Adams (once more demonstrating bad political judgment) with some background encouragement from Cousin John, who intensely resented Washington's soaring popularity. Conway was a loudmouth whom the real plotters manipulated. It soon became apparent that the cabal lacked a serious following in the army or in Congress. But for a few months, Washington's headquarters was in frequent turmoil, responding to it.

If the cabal had succeeded and Gates had become the American commander in chief, the Revolution would have almost certainly ended in a whimper. In no way could the short fussy Englishman, called "Granny" by his troops, have replaced Washington as an inspiring figure. Worse, in 1780, when Gates led an army into the South to repel a British invasion that had already captured Charlestown and most of South Carolina, he met a catastrophic defeat at Camden. On the fastest horse he could find, Horatio did not stop retreating until he was 160 miles from the battlefield.

A frantic Congress, its Continental dollars degenerating into wastepaper, the Southern states about to be overrun, might well have turned to a general with a reputation as a fighter: Benedict Arnold. By this time, however, the disgruntled hero of Saratoga was deep in correspondence with the British high command about how to best betray the American cause. Imagine his delight if he had been made commander in chief of the Continental Army! He would have been able to fulfill the ambition he hinted at when he signed some of his early letters to the British "General Monk." The pen name suggests Arnold saw himself as a reincarnation of General George Monk (or Monck), who switched sides in 1660 after the death of Oliver Cromwell and backed the restoration of the Stuart monarchy. No doubt Arnold was thinking of the wealth and titles that a grateful Charles II heaped on Monck.

Even without this gift from Congress, Arnold's plotting came close to unraveling the Revolution. His plan to surrender the key fortress of West Point to the British in the fall of 1780 went awry only because the chief of British intelligence, Major John André, was captured by some wandering American militiamen while returning to British-held New York with the plans for the fortress in his boot. A seizure of West Point would have given the British their long-sought control of the Hudson River, enabling them to isolate New England from the rest of the colonies. Such a blow, coming in a year when the American Army had been shaken by a serious mutiny in its winter quarters, the South was being overrun by British and loyalist armies, and the depreciation of the Continental dollar had reached the nadir of total collapse, could well have been the *coup de grace* that the British sensed was within reach.

*What if the British had destroyed the French expeditionary force within days of its arrival?*

Another moment when the war hung in the balance was rescued by George Washington's talent for espionage. With some help from a Long Island–born cavalryman, Major Benjamin Tallmadge, Washington was his own intelligence chief. He operated several networks inside New York. One of these, known as the Culper ring, smuggled him alarming news in July of 1780. The British were putting 6,000 men aboard ships for a pre-emptive strike at the French expeditionary force that had just landed at Newport, Rhode Island.

Nothing would have more certainly ended the war than the destruction of this 5,500-man army. Rampant inflation and war weariness were eroding the Continental Army's morale. Recruiting new men was becoming impossible because of the worthless currency. Thus far, the French alliance had been a series of bitter disappointments for the allies. A 1778 attempt to capture British-held Newport ended in a fiasco. A 1779 assault on Savannah was repulsed with severe losses. A devastating defeat such as the British hoped to inflict would have knocked a discouraged France out of the war.

Washington could not outmarch the British fleet in a race to Newport. He fell back on his spymaster's role. A double agent approached a British outpost with a packet of papers, which he claimed to have found on the road. It contained detailed plans for a massive American attack on New York. The British transports and their escorting men of war were already heading down Long Island Sound for the open sea. Signal fires were lit at strategic points on the shore (Long Island was in British hands) and the fleet hauled into Huntington Bay to receive the "captured" American war plans, rushed there by hard-riding horsemen. The dismayed British abandoned the descent on Newport and rushed back to New York, where they hunkered down in their numerous forts for an attack that never came. By the time the British realized Washington had gulled them, the French had fortified Newport, making a successful assault impossible.

The failure to knock the French out of the war forced the British to maintain a serious army in New York, complicating their new strategy, to conquer the South.

### What if Daniel Morgan had lost at Cowpens?

While a stalemate prevailed in the North, the South continued to slide into British control. Georgia had returned to royal allegiance in 1779. The capitulation of Charleston in the spring of 1780, with its 5,000-man garrison, more than balanced Burgoyne's surrender at Saratoga. After the Camden rout, the Southern Continental Army dwindled to some 800 half-starved men. The new commander, Major General Nathanael

Greene, tried to persuade guerilla leaders such as Thomas Sumter to operate under his control, with no success.

Greene saw that the British would snuff out these pickup bands one by one. Under burly, aggressive Lieutenant Colonel Banastre Tarleton, the royal army had perfected a quick strike force, the British Legion, a mix of cavalry and infantry, that could travel as much as seventy miles a day, often catching the guerillas in their camps. The tough policy of requiring men to serve in the royal militia or have their crops and houses burned was also proving brutally effective. By the end of 1780, South Carolina's resistance was at the vanishing point. The British were discussing a quick conquest of North Carolina and an assault on Virginia.

In a gesture that was half strategic and half despairing, Greene ordered Daniel Morgan, now a brigadier general, to take 600 regulars and the remnants of the American cavalry, about 70 men under Lieutenant Colonel William Washington (George's second cousin) and march into western South Carolina in an attempt to rally the prostrate state. The British commander, Lord Cornwallis, dispatched Tarleton and his British Legion to finish off Morgan's feeble foray.

There seemed little doubt that the redheaded cavalryman would do the job. Scooping up reinforcements en route, Tarleton headed for Morgan at his usual pace, ignoring the cold December rain that turned the roads to gumbo. The Old Wagoner, as the muscular, six-foot-two Morgan was called, saw no alternative but headlong retreat. Barely 300 militia had responded to his pleas. As Morgan approached the Broad River, Tarleton's scouts were only about five miles behind him. The Broad was in flood and Morgan realized he might lose half his little army if he tried to cross it.

Nearby was a patch of rolling lightly wooded ground called The Cowpens, where local farmers used to winter cattle. Morgan decided to make a stand in this deserted pasture. A last desperate exhortation persuaded another 150 militia to join him. The big Virginian drew up a battle plan that made maximum use of these temporary soldiers, without depending on them too much. He positioned the amateurs in two eche-lons well forward of his Continentals. They were told to give him "two fires" and then they could run for their lives—which was what they would do anyway.

About 150 yards behind the second line, Morgan took personal com-mand of his Continentals on a low ridge. Behind them, sheltered by the rise, he held William Washington and his cavalry in reserve. Morgan spent the night going from campfire to campfire, explaining his battle plan to every man—assuring them that if they did their jobs, the Old Wagoner would crack his whip over "Benny" Tarleton in the morning.

Tarleton arrived on the battlefield at dawn on January 17, 1781, af-ter an all-night march. Without giving his tired men a chance to pause even for breakfast, he ordered them into line of battle and advanced. That was his first blunder. His second was ignoring the way the militia marksmen emptied the saddles of his flanking cavalry and cut down a ru-inous number of his officers at the head of their companies.

The militia raced for the rear, giving Tarleton the impression the bat-tle was as good as won. But he soon collided with the Continentals, who poured volley after volley into his ranks. The British commander threw in his reserve, the 71st Highlanders, to outflank them. To meet this threat, the Americans ordered their flank companies to fall back and face the Scots, a standard battlefield maneuver known as "refusing" one's flank. In the confusion, the whole American line began to retreat and Tarleton, thinking a rout was imminent, ordered a bayonet charge. Cheering fero-ciously, the redcoated line surged forward.

But Morgan was still in command of the situation. He got a message from William Washington, now out on the British right flank: "They are coming on like a mob. Give them one fire and I'll charge them." Morgan shouted the order to the Continentals, who turned, fired from the hip and charged the onrushing British with the bayonet. Simultaneously, the cavalry hit them in the rear, slashing men with their fearsome sabres.

The British, exhausted and with many companies leaderless, panicked. Some threw down their guns and surrendered; others ran. In five minutes the battle was over. Morgan had won a victory that destroyed Tarleton's army and dramatically reversed the tide of the war in the South. If Tarleton's frontal assault had succeeded, there is little doubt that North and South Carolina would have followed Georgia into royal government. Virginia, which was showing ominous signs of war weariness, was equally vulnerable, and Maryland, too, would have been sucked into this defeatist vortex. With the virtually bankrupt French government already sending out feelers for a peace conference, the British might have ended the war in possession of the entire South. In a few years they would have undoubtedly launched a renewed assault on the precariously independent Northern colonies from this base.

*What if Washington had refused to march to Virginia to trap the British at Yorktown—or the British had escaped after the siege began?*

After fighting a costly battle against a revived Continental Army at Guilford Court House in North Carolina, the British Southern commander, Charles, Lord Cornwallis, retreated to the coast and decided to discard the state-by-state strategy the Royal Army had been following. Only if wealthy, populous Virginia was reduced would the South surrender. Marching north and taking command of troops raiding the Virginia coast, the earl found no resistance worth mentioning from a tiny American army under Marquis de Lafayette.

But Cornwallis met a great deal more opposition from the British commander in chief, Sir Henry Clinton, who felt the earl had invaded his bailiwick and was in danger of losing the lower South to the resurgent Nathaniel Greene. An exchange of acrimonious letters let Cornwallis know who was running the war—and he glumly retreated to a small tobacco port, Yorktown, at the tip of the peninsula of the same name, with orders to fortify it and ship most of his army to Clinton in New York.

The earl nastily informed Clinton he would have to keep the entire army of 7,500 men to build the required fortifications. So the war spiraled to the late summer of 1781, still stalemated in the North and only slightly less deadlocked in the South. More and more, it was obvious that whoever struck the next blow—a victory on the level of Saratoga or Charleston—would win by a knockout.

Outside New York City, George Washington and the Comte de Rochambeau, the commander of the French expeditionary force, conferred about where to strike this blow. Washington wanted to attack New York. But his army, even with French reinforcements, was too weak. The French commander argued for a march south to try to trap Cornwallis at Yorktown. Washington dismissed it as a waste of time and energy as long as the British Navy controlled the American coast. They would rescue Cornwallis before the Allied army could force him to capitulate.

Rochambeau informed Washington that the French West Indies fleet had orders to sail north to escape the hurricane season. Why not tell them to head for the Chesapeake—while they did likewise with their soldiers? Washington reluctantly assented, although he still thought the British Navy would rout the French fleet, as they had so often in the past. He also worried that a substantial number of his unpaid war-weary soldiers would desert rather than make the march.

If Washington had refused to march to Yorktown, the French would probably have given up on him. The Revolution looked moribund. The Continental dollar was so worthless, it took, Washington gloomily noted, "a wagonload of money to buy a wagonload of hay." Recruiting officers reported zero interest in army service. The French were ready to withdraw their expeditionary force and throw in the diplomatic equivalent of the towel.

Instead, Washington marched south and a series of miracles occurred. Desertions were few, thanks to a hasty infusion of hard money from the French army's military chest, and the French fleet arrived just in time to trap Cornwallis at Yorktown. The British fleet sallied from New York to rescue the earl and his men. On September 5, in the little known

Battle of the Chesapeake Capes, the Royal Navy, commanded by a third-rate admiral named Thomas Graves, did everything wrong and the French did a few things right. The badly battered British limped back to New York and Cornwallis remained trapped on the tip of the Yorktown peninsula, a prime target for Allied siege guns.

If Graves had won the sea fight off the capes and rescued Cornwallis, American disillusion with the French would have been little short of overwhelming. The discouraged Continental Congress might have told their diplomats to get the best deal they could manage from the British in the looming peace negotiations. The Americans might have been forced to surrender large chunks of New York and most of the South. The British would also have probably claimed the trans-Appalachian west, where their Indian allies were waging a sanguinary war. The American alliance with France would have collapsed, exposing the infant republic to a world in which England remained the dominant power.

In New York, a frantic Sir Henry Clinton proposed to Admiral Graves a rescue plan that called for putting most of the army on navy ships and fighting their way into the Chesapeake to join Cornwallis. Together they would launch an all-out attack on Washington and Rochambeau that would decide the war. Alas for Sir Henry, Admiral Graves had no stomach for such a venture. He insisted he had to repair his damaged ships first. This led to a series of excuses and delays that dragged on for weeks.

On October 13, the fleet was supposed to sail—when a tremendous thunderstorm swept over New York harbor. Terrific gusts of wind snapped the anchor cable on one of the ships of the line, smashing her into another ship and damaging both of them. Once again Admiral Graves decided he could not leave until the damage was repaired. It was not the first nor would it be the last time that weather played a crucial role in the struggle for independence.

By October 15, French and American artillery had pounded Cornwallis's defenses to a shambles. Picked troops had captured two key redoubts, which enabled them to enfilade his lines. The moment approached when the Allies would launch a decisive frontal assault. A desperate Cornwallis decided on a daring getaway plan. Across the York River in Gloucester was a British outpost. Only about 750 French troops and some Virginia militia were stationed on its perimeter, largely to prevent foraging. Perhaps remembering Washington's escape from Brooklyn Heights, Cornwallis decided to ferry most of his army across the river on the night of October 16 and break out of the Gloucester lines at dawn. By forced marches, they would head north to the mouth of the Delaware, where they could easily contact British headquarters in New York.

As the Allied guns continued their relentless pounding, Cornwallis relieved the British light infantry in the front lines and marched them to the water's edge. There they boarded sixteen heavy flatboats manned by sailors of the Royal Navy. They were joined by the elite Foot Guards and the better part of the equally elite Royal Welch Fusiliers. It took at least two hours to make the trip back and forth across the broad river. Around midnight the boats returned and a second contingent embarked.

About ten minutes later a tremendous storm broke over the river. Within five minutes, there was a full gale blowing, as violent, from the descriptions in various diaries, as the storm that had damaged the British fleet in New York. Shivering in the bitter wind, soaked to the skin, the exhausted soldiers and sailors returned to the Yorktown shore. Not until two A.M. did the wind moderate. It was much too late to get the rest of the army across the river. Glumly, Cornwallis ordered the guards and the light infantry to return. About 7 A.M. on October 17, the earl, his second in command, Brigadier Charles O'Hara, and their staffs went to the forward trenches and morosely studied the sweep and scope of the allied bombardment. The commander of the artillery informed them that there were only 100 mortar shells left. The sick and wounded multiplied by the hour.

Cornwallis asked his officers what he should do. Fight to the last man? Every officer told him that he owed it to his men to surrender. They had done all that was expected of them, and more. Silently, Cornwallis nodded his assent. He turned to an aide and dictated a historic letter.

> Sir, I propose a cessation of hostilities for twenty-four hours, and that two officers may be appointed by each side . . . to settle terms for the surrender of the posts at York and Gloucester.

Not a few military authorities think Cornwallis's getaway might have succeeded, if it were not for that storm. Without the previous storm in New York harbor, Sir Henry Clinton might have embarrassed Admiral Graves into sailing on October 13. That would have gotten him to the Chesapeake before Cornwallis signed the articles of surrender on October 19. Either alternative would have created the possibility of a far different outcome. A Cornwallis getaway would have left the French and Americans frustrated and hopeless, facing a stalemated war they no longer had the money or the will to fight. American independence—or a large chunk of it—might have been traded away in the peace conference. A Clinton invasion of the Chesapeake would have triggered a stupendous naval and land battle that might well have ended in a British victory—enabling them to impose the harshest imaginable peace on the exhausted Americans and shattered French. Instead the Allies had landed the knockout blow.

*What if George Washington had failed to stop the Newburgh Conspiracy?*

As the war wound down to random clashes between small units in the South and West and along the northern border of New York, the American Revolution confronted one last crisis that might have made the long struggle all but meaningless. Once more the cause was rescued by that man for all seasons, George Washington.

As 1783 began, word arrived from Europe that Benjamin Franklin and the other American negotiators in Paris had signed a triumphant peace, recognizing the independence of the United States and extending American sovereignty to the east bank of the Mississippi. All that was needed now was a peace treaty between France and England. But this good news did not produce diapasons of joy inside the Continental Army.

On the contrary, this glimpse of peace just over the horizon aroused in the officer corps a surge of sullen fury. Congress had not paid them for years. In 1780, they had been promised half-pay for life. Now Congress no longer needed them and was reportedly going to welch on this agreement. Antagonism between the lawmakers and "the gentlemen of the blade," as some hostile New England congressmen called the officers, was not new. The officers decided to settle matters while they still had guns in their hands.

The officers dispatched a delegation to Congress led by Major General Alexander McDougall of New York. Choosing McDougall as a spokesman was a statement in itself. In the early 1770s, this abrasive demagogic New Yorker had been second only to Sam Adams as an agitator. The officers wanted an advance on their back pay, a solemn commitment to pay the balance eventually, and negotiation to settle the promise of half pay for life either by a lump sum payment or full pay for a number of years.

When McDougall met with James Madison, Alexander Hamilton, and other congressmen on January 13, 1783, Madison thought his language was "very high colored." Another member of the military delegation, Colonel John Brooks, warned that a disappointment would throw the army into "extremities." On February 13, Alexander Hamilton, who had retired from the army after Yorktown, wrote Washington an urgent letter, warning him that the situation was close to exploding.

Hamilton's letter arrived just in time. A dangerous conspiracy was simmering between officers at Newburgh and the army delegation in Philadelphia. Among the leaders was Major John Armstrong, aide to Washington's old enemy, Major General Horatio Gates. From Philadelphia, Armstrong wrote Gates that if the troops had someone like "Mad Anthony [Wayne] at their head," instead of Washington, "I know not where they would stop," especially if they "could be taught to think like politicians."

Soon Armstrong and another Gates man, Pennsylvanian Colonel Walter Stewart, began circulating anonymous "addresses" in the camp at Newburgh, calling on the army not to disband "until they had obtained justice." Next came another anonymous letter, urging the officers to meet and resolve to do something about a country that "tramples on your rights, disdains your cries, and insults your distresses."

Forewarned by Hamilton's letter, Washington's reaction to these Newburgh addresses was immediate and fierce. He condemned the unauthorized meeting and announced his determination to "arrest on the spot the foot that [is] wavering on a tremendous precipice." The dawn of peace had made him acutely aware that they were setting precedents for a new country. If the army got away with bullying Congress, it would cause America endless tragedies in the future.

On March 13, 1783, Washington convened a formal meeting with the officers in a large building in the Newburgh camp called The Temple. It was used as a church on Sundays and as a dance hall on other occasions. The commander in chief gave a passionate speech, pleading with the men, "as you value your own sacred honor," to ignore the anonymous letters calling for a march on Congress. He urged them to look with "utmost horror and detestation" on any man who "wishes, under any specious pretenses, to overturn the liberties of our country."

The men listened, but their faces remained hard. They were still angry. Washington closed with a plea that the officers conduct themselves so that their posterity would say, "Had this day been wanting, the world had never seen the last stage of perfection to which human nature is capable of attaining." Still, the resistance in the room remained almost palpable.

Washington drew from his pocket a letter from Congressman Joseph Jones of Virginia, assuring him that Congress was trying to respond to the army's complaints. After a moment's hesitation, he pulled out a pair of glasses. Only his aides had seen him wearing them for the previous several months. "Gentlemen," he said. "You will permit me to put on my spectacles, for I have not only grown gray but almost blind in your service."

A wave of emotion swept through the officers. More effectively than all Washington's exhortations, this simple statement of fact demolished almost every man in the hall. Many wept openly. Washington read the congressman's letter and departed, leaving the men to make their decision without him. They voted their thanks to the commander in chief, repudiated the anonymous letters, and expressed their confidence in Congress.

Washington's report on the Newburgh meeting reached Congress just in time to prevent the lawmakers from declaring war on the army. James Madison noted in his journal that the dispatch dispelled "the cloud which seemed to have been gathering." Congressman Eliphalet Dyer of Connecticut proposed that they offer the soldiers a deal—commutation in the form of five years pay in securities redeemable when the U.S. government achieved solvency. The officers accepted and the worst crisis yet in the brief history of American liberty was over.

Washington's use of the word "precipice" in describing the Newburgh confrontation was not an exaggeration. If he had failed to change the army's mind, the Revolution could have unravelled. The army might have marched on Congress to dictate terms at the point of a gun. The states, especially the large ones such as Virginia and Massachusetts, would almost certainly have refused to approve such a deal. If the army had attempted to force their compliance, civil war would have erupted. The shaky American confederation might have collapsed and the British, still with a fleet and army in New York, would have been irresistibly tempted to get back in the game. It is hard to imagine any of the states returning to the empire but some with strong loyalist minorities, such as New Jersey and New York, might have formed defensive alliances with the British to protect themselves against the rampaging Continentals. Such a foot in the door would have proved ultimately fatal to American independence.

✦ ✦ ✦

Many years later, George Washington reportedly corresponded with Charles Thomson, the secretary of the Continental Congress, about writing their memoirs. Thomson had been present at virtually every session of the Congress, from its inception in 1774 to its dissolution in 1788. Between them the two men probably knew more secrets than the entire Congress and the Continental Army combined. They decided that memoirs were a bad idea. It would be too disillusioning if the American people discovered how often the Glorious Cause came close to disaster. They jointly agreed that the real secret of America's final victory in the eight-year struggle could be summed up in two words: Divine Providence.

## ✦ IRA D. GRUBER ✦

# GEORGE WASHINGTON'S GAMBLE

By late December of 1776, the British had driven George Washington's dwindling and demoralized forces out of Manhattan and across New Jersey. The enlistments of all save 1,400 of Washington's men were due to expire by the end of the year. Nearly all were suffering from shortages of food, clothing, blankets, and tents while thousands of ordinary citizens in New Jersey were accepting British offers of pardon. The Continental Congress, anticipating the loss of Philadelphia, had withdrawn to Baltimore. It was, as Thomas Paine said, a time to "try men's souls."

If at that moment Washington's desperate attacks on the British outposts at Trenton and Princeton had failed, and if the British had destroyed his army, the rebellion might well have collapsed. Indeed, had Congress in those circumstances been tempted to seek a negotiated peace, they would have found the British offering surprisingly attractive terms (a proposal for replacing Parliamentary taxation with limited colonial contributions for imperial defense). Such terms in such circumstances might have appealed to many Americans.

But if stakes were high at Trenton and Princeton, it should still be asked whether Washington was in danger of losing his desperate gamble. Perhaps not at Trenton, where he had the advantages of surprise, superior numbers, and well-coordinated attacks, and where he gained a complete victory over a Hessian garrison besotted from celebrating Christmas. His successful attack on the British at Princeton little more than a week later—on a larger and better-prepared enemy—could much more easily have gone disastrously wrong. Had Washington been detected during his long night's march around Lord Cornwallis's flank, had the garrison at Princeton been united when the Americans arrived, or had that garrison been able to hold out longer, Cornwallis might have arrived to overwhelm Washington's exhausted men. And had those men been crushed at Princeton, Washington's reputation, the remainder of American forces, and the rebellion might have collapsed in all too rapid succession.

✦ *Ira D. Gruber is professor of history at Rice University.*

## DAVID McCULLOUGH

# WHAT THE FOG WROUGHT

*The Revolution's Dunkirk, August 29, 1776*

For all that can be said for a deterministic view of history—for the inevitability of what T. S. Elliot called "vast impersonal forces"—chance and luck (two related but altogether different phenomena) also play a part. How else to explain the events of mid-August 1776, when, badly beaten at the Battle of Long Island (Brooklyn, actually), George Washington and his small army faced what seemed to be certain annihilation by a larger British army, one of the world's best. As David McCullough points out, nothing less than the independence of the United States was at stake. But the whims of weather were beyond prediction then, as they often still are. Perhaps in this case the most you can say about inevitability is that Washington almost always had the knack of seizing the right moment.

✦ *David McCullough is one of the most deservedly popular historians of our time. His* Truman *won the National Book Award and Pulitzer for biography;* The Path Between the Seas, *his account of the building of the Panama Canal, also won the National Book Award for History. His other books include* The Johnstown Flood,

*THE GREAT BRIDGE, and MORNINGS ON HORSEBACK. Millions know him as the host, and often the narrator, of television shows like THE AMERICAN EXPERIENCE. The past president of the Society of American Historians, McCullough has also won the Francis Parkman Prize and the Los Angeles Times Book Award. He is at present at work on a biography of John and Abigail Adams.*

The day of the trial, which will in some measure decide the fate of America, is near at hand," wrote General George Washington in mid-August 1776 from his headquarters in New York.

The Declaration of Independence had been signed in Philadelphia only days before, on August 8—not July 4, as commonly believed—and for six weeks an enormous British expeditionary force, the largest ever sent to dispense with a distant foe, had been arriving in lower New York Harbor.

The first British sails had been sighted at the end of June, a great fleet looking, as one man said, like "all London afloat." It was a spectacle such as had never been seen in American waters. And the ships had kept coming all summer. On August 13, Washington reported an "augmentation" of ninety-six ships on a single day. The day after, another twenty dropped anchor, making a total of more than 400, counting ten ships-of-the-time, twenty frigates, and several hundred transports. Fully thirty-two thousand well-equipped British and hired German troops, some of the best in the world, had landed without opposition on Staten Island—an enemy force, that is, greater than the whole population of Philadelphia, the largest city in the newly proclaimed United States of America.

The defense of New York was considered essential by Congress, largely for political reasons, but also by General Washington, who welcomed the chance for a climactic battle—a "day of trial," as he said. Yet he had scarcely 20,000 troops and no naval force, not one fighting ship or proper transport. His was an army of volunteers, raw recruits, poorly armed, poorly supplied. The men had no tents—to cite one glaring deficiency—and few were equipped with bayonets, the weapon employed by the British with such terrifying effectiveness. As a surgeon with Washington's army wrote, "In point of numbers, or discipline, experience in war . . . the enemy possessed the most decided advantage; beside the importance of assistance afforded by a powerful fleet."

Among the considerable number of the men who were too sick to fight was Washington's ablest field commander, Nathaniel Greene. Few American officers were experienced in large-scale warfare. Washington himself until now had never led an army in the field. The battle to come was to be his first as a commander.

With no way of knowing where the British might strike, Washington had chosen to split his troops, keeping half on the island of Manhattan, while the rest crossed the East River to Long Island, to dig in on the high bluffs on the river known as Brooklyn Heights—all this carried out in disregard of the old cardinal rule of never dividing an army in the face of a superior foe. When, on August 22, the British began ferrying troops across the Narrows to land further south on Long Island, about eight miles from the little village of Brooklyn, Washington responded by sending still more of his army across the East River, which, it should be noted, is not really a river at all, but a tidal strait, a mile-wide arm of the sea with especially strong currents.

"I have no doubt but a little time will produce some important events," Washington wrote in classic understatement to the president of Congress, John Hancock.

In fact, it was a situation made for an American catastrophe. With at most 12,000 troops on Long Island, Washington faced an army of perhaps 20,000. Should there be no stopping such a force, he and his amateur soldiers would have to retreat with the river to their backs. Which is just what happened.

The furious battle of Long Island was fought several miles inland from Brooklyn Heights on Tuesday, August 27, 1776. The British, under General William Howe, outflanked, out-fought, and routed the Americans in little time. The British officers under Howe included James Grant, Henry Clinton, Lords Cornwallis and Percy, and all performed expertly. As John Adams was to conclude succinctly, "In general, our generals were outgeneralled."

Astride a big gray horse, watching from a hillside, Washington is supposed to have said in anguish, "Good God! What brave fellows I must this day lose!" By later estimates, his losses were higher than he knew; more than 1,400 killed, wounded, or captured. Two of his generals had been taken captive. Many of his best officers were killed or missing. British use of the bayonet had been savage and on men who had surrendered as well, as one British officer proudly recorded, explaining, "You know all stratagems are lawful in war, especially against such vile enemies of the King and country." Washington and his exhausted men fell back to the fortifications on the Heights, waiting as night fell for a final British assault, the river to the rear.

And right there and then the American cause hung in the balance. The British, as Washington seems not to have realized—or allowed himself to think—had him in a perfect trap. They had only to move a few warships into the East River and all escape would be sealed. Indeed, but for the caprices of weather, the outcome would have been altogether different.

What actually happened was extraordinary. What so obviously could have happened, and with the most far-reaching consequences, is not hard to picture.

To be sure, the individual makeup of the two commanders played a part. On the day following the battle, influenced no doubt by his experience of the year before at Bunker Hill, General Howe chose not to follow up his victory by storming the American lines on Brooklyn Heights. He saw no reason to lose any more of his army than absolutely necessary, nor any cause to hurry. William Howe almost never saw cause for hurry, but in this case with reason—he had, after all, Washington right where he wanted him.

For his part, Washington appears to have given no thought to a withdrawal, the only sensible recourse. All his instincts were to fight. On

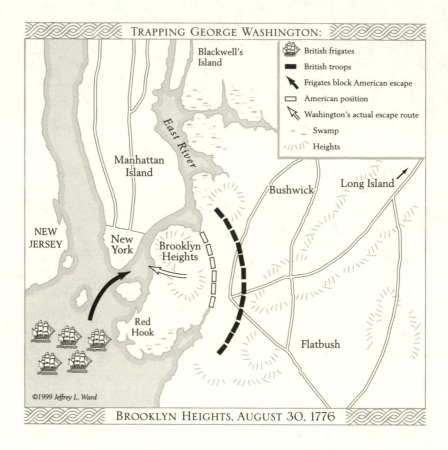

TRAPPING GEORGE WASHINGTON:

Blackwell's Island

British frigates
British troops
Frigates block American escape
American position
Washington's actual escape route
Swamp
Heights

East River

Manhattan Island

Bushwick

Long Island

NEW JERSEY

New York

Brooklyn Heights

Red Hook

Flatbush

©1999 Jeffrey L. Ward

BROOKLYN HEIGHTS, AUGUST 30, 1776

Wednesday, August 28, and again on Thursday, August 29, his food supplies nearly gone, his time clearly running out, he ordered that still more reinforcements be rowed over from New York, a decision that seems almost incomprehensible.

His men, for all their bravery and devotion to him, were worn out, hungry, and dispirited. And it had begun to rain. On August 29, the temperature dropped sharply and the rain came in torrents on the unsheltered army. During the afternoon, according to a diary kept by a local Brooklyn pastor, "Such heavy rain fell again as can hardly be remembered." Muskets and powder were soaked. In some places men stood in flooded trenches in water up to their waists. Expecting the enemy to at-tack at any moment, they had to keep a constant watch. Many had not slept for days. A New York man who saw them after it was all over said he never in his life saw such wretched, exhausted-looking human beings.

Washington's presence along the lines and his concern for the men were felt day and night. Seldom was he out of the saddle. On both August 28 and August 29, he appears to have had no rest at all.

But in their misery was their salvation. The driving rain and cold were part of a fitful, at times violent, nor'easter that had been blowing off and on for better than a week, and for all the punishment it inflicted, the wind had kept the British ships from coming upriver with the tide. For the new nation, it was an ill wind that blew great good, so long as it held.

Meantime, as the British historian Sir George Otto Trevelyan would write, "Nine thousand [or more] disheartened soldiers, the last hope of their country, were penned up, with the sea behind them and a tri-umphant enemy in front, shelterless and famished on a square mile of open ground swept by fierce and cold northeasterly gale . . ."

In a letter to John Hancock written at four o'clock in the morning, August 29, the crucial day, Washington reported only on the severity of the weather and the lack of tents that Congress had failed to supply, but said nothing of a retreat. He had seen five British ships attempt to come up the river and fail; and so he appears to have been banking on no change in the wind. Possibly he believed, too, that obstructions in the harbor—hulks sunk as hazards—had truly blocked the passage of all but small craft, a notion that was to prove quite wrong. In any event, having been out-flanked on land, he stood perilously close to being outflanked by water.

The decision that so obviously had to be made came only later in the day, after it was learned that the British, under the cover of dark, were ad-vancing by "regular approaches"—working through the night, throwing up entrenchments nearer and nearer the American lines—and after Washington at last accepted the likelihood of the British fleet at his back. Importantly, as he himself was to emphasize, the decision came on "the advice of my general officers."

According to one first-hand observer, it was General Thomas Mifflin, a self-assured thirty-two-year-old "fighting Quaker" from Philadelphia, who was the most emphatic. Mifflin, who had come over from New York with the last reinforcements only the day before, had been the one who, on his night rounds, discovered that the British were digging their way forward. Immediate retreat was imperative, the only remaining choice, he told Washington. Lest anyone question his character for making such a proposal, Mifflin asked that he be put in command of the rear guard, by far the most dangerous of assignments in a retreat.

With the rain still pounding down, Washington and his generals gathered for a council of war in the Brooklyn Heights summer home of Philip Livingston, a signer of the Declaration of Independence, who was in Philadelphia attending Congress. The time was early afternoon. The purpose of the meeting, as stated in the official minutes, was "whether under all circumstances it would not be eligible to leave Long Island." Two of the reasons given for an affirmative resolution were that the northeast wind might shift and that the consoling thought of obstructions in the harbor was now considered erroneous.

So it was decided. Preparations were set immediately in motion. An order from Washington went over to New York to collect every boat "from Hellgate on the [Long Island] Sound to Spuyten Duyvil Creek [on the Hudson] that could be kept afloat and that had either sails or oars, and have them all in the east harbor of the city by dark."

It was said the boats were needed to transport the sick and bring still greater reinforcements over to Brooklyn. Officers on the Heights, meanwhile, were to be ready to "parade their men with their arms, accoutrements and knapsacks at 7 o'clock at the head of their encampments and there wait for orders."

In all, it was a straightaway lie by Washington, intended to keep the truth from the men until the last moment—and thereby reduce the chance of panic—and hopefully to deceive the British—and the innumerable British spies in New York—once the roundup of boats was under way.

Most of the troops took the order to mean they were to go on the attack. A young captain of Pennsylvania volunteers, Alexander Graydon, would recall men taking time to write their wills. He, however, sensed something else was afoot. "It suddenly flashed upon my mind that a retreat was the object, and that the order . . . was but a cover to the real design." Yet who was to say? None of the other officers who listened to his theory dared believe it. Never in years to come could he recall the long wait without thinking of the chorus in Shakespeare's *Henry V,* describing the "weary and all-watched night" before Agincourt.

The first boats began crossing as soon as it turned dark. How it was all managed is almost beyond imagination. Every conceivable kind of small craft was employed, manned by Massachusetts men—soldiers from the ranks but sailors and fisherman by trade—from Marblehead and Salem, under the command of General John Glover and Colonel Israel Hutchinson. It can be said that the fate of the American army was in their hands. How readily the night could turn disastrous on the water, no less than on land, was more apparent to them than to anyone.

Everything was to be carried across—men, stores, horses, cannon. Every possible precaution had to be taken to keep silent—oars and wagon wheels were muffled with rags; orders were passed on in whispers. Every boat that pushed off, every crossing, was a race against time, and in black night and rain.

At one point, all seemed lost. Sometime near nine, the northeast wind picked up at ebb tide. The wind and current were more than sail could cope with, even in expert hands, and there were too few rowboats to carry everyone across before daylight. But in another hour or so, the wind mercifully fell off and shifted southwest, becoming the most favorable wind possible; and so the exodus resumed, all boats in service.

It went on hour after hour almost without a hitch. If ever fortune favored the brave, it was that night on the East River. Washington, who had proven considerably less than impressive in his first battle command, handled this, his first great retreat, with a steadiness and dispatch that were masterful. As untrained and inexperienced as his men may have been, however wet and miserable, they more than rose to the occasion. They stood for hours waiting their turns, then when told, moved off as silent ghosts, heading down the slopes to the river in pitch darkness, to the Brooklyn ferry landing, which was about where the Brooklyn Bridge now stands.

As the night progressed, and one regiment after another was withdrawn, the front lines grew perilously thin, to the point where there was almost no one left to stop an attack, should the enemy discover what was happening. It was the rear guard under Mifflin that had to stay to the last, keeping campfires burning and making sufficient noise to maintain the illusion of the full army in position.

The one hitch happened about two in the morning, when somehow Mifflin received orders to withdraw, only to learn on the way to the landing that it had been a dreadful mistake and that he and his men must return at once to their posts. "This was a trying business to young soldiers," one of them later wrote. "It was nevertheless complied with." They were back on the line before their absence was detected.

Another officer, Colonel Benjamin Tallmadge would recall, "As the dawn of the next day approached, those of us who remained in the trenches became very anxious for our own safety . . ."

Troops in substantial numbers had still to be evacuated and at the rate things were going, it appeared day would dawn before everyone was safely removed. But again "the elements" interceded, this time in the form of pea-soup fog.

It was called "a peculiar providential occurrence," "manifestly providential," "very favorable to the design," "an unusual fog," "a friendly fog," "an American fog." "So very dense was the atmosphere," remembered Benjamin Tallmadge, "that I could scarcely discern a man at six yards' distance." And as daylight came, the fog held, covering the entire operation no less than had the night.

Tallmadge would recall that when the rear guard at last received word to pull out, and "we very joyfully bid those trenches adieu," the fog was still "as dense as ever."

When we reached Brooklyn ferry, the boats had not returned from their last trip, but they very soon appeared and took the whole regiment over to New York; and I think saw General Washington on the ferry stairs when I stepped into one of the last boats . . .

When the fog lifted at about seven o'clock, the British saw to their astonishment that the Americans had vanished.

Amazingly, the entire force, at least 9,000 troops, possibly more, plus baggage, provisions, horses, field guns, everything but five heavy cannon that were too deep in the mud to budge, had been transported over the river in a single night with a makeshift emergency armada assembled in a matter of hours. Not a life was lost. It is not even known that anyone was injured. And as Tallmadge remembered, Washington, risking capture, had stayed until the last boat pushed off. As it was, the only Americans captured by the British were three who stayed behind to plunder.

The "day of trial" that Washington had foreseen deciding the fate of America had turned out to be a night of trial, and one that did truly decide the fate of America as much as any battle.

It was the Dunkirk of the American Revolution—by daring amphibious rescue a beleaguered army had been saved to fight another day—and tributes to Washington would come from all quarters, from those in the ranks, from officers, delegates in Congress, and from military observers and historians then and later. A British officer of the time called the retreat "particularly glorious." A latter-day scholar would write that, "A more skillful operation of this kind was never conducted."

But what a very close call it had been. How readily it could have all gone wrong—had there been no northeast wind to hold the British fleet in check through the day the Battle of Long Island was fought, not to say the days immediately afterward. Or had the wind not turned southwest the night of August 29. Or had there been no fortuitous fog as a final safeguard when day broke.

What the effect would have been had British naval forces come into play off Brooklyn Heights was to be vividly demonstrated just weeks later, when, with favorable wind and tide, five warships, including the *Renown* with fifty guns, sailed up the East River as far as Kips Bay and from 200 yards offshore, commenced a thunderous point-blank bombardment of American defenses on Manhattan. "So terrible and so incessant a roar of guns few even in the army and navy had ever heard before," wrote a British naval officer. Earthworks and entrenchments were destroyed in an instant, blasted to dust, while American troops fled in terror.

Had such overwhelming power been brought to bear at Brooklyn, the trap would have been closed tight. Washington and half the Continental Army would have been in the bag, captured, and the American Revolution all but finished. Without Washington there almost certainly would have been no revolution, as events were to show time and again. As the historian Trevelyan would write, "When once the wind changed and leading British frigates had . . . taken Brooklyn in the rear, the independence of the United States would have been indefinitely postponed."

Significantly, the same circumstances as at Brooklyn were to pertain again five years later, in 1783, except that the sides were switched, when American and French armies under Washington and Rochambeau had the British trapped at Yorktown, a French fleet at their back, sealing off any possible escape and leaving the British commander, Cornwallis, and more than 7,000 men no choice but to surrender.

"Oh God! It is all over!" Lord North, the British prime minister, is said to have exclaimed on hearing the news from Yorktown. It is what might well have been heard in the halls of Congress or any number of places the summer of 1776 had there been no fateful wind and fog at Brooklyn.

## ALISTAIR HORNE

# RULER OF THE WORLD

## Napoleon's Missed Opportunities

Even if you have to admit that Napoleon was the dominant personality of the nineteenth century, there remains something more than faintly unappetizing about the man. He is the consummate come-lately, who did not hesitate to sacrifice a generation of Europeans in the pursuit of personal glory. The lives of overreachers are ready-made for counterfactual speculation, and Napoleon's more than most: We would not see his like again until Hitler. He was a man who did not know when to stop, and who can say what destination he might have taken if he had.

In this chapter, the British historian Alistair Horne examines some of the tantalizing might-have-beens of Napoleon's career. Could he have brought off an invasion of England in 1805? Was he right in selling the Louisiana Territory to the infant United States? In the campaign that led up to his most famous victory, Austerlitz, how close did the Great Gambler come to defeat in Central Europe? And what would have been the result? (Curiously, it might have forestalled a united Germany and a century of trouble.) What if Napoleon had decided not to invade Russia but had

201

*driven through Turkey and the Near East instead—Alexander the Great's route of conquest—to threaten British India? What if the Duke of Wellington had taken command of the British Army in North America that was offered him? He might have won the War of 1812 for England but he would have been absent from Waterloo: That may have made all the difference. Can we say what Europe—and, indeed, the world—would have been like if Napoleon had realized his "miracle" at Waterloo?*

✦ *Alistair Horne is the author of two books about Napoleon—NAPOLEON: MASTER OF EUROPE 1805–1807 and HOW FAR FROM AUSTERLITZ? He has written such noteworthy studies as THE FALL OF PARIS: THE SIEGE AND THE COMMUNE 1870–1871, THE PRICE OF GLORY: VERDUN 1916, TO LOSE A BATTLE: FRANCE 1940, and A SAVAGE WAR OF PEACE: ALGERIA 1954–1962. He has been awarded both the British CBE and the French Legion d'Honneur for his historical works, and is Doctor of Literature at Cambridge University.*

Over Napoleon's extraordinary career, which lasted some twenty years, there were various times when history might have turned out differently: There were options that either he or his opponents could have taken up and moments when, had he made alternative choices, Napoleon might have remained on top to the end. What, for example, would have happened had he won at Waterloo? And what might the world have looked like today in the event of a definitive Napoleonic victory?

Napoleon was, as the historian George Rudé has written, "a man of action and rapid decision, yet a poet and dreamer of world conquest; a supreme political realist, yet a vulgar adventurer who gambled for high stakes." He had the good fortune to come on the scene in a period of revolutionary exhaustion, and it is hardly surprising that the dominant personality of his time would control the future of Europe—and the world—for so long.

The Directory, which succeeded Robespierre's Terror of 1792 to 1794, was a weak and divided government—perhaps a bit like Gorbachev and Yeltsin coming after the years of Stalinism—and 1799 could possibly have been a year of hope and reconciliation for the warring nations of Europe, at war since the Revolution had submerged France. But four years earlier, a twenty-six-year-old one-star general had made his name by the "Whiff of Grapeshot," which quelled the Paris mob. While still under thirty, Napoleon Bonaparte had won his first great military victories in Italy, between 1796 and 1797, and with the "Brumaire" coup on November 9, 1799, he found himself the de facto ruler of France; shortly afterward a national plebiscite confirmed his supremacy by making him consul for life. His rise to power in fact wrecked any prospect of an early settlement with England, especially after he persuaded the Directory to send him on his ill-fated expedition to Egypt. Up until 1803, the French perceived Napoleon as a peacemaker, but afterward saw him as a conqueror and the founder of a new empire. In the years until things visibly began to go wrong, they happily went along (indeed, much as the Germans had during the years of Hitler's easy conquests).

The brief Peace of Amiens (in the words of Winston Churchill, "the tourist season was short!") in 1801 offered statesmanship an early opportunity for a negotiated settlement. But neither Pitt's Britain, smarting from her reverses and determined not to lose Malta, nor Napoleon—proven supreme on land even though the Royal Navy had thwarted him everywhere at sea—were ready for it. No compromise peace was possible so long as an implacable Pitt faced a Napoleon unvanquished on land.

During the Peace, Napoleon busied himself internally with his first social and legislative reforms for France, but his thoughts were on further external conquests. Abroad, he pulled off the supreme coup of selling the Louisiana Territory to the young United States, thereby ensuring that she would at least remain benevolently neutral in the global conflict with England, if not an ally. Of course, here he could have clung on to these vast former territories of Imperial Spain; but this would almost certainly have brought him into conflict with the Americans—an enemy neither he nor Pitt wanted.

This fact of life had been proven over the course of the costly wrestling for the colonial islands of the Caribbean, stretching back into the Ancien Régime. (In the eighteenth century, it should be noted, these islands were considered to be by far the most valuable real estate in the New World.) Over the twenty-two years that the wars with France lasted, nearly half of Britain's total death toll had died in Pitt's campaigns in the West Indies, most of the casualties falling to the deadly yellow fever. In 1802 an expedition sent by Napoleon to reconquer the sugar-rich island of Santo Domingo (now Haiti) was decimated by the disease, with the commander, General Leclerc (the husband of Napoleon's sister Pauline), himself succumbing to it. Only three thousand of the original 34,000 sent there returned; nevertheless, Napoleon's restless eyes repeatedly turned to those lost jewels in the Caribbean. But, with the sale of the Louisiana Territory and the failure of the Santo Domingo operation, his options in the New World were effectively terminated—to the huge relief of Washington.

Equally, post-revolutionary France did not have the naval strength to maintain a presence in the New World. Such an endeavor would have made the Napoleonic navy a ready prey to the British. Thus this was never a viable option. Indeed, at almost every turn in Napoleon's career one sees possible options seriously conditioned by his naval inferiority vis-à-vis Britain. Wracked by mutinies, with most of its officers drawn from the purged upper classes, its ships decaying, the French Navy never recovered and was never to recover from the Revolution. In 1798, while Napoleon won on land in Egypt, offshore a young Nelson had annihilated his ships; three years later the lesson was repeated at Copenhagen. Despite this, in July 1803, Napoleon announced the creation of a "National Flotilla," with the express purpose of invading Britain. Historians continue to argue as to whether he ever really intended to; but the evidence seems to be that, like Hitler, he would have done it if he could.

Also as with Hitler, had he been able to land substantial forces, the defenders, with then vastly inferior numbers, would have been swamped. Already in 1797, an abortive attempt had been made to invade Ireland, but it was disrupted by storms. The following year, encouraged by France, Ireland exploded in a violent revolt. This was crushed, and so was a French landing two months later. Thus, as an option for Napoleon, attractive as it might seem on paper, Ireland proved no more than a blind cul-de-sac—at least so long as the Royal Navy commanded the sea approaches to England. Back in the reign of hated King John in the early thirteenth century, a French ruler invited by dissident barons had briefly held sway at Westminster; but the following year an upsurge of patriotism had led to the complete annihilation of the French fleet in the Battle of Calais. Without seeming to make too chauvinist a point, ever since then France—though often mighty on land—has seldom prospered at sea in conflict with Britain.

**THE FLOATING SUMMIT, 1807**

*On a raft in the middle of the River Nieman in East Prussia, Napoleon (center right) meets with Tsar Alexander of Russia to divide Europe. Had his career of military conquest ended there, in June 1807, Napoleon might have established himself as the permanent master of the continent.*

(Anne S. K. Brown Military Collection, Brown University Library)

Napoleon, nevertheless, set to building a vast fleet of over a thousand invasion barges. But, flat-bottomed and keelless, although ideal for landing on British beaches and estuaries, they swamped in anything but the lightest of seas, and the French suffered terrible loss of life in trial exercises. Britons took the threat seriously, but the then "Ruler of the Queen's Navee," Admiral "Jarvie" St. Vincent, was right when he declared: "I don't say the French can't come. I say they can't come by sea!" Napoleon had himself admitted after the Egyptian Campaign that, "If it had not been for the English I should have been emperor of the East, but wherever there is water to float a ship, we are sure to find [them] in our way." Although Pitt had no army worth the name at the time, it was British gold financing the continental foes of Napoleon and her fleet that repeatedly blocked Napoleon's ambitions.

By the reopening of hostilities in 1804, Nelson had fifty-five ships-of-the-line to France's forty-two, of which only thirteen were ready for active service. But, in the summer of 1805, Napoleon played his most daring card with the ruse of sending Admiral Villeneuve and his rickety fleet on a 14,000-mile voyage of deception to draw off Nelson to the West Indies—just long enough for the French Channel fleet to gain sufficient time for achieving local supremacy. With his habitual optimism, Napoleon reckoned that twenty-four hours would be enough. "We are ready and embarked," he told his admirals. Through the summer of 1805, Pitt's England, like Churchill's of the summer of 1940, waited with baited breath for the threatened invasion. On the cliffs of Boulogne, in August, Napoleon cursed the "foul wind," and his admirals. Both failed him. The right twenty-four hours never came. Once more, like Hitler, Napoleon cut his losses and marched eastward. By the end of August, a vast *Grande Armée* 200,000 strong was heading toward Austria, to meet a combined Austrian and Russian threat mustering there.

Britain was safe. But could "Invasion 1805" have worked? Was it ever a serious option? To Napoleon the arch-gambler, ever profligate with the lives of his troops, it may have seemed a risk worth taking. But at best, given the overall superiority of the Royal Navy in seamanship, ships, and commanders, it would have been a gamble with the dice heavily loaded against him—in an element that he and his marshals, so invincible on land, never understood, and would never understand. To quote the famous words of America's Admiral Mahan about Nelson's victory at Trafalgar two months later: "Those distant, storm-beaten ships, upon which the Grand Army never looked, stood between it and the dominion of the world."

The truth of that remark would pursue Napoleon all the way to St. Helena.

After some incredibly rapid marches and brilliant maneuvering across Europe, on December 2, 1805, Napoleon won his greatest victory of all at Austerlitz. Deep in the heart of Europe, in what is now the Czech Republic, with only 73,000 men and 139 guns, he pulverized the joint Austrian and Russian forces of 85,000 men and nearly twice the number of cannon. Napoleon planned superbly and knew exactly what he was doing, both at Austerlitz and earlier at Ulm. Yet, here too, in the middle of hostile territory, the risks were immense; the what ifs proliferate.

If the slow-moving Russian steamroller had reached Austria's General Mack before he was encircled at Ulm . . .

If the Prussians had entered the war in time to attack Napoleon's long-extended flanks . . .

If Russia's General Kutuzov had refused battle at Austerlitz (as he was to do with such success in Russia in 1812) . . .

Finally, if Napoleon had conducted at Austerlitz as untidy a battle as he was to fight against the much more outclassed Prussians at Jena the following year . . .

Here, particularly, in tactical terms, it seems to me that there was an option for history to have taken a different course, for events to have gone decisively against the gambler. At one moment in the Battle of Austerlitz the issue looked closely in the balance. All depended on the speed of Napoleon's top general, Davout, marching at all haste up from Vienna. But suppose, instead of Davout, the vain, incompetent, and slow-moving "Belle-Jambe" Bernadotte had been placed in that position? Bernadotte, whose deplorable conduct was to come so close to wrecking the victory at Jena in 1806, and whom Napoleon actually ordered off the field of Wagram in disgrace in 1809?

Defeated, his *Grande Armée* wiped out in the center of Europe a thousand kilometers from Paris, himself probably a captive, it is difficult to see how Napoleon could have survived failure at Austerlitz. Meanwhile, two months earlier, in October, Nelson had inflicted on him the decisive defeat of his career at the other end of Europe. From Trafalgar onward this failure to gain freedom of action on the high seas was to limit his every maneuver and option—a factor that it is impossible to overstate.

There is yet another what if option that would have followed from a French defeat at Austerlitz. The peace that was to come after Waterloo, and lasting a century, would not then have been a *Pax Britannica*. Won by feat of Russian and Austrian arms under Kutuzov, it would have been their peace, in fact Tsar Alexander's, to dictate. With such an outcome in 1805, the Habsburg Empire, ramshackle though it was, would have emerged strengthened; Russia, characteristically, would have retired behind her frontiers, possibly expanding southward at the expense of Ottoman Turkey. The big difference would have been in the development of Prussia. Not challenged by war, it would have found no motive for uniting the German states under its mantle and would have remained an insignificant entity, unlikely to threaten the peace of Europe in later generations. The European *status quo ante* of the eighteenth century would effectively have been restored.

As already mentioned, the Battle of Jena-Auerstädt (against the Prussians) the following year was a much less tidy affair; so too were the bloody battles—the last round against the Russians—of Eylau and Friedland. But by then the dice were heavily cast on Napoleon's side; success generates success, victory procreates victory. If anything, on the wider spectrum of history, Napoleon's triumphs of 1805 to 1807 were just too complete—the humiliation of his continental enemies—Austria, Russia, and Prussia—too great for them to lie down complacently without thoughts of revenge. If he had not won so resoundingly on Austerlitz's Pratzen Heights, might there have been no Waterloo ten years later? By 1807, Napoleon's best hopes for the future now lay, not on the battlefield, but in diplomacy—notably in the skilled hands of that Henry Kissinger of his times, Charles-Maurice de Talleyrand-Périgord, the self-defrocked former bishop, who was now his minister of foreign affairs.

Certainly it can be argued that, had Napoleon's head not become so swollen by such a run of apparently endless victories, Talleyrand might now have had an easier time. But, as Prussia's victory over France in 1871 was to prove, excessively successful generals do not make the best negotiators of peace. On June 19, 1807, Murat's cavalry reached the River Niemen, the Russian frontier over 1,000 miles from Paris. There the French were met by Tsar Alexander's envoys, sent to beg for an armistice.

The following week the two potentates met on board a raft hastily assembled in the middle of the river—to settle the future of the continent. As Napoleon stood on that raft, only thirty-seven, he was truly Master of Europe; but to his undoing, perhaps, he also saw himself, in the contemporary phrase of Tom Wolfe, "Master of the Universe." From Gibraltar to the Vistula and beyond, he now ruled either directly or through vassals who were his creations. "He dominated all Europe," wrote Winston Churchill:

> The Emperor of Austria was a cowed and obsequious satellite. The King of Prussia and his handsome queen were beggars, and almost captives in his train. Napoleon's brothers reigned as kings at The Hague, at Naples, and in Westphalia . . .

Before Austerlitz, Napoleon had been an object of fear; after Tilsit, he held Europe spellbound with terror. His conquests over the past ten years surely rivaled those of Alexander the Great; but where Alexander had simply marched across great spaces of defenseless Persia or India, massacring helpless populations who offered small challenge, Napoleon had marched a thousand miles across a hostile Europe, conquering great nations and powerful armies as he went. However, the parallel grows alarming: Alexander had aimed at nothing less than reaching the "End of the World." He was incapable of stopping. If only he had stopped at Persepolis. But India ruined him, the deserts of Persia killed him.

Could Napoleon now stop? Aboard the raft on the Niemen he had the option. It was his best chance to halt and consolidate his achievements. Perhaps he could have been satisfied merely with being king of Italy, uniting its disunited states; as a Corsican he was, after all, more akin to the Italians than the French, while Milan—with its statues and avenues named after Napoleon—still always strikes the visitor as being one of the few conquered cities where his name remains hallowed.

Or he could have devoted his vast energies entirely to the reconstruction of France, and the glorification of Paris: "If I were the master of France," he declared in 1798, "I would like to make Paris not only the most beautiful city in the world, the most beautiful that ever existed, but also the most beautiful that could ever exist."

And, later, regretfully: "I wanted Paris to become a city of two, three, or four million inhabitants, that is, something wonderful, powerful, and never experienced before our time . . . If the heavens had granted me another twenty years and some leisure, you would have looked in vain for the old Paris."

But few of his grandiose building projects were ever completed, and this dream of turning Paris into a gigantic monument to the fame and greatness of his rule was to be forever denied to him by military ambition.

Thus Tilsit turned out to be his last option before the tide turned irrevocably against him. The next time he ventured on to the River Niemen, just five years later, he would be on the road to his first great defeat, and the beginning of his eclipse.

The wily but astute Talleyrand comprehended the danger, saw the option now facing his chief. Talleyrand profoundly disapproved of the humiliating terms Napoleon had insisted on exacting on his defeated opponents. The terms imposed on the proud Prussians—heavy reparations and dismemberment of all their territories west of the Elbe—were particularly draconian. They would prove unacceptable and the stimulus for the national regeneration that would help defeat France from 1813 onward. Far more lethal, the all-powerful Prussia emerging from the German unification in the teeth of Napoleon's onslaught would lay the foundations for the catastrophes to overtake France at the hands of heirs of the unforgiving Prussians—in 1870, 1914, and 1940.

As far as Austria was concerned, Talleyrand had hoped that generous terms after Austerlitz would have made Austria a bulwark against Russia and ensured a balance of power in Eastern Europe. (The unfortunate Russo-Austrian alliance of 1805 had been, after all, both unnatural and unhistoric.) But she, too, was left, like Prussia, prostrate and dreaming of revenge.

At Tilsit, Russia became, nominally, Napoleon's ally. But she, too, had been humiliated, and she chafed at the creation of a Polish state, the Grand Duchy of Warsaw, set up by Napoleon on what Russia historically considered to be a Russian satellite, and on her very borders—reacting to it much as Yeltsin would greet the move eastward of NATO in the 1990s. It was therefore a thoroughly artificial new friendship, based on ephemeral self-interest and continuing hostility to Britain. To this end, Napoleon pushed a reluctant tsar into his "Continental System," the counterblockade that was aimed at strangling Britain.

None of this was what Talleyrand had striven for: Above all he wanted an end to the fifteen years of war that had been impoverishing France since the Revolution. He saw Tilsit, which left France no real friends in Europe, as perpetuating that war. He was right. In frustration and disgust, Talleyrand now defected, in effect offering his services to the tsar. It was an act of questionable treachery—which Talleyrand himself dismissed as "a matter of dates"—in an endeavor to bring down his master before he brought down France. Meanwhile, in Paris, news of Tilsit was welcomed with rather more pageantry and festivity than reality.

What could Napoleon, in fact, have achieved at Tilsit, had he followed the advice of Talleyrand? Through persuasion and diplomacy rather than military coercion, he could have imposed the uniformity of the admirable administrative aspects of the Napoleonic system across Europe. Such uniformity would, in the course of time, have probably effected a stranglehold on markets essential to British prosperity more effectively than the universally unpopular rigidity of his "Continental System"—which was to hurt his continental partners more than Britain.

In strategic terms, he might well have wooed the tsar to support him in a drive through Turkey and the Near East, to threaten the very roots of British power in India. It was, after all, not many years since France had been a power on the subcontinent. This was a dream often in the back of Napoleon's mind, ever since the abortive Egyptian Campaign of 1798, and here he would almost certainly have found sympathy in Russia, her ambitions in Central Asia being constantly at odds with Britain's. By moving chiefly overland he would have neutralized the ubiquitous menace of the Royal Navy. In the Near East he would have encountered no serious opposition; quite possibly, he would have found a role for Islam to play within the empire—provided it toed the line, politically, like other religions.

Yet one needs recall the fate of the legions of Alexander the Great. The terrible deserts of Persia and Baluchistan destroyed them, and distance coupled with disease might have done the same for Napoleon—as indeed the wastes of Russia did. Flying in the face of British seapower, his dangerously extended lines of communication were bound to be vulnerable at one point or another—perhaps at the Bosphorus, or to an expeditionary force judiciously landed in the Levant. Then, too, for how long would the Turkish warriors of the Ottoman Empire prove malleable allies, or vanquishable foes?

What this all might have meant for the Jews of Palestine invites speculation. In France, Napoleon had expressed serious (and, by the standards of the day, advanced) desires for a liberal-minded emancipation of French Jewry. At the bitter Siege of Acre in 1797 (where he had been partly frustrated by the Royal Navy), he had issued a proclamation declaring solemnly that Jewry had "the right to a political existence as much as any other nation," which was never to be forgotten. If Napoleon had had his way in the Middle East, might it have led to the realization of Jewish aspirations in Palestine over a century before the creation of the state of Israel? On the other hand, one has to recall what a gulf there was to lie between Napoleon's promises to the Poles and their fulfillment. Napoleon was impatient at having to honor undertakings once their geopolitical value had passed.

At Tilsit, however, Napoleon exchewed all these options—and the defection of Talleyrand marked a major turning point in his fortunes. As he was himself to confess in exile on St. Helena, Tilsit was perhaps his finest hour.

Attempts to seal up holes in his "Continental System" led Napoleon, within months of Tilsit, to commit his greatest strategic error to date. Portugal, Britain's oldest ally, remained her last foothold on the continent. Napoleon determined to expunge it; but in marching through Spain he created a problem for himself that was both intolerable and insoluble. This took the form of a guerrilla war that was almost impossible to win. The intractable Spanish irregulars were backed by an originally small expeditionary force of 9,000 men commanded by Sir Arthur Wellesley (later to become the Duke of Wellington). In Napoleon's self-inflicted wound that came to be known as the "Spanish Ulcer," Britain now had her "Second Front." By the end of 1809, no less than 270,000 of Napoleon's best troops were committed to the Peninsular War—or three-fifths of his total forces. This automatically, and fundamentally, altered his relations with Russia. From Tsar Alexander having been the defeated client at Tilsit, within a year it was Napoleon who was now asking for favors—notably that Russia keep Austria on a leash.

Meanwhile, Austria was energetically rearming to avenge Austerlitz.

Could Napoleon have played it differently in the Iberian Peninsula? Of course. He could simply have kept out of Spain, sealing her borders at the Pyrenees and leaving the proud and nationalist Spaniards to deal with any British adventure there. (They were, after all, still resentful of Nelson's destruction of their fleet, too, at Trafalgar. They were as likely to turn on a British invader interrupting their Iberian slumbers as they did on the French.) The trouble was that Napoleon never knew when to stop. Meanwhile, at home increasing hardship, discontent, and sinking morale meant that, in the time-honored manner of dictators, he felt he had to distract the populace by seeking ever-fresh draughts of *la Gloire*.

In the summer of 1809, Napoleon found himself at war with a resuscitated Austria. At Wagram, on the outskirts of Vienna and not far from Austerlitz, he won his last victory—though largely through dependency on foreign levies from the Saxons and Italians, hardly reliable in adversity. Unlike Austerlitz, Wagram could neither be termed a decisive or definitive victory. Austria would soon be rearming once more. The shadows were drawing in, the opposing generals were learning.

With each succeeding year, the Royal Navy's blockade of European ports extended and perfected itself, tightening the grip. There were repeated domestic economic crises in France in 1806, 1810, and 1811: Napoleon should have read the warnings. In 1810 over 80 percent of British wheat imports had slipped through Napoleon's fingers, some even coming from France herself; while, to keep the *Grand Armée* supplied with greatcoats and boots, his own quartermasters had to covertly run the British blockade. By that same year, only 3 out of 400 of Hamburg's sugar factories remained in business. But it was Russia that was most hurt and angered by the blockade; by the summer of 1811, ships in Russian ports included 150 British vessels flying the American flag. Such defiance of his System was intolerable to Napoleon, and the war clouds gathered—with a bread crisis in January 1812 providing him with an extra motivation for marching East.

The year 1811, however, was also one of the most dangerous for Britain, when a bad harvest coincided with economic crisis. Then, in 1812, a heaven-sent opportunity seemed to fall into Napoleon's lap. In June, the U.S. Congress declared war on Britain. What was to be one of the silliest (and, from the British point of view at least), most unwanted conflicts history has to offer was a direct consequence of British arbitrary measures stemming from the blockade of Napoleon's Europe. Here was an opening for Napoleon of a different order; but by the time he might have taken advantage of it, he was embroiled in Russia, defeated, and reeling back on France.

What if Napoleon had had his eyes focused on the West in 1812, instead of the East; What if he could have thought in diplomatic instead of purely military terms; What if he had still had Talleyrand at his side. Talleyrand had actually lived in the U.S. for two years—in Philadelphia, during the French Revolution—and therefore knew a little about American motivations? Because of his failure to command the seas, once again, there was little Napoleon could have done militarily to lend support to the Americans. But a Talleyrand would have lent diplomatic and moral support to fan the very real resentment against the arrogance on the high seas of the former colonial power, Britain. The game was certainly worthwhile. Let us consider one possible result. In November 1814, the Duke of Wellington was invited to take over Britain's armies in North America. Disapproving strongly of the war, he refused—as he might not have done if Napoleon had been meddling on the American side. His decision was fortunate for Britain. The fighting against those former colonies ended in a draw a few weeks later. But: if Wellington had taken a different view, or if the American war effort had been more wholehearted, sufficing seriously to threaten Canada, and Quebec especially, then Wellington could well have been three thousand miles away when Napoleon launched his supreme bid against the Allies in June 1815.

Of course, there is a possibility that Wellington might have inflicted a decisive defeat on the Americans. Would the British then have been tempted to retake substantial parts of their former colonies, as reparations? To reverse 1775? The hypothesis is hardly likely: With no desire to become re-embroiled in the New World, Britain was lukewarm in prosecution of the War of 1812. Her main priority was Napoleon.

As it was, some of Wellington's badly needed regiments at Waterloo were only just reaching Belgium from across the Atlantic on the very eve of that battle. The consequences of Wellington's own absence would have been readily calculable—and what a sublime opportunity for Napoleon!

But by November 1814, the sand had all but run out for him. Failing to do the one thing that might have turned the scales against the tsar, liberating the Russian peasants from serfdom, Napoleon had marched to destruction to Moscow and back. Out of 600,000 troops that crossed the Niemen in June of 1812, only a broken 93,000 straggled home. The limits of his empire returned to what it had had been before Tilsit. Meanwhile, at his rear Wellington was grinding relentlessly through Spain toward the frontiers of France itself.

Option: Napoleon should never have left the war in Spain at his rear—just as Hitler in 1941 foolishly attacked Stalin leaving Britain still undefeated. Better still he should not have been in Spain at all; secondly, he should never have moved into Russia. The following year, 1813, came the Battle of the Nations, with a resurrected Prussia, Austria, and Russia coalescing in the greatest concentration of force seen in the whole of the Napoleonic Wars to corner and defeat the *Grand Armée* decisively at Leipzig.

The crushing defeats of 1814, on France's own soil, followed. Yet even then it was not too late for Napoleon to have stopped: The Allied terms on offer, generous by the standards of the day, would at least have preserved the historic and geographical integrity of France. But Napoleon chose to fight on, brilliantly, vainly awaiting his "Star" to produce a miracle. But no miracle came and he abdicated in April 1814. He went into his first imposed exile on Elba, an island near Corsica. Then, after ten months he slipped away, landed in the south of France, and marched north to Paris in the resurgence of the "Hundred Days." He seemed to have his miracle at last.

We arrive on the field of Waterloo, June 1815. In the oft-quoted words of the Iron Duke, it was indeed "the nearest-run thing you ever saw"—even with Wellington there. But without him at the helm—away in Canada, as might have been possible—Blücher, his stalwart Prussian ally, would almost certainly not have made his famous eccentric move to support his allies and—with equal certainty, Waterloo would have been lost.

On the other hand, such a victory would not have ensured Napoleon's ultimate triumph. There were vast fresh forces of Russians, Austrians, and Germans already moving toward France. A second battle, or perhaps several battles, would probably have followed Waterloo. But even if the ultimate engagement had ended in the likely defeat of Napoleon, with Britain out of the war, it would have been a *continental* and not a *British* victory. What followed would have, therefore, been a peace dominated by Metternich's Central European powers—by Russia,

Austria, and Prussia instead of Great Britain. The century ahead, would, inevitably have been a very different one. Would the victors, on past form, have fallen out, creating a period of uncertainty instead of the century of stability that Waterloo bequeathed the world? Or could they between them have cemented a different kind of "Concert of Europe"?

What about America in all this equation? Might such an alternative option have imposed on the youthful colonies an accelerated pubescence in world affairs? Suppose England had been decisively defeated in June 1815, or in the Middle East and India, or excluded successfully from Napoleon's "Continental System" at any time after Tilsit, what might this have meant for the young United States? One can predict, with some assurance, that necessity, adversity, and common interest would have brought the former colonies and a Britain shorn of her world power increasingly closer together—as was to happen in 1940.

The trouble with all these various options, these hypotheses, these what ifs, is that all hang subject to Napoleon's character. A greater and better man might have admitted, as Cassius said about Caesar in Shakespeare's *Julius Caesar*, "The fault, dear Brutus, is not in our stars, but in ourselves . . ."

Napoleon, however, could never bring himself to admit that any of his reverses were his own fault. Someone else was always to blame. Or, to quote Shakespeare again, like Hamlet he could count himself ". . . a king of infinite space, were it not that I have bad dreams."

The "bad dreams" that plagued Napoleon were the fantasies of endless military conquest. Like most conquerors before and after him he never knew when—or how—to stop. Wellington understood only too well: A conqueror was like a cannonball, he once observed; it must go on. This was what caused Talleyrand to despair and defect to the tsar. As I have suggested, Tilsit was the last best hope Napoleon had of attaching his name to an enduring peace; but it was his character that prevented him from reaching up and grabbing the opportunity. And, even so, how long would the defeated and humiliated nations of Eastern Europe—

Prussia, Austria, and Russia—have allowed him to enjoy it unchallenged? It is a question that cannot be answered.

Ninety years ago, a budding young British historian (later to become one of the most famous of his generation), named George Trevelyan, won the prize for a competition in London's *Westminster Gazette* with an essay entitled "If Napoleon had won the Battle of Waterloo." As Trevelyan saw it, the instinct of an emperor, victorious at Waterloo but exhausted by endless war and overwhelmed by the cries for peace that ran down the ranks of his army, would have been to propose a pact of "unexpected clemency" to his archenemy England. The results would be: Russia out of Europe, France dominant, the Germans remaining "the quietest and most loyal of all Napoleon's subjects" (this was written seven years before 1914), and Britain isolated.

Here were overtones of a Europe perhaps not entirely remote from the dreams of a Charles de Gaulle or a modern-day Brussels technocrat.

# ✦ CALEB CARR ✦

# NAPOLEON WINS AT WATERLOO

Suppose that the unfortunate Marquis de Grouchy had been able to complete the arguably unrealistic task that Napoleon assigned him on June 17, 1815, and had kept Prussia's Marshal Blücher from combining forces with England's Duke of Wellington the next day at Waterloo. In the best-case scenario for the French, Napoleon would have won that battle, and the allies would have been forced to make peace with the restored Bonapartist regime. What would that have implied for Europe and the world?

If we further imagine that Napoleon could have ceased behaving like a power-mad megalomaniac, we can entertain the thought that he would have become a reasonable player in the new congress system of diplomacy being devised by England's Viscount Castlereagh and Austria's Prince Metternich. This possibility had and has understandable attractions: If Bonaparte had been willing to become one among many players in the nineteenth-century balance of European power (which brought about the longest period of relative peace in that continent's modern history—a full hundred years) then the rise of the German empire—the event that eventually caused the destruction of the balance—would certainly have been prevented. General peace could, in such a scenario, have lasted well beyond 1914.

Unfortunately, to suppose such a result is to ignore the salient psychological compulsions that always drove the French emperor. The idea that Napoleon—an imperialist, but nonetheless a child of the French Revolution—would have been content to sit at a conference table with his former (and primarily reactionary) enemies and treat them as equals is improbable if not ludicrous. In all likelihood, he would instead have bided his time, built up his armies, and sooner or later made another play for continental domination. There is little if any evidence to suggest that Napoleon was alive to the suffering he personally brought on Europe for so many years or that he felt any responsibility for it; and so instead of delaying the calamities of 1914, Napoleon's victory at Waterloo would probably have advanced them some ninety or so years, and turned the nineteenth into just another century during which Europeans spent the better part of their time slaughtering each other at the behest of callous princes.

✦ *Caleb Carr's latest books are* THE ALIENIST *and* THE ANGEL OF DARKNESS.

## JAMES M. McPHERSON

# IF THE LOST ORDER
# HADN'T BEEN LOST

### Robert E. Lee Humbles
### the Union, 1862

One of the focal moments of the American Civil War, as well as a de-served staple of counterfactual history, is the finding of Robert E. Lee's Special Orders No. 191—the legendary "Lost Order." In September 1862, Lee's Confederate Army of Northern Virginia was in the process of crossing into Maryland, on his way to Pennsylvania. He had just battered Union forces at the Second Manassas; one more big victory might bring the Confederacy official British and French recognition. The Special Order, which he dispatched to his various commanders, was his strategic plan for the fall campaign. On the morning of September 13, an Indiana corporal named Barton W. Mitchell discovered in a cloverfield a bulky envelope containing three cigars and a copy of Lee's orders. The "Lost Order" was bucked up to Lee's Union opposite, General George B. McClellan. (Somewhere along the way, the cigars disappeared.) McClellan was offered a golden opportunity to divide and conquer the widely spread Confederate forces. But he frittered it away. The result was the bloodiest day of the Civil War, the Battle of Antietam—a narrow win on points for the Union but not the war-ending victory it might have been.

223

*So much for the facts. Now for the speculation. Let us assume, as James M. McPherson does here, that the Lost Order was not lost. Lee very likely would have continued north, all but unchallenged, and military logic tells us that in the Cumberland Valley of Pennsylvania a vast battle would have taken place. Where would it have been fought? McPherson has an answer equally logical—but hardly promising for the continued existence of the United States as one nation.*

✦ *McPherson is not just an expert on the Civil War but one of the finest historians writing today. He is professor of American history at Princeton University and the author of ten books, including* BATTLE CRY OF FREEDOM, *which won the Pulitzer Prize in History.*

Great possibilities rode with the Army of Northern Virginia as it began to cross the Potomac at a ford thirty-five miles upriver from Washington on September 4, 1862. Since taking command of this army three months earlier, General Robert E. Lee had halted the momentum of Union victory that had seemed imminent in May. At that time, the Army of the Potomac had stood only five miles from Richmond, poised to capture the Confederate capital. Coming on top of a series of Northern military successes during the previous four months, which had gained control of 100,000 square miles of Confederate territory in western Virginia, Tennessee, the Mississippi Valley, and elsewhere, the fall of Richmond might well have toppled the Confederacy. But Lee launched a series of counteroffensives that turned the war around. His troops drove Union forces back from Richmond in the Seven Days' Battles (June 25–July 1) and then shifted the action to northern Virginia, where they won the battles of Cedar Mountain (August 9), Second Manassas (August 29–30), and Chantilly (September 1). Dispirited Union troops retreated to the defenses of Washington to lick their wounds.

This startling reversal caused Northern morale to plummet. "The feeling of despondency is very great," wrote a prominent New York Democrat after the Seven Days' Battles. His words were echoed by a New York Republican, who recorded in his diary "the darkest day we have seen since [First] Bull Run . . . Things look disastrous . . . I find it hard to maintain my lively faith in the triumph of the nation and the law." Reacting to this decline in Northern spirits, President Abraham Lincoln lamented privately: "It seems unreasonable that a series of successes, extending through half a year, and clearing more than a hundred thousand square miles of country, should help us so little, while a single half-defeat [the Seven Days' Battles] should hurt us so much."

Unreasonable or not, it was a fact. The peace wing of the Democratic Party stepped up its attacks on Lincoln's policy of trying to restore the Union by war. Branded by Republicans as disloyal "Copperheads," the Peace Democrats insisted that Northern armies could never conquer the South and that the government should seek an armistice and peace negotiations. Confederate military success in the summer of 1862 boosted the credibility of such arguments. And worse was yet to come for the Lincoln administration. Western Confederate armies, which had been defeated in every campaign and battle from January to June 1862, regrouped during July and carried out a series of cavalry raids and infantry offensives in August and September that produced a stunning reversal of momentum in that theater as well. As the Army of Northern Virginia splashed across the Potomac into Maryland, Confederate armies in Tennessee launched a two-pronged counteroffensive that not only reconquered the eastern half of that state but also moved into Kentucky, captured the capital at Frankfort, and prepared to inaugurate a Confederate governor there.

Rather than give up and negotiate a peace, however, Lincoln and the Republican Congress acted dramatically to intensify the war. Lincoln called for 300,000 more three-year volunteers. Congress passed a militia act that required the states to produce a specified number of nine-month militia and impose a draft to make up any deficiency in a state's quota. The same day (July 17), Lincoln signed a confiscation act that provided for the freeing of slaves owned by disloyal (i.e., Confederate) masters.

Southern states had seceded and gone to war to defend slavery. Slaves constituted the principal labor force in the Southern economy. Thousands of slaves built fortifications, hauled supplies, and performed fatigue labor for Confederate armies. From the outset, radical Republicans had urged a policy of emancipation to strike a blow at the heart of the rebellion and to convert the slaves' labor power and military manpower from a Confederate to a Union asset.

By the summer of 1862, Lincoln had come to agree with this position. But so far as possible, the president wanted to keep the emancipation issue under his own control. On July 22, he informed the Cabinet that he had decided to use his war powers as commander in chief to seize enemy property to issue an emancipation proclamation. Emancipation, said Lincoln, had become "a military necessity, absolutely essential to the preservation of the Union. We must free the slaves or be ourselves subdued. . . . Decisive and extensive measures must be adopted. . . . The slaves [are] undoubtedly an element of strength to those who [have] their service, and we must decide whether that element should be with us or against us." Most of the Cabinet agreed, but Secretary of State William H. Seward advised postponement of the proclamation "until you can give it to the country supported by military success." Otherwise the world might view it "as the last measure of an exhausted government, a cry for help . . . our last *shriek*, on the retreat."

This advice persuaded Lincoln to put the proclamation in a drawer to await a more favorable military situation. Unfortunately, it deteriorated further as enemy armies began their invasions of Maryland and Kentucky, two border states that seemed ripe for Confederate plucking. Northern morale continued to fall. "The nation is rapidly sinking just now," wrote a New York diarist. "Stonewall Jackson (our national bugaboo) about to invade Maryland, 40,000 strong. General advance of the rebel line threatening our hold on Missouri and Kentucky. . . . Disgust with our present government is certainly universal."

Democrats hoped to capitalize on this disgust in the upcoming congressional elections. Republicans feared the prospect. "After a year and a half of trial," wrote one, "and a pouring out of blood and treasure, and the maiming and death of thousands, we have made no sensible progress in putting down the rebellion . . . and the people are desirous of some change." The Republican majority in the House was vulnerable. Even the normal loss of seats in off-year elections might eliminate this majority. And 1862 was scarcely a normal year. With Confederate invaders in the border states, the Democrats seemed sure of gaining control of the House on their platform of an armistice and peace negotiations.

Robert E. Lee was well aware of this possibility. It was one of the factors that prompted his decision to invade Maryland despite the poor physical and logistical condition of his army after ten weeks of constant marching and fighting that had produced 35,000 Confederate casualties and thousands of stragglers. "The present posture of affairs," Lee wrote to Jefferson Davis on September 8 from his headquarters near Frederick, Maryland, "places it in [our] power . . . to propose [to the U.S. government] the recognition of our independence." Such a "proposal of peace," Lee pointed out, "would enable the people of the United States to determine at their coming elections whether they will support those who favor a prolongation of the war, or those who wish to bring it to a termination."

Lee did not mention in this letter the foreign-policy implications of his invasion. But he and Davis were aware of those as well. The much-anticipated "cotton famine" had finally begun to have a serious impact on the British and French textile industries. An end to the war would reopen foreign trade and bring a renewed flow of cotton from the South. Powerful leaders and a large part of the public in both countries sympathized with the Confederacy. The French emperor, Napoleon III, flirted with diplomatic recognition of the Confederacy, but was unwilling to take the initiative without British cooperation.

When the war had seemed to be going in the North's favor during the first half of 1862, foreign governments backed off from any overt dealings with the Confederacy. When news of the Seven Days' Battles reached Paris, however, Napoleon instructed his foreign minister to *"Demandez au gouvernement anglais s'il ne croît pas le moment venu de reconnaître le Sud."* ("Ask the English government if it does not believe the time has come to recognize the South.")

British sentiment seemed to be moving in this direction. The United States Consul in Liverpool reported that "we are in more danger of intervention than we have been at any previous period . . . They are all against us and would rejoice at our downfall." The Confederate envoy in London, James Mason, anticipated "intervention speedily in some form." The news of Second Manassas and the invasions of Maryland and Kentucky gave added impetus to the Confederate cause abroad. Britain's chancellor of the exchequer in a speech at Newcastle in October, declared, "Jefferson Davis and other leaders of the South have made an army; they are making, it appears, a navy; and they have made what is more than either; they have made a nation."

More cautious, Prime Minister Viscount Palmerston and Foreign Minister Lord John Russell nevertheless discussed a concrete proposal for Britain and France to offer to mediate an end to the war on the basis of Confederate independence—if Lee's invasion of Maryland brought another Confederate victory. Union forces "got a complete smashing" at Second Manassas, wrote Palmerston to Russell on September 14, "and it seems not all together unlikely that still greater disasters await them, and that even Washington or Baltimore may fall into the hands of the Confederates. If this should happen, would it not be time for us to consider whether in such a state of things England and France might not address the contending parties and recommend an arrangement on the basis of separation?" Russell responded three days later, concurring in the proposal for mediation "with a view to the recognition of the Independence of the Confederates." If the North refused, then "we ought ourselves to recognize the Southern States as an independent State."

The Lincoln administration was acutely sensitive to the political and diplomatic dangers posed by Lee's invasion. But the military crisis had to be dealt with first. The Union army that fought and lost Second Manassas (Second Bull Run) was an ill-matched amalgam of troops from Major General John Pope's Army of Virginia, Major General Ambrose Burnside's IX Corps transferred from North Carolina, and parts of Major General George B. McClellan's Army of the Potomac transferred from the Virginia Peninsula. There was no love lost between Pope and McClellan, who was sulking because of the withdrawal from the peninsula and who considered himself unjustly persecuted by the administration. McClellan dragged his feet about sending troops to Pope's aid, and two of his strongest corps, within hearing of the guns along Bull Run, never made it to the battlefield.

Lincoln considered McClellan's behavior "unpardonable"; a majority of the Cabinet wanted to cashier the general. But Lincoln also recognized McClellan's organizational skills and the extraordinary hold he had on the affections of his soldiers. Lincoln therefore gave McClellan command of all the Union troops in this theater, with instructions to meld them into the Army of the Potomac and go after the rebels. To Cabinet members who protested, Lincoln conceded that McClellan had "acted badly in this matter," but "he has the Army with him . . . We must use what tools we have. There is no man in the Army who can lick these troops of ours into shape half as well as he . . . If he can't fight himself, he excels in making others ready to fight."

McClellan confirmed both Lincoln's confidence and his lack of confidence. A junior officer wrote that when the men in the ranks learned of McClellan's restoration to command, "from extreme sadness we passed in a twinkling to a delirium of delight . . . Men threw their caps in the air, and danced and frolicked like schoolboys . . . The effect of this man's presence upon the Army of the Potomac . . . was electrical, and too wonderful to make it worthwhile attempting to give a reason for it." McClellan did reorganize the army and "lick it into shape" in a remarkably short time, making it "ready to fight." But then he reverted to his wonted caution, estimating enemy strength in Maryland at two or three times Lee's actual numbers and moving north at a snail's pace of six miles a day as if he were afraid of finding rebels.

McClellan clamored for reinforcements, particularly the 12,000-man garrison at Harpers Ferry. But General in Chief Henry W. Halleck refused to release these troops. That refusal created both a problem and an opportunity for Lee. The garrison threatened his line of supply through the Shenandoah Valley. So on September 9, Lee drafted Special Orders No. 191 for the dispatch of almost two-thirds of his army in three widely separated columns under the overall command of Jackson to converge on Harpers Ferry and capture it. The opportunity: a large supply of artillery, rifles, ammunition, provisions, shoes, and clothing for his ragged, shoeless, hungry troops. The problem: McClellan might get between the separated parts of his army during the three to six days it would take to carry out the operation and destroy the fragments of the Army of Northern Virginia in detail.

But two of Lee's hallmarks as a commander were his uncanny ability to judge an opponent's qualities and his willingness to take great risks. To Brigadier General John G. Walker, commander of one of the columns to converge on Harpers Ferry, Lee explained the purpose and plan of his campaign. After capturing the garrison and its supplies, the army would re-concentrate near Hagerstown. "A few days' rest will be of great service to our men," Lee said. "I hope to get shoes and clothing for the most needy. But the best of it will be that the short delay will enable us to get up our stragglers," who from exhaustion, hunger, and lack of shoes had not been able to keep up with the army. Lee believed that there were "not less than eight to ten thousand of them between here and Rapidan Station"—a fairly accurate estimate. When they rejoined the army and were resupplied, Lee intended to tear up the Baltimore and Ohio Railroad and then move to Harrisburg and destroy the Pennsylvania Railroad bridge over the Susquehanna, thus severing the Union's two east-west rail links. "After that," Lee concluded, "I can turn my attention to Philadelphia, Baltimore, or Washington, as may seem best for our interests."

Walker expressed astonishment at the breathtaking boldness of this plan, which would leave the Union army at his rear. "Are you acquainted with General McClellan?" Lee responded. "He is an able general but a very cautious one . . . His army is in a very demoralized and chaotic condition and will not be prepared for offensive operations—or he will not think it so—for three or four weeks. Before that time I hope to be on the Susquehanna."

Even as Lee was offering these observations, however, his adversary had an extraordinary stroke of luck. On September 13, two Union soldiers resting in a field near Frederick, where the Confederates had camped a few days earlier, found a copy of Lee's Special Orders No. 191 wrapped around three cigars where they had been lost by a careless

Southern officer. Recognizing their importance, the Yankee soldiers took them to their captain, who forwarded them up the chain of command until they reached McClellan. A Union staff officer vouched for the genuineness of the document, for he had known Lee's adjutant, Robert H. Chilton, in the prewar army and recognized his handwriting.

The orders gave McClellan a picture of the division of Lee's army into five parts, each at least eight or ten miles from any other while the most widely separated units were thirty miles apart with the Potomac River between them. No Civil War general ever had a better chance to destroy an enemy army in detail before it could reunite. To one of his subordinates, a jubilant McClellan declared: "Here is a paper with which if I cannot whip 'Bobbie Lee,' I will be willing to go home."

As usual, however, McClellan moved cautiously. He did drive Confederate defenders away from the South Mountain passes on September 14. But Harpers Ferry fell to Jackson on the fifteenth and Lee was able to concentrate most of the Army of Northern Virginia near Sharpsburg before McClellan was ready to attack on September 17. After an all-day battle along the ridges above Antietam Creek, Lee was compelled to retreat across the Potomac on the night of September 18. Without the discovery of the lost orders, perhaps even this limited Union victory would not have occurred.

✦ ✦ ✦

The odds against the sequence of events that led to the loss and finding and verification of these orders must have been a million to one. Much more in line with the laws of probability is something like the following scenario. Knowing that most residents of western Maryland were Unionists, Lee imposed tighter security on the army than when in friendly Virginia, to prevent penetration of his camps by any local civilians who hung around the edge and undoubtedly included several spies among their number. Lee instructed his adjutant to deliver Special Orders No. 191 directly to the relevant corps and division commanders. They were to read them in Chilton's presence and commit them to memory, after which all copies of the orders were burned except one, which Lee kept in his possession. In this way there could be no leaks.

Because of an inept defense of Harpers Ferry by its Union commander, Dixon Miles, and because of McClellan's failure to advance rapidly, the garrison surrendered 12,000 men and mountains of supplies to Jackson on September 15. Meanwhile, Jeb Stuart's cavalry performed outstanding service, bringing up stragglers and guarding the passes through the South Mountain range against the ineffectual probes of Union horsemen trying to discover the whereabouts of Lee's main force. On September 16, McClellan arrived at Frederick, which the rebels had vacated a week earlier. By then Lee had reconcentrated his army at Hagerstown. Thousands of stragglers had rejoined the ranks, and thanks to the captures at Harpers Ferry, the Army of Northern Virginia was well equipped for the first time in two months.

After a further pause for rest, while McClellan remained in the dark about Lee's location and intentions, the rebels moved north into Pennsylvania. They brushed aside local militia and the outriders of Union cavalry who finally located them. Spreading through the rich farmland of Pennsylvania's Cumberland Valley like locusts, Lee's army—now 55,000 strong—was able to feed itself better than it had in Virginia. On October 1, the van reached Carlisle. Lee sent a strong detachment of cavalry and part of Jackson's swift-marching infantry twenty miles farther to the railroad bridge at Harrisburg, which they burned on October 3. The Confederate commander also sent his Maryland scouts back into their home state to locate the Army of the Potomac. They found it near Emmitsburg, just south of the Pennsylvania border, marching northward with a determined speed that suggested McClellan finally meant to find Lee and fight him.

Those scouts also reported to Lee that they had discovered a series of hills and ridges around a town named Gettysburg where numerous roads converged, enabling an army to concentrate there quickly and fortify the

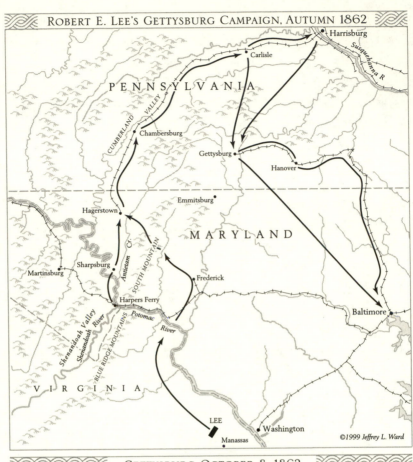

## ROBERT E. LEE'S GETTYSBURG CAMPAIGN, AUTUMN 1862

Harrisburg

Susquehanna R.

Carlisle

P E N N S Y L V A N I A

CUMBERLAND VALLEY

Chambersburg

Gettysburg

Hanover

Emmitsburg

Hagerstown

M A R Y L A N D

Baltimore

Antietam Cr.

Sharpsburg

Frederick

SOUTH MOUNTAIN

Martinsburg

Harpers Ferry

Potomac

River

Shenandoah Valley

Shenandoah River

BLUE RIDGE MOUNTAINS

V I R G I N I A

LEE

Washington

Manassas

©1999 Jeffrey L. Ward

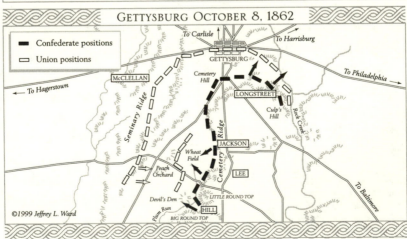

## GETTYSBURG OCTOBER 8, 1862

■ Confederate positions
□ Union positions

To Carlisle

To Harrisburg

GETTYSBURG

To Philadelphia

McCLELLAN

Cemetery Hill

To Hagerstown

LONGSTREET

Seminary Ridge

Culp's Hill

Rock Creek

JACKSON

Wheat Field

Cemetery Ridge

LEE

To Baltimore

Peach Orchard

Devil's Den

LITTLE ROUND TOP

Plum Run

HILL

BIG ROUND TOP

©1999 Jeffrey L. Ward

high ground. On October 4 Lee ordered his army to Gettysburg. They arrived there only hours before the enemy, and by October 6 the Army of Northern Virginia was dug in on the hills south of town.

McClellan came under enormous pressure from Washington to attack the invaders. "Destroy the rebel army," Lincoln wired him. From the Union position on Seminary Ridge, a reluctant McClellan surveyed the Confederate defenses from the Round Tops on the south along Cemetery Ridge northward to Cemetery and Culps Hills. McClellan evolved a tactical plan for a diversionary attack on the morning of October 8 against General James Longstreet's corps on the Confederate right. When Lee shifted reinforcements to that sector, the Yankees would launch their main assault through the peach orchard and wheatfield against the Confederate left center on low ground just north of Little Round Top, held by Jackson's corps. If successful, this attack would pierce a hole in the Confederate line, giving Union cavalry massed behind the center a chance to exploit the breakthrough. Napoleonic in conception, this plan had a crucial defect: It left Union flanks denuded of cavalry.

At dawn, the Union I and IX Corps carried out the diversionary attack on Cemetery and Culps Hills. Lee saw through the feint, however, and refused to shift his reserves, A. P. Hill's light division, to that sector. Longstreet held firm, so when the Union II, VI, and XII Corps attacked through the peach orchard and wheatfield, they found Jackson ready for them. Fierce fighting produced a harvest of carnage unprecedented even in this bloody war, with neither side gaining any advantage.

About 3:00 P.M., Stuart reported to Lee that the Union right was uncovered. Lee immediately ordered Hill to take his division south around Round Top and attack the Union flank in the wheatfield. Undetected by the Union cavalry, which was massed more than a mile to the north, Hill's 6,000 men burst from the woods and boulders of Devil's Den screaming the rebel yell. Many of them wore blue uniforms captured at Harpers Ferry, which increased the surprise and confusion among Union troops of the XII corps. Like a row of falling dominoes, the exhausted and decimated Union brigades collapsed. With perfect timing the rest of

Jackson's corps counterattacked, smashing the fragments of Union regiments that had rallied to resist Hill. As the fighting rolled in echelon toward the North, Longstreet's corps joined the counterattack at 4:30 P.M.

McClellan had kept his favorite V Corps in reserve. Steadied by Brigadier General George Sykes's division of regulars, they held back the yelling rebels for a brief time. But as the sun dipped below the South Mountain range, the V Corps also broke. In a desperate attempt to rally them, McClellan rode to the front. "Soldiers!" he shouted. "Stand fast! I will lead you!" As he drew his sword, a minié ball smashed into his skull and toppled him dead from his horse. Word of McClellan's death spread like lightning through the thinned and scattered ranks of Yankee units that were still fighting. The last remnants of resistance winked out. Thousands of dejected bluecoats surrendered; thousands more melted away into the dusk, every man for himself. The Army of the Potomac ceased to exist as a fighting force.

News of the Battle of Gettysburg resounded through the land and across the Atlantic. "My God! My God" exclaimed Lincoln in the White House. "What will the country say?" It said plenty, all of it bad. Peace Democrats redoubled their denunciations of the war as a wicked failure. "All are tired of this damnable tragedy," they cried. "Each hour is but sinking us deeper into bankruptcy and desolation." Even staunch patriots and Lincoln supporters like Joseph Medill, editor of the *Chicago Tribune*, gave up hope of winning the war. "An armistice is bound to come during the year '63," he wrote. "The rebs can't be conquered by the present machinery." Captain Oliver Wendell Holmes Jr. of the 20th Massachusetts, which had suffered 75 percent casualties at Gettysburg, wrote in November that "the army is tired with its hard and terrible experience. I've pretty much made up my mind that the South have achieved their independence."

In Kentucky, Union and Confederate forces had clashed in the indecisive Battle of Perryville on the same day (October 8) as the Battle of Gettysburg. Encouraged by the news from Pennsylvania, Confederate commanders Braxton Bragg and Edmund Kirby-Smith decided to continue their Kentucky campaign. Having already occupied Lexington and Frankfort, they began a drive toward the prize of Louisville as the Union army under Major General Don Carlos Buell, discouraged by the reports of McClellan's defeat and death, fell back listlessly. In Pennsylvania, after a pause for consolidation of his supply lines, Lee began an advance toward Baltimore. Newly emboldened pro-Confederate Marylanders openly affirmed their allegiance. Although reserve troops manning the formidable defenses ringing Washington dissuaded Lee from attacking the capital, there was no Union field army capable of resisting Lee's movements.

Hesitant to goad last-ditch resistance by attacking a major city, however, Lee paused to await the outcome of Northern congressional elections on November 4. The voters sent a loud and clear message that they wished to end the war, even on terms of Confederate independence. Democrats won control of the next House of Representatives and the peace wing established firm control of the party.

At almost the moment the election results became known, the British minister to the United States, Lord Lyons, presented Secretary of State Seward with an offer signed by the governments of Great Britain, France, Russia, and Austria-Hungary to mediate an end to the war on the basis of separation. "We will not admit the division of the Union at any price," Seward responded. "There is no possible compromise." Very well, responded Lyons. In that case Her Majesty's Government will recognize the independence of the Confederate States of America. Other European governments will do the same. "This is not a matter of principle or preferences," Lyons told Seward, "but of fact."

Despite Seward's bluster, he was a practical statesman. He was also a student of history. He knew that American victory at the Battle of Saratoga in 1777 had brought French diplomatic recognition of the fledgling United States, followed by French assistance and intervention that proved crucial to the achievement of American independence. Would history repeat itself? Would British and French recognition of the Confederacy be followed by military assistance and intervention—against the blockade, for example? As they pondered these questions and absorbed the results of the congressional elections, while Confederate armies stood poised for attack outside Baltimore and Louisville, Lincoln and Seward concluded that they had no choice.

On a gloomy New Year's Day 1863, a melancholy Lincoln called Republican congressional leaders and state governors to the White House. "This is not the duty I had hoped to discharge today," he told them. "Last July I decided to issue a proclamation freeing the slaves in rebel states, to take effect today," he continued sadly. "There is no chance of that now. Would *my word* free the slaves, when I cannot even enforce the Constitution in the rebel States?" Instead, "We are faced with a situation in which the whole world seems to be against us. Last summer, after McClellan was driven back from Richmond, I said that in spite of that setback, 'I expect to maintain this contest until successful, or till I die, or am conquered, or my term expires, or Congress or the country forsakes me.' Gentlemen, the people expressed their opinion in the last election. The country has forsaken us, and the next Congress will be against us. Whether or not we admit we are conquered, we must admit that we have failed to conquer the rebellion. Today I will issue a proclamation accepting the insurgents' offer of an armistice. Secretary Seward will accept the good offices of foreign powers for mediation." The president's voice choked as he concluded: "Gentlemen, the United States no longer exists as one nation, indivisible."

STEPHEN W. SEARS

# A CONFEDERATE CANNAE AND OTHER SCENARIOS

*How the Civil War Might Have
Turned Out Differently*

The what ifs of the American Civil War may be more difficult to gauge than those of our Revolution—already the times and the technology of war were more complex—but they are plentiful enough. A nation permanently divided was a real prospect during the first two years of the war, and one that certainly fueled Southern ardor for battle. If, as James M. McPherson speculates in the previous chapter, the Lost Order hadn't been lost, that might have been the inevitable outcome of Robert E. Lee's first invasion of the North. Or, as Stephen W. Sears describes in this chapter, if Robert E. Lee had pulled off a double envelopment of a large part of George B. McClellan's Union army on day six of the Seven Days' Battles in June 1862, it might well have led to the end of hostilities and negotiations for "an arrangement upon the basis of separation." But the rebellion (as the North thought of it) might just as easily have ended not long after it began. Sometimes, Sears notes, if there is any inherent logic to military operations, outcomes should have gone another way. Sometimes, too, the difference can be as slight as the path of a bullet and whether its target gets out of the way in time. As we have seen before, milliseconds can influence cen-

*turies. But in other cases, an event that seems likely to bring a swing in historical direction—Sears offers by way of example the victory of McClellan over Lincoln in the presidential election of 1864—may produce the curious phenomenon of the "second order counterfactual." In other words, enormous change can in the end, merely lead us back to where we might have been all along.*

✦ *Stephen W. Sears is one of the foremost historians of the Civil War. His books include* LANDSCAPE TURNED RED: THE BATTLE OF ANTIETAM, GEORGE B. MCCLELLAN: THE YOUNG NAPOLEON, CHANCELLORSVILLE, *and, most recently,* CONTROVERSIES & COMMANDERS: DISPATCHES FROM THE ARMY OF THE POTOMAC.

The Civil War—like every war—was marked by a number of pivotal moments, moments in which the balance tipped suspensefully to produce a victor or a vanquished and subsequently a crucial change in the war's direction. At these moments it was the decisions or actions of soldiers and statesmen (and in one instance here, voters) that resulted in the consequences that history records for us. But outcomes and consequences could just as easily have gone another way—sometimes, if there is any inherent logic to military operations, *should* have gone another way.

Each of the five scenarios that follow held the promise (at that moment, at least) of affecting the war profoundly or, in the case of the last one, the aftermath of the war. None of them requires a great leap of imagination to believe its premise. Without improbably distorting actual events—in the first scenario, for example, Jefferson Davis was a witness to the 1861 fighting at Bull Run—and without putting unspoken words into the mouths of the actors, then, imagine that at this handful of critical Civil War moments it turned out this way instead of that way . . .

### Battle at Bull Run, or the Rebellion of '61

"You are green, it is true," Mr. Lincoln said to Irvin McDowell, commander of the newly recruited Federal army at Washington, "but they are green, also; you are all green alike." It was a remarkably prescient observation. On July 21, 1861, when McDowell's raw troops joined battle with the equally raw troops of the newly proclaimed Confederate States of America, along the banks of Bull Run west of the capital, the outcome would be decided by which of these green armies broke and ran first.

The decisive moment occurred in late afternoon. After six hours of confused maneuvering and bloody fighting, the men of both armies were nearing the limit of their endurance. The Confederates, pressed slowly but steadily back by General McDowell's flanking movement, formed a last-ditch defense on Henry House Hill. At the core of their line was a brigade of Virginians being held rigidly to their task by a flinty brigadier named Thomas J. Jackson. Charge and countercharge swept across the hilltop, but the Virginians stood fast. Then, suddenly, a Federal volley found General Jackson and he was down, struck by three bullets, his left arm mangled. He was carried to the rear and out of the battle, his moment of glory fated to be forgotten.

Without Jackson's stalwart leadership as a rallying point, his Virginians began to waver. Seeing this, the regiments on both their flanks gave way. Once again the Federals came on, and this time they would not be stopped. The center of the Confederate line broke open and fell away. Abruptly everyone was running for the rear and safety. Behind the shattered front, fearful teamsters jammed their supply wagons into the crossroads village of New Market, where shells from the U.S. batteries found them and turned the jam to pandemonium. Fear was transmuted into panic. "The larger part of the men are a confused mob, entirely demoralized," the field commander of the beaten army had to admit. "It was the opinion of all the commanders that no stand could be made . . ."

That in the end proved crucial—there was nowhere close by for the routed Confederates to take a stand, no natural barrier behind which the panicked men might be calmed and rallied. Had the battle gone the other way, had it been the raw Federals who broke and ran, they would have had the nearby Potomac and Washington's rudimentary defenses as a rallying point. As it was, for the Confederates fleeing the battlefield, the closest major defensive feature where they might attempt a stand was the Rappahannock, some twenty-five miles to the south. Hardly more than a corporal's guard would reach the river.

The Federal brigades that had done the fighting were as disorganized in victory as their foes in defeat. However, General McDowell had two divisions available in reserve to throw into the pursuit. As the flight continued through the night, exhausted, discouraged rebels by the thousands threw down their arms and surrendered to the pursuers. The most noteworthy prisoner was the president of the Confederate States. Jefferson Davis had rushed up from Richmond to witness the battle, and he was captured as he rode out into the mass of fleeing rebels to try and halt the rout.

By the second day after the battle, the ranking rebel generals, Joseph E. Johnston and P. G. T. Beauregard, had dragged what remained of their forces across the Rappahannock. On the twenty-first they had given battle at Bull Run with something over 30,000 men; hardly a quarter of that number now remained under effective command. Even though they were joined by a reserve force from Fredericksburg, just then the armed might of the Confederate States totaled barely 10,000 troops. McDowell and his legions, forming up opposite along the riverbank, were being reinforced hourly by fresh regiments from the North. No fresh regiments were forthcoming from the South.

It was only too clear to Johnston and Beauregard that within a matter of days, perhaps within a matter of hours, the enemy in overwhelming force would plunge across the Rappahannock to stamp out what remained of the rebellion's armed forces. With President Davis languishing in Old Capitol prison in Washington, the two generals took decision-making into their own hands. Neither was a revolutionary; both were traditionalists in matters of military form: When every choice promises only defeat, there is but one honorable choice. They sent to McDowell under a flag of truce to request an armistice. With a nod of approval from President Lincoln, McDowell granted it. So ended the military phase of what would come to be known as the Rebellion of '61.

Diplomacy now replaced arms. Stepping again into the limelight were Kentucky Senator John J. Crittenden and the Senate's Committee of Thirteen, who had labored fruitlessly for a compromise settlement between the Secessionists and the Unionists at the turn of the year. This time the Southerners had to play their hand without trumps. From the White House, Mr. Lincoln dictated the terms of settlement. The eleven

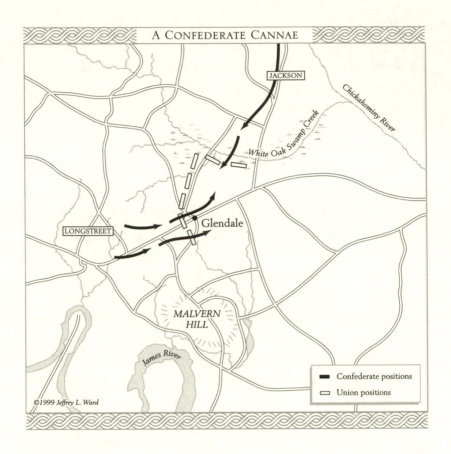

A CONFEDERATE CANNAE

JACKSON

Chickahominy River

White Oak Swamp Creek

LONGSTREET

Glendale

MALVERN
HILL

James River

Confederate positions

Union positions

©1999 Jeffrey L. Ward

states of the Confederacy must rescind their articles of secession and re-join the Union. Their armed forces must disband, and all federal property be restored. While of course slavery would not be interfered with in those states where it had been constitutionally established, its extension beyond their borders would henceforth be strictly prohibited. The Congress would enact the necessary legislation, and the Committee of Thirteen was charged with crafting a long-range plan for compensated emancipation.

With the remnant of the C.S.A. army firmly in McDowell's grip, and with the memory of the debacle at Bull Run fresh in every mind, Richmond had no choice but to accept the terms of settlement and recon-struction. There was agitation in the North for the leaders of the Rebel-lion of '61 to be hanged for treason, starting with Mr. Davis. President Lincoln would have none of it. After all, with further warfare now averted, he faced a presidential term certain to focus on the most delicate political negotiations aimed at finding a peaceful way out of the morass that was American slavery. An embittered former Confederacy would make that task all but impossible. "Let 'em up easy," was Lincoln's homely injunction.

Of course it did not happen that way. Only nicked by a bullet, Gen-eral Jackson famously held steadfast to the position on Henry House Hill—"There is Jackson standing like a stone wall!"—and in the end it was McDowell's green troops who broke and ran. The victorious Con-federate army—in due course to be christened the Army of Northern Virginia—looked forward to winning independence for the South in its next campaign.

That next campaign was fought on the Virginia Peninsula, where McDowell's replacement, George B. McClellan, advanced on Richmond. The Peninsula Campaign reached its climax in the Seven Days' Battles, which opened in the last week of June 1862. Robert E. Lee—who had re-placed Joseph E. Johnston, wounded at Seven Pines—attacked McClel-lan relentlessly, driving him back from the gates of Richmond. On June 30, at the crossroads hamlet of Glendale, Lee delivered what he intended to be the decisive blow of the campaign.

### General Lee Achieves His Cannae

As Lee's biographer, Douglas Southall Freeman, would put it, General Lee "had only that one day for a Cannae . . ." It was day six of the Seven Days', and McClellan's Army of the Potomac was in rapid flight toward the James River. The routes to the river funneled through Glendale. Hot on McClellan's heels came Stonewall Jackson with four divisions. Thrust-ing in toward the flank of the retreating Yankees were three divisions under James Longstreet. Although McClellan's army was the larger of the two overall, at the Glendale chokepoint it was Lee who could bring superior force to bear against the extended enemy columns. A flank attack there by Longstreet held promise of cutting the Federal army in half; indeed, Hannibal's classic conquest at Cannae in 216 B.C.—history's watchword for a crushing military defeat—might be duplicated. Porter Alexander, that most astute of Confederate historians, said there were but a handful of moments in the Civil War when "we were within reach of military successes so great that we might have hoped to end the war with our independence. . . . This chance of June 30th '62 impresses me as the best of all."

As it happened, Lee missed this best chance by the slimmest of margins, and the Yankees escaped to fight another day. After watching Longstreet's flank assault come up just short, Lee wrote bitterly, "Could the other commands have co-operated in the action the result would have proved most disastrous to the enemy." The primary offender was Stonewall Jackson. Sunk in a state of profound lethargy that day, Jackson failed to move against the Federal rear guard, which was thus able to send strong reinforcements in the nick of time to seal off Longstreet's breakthrough.

The day might easily have taken a different course. In fact, had Jackson been his usual self on June 30, 1862, it almost certainly would have taken a different course.

✦   ✦   ✦

After three months' intensive campaigning in the Shenandoah Valley, after his dash to the Peninsula and straight into the Seven Days' fighting there, Stonewall Jackson was utterly exhausted. On day five—Sunday, June 29—with his command held inactive under Lee's orders, Jackson recognized the perilous state of his own physical and mental health. Abandoning his usual strict Sabbath evolutions, he gave orders that he was not to be disturbed and slept half the clock away. Consequently, when he faced the pivotal events at Glendale on June 30, Stonewall Jackson was refreshed and alert and eager for the test.

That morning Jackson caught up with the Yankees' rear guard, under William Franklin, at a broken bridge over the White Oak Swamp watercourse north of Glendale. Jackson's reconnoiter uncovered the considerable strength of the enemy position and set his thoughts (as usual) to a flanking movement. Enterprising subordinates found two downstream fords where infantry might cross. Jackson pounced on the opportunity. Under cover of a tremendous artillery barrage at the bridge site, he directed three brigades to cross and take Franklin's Yankees in flank and rear.

As Franklin's rear guard joined battle against this threat, Lee directed Longstreet to launch his offensive against the Federals defending the Glendale crossroads to the south. Soon the hard-pressed Glendale defenders were calling on Franklin for help. He could send them none; indeed, he even refused to return two brigades sent him "on loan" from Glendale earlier.

Longstreet smashed cleanly through the center of the extended Union line. Pushing aside the inconsequential reserves, he turned his spearhead northward, toward Franklin's embattled rear guard. When Franklin turned to meet this new threat, Jackson stormed the White Oak Swamp crossing in full force. A good half of the Federal army was cut off and engulfed by converging forces.

The Federals' plight was made all the worse by a muddled high command. Before the battle opened, General McClellan, distraught and demoralized by the turn his campaign was taking, had deserted his troops at Glendale and ridden off to join the army's advance guard on the James, well distant from the fighting. He left no one in charge, and so the defense of the "Glendale Pocket" became simply every general for himself.

"Fighting Joe" Hooker, south of the break in the line, got his division away. Phil Kearny boldly attacked and broke through the closing ring. Their two divisions, along with the four that earlier had reached Malvern

Hill on the James, now comprised the fighting strength of the Army of the Potomac. Darkness found the other five divisions trapped at Glendale and in the margins of White Oak Swamp. Lee tightened the ring during the night, and the next day, July 1, accepted the Federals' surrender. Including battle casualties, Glendale cost the Yankees 46,000 men and all their equipment. General Lee had achieved his Cannae—or at least half of it.

McClellan scrambled away to Harrison's Landing on the James with what remained of his forces. Already convinced that Lee's army was 200,000 strong (more than twice its actual count), the Young Napoleon was unstrung by the reports from Glendale. His grand campaign had ended in a Waterloo. Telling his second in command, Fitz John Porter, to surrender on the best terms possible, he sailed off in a gunboat for exile. He would not gain even that haven. Court-martialed on charges of dereliction of duty at Glendale, McClellan was convicted on the furious testimony of Generals Hooker and Kearny and cashiered.

As for General Lee, he was treated to a Romanlike triumph in Richmond. Calmly he recruited his army and re-equipped it with the rich military spoils seized from the Army of the Potomac. He knew he now faced only loud-talking General John Pope and his Army of Virginia, a patchwork assembled from the remaining Federal forces in the East. In late July, Lee set off northward. His instructions to Stonewall Jackson, leading the spearhead, were to "suppress" the braggart Pope.

The outmanned Pope did not wait to be suppressed, but fled to the defenses of Washington. Lee followed rapidly and put the city and its ragtag collection of defenders under siege. The Potomac was closed both above and below the capital, and all rail connections severed. Then, laboriously, the Confederates began to bring up the massive siege train they had seized from McClellan on the Peninsula. Watching all this from London, Prime Minister Palmerston addressed a note to his foreign secretary. The Federals had received "a very great smashing," he noted and asked, "Would it not be time for us to consider whether in such a state of things

England and France might not address the contending parties and recommend an arrangement upon the basis of separation?"

The British-French offer arrived aboard the next packet, and behind
it, the Lincoln administration knew, lay the threat of full recognition of
the Confederacy by Europe's powers. The administration realized, too,
that if it brought forces from the Western theater to try and lift the siege
of Washington—a dubious prospect at best against the brilliant Lee—the
Rebels there would march straight to the Ohio and into the heartland.
When in September General Lee sternly granted but three days to evacuate all civilians from the capital before he opened with his siege guns,
the reply was a call for a suspension of hostilities so as to negotiate "an
arrangement upon the basis of separation." Lee's Cannae had now produced everything he expected of it.

+ + +

The most celebrated tactical surprise of the Civil War was, of course,
Stonewall Jackson's successful flanking march and attack on Joe Hooker
at Chancellorsville. Looking back on it, Hooker was unrepentant about
his management of the battle. Jackson's movement, he wrote afterward,
"under the circumstances admitted of not a ray of probability of successful execution. Ninety-nine chances out of a hundred Genl Jackson's
corps would have been destroyed." To be sure, Hooker was hardly an un-
biased observer. Yet he had a point. General Hooker had taken specific
steps to avoid and to counter just such a surprise attack that May 2,
1863. If those orders to guard his right had been carried out as he intended them to be, how different the outcome might have been.

### The Victor of Chancellorsville

On the morning of May 2, the sixth day of his campaign, Joe Hooker was
brimming with confidence. Having fixed Lee in place at Fredericksburg
with a holding force and then secretly crossed the Rappahannock up-

stream with his main body, his campaign plan showed every sign of working perfectly. He had drawn Lee out of his imposing fortifications and was threatening his flank and rear. The plan now was to force Lee to attack him in his chosen position, around the Chancellorsville crossroads.

Hooker's forces were posted in expectation of a defensive battle. His weakest corps, the Eleventh, with its less-than-stellar commander, O. O. Howard, held the right flank, farthest from the expected scene of action. To be on the safe side, however, Hooker had ordered up from the Fredericksburg front John Reynolds's First Corps, one of the best in the army, to brace Howard's position. To this point in the campaign the one serious malfunction had been in communications between the two wings of the army—couriers got lost in the woods, and the telegraphic link to the Fredericksburg front failed to work. But in this instance, for a welcome change, the link worked perfectly. Reynolds received his orders promptly, and by midafternoon on May 2 the First Corps was solidly anchoring the army's right flank.

During the morning an enemy column was sighted crossing an opening in the woods off to the south, and word of it was passed up to headquarters. Hooker was quick to warn Howard: "We have good reason to suppose that the enemy is moving to our right." Look to your exposed flank, Howard was told; mass your reserves "in order that you may be prepared for him in whatever direction he advances."

Otis Howard had only recently been promoted to command of the Eleventh Corps, and it seems that in this first action he determined to be especially conscientious about obeying orders. At the end point of his line, then, he quickly formed a long right angle facing west, throwing up log breastworks and posting his artillery. To the rear he positioned substantial reserves of men and guns. In early afternoon, as the First Corps began arriving on the scene, he made sure his line was securely tied to Reynolds's. When Howard replied to Hooker's warning, "I am taking measures to resist an attack from the west," he meant every word of it.

At 5:30 that afternoon, when Stonewall Jackson gave the word to his flanking force—"You can go forward then"—his first wave of attackers

250

struck like an avalanche. Howard's line bent and in places even broke, but there was no surprise and no panic. Reserves, already on the alert, were moved into the gaps. Reynolds, too, absorbed the blows, and then pitched into the flank of the attackers. By the time darkness finally ended the fighting, Jackson could claim gains of only some 200 yards. When that night he was accidentally felled by a volley from his own men, he was searching in vain for some gap in the solid enemy front.

May 3, the pivotal day of the campaign, went all Joe Hooker's way. Cavalryman Jeb Stuart, who took over for the wounded Jackson, attacked repeatedly but fruitlessly in an attempt to close the huge gap between the two wings of the Confederate army. Coolly meeting these assaults, Hooker parried every blow of Stuart's and then counterattacked with two fresh corps. Stuart reeled back in defeat.

No choice remained for Lee now but to give up the fight and order a withdrawal. Taking severe losses in extricating his army from the Chancellorsville front, he fell back south toward Richmond along his railroad supply line. Hooker pursued, and the continuous fighting that spring of 1863 came to be known as the Overland Campaign—Lee stubbornly defending each river line between Fredricksburg and Richmond, Hooker patiently outflanking each line. By July, Lee and his proud Army of Northern Virginia were pinned in the trenches before Richmond. Joe Hooker, now promoted to lieutenant general, confidently managed the besieging army.

That July 1863 saw Grant's capture of Vicksburg and the opening of the Mississippi. By November, under Grant's management, the Chattanooga gateway to the Deep South was in Union hands. In the face of Hooker's steady successes in the East and Grant's in the West, Confederate morale sagged. Quickly pressing his advantage, Grant marched straight for Atlanta, took it, then cut a swath through Georgia to the coast. Spring 1864 witnessed the final campaigns. While Grant drove north through the Carolinas, at Richmond Hooker snipped off Lee's rail supply lines one by one. On April 9, 1864, at Appomattox Court House, Lee's desperate effort to escape fell short, and he surrendered to Joe

Hooker. Soon afterward, Joe Johnston surrendered to Grant in North Carolina, and the great rebellion was history.

Grant's and Hooker's partisans urged their heroes to seek the presidency in the fall. But Grant had already assured Mr. Lincoln that he would not challenge his reelection. Nor would Joe Hooker, who expressed only contempt for politics. "I will not accept if nominated and will not serve if elected," he announced loudly.

Historians of the war would rank Grant first among the Union's generals, but by consensus they credited "Fighting Joe" Hooker with conducting at Chancellorsville the most perfectly executed campaign of the entire three-year war.

✦ ✦ ✦

On August 24, 1863, President Davis telegraphed Robert E. Lee to come to Richmond from his camps on the Rappahannock to consult on grand strategy. In the East, Lee's army, despite its Gettysburg defeat, seemed able to stand off any fresh Federal threats. But in the Western theater, particularly in Tennessee, the Confederacy was in dire straits. Mr. Davis wanted Lee to send troops west from his army—and he wanted Lee himself to go West with them and take over command of the Army of Tennessee from the incompetent Braxton Bragg. As Davis put it, Lee's "presence in the western army would be worth more than the addition of a corps."

While properly deferential to the president, Lee made it clear that he was not interested in the Western command. "I did not intend to decline the service," he told Davis, "but merely to express the opinion that the duty could be better performed by the officers already in that department." At the time, Davis seems to have felt it would be a mistake to force any such change on his unwilling (and indispensable) lieutenant, and he let the matter drop. Instead, it would be Longstreet who commanded the troops sent West, and the Army of Tennessee continued its march to grim ruin under Braxton Bragg.

What if, however, Davis had adopted his commander in chief's stance and *ordered* Lee to go West, "for the good of the service"? Might the war in that theater then have taken a different course? . . .

### A New General for the West

Mr. Davis, having somewhat nervously exercised his ultimate authority in the matter of this momentous command change, was wise enough to leave it up to General Lee what troops he would take West with him, and, more important, who would command the Army of Northern Virginia in his absence. Of that army's three corps commanders, James Longstreet, A. P. Hill, and Dick Ewell, only Longstreet had Lee's full confidence. Lee promptly chose him for the place.

Paradoxically, it was Longstreet who had argued long and vigorously for sending his corps from the Army of Northern Virginia to the Army of Tennessee—hoping, in the bargain, to be awarded command of the Western army himself. Now, thrust into Lee's place instead, he was insistent on having his trusted corps remain with him. Lee agreed, and rather than Longstreet's corps going West, it was the corps of Dick Ewell. Ewell's first battle as corps commander had been Gettysburg, where he had acted indecisively. Lee thought it best to take Ewell West with him and through careful supervision perhaps embolden him. Ewell had earlier performed capably enough under Stonewall Jackson's tight control; perhaps all he needed was a shorter rein.

Lee had expressed concern that the Western army's high command might not accept him as an "outsider." He need not have worried. Bragg had so alienated his lieutenants that they welcomed Lee with open arms. When he took over the command, he found immediate opportunity to employ his aggressive martial nature. Bragg's army had been maneuvered out of Chattanooga and out of Tennessee entirely, yet now the incautious Federals under William Rosecrans were ripe for a counterstroke. Bragg had planned such a stroke, but it was Lee who carried it out, at Chickamauga. On September 20, the second day of the battle, acting on a direct order from Lee, Dick Ewell's reinforcing corps from the East delivered the decisive blow. Rosecrans's Army of the Cumberland was split in half and by nightfall was retreating helter-skelter for Chattanooga.

Early the next morning, the Confederate cavalryman Nathan Bedford Forrest ranged ahead to Missionary Ridge overlooking Chattanooga and saw the chaotic situation of the fleeing Federal columns. He hurried dispatches back to headquarters: "I think they are evacuating as hard as they can go . . . I think we ought to press forward as rapidly as possible." With a single brigade of infantry, Forrest promised, he could take Chattanooga: "Every hour is worth a thousand men."

Braxton Bragg had been wont to let such shining opportunities slip away. Not Robert E. Lee. He recognized in Forrest the same sure judgment that marked Jeb Stuart in the Eastern army, and he leaped at the advice. He rushed forward every man who could carry a gun. The army would outrun its supplies, he was warned. They could resupply from captured Yankee stocks, said Lee, just as he had resupplied his Army of Northern Virginia in the Chancellorsville victory.

Over the next few days, the battered Army of the Cumberland was decimated. For one of the few times in the war, a victory in the field turned into a virtual battle of annihilation. George Thomas, whose stubborn stand at Chickamauga had been the one bright spot for the Union in that battle, stubbornly directed the retreat of the remnant of Rosecrans's army after that general was captured. Lee regained Chattanooga, and in eastern Tennessee, the now outmanned Federal force under Ambrose Burnside beat a hasty retreat. By October, Tenneessee, vital gateway to the Deep South, was once again securely in Confederate hands.

Having restored affairs in the Western theater, at least until the next campaigning season in the spring, General Lee petitioned Davis to give the Army of Tennessee to Joseph E. Johnston and to let him return to his beloved Army of Northern Virginia. Longstreet had done well enough checkmating General Meade's halfhearted moves in Virginia—the Army of the Potomac, too, had had to dispatch troops to the Western theater— but Lee considered Longstreet far too defensive-minded. Robert E. Lee still believed that Confederate independence could only be achieved in the Eastern theater, and he wanted to direct that effort. Mr. Davis could hardly refuse his most spectacularly successful general.

Alas for the Confederacy, there was only one Robert E. Lee—and also only one cautious-to-a-fault Joe Johnston. In the spring of 1864, the Union might be forced to start all over in Tennessee, but this time it was U. S. Grant who was in charge of the effort from the beginning. With his force and Sherman's, along with Thomas's tattered command reinforced to corps strength from Northern reserves, Grant reprised the brilliant maneuvering he had displayed at Vicksburg. First, he feinted the nervous Johnston right out of Chattanooga, then without pause he pressed him back relentlessly toward Atlanta. As early as September 2, 1864, Grant would telegraph President Lincoln, "Atlanta is ours, and fairly won."

Lee's command presence in the Western theater and his bright victories at Chickamauga and Chattanooga were now all for naught—gone with the wind, it would be said. In the end, all he achieved was to bring U. S. Grant to the fore, unfettered and where he was needed most.

✦ ✦ ✦

In late August 1864 the Democrats met in convention in Chicago to nominate their candidate for president. It was all but certain that General McClellan would be the nominee, and even among Republicans there were many who expected the general to be elected. One of those was Abraham Lincoln. A few days before the convention, he had his Cabinet members sign a "blind memorandum," the contents of which only he knew. He did not expect to be re-elected, he wrote, and therefore it must become the administration's duty to save the Union before the new president-elect's inauguration, "as he will have secured his election on such ground that he can not possibly save it afterwards."

The Democrats, however, proceeded to commit political suicide. At the convention, a peace-at-any-price Copperhead faction, outmaneuvering the McClellanites, seized control of the platform committee and rammed through a peace plank that termed the war a failure and called for an armistice without conditions. The general, duly nominated, found himself a war Democrat running on a peace platform. Although he repudiated the peace plank, it was a fatal handicap. The soldier vote, in particular, turned overwhelmingly against him. Sherman's capture of Atlanta made a sham of the Democrats' war-is-a-failure argument. On November 8, McClellan lost by 2.2 million to 1.8 million in the popular vote, and by 212 to 21 in the electoral college.

What if, however, the Democrats had acted sanely at Chicago? What if the majority at the convention kept control of events and wrote into the platform a strong war plank for General McClellan to run upon? Surely that would have made a difference on November 8.

## Our Seventeenth President

George McClellan proved not to be as politically naive as many had thought. He understood what needed to be done to exploit the pessimism in the North and gain him the presidency. First and foremost, he had to take both New York and Pennsylvania, the two most populous states, with fully half (plus one) of the 117 electoral votes he needed for victory. The Democrats also had traditional strengths in the border states—Maryland, Delaware, Kentucky, Missouri. They were thought to have good prospects in two New England states—Connecticut and New Hampshire—and in New Jersey, McClellan's adopted state. Finally, Indiana and Illinois, with their substantial Southern constituencies, were worthwhile campaign targets. If General McClellan could capture New York and Pennsylvania, he would need but 58 more electoral votes; these "focus states" contained 79.

Sherman's capture of Atlanta, coming on the heels of McClellan's nomination, was immediately made the occasion for high celebration by war Democrats. As one party leader put it, they must be sure that McClellan people "burnt as much powder as the Republicans in celebrating the victories announced from time to time." McClellan wrote Sherman, "Your campaign will go down in history as one of the memorable ones of the world," and made sure the press got copies. The Democrats' strategy was to present General McClellan, the senior general on the active list, driven from command after his great victory at Antietam by a radicalized Republican administration, as a superbly qualified commander in chief in contrast to the bumbling civilian Lincoln. McClellan would see the war through surely and swiftly and professionally. One of his staff members told the press, "The General stated that should he be elected, he expected to be very unpopular the first year, as he should use every power possible to close the war at once, should enforce the draft strictly, and listen to no remonstrance until the rebellion was effectually quashed." That attracted much favorable notice among soldier voters.

Democratic campaigners hit hard at what they called the tyrannies of the Lincoln administration, with its trampling of such individual liberties as the habeas corpus privilege. They pointed to "abolitionist fanaticism" and social and economic chaos and costly trickeries in financing the war. It was pointed out that the Army of the Potomac, McClellan's old command, was bogged down in trench warfare under his successors, and after a bloody summer of staggering casualty lists was no closer to Richmond than McClellan had been in 1862. McClellan had opposed emancipation, but had done so privately; now both he and the platform were silent on the slavery question. Personally he was most comfortable focusing on the soldier vote, including the McClellan Legion, organized on the home front from thousands of discharged soldiers and men on sick leave and furlough.

In October, there were bellwether state elections in Ohio, Indiana, and Pennsylvania. In Ohio the notorious Copperhead Clement Vallandigham, who had attempted to disrupt the Chicago convention, was fresh in voters' minds and Republicans held the state. But Democrats scored narrow victories in Indiana and Pennsylvania; in the latter the soldier vote went decisively for the obviously still-popular onetime commander of the Army of the Potomac.

Both sides predicted a close outcome on November 8. Even Mr. Lincoln conceded New York and Pennsylvania to McClellan, although calculating a narrow six-vote electoral victory for himself. McClellan wrote ten days before the election, "All the news I hear is *very* favorable. There is every reason to be most hopeful."

The general's forecast was the more accurate of the two. On Election Day he lost in the popular vote, but won nine states in the Electoral College, 120 to 113. He gained both New York and Pennsylvania on the soldier vote, especially from Army of the Potomac loyalists. He picked up Delaware, Kentucky, and New Jersey, and had paper-thin margins in Connecticut and New Hampshire. His war stand gained him Indiana and Illinois. Election analysts pointed to the strong war plank in the Chicago platform as the decisive factor for the Democrats.

It would be nearly four months until president-elect McClellan was inaugurated, but he promptly made a point of visiting or sending strongly worded statements to Union army commanders that come March 4 the new president intended to be a vigorous, active commander in chief. In effect, he would once again be general in chief of all the armies, only this time without any superior to contradict him. So it happened. When Lee surrendered his army at Appomattox Court House on April 9, 1865, President McClellan was there at Grant's side.

By then, Abraham Lincoln was home in Springfield, Illinois, yet another in a string of one-term presidents going back to the time of Andrew Jackson. Lincoln would be remembered favorably as a president who had stood fast for the Union in 1861, and who spoke and wrote well, but in the end as a president who could not persuade the people to let him see the war through on his own terms.

Ironically, his successor, who in Lincoln's August blind memorandum was predicted to be incapable of saving the Union, saved it probably as effectively as a reelected Lincoln could have. To be sure, President McClellan faced several months of battle with the still-Republican Thirty-Eighth Congress over the process of reconstructing the Union. However, George McClellan had always done better fighting his battles with words and on paper than on battlefields, and so it would prove now.

# VIETNAM IN AMERICA, 1865

Soon after dawn on Sunday, April 9, 1865, General Robert E. Lee's hungry, exhausted Army of Northern Virginia was surrounded by the overwhelming Federal forces of U. S. Grant near Appomattox, Virginia. Sitting on a log with a trusted subordinate, General Porter Alexander, Lee said he saw no way out except surrender.

Shocked, Alexander urged an alternative—that Lee order his army "to scatter in the woods and bushes . . ." to spare "the men who have fought under you for four years . . . the mortification of having you ask Grant for terms and having him reply, 'Unconditional Surrender. . . .'" Two-thirds of Lee's troops, Alexander estimated, would "scatter like rabbits and partridges," could not be caught, and could carry on the war.

That would be only about 10,000 men, Lee replied, a number "too insignificant to accomplish the least good." But suppose, he said, that "I should take your suggestion . . . The men would have no rations and would be under no discipline . . . they would have to plunder and rob . . . the country would be full of lawless bands . . . and a state of society would ensue from which it would take the country years to recover. Then the enemy's cavalry would pursue . . . and wherever they went there would be fresh rapine and destruction.

"No," the old general said. "We have now simply to look the fact in the face that the Confederacy has failed." The men should "quietly and quickly" go home, "plant crops and begin to repair the ravages of war." As for himself, "you young men might afford to go bush-whacking [but] the only proper and dignified course for me would be to surrender myself and take the consequences."

Thus did Robert E. Lee, revered for his leadership in war, make perhaps his greatest contribution—to peace. He spared the country the divisive guerrilla warfare that undoubtedly would have resulted from Alexander's despairing idea—a mean and destructive struggle that would have delayed national reconciliation for years to come.

✦ *Tom Wicker, a former columnist for the* New York Times, *is the author of several historical novels.*

ROBERT COWLEY

# THE WHAT IFs OF 1914

*The World War That Should Never Have Been*

The conventional, and lasting, impression most of us have of World War I is the lethal stasis of the Western Front trenches. But we can now see that many questions about the kind of war it would be had been answered by the time the first trenches were dug in the fall of 1914, a time that was in fact consumed by movement and maneuver. The trenches merely ratified what the events of the first months had largely decided, pointing the century in a direction that seemed unthinkable when the year began.

Those first months of the war in 1914 reveal all manner of counterfactual outcomes. What would have happened if Great Britain had stayed out of the war? Could Germany have won? And might the world have been the better for a German victory? Could the war have ended about the time Europeans originally thought it would be over: before the leaves fell? What if the United States had never been drawn in? What would our century have been like without World War I—or with a smaller and shortened version that involved only continental powers? Most important: Did the war have to become a world war?

*Even as one century ends and another begins, we are still haunted by the traumas of those years, traumas that would forever alter the balance of world power and permanently influence the way we live. What would a world without those traumas have been like? History, to paraphrase James Joyce, is a nightmare from which we are trying to awaken.*

✦ *Robert Cowley, the founding editor of* MHQ: THE QUARTERLY JOURNAL OF MILITARY HISTORY *and the editor of this book, is an authority on World War I. With Geoffrey Parker, he edited* THE READER'S COMPANION TO MILITARY HISTORY.

I t was the worst of wars in the best of times. "The First World War was a tragic and unnecessary conflict," says the opening sentence of John Keegan's book on the Great War—as it was known until a greater one came along. "It was nothing less than the greatest error of modern history," says the last of Niall Ferguson's *The Pity of War*. As we approach the millennium and the end of a century of almost nonstop violence, this assessment increasingly prevails.

Could the First World War have been avoided? Could it have been confined to a scale that was not worldwide in its events and its influence? Could it have been shorter by years, with the saving of millions of lives? And could our century's saddest story have had a different ending?

To each question except, probably, the first the answer has to be yes. Some kind of outbreak was bound to happen: People then did not think in terms of extended cold wars. The nations of Europe had spent too long in dangerous opposition; the habit of diplomatic risk-taking, of violence barely suppressed that manifested itself in the arms race, was too ingrained. The conflict of nationalisms, the competition for markets and colonies, the clash of strategic agendas and hegemonic aspirations would not be denied. The war to come became an accepted part of European fantasy life; it obsessed popular literature. The question was less whether a continental civil war—which is what was shaping up—would explode, than when it would happen, what form it would take, and who would emerge on top. The basic underpinnings of European society, with its colonial extensions, would surely remain unchanged: Few doubted that victory would be worth the briefly maximum effort. And fewer still imagined that the convulsion would be so enormous and all-consuming, or would last so long and change so much. That is where error and miscalculation—often needless and repeated—came in.

North Sea

BRITAIN

Amsterdam

The Hague

Rotterdam

Zeebrugge

Ostend

Arnhem

HOLLAND

Dover

Dunkirk

GERMANY

Calais

Bruges

Antwerp

Düsseldorf

Boulogne

Ypres

Montreuil

Lille

Brussels

Maastricht

Cologne

Arras

BELGIUM

Namur

Liège

Cambrai

Coblenz

Somme R.

Maubeuge

FRANCE

Rhine R.

LUXEMBOURG

Trier

Sedan

Rheims

Paris

Verdun

Saarbrücken

Speyer

Alsace-Lorraine

Toul

Nancy

Strassburg

Epinal

Mulhouse

Belfort

Territory to be annexed outright in the event
of a German victory

Future possible annexations to be obtained at
the Peace Conference

The "Tributary State" of Flanders-Wallonia, to
be under German political and economic
supervision

"Strongpoints," or fortified towns, to be under
German control

Area to come within a German Customs
Union, and to subordinate its economic life
to that of Germany

Western boundary of German strategic
control, within which the existing French
fortresses were to be dismantled

©1999 Jeffrey L. Ward

Based on a map in *Atlas of World War I, Second Edition* by Martin Gilbert.
©1970, 1994 by Martin Gilbert. Used by permission of Oxford University Press, Inc.

If there is a great divide in modern history, it has to be the First World War. But that historical divide did not have to be one. The war might have proved great, but it did not have to turn into a world war—as recent historians, most notably Ferguson, have begun to maintain. That metamorphosis is the key to much of what follows. If England had stayed out, or delayed its involvement, the struggle on the continent might well have been suspended by mutual agreement of the combatants toward the end of 1914—not long after the leaves fell. Germany could have won on points, as it were, maintaining a dominant position on the continent, first among nominal equals—while the decline of the British Empire might have been postponed for decades. "The American Century," which really dates from our involvement in the First World War, might also have been postponed. Would Communism have prevailed in Russia? Probably not. And if there had been no real First *World* War—the emphasis on "World" is deliberate—could there have been a Second, with its atomic conclusion? (Given humankind's prurient hanker for extreme military solutions, the Bomb, was bound to have been dropped sooner or later.)

Let us now consider several alternative scenarios, all of which might have denied these results—though no doubt bringing about others that we cannot even dream of.

### England Stays Out

As the continental storm gathered in the last week of July 1914, and the major powers edged toward mobilization, the likelihood that Great Britain would go to war was slight. France, indeed, was pressuring it to make a commitment against the Central Powers. But since the defeat of Napoleon, Britain had deliberately kept itself aloof from continental involvements, and this crisis seemed no different. European entanglements would only diminish Britain's worldwide influence, power, and economic predominance.

Though Austrian Archduke Franz Ferdinand and his wife were assassinated in Sarajevo on June 28, it was not until Friday, July 24 that the

Liberal government of Herbert Asquith held its first cabinet meeting of the month specifically to discuss foreign affairs. The principal concern that day, it should be noted, was Ireland and the continuing fracas over home rule, which was perceived as the most acute threat to the Asquith government. As the tedious afternoon meeting was about to break up, the foreign minister, Sir Edward Grey, asked the ministers to stay for a few minutes. The quiet, somewhat secretive widower, whose eyesight was failing, described in his perpetually tired voice the ultimatum that Austria-Hungary had just presented to the Serbian government, the alleged conspirator in the assassinations. The ultimatum was a clear assault on Serbian sovereignty; refusal would be grounds for war. But an attack on Serbia would draw in Austria's ally, Germany, on one side, and Serbia's ally, Russia, and Russia's ally, France, on the other. The ministers listened to Grey, and then went their weekend ways.

In a letter Asquith wrote that night, he spoke of a coming "Armageddon" on the continent. "Happily," he added, "there seems to be no reason why we should be anything more than spectators." As the new week began, and military timetables for mobilization now took precedence over the qualms of continental politicians, England hung back. On July 29, a Wednesday, Austrian artillery dug in on the right bank of the Danube and began to shell the Serbian capital, Belgrade. Grey, meanwhile, gave little hint to the Germans of his intentions—which they took as confirmation that Britain would not go to war if they went ahead with their long-planned sweep through Belgium and into France. The evidence seemed to indicate that Great Britain would maintain its traditional hands-off policy. Had not the chancellor of the exchequer, David Lloyd George, told Parliament the very day that the Austrians delivered their ultimatum to Serbia that England's relations with Germany had improved so markedly that he could foresee "substantial economy in naval expenditures"? Asquith recognized that the majority of his party wanted to steer clear of the approaching conflict—and, more to the immediate point, a majority of his Cabinet. To abandon neutrality now was to risk the fall of his government. Even as late as Friday, July 31—as Austria, Russia, Turkey, and France mobilized—Asquith was still planning to make a speech at Chester on the next morning, after which he would catch a train to spend the rest of the weekend with his friend, Lord Sheffield.

Recapitulating the chronology of those next days, you can almost believe—if only for a moment—that England will not budge from the sidelines. The 947,000 young men from Great Britain and the empire will not die: The bodies will not pile up on the wire of Thiepval or sink into the mud of Passchendaele. The war will be confined to the continent; it will not become a global affair, with India, Australia, South Africa, and Canada involved. The United States, too, will stay out: Its minorities and majorities may root for one side or the other but its love/hate relationship with England will not be replaced by the alliance that has proved the most enduring strategic tryst of the century. The empire will not need us. Its strength undepleted by a war in which it played little part, it will remain the dominant presence on the globe far beyond 1945—a date that will have no special meaning in history.

But Asquith never made it to Chester for his date with Lord Sheffield and Great Britain did go to war on the evening of August 4, eleven days after Grey first broached the news of the Austrian ultimatum. The weekend still belonged to the antiwar faction. On Saturday morning, August 1, Grey had to report to the French ambassador, "We could not propose at this moment to send an expeditionary military force to the continent." He was convinced that any guarantee to France would cause the Cabinet to break up. Meanwhile, Germany began to mobilize. Financial panic swept the city. The Cabinet held crisis meetings. It seemed to be leaning toward a declaration of neutrality—which was only prevented by Grey's threat to resign. If neutrality was the government's position, he did not feel that he could support it. Over billiards, the hawkish young first lord of the admiralty, Winston Churchill, did persuade Asquith to mobilize the navy, as a protective measure: They had just learned of Germany's declaration of war against Russia. That same evening, in a mix-up, German troops marched into Luxembourg, and then retreated: The full-fledged invasion had to wait for the next day. ("A question has haunted the annals of history ever since," Barbara Tuchman writes. "What ifs might have followed if the Germans had gone east in 1914 while remaining on the defensive against France?")

Two Cabinet meetings took place that Sunday, and right until the second adjourned at 8:30 in the evening, Asquith's government seemed ready to fall. This is the possibility that tantalizes—no, agonizes—us. Four ministers offered their resignations, and if one magnetic individual among the undecideds—Lloyd George is the most likely candidate—had come forward to lead, more surely would have followed him. But Lloyd George himself wavered and instead pleaded with the resigners to hold off making their decision public.

A night's sleep, apparently, did wonders for belligerence—that, and a big assist from the Germans. On Monday morning, August 3, a bank holiday, Asquith learned of their ultimatum to Belgium, demanding the unopposed passage of the thirty-four divisions of General Alexander von Kluck's First Army. It could not have come at a worse moment. The idea that 400,000 German troops would be marching not just through a corner of Belgium but the whole country suddenly brought home the threat to England: Surely the French Channel ports of Calais and Boulogne would be menaced. And the kaiser's legions would be less than thirty miles away. Abruptly, the momentum began to swing toward war. Crowds waving small Union Jacks gathered from Trafalgar Square to the Houses of Parliament. The German ultimatum apparently came as something of a relief to the vacillating Asquith, who feared that nonintervention would cause a split in his government more intractable than intervention. The door was open for a Tory takeover—and, indeed, Churchill had already made discreet overtures to the Conservative Party. If too many members of Asquith's cabinet resigned, Churchill asked, would the opposition "be prepared to come to the rescue of the Government . . . by forming a Coalition"? (In the end only two ministers did resign.) As happened too often in those days of crisis in both England and the continent, politicians seemed more afraid of what would happen to them if they *didn't* go to war than if they did. That afternoon, in the House of Commons, Grey rose to speak for the Government. "Today," he began, "it is clear that the peace of Europe cannot be preserved . . ."

By the end of the next day, England was at war. But what would have happened if there had been wholesale resignations and the Asquith government had fallen?

Even if it had been replaced by a Coalition government that favored going to war, a delay of a week or more would have changed everything. There would have been no rearguard actions at Mons or Le Cateau, where the British Expeditionary Force (BEF) were blooded in the first encounters with a continental enemy since the Crimean War. And England might have hesitated to send the 80,000 men and 30,000 horses of its tiny army, concentrating instead on closing the sea approaches to Germany. If, on the other hand, new elections were called, the decision to go to war would have been put off until the fall. How could there have been a declaration of war *before* a general election? (Also, as it became obvious that the German wheel was not immediately menacing the channel ports, the demand for action might have been defused.)

Even without British help, the French may have been able to stop the Germans. You can debate that outcome endlessly. Their *élan* had not yet been sapped (as it would be in 1915, after the slaughters of the Artois and Champagne). And for all the general officers who were *limogés*—fired and sent back to the garrison town of Limoges—there were good commanders on the rise, men like Ferdinand Foch and Louis Félix François Franchet d'Esperey, who were more than a match for their German opposites. The French army was better than most people think, despite its cruel early setbacks. England may only have joined the war when the Germans actually did come close to taking the channel ports, later in the fall. But by that time the possibility of a deal may have surfaced, and one we shall presently consider.

Still, the outcome of the war may have been ordained that Tuesday night. Germany could probably win a continental war; it could not win a world war. But Germany would not begin to feel the weight of world involvement until later in the fall. Time, for the moment, was on its side.

## Germany Wins the Marne . . . If There Is a Marne

The novelist John Bayley speaks of "the non-inevitability of events that we nevertheless know are bound to come." That was true about Great Britain's entry into the war—and it may have been even more so about the next major episode in Western Europe that summer. It's easy to view the confused series of actions, large and small, that go under the rubric "Battle of the Marne," as a clash of vast impersonal forces (and, at the start, rather equal ones), a collision of momentums. But in fact few events have so turned on command decisions, and on the frailties (more often than the strengths) of the men who made them, many of whom were in their mid- to late-sixties.

With notable exceptions, energy was in short supply among the generals of both sides. And command energy was precisely the ingredient needed for such a nonstop operational confrontation (what we used to call a campaign), whose results in those first wild days of war were often decided far behind the lines. But right up until the final days of the Marne, when forces began linking up and troops dug the first trenches, you cannot really speak of lines. Fronts were established, only to disintegrate bloodily. Combat became a struggle of perpendiculars rather than horizontals, of endless dusty marching columns probing for flanks to turn or gaps to enter—while other marchers retreated in equally long lines from the probers. There were times when opposing divisions marched parallel to one another. In the month that the Marne lasted, the two sides covered an average of 12.5 miles per day. This was not World War I as we now think of it. Generals, who rarely stayed put themselves, had all they could do to keep in touch with their own men, let alone the enemy. No one was more in the dark than the staffs of the highest commands, the German OHL and the French GQG.

If the long marches had gone as originally planned, Germany could have won. It should have won, and thus spared us many of the agonies of the next eighty-five years.

The unbroken string of German triumphs in August 1914 reminds you of the opening days of Barbarossa a generation later: Paris, whose northern outskirts were explored by cavalry patrols, could have been the chimeric Moscow. The wide enveloping movement of the Schlieffen Plan—named after its originator, Count Alfred von Schlieffen—with its weight concentrated in its right wing, swung through Belgium and hammered down to the plains of northern France: On a map, its legs, each belonging to an army, extend like those of a giant crab—a kaiser crab, as it were. The French, preoccupied with their own offensive Plan 17, a battering ram aimed at the German border—and beyond it, the Rhine and its industrial centers—were caught off guard. By the time they began to shift their forces westward, it was almost too late.

The twelve supposedly impregnable forts circling the Belgium border city of Liège were the first to fall, pounded to submission by the monster howitzers of Krupp and Skoda. Brussels fell without a struggle. Meanwhile, the French, paying little heed to the unfolding disaster, attacked from the Ardennes to Lorraine: The Battle of the Frontiers, which lasted for eleven days in the middle of August, cost them an estimated 300,000 men. When a French army finally did advance into Belgium, it was nearly overwhelmed in the Battle of Charleroi (August 22–23). Another of the Belgian fortress cities, Namur, surrendered on the twenty-third, the same day that the tiny British army, then just five divisions strong, made its vain, valiant, delaying action along the canal and the slag heaps of Mons. They managed to check the German advance in their sector by a single day. On August 24, that advance reached, and crossed, the borders of France itself, only hours behind the Schlieffen Plan's tightly mandated schedule.

It is at this point that we arrive at a historical crossroads. Suddenly, as Winston Churchill wrote in his account of the Marne, "The terrible ifs accumulate." The next nine days—August 24 to September 1—would be crucial, and they probably decided the outcome of the war. Had the German victories up to now been too easy, the scythelike sweep of their seven armies in the West too seemingly invincible?

Remember that the original plan called for the right wing to deliver the killing punch: The tip of the scythe always cuts the most hay. Legend has it that in 1913, as Schlieffen lay dying, his last words were, "Make the right wing strong!" The place of honor went to the German First Army, commanded by General von Kluck, who was the best general Germany then had in the West. While the other armies pressed southward, his assigned task was to sweep in a semicircle around Paris, to net the French in a great trap. According to the German scheme, carefully worked out and elaborated for years, a decision would be achieved by the thirty-ninth day of battle.

But Schlieffen's successor as chief of staff, Helmuth von Moltke, the nephew and namesake of the great Moltke, military mastermind of the three wars that had made Germany a nation two generations earlier, had already begun to make alterations in the plan. "Gloomy Julius," as he was called behind his wide back, never ceased worrying about the Russian threat. Long before the war started, he moved four and a half corps, 180,000 men, to the East; all came for the right-wing armies. He wondered if he had done enough. He also worried, as his predecessor had not, about a French advance into Germany. Schlieffen's notion was to let the French gobble up as much territory as they could: They would simply be caught in a sack, making their destruction that much easier. But pride dictated to Moltke that as little German soil as possible be surrendered, even for the best strategic reasons. So he strengthened his left wing, again at the expense of the right. Finally, Schlieffen's plan called for clipping through of the poodle tail of Holland around Maastricht. That would have alleviated the awkward squeezing of the two right-wing armies in Belgium at the beginning of the campaign and would have made possible a wider swing. The army of the far right—Kluck's—would have reached the channel and enveloped Lille before heading south to Paris. Strangely, Moltke the Younger had ethical qualms about violating Dutch neutrality.

Had he adhered to Schlieffen's bold amoral scheme, there would have been no "race to the sea" that followed the Marne—and, needless to say, no Ypres. The channel ports of Dunkirk, Calais, and Boulogne would have belonged to the conquerors. Though the German military did worry about the possibility of a blockade by the British navy, it discounted the ability of the British army to influence outcomes.

Those decisions weakened the German effort, but not fatally. Moltke was uncomfortable taking the kind of risks Schlieffen endorsed. Only risks, as it proved, could have won him a war. The one he did take, on August 22, was the wrong one at the wrong time. But then it did not even seem a risk when he took it—if anything, a stroke of unaccustomed brilliance and one that would forever put his stamp on the brief and glorious campaign to finish off France once and for all.

On August 14, in the opening salvo of Plan 17, the French had crossed into Lorraine, one of the provinces lost to Germany in 1871. Bands struck up the *Marseillaise* as the troops in the lead tore down the striped posts that marked the boundary. The French advanced; the Germans retreated, with only a mild show of resistance. The sack yawned invitingly. So far everything followed the Schlieffen script, a bit like a game of *Kriegspiel*.

On the nineteenth and twentieth, around the towns of Sarrebourg and Morhange, the invaders abruptly came up against prepared defenses—the trenches, barbed wire, and concealed machine-gun nests that would soon become the basic stuff of the Western Front. The Germans literally mowed down the French infantry in swathes, and then followed up with attack after attack on the reeling enemy. The French broke, streaming back to fortified positions on the ridges around Nancy—the Grand Couronné—from which they had started a week earlier. (There was momentary talk of abandoning Nancy: The French supreme commander, General Joseph Joffre, wouldn't hear of it.) Meanwhile, the Germans, initially slow in pursuit, now saw a matchless opportunity of their own.

Much of what follows took place not on the battlefield but on the telephone, and this may be the first time in history that the device assumes the role of a major counterfactual *deus ex machina*. As reports of the French debacle in Lorraine deluged the temporary OHL headquarters in the Rhine city of Coblenz, what military sugarplums danced in Moltke's head? Did it seem to him that the war in the West was as good as over? Should he exploit success to strike while French forces were on the verge of disintegration? Could he afford to lose the opportunity? A direct attack on the heights around Nancy and the fortress systems of Épinal and Toul would violate the Schlieffen scheme but the result might be another Cannae. Great pincers would squeeze the entire French line from both left and right, duplicating the model of Hannibal's legendary double envelopment of the Romans in 216 B.C. That was an August battle, too.

OHL was already discussing the idea on August 22 when a call came in from General Krafft von Dellmensingen, the chief of staff of the German Sixth Army, victors at Morhange. He was pressing for permission to finish off the French, and the sooner the better.

"Moltke hasn't decided yet," the OHL's chief of operations, a Colonel Tappen, told Krafft. "If you hold the line for five minutes I may be able to give you the orders you want."

It didn't take that long. A couple of minutes later, Tappen was back on the line with Moltke's decision: "Pursue direction Épinal."

Gone was Schlieffen's sack. Gone were the two to three corps—as many as 100,000 men—who might have reinforced the right wing when they were most needed. The rolling stock held in readiness in the Lorraine sector could have moved them west in a matter of days. Though we will never know the final casualty figures, which increasingly the German high command began to conceal, the battles around the Grand Couronné were apparently a disaster as great as Morhange had been for the French. Entrenched on steep commanding ridges, French troops hurled fire on the tight German waves as they attempted to cross the plains below. This time it was Moltke who had been drawn into a sack. And it was Joffre who, long before the battles died down on September 10, felt confident enough to remove whole divisions from the Grand Couronné and send them westward, to help tip the balance of the Marne.

But even after Moltke had made his spur-of-the-moment command to "pursue direction Épinal," a German victory was not just possible but still probable. Then, four days later, there would come another of those history-altering phone calls.

The Russians, who had mobilized with a speed that surprised OHL, had invaded East Prussia—territory that now belongs to Poland—and as German refugees swarmed back, panic began to spread. Brigadier General Erich Ludendorff, the hero of Liège, was now the chief of staff of the German Eighth Army, joining General Paul von Hindenberg; a famous military partnership was born. Already the two men felt that they had blunted the Russian thrust—and were in fact on the verge of the epic German victory of the Great War, Tannenberg.

On the night of August 26, at his headquarters in East Prussia, Ludendorff received a call from Colbenz: Once more it was Colonel Tappen on the other end. He told a surprised Ludendorff that he was sending three corps and a cavalry division as reinforcements. Ludendorff replied that they weren't needed—and besides, they could not possibly arrive soon enough to affect the battle in progress. Tappen said that Moltke was adamant, and that was that. Two nights later another call came in: The troops were on their way, but there would be only two corps plus the cavalry. To that extent wiser heads had prevailed. That meant that 80,000 more men would not be available to bolster the right wing. (As Ludendorff had predicted, the two corps arrived days after the Russians had been destroyed. Just before he died in 1916, Moltke, truly a broken man, would concede that the dispatch eastward of those two corps was his biggest mistake on the Marne.) There were now at least four corps unavailable to reinforce the most sensitive part of the operation. Add two more to that number: One corps detached from Kluck's army to guard the Belgians holed up in Antwerp and a second assigned to reduce the French fortress of Mauberge, on the Belgian border. That was a total of six corps, or upward of 250,000 men, the equivalent of an entire army.

Three telephone calls had changed everything. The first two may have thrown victory away; the third, an afterthought, at best assured stalemate. The decision in front of Nancy, which involved more men and saw a fundamental change, not just a weakening, in the Schlieffen Plan did the greatest damage to German hopes. (The Grand Couronné may be the most important overlooked battle in history.) If Moltke had not gone for a Cannae, that peculiarly German military obsession, and had reinforced the right wing instead, Kluck's First Army could have continued its hook around Paris, skirting the forts to the west and south of the city, and then turning north again in a grand knockout blow. Other than the fortress garrisons and the jury-rigged army then being assembled in Paris, there was no substantial force to dispute Kluck's progress through the countryside. Already the French government was preparing to flee to Bordeaux, and it was clear that France could not take many more reverses. The rope, stretched to the limit and beyond, threatened to snap. Would the scenario of 1870 to 1871, with its collapse and revolution, repeat itself?

Speed was essential for the Germans. The enemy must not be given a chance to recover. A victorious army can overlook fatigue—and both officers and men of Kluck's army were very tired indeed. The lean meanness of the German command was beginning to create unnecessary stress. With too few in charge forced for too long to work twenty-hour days, details were falling between the cracks. "In war as in business," the military historian Dennis E. Showalter points out, "there is a certain advantage to redundancy." Moreover, in the absence of rail lines—destroyed by the retreating French and Belgians—and reliable motor transport, supplying men with food and ammunition was a problem, and only became more so as distances increased. Communications, too, were strained. Once in French territory, army commands could not depend on the telephone. Moltke, far away in Coblenz and then, after August 29, in Luxembourg

276

City, mainly used the wireless to communicate with the Western armies—though messages were delayed by congestion at the other end (and by the time needed to decode them) or interfered with by a French station on the Eiffel Tower. Schlieffen's thirty-nine days after mobilization would come none too soon.

Let us imagine, then, that Moltke had not only managed to restrain himself after Morhange but, at the last moment had decided not to send the two corps eastward. What might have happened next? Kluck's reinforced progress continues. The forts of Verdun are surrounded—that nearly did happen at the beginning of September—and neutralized. Rheims falls—it actually was occupied briefly. And now the German center armies turn to meet Kluck's right uppercut. Moltke gets his Cannae after all. The chances are that the truly decisive battle of the war might have been fought in the Seine Valley, southeast of Paris, perhaps in the gently wooded region around Fontainebleau, so favored by generations of French artists. The scenic oils this time would have been painted by Germans.

That is the best-case scenario for the kaiser's armies in the West. Great Britain's brief contribution to the fighting would prove largely irrelevant. The war would remain a continental affair, though it would not make relations between Britain and Germany easier—especially if the Germans insisted on turning the channel ports into fortified enclaves. Meanwhile a bit more of France, including Nancy, and some of Belgium would be incorporated into the Reich. Historians like Niall Ferguson have suggested that Germany would have initiated a Central European Economics Union (which it would dominate—a bit as it has done with the EEC at the turn of the new century). France would pay huge reparations, enough to keep it underarmed and angry for another generation. Anti-Semitism, ever the bane of defeated European nations, would become a problem for it and not for Germany. There is a brighter side, though, beyond the survival of the million Frenchmen who otherwise would die in the next four years (not to mention many of the best and brightest of the other combattants). Victory in World War I hid France's

277

backwardness. Perhaps the nation would not have been doomed to "the long nineteenth century" that only ended after another world war and a four-year-long German occupation. Perhaps the economic renaissance of that second postwar era would have been forced on it earlier.

## If the Lost Map Hadn't Been Lost and If Sir John Had Taken French Leave

Could Germany still have won the battle for France at this point? Perhaps—though its options were narrowing, and increasingly the outcome depended on the actions (and reactions) of the other side. Would the French break, as they did a generation later? There were instances those days of retreat turning into panic, in which not even gun-wielding officers could stop the rush to the rear. Bands of deserters roamed the country, pillaging. A million people, a third of the population of Paris, had fled the capital, along with the government. General Joseph Gallieni, the military governor of Paris, was prepared to reduce the city to a shell if the Germans fought their way into it. He would order the dynamiting of all bridges across the Seine; not even the Eiffel Tower would be spared. The perception of catastrophe distorted the reality. That was the real danger. One more defeat might prove fatal. At the moment the French thought they were experiencing the worst, the worst was in fact over.

On August 30, Kluck made his famous decision to wheel his columns to the east of Paris. The Schlieffen Plan was all but discarded now. Kluck hoped to take by forced marches the flank of the French fleeing in front of him. He also worried about leaving a gap between his army and the German Second Army to his left, which he surely would have done if he had continued on his original course. He paid little or no heed to a new danger: General Michel-Joseph Maunoury's Sixth Army being cobbled together in Paris. The French, for their part, still assumed that Kluck's army had not changed direction. It was at this point that chance, that great leveler of historical forces, intervened.

We have now arrived at September 1, 1914, which has to be another of the counterfactual crossroads of the Marne. Late in the day, a German dispatch car ran into a French patrol in the forested country near Coucy-le-Château, an area dominated by the huge medieval castle of the Lords of Coucy. (In an act of cultural desecration, the Germans would blow it up during their retreat in 1917.) The patrol opened fire, killing everyone in the car. Among the dead was a cavalry officer who carried a saddlebag filled with food, clothing, and papers, all splashed with his blood. When French intelligence officers emptied the bag, they discovered a map. Under more bloodstains they could see numbers and pencil lines—the numbers belonging to corps in Kluck's army and the lines indicating the change of direction, to the southeast.

It was a loss that was as potentially devastating as the loss of Robert E. Lee's Special Orders No. 191 before Antietam. The French could plainly see not only where Kluck was headed but the flank that he offered them. Air reconnaissance and radio intercepts confirmed the map's revelation. When the Sixth Army did smash into that flank on September 5, it ended Kluck's hope of victory. It was all he could do to survive. The able Kluck did, by prodigies of maneuver, successfully defend the flank—but in doing so he created a worse problem for himself. We'll get to that in a moment. If the map had not been lost, Kluck might have gained a couple of precious extra days. He might have been able to reverse his advance, which had gotten dangerously far ahead of the adjacent Second Army, and his survival would not have been so precarious. The lost map of Coucy-le-Château didn't cost the Germans the war in the West. Stalemate still would have resulted, but it would have been a stalemate far more favorable to them. A Paris that was twenty-odd miles distant would be much easier to reduce and capture than one that was eighty or a hundred, as it would be when the Westen Front began to firm up as a solid line days later. That nearness would have altered German operational choices in the months to come and might have meant that they would not have remained on the defensive for so much of the war in the West. Who knows? It might have been 1870 all over again, with Paris encircled, though history tends not to repeat itself. In a world where counterfactual scenarios are forever possible, humans are also forever condemned to make new mistakes, and the future to take unpredictable turns.

Accident is one thing; intent is another. September 1 saw the resolution of another might-have-been, and one potentially more damaging to the Allied cause than the Lost Map had been to the Germans. The commander of the British Expeditionary Force, Sir John French, had apparently given in to the general panic. From the beginning, the relationship of the little field marshal with his allies had been uneasy, and Sir John—who spoke only English—was deeply suspicious of their intentions. Would his troops be thrown, willy-nilly, into a sanguinary update of Plan 17? He was a man fatally afraid of being taken advantage of and now thought only of getting his army out of harm's way, with the least damage possible to his own reputation. Joffre, eager to stabilize his line at last, had met with his British opposite on August 29 and pleaded with him to hold fast. Sir John refused. He made it clear that his army, which had lost 15,000 men in a week of fighting retreat, now needed ten days out of the line in which to rest, reequip, and wait for reinforcements. Managing to contain his rage, Joffre thanked Sir John. This not only meant that his retirement would have to continue, but that he faced the prospect of a gap opening in his line. Even entreaties by the president of France, Raymond Poincaré, to the British ambassador, and passed on to Sir John, failed to budge him. French had, in fact, told his officers to prepare for a "definite and prolonged retreat due south, passing Paris to the east and west." Moreover, he was floating an even more ominous trial balloon: withdrawal to the British base—which was then the port of Saint-Nazaire, at the mouth of the Loire. There was talk of reembarking the army for England, with the idea of landing on the continent and resuming the war later in the fall—if, that is, there still was a war.

Back in London, the British secretary of state for war, Lord Kitchener, read French's telegrams with mounting dismay. On August 31, he telegraphed back to ask whether the contemplated withdrawal wouldn't leave a gap in the Allied line, causing the French to become fatally discouraged. There was a counterfactual ring to his words. Then he persuaded the prime minister to call an urgent Cabinet meeting. Sir John could not be allowed on his own to determine a matter of national policy, the military alliance with France. At this moment, the possibility of losing the war may never have seemed closer. Late that night, Sir John's reply to Kitchener's telegram came in: "I do not see why I should be called upon . . . to run the risk of absolute disaster . . ."

Kitchener, who was standing by as French's message was decoded, made up his mind. Asquith called another hasty Cabinet gathering and Churchill ordered the firing up of a fast cruiser at Dover. Kitchener left London in the middle of the night and was in Paris by midday on September 1. He arrived at the British embassy wearing his blue field marshal's uniform—which the supersensitive French immediately took as an insult. Was Kitchener, who did not outrank him, trying to pull rank? French immediately complained about being called away from his headquarters "at so critical a time." There were others present at the meeting, but the tone of the discussion soon grew heated, and the two field marshals went into another room and presumably closed the door. Somehow, an agreement was struck: French's troops would return to the fighting line, where they would remain "conforming to the movements of the French army." French left in a huff, but Kitchener had accomplished his mission.

What if Sir John French had taken his troops out of the line and marched them to Saint-Nazaire, some 250 miles away? The notion that they would have been refitted, reinforced, and readied back in England for new service on the continent is preposterous. The chances are that British troops never would have returned—and it's hard to see how the political leaders, whoever they now were, would have dealt with a fading war spirit that, like a siren, had been recently cranked up to such a high pitch. Certainly the Asquith government could not have survived (though the empire would have profited in the long run). What would the brief ignominious role of the British have done to relations with France over the next decade or more? France may have become the loser because of it. A British withdrawal that came at the worst psychological moment—which September 1 was—might have made all the difference. How could France ever forgive Great Britain's desertion? Put it another way: Sir John's failure of nerve could have handed Germany its last chance to win the war in the West. Better that England had never become involved in the first place.

There was a sequel. Kluck, we remember, had brilliantly parried the thrust of Maunoury's Sixth Army in what came to be known as the Battle of the Ourcq. The taxis of the Marne notwithstanding—they did transport needed men from Paris—Kluck actually had the upper hand in that part of the vast Marne encounter that sprawled for five days along a 200-mile front. But to do so, he was forced to borrow the two corps that had filled the space between his First Army and Karl von Bülow's Second. He thought he could get away with it, and he nearly did. But on the last day of the Marne, the British Army, about the size of those two German corps now detraining in East Prussia, marched into the thirty-mile gap. Though it penetrated only a few miles, it had, as Winston Churchill wrote, "probed its way into the German liver." Flanks were threatened; the Germans panicked. Soon retreat spread along the entire front. The first trenches were dug. The original invasion plan called for a decision between September 6 and September 9—the thirty-sixth to the thirty-ninth day after mobilization. That happened, but not the way the Germans expected. Churchill invoked the words of the Roman emperor Caesar Augustus when he learned of the massacre of his legions in the Teutoburg Forest 1900 years earlier: "Well might the kaiser have exclaimed, 'Moltke, Moltke, give me back my legions!'"

### The Brigadier and the Private

This story involves two people who never met, a British officer and a common soldier in the German army. But their lives may have touched on 1914's terminal day of crisis, October 31. In one case, history might have changed; in the other, it did.

In the weeks that followed the Marne, the opposing armies marched and fought their way northward on parallel courses, each trying without success to outflank the other. "The race to the sea" left only stalemate in its wake, as the line closed behind it. By late October, the one remaining opening, which the Allies were fast plugging, presented itself around the Belgian town of Ypres, a little more than ten miles from Dunkirk and the North Sea. Around a narrow and ever-constricting salient, there took place the year's final desperate battle.

For the Germans, a breakout at Ypres offered the prospect of the last great prizes of 1914: The channel ports of Dunkirk, Calais, and Boulogne. Their capture would not only neutralize the channel but would lengthen and otherwise inconvenience the passage of troops and materiel from England to France—if much of a British army existed after a defeat at Ypres. (Sir John French was once again seriously contemplating evacuation; but now it was Joffre who emphatically vetoed the idea.) For the second time in two months, Great Britain's contribution was at risk—though at this point the French were better able to carry on without their ally. But beyond those considerations, the bagging of the channel ports would give a tremendous boost to morale back home: The German people would have something to show for their futile and costly exertions in the West.

After twelve days in which wave after wave of German attacks broke on the thinning lines of French and British defenders, a decision seemed at hand. It happened at a place called Gheluvelt, a cluster of brick buildings on a ridge five miles to the east of Ypres. Shortly before noon on October 31, the British line here disintegrated. The defenders were outnumbered by as much as ten to one, and ill-trained but fanatically eager German reserves swept over them. A breach a mile wide opened. All it would take was for the ample reinforcements close at hand to burst through and spread out fanwise, destroying whatever remained of British cohesion. But the German troops stopped to wait for orders. None came. The early afternoon found 1,200 men, many belonging to the 16th

Bavarian Reserve Regiment, milling around the grounds of a nearby château and doing a bit of looting. But sooner or later that afternoon, the staffs would get it together, orders would go out, and those troops—and thousands more—would begin their inexorable progress forward.

Meanwhile, in a woods about a mile away, a British brigadier made a decision that quite possibly altered the course of the war. He was named Charles Fitzclarence, and he was obviously destined for greater things if a bullet hadn't permanently interrupted his career a few days later. Fitzclarence, who learned about the disaster at Gheluvelt from stragglers, rounded up the only reserves he could find, some 370 men from the 2nd Worcester Battalion, and sent them forward over a mile of undulating pasture. German artillery caught them in the open, killing or wounding more than a quarter of their number; but still they went forward. The Worcesters crashed onto the lawn of the Gheluvelt château, scattering the Bavarians. They rooted them out of hedges and fired at their receding backs. That ended the German advance. The gap to Dunkirk was plugged. Thanks to the brigadier, Great Britain would hold that day—and would stay in the war that bankrupted it.

There is a final circumstance, which no historian seems to have pointed out. Of the hundreds of Bavarians flushed out of the chateau grounds, one may have been a private from Austria, lately removed to Munich—Adolf Hitler: Two days earlier he had gone into action with the 16th Bavarian Reserve Regiment, which had taken terrible losses. Those men at the château pretty much represented what was left of its combat strength. Given Hitler's almost magnetic attraction to a fight, it's hard to think that he wasn't there. But German memoirs and regimental histories are silent on the episode. They neither seem to recognize, nor to admit, how close the Germans were to a breakthrough that day, nor do they mention the debacle at the chateau. That would hardly have suited history as propounded by the Nazis, and especially history that involved their own führer. But what if Hitler had been cut down in flight, or captured? History—the real version—would have been deprived of one of its true monsters. In this case, we hardly need to elaborate on the calamities that a single bullet might have denied.

That possibility has to be the most intriguing might-have-been of 1914.

*Postscript: Falkenhayn's Despair*

Immediately after the Battle of the Marne shut down, Moltke was removed—though for public relations reasons his successor, Erich von Falkenhayn, who was also the Prussian war minister, compelled him to remain at headquarters as titular chief of staff for another two humiliating months. But the new man hardly had better luck. On November 18, after the disaster of Ypres, Falkenhayn, deeply depressed, met in Berlin with the German chancellor, Theobald von Bethmann-Hollweg. He told Bethmann flatly that the war could no longer be won. He saw no way for Germany to reduce its adversaries "to such a point where we can come to a decent peace." If a negotiated settlement of some sort wasn't concluded soon, the country faced a dreary prospect: "The danger of slowly exhausting ourselves." Falkenhayn suggested overtures to Russia first, with no annexations asked. France, he was sure, would follow.

Bethmann-Hollweg turned him down. He was still convinced, he said, that Germany could, and would, win the war. Moreover, a deal with Russia and France would mean a deal with Great Britain—which, as the weeks passed, the Germans had come to regard as their real enemy, the true threat to their aspirations. Even as hostility toward England had undone Napoleon at Tilsit in 1805, so it would blind Germany in 1914. Can we extrapolate, too, a hint that Bethmann-Hollweg was afraid to face down what would surely be the blustering rage of the kaiser? Whatever his reasons, his refusal represented an irrevocable death sentence for a generation.

Soon the British Empire's legions would be arriving on the continent from the four corners of the globe. One naval battle had been fought just days before off the coast of Chile and in a few days to come, another would be fought off the Falkland Islands. In January, Turkey would briefly menace the linchpin of the British Empire, the Suez Canal—and would itself be invaded that next spring at Gallipoli. A German submarine would torpedo the liner *Luisitania*—now, there was a true accident of history—killing 128 Americans and guaranteeing the eventual entry into the war of the Great Neutral. Even as Falkenhayn made his vain pitch, the war was beginning to drag in the entire world. That day may have witnessed the last slim chance to halt its spread.

"A singular fact about modern war is that it takes charge," Bruce Catton notes. "Once begun it has to be carried to its conclusion, and carrying it there sets in motion events that may be beyond men's control. Doing what has to be done to win, men perform acts that alter the very soil in which society's roots are nourished."

Think what even a truncated war would have meant to the twentieth century. Let us say that German overtures to Russia had succeeded. Russian losses at the end of 1914, though substantial, were hardly crippling. Peace would have allowed its industrial economy, which was already showing signs of significant growth, to flourish; at the same time, some measure of democracy was taking hold. Lenin would have remained sulking in his impoverished Swiss exile: There would have been no German-arranged sealed train to carry him and his political pestilence to the Finland Station. It follows that without Lenin there would have been no Stalin, no purges, no gulags, no Cold War.

We have already considered Great Britain and France—but what of the United States? If an armistice had come at the end of 1914, our country would have remained for years what it was then: a crude, boisterous, and not always charming provincial cousin. No American boys would have crossed our Rubicon, the Atlantic. The question asked by the popular song was on the mark: "How're ya gonna keep 'em down on the farm, after they've seen Paree?" The "American Century" would have to wait, depending not on wars but on markets. The year 1918 would not have found the world's most powerful nation, Great Britain, deep in debt to us.

The long nineteenth century would surely have continued for decades, not only in France but everywhere. Europe would have retained its position of benignly condescending dominance. Take, for example, the world of letters. How much talent, barely revealed or never discovered, dissolved in the earth of all those obscenely neat Great War cemeteries? Alain-Fournier's novel *The Wanderer* or the poems of Wilfred Owen— both men gunshot victims—give us some indication of what we lost. Literary leadership was only ceded to America by the default of death. There would have been a Hemingway but no *Farewell to Arms*. "Troops went by the house and down the road and the dust they raised powdered the leaves of the trees . . ." Perhaps he would have found another way to deliver the most luminous opening paragraph of our century.

Without the events of 1914, we would have skipped a more sinister legacy, and one that has permanently scarred our lives: the brutalization that trench warfare, with its mass killings, visited on an entire generation. What men like Adolf Hitler learned in that first Holocaust, they would, as John Keegan has written, "repeat twenty years later in every corner of Europe. From their awful cult of death the continent is still recovering."

There are times when you can measure the lasting effects of a trauma only by imagining their absence.

# BISMARCK'S EMPIRE: STILLBORN

"There is a dynasty on its way out," Bismarck remarked as he observed the retreat of Emperor Napoleon III after the defeat of the French army at Sedan on September 1, 1870. Less than two months later, French marshal François Achille Bazaine surrendered to the Prussians at Metz, with 6,000 officers and 173,000 men. Three months later, on January 18, 1871, the German empire was proclaimed in the Hall of Mirrors at Versailles.

The French defeat was not inevitable. The French armies were ample, and their equipment, in certain respects, was superior to that of the Prussians. The new French rifle, the chassepot, increased the number of rounds an infantryman could carry and substantially improved his range. The French also possessed the mitrailleuse, an early version of the machine gun, which carried a bundle of twenty-five barrels, each detonated by turning a handle. The French capitulation resulted very simply from poor leadership.

Holed up at Sedan and later at Metz, the famed *furia francese* was never unleashed. Even when the two German armies swept on and invested Paris under the direction of Graf Helmuth von Moltke, the French commander in the capital, with a larger force, showed himself paralyzed and allowed himself to be surrounded.

With Napoleon III nominally in command before Sedan, the French military was directionless. Had the French armies taken the offensive early, had they broken out of their fortresses, the Prussians might well have been stopped in their tracks, and the German empire, as we know it, would not have existed.

Without Bismarck's German empire, there would have been no Wilhelmine

Germany, no pursuit of power for its own sake, no French revanchism over Alsace-Lorraine, and no First World War. In which case, there would have been no Treaty of Versailles in 1919, no Second World War. Had there been no First World War, there would have been no Bolshevik Revolution, no Soviet Union, and therefore no Cold War. The course of history for the last 150 years, the horrors of the century of total war, our century, would have been irrevocably changed. Instead, an inept, posturing nephew of the greatest military commander in modern times became the unwitting destroyer of the primacy of Europe.

✦ *James Chace is the editor of the* World Journal *and professor of international relations at Bard College. He is the author of the biography,* ACHESON.

# THANKS, BUT NO CIGAR

One chilly November afternoon in 1889, a fur-coated crowd assembled in Berlin's Charlottenburg Race Course to enjoy a performance of Buffalo Bill's Wild West Show, which was touring Europe to great popular acclaim. Among the audience was the Reich's impetuous young ruler, Kaiser Wilhelm II, who had been on the throne for a year. Wilhelm was particularly keen to see the show's star attraction, Annie Oakley, famed throughout the world for her skills with a Colt .45.

On that day, as usual, Annie announced to the crowd that she would attempt to shoot the ashes from the cigar of some lady or gentleman in the audience. "Who shall volunteer to hold the cigar?" she asked. In fact, she expected no one from the crowd to volunteer; she had simply asked for laughs. Her long-suffering husband, Frank Butler, always stepped forward and offered himself as her human Havana-holder.

This time, however, Annie had no sooner made her announcement then Kaiser Wilhelm himself leaped out of the royal box and strutted into the arena. Annie was stunned and horrified but could not retract her dare without losing face. She paced off her usual distance while Wilhelm extracted a cigar from a gold case and lit it with a flourish. Several German policemen, suddenly realizing that this was not one of the kaiser's little jokes, tried to preempt the stunt, but were waved off by His All-Highest Majesty. Sweating profusely under her buckskin, and regretful that she had consumed more than her usual amount of whiskey the night before, Annie raised her Colt, took aim, and blew away Wilhelm's ashes.

Had the sharpshooter from Cincinnati creased the kaiser's head rather than his cigar, one of Europe's most ambitious and volatile rulers would have been removed from the scene. Germany might not have pursued its policy of aggressive Weltpolitik that culminated in war twenty-five years later.

Annie herself seemed to realize her mistake later on. After World War I began, she wrote to the kaiser asking for a second shot. He did not respond.

✦   *David Clay Large has just completed a history of the city of Berlin.*

### ✦ DENNIS E. SHOWALTER ✦

# THE ARMISTICE OF DESPERATION

World War I is increasingly recognized as the defining event of the twentieth century, with its total wars, its genocides, its weapons of mass destruction. What might have resulted if the war had ended in a matter of weeks, as virtually all the experts predicted?

A quick decision would have had to come in the West, in 1914 the only possible theater for mass industrial war. The most plausible scenario begins with more aggressive leadership at all levels of the French and German armies. By the end of 1914, France had suffered almost a million casualties; German losses in the same period were around three-quarters of a million. These were the highest ratios of the whole war. What if generals and regimental officers had driven their men forward even more ruthlessly during the battles of the Frontier and on the Marne? What if the Germans had been even more willing to exchange lives for ground in the Ypres Salient?

This reaction fully accorded with existing doctrines of the offensive. It might have achieved some tactical victories—a more precipitate German retreat after the Marne, for example, or the capture of Ypres in a final desperate lunge. These victories, however, were unlikely to be exploited by their survivors. Attacks of this intensity instead would have depleted, perhaps exhausted, already limited ammunition reserves to a point that force more and more reliance on numbers that were vulnerable and courage that went unrequited. A 20 or 25 percent increase in casualty rates seems a reasonable immediate consequence in the battlefield environment of 1914. Administrative systems, particularly medical services, might have buckled under the strain, destabilizing the "cultures of competence" that hold armies together by regularly providing food, care, and mail. Morale in the line, at the rear, and on the home front was likely to waver, if not collapse, as losses increased exponentially with each week—to no end. Gridlock on the fighting line, revolution at home—such a sequence of events was in fact feared by prewar decision-makers. Facing its reality, the combatants might well have negotiated an armistice of desperation.

The titular "victor" is unimportant. Europe's great powers undertook World War I for negative, not positive, reasons. Even Germany's war aims in 1914 were a cobbled-together post facto shopping list. The scales of destruction and disorder accompanying a quick end to an unwanted apocalypse were likely to generate at all levels a renewed sense of Europe as a community—and a consequent sense of what it took to sustain that community. International order would be stabilized, with regional powers no longer given the kind of latitude the Balkan states enjoyed between 1911 and 1914. Germany and Russia in particular were likely to undertake domestic housecleanings. In the Second Reich, the diminished prestige of kaiser and army favored the introduction of a genuine parliamentary government. Russia, never suffering the exsanguination of 1915 to 1916, was in a position to continue its economic and political development.

As for Vladimir Lenin, in this alternate world he died an exile in Switzerland. Adolf Hitler became a familiar figure in Munich's bohemian circles. Picasso never created *Guernica*, and Albert Einstein spent a long and fruitful life as a physicist and philanthropist. It was a Europe safe for men with briefcases and potbellies, whose younger generations occasionally bemoaned its ordinariness. But while memories of the Six Months' War of 1914 to 1915 endured, older heads thanked God and the fates that they no longer lived in interesting times.

✦   *Dennis E. Showalter is professor of history at Colorado College and the president of The Society for Military History.*

JOHN KEEGAN

# HOW HITLER COULD HAVE
# WON THE WAR

*The Drive for the Middle East, 1941*

Adolf Hitler may be the perfect example of how an individual with a genius for the main chance can—through determination close to madness, and more than a little luck—alter history. You can argue that if Hitler hadn't survived the First World War, someone else in a Germany ravaged by defeat, hyperinflation, and world depression, would inevitably have come forward to start the Second. In this deterministic view, people like Hitler are not causes but symptoms. But who? None of those around him had the same sort of evil charisma. The conditions he fed on may have been largely unavoidable but the Nazi revolution he created and led was not. Nor can a phenomenon so focused on one man and his whims evolve in a predictable pattern. Hitler's mind was a virtual Pandora's box of what ifs. Today we tend to forget how close he came to imposing his Triumph of the Will on much of the world: The scenario that John Keegan describes here could very well have happened. Hitler, like Napoleon, seriously contemplated a campaign through the Near East, following the route of another conqueror, Alexander the Great. In actuality, both Hitler and Napoleon came to fortunate grief in Russia. What if, in 1941, Hitler had put off *his invasion of the Soviet Union for a year and had gone for the prize that might have given him the edge against the beleaguered Allies: Middle Eastern oil?*

✦ *John Keegan, who spins the frightening possibility that follows, is one of our finest military historians, the author of such notable books as THE FACE OF BATTLE, THE PRICE OF ADMIRALTY, and, most recently, THE FIRST WORLD WAR. He is defense correspondent for the DAILY TELEGRAPH in London and in 1998 delivered the BBC's Reith Lectures.*

W hat if, in the summer of 1941, Hitler had chosen to make his major attack not into Soviet Russia but across the Eastern Mediterranean, into Syria and the Lebanon? Would he have avoided the defeat he suffered outside Moscow that winter? Might he have won a strategic position that would have brought him eventual victory?

The inducement was strong. Had he been able to solve the logistical difficulty of transferring an army from Greece to Vichy French Syria, he would then have been well placed to strike at northern Iraq, a major center of oil production, and thence at Iran, with even ampler oil reserves. The establishment of a strong military presence in northern Iran would have positioned his forces close to the Soviet Union's own oil production centers on the Caspian Sea, while a drive into Southern Iran would have given him possession of the Anglo-Iranian Oil Company's wells and vast refinery at Abadan. From eastern Iran, moreover, the route lay open toward Baluchistan, the westernmost province of British India, and thence to the Punjab and Delhi. The occupation of the Levant—Syria and Lebanon— would, in short, have placed him astride a network of strategic highways leading not only to the main centers of Middle Eastern oil supply but also to entry points giving onto the most important imperial possession of his last remaining European enemy, Britain, and also the southern provinces of his chosen ideological opponent, Stalin's Russia.

By the spring of 1941 Russia had become a strategic obsession to Hitler. After his defeat of France in 1940, he had, for a few weeks, persuaded himself that he could assure Germany's dominance of Europe by negotiating a peace with Britain. With Britain neutralized, he could have consolidated his military position and taken his time in choosing future strategic options. The defeat of the Soviet Union was foremost among them. In the aftermath of the French armistice in June, however, he did not expect to have to make an immediate call on his military resources. His appreciation of the situation was that Britain would, in a spirit of realism, accept that Nazi Germany enjoyed an unassailable superiority and consequently submit to its military dominance.

Churchill's refusal to admit realities, as seen from Berlin, and to persist in resistance, caused Hitler in July, even while he was committing the Luftwaffe to what would become known as the Battle of Britain, to reposition the ground forces of the Wehrmacht eastward, toward the new frontier of the Soviet Union as defined after its annexation of half of Poland in September 1939. At the same time, he reversed his recently taken decision to demobilize thirty-five of the infantry divisions that had fought in the Battle of France and to double the number of panzer divisions from ten to twenty. He also arranged for his war production office, during August, to select the site for a new führer headquarters in East Prussia, while in September his personal operational staff, OKW, submitted an outline plan, "Fritz" for "an offensive against the Soviet Union."

All these measures were, however, precautionary. He had certainly not yet firmly decided to attack Russia and was, indeed, still ready to negotiate an extension of the Ribbentrop-Molotov Pact of August 1939 for the further settlement of spheres of interest in Eastern Europe, as long as the terms were satisfactory to him. Molotov would come to Berlin in November to continue discussions. In the meantime, Hitler embarked on a program of diplomatic rather than military measures as a means of consolidating his power over Eastern Europe short of the Soviet border.

His instrument was the Tripartite Pact, signed between Germany, Italy, and Japan on September 27, 1940, binding any two to come to the aid of a third if it was attacked. The pact was not exclusive. Others might join and Hitler, in the autumn of 1940, decided that the uncommitted states of Central and southern Europe should. Hungary and Romania, both strongly anti-Russian and pro-German, and the puppet state of Slovakia signed, before the year was out. Pressure was then put on Bulgaria and Yugoslavia to join also, as they would the following March.

His Russian diplomacy worked less smoothly. Despite the evidence of Nazi Germany's military mastery over most of the continent and the strong suspicion that Stalin's military purges of 1937 to 1938 had gravely damaged the Red Army's fighting power, Stalin insisted upon treating Hitler as an equal throughout the complex second half of 1940. When Molotov, the Soviet foreign minister, arrived in Berlin on November 12, he proposed that the Soviet Union be allowed to annex Finland, as it already had the Baltic States, that it should guarantee Bulgaria's frontiers, despite already having taken a large slice of Bulgarian territory, that its rights of exit from the Black Sea to the Mediterranean, through the Turkish Bosphorus, should be enlarged, and that it should also be given new maritime rights in the Baltic. Hitler was outraged. When, after his departure, Molotov sent the draft of a treaty outlining Soviet requirements, Hitler order Ribbentrop to make no reply. Instead, on December 18, he signed the secret Führer Directive 21, which would become the blueprint for Operation Barbarossa, the invasion of Russia.

Between the inception of Barbarossa on June 22, 1941, and Hitler's rejection of Molotov's November proposals, many disturbing events were to intervene. To Hitler, the most irritating were those initiated by his fellow dictator, Benito Mussolini, in an attempt to establish Italy's claim to be Nazi Germany's equal as an actor on the stage of grand strategy. Mussolini had delayed his entry into the Second World War until the hard tasks in the West—the defeat of France, the expulsion of Britain from the continent—had been achieved. Mussolini had then struck easy victories. In September 1940, he invaded British Egypt from Libya. On October 28 he launched, from recently occupied Albania, an offensive into Greece, Britain's last ally on the European mainland. Both enterprises proved fiascoes. A British counteroffensive in December humiliated Italy's Libyan army, while the Greeks, outnumbered though they were, rapidly moved from defense to attack and, in a winter campaign, captured half of Albania from its Italian occupiers.

Worse was to follow. Having browbeaten the Yugoslav government of Prince Regent Paul to subscribe to the Tripartite Pact on March 25, the

Germans were confronted two days later by a patriotic military coup, which rejected the pact and made common cause with the British and Greeks, who were still united in opposition to the settlement of southern European affairs in Germany's favor. Hitler had, in February, been obliged to send troops to Italian Libya, the nucleus of the soon-to-be-famous Afrika Korps, under Erwin Rommel, to rescue the Italians from a worse defeat. He now decided to interrupt his deployment of forces for the inception of Barbarossa by instructing a subordinate operation, Marita, that would bring Yugoslavia and Greece under his complete control.

Marita was in part provoked by a British initiative. In November 1940, the Greek government, attacked by the Italians a week earlier, had accepted the deployment of R.A.F. squadrons to the Peloponnese. In March 1941, it went further. Even though it risked provoking Hitler, it agreed to welcome four British divisions, detached from the Western Desert Force in Libya, where they had recently taken part in Wavell's spectacular defeat of the Italians. The arrival of the British divisions on March 4 did indeed gall Hitler. It was also the development that encouraged the Yugoslav patriots to repudiate the Tripartite Pact, a bold but disastrous gesture. On April 6, Yugoslavia was invaded simultaneously from five directions, by the Italians from Albania, by the Hungarian army, and by German forces based in Austria, Romania, and Bulgaria. The Yugoslav army collapsed immediately, freeing the Germans and Italians to switch their troops southward into Greece.

The Greeks and their British allies sustained a longer resistance than the hapless Yugoslavs. Their defensive positions were, however, also outflanked from the start, particularly by the strong German army based in Bulgaria under the Tripartite Pact. One line after another was turned until, on April 27, the British survivors of the campaign succeeded in making their escape from southern Greek ports, leaving many prisoners and almost all their heavy equipment behind them.

Marita was another triumph for Hitler. At almost no cost, he had completed his conquest of mainland Europe, leaving only Sweden,

Switzerland, and the Iberian Peninsula outside his control or that of his allies. The Soviet Union alone remained to challenge his power. The plans for its invasion and defeat were written, however, and it only required his word to set the Wehrmacht in motion toward Moscow.

But was the road to Moscow the right direction to take? The destruction of the Soviet Union was the strategic and ideological project closest to Hitler's heart. It may be thought in retrospect, however, that a direct offensive across the Soviet frontier was not the best means of bringing the result about. In the long run, of course, the Wehrmacht would have to fight and defeat the Red Army. Military victory was, nevertheless, only one of the objects of Barbarossa. Another, almost equally as important if he were to sustain his effort and achieve the final defeat of Britain, was to secure the Soviet Union's enormous natural resources—above all its oil output. The Romanian oil wells apart, and they were insufficient to supply his needs, the supplement of oil exported from Russia under the terms of the Ribbentrop-Molotov Pact being essential, he had no source of oil directly under his control. He needed oil urgently.

Yet ample oil lay close at hand, all the closer since he had completed the conquest of Greece. Iraq, Iran, and Saudi Arabia were the world's largest providers of oil and a direct route toward their fields and refineries lay just across the eastern Mediterranean through Syria. If Turkey's neutrality were to be violated, a land route was available as well. The Levant was weakly defended. The Vichy French army in Syria and Lebanon numbered only 38,000, without modern equipment or air cover. The British army in Palestine, Egypt, and Libya numbered only seven divisions and was already locked in combat with the Afrika Korps, which buttressed a larger Italian army. Militarily, if the German-Italian forces in the Middle East were strengthened, the area was ripe for plucking. There was even the makings of a local pro-German client regime. On April 3, Rasid Ali had overthrown the pro-British government in Iraq and asked for German help. German aircraft arrived at Mosul on May 13, having staged through Syria, the Vichy French garrison feeling powerless to impede. Though Rasid Ali was swiftly overthrown by a British force operating from Transjordan—and the Vichy garrison of Syria and Lebanon defeated in a bitter three-week war in June and July—Hitler was sufficiently encouraged by the evidence of his enemies' strategic fragility in the Middle East to issue Fürher Directive 30, on May 23, outlining a project to support the "Arab Freedom Movement," in conjunction with a German-Italian offensive toward the Suez Canal. On June 11, Führer Directive 32 anticipated, among other operations, the assembly of forces in Bulgaria "sufficient to render Turkey politically amenable or overpower her resistance."

Both Directives were posited, however, on the supposition that Barbarossa would have already been launched. What if, as an alternative, the thrust into the Middle East from Bulgaria and Greece had been chosen as the principal operation for 1941? There might have been two variants.

The first would have avoided the violation of Turkish neutrality and used territory already Axis—the Italian Dodecanese islands off the Turkish coast, other Greek islands, or British Cyprus—as stepping-stones to Vichy Syria. Italian Rhodes, for example, might have been chosen as a staging point for an airborne assault on Cyprus, employing the 7th Airborne Division, in practice uselessly thrown away in the descent on Crete on May 20. Behind an airborne bridgehead in Cyprus and employing local shipping protected by German airpower, a sizable amphibious assault force could have been built up for landings in Syria and Lebanon. Once a secure foothold had been established in the French Levant, mobile columns could have raced across the desert to northern Iraq and a strong lodgment area created from which reinforcements might have begun the conquest of southern Iraq, Iran, and Saudi Arabia. The oil wealth yielded would have solved all Hitler's difficulties in maintaining his military machine. By the end of 1941, with a force of perhaps only twenty divisions, no more than he pushed toward the Russian Caucasus via the Barbarossa routes in 1942, he would have secured a position from which to threaten Stalin's oil-producing centers on the Caspian Sea, having bypassed the major geographical obstacles defending it. Barbarossa might have been

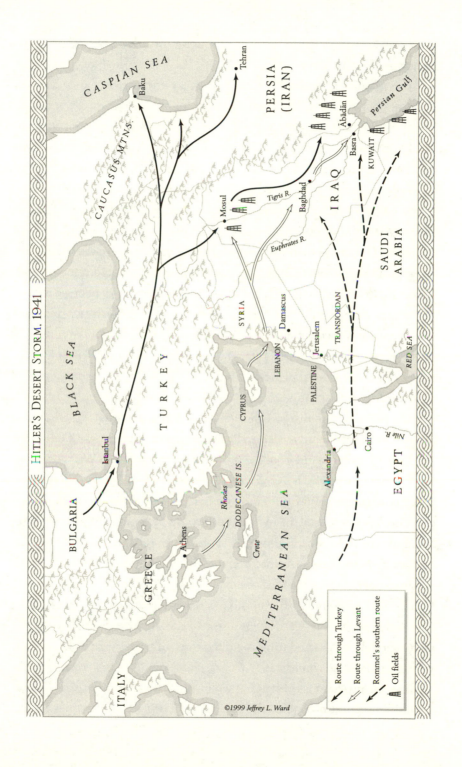

HITLER'S DESERT STORM, 1941

CASPIAN SEA

Baku

Tehran

PERSIA
(IRAN)

Persian Gulf

CAUCASUS MTNS.

Mosul

Tigris R.

Baghdad

I R A Q

Ābādān

Basra

KUWAIT

Euphrates R.

SAUDI
ARABIA

BLACK SEA

T U R K E Y

SYRIA

Damascus

TRANSJORDAN

Jerusalem

Istanbul

PALESTINE

LEBANON

RED SEA

BULGARIA

CYPRUS

Nile R.

Cairo

Rhodes

DODECANESE IS.

Alexandria

EGYPT

GREECE

Athens

Crete

ITALY

M E D I T E R R A N E A N   S E A

©1999 Jeffrey L. Ward

Route through Turkey

Route through Levant

Rommel's southern route

Oil fields

launched, in consequence, in 1942 in much more favorable military circumstances.

This scenario depends for its success on the assembly of sufficient shipping in the eastern Mediterranean to transport the force required. That it could have been adequately protected by airpower against British naval attack is demonstrated by the failure of the Royal Navy to sustain the landings in the Dodecanese in the autumn of 1943. What seems more problematic is the availability of maritime transports. Hitler, in Directive 32, wrote of ". . . chartering French and neutral shipping." The reality was that the British had already acquired most available vessels, forcing the Germans during the assault on Crete, for example, to depend on a fleet of wholly inadequate coastal craft to transport its ground forces. The probability is, therefore, that a strategy that depended on using island "stepping-stones" toward the Levant, attractive as it looks, would have foundered for want of shipping capacity.

A strategy that took as its starting point the violation of Turkish neutrality might, on the other hand, have worked very well. Turkey's record of neutrality during the Second World War is stoutly honorable. Wooed by the Germans, the British, and the Russians, it consistently refused to make concessions to any, despite its patent military weakness. The Turks are doughty fighters. They lacked during the Second World War, however, any sort of modern military equipment. Had Hitler decided, therefore, after the conquest of the Balkans, but before Barbarossa, to use Bulgaria and Greek Thrace as a springboard to invade European Turkey, capture Istanbul, cross the Bosphorus, and capture Anatolia, the Turkish mainland, it is difficult to see what could have stopped him. Stalin's forces, certainly, deployed as they were to defend the Soviet Union's new Eastern Europe frontier, were in no position to oppose such an initiative. The Wehrmacht, as it was to demonstrate in the Russian Steppe, was certainly capable of surmounting the difficulties of traversing the Anatolian terrain. A rapid advance to the Caucasus barrier, Russia's frontier with Turkey, would have secured the Wehrmacht's flank with the Soviet Union. From Anatolia, it could easily have irrupted into Iraq and Iran, thrust its tentacles southward into Arabia, and positioned its vanguards to envelop the Caspian Sea and menace Russian Central Asia.

Had Hitler used the Balkan victories of the spring of 1941 to align his forces for an Anatolian and Levantine victory, leading to wide conquests in Arabia and the securing of decisive positions on Russia's southern flank, it is difficult to see how a variant of Barbarossa, conceived as a pincer movement rather than a blunt frontal assault, would not have succeeded. As a by-blow, Britain's foothold in the Middle East would have been fatally undermined and its dominance of the Indian Empire dangerously threatened.

Fortunately, Hitler worked within a strategic vision limited by legalistic and ideological blindspots. Legally, he could find no quarrel with Turkey's stringently neutralist diplomacy. Ideologically, his fear and hatred of Bolshevism allowed him no freedom to choose an alternative to his desire to smash the Soviet Union by direct, frontal assault. He exulted in the great victories over Stalin in the summer and autumn of 1941 and never expressed regret, even when Russian shells were falling on his Berlin bunker in 1945, that he had set Operation Barbarossa in motion. How grateful we should be that, in the spring of 1941, he should not have chosen a more subtle and indirect strategy.

# WHAT A TAXI DRIVER WROUGHT

In 1931, a taxicab driver in New York City, looking for late-night fares, was making his rounds. It was a cold, shadowy night, and as he turned north on Fifth Avenue (which then ran two ways) he discerned a figure waiting for him to pass on the almost-deserted avenue. In a hurry to find one final fare, he ignored his instinct to slow and accelerated. He hit the rather dumpy man who, perhaps looking in the wrong direction, stepped in his way.

In its obituary the next day, the *New York Times* spoke of Churchill's contributions to British politics in the Great War: his getting the fleet ready and his work at the ministry of munitions in 1918, but the obituary writer could not resist the temptation to lay the failure of the Dardanelles expedition in 1915 primarily at Churchill's door. And not surprisingly the *Times* also underlined Churchill's life as one of great political and intellectual promise—promise that he never quite fulfilled.

American historians in a beleaguered democracy at the end of the twentieth century never put the blame for the great Nazi victory in the war of 1939 to 1947 on this by now obscure event. How could one assign the troubles of a nation to a taxi accident? After all, everyone agreed that history is entirely the result of great social movements and the actions of the millions who make up humanity—certainly not the product of the actions of a few great men. But some historians still did argue that Britain's surrender in the summer of 1940 by its prime minister, Lord Halifax, was not a reasoned and sensible recognition of Britain's hopeless strategic position, and that the turning over of the Royal Navy to the Kriegsmarine had not made sense. But they could not imagine how Britain might have acquired the strategy of leadership to defeat the Nazi conquerors of Europe. And so America's armed forces again prepared to meet the Nazi forces in South America, and the wars for survival never seemed to end.

The taxi injured but did not kill Churchill—a matter of inches and milliseconds saved his life. But that's a story we already know.

✦ *Williamson Murray is Professor emeritus of history at the Ohio State University.*

### ✦ DAVID FROMKIN ✦

# TRIUMPH OF THE DICTATORS

In the spring of 1941, Nazi Germany was poised to dominate the earth. France, the Low Countries, Norway, Denmark, Austria, Czechoslovakia, Yugoslavia, Greece, and much of Poland had been overrun by the Germans. All of Europe, save neutral Sweden and Switzerland, was in the hands of Hitler's friends and allies: dictators or monarchs who ruled fascist Italy, Vichy France, Franco's Spain, Portugal, the Balkan countries, Finland, and above all the Soviet Union.

A single German division under General Erwin Rommel, sent to rescue beleaguered Italians in Libya, drove Britain's Middle Eastern armies flying and threatened the Suez lifeline; while in Iraq a coup d'état by the pro-German Rashid Ali cut the land road to India. In Asia, Germany's ally, Japan, was coiled to strike, ready to take Southeast Asia and invade India. No need to involve the United States; by seizing the Indies, Japan could break the American embargo and obtain all the oil needed for the Axis Powers to pursue their war aims.

Hitler should have sent the bulk of his armies to serve under Rommel, who would have done what Alexander did and Bonaparte failed to do: He would have taken the Middle East and led his armies to India. There he would have linked up with the Japanese. Europe, Asia, and Africa would have belonged to the coalition of dictators and militarists.

The Nazi-Soviet-Japanese alliance commanded armed forces and resources that utterly dwarfed the military resources that the holdouts, Britain (with its empire) and the United States, could field. The English-speaking countries would have been isolated in a hostile world and would have had no realistic option but to make their peace with the enemy, retaining some autonomy for a time, perhaps, but doomed ultimately to succumb. Nazi Germany, as leader of the coalition, would have ruled the world.

Only Hitler's astonishing blunder in betraying and invading his Soviet ally kept it from happening.

✦ *David Fromkin is professor of international relations and history at Boston University*

## THEODORE F. COOK, JR.

# OUR MIDWAY DISASTER

*Japan Springs a Trap, June 4, 1942*

There is a story, no doubt apocryphal, that gamers at the Naval War College in Newport, Rhode Island, have many times replayed the 1942 Battle of Midway—but have never been able to produce an American victory. How to duplicate the luck of our dive-bombers, swooping down on the Japanese carriers at the very moments when all planes were down for refueling? Talk about the balance of a war shifting in a few moments. "Given the deadly suddenness of carrier warfare" Theodore F. Cook, Jr. has written, "How easily might it have been the U.S. Navy mourning the loss of three carriers and their splendid air crews in exchange for, perhaps, one or two Japanese flattops on June 4, 1942?"

What would have happened if the Japanese had won at Midway? With only one carrier left in the Pacific, how could we have resisted their advance? For the United States, the immediate prospects would have been bleak. The Japanese would have taken Midway Island itself. In an island-hopping plan of their own, they would have isolated Australia. And they would have initiated what they called "the Eastern Operation"—the invasion of Hawaii. How, in turn, would the United States have reacted? What would our new grand strategy have been? It is hardly likely that we would have allowed the Japanese to win the war by default. Cook suggests an ingenious alternative, and one entirely fitting for the world's greatest industrial power. Timetables might have been altered but in time the pattern familiar to us would have reasserted itself—that of the "second-order counterfactual." In other words, the atomic bomb.

✦ Theodore F. Cook, Jr. is professor of history at The William Paterson University of New Jersey. One of the foremost American authorities on Japanese military history, he is, with Haruko Taya Cook, the author of JAPAN AT WAR: AN ORAL HISTORY.

Incredible Victory," "The Turning Point," "Miracle at Midway," "The Battle that Doomed Japan" are among the many sobriquets used for the extraordinary events of early June 1942 that became the Battle of Midway. Admiral Chester W. Nimitz ordered a badly outnumbered American fleet, alerted by intercepts of the Japanese naval code to Admiral Yamamoto Isoroku's plans to invade Midway island in the central Pacific Ocean, to confront the aircraft carriers of Japan's Mobile Fleet, attackers of Pearl Harbor. The Americans destroyed them in a single day. Its striking power smashed, the Imperial Navy found itself suddenly forced into the strategic defensive. Allied commanders, from Ceylon to San Francisco could reasonably assume that the Japanese flood had crested. American victory at Midway secured the Allied grand strategy of seeking to defeat Germany first, and even allowed a counteroffensive against Japan to begin at Guadalcanal in August.

One month earlier, in May 1942, Admiral Yamamoto Isoroku, commander in chief of Japan's Combined Fleet, proposed an invasion of Midway Island (Operation MI) in the Central Pacific and simultaneous landings in the Aleutians far to the North at Attu and Kiska (Operation AL), as his next moves in the Pacific War. He was enraged and embarrassed by the raid, commanded by James Doolittle, made on Japan by medium-range U.S. Army bombers, launched from an aircraft carrier, that had avoided detection through the northern Pacific in April. In early May his plan to land Japanese troops at Port Moresby on the southeastern coast of New Guinea was thwarted at the Battle of the Coral Sea, even though his forces had inflicted more damage on their enemy than they suffered. Now Yamamoto pushed forward a design that would both plug the gaps in Japan's outer defenses, and, he felt certain, draw into battle and destroy the American carriers that had not been at Pearl Harbor, or knocked out at the Coral Sea. His plans were very elaborate, involving nine separate groups of ships, coordinating their movements across the vastness of the north and central Pacific.

Unfortunately for the Japanese, through the efforts of the code breakers working under the direction of Commander Joseph J. Rochefort Jr. at "Hypo," as the Pearl Harbor Navy's Combat Intelligence Unit at Pearl Harbor was known, the United States got wind of Yamamoto's impending operations. Its targets might have been anywhere, but as information streamed in, it seemed probable that Yamamoto meant to strike at Midway. Confirmation was needed. Rochefort's struggle to pry meaning out of intercepted communications coming in from all over the Pacific in the Imperial Navy's JN-25 code—only partially broken—culminated in an attempt to determine what geographic location corresponded to "AF," the objective of the future operation in an otherwise decoded message picked up in early May. It sparked debate and argument throughout Admiral Chester W. Nimitz's small circle of code-privy staff.

The story of how it was done has become the epic of the code-breakers fraternity; especially clever seems the remarkably simple ruse used to draw the Japanese into revealing the code word. Midway Island was ordered to broadcast a message on May 21, sent in the clear, that their condenser had broken down and that they would soon be short of fresh water; Pearl Harbor then sent a reply, also uncoded, that a water barge was on its way. Allied listening stations in Australia were rewarded the same day with a Japanese message dutifully reporting that "AF" was running short of water. This was decoded, translated, and flashed to Pearl immediately. It led to Nimitz's firm commitment to meet the enemy at the place—Midway—and the date—June 4—earlier intercepts had detected. He prepared a "flank attack," aiming to be waiting north of Midway Island within range of where the enemy was likely to appear, to allow his fleet, concentrated for this one operation, to get in a surprise blow on Yamamoto's fleet.

The outlines of what happened at Midway are well known. For operations aimed at Midway and the occupation of the Western Aleutians isles of Attu and Kiska, Yamamoto had 11 battleships, 8 carriers (4 of them carriers of the first rank, *Akagi, Kaga, Hiryu*, and *Soryu*, all veterans of the Pearl Harbor attack—the other two carriers in that attack were back in Japan recovering from the Battle of the Coral Sea early in May), 22 cruisers, 65 destroyers, 21 submarines, and over 700 airplanes. Nimitz was only able to send into action 3 carriers (including *Yorktown*, practically raised from the dead after the Battle of the Coral Sea by the dockyards of Pearl Harbor), 8 cruisers, 18 destroyers, and 25 submarines.

Alerted to both the objectives and timing of Yamamoto's massive operation, Nimitz, nevertheless, ordered his fleet, divided into two task forces built around aircraft carriers—Task Force 16 containing *Enterprise* and *Hornet* under Rear Admiral Raymond Spruance and Task Force 17 with *Yorktown* under Rear Admiral Frank Jack Fletcher, the latter in overall command, temporarily replacing Vice Admiral William F. Halsey, beached due to illness at this critical moment. They would be waiting for Vice Admiral Nagumo Chûichi's Mobile Force aircraft carriers when they approached Midway to bomb the island's defenses, preparatory to an invasion.

Ironically, both commanders had complete confidence in their own ability to surprise their enemy. Nimitz reinforced the Midway garrison with orders to prepare a nasty surprise for any imperial troops who sought to storm ashore, and rushed as many planes as possible—whether obsolete, oversized, or untested—to the island's airfield. He then ordered his carriers to their flanking position, designated "Point Luck." Historically, Nagumo had the more flawed appreciation of his situation. Just prior to the launch of his first strike against Midway Island, Nagumo prepared an assessment of the situation as follows that listed his premises:

1. The enemy fleet will probably come out to engage when the Midway landing operations are begun.
2. Enemy air patrols from Midway will be heavier to westward and southward, less heavy to the north and northwest.

3. The radius of enemy air patrols is estimated to be approximately 500 miles.

4. The enemy is not yet aware of our plan, and he has not yet detected our task force.

5. There is no evidence of an enemy task force in our vicinity.

6. It is therefore possible for us to attack Midway, destroy land-based planes there, and support the landing operation. We can then turn around, meet an approaching enemy task force, and destroy it.

7. Our interceptors and anti-aircraft fire can surely repulse possible counterattacks by enemy land-based air.

Hardly could he have been more wrong, and these assumptions contributed greatly to Nagumo's inability to adapt to radically different circumstances.

As it turned out, the Invasion Force, approaching from the southwest, was spotted first, on June 3, and was attacked to no effect by bombers from Midway. At first light the next day, the Japanese bombed the island, causing extensive damage, but they failed to catch the American aircraft on the ground. They were met by severe anti-aircraft fire, leading the air commander to request another strike on Midway. Nagumo, unaware American carriers were lurking near at hand—and haunted by the second-guessing that had dogged him since his supposed failure to follow up his Pearl Harbor success back in December with a crushing blow against storage facilities and depots—then authorized, at 7:15 A.M., the rearming of the aircraft kept in reserve for any American ships that might appear, for a second attack on Midway. While the crews labored to switch torpedoes and penetration bombs to weapons suited to land targets, Spruance's Task Force 16 was sighted where no enemy was expected. Despite the urging of some that he strike immediately at this dangerous and unexpected target, Nagumo ordered a second switch of armaments.

For his part, although still at extreme range, as soon as he got a fix on Nagumo's location, Spruance ordered his planes to attack. The U.S. attack was uncoordinated. The torpedo bombers, slow and vulnerable, found the enemy first, and were nearly annihilated, but they attracted most of Nagumo's fighters, and just as the Japanese commanders felt that their furious maneuvers had weathered another ineffective American attack, Spruance's dive-bombers found Nagumo's task force. Nine bombs virtually destroyed the Japanese fleet, knocking carriers *Akagi*, *Kaga*, and *Soryu* out of action, the bombers on their decks and hangers, caught before they could be launched, were consumed in the conflagration of fuel and exploding munitions that incinerated many of their crew and would lead to the loss of all three ships.

*Hiryu*, Nagumo's fourth carrier, escaped this attack and was able to launch planes later in the morning that found Fletcher's carrier, *Yorktown*, inflicting such serious damage that Fletcher was forced to change ships; he immediately relinquished overall command to Spruance, who ordered his now rearmed dive-bombers to strike back. They found *Hiryu* late in the afternoon, so seriously damaging the ship that she would be scuttled. Yamamoto's plans were ruined, and his last chance at revenge was lost when Spruance ordered a retirement, beyond the range of Japan's powerful surface fleet that sought a night action. Apart from a Japanese cruiser damaged in a collision, sunk by Spruance's aircraft the next day, the action was over. *Yorktown* was eventually sunk by the Japanese submarine *I-168* on June 7 as she tried to make it home. Yamamoto's grand design had ended in disaster, and the initiative had passed to the Americans.

✦ ✦ ✦

The might-have-beens of the battle have long tantalized students of the war in the Pacific. Bemoaning mechanical failures, querying small changes in the timing of events, and second-guessing command decisions in light of events known and unknown to the participants all have been common. A list of the most popular, given in Walter Lord's *Incredible Victory*, published in 1967, includes, for example: If only float plane No. 4, from the heavy cruiser *Tone* had gotten off on time, "they would have discovered the U.S. fleet before rearming for that second attack on Midway;" "If only the American dive-bombers had attacked a few minutes later, Nagumo's own strike would have been launched" (this is the famous "five minutes" claim that puts down Japan's defeat to timing); "If only the Japanese had attacked the American carriers as soon as they were sighted, instead of holding back until all the planes were ready." To this list could be added: What if American dive-bomber commander Wade McClusky had not decided to push on beyond his safe range to find the Japanese carriers; and what if Rear Admiral Frank Jack Fletcher, his carrier *Yorktown* sunk from under him, had not turned tactical command over to Rear Admiral Ray Spruance, who then pressed home the attack? These, and many other bold decisions, brave choices, and even colossal blunders might be credited as critical in bringing about the historic victory of the American fleet at Midway, but here I look at the period preliminary to the battle that played perhaps the greatest part in America's victory, and suggest that with a very small change, things might have turned out very differently.

### An Alternate Path? The Making of a Japanese Midway Victory

Few have doubted the importance of the battle in forging America's triumph over Japan. In the words of Admiral Chester W. Nimitz, America's overall naval commander in the Pacific Theater and the man most credited with leading the United States Navy to victory over Japan's fleets in the Second World War: "Midway was the crucial battle of the Pacific War, the engagement that made everything possible." The rest, they say, is history.

*But*, what if in mid-May 1942, a Japanese sailor, after transcribing a radio message he had just intercepted from Midway Island, had turned to his superior to ask, "Why are they broadcasting this message in the clear? Don't they care if we know that Midway is running short of water?" What if, acting on this kernel of suspicion, the young communications officer had passed along his doubts? What if more experienced cryptographers and cipher specialists in Tokyo had not dismissed the idea that Imperial Japan's codes could be broken; what if they had considered the possibility that the Americans could possibly be playing out an intelligence gambit. They might have reasoned, "If the Americans have been able to read some of our messages and are attempting to link potential objectives with cipher designations, would not this little message be an excellent way to trick us into confirming the code word for Midway?"

What if, with a red flag raised, naval staff at Imperial General Headquarters Tokyo broadcast the now famous message of May 19, 1942, referring to "AF" being short of water not merely as a routine signal (the decryption of which today occupies an almost sacred place in the history of signals intelligence and code breaking), but as the first salvo in a Japanese intelligence offensive designed to lure the Americans to battle on terms favorable to Japan?

A simple question, heightened alertness, and suddenly what historians have often described as the decisive U.S. advantage in the close-run Battle of Midway might well have become the Japanese side's key to a great victory in the central Pacific, dramatically altering the course of the Second World War.

To rewrite the history of the Battle of Midway is to tear up one of the most cherished of American war stories, for the decisions taken during it, the sacrifices made, and the glorious results achieved have become legend. Yet, intelligence that allowed the outnumbered American carriers to ambush Nagumo Chûichi's carriers after they had bombed Midway Island could well have yielded very different results. Had Admiral Yamamoto Isoroku known, or even strongly suspected, that the Americans were privy to his plans for "Operation MI," calling for the seizure of Midway before U.S. carriers could steam up from Hawaii, he could have used his heavy numerical superiority in both carriers and aircraft to set his own trap and bring on just the decisive battle he sought.

While it is of course possible that a Yamamoto who knew his plans were known to the enemy could have abandoned his Midway operation and gone after alternative targets—perhaps Australia, Ceylon, Dutch

319

Harbor off Alaska, or even Fiji and Samoa (identified in Operation Plan FS favored by his opponents in the navy). But the Midway plan was a sound one, at least in the mind of the commander in chief of the Combined Fleet. To abandon his own plan, in all its elaborate elegance, seems uncharacteristic of the man. The interplay of nine different task forces maneuvering to a planned-for endgame was something Admiral Yamamoto seemed to thrill in. Indeed, he assigned himself a key part in the battle that he initially envisioned; at sea in his flagship, the super-battle-ship *Yamato*, just a few hundred miles behind Nagumo's carriers, he could be on the kill if Americans followed the first script he had prepared for them.

If the Americans had, in fact, gotten wind of his operations, all the better, he might well have concluded, since knowing his objective, they surely would realize that Midway could not be allowed to fall into Japanese hands. The commander of a temporarily superior fleet, from a nation that could not hope to compete over the long-haul, sought no "fleet-in-being" strategy. But in the footsteps of Japan's Admiral Tôgô Heihachirô, victor of Tsushima over the Russians in 1905, and in the spirit of Britain's Nelson, whose words rang throughout the Imperial Japanese Navy's heritage, Yamamoto could not have wished for a better opportunity than a decisive battle at the place of his own choosing.

So, instead of re-scripting Combined Fleet's grand operation and creating entirely new roles for the Americans to act out in his drama, it seems that Yamamoto, even with more than an inkling that the Americans were waiting for him, would have adjusted his operational plan at the margins rather than curb his own strategic vision of what was to follow Midway. In the minds of Yamamoto and his chief of staff, Ugaki Matome, anticipated victory there would be the opening phase of an even grander plan. Beyond lay the Hawaiian Islands and their greatest prize, Pearl Harbor, on Oahu, spoken of as "The Eastern Operation." The stakes for which Yamamoto was playing included America's Pacific Fleet base itself.

What evidence would Yamamoto have had about American deployments and intentions before the battle? The answer to that question is probably, "not much," since the Americans were so anxious to keep secret both their whereabouts and capabilities. Calculating two U.S. carriers at sea, and even adding in a third carrier, *Yorktown*, (claimed, but not confirmed, sunk at Coral Sea) or *Saratoga*, whose precise whereabouts were unknown (at the time she was steaming west from San Diego), Yamamoto could count on superiority in numbers. Yamamoto could not be certain that the United States was reacting to his plans, even if he were alerted to that possibility, but he might have had his first confirmation of America's efforts, when it became necessary for Japan to cancel "Operation K" at the end of May. This was a night reconnaissance of Pearl Harbor by long-range Kawanishi flying boats (known as "Emily" by the Allies) from Kwajalein, the second one of the war. The planes were scheduled to be refueled by submarine *I-123* at the French Frigate Shoals, several hundred miles west of Oahu, until it was found that an American seaplane tender had taken up station there on the nights of May 30 and 31. The Japanese could still have executed the reconnaissance by ordering refueling operations shifted to nearby, and equally inhospitable, Necker Island so that the flying boats could go on their way to Pearl Harbor. There they would have found no American carriers, giving Yamamoto possible corroboration that Nimitz was trying to counter his moves as Japan closed in on Midway.

In our scenario, the battle might have developed like this: Yamamoto sets his submarine picket line between Hawaii and Midway several days earlier. The subs provide early warning that the Americans are coming when one catches a glimpse of Spruance's carriers moving toward the battle area on June second. Instead of relying on a perfunctory search for an enemy he did not expect to find, Admiral Nagumo, the alert predator, has all his escorts' float planes in the air before dawn searching determinedly for the enemy; his air groups are primed on deck, ready to strike at the first opportunity. "Point Luck," the location northeast on Midway designated as the rendezvous of Task Force 16 and Task Force 17, was to become a black mark on America's map of the Pacific, for to it—and to doom—sailed virtually all of America's striking power on that ocean.

Alerted to America's readiness to meet him at the outset, most of Nagumo's immediate pre-battle assumptions about his enemy are absent. Instead of planning a two-stage operation, where he had first to reduce and then seize an enemy island base before he could move against an enemy response, Japan's Mobile Force is no longer "a hunter chasing two hares at once," as Admiral Kusaka, Nagumo's chief of staff put it, and can unleash the veteran flight leaders to seek out the enemy fleet and destroy it. Not long after dawn on June 4, a contact report comes in to Nagumo: There are the Americans—two carriers and escorts. With full concurrence of his air staff, although at extreme range, Nagumo immediately gives orders to launch against the Americans, identified as *Enterprise* and *Hornet*. Balanced attack groups of Val bombers and Kate torpedo bombers, flown by magnificent air crews, and escorted all the way to their targets by half of Nagumo's Zero fighters, bear down on Spruance. The Japanese carriers, ready for an American counterattack, spot their fighters on deck, as the armoires prepare Nagumo's planes for a second strike.

Fortune does not always favor the large battalions, and good luck may not entirely desert the Americans; a report locating Nagumo's force from a Midway-based PBY Catalina flying boat comes in just as Task Force 16's radar picks up what may be incoming Japanese planes. Spruance, himself expecting and seeking contact, launches his own strike at this target. Ray Spruance has made a split-second decision under pressure. His radar gives him the chance to get his planes into the air rather than see them caught on his carrier's decks as the enemy arrives, but the position of the enemy fleet is beyond the round-trip range of many American aircraft; he will attempt to close the distance on their return trip, he tells them, knowing that many will have no chance to make it back. The fighters of TF-16's Combat Air Patrol, those not sent as escorts on the attack, meet the incoming enemy courageously, but they are knocked aside as Japanese Zeroes engage them aggressively, downing many, using their superior maneuverability to screen the Americans from the slower bombers. Few of the attacking bombers are turned aside before they reach the frantically turning American flattops. Within ten minutes, despite the desperate efforts of every antiaircraft gunner in the fleet, torpedoes have rammed home on both beams of *Hornet*, while *Enterprise* is ablaze from several huge holes on her flight deck. TF-16 is out of action; losses among the attackers are moderate. Heroic attacks and frantic actions still lie ahead, but this Midway battle would have already taken on the tones of an American disaster.

Even as Ray Spruance is transferring his flag from *Enterprise* while her captain tries desperately to save his ship, the planes of TF-16 are intercepted by a swarm of Japanese fighters as they approach Nagumo's carrier force. With great courage, most attempt to press home their attacks, but the slow-moving torpedo bombers are slaughtered; the dive-bombers are picked up by more Zeroes, waiting for them on high, which pursue them down their less-than-perfect bombing paths with murderous persistence; all this occurs while the ships of Nagumo's force are thowing up a curtain of ack-ack, maneuvering skillfully to avoid their attackers. As at Coral Sea, American bombers inflict severe damage on a Japanese carrier, let us say *Kaga*—the largest and most likely to attract the few attackers that can release their ordinance on target—but they are unable to finish her off. With their own mother ships devastated, these pilots will not get a second chance.

The curtain rises on the second phase of the battle soon thereafter. Fletcher in *Yorktown*, core of TF-17, learns of the sighting of Japanese carriers and wants to join the action, but he is not yet close enough to participate. His planes ready to go, and making flank speed to the west, he then gets the terrible news from Spruance of his ships' condition. It is no knock on Jack Fletcher to suggest that at this moment he would have been deeply divided on the course of action expected of him. The battle orders under which he is operating were ambivalent in such a situation.

American after-action reports will look askance at Nimitz's May 27, 1942, orders to Fletcher and Spruance that they were to, "inflict maximum damage on enemy by employing strong attrition tactics," striking from the northeast of the anticipated Japanese approach. Before they departed Pearl Harbor, Nimitz had also urged that they "be governed by the principle of calculated risk" and avoid attacking a superior force unless there was a good chance of inflicting greater damage. Viewed in the wake of a decisive defeat, do these orders not seem hopelessly contradictory, tying the hands of subordinate commanders? The enemy was known to be superior before the battle. Where is the "attrition" in retreat? Nimitz would seem to have left himself few options if his "flanking maneuver" were to prove a chimera, since with all of America's forces northeast of Midway Island, he was in no position to strike at the Japanese Midway Invasion Force steaming up from the southwest. If America's carriers were beaten, would not that leave Midway's reinforced garrison to the tender mercies of Yamamoto's battle fleet?

Jack Fletcher knows that Halsey would have hurled himself into battle, but he is not a "Bull" Halsey, likely to act before considering all the ramifications; nor can he easily abandon Spruance to an unanswered second strike from Nagumo. It is still midmorning; perhaps, Fletcher thinks, he himself has escaped detection and can get in a blow before the enemy finds him, evening up the score. Fletcher makes the decision to continue to sail west, rather than turn back for Pearl, hoping to narrow the range on Nagumo. A scout plane from the Japanese cruiser *Tone*, on its homeward leg, detects him. Fletcher launches *Yorktown*'s planes when he gets reports of "enemy carriers," hoping perhaps to catch Nagumo recovering his aircraft. America's last hope make their way to the Mobile Force's previous location, but can find only a crippled *Kaga* limping westward, escorted by two destroyers. Despite searching frantically for Nagumo's ships, which have made a sharp turn to the north to recover, they can find no fresh targets. The flight groups from *Yorktown* overwhelm the damaged Japanese carrier, dispatching her and one of her escorts in frustration.

While the American aircrews are pounding *Kaga*, Fletcher's flagship becomes the target of a ferocious attack in turn. Nagumo's other three carriers, having recovered their planes at the prearranged rendezvous to the north, launch their second strike against *Yorktown*, stalked by several floatplanes; she is a smoldering hulk by nightfall. Fletcher's planes are lost when they return to the site, though some of the aircrews who can make it back to all that remains of TF-17 are able to splash nearby. In a single day, *Hornet* had been sunk, *Yorktown* wrecked and scuttled by the same crew who had seen her saved just a few days before, while *Enterprise*, trying to make it home, the fires put out but her flight deck ruined, becomes an easy target for one of Japan's submarines, just as *Lexington* had been at Coral Sea; torpedoed, she sinks near dawn the next day, the fifth of June. With the Japanese navy's surface units closing in for night action to pick off any damaged vessels and American survivors of lost ships and ditched planes bobbing about in the waters near "Point Lucky," could not the "miracle of Midway" have become a massacre? Over the next few days, Japanese destroyers find many survivors, Americans and Japanese, though there is little joy for the prisoners, who find their rescuers interested only in what information they can provide about the defenses of Midway and Hawaii before they are killed. The loss has stripped America's naval air corps of its core of fine pilots and experienced aircrews, while possession of this "ocean battlefield" means many downed Japanese airmen will fly again.

The first consequence of American naval defeat would be the loss of Midway Island itself. Midway Island comes in for the attentions of Nagumo's planes from the Mobile Fleet, who soon reduced the island's airbase to rubble, its aircraft burned or expended in futile efforts to sink fast ships at sea. It is then pummeled by the big guns of the Support Group cruisers and then even the Main Force battleships under Admiral Yamamoto himself, hurling 16- and 18.1-inch shells against the coral. The American garrison, even reinforced as it was, can hardly resist for long unsupported, once Japanese troops go ashore. Yet it proves a bloody affair and a formidable warning for Japan of the dangers inherent in making opposed landings against the U.S. Marines in base-defense mode; the garrison adds "Midway" to the name of "The Alamo," "Wake," and "Bataan" in America's hagiography of last stands.

Nimitz finds himself in our scenario with just a single carrier in the Pacific: *Saratoga*, just in from San Diego. Of course, Halsey wants to steam off directly toward the enemy, "catch 'em gloating," might be the way he would have put it, but Nimitz is aware that the strategic defense he had planned has been ruined by his own impetuosity. He had gone on a hunch—no, a reasoned assessment based on intelligence estimates—but it was a very thin strand that had held it all together. There never seemed to be any consideration of whether the Japanese might have guessed his plans. Most of the fleet had been risked and now it was gone. How could expert strategic intelligence have produced such a catastrophic defeat? How could he have guessed right and still been defeated? He will not learn why until after the war.

### The Long War

On the morning after an overwhelming Japanese victory at Midway, what would the strategic situation have been and what alternatives would have presented themselves to the Japanese? Let us consider the possibilities.

The balance of naval power in the Pacific was heavily tilted in Japan's favor, and was likely to remain so for the remainder of the year 1942, and perhaps even the first half of 1943. At the beginning of June 1942, there were only six aircraft carriers in the American fleet; had Nimitz lost three of them at Midway, there was simply no way to make up the numbers in the short term. The remaining three carriers would not be augmented until the end of 1942 when the first of a new generation of *Essex*-class fast carriers was due to arrive. But the schedule for commissioning fleet carriers was six in 1943, seven in 1944, and three in 1945. In other words, assuming no losses, the most frontline carriers America's admirals could hope for was ten by the end of 1943. With U.S. carrier forces nearly an-

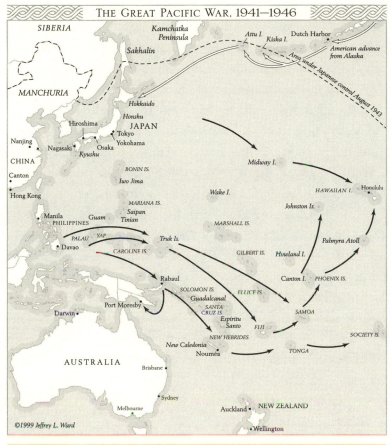

## THE GREAT PACIFIC WAR, 1941—1946

SIBERIA

Kamchatka
Peninsula

Sakhalin

Attu I.   Kiska I.   Dutch Harbor

*American advance
from Alaska*

Area under Japanese control August 1943

MANCHURIA

Hokkaido

Honshu

Hiroshima   JAPAN
  Tokyo

Nanjing    Osaka   Yokohama
  Nagasaki   Kyushu

CHINA

Canton

Hong Kong

BONIN IS.

Iwo Jima

Midway I.

Wake I.

HAWAIIAN I.   Honolulu

Johnston Is.

MARIANA IS.
Manila   Guam   Saipan
PHILIPPINES   Tinian

MARSHALL IS.

PALAU   YAP
Davao   CAROLINE IS.

Truk Is.

Palmyra Atoll

GILBERT IS.   Howland I.

Canton I.   PHOENIX IS.

Rabaul

SOLOMON IS.
Guadalcanal
SANTA
CRUZ IS.

ELLICE IS

Port Moresby

Darwin

Espíritu
Santo
NEW HEBRIDES
New Caledonia
Nouméa

FIJI

SAMOA

TONGA

SOCIETY IS.

AUSTRALIA

Brisbane

Sydney

Melbourne

Auckland   NEW ZEALAND

Wellington

©1999 Jeffrey L. Ward

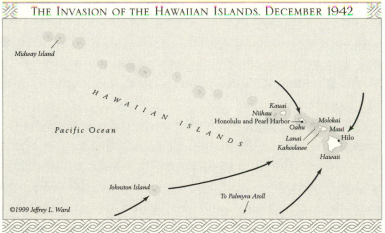

## THE INVASION OF THE HAWAIIAN ISLANDS, DECEMBER 1942

Midway Island

H A W A I I A N   I S L A N D S

Pacific Ocean

Kauai
Niihau
Honolulu and Pearl Harbor   Molokai
Oahu   Maui
Lanai   Hilo
Kahoolawe

Hawaii

Johnston Island

To Palmyra Atoll

©1999 Jeffrey L. Ward

nihilated at the Battle of Midway, the USN must either withdraw the few carriers still afloat from the Atlantic—stripping U.S. convoys there of air coverage and aborting U.S. training and planned offensive operations—or assume a completely defensive posture in the Pacific.

Japan was in a much stronger position. The victorious Nagumo force would hold the initiative if they had come off as well at Midway as the United States did historically. *Shokaku* and *Zuikaku*, the two carriers in the Pearl Harbor raid that were damaged in the Coral Sea battle and re-quired refitting and restaffing with new air units, were ready to rejoin the Mobile Fleet soon after Midway, and two more carriers would join the fleet in mid-1942, so available Japanese strength was likely to remain four or even five fleet carriers for future operations in the coming cam-paigns, even with refit and repair. Japan's numerical edge in the new measures of naval power, carriers, was secure for some time to come, while Yamamoto retained his battleship advantage—the old arbiter of sea warfare. It was not certain that even the huge number of American lighter warships, including light and escort carriers (eventually to number in the dozens), scheduled to arrive more than a year later, could be used to redress the balance.

Second, Australia was in jeopardy of being completely cut off, at least from the Pacific side, and the American fleet and army air corps were vir-tually powerless to intervene against Japanese efforts to sever communi-cations between the United States and Australia, at Fiji and then Samoa. The seven million people of Australia would find their land even more isolated than before, as the flow of supplies was pinched and General MacArthur's Southwest Pacific Command threatened to shrivel up even before it could come to life.

Third, the Indian Ocean was the one route still open to Australia, but a lifeline would have to be strung through India and Ceylon, both vul-nerable to Japanese attack at many points. Indian nationalism, evidenced by appeals for resistance to British rule and the calls for independence sweeping the subcontinent—while the British army is reeling back be-fore Imperial Japanese army troops in Burma—would surely make India seem less a stable base and more a potential future flash point in June 1942.

At the northern end of the Pacific, an advance up the Aleutians, perhaps even to Dutch Harbor, seems possible, assuming the landings planned for Attu and Kiska carried out with the Midway operation were successful. This move might prove of great importance pending the outcome of the more audacious Japanese plans to come. Dutch Harbor, just off the continental base of the Aleutian chain, is about the same distance from San Francisco as Honolulu (2,034 miles) and was vital to this theater of war, and if contained or perhaps even taken by Japanese troops, would have been defended by miserable cold weather, poor visibility, and heavy seas, placing a formidable barrier in the path of any U.S. alternative to the Central Pacific route to Tokyo.

In the southwestern Pacific, instead of an American "Operation Watchtower" to seize Guadalcanal in August 1942, Japanese advances in the Solomons might proceed nearly unchallenged. They could then threaten Allied outposts in Espíritu Santo, New Caledonia, or perhaps even Fiji and Samoa beyond. Although executed with thin margins for error and scant resources, each move could be supported by Japan's land-based aviation and made at Japan's initiative, and could only be challenged if America itself could somehow get the planes and fuel to the appropriate place to meet them.

Is it beyond the realm of possibility that panic contained after Pearl Harbor might have again swept the West Coast or spread to the corridors of power in Washington, D.C.? Again, a reassessment of the "Germany First" strategy that had become the foundation for the "Rainbow" war plan could well have been considered if the American fleet, the weapon needed to parry the Japanese thrusts, had been broken for a second time at Midway. If it seemed Japan could not be held off until Germany was defeated, what would the impact be on Allied Global Grand Strategy?

As bad as these prospects in the Pacific were, things could get a lot worse for the Americans. What if Hawaii itself was invaded next? Such an operation was not only contemplated but was in the advanced planning stage as the Midway operation was launched; to Yamamoto, at least, the "Eastern Operation" was the logical follow-up to his Aleutians and Midway strikes, hitting at the most significant real estate in the Pacific Ocean.

*Hawaii Invasion: Lei's for the Emperor*

Almost from the outset of the war, planning for an invasion of Hawaii stirred controversy at the highest level of Japanese military leadership. On January 14, 1942, Rear Admiral Ugaki Matome, chief of staff of the Combined Fleet and Yamamoto's right-hand man, confided in his diary that Japan had to make the attempt "to take Midway, Johnston, and Palmyra after June, send our air strength to those islands, and after these steps are completed, mobilize all available strength to invade Hawaii, while attempting to destroy the enemy fleet in a decisive battle." He knew many would likely oppose his plan, but among the reasons he listed for why it had to be executed were: "What would hurt the United States most is the loss of the fleet and of Hawaii"; "An attempted invasion of Hawaii and a decisive battle near there may seem a reckless plan, but its chance of success is not small"; "As time passes, we would lose the bene-fit of the war results so far gained. Moreover, the enemy would increase his strength, while we would have to be just waiting for him to come"; and "The destruction of the U.S. fleet would also mean that of the British fleet. So we would be able to do anything we like. Thus, it will be the shortest way to conclude the war." Ugaki noted too that "Time is an im-portant element in war. The period of war should be short. Though a pro-longed war is taken for granted, nobody is so foolish as to wish for it himself." Each of these reasons would still have seemed valid after a Japanese Midway.

That Hawaii was the next target for the Imperial Navy after the seizure of Midway is nearly certain. Thanks to the prodigious efforts of John Stephan of the University of Hawaii presented in his book, *Hawaii Under the Rising Sun: Japan's Plans for Conquest After Pearl Harbor*, we have a pretty good idea of what Japanese thinking was in 1941 and 1942 for a Hawaii operation and invasion. The Japanese faced formidable obstacles to success. Certainly a Japanese jump to Pearl Harbor would have been a tremendous gamble, but it would have become a much better wager with the U.S. carriers sent to the bottom and the Hawaiian islands partially isolated by free-ranging Japanese carriers and submarine forces to their east. Having come this far, Yamamoto surely would have made the attempt if he could pry out of the Imperial Army the divisions, aircraft, and supplies needed. Despite the risks, the potential benefits to Japan of a successful seizure of Oahu are hard to exaggerate, so much so that one can even argue that the only way Japan could have hoped to stave off defeat long enough for negotiations may have been with an all-out assault on the islands at the onset of war. But that is another path off our chosen counterfactual road.

Eastern Operation's invasion of Hawaii was planned to unfold over a period of months, in a series of stages, though had the victory at Midway been as complete as suggested in this scenario, calls would have been raised to speed up the timetable. To strike immediately would take advantage of American confusion (not to suggest panic) but it would also invite complete disaster. Oahu, the island where Pearl Harbor was located, could not be taken by storm; its fortifications, garrison, and air bases were formidable and would have to be reduced before any invasion could be attempted. The Japanese sword needed to be kept sharp through time in port and under refit and the carriers' aircraft and aircrews had to be rested and replaced. Yamamoto could not have continued to keep his fleet at sea, flitting from one "triumphant operation" to the next in preparation for a culminating battle for Hawaii, even were he able to find the fuel to do so. Moreover, the Japanese navy would have to secure the full commitment from the army to supply the men and planes needed for the job—not just the few designated before Midway. This would be no small task as they had opposed each of Yamamoto's offensives to this point in the war. But a great Midway victory might have made them enthusiastic supporters, though it seems that few in Japan

shared Yamamoto's view that the Americans would be willing to negotiate after Hawaii was in Japanese hands.

With a clear objective, a timetable, and the attention of the commander in chief of the Combined Fleet, Yamamoto Isoroku, the plan
most likely to have been attempted posited a strangling of Hawaii from
the west and southwest by a careful move against Palmyra Island as the
key air link leading on to the South Pacific, a completion of operations in
the FS Operation by taking Samoa, and the establishment of Japanese air
and sea bases in September. Thus the full-blown invasion of Hawaii
might be executed in late 1942, perhaps December. This plan had the advantage of allowing several more carriers to join the fleet and provided
for a rapidly accelerated program of converting seaplane tenders into aircraft carriers. Preparations for the Hawaii Campaign were grandiose, but
might have been just feasible if America's military forces were crippled
at Midway. Like a great scythe sweeping across the southwest and south
central Pacific, the first phases of the operation, following the theme of
the original Operation FS (Fiji-Samoa) proposed before the Midway invasion would sever the lines of communication and supply that tied Australia to Hawaii and the West Coast of the United States. New Caledonia,
Fiji, then Samoa were to be seized (perhaps even Tahiti beyond). Each
leap supporting the next. This would be accompanied by landings on
Johnston Island and Palmyra Island, another featureless point in the Pacific, leaving the Hawaiian Islands as the only U.S. territory left in the
Central Pacific.

American defenses in the Hawaiian Island chain had grown stronger
since December 1941, when U.S. Army troops had numbered 40,000
and probably exceeded 65,000 in April 1942. Even larger garrisons were
projected for Oahu, home of Honolulu and Pearl Harbor, and for Hawaii,
the "Big Island," several hundred miles to the southeast. But these reinforcements would have posed immense problems for American commanders in the coming battle. Hawaii was not the rich island paradise of
the travel brochures and prewar navy recruiting posters; provisioning the
troops and feeding the civilian population, especially the large concen-

tration of people in Honolulu, would have been a nearly impossible task without easy access to maritime supply. Poor and underdeveloped, except for its pineapple and sugar plantations, the Hawaiian Islands were heavily dependent on imported food, and virtually all the supplies necessary to support the civilian economy, to say nothing of the massive needs of the military forces, had to be imported. Most supplies came from U.S. ports more than 2,000 miles across the Pacific to the northeast. Estimates of Hawaii's food supply on the eve of war were on the order of weeks, rather than months.

The utility of Pearl Harbor and other facilities depended on the local labor force. Moreover, 160,000 of the residents, more than 40 percent of the total population, were what the Japanese at that time called *dôhô*, meaning "compatriots" (a term embracing ethnic Japanese at home and abroad, regardless of their citizenship). It must be said that prewar U.S. Army planning for defense of the islands had rated the loyalty of second-generation Japanese (known as *nisei*) quite high; the Hawaiian Department even recommended recruiting *nisei* soldiers. Despite the Draconian practices employed on the West Coast, very few Japanese Americans or Japanese nationals attracted the attentions of U.S. security authorities— less than 1 percent of Hawaii's population of Japanese descent were interned. Nevertheless, Japanese planners were hoping for a mass rising of "fellow countrymen" when Imperial forces arrived and planned to make good use of a sizable number of Japanese with Hawaiian experience identified in Japan once the islands were conquered for the emperor.

What means had America to contest operations against Hawaii, to supply an expeditionary force there, or to sustain any large-scale operation from the West Coast? Air operations were impossible from the United States against Hawaii—no bomber or transport plane could fly there fully loaded until the B-29 in mid-1944. As we have seen, an overwhelming Japanese victory at Midway would have left no American carriers to contest a Japanese invasion and taking back Hawaii, should it fall to Japan, would have required a massive seaborne operation, on a scale the United States could only mount in late 1943. What a prolonged

Hawaiian campaign might win for Japan must be assessed against what the diversion of force and effort of a greatly outnumbered fleet would have cost the United States. Without a fleet-in-being operating out of "America's Gibraltar," Pearl Harbor, Hawaii Territory's capital, Honolulu, and the island of Oahu were not protected from attack. Its principle defense, besides the coastal guns protecting the harbor, were the planes on Oahu's airfields. Even in the age of air power and the capability of aircraft to strike far out to sea and patrol, keeping the planes aloft depended on supply by sea.

The most likely scenario for the final Japanese assault on the Hawaiian Islands would begin with a strong diversion aimed at Oahu and a carrier-covered landing on Hawaii Island in an effort to secure forward-base facilities at Hilo; rapid construction of airfields to support the bombardment of U.S. Army and Navy installations on Oahu would follow, as the Imperial Navy brought in its bombers and fighters from the south. A furious series of air battles would be fought, and while the Americans could be expected to do well and the Japanese planes and pilots would be operating themselves at the extreme end of a painfully thin line of supply, the Americans, without a fleet-in-being to truly threaten the Japanese, would likely not be able to sustain the struggle indefinitely. Spare parts, ammunition, replacement pilots, to say nothing of fuel and new planes would have to run the gauntlet from the United States and would be most vulnerable as they approached the islands where cargo ships could be intercepted by units of Japan's fleet. If no "rising" had occurred among the Japanese American population, it seems likely that civilian targets on Oahu would be subjected to merciless air attacks and the U.S. fighter force gradually whittled down. There is no doubt that a direct assault on the harbor at Pearl would have been suicidal, and it is likely that the American garrison would have made the northern beaches of Oahu—the most favorable landing sites—quite impregnable to direct assault. But it is possible that elite units of the Imperial Army, such as those used in airborne assaults in Indonesia, could have been employed after the American defenses were hammered by the battleships of Japan once the U.S. air defenses had been suppressed or exhausted. Japan's attacks across the beaches would take terrible casualties in their assaults, but with sufficient fire support from the fleet, they might overwhelm the defenders and force the ignominious surrender of another American Pacific bastion.

Nowhere in the Imperial archives can we find a plan to extend the Imperial sweep further eastward, but, while Japanese fleets or squadrons probably could not operate effectively far beyond Hawaii, occasional raids in force, or lucky cruiser strikes against a few high visibility transports bound for Hawaii in desperate U.S. efforts to reinforce the islands, could have been very bad for American morale. Also, Japanese submarine raids against the West Coast 2,000-odd miles to the northeast—like the shelling of isolated outposts—surely would have heightened tension there and perhaps even have been of some military utility. Hunting packs of Japanese subs, with supply subs as mother ships, or resupply vessels, might have threatened coastal traffic until long-range patrols were established, as they were in the Atlantic. Deploying a few submarines off Panama could disrupt shipping in a major way, even if they could not stay on station long, while a bold raid on the Panama Canal, employing aircraft carried by Japan's largest submersibles, flown on a one-way mission from close in, loaded with high explosives, could have wreaked havoc were they able to seriously damage even one of the locks; again the threat would likely have tied up even more American forces.

## 1942: Year of Decision

The added confusion of a U.S. catastrophe at Midway and Hawaii could well have forced the Joint Chiefs into even more difficult decisions about priorities between Europe and the Pacific. Around the world that summer of 1942, Allied forces were hard-pressed. On the steppes of Russia, German forces were sweeping toward Stalingrad on the Volga and into the Soviet Union's oil-rich Caucasus region. German's Afrika Corps in North Africa was at the gates of Egypt, while in the Atlantic the U-boat menace was growing ever-more deadly; German submarines had sunk

700,000 tons of Allied shipping in June, and losses would reach their peak of 802,000 tons in November. All claims for resources to meet these threats would have to be balanced by General George C. Marshall and President Franklin D. Roosevelt against Japanese threats to the West Coast. The fragile balance of the Anglo-American accords that gave primacy to Europe and the defeat of Hitler might well remain the stated strategic objective, but the harsh realities of the Pacific Theater could well override many commitments. What would be available for the Soviet Union and how could it be shipped there?

Profound shock, reviving the panic of December 1941, was surely possible throughout America in the aftermath of a Hawaiian debacle. Demands for increased commitment to the defense of the West Coast, leading to diversion of troops, artillery, and vital supplies, including aircraft to coastal defense, would be hard to resist with nothing between Japanese-held Hawaii and California. The few long-range patrol craft available to America at this time could well have led to the great strategic weapon in America's arsenal, the B-17 Flying Fortress heavy bomber, being diverted from a build-up in Britain for a future bombardment campaign against Germany, to coastal defense. Surely, the use of the B-17 in the Philippines and in operations out of Midway's limited airstrips had won no glory to the heavy bomber as a weapon against ships at sea, but what else was there? Calls to create a strategic bombing force based in Britain to attack Germany were less likely to get the support required when anti-ship strikes were still considered a major mission for America's long-range bombers and when the Pacific coast seemed to lie exposed to prowling Japanese forces.

Expansion of industrial production was certain, but a greater sense of immediate vulnerability might well have led to higher manpower calls for military service, with consequent waste in both resources and personnel. Certainly, an aroused America could out-produce the world, but would it do so in time? Could American economic mobilization possibly have been as deliberate as it was had the first great battle of the war ended in a defeat that seemed to make the threat to continental America even greater?

The possibility certainly exists that a 1942 rush to create a more massive U.S. Army, with perhaps more than 100 divisions, would have upset timetables, trashed production schedules, and made a mess of efforts to manage bottlenecks in manpower skills, training, and production. Admiral Ernest King and General Marshall would have been even more hard-pressed to decide priorities between the services were America pushed back on its own coast in the Pacific. While solid realists might have re-asserted control later in the war, time lost certainly would have slowed efforts to bring to bear America's real strength, its mechanical skill and industrial capacity for the production of quantity, quantity, and more quantity, delivered where most necessary, and everywhere else as well.

Despite the hopes of Yamamoto and perhaps some others in Japan's ruling élites that the capture of Hawaii might provide an opportunity to negotiate a settlement with the United States, this seems far-fetched. There is nothing in the history books to suggest that America would be particularly willing to cooperate with the conquerors of Honolulu. As the resounding words of President Roosevelt to Congress on December 8, 1941, made clear: "No matter how long it may take us to overcome this premeditated invasion, the American people in their righteous might will run through to absolute victory." Long and protracted battle for the islands could have worn down American strength to the point that even with Japan's fleet seriously depleted by the effort, the task of building the entire grand fleet needed to assault and retake the islands might have been judged not worth the time and effort.

It seems to me likely that the Central Pacific Offensive—envisioning the seizure of selected islands and atolls, using each as a base for the next and moving ever closer to Japan—long the dream of America's naval strategists, would have been rendered a relic by Japanese success in Operation MI, Operation AL, and the Eastern Operation culminating in an invasion of Hawaii. Rather than a massive D Day–type invasion against Hawaii, what we might well have seen was the alternative nightmare of Japanese strategic thinkers before the war—a determined United States advance via Alaska.

It is in this strategy that we can best understand Yamamoto's interest in the Aleutian islands at the time of the Midway operation. The only direct route to Japan available under the circumstances foreseen here would be the fog-shrouded, ice-clogged wilderness of the Alaska-Aleutians approach. The Great Circle Route, as it was called, ran from San Francisco to Manila and passed directly through Tokyo. But to make this approach work as a war-winning strategy would require building not just the Alcan Highway, begun in February 1942 to provide a direct overland route to central Alaska, but what we might figuratively call "the Alaska Super-Highway," a string of air bases, naval complexes, transportation nexuses, and depots all the way from western Canada and Seattle, Washington, to Dutch Harbor and beyond. This is the kind of project that America and Canada could handle if the need were determined great enough to complete it—thousands of miles of highway, rendered all-weather with awesome road-borne capacity emerging, supplying short-range leaps through the Aleutians, stretching across the northern Pacific's rim, culminating in Kiska and Attu in the western Aleutians, down through the northern Kurile Islands, wrested from Japan by sea assault covered by the new American Navy that would have been ready in the two years or so this could take.

Whenever one studies the Second World War and American power, one axiom seems to emerge: Whatever America had to build would have been built, drawing on a virtually limitless industrial potential; yet there are at least some flaws in such arguments that might make speculation more than idle. One is that the mobilization of America, begun well before Pearl Harbor and carried on thereafter was not pursued in an environment when ultimate victory in any theater could be doubted. Two American fleets lost in six months—the battle fleet smashed at Pearl Harbor and the carriers lost at Midway—certainly made for no "turning-the-tide" mentality that was historically so important in sustaining American spirit in the still-dark days of 1942. With the Philippines lost, the American flag swept from the western Pacific, the strategic riches of the Dutch

East Indies and Indochina lost to the Allies, the loss of a second fleet at Midway and perhaps the capture of Pearl Harbor by a Japanese invasion, might have shaken that resolve.

## Endgame

Would America have lost the war? Not likely, given American economic potential, but winning the war against Japan after a disaster at Midway would have been an even more daunting task. Making up the losses would only have been part of the problem, since with the initiative still in Japanese hands after June 1942, America would still have been on the strategic defensive, forced to allocate resources on the basis in large measure on what the enemy might attempt. This might have drained away enough to prolong the war in Europe, which, as we now know, could have allowed some of the German superweapons to come on-line earlier. The need to match German technical prowess in jet aircraft, and the threat posed by rockets, especially the V-2, might have greatly complicated European Theater operations. For millions languishing in death camps, their fate largely ignored by the Allies, Nazi Germany's "Final Solution," might well have moved even closer to its objective.

A lengthened war could also have meant prolonged Japanese control over East Asia. The captured suffering unspeakable deprivations under Japanese occupation throughout East and Southeast Asia would have seen that horror extended. Japanese mobilization of labor in China and Malaya might well have meant an even more astronomic death toll. In the end, of course, the final toll from a rain of atomic bombs on Japan, when at last the Home Islands were approached is even more terrible to contemplate than the ruin that was suffered in Japan in 1945. This assumes, of course, that speculative "Big Science" projects like Manhattan could have received funding in the face of other crises facing American industry and strategic planners forced to deal with a continued rampage of Japan through 1942.

✦ ELIHU ROSE ✦

# THE CASE OF THE MISSING CARRIERS

As the attacking Japanese planes swooped into Pearl Harbor on December 7, 1941, the U.S. Pacific Fleet appeared as sitting ducks. Almost, but not quite. The harbor was chock full of battleships, destroyers, submarines, and any number of auxiliary vessels, but the Pacific Fleet's three aircraft carriers were missing. The gods of war had thus given the U.S. Navy one small gift to assuage its impending humiliation: the *Saratoga* was in overhaul on the West Coast; the *Lexington* was delivering aircraft to Midway; and the *Enterprise* was on a similar mission to Wake.

All lived to fight another day. The *Lexington* was lost at the Coral Sea and the *Saratoga* earned seven Battle Stars in her subsequent career—important though not decisive contributions.

However, it was planes from the *Enterprise*, along with those of the *Yorktown*, that sank four Japanese carriers at Midway, turning the tide of that climactic battle and administering the coup de grace to Japanese hopes of invading Midway and Hawaii as well as aborting plans for operations against Ceylon and Australia. It was the single greatest Japanese naval defeat since Korean ironclads ravaged a Japanese fleet in 1592. As Samuel Eliot Morison observed: "Midway changed the whole course of the Pacific War." In a tantalizing what if, one might speculate upon the outcome of the battle had not the *Enterprise* been out of harm's way on December 7.

✦   *Elihu Rose teaches military history at New York University.*

## STEPHEN E. AMBROSE

# D DAY FAILS

*Atomic Alternatives in Europe*

Often, in military history, the dominoes fall where the wind blows them. We have seen that happen with the influence of weather in the preternatural wetness of 1529, the breezes that disrupted the Spanish Armada, and George Washington's fog-aided escape after the Battle of Long Island. But rarely have the whims of weather produced more far-reaching consequences than they did at D Day. June 6, 1944 witnessed not just a genuinely decisive military event, but, in a sense, a political one that determined which ideological path Western Europe would follow in the next half century. What if the Allied invasion of Normandy had been called off or had failed? What if the famous window—a brief break in the storm battering the continent—had not opened, and Dwight D. Eisenhower had withheld the go-ahead or had gone through with the invasion anyway? Would the storm have become for the Germans a force multiplier, giving them the edge that Allied deceptions—which caused Hitler and his generals to divert divisions to other possible invasion sites—had taken away? In this speculation by Stephen E. Ambrose, failure would have resulted in alternatives that ranged from unpleasant to frightening.

341

◆ *If history is enjoying a resurgence of popularity, one of those chiefly responsible is Professor Ambrose. He has written (at the latest count) twenty books, including multivolume biographies of Dwight D. Eisenhower and Richard M. Nixon, as well as his three most recent bestsellers, UNDAUNTED COURAGE, the story of the Lewis and Clark expedition, his two accounts of the end of World War II in WESTERN EUROPE, D DAY and CITIZEN SOLDIERS, and most recently, COMRADES.*

For what if history to work, there has to be a real chance that things could have turned out differently because of forces beyond human control—meaning, in most cases, weather. Some parts of weather can be predicted with certainty long in advance—tides and moon conditions—but others, such as wind, waves, and cloud cover can scarcely be guessed much more than twenty-four hours in advance, especially in an area of notoriously volatile weather such as the English Channel.

Overlord—the code name for the Allied invasion of Western Europe—was the most tightly planned offensive of the war. From the beginning, SHAEF (Supreme Headquarters Allied Expeditionary Force) counted on reasonable weather—moderate seas, low winds, scattered cloud cover. Heavy seas, high winds, a zero ceiling would make the assault impossible.

The invasion had originally been scheduled for June 5, 1944. The weather, which had been beautiful for the first three days of June, began to deteriorate. In the channel, a drizzle began to turn into a cold, penetrating rain. The final weather conference was scheduled for 4:00 A.M., June 4. Group Captain J. M. Stagg, whom Dwight D. Eisenhower described as a "dour but canny Scot," made the weather predictions, as he had every day for a month, spending half an hour or more with the SHAEF commander. Stagg had bad news. A low-pressure system was moving in. June 5 would be overcast and stormy. Eisenhower decided to postpone it for at least one day.

In the early hours of June 5, with the wind and rain rattling the windowpanes of the SHAEF headquarters, Stagg made the most famous weather prediction in military history. He thought the storm would ease off later that day, and that by Tuesday, June 6, the weather would be

343

## D DAY: THE WEATHER FACTOR

*Twice, weather might have caused an Allied disaster on the beaches of Normandy. A fierce gale let up just in time for the D Day invasion to go forward on June 6, 1944. The next possible day, June 19, brought an even more turbulent tempest, shown here battering the artificial harbor code-named Mulberry.*

(Corbis/Bettmann)

acceptable. The rain that was then pouring down would stop before daybreak. There would be thirty-six hours of more or less clear weather. Eisenhower asked for a guarantee; Stagg laughed and said the general knew that was impossible. Then Ike made his decision: "Okay, let's go."

Stagg's prediction was as much hunch as scientific. Though he was only twenty-eight, he had spent several years as a weather forecaster. Other weathermen, from the Royal Navy and the U.S. Navy, for example, disagreed with him—they thought the storm would continue. Stagg wrote in his memoir, *Forecast Overlord*, that even had he had access to modern satellite imagery, he still would have been guessing as much as predicting. A half-century after Overlord, when the BBC has satellites and reporting stations such as Stagg could not imagine, the weather predictions in May or June for twenty-four hours in advance are dead wrong about half the time.

So, what if the storm had continued into June 6? Eisenhower could have called the invasion back, although not easily. Had he done so, he would not only have given away the landing site, but June 19, the next date in which the combination of full moon and low tides was suitable, would witness the worst storm of the year to hit Normandy.

If, on the other hand, he had gone ahead with the invasion, the consequences may have proved disastrous. The landing craft would have been tossed about like toy boats in a bathtub. Men trying to go ashore from any craft that made it to land would have been vomiting, exhausted, suffering all the agonies of seasickness, incapable of fighting. There would have been no air cover and no paratrooper support, as the air drops would have been scattered to hell and gone), no supporting bombardment from the two- and four-engine bombers. The Navy might have been able to fire its big guns, but because of the rolling of the vessels in the waves, accuracy would have been limited. The German defenders, protected from the elements in their bunkers, would have delivered a deadly fire on the hapless Allied infantry.

Eisenhower would have had no choice but to order the follow-up landings canceled. He almost certainly would not have been able to withdraw the men from the initial waves: They would have been killed or captured, as had happened to the raiders at Dieppe in 1942, the war's first major amphibious landing in Europe. At nightfall on June 6, he would have issued his prepared-in-advance statement to the press: "The landings have failed . . ." The Allied fleet would have pulled back to England in disarray, its tail between its legs.

Then what? Eisenhower would have certainly lost his job, and this was something he knew, which was why he had prepared his statement accepting full responsibility for the failure. There was no sense bringing the entire high command down with him. But who could have taken his place? Bernard Montgomery was unacceptable to the Americans, who were making the major contribution. Omar Bradley would have been as tarred by the brush of failure as Eisenhower. George S. Patton, perhaps—he was being readied to take a field command after the landing was established and would not have been implicated in the failure. But Monty would have tried to exercise a veto over Patton's appointment. George C. Marshall, the U.S. Army chief of staff was a possible choice: He had originally hoped to lead the invasion but President Roosevelt felt that he was too valuable in Washington.

The Allied planners, meanwhile, would have been in despair. Despite failure, they still would have had an enormous force at their disposal of land, air, and sea forces. But it had taken more than a year to put the Overlord plan together. There was no alternative plan available. In retrospect, Normandy was the perfect choice; but the planners could not have tried there a second time. Where, then? The Pas de Calais beaches were far better defended than those in Normandy. Le Havre bristled with German guns. Reinforcing the South of France landings (Operation Dragoon) in mid-August would have been the most appealing option, perhaps the only way was to get the forces gathered in Britain into the battle in France. But such a diversion would have created immense logistical problems while leaving the bulk of the Allied army far short of the Rhine, not to mention Berlin. The liberation of southern France was not going to end the war, or even seriously threaten Hitler's empire in northwest Europe. Moreover, with his channel flank secure for the moment, Hitler would risk little in sending reinforcements south—not the case when Operation Dragoon actually took place. Something akin to the stalemate in Italy would have ensued in the Rhone Valley. Still, the south of France seems the most likely alternative.

Failure would have brought immediate political as well as military problems. I would guess that the Churchill government could not have survived—after all, it had bet the kingdom on Overlord. The successor government would have had a mandate—to do what? Prosecute the war more vigorously? Hardly possible. Negotiate with Hitler? Unthinkable. Muddle on and hope for the best? Most likely.

In the United States, meanwhile, Roosevelt—who had also bet the house on Overlord—would have been secure from a no-confidence vote. But he had a presidential election coming up in five months. Without a vigorous display of American military might—and where would that have come from?—he would have lost the election. The Tom Dewey Administration would have had a mandate—to do what? Prosecute the war in the Pacific with more vigor, that's what.

Failure on D Day would not have spared Hitler the problems of a two-front war, because of the Allied forces still intact in Britain, always posing a threat. Still, he would have been free to transfer at least some of his army in France to his Eastern front. Perhaps more important, he could have used the D Day failure to split the strange alliance of West and East. How hard would it have been for Goebbels and the Nazi propaganda machine to convince Stalin that the capitalists were ready to fight to the last Russian? It is not inconceivable that Hitler and Stalin would have groped their way back to 1939, when they were partners, and reinstated the Nazi-Soviet pact. It is also possible that Stalin might have overrun Germany, then France, and the war in Europe would have ended with the Communists in control of the continent. The Red Army would have been on the English Channel. It is hard to imagine a worse outcome.

With the mounting Soviet threat and Operation Dragoon stalled in the South of France, Britain and the United States would have increased the severity of the bombing raids over Germany. A climax would have come late in the summer of 1945, with atomic bombs exploding over German cities. What a finish *that* would have been.

After that, things get extremely murky, as they always do in what if history the farther one goes away from a single event. The vacuum in a Central Europe devastated by atomic bombs would have sucked in armies from the outside—the Red Army from the east and the Allied armies from Britain. Would they have clashed? If so, would the United

States have used a bomb or two against the Soviets? Or would they have cooperated (as they in fact did in 1945), drawing a line through Central Europe?

In the Pacific in the summer of 1945, with the United States expending her atomic arsenal against Germany and Stalin free to transfer some part of his armies from the German to the Japanese front, the Red Army would have invaded the northern Japanese home islands. In this scenario, Japan would have been spared the atomic bombs but subjected to a Communist dictatorship in the northern half of a divided country. This was exactly what Stalin was planning and would have done if the Japanese had not surrendered to the Americans first. Had Stalin gotten into Japan, who knows when, and if, the Russians ever would have left.

That the consequences of a failure on D Day would have been catastrophic is obvious; what they would have been is anyone's guess; what stands out for me is that one of the consequences would *not* have been a Nazi victory. Almost surely, however, one of the consequences would have been a Communist victory in Europe. A Communist Germany, France, Low Countries, and Italy would have meant no NATO and a possibility of a Communist Great Britain. Relations with the Soviet Union would have been impossibly difficult and dangerous. That is a terrible prospect—but it might have happened if the Germans had beaten us on the beaches of Normandy.

◆ ROBERT COWLEY ◆

# THE SOVIET INVASION OF JAPAN

We now know that the Soviet Union, whose armies had raced across Manchuria and down Sakhalin Island in August 1945, intended to invade Hokkaido, the northernmost of the Japanese home islands. That invasion would have taken place two months before Operation Olympic, our invasion of the south island, Kyushu. While Emperor Hirohito's surrender declaration awaited the official signing in Tokyo Bay on September 2, the Soviets continued to gobble up territory and were poised to make a leap to Hokkaido. That amphibious landing would have been an improvised affair, but no matter: Of Cold War confrontations that almost happened but didn't, none is more frightening in its potential for fatal mischief.

It's not just that the Soviets would, in just over two weeks and at minimal cost, have picked up a large share of the Japanese marbles that had taken the Allies almost four years and thousands of lives to gather. If their landing force had established so much as a beach hold on Hokkaido—and American raiders had apparently gone ashore there with little resistance that summer—the Soviets would have had a legitimate claim to the island, a significant (and no doubt troublemaking) role in the formal surrender preparations, and a zone of a partitioned Tokyo. Just think of the Cold War implications of a Berlin in the Pacific. (Looking on the positive side, we could have blockaded the Soviet zone of Tokyo in response to Stalin's blockade of Berlin in 1948, which might have ended that crisis—or created a more general one.) Consider, too, the deadening effect of a Soviet Hokkaido on Japan's reconstruction—or the inhibiting effect that a hostile occupying force on a home island would have had on our decision to intervene in

Korea, using Japan as a base. The chances for future regional and international conflict seem infinite.

We are lucky that the Pacific war ended when it did. If the war had gone on for even a week or two longer, the entire East-West geopolitical situation might have changed irrevocably. In retrospect, it begins to seem that when Harry S Truman warned Stalin to keep away from the Japanese home islands—and the Soviet dictator reluctantly called off the Hokkaido operation at the eleventh hour—our accidental president made one of his most important decisions, one that ranks with his decision to drop the bomb.

If he hadn't, I might not be writing these words today.

✦   *Robert Cowley is the founding editor of* MHQ: The Quarterly Journal of Military History.

## DAVID CLAY LARGE

# FUNERAL IN BERLIN

*The Cold War Turns Hot*

For forty-five years, the divided city of Berlin was at the center of what David Clay Large calls, "The surreal game known as the Cold War." On a number of occasions, that game could have taken much different forms than it did, and Large examines the most serious of those scenarios. What if the Germans and Russians had made a second pact in 1944? Should we have tried to reach Berlin before the Russians in April 1945? Could we have done so? How real was the threat of a Soviet invasion of Western Europe in the late 1940s? What would have happened if we had used force to resist the Berlin blockade in 1948? Or if, on the other hand, the Allied powers had decided to abandon the city? What were the dangers of making Germany a "neutral" state, with an independent army, as Stalin proposed in 1952? What if President Eisenhower had forbidden Francis Gary Powers's fatal U-2 flight? Or if we had used force to stop the East Germans from building the Berlin Wall? Could Berlin, Large asks, have become the Sarajevo of World War III?

✦ *David Clay Large is professor of history at Montana State University and the author of such books as* BETWEEN TWO FIRES: EUROPE'S PATH IN THE 1930S, WHERE GHOSTS WALKED: MUNICH'S ROAD TO THE THIRD REICH, *and the forthcoming* BERLIN: THE METROPOLIS IN THE MAKING OF MODERN GERMANY.

As the Cold War dragged on and on, with a kind of ideological permafrost settling over much of the world, many people on both sides of the divide came to perceive the situation as reassuringly "normal," almost as a condition that could not have been otherwise. Believing that no substantial change would come, they imagined that change had never been possible. Yet of course there was nothing immutable about the forty-year standoff we call the Cold War; on a number of occasions it might have evolved very differently than it did, especially in the early phases.

Nowhere were the opportunities for alternative development greater than in Germany, and particularly in Berlin, where the hot war in Europe had ended. Here the wartime partners-turned-adversaries stood toe to toe and tank to tank.

And yet it is quite possible that the surreal game known as the Cold War might never have gotten going at all—or, at the very least, that Germany might not have been its primary arena and most coveted prize. And if Germany had been removed from the game, the nature of the contest would have been very different, as would the relative strengths of the players.

### The Allies Take Berlin

Everyone knows that the Nazis made a "nonaggression" pact with the Soviets in August 1939, which allowed the Germans to embark on their aggression against Poland in the following month. Less well known is that Hitler considered making another pact—this one a separate peace—with the Soviets in the fall of 1944. After suffering a series of military reversals beginning with Stalingrad, the Wehrmacht was on the retreat in the

East. Hitler's Japanese allies were urging him to make peace with the So-viets so that he might concentrate all his forces against the United States and Great Britain. The führer had resisted such advice in the past, but now, given the reversal in his military fortunes, he briefly contemplated going back to the negotiating table with his one-time ally. Had he actu-ally sought discussions with Moscow, the Soviets might have been pre-pared to listen. After all, while formally pledging allegiance to the unconditional surrender doctrine of the Grand Alliance, they had re-cently promised a group of anti-Hitler officers (the so-called "National Committee for a Free Germany") that Germany could retain its borders of 1937 if the Reich suspended its operations against the USSR.

In the end, of course, Hitler decided that the best way to reverse the tides that were running against him was to launch his ambitious Ar-dennes offensive in the West. Stalin, smelling German blood, abandoned any further considerations of a separate peace. But what if the Germans and Russians *had* made a second pact in 1944, thereby allowing the Re-ich to focus all its energies on the West? We cannot know whether Hitler would have been able to bring the Western powers to terms (a similar scenario in 1918 had of course not yielded this result), but the Reich would at least have avoided being invaded from the east as well as from the west. And Russia, for its part, would not have been in a position to exact its pound of German flesh, or, indeed, to gain its foothold in Eastern Europe. Without an Eastern European empire, it is highly doubt-ful that the Soviets would or could have mounted a challenge to the West in the postwar era at all.

Another chance to avert the Cold War came in spring 1945, as Allied armies overran Germany from west and east. Alliance strategists had ear-lier agreed that the Red Army would take Berlin, for this seemed dictated by the logistical situation. Moreover, it was planned that Berlin would lie within the Soviet zone of occupation in Germany. But the Western armies had made such rapid progress after crossing the Rhine in March 1945 that a push on to Berlin seemed not only possible but, to some Western military figures, advisable. As is well known, Field Marshall

354

Montgomery pressed General Eisenhower for permission to lead a "single, full-blooded thrust toward Berlin." Eisenhower rejected this appeal, insisting instead on a broad-front march through Germany that would leave Berlin to the Russians. The British were furious over this decision, contemptuously referring to Eisenhower's deference to Stalin as "Have a Go, Joe," an expression used by London prostitutes seeking custom from American GIs. The Berlin question rose again in mid-April when the American Ninth Army reached the Elbe, only fifty miles from Berlin. The American commander, William Simpson, now pleaded for the chance to take the Nazi capital, which he estimated he could reach in one day. But again Eisenhower said no, not wanting to risk possibly high American casualties for a target he did not consider strategically significant. When he learned of his commander in chief's decision, General George Patton, who had seconded Simpson's plea, was incredulous. "Ike, I don't see how you figure that out. We better take Berlin, and quick—and on to the Oder!" Eisenhower countered that Berlin, with its wrecked infrastructure and hordes of displaced persons, would be more a liability than an asset. "Who would want it?" he asked. To which Patton replied: "I think history will answer that question for you."

For half a century arguments have raged over whether Allied armies could have beaten the Russians to Berlin. The answer is: probably not. For all his cocky bluster, Montgomery was a very cautious and slow-moving general; he was an unlikely candidate to win a race to any goal save a pedestal on which he could prop himself. Simpson was a more energetic leader, but the troops he had led to the Elbe were mere spearheads; the real strength was much farther back. To make the final rush to Berlin, he would have needed large quantities of gasoline, which was in short supply, and he would have had to cross several water barriers, which would have taken time. The Russians, on the other hand, were fifteen miles closer to Berlin than the Americans, and they had a vastly larger force— some 1,250,000 men and 22,000 pieces of artillery. True, it ended up taking the Red Army about two weeks to conquer Berlin from the moment they launched their final offensive, but they would undoubtedly have tried to accelerate their pace had they seen that the Americans were racing for the city.

However, this being an essay on hypothetical scenarios, let us assume for the moment that the Western armies *could have* beaten the Russians to Berlin, or, failing that, at least gotten there at roughly the same time. Would it have made much of a difference? Again, the answer is probably no—unless the changed military situation in Berlin were accompanied by a wholly different geopolitical strategy on the part of the Western powers. Contesting the Red Army's ambition to conquer Berlin would have made sense only if imbedded within a comprehensive determination to reverse the earlier agreements allowing the Soviets spheres of influence in eastern Germany and Eastern Europe. None of the Western leaders, not even Churchill, contemplated such a plan of action in 1945.

Yet this option, or something close to it, was what Patton and Montgomery envisioned and even openly advocated. Once the war against Nazi Germany was over, Patton spoke of "pushing on to Moscow," if need be with help from what remained of the Wehrmacht, while Montgomery called for the immediate establishment of "a flank facing east." In Patton's view, the United States had come to Europe to give the peoples there the right to govern themselves. The Nazis had denied them this right, and now the Soviets were threatening to do so. Thus America's "job" in Europe was not yet done. "We must finish the job now, while we are here and ready," he declared in May 1945, "or [finish it] later under less favorable circumstances."

Patton and Montgomery's scheme was sheer political fantasy in the context of the time, but if the will had been there to attempt such a course (and emphatically it was not), the prospects for its *military* success were by no means nonexistent. At the end of the war in Europe the western parts of the Continent were occupied by the largest coalition army the world had ever seen. The American force stationed in western Germany alone numbered 1.6 million men. The draining war against Japan was about to end and America was about to come into sole possession (at least for a time) of the atomic bomb. The Red Army, while thick on the

356

ground, had been badly beaten up in its final assault on the Reich, and it was so low on food and supplies that it had to live off the land (much to the detriment of its relations with the Germans). A Western military campaign to expel the Red Army from Eastern Europe would obviously have meant more "hot war" in Europe—a hideous concept to just about everybody—but, just as obviously, it would if successful have removed the basis for a subsequent "cold war" waged over divided Germany and Europe.

There was another, rather more modest, alternative open to the Western powers that would have undercut the Soviets' position in Eastern Europe without necessarily pushing them back (again to quote Patton) "to the Asiatic steppes where they belong." The Americans, British, and French might have insisted upon occupying their sectors of Berlin at the same time that the Soviets set up their occupation regime, which was their right, and then demanded genuine Four-Power administration over the entire city, which was also their right. This would have prevented the Soviets from forcing Communist-dominated political institutions on their sector, a tactic that informally divided the city. Without secure control in eastern Berlin, the Soviets' position in the rest of eastern Germany would have been much weaker, which in turn would have weakened their grip on Eastern Europe.

### 1948: The Soviets Push West or Get Tougher in Berlin

Would Have, Could Have, Should Have. By 1948, the opportunities to avert the Cold War had vanished, for the simple reason that it had already started, and the chance to deny the USSR a power base in Eastern and Central Europe had also been lost. Indeed, the balance of power in the region, at least in terms of conventional military strength, had now shifted dramatically in favor of the Soviets. According to American intelligence estimates (now known to have been exaggerated), the Soviet land army totaled 2.5 million men organized in 175 divisions. Eighty-four were said to be stationed in the Soviet Occupation zone in Germany and in other "satellite" countries. Against this force the West could muster only sixteen divisions stationed in Germany, Austria, the Benelux countries, and France. Because of rapid demobilization and budget cuts, the great American army that had invaded Hitler's Europe was no more. U.S. units on the Continent were undersized, badly equipped, and poorly trained. The forces of America's allies were even worse. Pentagon analysts regarded the Dutch and Belgian troops as practically useless and were also unsure of France, which had a strong Communist Party and extensive colonial commitments. (It was for this reason that the Americans were so anxious to rearm the Germans in the Western zones: *they* at least could be counted on to know how to fight.) It was believed in some quarters that the Russian superiority in conventional forces might allow their armies to cross the Rhine in five days and reach the channel in two weeks. "All the Russians need to reach the Rhine is shoes," said American Under Secretary of State Robert Lovett.

We know now that the Soviets had no plans for an invasion of Western Europe in the first years after the war. Stalin believed that his nation was not yet ready to fight the West. Someday, maybe. But what if the Soviets had not been so patient, or so prudent? What if they had in fact put on their marching shoes and made a dash for the Rhine, or indeed the channel, in 1948? Could they really have made it as easily as some Western analysts feared?

In addition to sturdy shoes, they would have needed antiradiation suits. Given the relative weakness of their conventional defenses, the Western powers were prepared to meet a Russian advance across Central and Western Europe with an immediate deployment of tactical and strategic nuclear weapons. Contingency plans worked out by the service branches of the American military variously envisaged air attacks with atomic weapons on Russian troops and lines of communication, followed by surface counterattacks launched from bridgeheads in Spain and Sicily (the army's option); atomic attacks on the Soviet Union by long-range strategic bombers (the air force proposal); or tactical atomic strikes by carrier-based aircraft on Soviet ground troops (the navy preference). Admiral D. V. Gallery, one of the American defense planners, expressed the hope that tactical atomic attacks on advancing Russian ground troops in Central Europe would obviate the need for an all-out strategic bombardment of the Soviet motherland. "When the Russian armies are stopped short of the Rhine," he wrote, "their leaders and people may see that they had better negotiate a peace or else they will be in for a large-scale atomic blitz. In this case, with their armies halted east of the Rhine, the threat of the blitz might have more effect than the actual blitz itself if their armies were overrunning Europe."

Even if it proved unnecessary to extend the American "atomic blitz" to the Soviet motherland, a tactical nuclear campaign against Russian troops would have yielded horrendous "collateral damage" in Central and Western Europe, the very regions that Washington was hoping to save. Appreciation of this fact fueled "better Red than dead" arguments across Europe, especially in western Germany, where folks began to worry that Washington and its allies intended "to fight World War III to the last German."

Of course, instead of putting on their marching shoes, the Soviets put the squeeze on Berlin, where the West was particularly vulnerable. In response to Western measures aimed at creating a new West German state (which Moscow, still hoping to control all of Germany, resolutely opposed), the Soviets began, in spring 1948, to interfere with Western rail and road traffic between West Berlin and western Germany. The Russians could do this easily because the Western powers had neglected to secure guarantees of unlimited access across the Soviet zone to their sectors in Berlin. Western Allied access was now restricted to three roads, two railroads, a canal, and three air corridors. In June 1948, following the introduction of a new West German currency to Berlin, the Soviets dramatically tightened their squeeze by cutting the land ties between western Germany and West Berlin. Contrary to popular mythology, however, the Soviets did not isolate West Berlin entirely; they continued to allow trade between the western sectors of the city and the Soviet zone, and also the passage of goods and people from East to West Berlin. They left these avenues open largely because their own occupation zone was heavily dependent on trade with West Berlin. Moscow's immediate goal with its somewhat leaky "blockade" was to sabotage the creation of a West German state; down the line Russia hoped that the West would see the folly of keeping garrisons in such a vulnerable place as West Berlin and would simply pull out.

The Soviet initiative produced a sense of crisis in the Western Allied capitals, especially in Washington, which was expected to take the lead in determining an appropriate response. George Kennan, head of the State Department's policy planning staff, recalled: "No one was sure how the Russian move could be countered, or whether it could be countered at all. The situation was dark and full of danger." The situation seemed so dangerous, in fact, that Congress called for an immediate evacuation of American dependents from Berlin, and some politicians advocated military withdrawal as well. Intriguingly, so did General Omar Bradley, the Army chief of staff. Even before the Soviets cut the land ties to West Berlin, Bradley asked General Lucius Clay, American commandant in Berlin, whether it made any sense for the United States to hold its position there at the risk of war : "Will not Russian restrictions be added one by one, which eventually make our position untenable unless we ourselves were prepared to threaten or actually start a war to remove these restrictions?" he asked. And he added: "Here we doubt whether our people are prepared to start a war in order to maintain our position in Berlin and Vienna." Clay, by contrast, believed that the Soviet tactics were simply a bluff to push the West out of Berlin, but if it proved necessary to go to war to "save" Berlin, he was prepared to do so. "If Berlin falls," he warned, "Germany will be next. If we intend to defend Europe against Communism, we should not budge."

As it turned out, the West did not budge from Berlin, but it is worth asking what might have happened had Washington and its allies abandoned the city in 1948, which many then saw as the wisest course. Whether or not holding West Berlin was *militarily* significant in the emerging Cold War, it was certainly *politically* important to do so. By

1948 Western prestige was very much on the line in Berlin, and a pull-back there would have weakened the Allies'—especially the Americans'—leverage throughout Europe and the world. Washington was committed to helping Western Europe recover economically and regain its political confidence, goals that presupposed America's retention of its own high standing. The loss of prestige and clout that would inevitably have accompanied an abandonment of Berlin would have been particularly disastrous for American policy in western Germany, for this would have greatly strengthened the considerable opposition within Germany to the creation of a West German state. Konrad Adenauer, who favored the establishment of a "Bonn Republic" closely tied to the West, would not have been able to prevail without strong American backing. The formal division of Germany in 1949 was unpalatable to many Germans, but without it all of Germany would have been open to continuing destabilization efforts by the Soviets and their German Communist clients. A Germany "up for grabs" would have been far more dangerous than a Germany divided, painful as the division was.

As we know, instead of abandoning Berlin, the Western powers responded to the Soviet blockade by launching a massive airlift that supplied the western sectors of the city with everything from food and coal to candy for the kids (but not, as another myth would have it, with *everything* the Berliners needed to survive). The airlift, however, was not the only option that the West considered to "break" the Soviet blockade. Before the lift was decided upon, General Clay urged a much riskier gambit: the dispatch of an armed convoy from western Germany across the Soviet zone to West Berlin. He asked General Curtis LeMay, commander of the U.S. Air Force in Europe, to provide air support in case the Russians started shooting—an eventuality that LeMay did not expect but believed would provide a fine opportunity for a preemptive strike on all Russian air fields in Germany. "Naturally we knew where they were," he said later. "We had observed the Russian fighters lined up in a nice smooth line on the aprons at every place. If it had happened, I think we could have cleaned them up pretty well, in no time at all."

Of course "it" did not happen, since the convoy idea was quickly dismissed as unworkable. As Bradley cautioned: "The Russians could stop an armed convoy without opening fire one it. Roads could be closed for repair or a bridge could go up just ahead of you and then another bridge behind you and you'd be in a hell of a fix." Had the U.S. military adopted Clay's strategy and stumbled into a "fix," the only way to have gotten out of it, short of surrender, would have been to send larger forces to the rescue, with all the risks of escalation that this would have entailed.

The airlift option that was eventually selected may have made more sense than Clay's convoy, but it was hardly without its own risks. There was considerable concern that the Russians might try to shoot down the Allied planes or obstruct the lift in some other provocative way. Such concerns took on added urgency when, before the full lift was even operational, a Soviet fighter buzzed and then smashed into a British transport plane approaching Gatow airfield in the British sector. Both aircraft crashed, killing the Soviet pilot and fourteen passengers and crew on the British plane. Fortunately there were no more incidents of this kind, and the Soviets never opened fire on any of the airlift planes. They did, however, announce in September 1948 that they would hold air maneuvers over the Berlin area, and this produced a new war scare in Washington because it was interpreted as a possible preliminary to aggressive measures.

Had the Soviets in fact used force against the airlift (which apparently they never seriously considered), war would certainly have erupted, for the United States (and the British) fully intended to answer fire with fire. President Truman reassured Defense Secretary James Forrestal, who was worried that America might back down, that he would order the use of the atomic bomb if push came to shove over Berlin. Coming from the man who had ordered the atomic attacks against Japan in 1945, this promise had some heft to it. B-29 aircraft capable of delivering atomic bombs were duly dispatched to Britain. Reiterating earlier contingency plans, the National Security Council directed that the U.S. military should assume that nuclear weapons would be deployed if war broke out. Had the big trigger indeed been pulled, Berlin, the place from which Hitler had orchestrated World War II, would have become the Sarajevo of World War III. And this new conflict, in turn, might well have managed to become what World War I was supposed to have been but was not: "The War to End All Wars."

In the end, the Soviets lifted the Berlin Blockade not only because of the Allied airlift, but because the West imposed a counterblockade against the USSR. By early spring 1949 the Western measures were effectively disrupting what was left of East-West trade in Central Europe, which was vital to the Soviet economy. If the Russians had been economically stronger—if, so to speak, they had possessed adequate butter to go along with their plentiful guns—they could have imposed a tighter blockade on Berlin and withstood the counterblockade from the West. They could then have put the Allies in a truly desperate situation, since the airlift, even at its peak, had been incapable of simultaneously satisfying West Berlin's total requirements for food, coal, and industrial goods. Even without firing a shot, the Soviets could have forced the Western powers to chose between abandoning their post in Berlin or using their air power to drop bombs instead of bon-bons.

## A Dangerous Reunified Germany in 1952

By the early 1950s, the Soviets were obliged to reconcile themselves to the existence of a separate West German state, but there was a real question whether they would tolerate an *armed* West German state operating within the Western alliance structure, which was a major foreign policy goal of the Americans and the Adenauer government in Bonn. Washington had concluded that the most effective way to deter any Soviet expansionist ambitions in Europe was to bolster the West's conventional defenses with the addition of West German troops. At the time this option was raised, many in the Western camp, and in West Germany itself, feared that the very threat of West German rearmament might incite the Soviets to launch a preemptive strike. The Russians, after all, had had some rather intimate experience with German aggression in recent years and were known to dread nothing more than a new *Drang nach Osten* on the part of their old adversaries. Instead of deterring another major war, it was feared, German rearmament might well provoke one.

Such fears seemed all the more credible because the opening of the German rearmament debate coincided with the outbreak of the Korean War, which was widely understood to have been authorized by Moscow, and which many in the West believed might presage a similar fate for Germany, another nation bisected along the Cold War fault line. German newspapers spoke of the Asian crisis as a "test run" for Central Europe. Fearing a "German Korea," West Germans wallowed in apocalyptic fears. Parliamentarians stocked up on cyanide capsules so they could kill themselves rather than fall into enemy hands. Adenauer himself requested two hundred automatic pistols for the defense of his office in case of a Communist attack. Polls showed that over half the West German population believed that if the Communists came over the border, the Western powers would simply abandon the infant Federal Republic.

The West Germans' angst was hardly eased by pronouncements from the new Communist regime in East Germany. The GDR's Stalinist dictator, Walter Ulbricht, declared that Korea proved that "puppet governments" like Adenauer's could not expect to maintain themselves. North Korean leader Kim Il Sung, Ulbricht said, had shown how to reunify Germany, adding: "If the Americans in their imperialist arrogance believe that the Germans have less national consciousness than the Koreans, they have fundamentally deceived themselves."

Ulbricht's threats, of course, were nothing but bluster, but what if he *had* tried to play the role of a German Kim Il Sung? What if his backers, the Soviets, had attempted to rerun the Korean experiment in Germany?

In the first place, Ulbricht would not have had the same advantages as his North Korean counterpart. The East German *Volkspolizei*, which consisted almost exclusively of Wehrmacht veterans, had been built into a military force by the Soviets, but it was not nearly as strong as the North Korean People's Army, which dwarfed the South Korean army in firepower. The Communists' adversary in Europe was considerably more formidable than their target in Korea. Unlike South Korea, West Germany was occupied by three major powers, two of which were geographically close to the region of occupation. The Federal Republic did not yet have an army of its own, but its regional and border police forces would have been a match for the *Volkspolizei*.

To make any significant progress, a Korean-style operation in Germany would have had to involve the Soviets acting not just as backers and suppliers but as active combatants—the role that the Red Chinese took on in Korea after General MacArthur's push to the Yalu River. Had the Soviets thrown their own troops into West Germany in the early 1950s they would have had a harder time of it than in the late 1940s, because since that era the Western powers, especially America, had beefed up their security forces in the region. On the other hand, of course, the Soviets now had a nuclear capacity of their own, having built up a small stockpile of atomic weapons since successfully testing a bomb in 1949. Although they were not yet capable of delivering atomic warheads over long distances, in the event of war their plans called for deployment of tactical atomic weapons on the battlefield and strategic strikes against those targets in the rear that they were capable of reaching. In other words, unlike the Korean War, a "European Korea" would undoubtedly have gone nuclear right from the outset, with the nukes raining in from both sides. Most of Europe would have ended up looking like Berlin in 1945, with the difference that the ruins would have been radioactive.

Stalin, as we now know, had no intention of trying to forcefully reunify Germany under Communism at the time of the Korean War. But until his dying day, which fortunately came soon, he hoped by political means to wreak havoc in the parts of Germany he did not control. This was the chief motive behind his much-debated diplomatic note of March 1952, in which he proposed to the Western powers the establishment of a reunified and rearmed Germany that would be cleared of all foreign troops and pledged to unconditional neutrality. Stalin never meant for his initiative to be accepted, for he considered a genuinely neutral Germany far too dangerous. For that matter, he believed that even a reunified Germany *allied* to the Soviet Union, but not *controlled* by Moscow, was too dangerous. After all, the Germany that had invaded Russia in 1941 had been Russia's own ally, not an ally of the West. The real target of Stalin's famous note, then, was not the Western powers but West German domestic opinion. The idea was to thwart the development of a West German army and to destabilize the Adenauer government by dangling before the West Germans the tantalizing prospect of reunification in place of West integration. If, with a little diplomatic subterfuge, Stalin could bring down Adenauer and sabotage West German rearmament, this would be a great gain for the Soviet cause.

When Stalin made his "offer" to the Western powers he was assured by one of his diplomats that it would be rejected, which eventually turned out to be the case. But for a brief moment it looked as if the West might actually discuss this proposal, and some Western diplomats thought it had merit.

Let us imagine, therefore, that what Stalin proposed had actually become a reality. Let us imagine that Germany had been reunified not in 1990 but in 1952, and reunified not as a member of NATO but as a "neutral" state with its own independent army. As we know, some Western leaders, most notably Margaret Thatcher and François Mitterand, were not exactly enthusiastic about German reunification in 1990, fearing that the new nation might behave "irresponsibly," might quickly break free of its Western moorings and sail off to some new and terrible adventure. No doubt such fears underestimated the extent to which democratic and peace-loving ideals had taken root in Germany over the past forty years. In the early 1950s, however, there had been precious little time for such values to take root, and a remilitarized Germany without firm Western ties in those days would have been a dangerous vessel indeed, perhaps like the *Bismarck* out for revenge. Stalin worried about a new *Drang nach Osten*, but the *Drang* could have gone in the other direction as well, or in both directions at once, moderation never having been the Germans' strong point. The risk here was not so much of the Cold War turning hot, but of the old hot war reheating. Had this happened, the Cold War antagonists might have been obliged to join forces once again to put out the fires.

### Khrushchev in Berlin

As it happened, Stalin's diplomatic gambit was dismissed too soon to have the effect on West German domestic opinion that he had hoped for, and of course Moscow was ultimately unable to prevent Bonn's joining NATO, which occurred in 1955. Even before that point the Soviets, despairing of having much impact in the Federal Republic, had begun focusing on the political and economic consolidation of their own portion of Germany. Yet it proved impossible for the economically strapped USSR to develop its East German satellite into a convincing competitor with West Germany. Over the years East Germany fell further and further behind the West economically, while its political and cultural life remained locked in Stalinist rigidity.

Losing hope for a better life in their own state, East German citizens began decamping by the thousands for the West. The refugees tended to be young, well educated, and highly motivated—the kind of folks that no state can afford to lose.

Trying to stem the flow, the East German government sealed off its border with West Germany in May 1952. Berlin, however, remained an avenue of escape because people could still travel relatively unimpeded from the Soviet sector to West Berlin, and from there it was possible to travel on to West Germany. Tens of thousands more East Germans did just that over the next few years.

In 1958, Nikita Khrushchev decided that the time had come to eliminate West Berlin as a bolt hole for GDR citizens (and as a spy hole for the Western powers). In November of that year he issued an ultimatum: If the Western powers did not agree within six months either to vacate West Berlin, or, as an interim solution, to transform it into a "free city" with no ties to the West, he would sign a treaty with the GDR giving that

## CONFRONTATION AT THE BERLIN WALL

*In 1961, East German troops in full battle dress stand guard while Communist workmen construct tank traps and reinforce the Berlin Wall. Had the edgy confrontation with the West turned violent, the result might have been World War III.*

(Corbis/Bettman—UPI)

state control over all access rights in and out of Berlin. He believed that this threat had credibility because the West was as vulnerable as ever in its isolated outpost. Berlin, Khrushchev liked to say, was the "testicles" of the West, on which he had only to "squeeze" to make his adversaries scream. Moreover, unlike during the first Berlin crisis, Russia now not only had nuclear weapons but the missiles and planes to deliver them to Western cities, including those of the United States. "The leaders of the United States," Khrushchev confidently told his advisors, "are not such idiots as to fight over Berlin."

Khrushchev was wrong about this. American and other Western leaders had no desire to fight over Berlin, but they *were* idiots enough to do so if the issue at stake was their remaining in the city. So if the Soviets themselves had been such idiots as to try once again to squeeze the West out of Berlin, either through a new blockade of their own or one orchestrated by the East Germans, the West would have responded force-fully. Reviving Clay's old convoy idea of 1948, the Pentagon planned to send a platoon-size force across the GDR to Berlin; if the East Germans (or the Soviets) stopped it, a division-size unit would follow. Should even this force run into trouble, an all-out attack would result in which, as Secretary of State John Foster Dulles told Adenauer, "We obviously would not forego the use of nuclear weapons." Indeed, Pentagon strategy called for the United States to use its nukes *first*, to get in its best licks be-fore the Russian rockets flew. The plan also called for extensive use of tactical atomic weapons against enemy targets in Germany. Once again, this would have cause a great deal of collateral damage. Dulles admitted to Adenauer that NATO estimates projected 1.7 million Germans killed and another 3.5 million incapacitated. Even a valiant cold warrior like the German chancellor blanched at the prospect of sacrificing so much to hold the door open in a city he had never liked anyway. "For God's sake, not for Berlin," he gasped.

Hoping for a peaceful resolution to the German crisis, President Eisenhower invited Khrushchev to Camp David in September 1959. The talks were convivial but did not bring much substantial progress; Khrushchev dropped the six-month time frame for a solution to the Berlin crisis, while Ike agreed to a Four-Power summit in Paris in the coming spring on the German problem.

As it turned out, any possible movement at the Paris Summit was scuttled in advance by a momentous event high in the skies over the So-viet Union: the Russians' downing of an American U-2 spy plane on May 1, 1960. Eisenhower had been extremely reluctant to sanction such flights in view of the impending summit, but the CIA had convinced him that one last reconnaissance sortie was necessary to check on Soviet ICBM bases. The Russians were incapable of knocking down a U-2, the CIA promised, and for that very reason they were unlikely to complain publicly about the flights. Alas, the Soviets succeeded not only in bring-ing down the plane but in capturing the pilot, Francis Gary Powers, who had disobeyed orders to blow up his aircraft and kill himself if he ran into trouble. Failing to extract a public apology from Eisenhower for violating Soviet airspace, Khrushchev walked out of the Paris Summit.

This unhappy turn of events prompts one to ask what might have happened if Eisenhower had acted on his instincts and forbade the U-2 flight. Or, even if the flight had gone ahead as planned, what might have been the result had Powers done what he was supposed to do in the event of trouble, thereby depriving the Soviets of any evidence of American skullduggery?

Here the most likely alternative scenario does not seem very dramatic. Khrushchev had not expected any progress at Paris and was actually looking for a pretext to pull out of the summit. Had he not been able to find another excuse to do so he would have undoubtedly repeated his demands, and perhaps pounded his shoe on the table (which was his want when he got mad), but there is no evidence that Eisenhower was prepared to offer any significant concessions.

The reason Eisenhower was not prepared to dicker on Berlin was that he had come to believe that holding the Western position in the city was symbolically imperative (if militarily difficult). The alternative scenario he conjured up if the West voluntarily gave up Berlin, or was forcibly kicked out, was very dramatic indeed. He saw the old German capital as the first of a proverbial row of dominos, which would inexorably start tumbling if the West abandoned the city. Once Berlin went, Germany would be next, and once Germany fell, all Europe would tumble, and with Europe in Soviet hands, America would be unable to remain a democratic nation. As Eisenhower put it: "If Berlin fell, the U.S. would lose Europe, and if Europe fell into the hands of the Soviet Union and thus added its great industrial plant to the USSR's already great industrial plant, the United States would be reduced to the character of a garrison state if it were to survive at all." In other words, the loss of Berlin meant a fascist America.

Khrushchev hoped to do better with the new American president, John F. Kennedy, who was thought to be skittish on Berlin, which he had barely mentioned in his election campaign. Shortly after being elected,

Kennedy had admitted that of all his foreign policy challenges, Berlin had the greatest potential of forcing a choice between "holocaust and humiliation." The Russian leader knew that fear of Soviet retaliation against Berlin had been a primary motive for Kennedy's failure to save the Bay of Pigs invasion. JFK's cut-and-run approach in that instance convinced Khrushchev that the young American leader would fold even faster if he found his tender parts in a vise over Berlin.

Khrushchev got his chance to squeeze Kennedy hard on this issue during their first face-to-face confrontation at the Vienna Summit in June 1961. That meeting had hardly gotten underway when the Soviet premier began to complain about Washington's "impossible" position on Berlin and Germany. He declared that by staying in Berlin, remilitarizing West Germany, and feeding Bonn's dreams of reunification, America was creating the preconditions for a new world war. Why did not Washington simply accept the fact that Germany was now divided and Berlin a legitimate part of the new East German state? Glaring at Kennedy, he said that he wanted to reach an agreement "with *you*," but if he could not, he would sign a peace treaty with the GDR. Then "all commitments stemming from Germany's surrender will become invalid. This would include all institutions, occupation rights, and access to Berlin, including the corridors."

Before coming to Vienna, Kennedy had been advised by Allan Lightner, the U.S. minister in West Berlin, to tell Khrushchev that the "Soviets should keep their hands off Berlin." This, in effect, is what he proceeded to do. While thanking the chairman for being so "frank," he reminded him that "the discussion here is not only about the legal situation but also about the practical facts, which affect very much our national security." America was in Berlin "not because of someone's sufferance," but because "we fought our way" there. If the United States and its allies were to leave West Berlin, "Europe would be abandoned as well. So when we are talking about West Berlin, we are also talking about Western Europe."

Having expected at least *some* give from Kennedy, Khrushchev became increasingly angry, lecturing him like a schoolchild on the high stakes at play in Berlin. The former Nazi capital, he said, was "the most dangerous place in the world." Upping his ante in metaphors and mixing them prodigiously, he warned that he was determined "to perform an operation on this sore spot, to eliminate this thorn, this ulcer." By signing a peace treaty with East Germany, Moscow would "impede the revanchists in West Germany who want a new war . . ." Slamming his hand on the table, he shouted: "I want peace. But if you want war, that is your problem."

Despite a regimen of amphetamines prescribed by a quack doctor for his Addison's Disease, Kennedy remained calm under the barrage. "It is you, and not I, who wants to force a change," he replied. America would not abandon Berlin. If, as a result, Moscow followed through on its threats and signed a peace treaty with East Germany in December, it would be "a cold winter," he said grimly.

Actually, it might well have been a *hot* winter, for if the East Germans had indeed gotten their treaty and then decided to celebrate it by kicking the Western powers out of Berlin, they would have had a major fight on their hands. Although Kennedy was actually quite ambivalent about Berlin, fuming in private that it seemed "particularly stupid to risk killing a million Americans over an argument about access rights on an Autobahn," he was (like Eisenhower) determined that West Berlin would not be lost on his watch. He would send armed troops down that Autobahn rather than abandon the city to a fate under Communism. There would be no Bay of Pigs on the banks of the Spree.

On the other hand, if a solution could be found in Berlin that did not involve Western abandonment of the city, Kennedy was all for it. He even sympathized with the Soviets' dilemma in Germany—with their frustration at watching their prize client being steadily drained of its best and brightest citizens and thereby becoming a liability rather than an asset to Moscow. "You can't blame Khrushchev for being sore about that," Kennedy admitted.

A "solution" to the Berlin crisis was found on August 13, 1961. In the early morning hours of that day, East German soldiers and police began stringing bales of barbed wire along the sector line between West and East Berlin. Immediately thereafter the wire was replaced by concrete blocks. The Cold War's most famous piece of architecture was taking shape before the eyes of an astonished—and frightened—world. If ever the tensions of prolonged political confrontation were to boil over into open conflict, this seemed to be the most likely moment.

There was in fact considerable pressure on the Western powers to take forceful countermeasures. West Berliners, including West Berlin's dynamic young mayor, Willy Brandt, were demanding action. The Allied garrisons in Berlin, they said, should immediately knock down the horrible wall, with tanks if necessary. Unable to do much about the wall themselves, West Berliners vented their frustration by attacking the Soviet War Memorial in the British sector just to the west of the Brandenburg Gate. The Soviet soldiers guarding the memorial might have been killed had British occupation troops not rushed to their rescue—one of the more ironic twists in that confusing and emotional time.

If the Western Allied garrisons had indeed decided to move against the East German wall builders, as the West Berliners were crying out for them to do, the Soviets were prepared to react forcefully. They had circled Berlin with troops and put their rocket forces on high alert. They hoped that these measures would be sufficient to deter the West from taking any military action, such as attacking the wall or sending troops over the East German border. But if the deterrent did not work, the Soviet forces had orders not just to protect the nascent wall but to crush the Allied garrisons and the entire Western enclave in Berlin. This they certainly could have done, for Western military strength in the city was paltry compared to Soviet might in the area.

The Western powers, however, had no intention of knocking down the Berlin Wall. This structure, after all, did not force them out of Berlin, it merely fenced the East Germans in. President Kennedy, we should remember, had never made any commitments to the entire city of Berlin, only to *West* Berlin. (Later, when he gave his famous speech in the city, he really should have said: *"Ich bin ein West Berliner."*) By stabilizing the situation in East Germany, the wall promised to defuse a very explosive situation. Moreover, while it was something of an embarrassment for the West to stand idly by while the wall went up, the thing was a much greater embarrassment for the East Germans and Soviets, who had been forced to put a fence around their "Workers' Paradise" to keep all the workers from running away. (Not that the Communists admitted to this humiliation: they called the wall an "antifascist protective barrier," insisting it was there to protect the security of the GDR.) In short, the West could not have asked for a greater propaganda coup, a more striking symbol of the bankruptcy—economic and moral—of their Communist adversaries. Once the surprise over the wall's erection had subsided, the primary reaction in the Western capitals was a combination of *Schadenfreude* and relief.

Of course, no Western leader could admit to feeling *relieved* over the erection of the Berlin Wall. There had to be some demonstrative handwringing and expressions of solidarity with the people of Berlin. The Western powers all lodged formal complaints with their former Soviet ally. President Kennedy ordered Vice President Lyndon Johnson to fly to West Berlin to reassure the folks that America was still with them. (Johnson at first refused to go, on the grounds that it was too dangerous.) General Clay, much beloved in West Berlin for his tough stand during the 1948/1949 blockade, was pulled out of retirement and dispatched to Berlin as Kennedy's personal representative in the city.

Sending Clay to Berlin turned out to be almost a little *too* demonstrative, for he was determined to show that the United States could still exercise its traditional rights in the city despite the new wall, which in fact he hoped to tear down. When the East Germans started demanding that Americans show passports to enter East Berlin, Clay sent armed jeeps to Checkpoint Charlie to force their way across the border. He followed this up by dispatching ten M-48 tanks to the checkpoint. Alas, the Soviets responded in kind. For several hours the machines stood muzzle to muzzle, with nothing but a flimsy guardrail between them. All the armor was fully loaded, ready to fire. The American commander on the spot admitted that he was worried that a "nervous soldier might accidentally discharge his weapon." After seventeen hours, during which rumors abounded that the shooting was about to commence at any moment, but during which the only killing was scored by a pretzel seller who unloaded all his wares to the tankers on both sides, word came from Washington to pull back. Again, the Soviets responded in kind.

Secretary of State Dean Rusk later dismissed this contretemps as "the silly confrontation at Checkpoint Charlie brought on by the macho inclinations of General Clay." The gesture was certainly macho, but hardly without danger. Had an American tank opened fire, either deliberately or by accident, the Soviets would certainly have fired back, and the wartime partners of yesteryear, who sixteen years before had famously embraced at the Elbe, would have plunged headlong into a slug-out on the Spree, with the chances very good of a much broader conflagration.

We now know that, aside from MAD (the "Mutually Assured Destruction" that a major nuclear exchange was likely to bring), few factors did more to keep the Cold War cold than the erection of the Berlin Wall. After it went up, the level of East-West tension in Europe went down. With the Wall's evolution into a seemingly permanent fixture on the political landscape—not to mention a lucrative tourist attraction and the world's longest art gallery—the primary sites of ideological contention, where the Cold War might yet have turned hot, tended to develop away from Germany and Europe.

# ARTHUR WALDRON

# CHINA WITHOUT TEARS

*If Chiang Kai-shek Hadn't Gambled in 1946*

Τhe last *what if* of this book has to be one of the most poignant. But for the stubborn gamble of one man and bad judgment of another—a genuine American hero—the worst of the Cold War might not have happened. No Korea, no Indochinese War, no Vietnam War, no Cambodia, no crises in the Formosa Strait, no Red Scare in America. More than 100,000 American lives would have been saved, not to mention those of countless Asians. The gambler was the Nationalist leader Chiang Kai-shek—who, at the end of World War II, vowed to eradicate the Communist Chinese presence in Manchuria. Against American advice, he threw in his best troops and in the spring of 1946 seemed on the verge of victory. Suddenly Chiang called a halt, pressured by General George C. Marshall, who was trying to broker peace between the Nationalists and Communists. Chiang's Nationalists *would never regain their momentum, and three years later they would be forced off mainland China. But what if there had been two Chinas, both on the mainland?*

✦ *Arthur Waldron, a specialist in the history of modern China, is a professor of international relations at the University of Pennsylvania and director of Asian studies at the American Enterprise Institute.*

Imagine the Cold War without a "Red China." With its major theater in Central Europe, and that under firm Soviet control, it would probably have been a lot less frightening. Without a Red China supporting him, Kim Il Sung would never have dared invade South Korea. Without a Red China providing active sanctuary, Ho Chi Minh's Communists would never have succeeded in Indochina. Without the division between Communist mainland and anti-Communist Taiwan, the Formosa Strait would never have burst into flame in the 1950s and the 1990s. Without its volatile Asian theater acting as sparkplug, the Cold War would have been far different and far milder.

But is such a possibility even thinkable? It is—because the key event, the Communist conquest of China, would probably never have occurred without the fatal mistake that the nationalist Chinese leader Chiang Kai-shek made in the early summer of 1946.

Late the previous year, after the surrender of Japan, the generalissimo had begun to airlift his best troops into Manchuria, which the Communists had made their stronghold. The Reds resisted, but were no match for the Nationalists' battle-hardened veterans, who moved quickly north, smashing Communist resistance at Sipingjie in May 1946, after a month of fighting. Southern Manchuria was now recovered and the Communists were on the run: On June 6 the Communist commander, Lin Biao, was ordered to prepare the abandonment of Harbin, the security key to the north. But with advanced units already in sight of the city, Chiang Kai-shek halted his attack. It was an error from which he would not recover: He lost his momentum, the Communists had time to regroup and reorganize. His army never reached Harbin. Three years later it was thoroughly beaten and its remnants fled to Taiwan. Chiang had grasped the proverbial defeat from the jaws of victory—with enormous consequences for the rest of Asia felt to this day.

What explains Chiang's action? In two words: American pressure. Chiang's mistake was effectively forced on him by the revered U.S. Army General George C. Marshall, who was then in China on the mission impossible of brokering peace between the Communists and Nationalists. And what of Marshall? He is rightly valued as a soldier and statesman, but in China he was miscast and outmatched. This brave and honorable man walked uncomprehending into the snake pit of Chinese politics. He intended to bring peace, but what he really began was the Cold War in Asia. It was all a terrible surprise.

No one expected the Communists to win in China when Japan abruptly surrendered—reeling under the twin blows of Soviet invasion of Manchuria and U.S. atom bombing of the home islands. When hostilities suddenly ceased, the Communists were mostly holed up in their wartime base at Yanan, far away from the fighting in northern Shaanxi, and in any case lacked heavy military forces. All the foreign powers—the USSR included—recognized Chiang Kai-shek's government at Chongqing as China's sole legitimate authority.

Stalin certainly did not expect the Communists to win. At Yalta he had agreed to secret provisions that gave his forces in Manchuria a privileged administrative and military position and made no reference to Chinese sovereignty in the area. In fact, many people expected Moscow simply to annex the territory, over which Russia and Japan had been struggling since the end of the nineteenth century, and which, in hostile hands, posed a major threat to the Soviet Far Eastern province and the great military port at Vladivostok.

Such reallocation of territory had already been agreed to meet Soviet demands in Europe. Why not in Asia as well? Perhaps the clearest signal came in the wartime best-seller *People on Our Side*, by the fellow-traveling American journalist Edgar Snow. He was almost certainly acting on inside information when he warned his readers to expect Moscow to make just such changes in northeast Asia.

The problem was that the Chinese government would bitterly resist such a solution. Having gone to war with Japan over Manchuria in the first place, it could hardly stand by while the Soviets simply took over Japan's role. So instead of focusing on China proper, where he had problems enough, Chiang Kai-shek and his government turned their attention to the northeast.

Chiang Kai-shek now made his reputation as a soldier in 1925 to 1928 when he recognized a brief window of opportunity in China's north and gambled his southern army on a lightning invasion—the so-called "Northern Expedition," which overthrew the military government in Beijing and established the Republic of China regime at Nanjing. It was a classic *suzhan sujue* operation—"rapidly fought and rapidly decided"—which had long been the preference of Chinese strategists. Assessing the tendencies and propensities of the situation *(shi)* he identified a moment of opportunity *(ji)* and unleashed a strategem *(mou)* designed to use it to win—striking fast, winning a key victory at Wuhan against the north's best, and then snowballing to victory. Chiang was only the second leader ever to conquer China from the south; no mean achievement. His strategy for Manchuria in 1946 rested on the same basic concept.

But Chiang was also controversial and, although Washington was his indispensable ally, he was disliked by many Americans. He spoke not a word of English and was stiff and reserved with foreigners: "Vinegar Joe" Stillwell, the American commander in the China-Burma-India theater, despised him, calling him "the Peanut." Under Chiang's leadership, China had been ruined in a war of futile resistance to Japan—and Chiang was personally blamed for rampant corruption, black marketeering, and violence. The untried Communists looked better to many people, including lots of intelligent and articulate foreigners.

As for the Communists in remote Yanan, strategic opportunity knocked in August 1945 when the Soviet Red Army swept into Manchuria. Strategically, Yanan was nowhere: The Communists had gone there to escape the Nationalist "bandit extermination" campaigns of the 1930s. Its great advantage was proximity to the Mongolian People's Republic, at that time a wholly owned subsidiary of the USSR, effectively under Soviet secret police control—and a final sanctuary should the Nationalists threaten again.

Manchuria was altogether different. Strategically, the territory had always been a key to the control of China proper: the jumping-off place for conquest dynasties, most recently in 1644 when the Manchus, who had given the territory its name, sent their armies through the passes to Beijing and beyond—to establish the great Qing dynasty, which lasted until 1912.

So the decision was easy to move the Communist administration and army into Manchuria behind the Soviet forces. Indeed, the Soviets helped with the move, some of which took place along Soviet-controlled railway lines. But there was a problem. The Soviets paid lip service to the idea that Manchuria was legitimately a part of Nationalist China—and did not recognize the Communists officially at all.

But Red Chinese and Soviets were all Communists—brothers in the international Party—so ways were found to coexist. The Chinese forces were given quarters outside the capital city; they were renamed "local self-defense forces," and their liaison with the Soviets, though good, was "informal." And the Soviets prevented Nationalist forces from entering Manchuria to accept the surrender of the Japanese there.

With the Soviets in control militarily, the Chinese Communists settled down in Manchuria, putting their primary effort into developing a strong civil administrative network. They did not initially concentrate on building up their army. Instead they opened party headquarters in every Manchurian village and town. Probably they expected the Soviet forces to shield them indefinitely.

Meanwhile, the Nationalists—panic stricken about ever getting the Soviets out of Manchuria—embarked on an intensive diplomatic campaign to secure Soviet withdrawal, which eventually succeeded. The stage was set for Chiang Kai-shek's fatal decision.

Suppose Chiang had not contested Soviet and Chinese Communist control of Manchuria? How might Asia have developed? The answer is that something like an East Asian East Germany—a "Chinese Demo-cratic People's Republic"—would almost certainly have emerged in Manchuria, in addition to the Korean Democratic People's Republic that was actually installed in Pyongyang by Soviet troops. But unlike the "People's Republic of China"—that Mao Zedong and his army established in 1949 after a long civil war, this northeastern Red China would have been firmly under Moscow's thumb.

Many Chinese Communist leaders had been educated in the Soviet Union; more still looked to the USSR as the model for China, believing, as Zhou Enlai put it, that "the present of the USSR is the future of China." Even Mao—uneducated, untraveled, and without Soviet connections—instinctively "leaned to one side," toward the USSR, early in the Cold War. So the Chinese Party leadership would almost certainly have settled for—more than that, welcomed—the opportunity to function like Ulbricht's Germans to create a Socialist China under Soviet auspices. They expected as much: That is what their emphasis on adminis-tration tells us.

And if Mao had proved intransigent, as Tito did in Yugoslavia? When East European Communists proved difficult, they often disappeared or were "suicided" or otherwise gotten rid of. The same would probably have happened in a Soviet-influenced Chinese client state. Mao's control of the party was by no means absolute. Plenty of Communists hated him. In the early 1950s the USSR evidently supported plots in Manchuria against Beijing. Those failed. But under these circumstances, Moscow would probably have gotten its way. Yugoslavia, after all, was geographi-cally well defended and had its own army—which was never under So-viet control. But Manchuria was almost surrounded by the USSR and Soviet naval and military facilities had been guaranteed even by the Na-tionalists.

Moreover, the Red China in Manchuria would almost certainly have done well—at least initially. Unlike much of the Chinese heartland, Manchuria was rich: Its land was fertile and not overpopulated; its re-sources, including coal and steel, were abundant; an extensive industrial plant, built by the Japanese, was already in place; a superb port at Dalian linked it to the maritime world, while the Chinese Eastern railway linked up with the Soviet rail network. Its economy was already developed.

As the Chinese civil war heated up, American advisers to Chiang Kai-shek advised him not to try to take Manchuria. They recognized that it would be a risk to reach too far and might well undermine his good chances of keeping control of China proper. Moscow probably expected the United States to keep Chiang in line on this point and thus assure a non-Communist regime in China proper. Such a situation would push the Communists in Manchuria into Moscow's arms.

Good boundaries make good neighbors. That was clear as World War II ended in Europe, and the Allied and Red Armies advanced up to—but not beyond—agreed lines of demarcation. Local hotheads—whether Communist or anti-Communist—had no luck in embroiling the great powers in conflict. The only dangerous ambiguities were over Berlin—and Yugoslavia, for reasons of its own. Otherwise what could have been a collision of two massive armies proved remarkably quiet.

Had the Asian issues been hashed out as carefully in advance, the same might have happened there. The partition of China into a small Communist and a large non-Communist state could have been agreed by the powers in a way that would have removed from Mao's hands—as from Kim Il Sung's and Ho Chi Minh's—the leverage to bring great power patrons into local disputes. The result would have been a more peaceful Asia.

"You started it!" That was one of the Communist charges leveled as China's civil war escalated into massive fighting between 1945 and 1949—and it had merit. For Chiang's Manchurian expedition was the flare that set the whole country aflame.

At the war's end, Chiang's best troops were in the China-Burma-India theater (CBI). Veterans of the losing and then winning campaigns against the Japanese in the Southeast Asian jungles, they had been reequipped and trained by the Americans in India. They also had some of the brightest and bravest Chinese officers, notably General Sun Lijen, a graduate of the Virginia Military Institute. The New First and New Sixth armies were put into Manchuria: These forces were as tough as well-tempered steel, incomparably stronger than anything the Communists had. Furthermore they had powerful artillery that far outmatched the lightly armed Communist guerrilla forces.

Chiang also had an air force. He shared the Chinese fascination with the most advanced military technology and from the start of the war with Japan had temperamentally favored the airpower visions of General Claire Chennault over the earthbound soldiering urged by Roosevelt's envoy, Stillwell.

So a plan modeled on the "Northern Expedition" of the late 1920s began to take shape in Chiang's mind. The Communists in Manchuria were not expecting war. If the Soviets could be persuaded to withdraw and then the heavy divisions from CBI thrown in, the Nationalist armed force would almost certainly cut through the Communists in Manchuria like the proverbial knife through butter. Meanwhile, airpower could overcome the nemesis of land war in Asia—logistics. Using air transport, Chiang ought to be able to leapfrog his forces behind the Communists and connect and resupply scattered garrisons in the vast territory.

It was a vision not unlike the one that the United States would take to Vietnam two decades later, and initially it seemed to work. The Soviets agreed to withdraw and the Nationalists poured in, first by air, starting in the autumn of 1945. They rolled over all before them. The Communist forces were caught by surprise, unprepared and unequipped for this kind of battle. Up and along the railway line, the Nationalist forces moved north. At Sipingjie, a key junction midway up Manchuria, they fought a month's pitched battle before the Communists cracked: Lin Biao, their commander, threw human wave after human wave against the Nationalist firepower, including 100,000 factory workers from Changchun, a truly desperate throw. By May 18, 40,000 Communists—half their force—were dead and Lin fled to the north.

What followed next is rather like Hitler's famous "Halt Order," which stopped the Wehrmacht as it closed in on the defeated British at

Dunkirk—turning what should have been a decisive German victory into a strategic defeat.

General Marshall was at this point attempting the impossible task of brokering a coalition government between Mao's Communists and Chiang's Nationalists. Nowhere had it been agreed that Chiang would not invade Manchuria. But the Communists at the talks objected vociferously, maintaining that by his surprise attack Chiang had undermined the trust and cooperation necessary for a peaceful resolution. Marshall secured one truce in January but it broke down quickly; now the Communists pressed him to act, for they realized that he—and not their own army—was the only force left that could stop Chiang.

Marshall listened. With all the power of a sole ally, rich and overwhelmingly strong in a ruined world (and in his own mind, some unrealistic ideas), Marshall pressured Chiang to halt his advance—and Chiang did.

When his incredulous commanders begged him to reconsider, telling him that Harbin in Nationalist hands ensured a total victory over Communist military forces in Manchuria, Chiang became very angry. To his supreme commander he said, "You say that taking the city will be easy, but if you knew the reasons why we can't take it, then you would understand why not taking it is not easy at all." Later Chiang would call this the worst mistake he ever made in dealing with the Communists.

Had the Chinese leader refused Marshall's request, one can imagine him actually succeeding in his attempt to deliver a knock-out blow to the Communists and presenting the world with a fait accompli that would have won not only Washington, but Moscow as well, to his side. Or one can imagine his initial triumph going bad, as the Communists reorganized and attacked his extended supply lines. One thing is certain, though: The decision to halt would remove the one chance Chiang had of actually winning the war militarily.

The military momentum of the Nationalist advance was lost. Like Sisyphus, the Nationalist army pushed almost to the top but not quite—and then began to fall back. Suppose, now, that Chiang had not contested

Manchuria. His forces concentrated in China proper would have been much stronger—probably decisively so. Furthermore, his relations with both the Soviet Union and the United States would have been greatly improved. Marshall's fury would then have turned on the Communists if fighting continued in China proper while the Soviets, seeing that Chiang was willing to allow them effective control over the northeast, would probably have cooperated with him to corral the Chinese Red Army and government within the northeast territory.

Mao's forces would have been effectively at the mercy of the Soviet garrisons in Manchuria and as their administration and economy developed, increasingly integrated with Soviet authority and economy in Siberia and the Far East.

Furthermore, this would have been to the liking, if not of Mao himself, who dreamed of ruling all of China, certainly of most of the leadership. Revolution across China would, in any case, not have been ruled out—only postponed until, as the Soviet economists confidently predicted, a global collapse of capitalism dropped the remaining non-Communist states into their lap, like the proverbial ripe fruits.

Such had been Stalin's argument when the French Communist party asked about taking power after the defeat of the Nazis. Wait a few years, he said, relying on the prognostications of his economic gurus. A world crisis is coming. In the meantime, don't unnecessarily stir up the British and the United States.

But of course the gurus were wrong. The global depression that he and others, including many American economists, expected would follow the Second World War as the Great Depression had followed the First, never happened. Instead the free-market economies revived, first slowly, then—as was remarked at the time—miraculously. In Germany came the *Wirtschaftswunder*, or "economic miracle," and in Japan a remarkable climb from the geegaws manufactured in the occupation period to the highest of high tech and high quality production. Hong Kong, a sleepy and underpopulated colonial port adjoining southernmost China, rocketed from abject poverty to relative affluence—until by the end of the century its per capita income surpassed that of Britain, its erstwhile colonial master.

Suppose that Chiang had not invaded Manchuria and that instead a stable partition had taken place. Shanghai—the greatest economic center of East Asia—would have been free to trade in the 1950s, instead of shut tight by both the antiforeign Chinese Communist regime and the Cold War Western embargo. The immense markets and resources, human and material, of the Yangzi valley would have joined in the Asian economic miracle. When China abandoned the worst of Communist economic policy in the 1980s and opened to world trade the results were staggering—double-digit growth rates, massive exports, record-breaking economic boom. It could all have happened twenty years sooner, if the Nationalists had continued to hold China proper.

And that boom would have transformed the strategic equation in China just as it did in Germany and Korea. In Korea the north had traditionally been industrial and the south agricultural, so partition initially favored Pyongyang. But South Korea eventually outstripped the north totally—so that by the 1990s the Communist half was a starving wreck, while the southern was a prosperous democratic state. Likewise the failure of the East German economy and West Germany's success prepared the way for the unification of the two states after 1989.

Manchuria was the Chinese center of heavy industry, of mining, of steelmaking. Initially China proper had nothing to match it. But suppose partition had worked. By 1960 or 1970 the south of China would almost certainly have been surging ahead. Like the industrial resources Communism inherited or created elsewhere, Manchuria would soon have turned into a rusting junkyard under socialist management; just as surely, South China would have become a "dragon economy."

Chiang and the Nationalists would have been more than compensated for their initial sacrifice. By the time the generalissimo died in 1975, his China would have decisively dwarfed the "Red China" in the northeast.

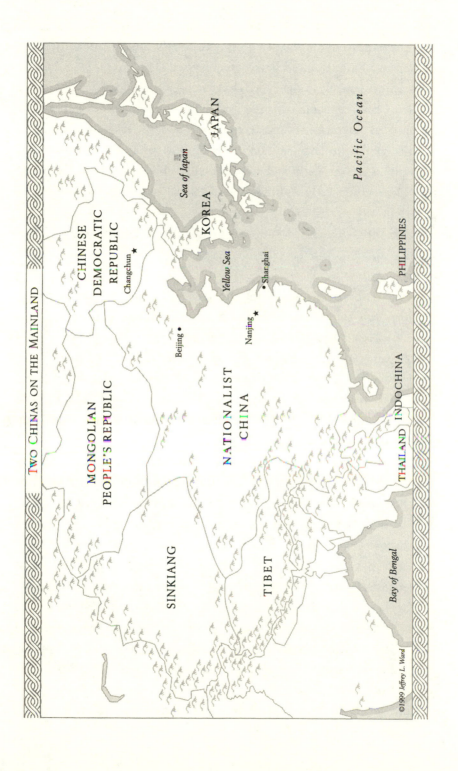

CHINESE
DEMOCRATIC
REPUBLIC

Changchun ★

KOREA

Sea of Japan

JAPAN

Pacific Ocean

MONGOLIAN
PEOPLE'S REPUBLIC

Beijing ●

Yellow Sea

● Shanghai

Nanjing ★

NATIONALIST
CHINA

PHILIPPINES

SINKIANG

TIBET

THAILAND

INDOCHINA

Bay of Bengal

©1999 Jeffrey L. Ward

The pattern of current relations between the small Nationalist-ruled Taiwan and Beijing would have been reversed. The leverage would have been almost entirely in the hands of the non-Communist China proper—as "Red China" became dependent on its prosperous southern neighbor for markets, investment, and technology—and increasingly affected by cross-border radio and television and the greater degree of freedom in the south. Like the German Democratic Republic facing West Germany, the "Democratic People's Republic of China" would have been beleaguered by the 1970s.

But there was no partition. Chiang threw his troops into Manchuria—and almost as soon as that move was made, his dream began to crumble.

The "halt order" was arguably the biggest setback, but other dangers lay just below the surface. Above all it was unrealistic to expect the Communist forces simply to roll over and play dead. Manchuria was their chosen territory, for which they had no choice but to fight—"death ground," as Sun Zi calls it. And fight they did. Tens of thousands of Communists died in the long attritional battle that followed from 1946 to 1948. Lin Biao, the Communist commander, shed rivers of blood to stop the Nationalist advance by putting soldiers in its path.

Lin and the Communists also did what had to be done to improve their forces and match the Nationalists' advantages. Soviet and abandoned Japanese artillery were incorporated into Communist forces; an artillery school was created. As the Communist forces became heavier, the battles became costlier for all. Chiang's troops could no longer count on outclassing their opponents; with antiaircraft artillery directed against Nationalist air transport, the key lines of communication that linked the Nationalist-held cities in Manchuria were cut. Hundreds of thousands of Chiang's best troops were effectively hors de combat. They were tied down, in futile attritional defense of an overextended position, wasting away and unable to concentrate or participate in the active war that would lead to decision.

In Manchuria, the Communists had two critical advantages. First, this was their primary theater—the key, as they well understood. They could concentrate on it—while Chiang had to chase all over the territory of China whenever the Communists launched an attack. Second, the Soviet position in north Manchuria provided active sanctuary for the Communist forces. They could be supplied easily and take refuge when necessary. The Nationalist lines of communication, by air and sea, were by contrast fragile and easily broken.

The Communists drove these advantages home. They stirred up guerrilla insurgency in Shandong to draw off Nationalist forces that could otherwise have gone to Manchuria. They pinned down Nationalist forces all over China in positional defense—and then, as they strengthened their own conventional strength, gradually chewed them up.

The result was like a termite attack on a once-strong building. Appearances were not bad for the Nationalists from 1945 to 1947. Seemingly impressive victories were scored; the appearance of rule existed over most of China's territory. But the military ratios were moving against them. As time passed they were growing weaker and the Communists stronger. In 1948, Manchuria was lost as hundreds of thousands of Nationalist troops, cut off and isolated in dozens of garrisons, had no choice but to surrender. In China proper they could have been the margin of victory. Now the tide turned the other way. In 1949, a powerful series of blows from the now-superior Communist forces brought the whole Nationalist military edifice crashing down.

The shock of the Communist victory in China—the famous "loss of China"—kick-started the McCarthy period, the roughest part of the Cold War in the United States, and it was followed—literally a few months later in June 1950—by the North Korean invasion of South Korea. This crisis was far worse than anything that had happened in Europe and it threw relations with Moscow into deep freeze.

We now know that the astonishing Communist victory in China inspired Kim Il Sung in his blitzkrieg against Seoul. We also know that Stalin and Mao signed off on the Korean invasion, both persuaded that Kim Il Sung might well succeed. Having sat back and done nothing as

China fell, after all, how likely was Washington to do anything when little South Korea was under attack? But a successful partition in China would probably have meant that Kim would never have made his plan. And had he, surely the partition in China would have been a very strong argument against it? The Korean War made the Cold War icy—but without the Manchurian gamble, no such war would ever have been fought.

The defense of Taiwan also drove a wedge between Moscow and Washington. Without a Communist victory in China, this problem would never have existed.

Finally, with an anti-Communist China on its borders, Vietnam would never have gone Communist. Chinese advice and supply, as well as active sanctuary, were critical to the Vietminh victory over the French at Dien Bien Phu. Without a divided Vietnam there would never have been an American role in Vietnam—and the exacerbation of the Cold War that followed. Indeed, the "wars" in the Cold War were almost entirely in Asia, and they grew out of the big Asian Communist victory in China. Asia was the motor that moved the Cold War from crisis to crisis.

A milder Cold War. A bigger and stronger non-Communist world. An earlier and more rapid economic recovery in Asia. A huge Eastern European-style bankruptcy on the USSR's eastern borders, as well as in the Red Chinese state. It all probably adds up, in our counterhistory, to an earlier collapse of Communism and a more decisive end to the Cold War.

Keeping the Red Chinese client state afloat would have drained Moscow's coffers. The Communist regime would have grown weaker. Had Mao been eliminated, a far less charismatic leadership would have been in place, one supported by the Soviets.

By the 1970s, the stage would have been set for "Free China" to absorb "Red China" economically, politically, socially—in every respect, just as dramatically as West Germany swallowed East Germany, and perhaps sooner. What an irony that would have been—for Chiang Kai-shek and his regime would then have achieved their long-standing goal of national unification, precisely as the result of an action—not invading Manchuria—that at the time they thought would have split their country irrevocably.

# A QUAGMIRE AVOIDED?

If President Eisenhower had approved Operation Vulture to rescue the encircled French fortress of Dien Bien Phu, the French might have won the battle and the war, averting a second Vietnam War, in which America was mired for a dozen years. Dien Bien Phu was a small mountain outpost in northern Vietnam, on the border with Laos. French forces occupied the town in late 1953 to cut off Vietminh supply lines and to maintain a base against enemy raids. General Giap, the Vietminh military leader, saw this isolated base, close to the borders of China and Laos, as a sitting duck. He proceeded with classic encirclement tactics, surrounding the French with 40,000 men, cutting off all the roads into the base, so that it could only be supplied by air, and bringing up heavy artillery to pound the French lines. Operation Vulture contemplated sending B-29s from bases in Okinawa and the Philippines to carpet bomb Vietminh positions around Dien Bien Phu. In January 1954, the French did appeal to Ike for twenty B-26 bombers and 400 technicians, and he gave them half those numbers. In March, the president agreed to furnish the French with some C-119 Flying Boxcars that could drop napalm and reveal Giap's artillery positions. But when the French asked for two or three atomic bombs, Ike said no. The mantra in Congress was "No more Koreas." Officers in the Pentagon had already formed a betting pool on when the fort would fall. It surrendered on May 7, in one of those decisive defeats that radiates far beyond the military importance to break the will of a nation and force the conclusion of a war. Two months later came a cease-fire and the partition of Vietnam. A decade later came America's turn to fight a war in Vietnam.

✦ *Ted Morgan, who served in the French army, is the author of* A COVERT LIFE, *a biography of the Communist leader (and later, CIA agent) Jay Lovestone.*

## ✦ ROBERT L. O'CONNELL ✦

# THE END

How quickly we forget. Having passed most of our lives in the shadow of the nuclear standoff and only recently found our way out of the Cold War and into the sunlight, we succumb to sweet oblivion. Who today seriously asks: "What if the sword had dropped?" Should the Cuban Missile Crisis be broached, wise heads stand ready to reassure us that its real lesson was how well deterrence and strategic communication really worked. Perhaps. But they fail to mention another crisis of a similar magnitude—an event in which there was not only no communication, but, in fact, one side barely knew what was happening.

In early November 1983, during a NATO exercise known as Able Archer, American and British monitors were astonished to note a sharp increase in the volume and urgency of Eastern bloc communications, signs indicative of warnings sent of an imminent nuclear attack. It was no mirage. The occupants of the Kremlin were on the edge of believing that the West was about to launch a preemptive nuclear strike.

The delusion went back to the early 1980's when Vladimir Kryuchkov, then head of the KGB and future leader of the failed against Gorbachev, became convinced that the Americans were planing a surprise attack—presumably with their new Pershing II missiles, whose earth-penetrator warheads and short flight times seemed tailor-made for a decapitating first strike. On his advice, the Soviet Union's leadership mobilized their intelligence assets in an antic campaign to find signs of war preparations.

These fears were without substance. The Pershing II's were yet to be deployed and had never been tested at ranges necessary to hit Moscow. This didn't matter to the antique leaders of the Kremlin presiding over a crumbling empire—particularly their chairman Yuri Andropov, graduate of the KGB and a sick man. They responded to their system's mounting troubles with anger and unbridled suspicion.

U.S.-Soviet relations continued to spiral downward. By June 1983, Andropov described them as "marked by confrontation unprecedented in the entire postwar period." Less than two months later, a Russian interceptor deliberately shot down a passenger-laden Korean airliner, supposedly on a spy mission. By November, Andropov was near death, and just who was in charge is open to question. But apparently his colleagues in the Kremlin viewed Able Archer as potentially the last straw.

Days passed and nothing happened. Able Archer wound down and still nothing happened. One by one the Eastern bloc units stood down from their alert. Gradually, it must have dawned on the Soviet leaders that they would live to see 1984. Meanwhile, in the United States, years would pass before there was an understanding of why the East had reacted in such a bizarre fashion. Once again, we had been eyeball to eyeball—only this time one side was hallucinating and the other was dozing. We did make it through, but history had been on cruise control. The war scare of 1983 might have been the end.

✦ *Robert O'Connell is the author of a history of the origin of war,* RIDE OF THE SECOND HORSEMAN.

〰〰〰〰〰〰〰〰〰〰〰〰〰〰〰〰〰〰〰〰〰

# INTRODUCTION

One of the troubles with history as it is studied today is that people take it too se-riously. I don't mean to say that history isn't serious business, or that history doesn't matter. History is not, to invoke the ghost of Henry Ford, "the bunk." We need history. "Life must be lived forward," the philosopher Kierkegaard observes, "but can only be understood backwards." But that understanding should not be treated like an exigent dose of milk of magnesia. I have real qualms about the way history is dispensed.

The solemnity of history assails us from the time we are schoolchildren. We are force-fed history as social studies, an approach in which all races, nationalities, and sexes are given equal time: Everyone must be included, no one can be of-fended. This surrender to special interests is not just distorting but boring. History involving great people or pivotal events is out of fashion. Broad trends, those waves that swell, break, and recede, are everything these days. We are left with the impression that history is inevitable, that what happened could not have hap-pened any other way, and that drama and contingency have no place in the gen-eral scheme of human existence.

What is too often lost is a sense of history as narrative, a vast and ever-evolving novel. A young woman I know was taking a course at an Ivy League university about women in pre-Revolutionary America. After we'd discussed matters such as compensation and race and gender roles, I casually asked if she had ever read Francis Parkman. "Who's Parkman?" she asked. I would have been more bothered by her answer if I didn't know that the best historians today tend not to be just fine writers but engaging storytellers. There is no reason why history can't entertain, especially when the object is to turn people on to a subject whose presentation at some point early in their lives may have turned them off. Parkman, remember, was the quintessential storyteller.

These thoughts bring me to the present volume, the sequel to What If?, which appeared two years ago. The time has come for a new set of answers to the historian's favorite secret question. That first book was entirely military. Armed confrontation provides counterfactual history with its most natural arena—but it is by no means the only one. Nonmilitary events also have a place in any examination of what might have happened. Consider four moments of the greatest magnitude in human history, as we do in these pages. What if Jesus had not been crucified and Pontius Pilate had decided to set him free? What if Martin Luther had been burned at the stake for his heretical views—and what if his chosen instrument of combat, the printing press, had not yet been invented? What if, more than half a century before Columbus, Ming emperors had not called back the huge fleets of the eunuch admiral-explorer Zheng He but had allowed him to continue his voyages along the African coast? What if the Chinese and not the Spanish had discovered the New World? Or what if, in 1917, the Germans had not sent Lenin to Petrograd on the famous "sealed train"—what if he had arrived in Russia too late to lead a successful revolution?

But consider too a seemingly trivial rebuff that would have enormous consequences, namely the rejection of Franklin Delano Roosevelt's offer of marriage to a beautiful debutante (who happened to be a Republican). There is also the phenomenon we might call a reverse counterfactual. Suppose, as William H. McNeill does, we were to subtract something as ordinary but essential to our everyday lives as the potato. How very different history might have been.

The reader will find an ample share of military might-have-beens; they are, quite simply, irresistible. Josiah Ober has love, under the sponsorship of Antony and Cleopatra, winning out at Actium. William doesn't conquer at Hastings and the Franco-Roman world that he represents loses more than a battle in Cecelia Holland's essay. Hitler follows his instincts and not the pleas of Neville Chamberlain to preserve peace in our time, invading Czechoslovakia in October 1938. The result, Williamson Murray tells us, would undoubtedly have been a general European War but a war that soon would have put Germany at a disadvantage. But two years could make all the difference. Andrew Roberts asks, what would have been the result if Lord Halifax and not Winston Churchill had become prime minister of Great Britain in 1940, as nearly happened. Would the Cold War have been averted and a million lives saved, Caleb Carr suggests, if Eisenhower had not "turned off" George S. Patton's gas early in the fall of 1944? Richard B. Frank explores the possibility that Japan might have tried to hold out, with disastrous consequences for the world, if we had not dropped two atomic bombs.

That these scenarios have entertainment value is undeniable, but their purpose is also to provoke. There is no better way of understanding what did happen in history than to contemplate what very well might have happened. Counterfactual history has a way of making the stakes of a confrontation stand out in relief. It can point out the moment that was truly a turning point—or the moment when the shading of an event edged from unfortunate to tragic. Plausibility is the key. Every day we make choices that, insignificant as they may seem at the time, can alter our lives, sometimes in drastic and unforeseen ways. History is merely the sum of millions of human decisions—which may be the decision to elevate the one person who makes the decisions for all of us. But history too may depend on a single accident—which has the power to abrogate all those thousands and millions of individual decisions. What if the arrow that killed the English King Harold at the Battle of Hastings had missed? What if, in February 1933, Giuseppe Zangara, bent on assassinating the president-elect, Franklin D. Roosevelt, had shown up at the Miami rally a few minutes earlier? These are the things that can't be quantified, no matter how diligently some historians try to change an art into a science. The only fixed rule of history is that there are no rules. This very rulelessness is what makes the study of history so full of surprise and fascination.

VICTOR DAVIS HANSON

# SOCRATES DIES AT DELIUM, 424 B.C.

## The consequences of a single battle casualty

*That the foundations of the Western intellectual tradition may rest on a military moment is a notion that some may find unsettling; its potential consequences are even more so. According to Victor Davis Hanson, philosophy as we know it was "nearly aborted"—his verb is hardly too strong—one late autumn afternoon in 424 B.C., in "an accidental battle in a failed campaign in a backwater theater of the Peloponnesian War," the twenty-seven-year-long struggle between Athens and Sparta. At the Battle of Delium, a ragtag Athenian contingent confronted a larger force from Thebes, an ally of the Spartan confederacy. One middle-aged infantryman from Athens was Socrates, a philosopher whose reputation was as yet uncertain. Service in war was an obligation of citizenship, and Greek men from the ages of eighteen to sixty could expect to experience in their lifetimes at least two or three episodes of concentrated terror; Socrates had already fought in two campaigns. What if he, like several hundred of the men he fought with at Delium, had been ridden down and skewered as he tried to flee to Athens? What if Socrates had not lived another quarter of a century, the period of his greatest influence? Or if he had not been alive to meet, and teach, the young Plato—who, without Socrates, might have become a politician or a poet and not a philosopher? Beyond leaving an excessive number of corpses to rot, that encounter at Delium may have decided nothing. Still, if it had counted one more Athenian victim, as Hanson says, "the entire course of Western philosophical and political thought would have been radically changed."*

VICTOR DAVIS HANSON is a professor of classics at California State University, Fresno, and the author of eleven books on subjects ranging from Greek military and rural history to the history of warfare and contemporary agriculture. His most recent books are *The Land Was Everything*, *The Soul of Battle*, and *Carnage and Culture*.

## A NIGHTMARISH RETREAT

THE CLASSICAL GREEKS saw no contradiction between a life of action and contemplation, even in the extreme polarities between military service and philosophy. War, the philosopher Heraclitus says, is "the father of us all." Plato proclaims that fighting "always exists by nature between every Greek city-state." A number of Greek writers, thinkers, and statesmen fought in the phalanx. The lyric poet Archilochus was killed in battle on the Aegean island of Thasos. The poets Tyrtaeus, Alcaeus, and Callinus, the playwrights Aeschylus and Sophocles, the democratic leader Pericles, the historian Thucydides, and the orator Demosthenes all took their slot in the files of the phalanx or on the banks of a trireme. At the siege of Samos (440 B.C.), Melissus, the Samian philosopher and student of Parmenides, led his ship into battle against Pericles' fleet. Sophocles was also at sea there, among the elected high command of Athenians who came to enslave the island. The philosopher and mathematician Archimedes died in the storming of Syracuse, in his final hours employing his novel military machines against the Roman besiegers.

It is not so surprising, then, that Socrates, the father of Western ethical philosophy, and veteran of the fighting in the campaigns of Potidaea and Amphipolis, found himself in a most dangerous place in the fall of 424 B.C. The aging forty-five-year-old hoplite fled for his life from an abject infantry disaster near the small border sanctuary of Delium, one nondescript, potbellied, middle-aged soldier amid a routed Athenian ragtag force of old men, irregulars, resident aliens, and inexperienced youth.

Delium, an accidental battle in a failed campaign in a backwater theater of the Peloponnesian War (431–404 B.C.), is a little-known and little-studied event. Nevertheless it was an unmitigated Athenian military disaster—the largest infantry battle fought near Athens since Marathon sixty-six years earlier, and a catastrophe in which nearly 15 percent of all Athenian infantrymen assembled there were killed in a few hours. No doubt an even far larger number were wounded or captured.

In the seventh year of the Peloponnesian War, the Athenians wished to end their two-front conflict with the Peloponnesians to the south and the Thebans to the north, and so in fall 424 B.C. they invaded Boeotia on their northern border. Unfortunately, they had devised an overly ambitious and unworkable plan of combined naval and infantry maneuvers in hopes of deploying two separate contingents inside Boeotia at the front and rear of a Theban army. The contemporary historian Thucydides records that the Athenian general Demosthenes had sailed earlier during the summer, intending to raise democratic insurrection throughout the Boeotian countryside by an unexpected amphibious landing. Then, aided by partisans, he was supposed to make his way east toward the sanctuary and small village of Delium—on the very day the other general, Hippocrates, and his Athenian hoplites, among them Socrates, marched out from Athens.

The idea was to crush the Thebans between two pincers, and thereby turn the entire Boeotian countryside into a democratic satellite of Athens in its war against Spartan oligarchy. But Demosthenes' naval assault to the west at the coastal Boeotian town of Siphae was timed too early. Once his plans were betrayed to the Boeotians, he was of little value in drawing off opposition from the Athenian land troops marching up from the south, and so he gave up the campaign. The result was that Socrates and his friends lost the element of surprise, were without help, and were soon to be confronted by the main army of an aroused and angry Thebes.

Hippocrates, a young nephew of Pericles and the general in charge of this rather motley expeditionary force, quickly turned his men toward home, stopping to have his Athenian infantry occupy the sanctuary of Apollo at Delium, cutting down surrounding vineyards and in general cannibalizing nearby farmhouses for the flotsam and jetsam with which to build his barricade. After ravaging the countryside, Hippocrates left a small force at the now garrisoned Delium and then led some 7,000 heavy infantrymen a few thousand yards back home toward the border of Attica.

When the Theban army finally arrived, the Athenians were ready to disband and apparently felt the campaign had failed—much to their relief. Thucydides says that a large throng of unarmed citizens and foreigners had followed the Athenian hoplite infantry from home, but had earlier dispersed, leaving few to stay with the army. In contrast, the Thebans had at least 7,000 hoplites, but also 10,000 light-armed troops, 1,000 cavalry, and an additional 500 skirmishers. When the battle commenced, Socrates and his friends would find themselves outnumbered by over two to one.

Without warning, the pursuing Theban army suddenly came up over a small hill and caught the assembled Athenian infantry off guard, still listening to a prebattle harangue from Hippocrates. Thucydides adds that water courses limited the field of operations. His description of the actual fighting is brief. Despite the uphill run, the Athenian right wing under Hippocrates nevertheless quickly cut down the Boeotian confederates opposite them on the enemy left. All along the Boeotian phalanx these panicked confederate allies fell back in the face of the Athenian upward assault. An Athenian victory looked certain. Yet at the same moment on the other side of the battlefield, the Theban general Pagondas and the reinforced Theban center and right wing held fast and soon went on the attack against the Athenian left. Delium thus unfolded as most typical hoplite battles of the age—a question of whether the strong right wing of an army could win the engagement before its own left weaker horn would collapse and lose it.

In fact, the unfortunate villagers of Thespiae on the extreme left of the Boeotian phalanx soon were at the point of annihilation from the Athenians under Hippocrates. Socrates was probably posted here along with his friends and associates—Laches (the eponymous subject of a Platonic dialogue), Alcibiades (his notorious young wayward student), and Pyrilampes (stepfather of Plato). Many in the army were middle-aged and well past forty (e.g., Socrates, Laches, Pyrilampes), perhaps because the campaign was envisioned as a short one while thousands of other frontline Athenian troops that late summer and fall were deployed elsewhere throughout the Aegean.

In any case, Thucydides tells us that in the first stage of the battle the Boeotian allies of Thebes in fact broke before the Athenian uphill charge, some trying to flee, others bumping into those attempting to fight and hang on. Meanwhile, far across the battlefield, Pagondas "gradually at first" pushed the weak Athenian left downhill and was systematically, as planned, clearing the battlefield through the advantage of favorable terrain and superior muscle. Only when the Thespian slaughter on his left horn threatened to pour Athenian hoplites to his own rear did Pagondas dispatch a reserve of Boeotian cavalry to the left to come up over the hill to the rear of the victorious Athenian right.

This was the key point in the entire battle. An apparent Athenian triumph was transformed into abject defeat in a matter of seconds. The successful Athenians under Hippocrates now wrongly surmised that an entirely new army was upon them. "On their sudden appearance over the hill," Thucydides writes, "the victorious Athenian wing thought an entirely fresh army had arrived, and thus simply took to panic." It was probably here—amid the stunned Athenians and their general who were suddenly transformed into panicked runaways—that Socrates began his famous trek back toward Athens.

Hippocrates was probably killed at this juncture, and soon the entire Athenian army took off at a run to the rear for safety—either nearby Mount Parnes, the fortified sanctuary at Delium proper and the refuge of Athenian triremes, or the woods in the flat Oropus borderland between Attica and Boeotia. Thucydides adds that some opportunistic enemy Locrian horsemen arrived for the spoils and now joined the Boeotian predators in the open-ended killing spree. Remember, there were already present over 10,000 light-armed Boeotians, in addition to 1,000 cavalry and another 500 peltasts, or skirmishers. With the Locrian reinforcements and the victorious hoplites, there may well have been a sizable swarm of 15,000 or so enemy pursuers, many of them either mounted or agile, lightly equipped auxiliaries. The routed Athenians, without much cavalry support or supporting

BOEOTIA AND ATTICA, 424 B.C.

Aegean Sea

N

*Euboean Sea*

*Euboean Sea*

Delium

Oropus

*Thebes*

BOEOTIA

**Mount Parnes**

SOCRATES' POSSIBLE
ESCAPE ROUTES

ATTICA

0 Miles 50
0 Kilometers 50

*Athens*

Saronic
Gulf

ANCIENT GREECE

0 Miles 100 200
0 Kilometers 200

THESSALY

*Euboean Sea*

Aegean
Sea

Thermopylae

Delium

BOEOTIA

Oropus

Thebes

**Mount Parnes**

Athens

ATTICA

PELOPONNESUS

N

Sparta

MESSENIA

LACONIA

*Ionian
Sea*

© 2001 Jeffrey L. Ward

skirmishers, and struggling to fling away their heavy armor, were vastly outnumbered, slower, confused, and in many cases lost in the growing twilight.

Socrates wisely avoided both the route to Delium and the high ground of Parnes, and so found safety in a third way through the forested Oropus. The disaster of this "home guard" must have quickly taken on mythic proportions and been recounted constantly throughout Athens: Hippocrates, nephew of Pericles, stepbrother of Alcibiades, and general of the army, killed; Alcibiades' bravery during the retreat soon to inaugurate his meteoric political career; Laches' less than courageous behavior in the flight from Delium foreshadowing his demise at the subsequent battle of Mantinea (418 B.C.), where he also fled the field; and Plato's own stepfather and great-uncle, Pyrilampes, captured when Plato was but a mere toddler.

In three later dialogues—*Laches*, *Symposium*, and *Apology*—Plato makes direct mention of Socrates' gallantry in the flight, how he backpedaled and made an orderly withdrawal toward the borderland of Oropus, accompanied by both Laches and Alcibiades. Indeed, in *Laches*, Socrates is made to lecture about the proper technique of attacking and fending off blows when in isolated combat, with a clear allusion to his own nightmarish experience after Delium. In this dialogue of the same name, Laches brags of Socrates that "if others had been willing to be like him, our city would now be upright and would not then have had such a terrible fall." In the last speech of his life, Socrates reminds his accusers in Plato's *Apology*—his defense to a criminal prosecution on trumped-up charges of impiety that led to his execution—that in three terrible battles he had kept rank and not left his position. And in Plato's *Symposium*, Alcibiades gives a description of the acute danger in which Socrates found himself during the general rout after Delium:

> I happened to be riding, he was serving as a hoplite. As the army was scattered he was retreating with Laches when I happened on him; at first sight I told them to keep their courage up as I told them I would not abandon them. Then I had even a finer view of Socrates than at Potidaea. For my part I was less afraid since I was mounted. First off I noticed how much more in control of his senses he was than Laches,

and how—to use your own phrase, Aristophanes—he made his way there just as he does here in Athens "swaggering and glancing sideways." So he looked around calmly at both his friends and the enemy; he was clearly giving the message to anyone even at a distance that if anyone touched this man, he quickly would put up a stout defense. The result was that he and his partner got away safely. For it is true that attackers do not approach men of this caliber but instead go after those fleeing headlong.

Centuries later, Plutarch, in his life of Alcibiades, also recalls this widely circulated story that Alcibiades rode past Socrates and his isolated contingent who were in dire straits. But in Plutarch's version, Alcibiades' mounted presence saves the life of Socrates as the enemy "was closing in and killing many." In his *Moralia*, Plutarch adds a slightly different twist— that Socrates' choice of escape alone saved him and his friends, as most other Athenians who headed over the mountains were ridden down and slain, while those who reached Delium were eventually besieged.

The disparate ancient evidence, nevertheless, points to two salient facts about Socrates' retreat—that Delium was a horrific Athenian catastrophe where hundreds were mercilessly hunted down and killed right on the border of Attica, and that Socrates' courage and good sense brought him out alive when most around him were killed. Clearly the philosopher himself was nearly almost ridden down and speared in the chaotic rout.

When we add the macabre fact that the corpses of over 1,000 Athenian dead—no doubt the majority hunted down in the dark and found randomly for miles without armor and with stabs to the back—were collected by the enemy, but then left to rot in the autumn sun for nearly three weeks, the flight from Delium must have been ingrained in the collective Athenian and Boeotian memory as a grotesque event in which human detritus littered well-traveled local paths. Again, we have no idea how many thousand more eventually died of their wounds or were captured.

In the fall of 424 B.C., the forty-five-year-old Socrates came within a hair's breadth of being killed. Had the middle-aged philosopher been speared by an anonymous Locrian horseman, or if his small band had been overtaken by pursuing Theban infantry, or if he had chosen to flee toward either Delium or Mount Parnes, where most of his terrified comrades were killed, the entire course of Western philosophical and political thought would have been radically altered.


## SOCRATES WITHOUT PLATO

Would Socrates' ideas have survived without Plato? Plato, approximately forty-two years Socrates' junior, was probably about five at the time of the battle of Delium. Had Socrates been killed, then the entire nature of Plato's dialogues would have been radically changed and with it the nature of Western thought itself. Even had a mature Plato written philosophical treatises, his dialogues—if there were to be any dialogues at all, since the original genre is patterned directly after Socratic oral dialectic—would have largely been non-Socratic both in form and content. In his autobiographical *Seventh Letter*, Plato says that he was naturally gravitating toward a life of politics until his association with Socrates, and his disillusionment over the philosopher's execution prompted him to turn to philosophy and reject an active life in government.

Much of Plato's singular literary genius draws inspiration from the magnetic character of the aged Socrates, who wandered the streets of Athens, engaging the strong, smug, and secure in tough question-and-answer sessions, and who in the process made such an impression on the adolescent Plato. Plato probably came under Socrates' tutelage sometime in his twenties, roughly in the last decade of the Peloponnesian War (e.g., 410–404 B.C.); the popular tradition relates that before their meeting, Plato was more interested in politics and poetry than philosophy. The influence of the elder Socrates on the young student remained profound until the old man was executed when Plato was twenty-eight.

Socrates is the chief interlocutor in the majority of the Platonic dialogues and the hero of the masterpiece *Apology*, which chronicles his final defense on charges of impiety and moral corruption before an Athenian jury. Socrates' concern that philosophy should deal with ethics, not mere natural inquiry or cosmology of earlier formal speculation, characterizes nearly all of Plato's early work. The idea in Plato that from knowledge comes virtue, and that morality can be taught through rational choices and the suppression of desire, seems to be derived from the thought and actual practice of the historical Socrates. And the notion of Socratic duality— men have souls whose integrity they must not endanger by a surrender to the appetites; the world we sense and live in is but a pale imitation of a divine and perfect counterpart—forms the basis of Plato's investigations into morality, language, the hereafter, politics, and the fine arts.

Quite clearly, had Socrates been killed that evening in autumn 424 B.C., Plato would never have had any firsthand association with the philosopher. Plato's interest in philosophy—if he even would have eventually developed such an interest from other contemporary thinkers—would have had little to do with Socrates. The latter himself wrote nothing; he founded neither a school nor institutional framework to keep alive his work. Socrates received no money for his teaching. The question then arises—in a world where Socrates never met Plato, would we now know anything about the itinerant philosopher and his thoughts at all?

Could there have been any other contemporary record of Socrates without Plato? Our other main source of Socrates' thought is preserved in the works of the historian and essayist Xenophon, whose dialogues *Memorabilia, Apology, Symposium,* and *Oeconomicus* feature Socrates as the main questioner on topics as varied as love, agriculture, politics, and his own career as combatant against the sophists. But like Plato, Xenophon also grew up under the influence of a post-Delium Socrates. He was born sometime around 430 B.C., and was probably at most a year or two older than Plato, making him only six or seven when Socrates was nearly killed at Delium. Consequently, a Socrates dead when Plato was five and Xenophon six or seven, rather than both in their late twenties, makes it likely that none of the works of either Plato or Xenophon would have centered around the lively presence of Socrates as interlocutor, their tough questioner and role model who serves as the fountainhead of their own ideas.

The famous orator and educator Isocrates claimed to be an adherent of

Socrates and he is mentioned favorably in Plato's *Phaedrus* as a star student of the old philosopher. But Isocrates was born in 436 B.C., eight years before the battle of Delium, making him nearly a generation younger even than both Plato and Xenophon. Had Socrates been killed in 424 B.C. when Isocrates was still a boy, the older philosopher would probably have had no indirect influence on the young orator, whose thought seems derivative from Socrates, especially the latter's disdain for radical democracy. It would have robbed Isocrates of any indirect knowledge of a quarter century of Socratic anecdotes and teaching, and his ideas probably would have had little place in Isocrates' massive corpus of work, which was influential in its criticism of both the sophists and radical democracy.

How, then, would we know anything of Socrates' thought without the testimony of Plato and Xenophon? Aristotle, of course, refers to Socrates often, but much of what he criticizes is derived from Plato and Xenophon, inasmuch as he was born (384 B.C.) twelve years after Socrates was executed (399 B.C.). We can assume that a Socrates dead at Delium would also have played almost no role at all in Aristotle's own thinking for a variety of reasons: There would have been no mention of Socrates in either Xenophon or Plato; Socrates would have died not twelve but instead thirty-seven years before Aristotle's own birth. Moreover, a dead Socrates would have been deprived of a final twenty-five years of life in which his own thinking reached maturity. These were the years that gave his ideas a chance to filter through talk of the dinner party or the symposium and private recollection of the last quarter of the fifth century B.C. in Athens. Most likely, a dead Socrates at Delium would not even have appeared by name in Aristotle's entire corpus—much of which gains its power for its deliberate posture against the politics and theology of both Socrates and Plato.

Were there other writers and philosophers besides Xenophon, Plato, Isocrates, and Aristotle who might have captured for posterity Socrates' unique ideas before he marched out at Delium? Thucydides, the contemporary historian and chief source for the battle of Delium, does not mention Socrates in his history at all, an omission that sometimes puzzles scholars. We also have no public or private Athenian inscriptions that mention him by name. Instead, there survive in association with Socrates only a few names of other philosophers who, like Xenophon and Plato, were self-proclaimed followers of the unique Socratic emphasis on philosophy as ethics, and who dedicated themselves to ensuring his memory as a great man who fought, rather than joined, the contemporary sophists, who unlike Socrates took money for their instruction and advocated moral relativism and situational ethics rather than an absolute code of good and evil that might transcend conditions of the moment. The chances, however, that any of these writers would have developed a sizable Socratic corpus of work had the philosopher died in 424 B.C. are small, if nonexistent.

The rather obscure Antisthenes, for example, may have been the same age as Socrates, and even known him well before Delium. Fragments of Antisthenes' work survive and suggest he was especially interested in the Socratic lifestyle, or at least the need for the man of contemplation to set himself apart from society and the temptations of the flesh. But we should doubt that Antisthenes would have kept alive the ideas of a middle-aged, rather than seventy-year-old, Socrates. For one thing, he seems to have written largely to combat Plato, and thereby may have not authored anything had Plato never met Socrates. Plato names Antisthenes as present at Socrates' last hours, and much of what little we know about his work seems prompted by Socrates' martyrdom and the fate of philosophical stalwarts who oppose the mob. Had Socrates died at Delium, then, Antisthenes would not have found his striking model of principled resistance to the ignorant crowd. Finally, we have only fragments of Antisthenes' work: Although he seems to have been known to Aristotle and a few others, the chances that his work in changed circumstances would have survived classical antiquity seem remote. There is no reason to think that had Socrates died at forty-five rather than seventy, we would know any more of him through Antisthenes than the tiny scraps of his work we now possess.

Aeschines of Sphettos wrote seven Socratic dialogues. The theme of many of them, apparently, was a defense of Socrates' association with the dissolute Alcibiades. None of these dialogues survives, except for a few fragments and quotations. But since Aeschines was roughly the same age as

Plato and Xenophon, like the latter two, he met Socrates only *after* Delium—and thus probably would not have devoted his life to a philosopher who did not write and whom he would never have met. In short, without a direct Socratic connection, we have little reason to believe any of Aeschines' work would have survived had Socrates died in 424 B.C.

Phaedon of Elis is just a name. Mere scraps of quotations of his two Socratic dialogues are extant. A near contemporary of Plato and Xenophon, he too was a small boy at the time of Delium. Nothing remains either of the work of Aristippus or Cebes, who both purportedly wrote panegyrics of Socrates. Thus we are left with the conclusion that most Socratic followers who were inspired to write about their mentor did so only after meeting him in the period *after* the battle of Delium—when they were of an age to wander along after the itinerant interlocutor. Many adherents seem to have been prompted to write after Plato began his early dialogues surrounding Socrates' death, either to enhance or reject the Platonic testimony. Socrates' other admirers, whose works are essentially lost, seem to have been influenced especially by his last courageous stand against his accusers in 399 B.C., in addition to the striking contrast between the grandfatherly philosopher and their own youthful zeal and impressionability. But in any case, the works of these lesser-known Socratics were either scarcely known or not highly regarded, and so there is no reason to believe they would have survived had Socrates died a quarter century earlier.

We are left with an inescapable conclusion: Almost everyone who wrote anything about Socrates and his thinking came of age *after* the battle of Delium. Socrates' influential students seem to be nearly all acquaintances from his late forties, fifties, and sixties. Had he died at the battle in 424 B.C., the later Western tradition of philosophy would probably have known almost nothing positive about either his life or thought.

We do, however, have at least one contemporary source for the life of Socrates who knew him well *before* the battle of Delium, a critic who has left us a gripping portrait a mere year after the battle—the dramatist Aristophanes. The picture of Socrates in his *Clouds* (423 B.C.) is not pretty, but a vicious caricature of a middle-aged huckster. Indeed, because of

Aristophanes' influential status, and since he portrayed Socrates on the stage before thousands of Athenians, both Plato and Xenophon spent their entire lives trying to counteract that apparently commonly embraced Aristophanic portrait of Socrates as sophist.

Some scholars have suggested that Socrates' hagiography in the works of both Plato and Xenophon was partly meant as a response to the vehemence of Aristophanes' earlier slander. Other comic poets—Ameipsias and Eupolis especially, whose works are now lost, but who were widely popular during the 420s—also caricatured Socrates on stage and reinforced the devastating portrayal of Aristophanes, whose lasting vilification so bothered Plato and Xenophon.

In Aristophanes' comedy *Clouds*, often considered his masterpiece and produced on the stage in 423 B.C., Socrates is the worst of the sophists, a leader of that infamous collection of slick tricksters who made a living by filling the heads of an idle rich elite with word games and relativist morality, and who were purportedly responsible for the cultural decline of Athens and its increasing lethargy and decadence during the long war with Sparta. In the drama, Socrates attempts to "make the weaker argument stronger." He is a windbag, whose superficial cleverness with words is attractive to untrained minds who are willing to pay for a foolish veneer of learning.

So influential was Aristophanes' invective that in the last speech of his life, as reported in Plato's *Apology*, Socrates attempts to defend himself from the popular prejudice incurred from the attacks of the comic poets. One tradition has it that he watched the comedy, and purportedly stood up during a presentation of *Clouds* to assure the audience he was not bothered by the caricature—an opportunity that also would never have transpired had he died along with hundreds of his comrades a year earlier at Delium.

Without Plato's and Xenophon's earlier acquaintance with Socrates, neither writer would have had any zeal to counteract the more prevailing Aristophanic view. Unlike themselves, the playwright at least had met and known Socrates for a good many years. It is highly likely, then, that our present-day Socrates would largely have remained a creation of Aristophanes and thus survived in history as little different from the notorious

Gorgias, Hippias, Protagoras, and other sophists whose writings are lost, but whose reputations have generally been sullied by nearly all their contemporaries. Socrates would not have been the hero of Plato and Xenophon, impressionable youths who both idealistically worshipped the aged philosopher whom they watched at seventy be unjustly killed by an ignorant mob. Instead, he would have remained the rascal of the cynical and jaded Aristophanes, joining the scoundrels Cleon and Alcibiades, whose reputations as knaves par excellence were cemented forever on the Athenian comic stage. Had Socrates died that afternoon in 424 B.C., whatever and whoever he was until the age of forty-five when he stalked the battlefield of Delium would mostly be unknown and of little interest to us outside the rather devilish creation of Aristophanes.

Finally, it is impossible to gauge the development of Socrates' own thought at age forty-five, inasmuch as he wrote nothing, and Plato's work gives us almost no clue to any chronological evolution in Socratic reasoning. Nevertheless, there is some evidence that his real development as a first-class thinker came during the last twenty-five years of his life, when he attracted the best minds of Athens to his side, such as Alcibiades, Agathon, Plato, Xenophon, and Isocrates. Other near-contemporaries of Socrates, who appear in Plato's dialogues as his close friends are, curiously, often non-Athenian—Phaedon of Elis, Echecrates of Phlius, Simmias and Cebes of Thebes, Aristippus of Cyrene, Euclides and Terpsion of Megara. And these men are interested not so much in ethical questions, but rather in natural philosophy and cosmology—especially Orphic thought, the teaching of Pythagoras, the ontology of Parmenides, the natural inquiry of Empedocles, and the radical views of Anaxagoras. When and where did Socrates meet these other disciples, who seem somewhat different from his later and more famous Athenian adherents?

Perhaps before the outbreak of the Peloponnesian War (431 B.C.), Socrates was even better known outside of Athens, and as an itinerant natural philosopher in the earlier pre-Socratic tradition of speculating about the nature of matter, the cosmos, and the soul. Later, with the outbreak of the war and the difficulty of these former associates to travel freely and to live in Athens (Elis, Thebes, and Megara were all at war with Athens), an older and more Athens-bound Socrates turned his attention increasingly away from these earlier concerns of cosmology to personal ethics, rhetoric, and politics—issues of vital interest as he watched his home city tear itself apart in open assembly during the war. A new following among wealthy, young, and impressionable Athenians suggests a more mature Socrates in his late forties and fifties, who traveled less and focused his philosophy on more germane concerns of everyday life. Thus, not only would we have known little about Socrates had he died in the darkness of Delium, but what little information that would have survived would suggest to posterity a picture of a rather obscure natural philosopher, who only very recently had turned his attention to ethical inquiry inside Athens, and so caught the attention of Aristophanes and the comic poets. The original faultline of Western philosophy—pre-Socratic as cosmology and natural inquiry; Socratic as ethical and moral thought—would never have existed.

## PLATO WITHOUT SOCRATES

Can we speculate about Plato's own career without the influence of Socrates? If we would now know very little of Socrates without Plato, what would we know of a non-Socratic Plato, of a philosopher who never met Socrates at all? His most famous treatises—*Euthyphro, Apology, Crito,* and *Phaedo,* the tetrad that surrounds the trial and death of Socrates—would vanish. But even more important, at least a third of Plato's earliest work, the so-called Socratic dialogues, would probably not have been written or at least not written in their present form. Scholars have spent the past century trying to arrange Plato's thirty-one dialogues into some sort of chronology by date of composition—a difficult task given that Plato probably wrote over a fifty-year period and told us little about his own life as an author. But on stylistic grounds, philosophical content, and contemporary references to historical events there is now a rough consensus of "early" work (*Apology, Crito, Laches, Lysis, Charmides, Euthyphro, Hippias Major* and *Minor, Protagoras, Gorgias,* and *Ion*) written in Plato's thirties and forties (i.e., 390s

B.C.), which are rather distinct from twelve subsequent "middle" dialogues (written in the 380s and 370s B.C.) and a final eight "late" works (composed in the 360s and 350s B.C.)

The first group of dialogues are usually considered to deal primary with moral issues and the need to establish proper definitions of ethical problems—in contrast with Plato's middle and later interests that turn to metaphysics, ontology, and epistemology. In addition, Socrates is the primary figure of Plato's first eleven dialogues, but he seems to fade somewhat in importance in later texts; indeed, in the *Laws*, considered one of Plato's last treatises, he does not appear at all. Some scholars even believe that Plato began his early dialogues while in his twenties, at a time when Socrates was still alive (e.g. 408–399 B.C.). In any case, it seems likely that at least eleven of his most important works were written within a decade and a half of Socrates' death, employed Socrates as chief questioner, and dealt with concerns made famous by Socrates during the last years of his life. Had Plato never met Socrates, then these eleven dialogues either would not exist or would not exist in their present form.

Plato's middle and later dialogues, in contrast, when the memory of Socrates was decades past, show increasing interest in the work of Parmenides, Protagoras, and Empedocles, and draw directly on their notions of causation, change, sensation, cosmology, and reincarnation. Like the younger Socrates, Plato seems to regard these earlier thinkers—who unlike Socrates wrote substantially—the most influential philosophers of the Greek tradition. As Plato matured, as the memory of life and conversations with Socrates dimmed, and as the value of the written philosophical texts of others was more appreciated, Plato seems to have diverged from Socrates in important areas of philosophy and to have drawn on these earlier giants. Thus an irony arises: The philosophical interests of the elder Plato resemble somewhat the thought of the younger Socrates, suggesting that the last two decades of Socrates' life were an exceptional period in the history of Greek philosophical thought, devoted far more to the practical and ethical, and attuned to debunking the false knowledge prevalent in the streets of Athens. Had Socrates died at forty-five in 424 B.C. at Delium, it is likely that at least a third of Plato's most interesting work would either be gone or not exist in its present form. Rather, his entire corpus might better resemble his middle and later dialogues and thereby belong more to the mainstream of Hellenic cosmological and ontological speculation.

Finally, Plato seems to have sensed that Delium was a momentous event in Socrates' life, one that was related over and over to the younger student by a variety of associates. Not only is the battle mentioned three times in his work, but there are a number of veiled allusions that arise unexpectedly elsewhere as well. In the utopian *Laws* and *Republic,* the nightmare of Delium is never far away; both the disgrace of the Athenian loss and the Theban sacrilege in the battle's aftermath offer implicit lessons for the military reformer. In the *Laws,* for example, Plato urges regular peacetime military drill, regardless of weather, and lasting for an entire day (Delium atypically took place in the late afternoon of November). All residents— men, women, and children—are to join in, but in an ordered and disciplined manner (surely unlike the chaotic mass levee at Delium). There, as in the *Laches,* soldiers are to learn set moves to avoid individual blows. Such exercise will be especially valuable when the fighting is fluid "and the ranks broken and it is necessary to fight one on one, either in pursuing after someone who is defending himself or in retreating yourself and beating off the attack of another"—as Socrates must have learned at Delium.

In his utopia of the *Republic* the infamous retreat and carnage of Delium also drew his attention. Fathers (does he have his stepfather Pyrilampes in mind?) are to take their sons out to the battlefield to make them watch the fighting, with the guarantee that the "older guides" can direct them away in safe retreat "if the need arises." Those who are caught alive (again, like his stepfather?) are not to be ransomed but left to the desires of the enemy. In contrast, the courageous—i.e., the Socratic—shall be given military prizes for their heroism. Plato continues that the dead shall not be stripped nor desecrated, and insists that the corpses of the defeated must be returned to their countrymen for a decent burial (in contrast to the notorious Theban behavior). Nor should the Greeks (as the Thebans did after Delium) display the weapons of the defeated in sanctuaries as dedicatory offerings, but instead regard such desecration as a "pollution." Although Plato himself may have seen brief military service for two years during the Corinthian

War (394–95 B.C.), his discussions of war in large part draw on the experience of Socrates and are predicated on both his presence and survival at Delium.

## SOCRATES' DEATH AT DELIUM AND THE LATER WESTERN TRADITION OF PHILOSOPHY AND POLITICS

One of the most moving texts in Western literature is Plato's *Apology*, the account of Socrates' final rebuttal before his peers in the Athenian jury. The influence of Plato's version of the speech has been enormous in the past two and a half millennia. Two fundamental traditions in the practice of Western philosophy followed from that majestic defense. First, is the accepted notion that society will kill those who question its authority and values, and thus the role of the true philosopher is properly to be tragic, inasmuch as an outsider he will inevitably meet with the revenge of the masses if he remains true to his ideas. Second, democracy—not oligarchy or autocracy—killed Socrates. In large part because of the trial and execution of Socrates, Athenian democracy suffered a terrible reputation among subsequent political and philosophical thinkers, from Cicero to Machiavelli to almost every subsequent major philosopher, until the late eighteenth-century revolutionaries in France and America.

In addition, the early Christian apologists of late antiquity, many responding to the renewed interest in Socrates among the Neoplatonist renaissance, who emphasized the mystical nature of Plato's work, found the parallel with the martyr Jesus especially unmistakable—both men were teachers who wrote nothing but were quoted widely by a close cadre of disciples; both were dragged before the mob, publicly humiliated, and then executed by lesser men who represented a frightened and paranoid establishment. In the early Christian apologists' view, Socrates' courageous end—and his advocacy of preferring to be hurt rather than to hurt others—was confirmation of his prescience: he surely had a blessed premonition of Jesus—and therefore, like Jesus, preached that we do not die with our bodies, but rather have an eternal soul that lives on after us. Socratic thought, via Plato, became critical to the early exegesis of the Christian Church.

Thus, there would have been no image of Socrates as pre-Christian pagan martyr had he died at Delium. Rather than a tragic man of conscience, he would have been a rather nondescript Athenian patriot and sophistic thinker who died during a bloodbath. In that sense, Socrates would have been embraced by, rather than at odds with, Athenian democracy. Nor would we have such a negative appraisal of Athenian democracy itself, had it honored Socrates as a fallen warrior of 424 rather than executed him as the perceived subversive agitator and tutor to the right-wing revolutionaries of 404 B.C. who for a time overthrew the government. Most of the animus of the democracy toward Socrates did not, as alleged, derive simply from his radical philosophizing as much from charges that his former students and associates toppled democratic government while he stood idly by.

In conclusion, Socrates fought in three battles, but it is his brush with death at Delium that captured the popular imagination of contemporary Greeks, a battle that was a nightmarish slaughter right on the border of Athens. That obscure battle has had a number of other ripples in Greek history: the shameful treatment of the Athenian dead later prompted Euripides' tragedy *Suppliants*, a play in which the Thebans are chastised for not burying the corpse of Polynices; Thebes itself underwent an artistic and architectural renaissance from the sale of the vast Athenian booty looted after the battle; and Alcibiades might have never convinced his peers to sail to Sicily nine years later without the heroic capital the young firebrand earned in his first battle at Delium.

Yet perhaps the chief significance of the battle is the philosopher's close escape from Theban pursuers. On that autumn late afternoon in 424 B.C., Western philosophy as we know it was nearly aborted in its infancy. Had Socrates been speared or ridden down by the enemy, today we would know almost nothing about him. The philosophical tradition would claim him only as an early and rather obscure cosmologist and natural philosopher in the tradition of Pythagoras, Parmenides, and Empedocles—or perhaps a budding sophist. But unlike his other contemporaries, there would not even be fragments of Socrates's own written work.

There would have been no Platonic or Xenophonic Socrates. Plato's own work—even if Plato would have gone on to write about philosophy without the tutelage and inspiration of Socrates—would be far different and probably exist as rather abstract utopian and technical theory with far less concern with everyday ethics or politics in general. A large percentage of Xenophon's work would never have been written. *Clouds* by Aristophanes, not the *Apology* by Plato, would be the sole source of information about Socrates the man, a character not much different from the other rogues who inhabit the Athenian comic stage. A dead Socrates at Delium would mean today there would not be a book in any library or bookstore on Socrates, and Plato himself might be as little-known to the general reader as a Zeno or Epicurus.

More important, Socrates' death at seventy—why and how he was killed—have had fundamental repercussions in the Western liberal tradition. Had he fallen to a spear thrust in the twilight of Delium in middle age and not been led away by a jeering and ignorant mob as an old man, the entire image of the philosopher would be radically different today, and the heritage of democracy far brighter. Twenty-five hundred years after the birth of Athenian democracy, much of the abstract criticism of popular government, ancient and modern, derives from the logic and emotion of Plato—whose political instincts were formed by the life and death of Socrates. In addition, the easy association between Socrates, martyr and founder of Western thought, and Jesus, who died on the cross to establish Western religion, would also not be so obvious. Neoplatonism as the early Church understood it through Plato would have had no ethical foundation without a live Socrates after 424 B.C. Quite simply, had a Locrian horsemen ridden down Socrates that late November afternoon, our present ideas about both Christianity and democracy would be radically different.

JOSIAH OBER

# NOT BY A NOSE

*The triumph of Antony and Cleopatra at Actium, 31* B.C.

To what extent does love exert a role in counterfactual history? Some would dismiss that as a purely Gallic question. Indeed, Josiah Ober notes here, the seventeenth-century French philosopher Blaise Pascal opined that if the Egyptian queen Cleopatra had possessed a less comely nose, "the whole face of the earth might have been changed." Would unpleasing looks have kept the soldier-politician Mark Antony, one of the most powerful men in the known world, from losing his heart to her, thus taking the first steps on the path to defeat at Actium and, as a consequence, the elevation of the first emperor of Rome, his rival Octavian Augustus? Was love the culprit?

To Pascal (and earlier, Shakespeare), the answer couldn't be clearer. "He who would fully know human vanity has but to consider the causes and effects of love," Pascal wrote in his Pensées. The causes of an infatuation might be trifling but the effects could be fearful, moving "earth, princes, armies, the whole world." Pascal was no doubt being hard on love, as well as on Antony and Cleopatra, but such concerns have made for an enduring tale of human folly. Why not say it? Cleopatra, apparently, was no beauty. Was this the nose that launched a thousand ships? No matter. She had other more fetching attributes. According to the Greek biographer Plutarch, who wrote within a century of Actium, "Her beauty (as it is reported) was not so passing, as unmatchable as other women, nor yet such as upon present view did enamor men with her; but so sweet was her company and conversation that a man could not possibly but be taken." Cleopatra *was captivating in another respect. Sex in the ancient world had its practical uses, as golf does in ours. In the ornate tents, barges, and bed chambers of the high and mighty, deals were made and alliances, political and dynastic, were cemented: Lack of virtue was its own reward, and Cleopatra was for much of her life a winner.*

*No Actium? No gilt-edged suicides? Ober considers some of the alternatives. With Antony and Cleopatra securely enthroned and their progeny guaranteed a future, their capital, Alexandria, might have been the other eternal city of the world. The whole evolving nature of religion would have been different: remember, Actium was fought in 31 B.C., at the threshold of the Christian era.*

JOSIAH OBER, the chairman of the Department of Classics at Princeton University, is the author of *The Anatomy of Error: Ancient Military Disasters and Their Lessons for Modern Strategists* (with Barry S. Strauss), *The Athenian Revolution*, and *Political Dissent in Democratic Athens*.

O
N A BARREN HILL on the western coast of Greece, above the site of the ancient city of Nicopolis ("Victory City") and some seventy-five kilometers by sea southeast of the popular Greek island of Corfu, there stands a unique and seldom-visited ancient monument. The monument takes the form of a low parapet, well built of massive stone blocks. On the face of the wall the occasional visitor who stumbles upon this place is struck by the deep and peculiar cuttings. Careful work by archaeologists has shown that the cuttings were specifically designed to accommodate the sawn-off ends of great oared warships; when the monument was still intact the wall bristled with delicately arched and highly decorated wooden ship sterns. This is a monument to a great naval victory.

The wall is Roman, dating to the age of the emperor Augustus. The ships that were mutilated to create this monument once belonged to Mark Antony. The monument was built by Antony's one-time partner, brother-in-law, and rival for the role of chief man in the Roman empire: Octavian, later to be called Augustus Caesar, the first emperor of Rome. Octavian Augustus erected this monument and founded the city of Nicopolis as lasting memorials to his most important naval victory, the Battle of Actium (31 B.C.), at which Antony—along with Antony's ally and lover, Queen Cleopatra VII of Egypt—was decisively defeated. Actium richly deserves its reputation as one of the turning-point battles of Western history.

Actium was not the first important battle fought between armies of Romans on Greek soil. As part of the Roman province of Macedonia, Greece had served as unwilling host to several sanguinary clashes between Roman citizen-armies, led by ferociously ambitious Roman politician-generals. Greece had the unhappy distinction of marking the boundary between the western Roman Empire, centered in Italy and extending to Spain, and the eastern Roman Empire, which extended well into Anatolia (modern

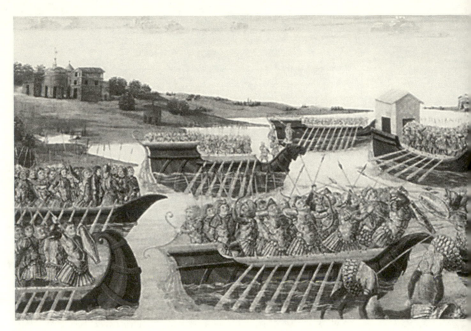

ACTIUM: EMPIRE LOST, EMPIRE ESTABLISHED

*The Italian Renaissance artist Neroccio de' Landi did this fanciful tempera of the Battle of Actium, where Octavian (who would soon proclaim himself the Emperor Caesar Augustus) defeated*

Turkey) and as far east as Syria. Cornelius Sulla had consolidated his position by victories in Greece in the mid-80s B.C. before returning to Italy to smash the supporters of Marius. Then Julius Caesar had crushed his rival, Pompey the Great, at Thessalian Pharsalus, in northeastern Greece. Next, at Macedonian Philippi, Octavian and Antony, at that time still allies, had eliminated the threat posed by Julius Caesar's assassins, the "Liberators," Brutus and Cassius. But Actium was the finale.

At Actium, Octavian defeated his last serious rival and so could finally proceed with his master plan: No longer would the aristocratic Senate dominate an ancient republic; rather the Senate would now be a rubber stamp for a new imperial form of government, a kingdom in all but name in which true power would be vested (if still somewhat covertly) in a single man. Actium also spelled the end of 300 years of Macedonian rule over an independent Egypt. After the battle, Octavian pursued Antony and

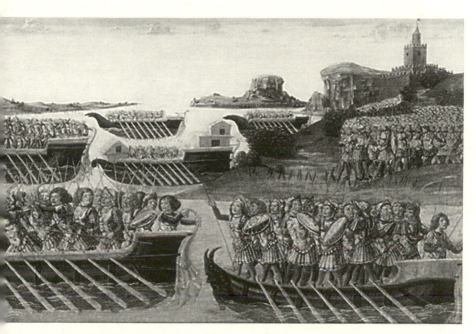

*Antony and his ally and lover, the Egyptian queen Cleopatra.*

(Neroccio de' Landi, 1447–1500, and workshop, *The Battle of Actium*. North Carolina Museum of Art, Raleigh, Gift of the Samuel H. Kress Foundation)

Cleopatra to Egypt. When Cleopatra committed suicide by asp bite rather than accepting the fate of passively marching in Octavian's triumphal parade, the last of the great Hellenistic Greek kingdoms passed into the control of the Roman state. Or, more precisely, into the private estate of the Roman emperor.

With Octavian's victory at Actium, the Roman conquest of the eastern Mediterranean was complete, and the long reign of the Roman emperors was inaugurated—for good (Claudius, Marcus Aurelius) and for ill (Caligula, Nero). And ever since, historians have speculated: Must it have gone that way? After all, Octavian, for all his political acumen, was not noted for his military talents; whereas Mark Antony was among the most skillful generals of his day. Antony brought a vast army and an imposing navy to Actium. How are we to account for Octavian's victory in this epoch-making confrontation? What factor might have tipped the scales of

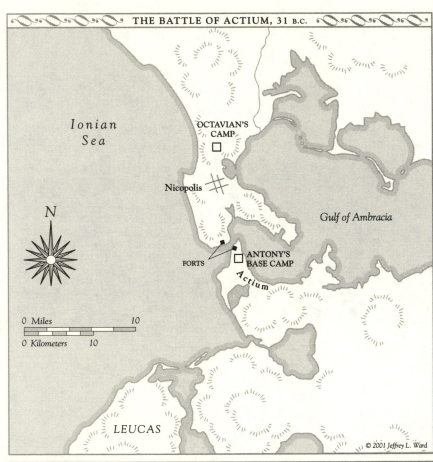

**THE BATTLE OF ACTIUM, 31** B.C.

*Ionian
Sea*

OCTAVIAN'S
CAMP

Nicopolis

*Gulf of Ambracia*

FORTS

ANTONY'S
BASE CAMP

*Actium*

0 Miles          10

0 Kilometers   10

LEUCAS

© 2001 Jeffrey L. Ward

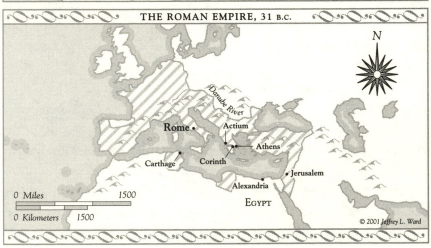

**THE ROMAN EMPIRE, 31** B.C.

N

*Danube River*

Rome

Actium

Athens

Carthage

Corinth

Alexandria

Jerusalem

EGYPT

0 Miles          1500

0 Kilometers   1500

© 2001 Jeffrey L. Ward

war in the other direction, and what might the world have looked like in the aftermath of an Antonine victory?

In one of the most celebrated counterfactual speculations in Western literature, Pascal suggested (in his *Pensées*) that if Cleopatra had been born with a somewhat larger nose, Mark Antony would have defeated Octavian at Actium, and thus the entire course of Roman imperial history (and so, of Western civilization) would have been altered. Pascal's classic "what if?" is predicated on the assumption that Antony was madly in love with Cleopatra, and that his wild passion for her fatally clouded his judgment as a general and a politician. Love, then, was the key factor in Antony's miscalculations in the years leading up to the decisive encounter on the western coast of Greece: Rome was saddled with a long series of emperors because Antony lost his heart over a cute nose.

Pascal's whimsical thought experiment is memorable, enjoying all the parsimonious elegance of "for want of a nail . . ." yet with the added elements of romance and tragically flawed historical characters. Ironically, however, the ancient accounts of Cleopatra do not describe her as a great beauty. Plutarch, who wrote biographies of both Julius Caesar and Mark Antony, claims that Cleopatra's musical voice and great force of character rendered her delightful company, but the biographer notes that she was not particularly good-looking. Indeed the only surviving contemporary portraits of her, on coins minted under Cleopatra's own authority in Egyptian Alexandria, depict the famous queen with a sharp jutting chin and a very prominent hooked nose.

Yet even if we leave out the most obviously problematic elements of Pascal's scenario (the assumptions that male passion must be stimulated primarily by a woman's physical beauty; that women with large noses cannot be regarded as beautiful; and thus that Antony would not have been passionately misled by a large-nosed Cleopatra), his counterfactual is subject to correction on its most basic (and perhaps most attractive) grounds: that is, on the notion that the course of human history was changed by romantic love.

There is no doubt that Antony and Cleopatra were physically intimate (he acknowledged as legitimate his three children by her), or that they contracted a lasting and fateful alliance. But a properly critical reading of the ancient sources leads quickly to the conclusion that there is little reason to suppose that Antony's failure at Actium was a product of foolish infatuation. The real story, patiently restored by a generation of Roman historians, is less elegant, perhaps less romantic, but more satisfyingly complicated and ultimately more historically interesting. The real story of the events leading up to the great battle of Actium suggests that Pascal was right in suggesting that Octavian's victory was far from inevitable—but quite wrong to predicate that somewhat unlikely victory on the biological accident of a petite nose.

The decades leading up to the battle of Actium featured some colorful historical characters, but the era was haunted by a pale ghost: the spirit of Julius Caesar. Caesar had precipitated the second phase of Rome's civil wars when he crossed the Rubicon in arms in 49 B.C. He subsequently defeated his rivals in a series of brilliant campaigns, only to end up assassinated by a group of his closest friends on the Ides of March 44 B.C. Caesar had never declared himself emperor, but the assassins had feared that he was about to do so. He had certainly prepared the way for a new form of government in Rome, one that would take account of the dramatic growth of Roman power and the outstanding political importance of those who could command the loyalty of Rome's highly trained legions. Caesar rose to power on the strength of his undeniable military genius. He had built a reputation as an indomitable warrior, having fought successfully on disparate battle grounds: from naval incursions on the coasts of Britain to prolonged sieges in the towns of Gaul to great set battles in Germany, Greece, and Anatolia to running street fights in Egyptian Alexandria.

It was during Caesar's mopping-up campaign in Alexandria in 48 B.C. that the tough-minded fifty-two-year-old civil warrior had encountered twenty-one-year-old Cleopatra VII, who was then in the middle of her own civil war with her brother and sometime husband, Ptolemy XIII. Cleopatra and her brother were descendents of Ptolemy I, a Macedonian nobleman who had fought for Alexander the Great. After Alexander's death in 323 B.C. Ptolemy I seized the throne of Egypt by force of arms. The throne had been occupied by his linear descendants ever since—and they had taken up the practice of brother-sister marriage early on in order to ensure that ruler-ship of Egypt would remain a Ptolemaic family affair. Not surprisingly the family was not a happy one and young Cleopatra immediately grasped the advantages to be gained by contracting an alliance with the de facto ruler of the most powerful state the ancient world had ever seen. Accordingly, she arranged an introduction (reportedly by having herself smuggled into Caesar's apartments concealed inside a carpet). Making a quick assessment the situation, Caesar declared for Cleopatra. Ptolemy XIII was soon dead and with Caesar's legions behind her, Cleopatra was named undisputed queen of Egypt. She accompanied Caesar on a well-publicized tour down the Nile and, hardly coincidentally, the son she subsequently bore was nicknamed Caesarion—Little Caesar.

No doubt Julius Caesar found the young heiress to the throne of the Ptolemies attractive, but Egypt was much too important a place to allow ro-mantic sentiment to decide questions of long-term leadership. As a leading Roman aristocrat, Caesar had a wide choice of sexual partners, and he was much too serious a politician to throw his support behind anyone he re-garded as less than fully competent. Cleopatra was young, indeed, and a woman, but she had all the other prerequisites to be a successful client-ruler at the fringes of Roman authority. She had the right Ptolemaic bloodline, and so was likely to be accepted by her Egyptian and Greek-speaking sub-jects. And she had demonstrated in the civil war that she had the ruthless determination to do whatever was necessary to gain and hold power: she would never be swayed by family sentiment to spare a potential rival.

But Cleopatra had more than birthright and ruthlessness, she had an es-pecially clear apprehension of what it took to rule the diverse peoples of Egypt—native Egyptians, Greco-Macedonians, and Jews were only three of the most prominent ethnicities. Each ethnic group resident in Egypt had its own historical relationship to the Ptolemaic throne and its own religious rituals. Several had their own quarter in the thriving capital city of Alexan-dria, and their own strongholds in the vast agricultural hinterland formed by the annual flooding of the Nile. Unlike any of her monolingually Greek-speaking royal ancestors, Cleopatra learned at least some of the multiple languages used in her kingdom: she was the first Macedonian ruler of Egypt to speak Egyptian. Cleopatra was intensely aware of the complex set of political, social, economic, and especially religious roles that a successful ruler of Egypt (and client of Rome) would be required to play. And she played these with great finesse: appearing in Egyptian costume in the guise of the goddess Isis for her native Egyptian subjects, promoting Dionysian festivals for the Greeks, and leaving the Jews alone to practice their distinctive rites.

Cleopatra clearly grasped two vital political facts from the very beginning: First, in the age of Julius Caesar (and his successors) the single key factor in the flourishing of Egypt (and thus the ruler of Egypt) was retaining the favor of Rome—and this meant gaining and retaining the favor of powerful Romans. In Caesar's Rome, politics were very personal indeed—alliances were often made on the basis of kinship. And thus whatever she actually felt for Caesar (and there is no reason to deny that she found him good company: Caesar was a highly cultured man and a brilliant speaker as well as a great general), Cleopatra's best move was to contract an alliance with Rome's most powerful man. If possible, it should be the sort of intimate alliance that would result in progeny. Caesar might never acknowledge, in public and in Rome, that he had a son by the Egyptian queen. But Romans were very serious about ties of blood, and Caesar might be expected to look favorably upon a line of succession that would place his own bastard son on the throne of Egypt.

Second, Cleopatra realized that Egypt was both valuable and a potential problem to the Romans because of its wealth and relative security against invasion by land or sea. That wealth and defensible location helped the Ptolemaic rulers of Egypt to weather the fierce and protracted wars of succession that had dragged on for long generations after the death of Alexander. The Romans, for their part, had demonstrated an almost inexhaustible capacity to tap the accumulated wealth of the ancient world—paying the legions, sponsoring the festival games, and feeding the growing population of Rome took a huge amount of money. That constant appetite for wealth had contributed to the complex process by which Rome had absorbed much of the Mediterranean world, and all of the other great Hellenistic kingdoms, into the empire as provinces. Egypt, still technically independent, was a tempting prize. But also a dangerous prize: every Roman province required a provincial governor, and the competitive Roman aristocrats who dominated the Senate had long been worried about allowing any one of their number to take control of what might quickly become a private fiefdom. And so, Egypt had remained independent, but that independence required playing the game of Roman politics with skill, while making it clear that Egypt's wealth was always available to Rome (or to the right Romans) without the necessity of a war of annexation.

The bottom line, for Julius Caesar, was that Cleopatra was a good choice as queen of Egypt, from every perspective: good for Rome, and good for Caesar. That she was delightful company and bore him a son was icing on the cake, no doubt very tasty icing, but never to be confused with the cake itself.

The assassination of Julius Caesar in 44 B.C. threw many career plans into violent disarray and opened up a whole new field of play. The assassins quickly discovered that their "liberation" of Rome from "Caesar the tyrant" was much less popular with the other Romans than they had hoped. They quickly retired to the eastern empire, where they sought to raise money and recruit legionary armies. The most startling single career move was made by Octavian, Caesar's nineteen-year-old adopted son, who got the news of the killing while studying in Greece. Octavian reacted quickly. Sailing to Brundisium on the heel of Italy, he proceeded by road to Rome, picking up a huge retinue of his adoptive father's mustered-out troops along the way. Octavian arrived in Rome as a young man to contend with: that is to say, as a young man at the head of a personal army. Meanwhile, Mark Antony, one of Caesar's most promising lieutenants, had set himself in the forefront of the pro-Caesar loyalists—in part with a rousing public speech in the forum, made famous by Shakespeare ("Friends, Romans, countrymen . . ."). But Antony had dangerous enemies in the Senate, and he soon found himself declared a public enemy and embroiled in a war against senatorial forces in northern Italy. Octavian was dispatched by the Senators (who supposed they could use the youth to their own ends) to help the generals fighting against Antony. But Octavian and Antony found they had interests in common (for the time being at least). In conjunction with a third, well-armed partisan of Caesar, Marcus Lepidus, they joined their forces, forming the Second Triumvirate (the First Triumvirate, an alliance of Julius Caesar, Pompey the Great, and Marcus Crassus, had dominated Roman politics in the 50s B.C.).

The first duty of the triumvirs was to take revenge upon the assassins, who had by now assembled a considerable force in the East, in large part by extorting "taxes" from the unhappy provincials and by squeezing the client kingdoms of the East. Cleopatra, whose own early career had been so closely tied to Caesar's ascendant star, found herself in a very difficult position. Should she declare openly for the triumvirs and defiantly refuse to allow any fragment of the wealth of Egypt to be sent to build the armies of the so-called Liberators? Or should she play a more subtle game and wait to see who emerged as Rome's next preeminent strong man? In the end, she fended off the most pressing of the financial demands of the Liberators with pleas, not of loyalty to Caesar's memory, but to poverty: It seems that Egypt was suffering from both famine and disease and this prevented her from sending the assassins the ships and men they demanded. Meanwhile, Cleopatra covertly raised her own fleet and set out to sea, ostensibly to bring aid to the triumvirs. But bad weather intervened and the fleet returned to Alexandria without making contact with either friend or foe. Cleopatra was straddling the fence, waiting for the next decisive move in a game that would decide her own fate and that of Egypt. She saw that she could not yet hope to influence the game's outcome and the realization taught her an important lesson: Cleopatra would not again willingly allow herself to be a pawn, passively awaiting what fate might bring.

The forces of the triumvirs, well generaled by Antony (Octavian conveniently fell ill and so missed the military action), were victorious at Philippi. In the aftermath of the battle Antony and Octavian effectively divided control of the empire between them, with Antony taking as his primary sphere the East and Octavian the West.

There were scores to be settled in that summer of 41 B.C. Those Roman clients who had aided the Liberators must be punished; those who had resisted would be rewarded. But what of those who had sat on the fence? Just how they would fare would be up to one-sided negotiations with the new master of the Roman East. And so Mark Antony, stationing himself at Tarsus (in Cilicia on the southeastern Mediterranean coast of Anatolia), summoned the queen of Egypt to answer charges that she had secretly aided the cause of the Liberators.

Thus was set the stage for one of the most famous meetings in history: Cleopatra arrived at Tarsus on a sumptuous barge, invited Antony to dinner, and quickly persuaded him that (whatever she had done or had not done during the war between the triumvirs and the Liberators), he would be much better off with her as an active ally than as a deposed client-ruler. Presumably Antony and Cleopatra became lovers at that time; certainly Antony spent the winter in Alexandria, as the queen's guest. But as in the case of Caesar and Cleopatra, the sexual attraction was only one aspect of a larger political game, a game that would determine the course not just of individual careers, but of the Western world.

Antony needed the active support of the wealthy ruler of Egypt to defend and pursue his own and Rome's interests on two fronts. in the East, Antony was concerned with the expansionist tendencies of the Parthians, a bellicose semi-Hellenized people whose loose-knit kingdom stretched from Mesopotamia and the mountainous highlands of Persia eastward into central Asia. The Parthians had taken advantage of the disruptions of the Roman civil wars to push into Roman-occupied Syria, and their incursion potentially threatened the security of the entire eastern empire. The Parthians were a military force to be reckoned with: in 52 B.C. at Mesopotamian Carrhae they had handed Julius Caesar's triumviral colleague, Marcus Crassus, one of the worst and most humiliating defeats of recent Roman military history. Parthian mounted archers had chopped Crassus's infantry to shreds in the open plains of Mesopotamia. The legionary standards, the sacred "Eagles," that were lost at Carrhae had never yet been recovered. There was no doubt that a major campaign against the Parthians must be a central feature of Antony's Eastern sojourn; and no question but that it would be a difficult and expensive campaign. But events in Italy soon complicated the immediate goals (raise money [especially from Egypt], gather and train troops, shore up tottering client states, plan an invasion route that would avoid the open plains, and force the Parthians to come to terms). While Antony had been occupied in the East, some of his relatives had taken it upon themselves to raise an army and attack forces loyal to Octavian. Worse yet, they made a mess of it; the "Antonine" forces were besieged and compelled to surrender in midwinter of 40 B.C.

Antony was thus pulled in two directions: He was eager to begin operations against the Parthians, but if he did not want an open break with Octavian (a break that could only lead to more civil war, and so to more inroads on Roman-held territory by the Parthians), he must go to Italy and take the lay of the land. When he got there he found a complicated situation; along with everything else, one of the sons of Pompey the Great, Sextus Pompey, had raised a navy and was emerging as an independent military factor, potentially threatening Italy's vital lines of supply. Sextus knew that there had been trouble between the triumvirs and offered Antony an alliance against Octavian. But Sextus was an unsavory character with no reputation for sticking by his agreements. Antony stuck by Octavian, sealing their renewed alliance by marrying his partner's sister, Octavia. The de facto division of the empire was renewed as well, with Octavian inheriting the responsibility for looking after matters in Italy, and Antony taking on full responsibility for the Parthian threat. While still in Rome, Antony proved his loyalty by intervening when Octavian was threatened by a mob furious over elevated taxes. Meanwhile, Antony's loyal lieutenant, Ventidius, was pushing the Parthians out of Syria. Antony could return East with a sense of being on top of things; accompanied by his new wife he took up residence in Athens and began preparations for the great Parthian campaign. It appeared, for a while, as if the Second Triumvirate might prove durable.

That appearance was deceptive. Octavian's ambition was not limited to the western empire, but he needed to rack up some dramatic military victories if he were to prove himself Antony's equal in the eyes of the Romans—and especially of the legionaries. Octavian did not have a brilliant military mind; his greatest skills were in the area of politics and shaping public opinion. But he also proved highly adept at attracting talented and loyal people to his side. Among his most important "human resource assets" was Marcus Agrippa, a member of an obscure Roman family who proved to be outstanding at organizing and conducting large-scale naval operations.

Octavian set his sights on Sextus Pompey; crushing the last independent naval operation in the Mediterranean, and thereby assuring his own capacity to control the vital grain supply to the city of Rome, would be a public relations coup. But it would take some doing, not least because Antony was opposed to making war on Sextus, with whom the triumvirs had signed a pact. Ignoring his partner's requests that he desist military operations, Octavian launched an ambitious campaign against Sextus. He immediately ran into difficulties, losing many of his ships to the sudden and violent storms that plague Mediterranean shipping. Despite his irritation, Antony refused to take advantage of Octavian's weak position; instead of backstabbing, he came to Italy and offered his brother-in-law substantial material support. Yet Octavian proudly refused; Octavian knew that he would never cement a reputation as a victorious general if he remained in Antony's shadow. And so the campaign against Sextus continued with ever-higher taxes raised from an increasingly disgruntled Roman population. Antony began to perceive the shape of things to come: The triumvirate would survive only until Octavian felt ready to make his bid for the entire empire.

In 37 B.C., Antony finally turned his full attention to the Parthian campaign, an operation that had been delayed due to his abortive attempt to help out Octavian at the nadir of the campaign against Sextus. Despite their agreement to share Italy as a neutral military recruiting ground, Octavian clearly intended to block any attempt his erstwhile partner might make to raise funds or men in Italy. If he were to take on the Parthians, Antony needed to raise massive funding in order to recruit and train a really big army. And this meant a return to Egypt and Cleopatra.

The queen was ready to negotiate and a deal was struck: She would pay for his legions; Antony in turn granted Cleopatra control of certain client-territories under Roman control and he recognized as legitimate his twin children by Cleopatra: Alexander Helios ("the Sun") and Cleopatra Selene ("the Moon"). Cleopatra was by now in an even stronger position than she had been after the birth of Caesarion (now a boy of ten, and still very much in the succession picture): she was the consort of and the mother of the children of the most important Roman in the East. Cleopatra had played her key cards—Egypt's wealth and her own reproductive capacity—with great skill. If Antony fulfilled his promise as a general, the future of independent Egypt—and the future of its new/old line of Romano-Macedonian rulers—looked very rosy indeed.

The year 36 B.C. would prove decisive: Octavian's renewed campaign against Sextus Pompey and Antony's grand invasion of Parthian Mesopotamia unrolled in parallel dimensions, the one on sea and the other over land. But, contrary to all expectations, whereas Octavian's campaign went like clockwork (thanks to the careful advance planning of Agrippa), Antony's campaign against the Parthians proved to be an unmitigated disaster. The route of invasion, through Armenia and down the headwaters of the Tigris to the heart of Parthian territory, was well thought through—carefully avoiding the open desert terrain that had doomed Crassus at Carrhae. But the departure of the expedition from its Armenian base was unaccountably delayed, forcing Antony to push his infantry ahead of his siege-train in the march south. His ill-defended siege-train was captured by the highly mobile Parthian cavalry. And deprived of his siege engines, Antony failed to capture the key stronghold of Phraaspa, where he probably intended to winter his troops. The client-king of Armenia suddenly withdrew his vital cavalry units. The king of the Parthians refused to be bluffed into turning over the lost Roman standards. In the course of an inglorious Roman retreat north, the "finest army that any commander of that epoch gathered together" (Plutarch) was routed by the Parthians. Antony had lost some two-fifths of his force, perhaps 32,000 men total, mostly to hunger, weather, and disease.

Octavian's glorious naval victory and Antony's disastrous overland failure laid the groundwork for the decisive encounter at Actium five years later.

Antony's options narrowed considerably after his expedition into Parthia. The loss of men, material, and especially prestige in the eyes of his fellow Romans represented very serious setbacks. Before the Parthian disaster, Antony had been able to play a variety of roles simultaneously; now he would have to make some choices. It was no longer possible for him to act at once as Octavian's cooperative partner in the management of the Roman Empire, Octavian's sometime rival for supremacy in the Roman state, and a freelance potentate in the Hellenistic East. At least one of those roles would have to be dropped, and another would have to be prioritized. Antony's subsequent actions elucidate his decision: the facade of cooperative partnership was dropped and the role of Hellenistic dynast became primary. The rivalry with Octavian would continue, but now it would be carried out in terms of the forces of the East, led by Antony and financed by Cleopatra, versus the forces of the West, led by Octavian and financed by Roman taxpayers. Antony's decision was finalized by his refusal to accept fresh troops and supplies offered by his wife, Octavia: the troops were too few, the supplies too parsimonious in comparison with those he could expect from Egypt.

Acting very much as a Hellenistic dynast, Antony moved quickly to shore up his alliances with the lesser dynasts of Asia, especially the king of Media, who might prove an effective counterweight to the expansionist Parthians. He also moved decisively against the treasonous king of Armenia, defeating the Armenian forces in battle and capturing the king himself, who was taken back to Egypt in silver chains. In the aftermath of that victory, Antony held a grand celebration in Alexandria. It had overtones of the official Roman general's Triumph—a sacred victory parade that could only be celebrated in Rome. Moreover, again acting in his role as Hellenistic dynast, he formally granted control over various Asian territories to his young children by Cleopatra. Caesarion was declared joint ruler with his mother over Egypt.

In Italy, Octavian, master of spin, saw that Antony was playing into his hand. The grants of Asian territory, the notorious "Donations of Alexandria," could be sold to the Roman audience as proof positive that Antony had "gone Eastern" and had renounced his primary loyalty to "the Senate and People of Rome." Antony still had many partisans in Rome who clung to the memory of Antony as Caesar's loyal comrade. But Octavian's verbal attacks cleverly shifted attention from Antony to Cleopatra herself. Antony was not to be depicted as a monster, but as the drink-and-love besotted dupe of a diabolically clever and limitlessly ambitious Eastern witch. Octavian concocted a story to the effect that Cleopatra hoped to rule over the entire Roman Empire, establishing her sway over the city of Rome itself. And thus, loyalty to Antony could be recast as treason against Rome. Realizing the growing danger, the pro-Antony senators fled East. With their departure, Octavian enjoyed undisputed control of Rome. Among his first actions was to seize Antony's will from the Vestal Virgins, the sacrosanct priestesses in whose care Antony had left his testament. Portions were read out to the rump-Senate of Octavian supporters: among its scandalous provisions was Antony's request to be buried in Egypt, next to his queen. Proof positive, screamed the propaganda machine, that Cleopatra had seduced Antony into renouncing his Roman heritage.

By 32 B.C., there was no further doubt that the Roman civil wars had entered their next "hot" phase and both sides gathered their forces. With Cleopatra's financial backing, Antony was able to raise an impressive force: some nineteen legions—about 75,000 men, including veterans of the campaigns of Philippi and Parthia; 25,000 auxiliary infantry (non-Roman troops raised from around the Eastern empire); 12,000 cavalry; 500 heavy oared warships; and 300 merchant ships to carry supplies. Antony could not use this mighty force to invade Italy: that would play all too readily into Octavian's story about "Cleopatra the would-be Queen of the World." But it must have been with serious misgivings that Antony took up a defensive position at Actium and awaited Octavian's attack: The "defensive position in Greece" strategy made sense in terms of forcing his opponent to stretch supply lines across the Adriatic, but it had recently proved fatal to the hopes of Pompey the Great and the Liberators.

Fatal as well, as it turned out, for Antony. Octavian's campaign of disinformation mounted a crescendo: the war was a patriotic crusade. Not, of course, against his old friend Antony, but against the terrifying seductress Cleopatra. "All Italy," Octavian later boasted, "of its own volition, swore an oath of loyalty to me." Exaggeration to be sure, but indicative of the tenor of Octavian's public relations effort, an effort that eventually proved corrosive to the loyalty of many of Antony's fighting men and his key senatorial supporters. Antony's problem with maintaining morale in the face of Octavian's hostile propaganda was compounded by Cleopatra's presence in his own camp. As Antony's paymaster and most important ally, she meant to keep a close eye on operations. And we may suppose that her decision to put herself in the center of the action was sealed by the shadow of the period after the death of Julius Caesar, when she had had no choice but to sit on the fence, nervously awaiting the outcome of military events over which she had no control. But the Romans in Antony's camp understood none of this. They increasingly found it hard to deny that there might be some truth in Octavian's charges: Maybe that woman did have some unnatural hold over their commander. And if so, who were they really fighting for after all? For his part, Antony was finding that his role as Hellenistic dynast made it extremely difficult to work with traditional Romans—men who were used to giving commands to oriental potentates, not taking commands from them.

Meanwhile, on Octavian's side, Agrippa was displaying his usual efficiency as an admiral. The fleet headed out from Brundisium, via Corcyra, to establish a primary base at the future site of Nicopolis; Antony's main camp was due south, just across a narrow strait, on the Actium peninsula. By quickly establishing a secondary naval base in a harbor south of Actium, Agrippa bottled up the better part of Antony's warships in the Ambracian Gulf. Meanwhile, Antony's own attempts to force a land battle by using his cavalry to cut off Octavian's camp from its water supply fell short. The campaign was stalemated: Antony dared not offer battle by sea, nor Octavian by land. But defections and disease were decimating Antony's forces; time was clearly on Octavian's side.

By September 2, 31 B.C., Antony was desperate. His only hope of extricating himself from the increasingly dire situation was by risking open battle at sea with his 230 remaining ships. The resulting battle was hard fought, but Octavian had many more ships and the numbers told against Antony's forces. In the afternoon, as the wind came, a squadron of some eighty ships led by Cleopatra's flagship broke through the screen of enemy warships, raised sails, and made a dash south for Egypt. With Antony following, they made good their escape. Octavian's partisans would later say that Cleopatra's flight from the battle was precipitous; but it is more likely that the breakout was carefully planned. Cleopatra's ships, like Antony's, had deliberately carried sails into battle; normally ancient oared ships entered battles stripped of their heavy sails.

Despite Antony's escape, Octavian had won the battle, and decisively. Antony's land army broke camp and withdrew in good order through Macedonia. Octavian the politician knew enough not to press the issue. Rather than challenging Antony's intact land force to battle, he opened negotiations with them; Antony's defeated forces would be bought off. Octavian could afford it. With the whole of the wealthy Eastern empire about to fall to his hands, he had no further reason to worry about money. And fall it quickly did. Antony made no serious attempt to defend Egypt against the invasion that soon followed. He committed suicide by sword. Cleopatra, now Octavian's captive, followed her lover's example by deploying the famous asp. Egypt with all its material and cultural riches became Octavian's personal possession. The eastern and western ends of the Roman Empire were now reunited under the authority of a single man. Octavian was eventually given the name "Augustus Caesar" by his grateful subjects, and the age of the emperors began.

But none of this might have come to pass if the events had proceeded somewhat differently in the year 36 B.C.

Antony's failure at Actium had nothing to do with the size of Cleopatra's nose, and everything to do with the military disaster he suffered in Parthia in 36. It was the loss of men, arms, and prestige that precipitated his fatal decision to embrace the role of Hellenistic dynast, and thus to take on Cleopatra as an ally of equal standing—rather than treating Egypt as a client kingdom, which would enjoy a tenuous independence only for so long as it pleased Rome. That decision cannot have been made lightly— Antony knew enough Roman history to grasp just how hard it would be for an Eastern potentate (even one born Roman) to challenge the sway exercised by the city on the Tiber.

But what if Antony had been more successful in Parthia? There is every reason to suppose he could have been: He was a fine general, his large army was in excellent condition, and his basic strategy (securing Armenia, invading via the Tigris headwaters) was subsequently used successfully by Roman imperial generals. The Parthians would come to terms if pressed; they later turned over the lost standards in a negotiated settlement to one of Octavian's generals—a diplomatic coup that Octavian never tired of trumpeting.

Antony's key error in 36 seems to have been in the timing of the expedition's launch. We will never be able to penetrate the fog of Octavian's propaganda sufficiently to explain why in fact the expedition left Armenia so late in the campaigning season. But let us suppose that Antony had been just a bit more prescient in 38 B.C., and saw then that it would be a waste of time to seek to deflect Octavian from striking at Sextus Pompey. Let's suppose that he saw that it would be a further waste of time to seek to aid Octavian after the disastrous first naval campaign against Sextus. Let us suppose, then, that in 38 and 37 Antony stayed sharply focused on his own impending campaign against the Parthians, putting all of his considerable talents and energies into launching his forces as early as possible in the campaigning season of 36. If the departure had been on time, he would not have been constrained to leave his siege-train defenseless during the southern march. The stronghold of Phraaspa would have fallen to superior Roman siege craft before winter. And thus, there would have been every reason for the pragmatic Parthians to negotiate a deal similar to the one they in fact eventually negotiated with Octavian.

A victory in Parthia in 36 would have dramatically expanded Antony's subsequent options. The return of the standards lost by Crassus would have wiped away the shame of one of the greatest losses ever suffered by Rome's legions. Octavian could not possibly have denied his partner the right to celebrate a grand Triumph in Rome. The prestige of defeating the barbarous Parthians would have more than counterbalanced Agrippa's civil-war successes against Sextus Pompey in the eyes of the Roman people. Antony would have no difficulties recruiting men wherever he pleased. There would have been no realistic possibility of keeping him out of Rome—if, indeed, he wanted to spend time extending his influence in the city. But by the same token, there is no necessary reason to suppose that he would have chosen to spend the rest of his career in Italy.

"Marcus Antonius Parthicus—Mark Antony, Victor over the Parthians" might well have chosen to spend most of his time in the East. There can be little doubt that Antony genuinely enjoyed his life in Alexandria, including the company of Cleopatra. She was in every sense his intellectual peer, and had lived an exciting life in which her successes and failures were direct products of her own decisions. She had a bright sense of humor and was overall splendid company for a man with Antony's background and tastes. In brief, she was a good deal more interesting than most of the Roman women Antony would have known. And Alexandria was a genuinely fascinating, highly cultured city. Defeating the Parthians would have allowed Antony to enjoy Alexandria and Cleopatra's company on his own terms. Whatever their assumed level of equality when in private, he could have maintained a "properly" Roman political distance from the queen of Egypt in public. There would have been no need for the politically embarrassing spectacle of the "Donations of Alexandria"—at least not until Octavian had been dealt with once and for all.

Octavian would indeed need to be dealt with: Julius Caesar's adopted son was simply too ambitious, too power hungry to have allowed Antony to remain at a level of genuine parity. Eventually, and probably sooner than later, there would have been a break between them: the Battle of Actium (or some simulacrum thereof) was bound to be fought. Because Antony lost to the Parthians, events in the five years after 36 B.C. went almost entirely in Octavian's favor, and they fed his increasingly strident campaign of propaganda and disinformation. But that campaign of words and images would have had much less to work with had Antony been successful in Parthia. Rather than the sad dupe of Cleopatra, Octavian would be taking on the man who was unquestionably the premier general of his age. Even with the aid of Agrippa, master of naval operations, Octavian would be hard-pressed to come up with a winning strategy against such a figure and the high-morale army he would command. Even as it actually took place, the Actium campaign was not an easy victory for Octavian. Going up against an army and a general that did not suffer from the "Cleopatra factor" would have been a far greater risk.

Had Antony defeated Octavian's forces at Actium—most likely by forcing a land battle—he would need to return to Italy for at least a while. Like

Sulla in 86 B.C., Antony would need to mop up pro-Octavian forces. And he would need to arrange political matters in Rome to his own liking.

What might his arrangement have entailed? There is not much reason to suppose that Antony shared Octavian's monarchical vision for the Roman Empire—it is more likely that Antony would have purged the Senate of Octavian's partisans and packed it with his own. But then he might have left the aristocracy to rule (within the bounds set by the military strongman of the hour), as it had throughout the period of the Republic. Antony might have divided his time between Rome and Alexandria, between working to ensure the continuity of a stable "Antonine" aristocracy in Rome and establishing Egypt and its queen at the center of a stable group of quasi-independent client states in the East. On this model, Egypt would not have become a Roman province, nor would (for example) Judea. Cleopatra (and her heirs) would dominate the southeastern Mediterranean culturally and economically, careful never to act in any way that might appear to threaten Rome's supremacy. Antony had realized (and would teach his own political heirs) that active rulership of this very tricky part of the world—with its mosaic of religious commitments and cultural traditions—was best left to the Macedonian descendents of Ptolemy I, who had spent generations developing techniques for maximizing revenues while minimizing cultural conflicts.

The long-term historical effects of such an arrangement in the eastern Empire, especially if we imagine the politically astute, multilingual, culturally sophisticated Cleopatra as its behind-the-scenes architect, would have been profound. Mediterranean culture and commerce would have revolved around two great poles—Alexandria and Rome. Interchange between the two would have been constant and intense: Roman exposure to Greek culture would be primarily mediated through the multicultural filter of Egypt's capital city.

Egyptian-speaking Cleopatra would see that the weak point in Ptolemaic social policy had been the segregation of Egyptian and Greek cultures. In her own person she was a cultural fusionist, and with the Roman military to restrain open expressions of resentment on the part of any of her Greek subjects who felt that equity for Egyptians threatened their own privileges, Cleopatra would have been able to make significant inroads in the traditional exclusion of ethnic Egyptians from active participation in the life of the city.

Among the most striking social developments, especially from the perspective of traditional Romans, would be the relatively greater freedom enjoyed by women in Egypt. Under Ptolemaic rule, native Egyptian women, mostly living outside of Alexandria, had retained their traditional rights: they could go into law, inherit real estate, and operate businesses in their own name. Now that pattern of relatively greater gender equality could spread into the capital city. Among the Alexandrian elite, Cleopatra's own example would have provided the model for an expansion of educational, cultural, perhaps even political opportunities for women. An openly multicultural society in which women took on some of the roles traditional Romans had always supposed were uniquely the preserve of men, would have been highly attractive to certain Greeks and Romans—Antony's tastes in culture and society were hardly unique. Egypt would continue to benefit from the talents of immigrants eager to find a place in the relatively open culture that contrasted so starkly with most of the societies that had so far flourished around the Mediterranean basin. The culture that would have emerged within a few generations after Actium might indeed begin to look remarkably "modern" to the eyes of twenty-first-century readers.

Meanwhile, the "Egyptian zone" of the southeastern Mediterranean would remain a center of religious innovation—and a hotbed of imaginative interfaces between religion and state. The early Ptolemies had proved themselves to be open-minded and inventive in the religious sphere, creating a composite state religion based on the god Serapis, which had blended Greek and Egyptian elements. Cleopatra had strongly encouraged identification of herself with the highly popular Egyptian goddess Isis, but she was happy to mix the rituals associated with a variety of deities into the frequent religious celebrations in which she and Antony participated.

If Antony had won at Actium, Jesus of Nazareth, born just a short generation after the battle, would have come to manhood in a very different society—one administered by highly trained professional Ptolemaic bureaucrats, rather than nervous Roman amateurs like Pontius Pilate. Those Ptolemaic bureaucrats would have had a much closer sense of how Jerusalem politics worked: they might well have found some solution to local concerns about a self-proclaimed messiah that would not have required his crucifixion. They might, for example, have arranged for him to move to Alexandria, where the sophisticated, hellenized local Jewish population would not be scandalized by his audacious ideas. So Jesus might have grown old, gathering to himself a following attracted by his socioreligious message rather than by a dramatic martyrdom. If so, Christianity would have developed quite differently and Alexandria, not Rome, would be its center.

If the new religion found quick and wide acceptance within the realm, the flexible heirs of Cleopatra would have found a place for it in the festival life of the city, perhaps eventually putting Serapis on the back burner and (like the Roman emperor Constantine in the fourth century A.D.) promoting Christianity as the favored state religion. Let us suppose, for a moment, that Caesarion, son of Julius Caesar, had succeeded his mother on the throne, and (keeping it all in the family, as the Ptolemies were prone to do) had married Cleopatra VIII Selene, daughter of Antony and Cleopatra. They in turn might have had a daughter, who would surely (following highly conservative Ptolematic naming practice) also be named Cleopatra. This hypothetical Cleopatra IX might have come to the throne at the time that Christianity was officially incorporated into the Egyptian state religion, a religion in which the queen of Egypt must of course be a central figure. And so we might imagine that a woman with a remarkable ancestry, granddaughter of Julius Caesar, of Mark Antony, and (twice over) of Cleopatra VII, would become Founding High Priestess—"Lady Pope" of the Universal Alexandrian Church of Jesus the Uncrucified.

In any event, the world we live in would be very different, and perhaps not worse, if the stone-wall monument above Nicopolis had displayed pieces of the warships of Octavian rather than of those lost by Mark Antony at the battle of Actium.

CARLOS M. N. EIRE

# PONTIUS PILATE SPARES JESUS

## Christianity without the Crucifixion

*Take away the crucifixion and you have erased the central moment of the Christian religion. Is it blasphemous to wonder what would have happened if Pontius Pilate, the Roman procurator of Jerusalem, had not ordered Jesus of Nazareth to be nailed to a cross but had spared him? What sort of life might Jesus have led? And, more important, how might the faith that he founded have developed and what sort of influence might it have had? How might the Romans have turned it to their advantage?*

*That new religion, speculates Carlos M. N. Eire, the chairman of the Department of Religious Studies at Yale University, would have been monotheistic but hardly Christianity as we know it. In essence, it would have been a form of Judaism, but a form that persecuted those who disagreed with its interpretation of Jesus: those who refused to accept him as a prophet or, conversely, those who believed him to be the Messiah—in other words, the people we now know as Jews and Christians. For Rome, a crucifixionless Christianity might have been a blessing, as Eire explains, because such an official state religion could have helped the empire survive into our own time. Still, what would our world be like without an Easter or a Christmas?*

CARLOS M. N. EIRE is the T. Lawrason Riggs Professor of History and Religious Studies at Yale University and chairs the Department of Religious Studies. He is the author of *War Against the Idols: The Reformation of Worship from Erasmus to Calvin* and *From Madrid to Purgatory: The Art and Craft of Dying in Sixteenth-Century Spain*. A memoir of his childhood during the Cuban Revolution, *Kiss the Lizard, Cuban Boy*, is forthcoming.

THE PRISONER STOOD before the procurator, bruised and bleeding, his hands bound, and his head ringed with thorns. A crude crown, made by Roman soldiers.

A zero, ringed with thorns, on the head of this rabbi.

The crowd kept calling for crucifixion, but the procurator hesitated and stalled. He couldn't pass sentence. Not that sentence. Not yet. Maybe there was some other way to save this prisoner from death. He had already pronounced him innocent, and so had Herod, the local "puppet" king who ruled over Galilee, the prisoner's homeland.

He kept thinking about that message his wife had sent him, urgently, by means of a servant. Like many Romans, the procurator placed a lot of faith in dreams, especially those that spoke directly to present affairs. Dreams were messages from the gods. And here, in godless Judaea, where they worshiped only one measly deity who was very touchy, and overly jealous, the gods had spoken to his wife.

He couldn't get the message out of his mind, not just because it was troubling, but also because his wife was such a good conduit for messages from the gods. She didn't garble the messages, or get them wrong. She was good at it. Better than most.

"Have nothing to do with that righteous man," the message read, "for today I have suffered much over him in a dream."

He had already tried to free this prisoner by offering the crowd a choice between him and the notorious rebel Barabbas. Much to his chagrin, the crowd had chosen freedom for the accused murderer instead of the rabbi.

And the crowd called for the rabbi to be crucified, again and again.

Accursed place, this Palestine, to which he had been sent. How he longed for those balmy summer evenings in his native Tarraco, in Iberia, on the shores of Mare Nostrum—Our Sea, the Mediterranean. No better place on earth.

He had already ordered a severe scourging for the prisoner, thinking this would satisfy the crowd's thirst for punishment. Then he ordered that the rabbi be paraded before the crowd, arrayed in a gorgeous purple cloak—an ironic joke from Herod—with that stupid crown on his head. Maybe these morons would get the joke and leave the poor man be.

Pilate yelled to the crowd, "Behold your king!"

But the crowd still called for crucifixion. Morons, all of them.

His own judgment and conscience weighed in heavily against giving in to the crowd. And then there was message about the dream. He couldn't dismiss that so easily. No. Not at all.

Pilate spoke: "You brought me this man as one who was perverting the people; and after examining him before you, behold, I didn't find this man guilty of any of your charges against him."

The crowd yelled more loudly: "Crucify him! Crucify him!"

Pilate pronounced him innocent again. And the crowd grew increasingly hostile. "Crucify, crucify him!" Pilate spoke a third time: "Why? What evil has he done? I have found in him no crime deserving death; I will therefore chastise him and release him."

The crowd yelled all the louder. The noise unnerved Pilate, but his conscience unnerved him even more. If he were to release this man, would he have a riot on his hands? What would be the best thing to do here? Spare the life of an innocent man, who posed no threat to the empire, or sacrifice that life for the sake of peace in Jerusalem?

He hated riots. All that property damage. All those corpses, and all those casualties. He hated to lose any of his soldiers, especially.

He hated the thought of having to face his wife too and of having to tell her that he had disregarded her dream. He heard her voice in his own head, speaking clearly and very loudly from the future, any time some misfortune should befall them: "See! See! It's all your fault: I told you not to crucify that man in Jerusalem!" That was it. Yes. That clinched it.

Over the roar of the crowd, Pilate shouted at the soldiers as loudly as he could: "Release the prisoner. Release him now! Forget any additional punishment. He's suffered enough. Release him and escort him back to Galilee. Now!"

He placed his hand on the rabbi's shoulder as he walked by, and neither man said a word. Jesus looked Pilate straight in the eye with a look of total bewilderment. Pilate looked away and stared at his hand—the one with which he had touched Jesus. He stared at it for a minute or so, and at the blood on it. He called for water. "I need to wash my hands," he said to one of the guards.

The crowd went wild, but nothing much happened. A few tried to start a riot, but the soldiers took care of that quickly. Roman soldiers knew how to handle such situations. This was an easy crowd to control, compared to others they'd seen. A few cracked skulls, some broken bones, a few puncture wounds. A little bit of blood. That's all. The crowd dispersed within an hour.

Pilate went home early and told his wife about the hard day he'd had and how much he'd appreciated that message she sent him.

It turned out to be a beautiful, sunny spring afternoon. Pilate and his wife drank three jars of wine that evening. Wine from Italy they'd been saving for a special occasion. They toasted the glowing sunset in that godless land, thanked the gods for their messages, fell asleep early on their dining couches, and snored so loudly that the slaves began to laugh and woke them up.

And Jesus of Nazareth returned to Galilee, under escort. There, out in the hinterland, he continued to teach and preach, and to cure the sick, and astound the crowds that flocked to him like sheep. Every now and then he showed up in Jerusalem, especially at Passover—that is, until that rebellion against Rome when the Jerusalem temple was destroyed. After that, he stopped coming to Jerusalem.

Many around him thought Jesus was the Messiah, the savior promised by God to the Jewish people, and he did his best to keep them guessing. Some proclaimed this message, up until the day he died, crucified by his own aging body and its 1,001 infirmities.

And after his death? What?

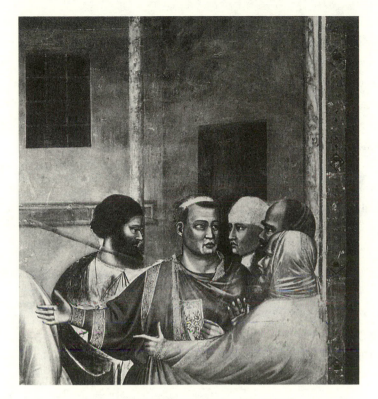

THE DECISION THAT MADE A RELIGION
*Pontius Pilate (second from left) discusses the fate of Jesus, in a fourteenth-century fresco by Giotto. Pilate would elect to crucify the troublesome religious leader, thereby presenting the Christian religion with its central unifying moment.*

(Giotto di Bondone, 1266–1336, detail from *The Mocking of Christ*, Scrovegni Chapel, Padua, Italy. Alinari/Art Resource, NY)

• • •

What if Jesus hadn't been nailed to a cross at Pilate's orders? What if he had lived a long, long life? Or even just ten more years? Or one? What if his person and message had been interpreted differently, as they surely would have been?

These are impertinent questions for a believing Christian—questions only an impious dog would dare ask, as John Calvin might have said in the sixteenth century. Believing that the world was saved through the crucifix-ion of Jesus is central to the Christian faith. For any believing Christian this counterfactual exercise is the ultimate blasphemy. The answer any tra-ditional Christian theologian would have to give to our "what if?" question is quite simple: If Jesus hadn't been crucified, there would have been no re-demption from sin and death, and the entire human race would be headed straight for hell.

Rewriting history with a different Jesus is a daunting enterprise. If you al-ter the central figure of the Christian religion, what might you end up with?

Religion is such an unpredictable factor in history, perhaps one of the most unpredictable. It is not entirely rational. Its very nature is to seek transcendence, and the coincidence of opposites. Paradox is always key. Sometimes, especially in the case of the Christian religion, the deepest and largest claims of truth are those that are most radically paradoxical.

This means that if you deal with the wild card of religion in any histori-cal narrative and try to rewrite history, you are balancing on a high tightrope, and often without a net. Finding "facts" to tweak in religious his-tory is not easy. Even single events, which could be considered pivotal facts, such as the crucifixion of Jesus, do not lend themselves readily to a counterfactual approach. This is because religion necessarily involves be-liefs, and beliefs are among the fuzziest of "facts."

Even the "minimal rewrite," that is, the changing of one small, highly plausible fact, is hard to carry off with confidence in religious history. One of the most common, and most plausible minimal rewrites in counterfac-tual history is that which kills off the protagonist earlier than he or she died in real history. The proposition may seem simple enough—but not when it comes to religion. Consider this: The minimal rewrite that kills off Jesus is impossible, since it is the fact that he was killed prematurely that started the Christian religion and remains the basis of an entire structure of belief, the cornerstone of thousands of institutions.

Any fact related to Jesus, then, is embedded in a thick bundle of para-doxes. Facts are inverted, folded into counterfacts, into beliefs. The prime "facts" the historian has to work with in the story of Jesus and the religion he founded are not bare historical facts, but beliefs. And here is the rub: Beliefs leave you with no clearly defined line between the objective and subjective.

Religion is all about interpretation.

And a figure such as Jesus of Nazareth is like a lightning rod that attracts interpretations. To speculate on what might have happened if anything at all had been different in the story of Jesus and his followers is to sail in an infinite ocean of possibilities.

So, what if Jesus had lived to a ripe old age? Or even just one year longer?

It could have happened, easily enough. Pontius Pilate did not have to condemn Jesus to death by crucifixion. This is what all the gospel accounts tell us. And the prime reason might have well been a procurator's desire to heed the warning given to him by his wife, for a complex set of reasons—or perhaps for a reason as simple and mundane as a husband not wanting to give his wife yet another chance to nag him for the rest of his life.

So, what might have happened if Pilate had listened to his wife?

Flash forward one year.

Jesus is still attracting huge crowds wherever he goes. It's not just what he says, but what he does that draws people to him. Especially the healing. When word comes that Jesus is near, the afflicted as well as the healthy flock to him. He moves from town to town, as always, never staying in any one place too long. Many of his relatives still think he is insane, but have given up on rescuing him from his delusions. Mary, his mother, remains at his side much of the time, and still supports and encourages him.

He still depends on twelve disciples to help him with his mission. Judas has been replaced by another man, handpicked by Jesus. As always, all twelve of them are confused and perplexed. What is Jesus trying to do? What is going on?

Jesus himself has a very clear sense of who he is and what he needs to do, but awaits the direction of the Father he always mentions. The Father doesn't always reveal His intentions, so Jesus goes from town to town healing the sick, preaching the coming of the Kingdom of God, expelling demons from those who are possessed by them, and, occasionally, it is rumored, raising people from the dead.

Jesus asks himself: "What happened last year?" He thought then that going to Jerusalem at Passover would have been the turning point, the ushering in of the Kingdom of God. He was ready to suffer and die. He didn't like the idea, but he was ready. He had even told his disciples he would be killed. Maybe the Father had heeded one of his prayers on the night he was arrested? "Father, if you are willing, remove this cup from me; nevertheless not my will, but yours be done."

The Father always acted in mysterious ways. When and how would his Kingdom come? He kept telling the disciples that even he, Jesus, didn't know. Only the Father knew.

But he knew he had to go to Jerusalem again at Passover. He had to. Maybe this time he'd be killed. He didn't know what would happen, but he had to go where the Father led him.

It was so different now. There was much less talk about the Messiah among his followers. Last year's arrest had shaken them up. They had all fled. Even Peter, their leader, had turned tail and denied him, as Jesus knew he would. The arrest, and the torture, and the trial had made many redefine their Messianic hopes, and their view of Jesus. Could the genuine Messiah allow himself to be handled so roughly, and come so close to death? Many were now saying that Jesus was merely a great prophet: another Elijah, another John the Baptist.

Jesus listened to what people said. He always did. And many believed he could read their minds.

So he went to Jerusalem again, not knowing exactly what would happen and yet knowing, in that peculiar way of his. This time, thanks to Pilate, no harm came to him. He preached the Kingdom, expelled demons, and healed the sick. And all of the religious elites who despised him could do nothing but wring their hands.

Those Roman soldiers were such good guards. Some were the very same men who had scourged him and beaten him up, but he had forgiven them, and they now had a very special affection for him.

He knew he had to descend into every hell, every single hell, and offer himself up in the place of every human bound by sin. But when would this happen? Not this year, it seems, he thought as he made his way back to Galilee with his disciples.

This scenario repeated itself many times over. Year after year he preached the Kingdom, celebrated Passover in Jerusalem, and waited for the Kingdom to come. He sacrificed his life, hour by hour, day by day, ministering to his people, tirelessly, waiting for the sacrifice to be offered, for his blood to be spilled. Year after year, he received protection from the Roman authorities. They liked what he had to say, despite all his talk about a Kingdom to come. The Romans knew that all of this Kingdom talk is like that of followers of Mithras, or Zoroaster, or even the Egyptian mother-goddess Isis. Spiritual talk, that's all. He taught people to turn the other cheek and forgive their enemies. What a wonderful message to preach to a subject people! Anyone who preached docile submission must be protected, especially if he also encouraged people to pay their taxes.

"Render unto Caesar what belongs to Caesar. . . ."


Emperors Tiberius, Claudius, Caligula, and Nero will hear of this Jesus and heartily approve of having him protected and so will their immediate successors. If only other subject nations could have such a prophet and teacher! So what if Jesus and his followers refuse to worship the gods of the empire? There's plenty of room for that Jewish God in the pantheon of all divinities. No one in their right mind would think that the Jewish God could totally displace all the other gods that exist and are worshiped. So what if this sect balks at worshiping the emperor? Better to allow these people to teach and practice submission than to insist on worship of the emperor. Only that crazy Caligula really believed he was a god, anyway. The others knew better. Any wise Roman knows that Jesus is a gift from the gods—a strange one, since he denies their existence, but a gift all the same. The gods have a strange sense of humor.

By the time he is sixty years old, Jesus has many more followers than he can handle or control. There are so many different ways in which his message and work are being interpreted. So many ways to interpret what Jesus has said and done. So many ways to interpret that change he made in the

Passover dinner ritual, in which he distributed matzoh and wine and said, "Take this and eat; this is my body. Take this and drink; this is my blood. Do this in remembrance of me." So many ways to interpret the Kingdom, too, and the New Covenant.

He can manage his disciples, for the most part, and they, in turn, those who are under their care. But the chain of command, though clear enough, stretches too far. And there is plenty of fraying and breaking away beyond that tight, narrow chain. Too much.

At one end he has those who still proclaim him to be the Messiah. Among these there is a whole spectrum of beliefs. Some see him as a spiritual savior; some have no clue as to what he can accomplish, but worship and revere him; some see him as a king in the making—a king who will establish a new order on earth. At the other end, he has followers who hate Rome with a passion and are waiting for him to lead a revolt. To these followers, he is a political leader.

In between these two ends, there are almost as many interpretations of who he is as there are people who follow him. Some believe he is a messenger from the spiritual realm who has come to reveal secret knowledge about the structure of the universe, and to expose and defeat the evil that resides in matter. Some of the intellectuals approach him as a sage and the founder of a new philosophical school. Some believe that he is a great prophet who has come to extend membership in the Chosen People to gentiles. Some constantly change their minds as to what he is, or what he is going to do. All they care about is the healing he imparts to bodies, souls, and minds, or the power he has over demons.

The world is so full of demons. They are everywhere, desperately trying to turn earth into hell. And Jesus has power over them. The demons fear him, and obey him. They leap out of the bodies of the possessed screaming and writhing and foaming at the mouth, and cursing Jesus and his Father. The important thing is that Jesus makes the demons tremble, and obey, and desist.

The most amazing thing of all: Simply invoking the name of Jesus makes the demons flee. You don't have to be Jesus, or even one of his handpicked disciples. You don't have to be touched by him or be appointed to this task.

You don't have to know everything he's said, or to understand it, or even agree with it entirely. All you have to do is have faith in him, invoke his name, and those stinking, accursed fiends bolt back to the nether regions from whence they came.

So many followers, so many views. So hard to control all these people and what they think and say. So impossible.

And then there are those disciples who have fanned out to all corners of the earth. Disciples traversing the entire Roman Empire, even as far away as Iberia and Britain. Disciples beyond the boundaries of the empire. Disciples in Ethiopia. Disciples in Armenia. Disciples in Persia. Disciples as far away as Scythia, Colchis, and the Indus River Valley. Rumors of disciples having made it all the way to the Middle Kingdom of China. And all those disciples in Rome, the seat of power.

These disciples have made tremendous inroads among the Jews who are scattered all over the world: the Jews of the Diaspora. There are so many opinions, and so many teachers, but also so many new disciples. Day by day their number grows throughout the world, and not just among his own people.

By now, also, a very large number of his followers are not Jewish by birth. There are many gentiles who believe that they can be counted among the Chosen People if they worship Yahweh, the True God of Israel, without observing all of the ritual and dietary laws required in the covenant with Moses. Jesus, they believe, has come to announce a new covenant—one that makes all nations children of Abraham. These beliefs were already in place before Jesus came along with his so-called new covenant. Jews had been carrying out missionary activity of this sort before, but now, with the presence of Jesus, and the wisdom he imparts, and the Kingdom he promises, and the cures and exorcisms effected in his name, the missionary activity has a keener sense of purpose. And Saul of Tarsus: what a dynamo, what a wonderful apostle to the gentiles!

Jesus loves to read Saul's letters. The man is truly inspired. By the time Jesus is sixty-six or so, all hell has broken loose on his corner of the earth. The Zealots in Palestine have openly rebelled against the Roman powers. A terrible war has swept over the land. In the end, the Jewish uprising is crushed. Jerusalem is besieged and captured by the Roman forces. The temple is destroyed, reduced to mere rubble. That gorgeous temple, gone, just as he had foreseen so many years ago. The very seat of God's presence on earth demolished. No more place to offer sacrifices to Yahweh, as required by His Law. So many Jews killed. Jerusalem, it is rumored, is awash with the blood of the slain. He knew it would happen, but that doesn't make the news any easier to bear.

Jesus is spared by the Romans. They know they can count on him to keep teaching submission and nonviolence.

Jesus weeps and sobs uncontrollably by the shores of the Sea of Galilee. He has managed to find a lonely spot where he can be by himself. Well, almost by himself. He always keeps some of his favorite disciples near him. That John, especially; he is the sweetest of them all, and the best friend anyone could ever hope to have. John is nearby, and Jesus can hear him weeping too. And those women. None of them are there now, but how could he live without them? They make life bearable when it is at its most unbearable, and they help to make him wiser. They are so far ahead of the men, and the men are too slow to realize it. They fill his life. He loves them so. No women at this spot, this time, though. Better not to let the women know you are crying uncontrollably. A few tears are fine: they can witness that, and have witnessed it hundreds of times, but unrestrained sobbing is another thing. No, that would reveal far too much and would cause more misunderstandings. Every tear is already counted and interpreted in so many ways. What would happen if the women saw this torrent, this infinite sea of tears that merges with all the water in the world, turning each and every drop into a grain of salt.

What if that one woman he loves more than all the others—the one who has so filled his soul for all these years—were to see him crying like this? No. She shouldn't see it. She might not be able to bear it. But John will understand. He always does.

There are really so few people he can trust and rely on. As they all fled once, so could they all flee again. All but John, and the women. Sometimes an awful thought crosses his mind too. Can he trust the Father? Can he rely on Him? Can he, really?

Abhorrent thoughts cross his mind all the time. He is tempted, sorely tempted, as are all human beings. Such an intolerable burden at times, the mind and the body. Wanting this, shunning that. So many appetites. So much that is forbidden, with good reason. So much that is unknown. So much that has to be taken on faith. So much mystery in history.

Such a disaster, such a holocaust. Was this the ultimate sacrifice that would usher in the Kingdom? The temple destroyed one more time, one final time? The end to animal sacrifices, forever? The Ark of the Covenant nowhere to be found? The Jewish people slaughtered yet another time, dispersed to the four winds?

Jesus cries out, as he has taught everyone to do: "Father, dear Father, our Father, who art in heaven, thy Kingdom come, thy will be done, on earth as it is in heaven."

What will his many, many followers say and do now? What shall he do now?

Fast forward, another thirty years or so.

Jesus is ninety-seven years old, and very frail. He can barely see now: he who once healed the blind. Cataracts. He can barely walk: he who once made the lame dance. His hearing is still fine, though. The Word incarnate, as John calls him, can hear just fine. He suffers from arthritis, and his mind is somewhere else most of the time. On some days he doesn't even recognize his favorite disciple, John, who is nearly as old as he is, but still attends to his needs. Jesus' disciples think that his mind is in heaven most of the day and night. He suffers terribly from a hernia that can't be repaired, and from constant indigestion, and a bladder he can no longer control. His hands and feet are so numb sometimes that he can't feel them at all. He looks as old as he feels too: thin, white hair, wrinkled, nearly transparent skin, spots all over his body, blue veins snaking all over too. No teeth left with which to chew.

He who healed so many has chosen not to heal himself, it is rumored.

Jesus wakes up to good news on the last day of his life on earth. He receives word that a woman he healed as a little girl more than sixty-five years ago has come to visit him with some of her great-grandchildren. Many still

461

believe he didn't simply heal her, but actually brought her back from the dead. He loves her visits, and the thought of seeing her again makes him rise from bed eagerly, for a change.

He thinks about the numbers that his disciples toss at him all the time: so many disciples here, so many there. He has followers all over the world, most of whom consider themselves members of the Chosen People. His followers don't all agree. As a matter of fact, more often than not the various sects are at each others throats. Jesus thinks of what might happen once he dies.

He knows what will happen. He's been praying for it not to happen since that awful Passover night, when he begged the Father not to take his life, the night before he was tried and tortured by Pontius Pilate.

"Holy Father, keep them in thy name, which thou hast given me, that they may be one, even as we are one."

He has been praying for it not to happen for over sixty years. He knows that all the divisions that exist already will only grow worse once he's gone. But he doesn't stop praying for it not to happen.

The Father works in mysterious ways.

So many people are now worshiping the one true God and following the spirit of Law of Moses rather than its letter. So many gentiles turned into Chosen Ones, spiritual children of Abraham. So many of them, in so many different places. In Rome alone, the numbers are amazing. In Alexandria, that most learned of cities, there are so many intelligent followers trying to make sense of his message according to the structures of thought invented by Greek philosophers. So many bright scholars trying to fuse Moses, Jesus, Plato, and Aristotle.

The future looks dim and promising at the same time. He is convinced that his physical death is not the end at all, but only the beginning. He thinks back on all his years on earth, ponders his long, long life, and all the pain and joy.

He has spent so much time these last few years reliving his childhood in Nazareth. Does he really talk about the carpentry shop that often? John, ever so thoughtful, has taken to bringing him baskets full of sweet-smelling sawdust. "Nothing like sawdust," says Jesus.

Jesus sleeps with the sawdust next to his head.

This is not what he expected. Not at all. He knew he'd have to empty himself, spend himself totally. But, this? Betrayed by Judas once upon a time. Yes, that was awful, but easier to comprehend. Betrayed by his own body now, and by the Father, maybe. That is not so easy to understand.

So much accomplished. So little accomplished.

He thinks of his visitor that morning. He can't wait to see that little girl, now a great-grandmother, and, as ever, he is eager to embrace the children.

It is then that he suffers a massive stroke, alone in his room, alone with the Father, and the Spirit he is always talking about too, the Spirit he so desperately wants to see take over the world.

"My God, My God, why have you forsaken me?"

Jesus dies within two minutes, his blood spilled, finally, inside his own head. No one is there to see him die, or hold his hand. It is John and the little girl turned great-grandmother who find the corpse. "Oh, look, he's asleep," says the old woman.

Jesus receives a humble, discreet burial, as he had requested many times.

No one, however, will be able to find his body after it is buried. It vanishes from the grave, mysteriously. John and his disciples are accused of stealing and hiding the body, but they claim they buried it properly. Those who witnessed the burial will speak up in their defense.

Three days later, though, some will claim to have seen him alive. The rumors will spread like wildfire. Most who claim to have seen him are in Palestine, but reports will later surface all over the known world. In Rome itself; in Colonia Agrippina, on the Rhine River; in Toletum, in Iberia; in Athens; in Carthage; in Edessa; in Seleucia, near ancient Babylon; in Nubia; far, far away in Varanasi, on the banks of the Ganges River; and even farther away, walking on the Wan-Li Cha'ng-Ch'eng, the so-called Great Wall of the Middle Kingdom. All of the reported sightings say that the resurrected Jesus looks as if he's thirty-three years old again.

And, oddest thing of all, no one dares to claim that they have a relic taken from his body.

Flash forward, about 230 years. The Emperor Constantine is seated on his imperial throne, taking part in the dedication of a new synagogue and shrine to the Apostle John, whose body has been brought to Rome. Constantine is about to make his conversion official. He is almost ready to undergo baptism, the rite of initiation into the New Covenant. He is about to become one of the Chosen Ones, as soon as Passover rolls around, in a couple of months.

This is a remarkable synagogue that Constantine has built, the grandest building in all of Rome. Imagine, having the body of the Apostle John, right here in Rome. Imagine all the pilgrims that will flock to this shrine, and all the miracles that will take place there. Imagine all the honor that will spill over to the emperor who built the shrine, brought the body to Rome, and was there at its consecration.

Constantine congratulates himself for having decided not to build that new capital city out east, on the site of that fishing village, Byzantium. What a dumb idea that was, in the first place. Good thing he didn't listen to those Greek advisers.

Constantine has put imperial muscle to work in unifying all of the followers of Jesus. All of those wrangling sects. Too many of them. Too untidy for the religion of the state. Unseemly for the Chosen People to disagree so much. Calling all of the chief rabbis together at Milan was one of the best ideas he ever had all on his own. They came up with a list of beliefs and defined the Truth for all time. Jesus has been proclaimed a prophet. The greatest prophet of all time. His New Covenant promises to make anyone who is baptized one of the Chosen People. The Messiah is yet to come, at some point in the future. Jesus has helped pave the way for him who will redeem and transform the earth for good. These New Covenanters think of themselves as God's Chosen Ones, since they worship Yahweh, but they despise those Jews who don't accept the teachings of Jesus and still follow the Law of Moses. They also despise those followers of Jesus who proclaim him to be the Messiah, and believe him to have been resurrected. The central rituals of the Chosen Ones are baptism, and the celebration of the New Passover meal, which is celebrated weekly, on the Sabbath. The council has also approved the veneration of the relics of Jesus and those of anyone who has led a holy life. Every synagogue is to have at least one relic enshrined under the pulpit from which the Scriptures are read.

Now that all of this has been defined, Constantine's troops can get busy closing down the synagogues of all those who don't believe the Truth as defined at Milan. Now all of his subjects will share the same faith, and be as one, just like the Prophet and Teacher Jesus, and the Father. Now his troops can descend upon those few misguided souls who still believe that Jesus was the Messiah, and that he rose from the dead. Deluded fools, turning Jesus into the Son of God. Now his troops can also go after those Jews who refuse to pay any attention at all to Jesus. Retrogrades, ignoring Jesus and following Moses instead. Now all those who believe falsely can be wiped off the face of the earth, for the glory of God and the well-being of the Chosen People and their empire.

A little persecution should take care of all those who believe what is wrong.

With the emperors residing at Rome, the western half of the empire remains strong and vibrant in every way, and the Roman cities of Western Europe grow and flourish undiminished by attacks from Germanic tribes. The German barbarians are held back east of the Rhine and north of the Danube and are gradually civilized by the missionaries that the Roman emperors send across the border. The same happens with the Scots and Picts, and the Celts of Ireland. The eastern half of the empire remains as strong as ever too, so the empire remains intact for a few more centuries, until the armies of the prophet Mohammed wrestle away much of the Near East and all of North Africa.

Centuries after Constantine, Roman civilization dominates all of the European continent, including those client states of the former barbarians that were outside the Constantinian borders of the empire, as far north as the Urals. All of these people profess belief in the One God of the ancient Jews. Anyone who doesn't agree with the orthodox religion defined by the rabbis, and approved by the Roman state, is persecuted, even in the client states of northern and eastern Europe. The evolution of the Roman Empire into a loose federation of nation states takes centuries, but is more or less complete by the year 1700 after the birth of Jesus. An evolved form of Latin remains the lingua franca of the entire continent, thanks to its use in all the rituals of the state religion. As to those lands discovered across the Atlantic

Ocean by the client state of the Norsemen in the ninth century, they will be Roman too. Conquered bit by bit, those two continents will be converted to the Roman religion, all the way down to Tierra del Fuego, by the year 1400. Missionaries make their way to Asia too, and contact with the East becomes ever stronger. Around 1250, Australia and New Zealand are discovered and colonized by the Chinese, who have learned a few lessons from the discoveries of the Norsemen.

But all that is in the distant future. Meanwhile the whole world has woken up and found itself Chosen, or so it seems. Chosen Ones, members of the New Covenant revealed to Jesus by God, according to the Council of Milan. Even those barbarian tribes north of the empire's borders are beginning to accept the new religion from Palestine and Rome, and they are becoming ever more civilized and docile. The old gods are dying fast. The old elite families of Rome continue to cling to the old religion, and the simple people mix the old with the new, but there is no denying the fact that the world has been transformed.

The temples to the old gods are vanishing quickly. Many have been turned over to the worship of the One Jewish God, Yahweh. The sayings of Jesus, and the narratives that tell of his life, are now being given the same attention by learned men as the writings of the greatest philosophers. Men and women are flocking to the desert to live lives of prayer and self-denial, just like the Essenes of old, the Jewish sect that had spawned John the Baptist, and influenced Jesus himself. Gladiators are a thing of the past, as are most of the old, cruel games of the arena. Crucifixions? Forget it. They've gone the way of wild orgies.

Some are very, very unhappy about the sexual ethics of this new religion. Will anyone ever be able to have any fun again?

As Constantine watches the long, intricate consecration ritual, he ponders the reconstruction of the temple in Jerusalem. Should he do it soon? Should he do it at all? This new Synagogue of John the Apostle in Rome is so nice, and it has cost so much to build. Isn't this enough for now? Isn't it enough that he has also brought to Rome the bed in which Jesus died, and the clothes he was wearing that final morning, along with all of his meager surviving wardrobe, and those coffers full of his hair and nail clippings?

And what about that most precious relic of all, the golden flask containing all the tears that Jesus ever shed, so lovingly collected by the women who followed him around all the time? Isn't all of this enough for now? Should he give in to the nearly endless requests he receives from all around the known world and rebuild the temple?

Constantine imagines what honor would devolve upon him if he were to rebuild the temple. He could go down in history as another Solomon, or maybe surpass him in fame.

The Temple of Constantine? It sounds so good. Maybe he should also move the capital of the empire from Rome to Jerusalem? Or, better yet, why shouldn't the temple be rebuilt at Rome instead of Jerusalem? Rome: the New Jerusalem? He should ask his advisers. He should ask the chief rabbis too. And he should check with his wife, first. Maybe she's had a dream?

## CECELIA HOLLAND

# REPULSE AT HASTINGS, OCTOBER 14, 1066

## William does not conquer England

*Hastings may come down to us mainly in the form of delicious trivializations like 1066 and All That (the "All That" being the rest of British history). But there is no getting around the date: The battle was one of those encounters—Salamis, Saratoga, Gettysburg, and D day come to mind—that, by determining futures, truly deserves to be called decisive. Hastings, in spite of (or perhaps because of) the mythic overlays of the victor's history, has the quality of good fiction, replete with the confrontation of two dominating protagonists. Here were two determined opponents, Harold Godwinson, who had occupied the English throne for a matter of months, and the man who came from across the Channel to wrest the crown from him: William the Bastard, duke of Normandy, known to posterity as the Conqueror. Not just a straightforward brawl in the typical medieval manner, Hastings was one of those rare struggles in which different styles of war-making face off: the defense-minded English infantry taking on the cavalry shock tactics favored on the Continent—although William also relied on archers and infantry (it was, a Norman knight later said, "a strange kind of battle"). Add to that another quality of a well-made plot, suspense, with an outcome that didn't become clear until the very end.*

*There was more, evident now as it was not a millennium ago. At that battle-field in October 1066, Cecelia Holland points out, two rival worlds collided. The one that emerged victorious would dominate not just the next English centuries but those of the Continent as well. England at the time belonged to a Scandinavian-*

468

centered sphere of influence that extended from the Viking fortress towns of Russia to the precarious settlements of Vinland on the North American coast (roughly from Newfoundland as far south as Maine). Opposed was the Franco-Roman world that William represented. He too was descended from Vikings, though his forebears had been settled for a couple of centuries in the country at the mouth of the Seine. Warriors with a knack for the political main chance, the Normans (from Normanni, Northmen) would carve out principalities as far away as Italy and the Holy Land. England, with its growing population, its grain, and its fine harbors, was the potential cornerstone for a Europe dominated either by the North or the South.

What if Norman arrows had not killed Harold and his brothers? What if the English infantry had stood firm behind its shields, and the waning light of an autumn afternoon had left them, and not William, masters of the field? Would the sequel of the battle have been played out, not that December in Westminister Cathedral, where William was crowned king of England, but at a later date in the woodlands of America?

CECELIA HOLLAND, one of our most acclaimed and respected historical novelists, is the author of more than twenty books.

IN THE NIGHT word came to Duke William that the English army was
approaching down the road from London. It was mid-October, with daylight precious, and William wasted none of it. At once he roused himself
and his men and began to get ready. In his hurry, in the dark, he put on his
hauberk backward, which several of the men around him were ready to interpret as a bad omen.

William brushed the matter off—as he had dismissed his stumbling, a
few days earlier, when he first set foot in England and fell flat on his face. "I
have seized England with both hands," he cried then, turning foul into fair.

William had been working for years toward this day, plotting and scheming and arranging. Yet not even he could have guessed that the battle he
was about to fight would become one of the most famous in history, or that
the victory would decide the fate of Europe for centuries.

With his officers, most of them friends or kinsmen, William heard Mass
and took Communion. He hung sacred relics around his neck. The blue
banner that the pope had consecrated for him fluttered out on the day's first
breeze, and in the cool gray of the English dawn William led his army, some
7,000 men, out to meet Harold Godwinson and his army, to settle the issue
between them.

This issue was the crown of England. William's claim to the throne was
specious at best, but he could take advantage of the circumstances. After
centuries of struggle against the Danes and Norse, England's leadership was
decimated. Now the Danes and Norse had momentarily lost their grip and
the kingdom was ripe for the taking. The English king, Edward the Confessor, who had died late in 1065, had left no son to succeed him; and Edward's
mother had been Norman, William's great-aunt Emma. William had even
been able to extort oaths and promises of support from Edward's chief man,

Harold Godwinson himself, the most powerful earl in England, when some years before Harold came luckily into William's hands in France.

The problem with all this effort was that the English crown was elective. When old saintly Edward died, the kingdom's council of elders turned to Harold Godwinson, whom they knew and who was half Saxon, anyway, if not of the house of great Alfred, and made him king. William proclaimed Harold a usurper and an oathbreaker—hence the relics and the blessed banner—and now the Norman duke was coming to get what he wanted.

On the day of the Battle of Hastings, William of Normandy was thirty-nine, a big, hot-tempered, shrewd, and vigorous man who had survived a terrifying childhood, wooed his wife by roughing her up, and mastered his whole duchy at the point of a sword. For his purposes he had assembled what was for the times an enormous force. Besides his own Normans, who had been fighting under his leadership for years, he had contingents of knights and infantry from Brittany, Belgium, and France, even from as far as Italy, including a corps of archers, who led the army down the road as it marched inland. After them heavier armed foot soldiers tramped along, wearing helmets and hauberks, the thigh-length mail coats the knights also wore, and carrying spears and swords. In the back of the army, with his knights, where he could see everything before him, William himself rode beneath the blue banner.

When the fighting started, William did not hold back and direct the action from a distance, like a modern general. William charged and struck and took blows like the rest of his men. In the end, as it had been all his life, he won or lost by the power of his own right arm.

Now he and his army climbed the road up a long hill. As his first ranks reached its crest, they looked out and saw the English.

Before them the road fell away to cross a narrow, marshy valley. Opposite, the land rose again into a treeless ridge, flanked on either side by swamp and forest. As William's army came up over the first hill, they could see the English in a mass pushing up through the forest onto the long height of that treeless ridge.

The road ran on across the valley, up that ridge, and on to London,

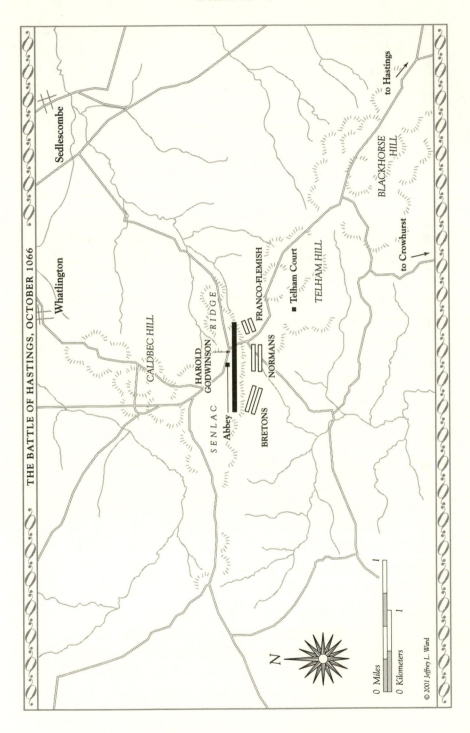

THE BATTLE OF HASTINGS, OCTOBER 1066

Sedlescombe

Whatlington

CALDBEC HILL

HAROLD
GODWINSON

SENLAC

Abbey

BRETONS

NORMANS

FRANCO-FLEMISH

R I D G E

Telham Court

TELHAM HILL

BLACKHORSE HILL

to Hastings

to Crowhurst

N

0 Miles          1

0 Kilometers     1

© 2001 Jeffrey L. Ward

England's heart. If William could take London, he could claim to hold the kingdom of England. But now, across the height of the ridge, where the road crossed, the English were building a wall of shields and bodies, to keep William of Normandy out.

There were thousands of these English, including a core of Harold Godwinson's own war band, his housecarls, bound to him by a personal commitment, and fighting under his gilded and jeweled banner, whose figure was a fighting man. Harold's two warrior brothers were part of this war band, and with the rest of these experienced, well-trained, and well-equipped soldiers formed the center of the shield wall.

Most of the other Englishmen were peasants, farmers and herdsmen, the fyrd, or militia, of the kingdom, bound by long tradition to arm themselves and answer Harold's summons for a set length of time, around a month. They could fight well, but they were untrained and not battle hardened and many had only a stick or a club to fight with.

Harold's army was stout and brave, but one-dimensional, without cavalry or archers. The housecarls carried tall shields, axes, and spears, but no bows; although they rode to the battlefield, they dismounted to fight. This limited what they could do. Yet on this day what they could do seemed good enough. On the crest of this hill King Harold had chosen an excellent position, making the most of his strengths.

The English army was a tough outfit. William's was the second invading force they had faced in less than four weeks. Halfway through the previous September, Harald Hardraada, the king of Norway, had landed with a sizable force in the north, near York, to take up again the endless Norse project of harrying England. Harold Godwinson had gathered his housecarls and marched up to meet him, picking up contingents of the fyrd as he went.

Harald Hardraada—the hard-counsel, or ruthless—was one of the most famous warriors in Christendom, a veteran of battles from Constantinople to Norway. He had with him his personal war band and several other freelance contingents of warriors, plus some rebellious English, and when a local army came out to challenge him, Hardraada's force made short work of them. Overconfident, Hardraada sent most of his men back to his ships and waited around at Stamford Bridge to receive the homage and hostages of the city of York, which had prudently gone over to him at once.

Harold Godwinson and his Saxon army got to Stamford Bridge before the homage. They caught the Norse king by surprise and annihilated him. When the rest of his army came up in support, too late, Harold crushed it also. Now, ranged up across the London road on Telham Hill, Harold Godwinson and his English army were ready for Duke William.

This day the sun was high on the hills of southern England. With blasts of horns, William's army advanced across the narrow valley toward the ridge; swamp on the left and forest on the right kept them from flanking Harold's position. William sent his archers up the slope first, to shower the English with arrows; shooting uphill and against the massive shield wall, the archers had little effect, and they fell back as the heavier infantry moved forward. Behind them, William's mounted knights spurred their horses to a gallop.

From the shield wall came the roars and screams of the English. Taking advantage of the height of their position, they threw spears and axes and stones fixed to chunks of wood onto the approaching Normans. The infantry faltered under this hail. William, in the center, charged his knights up into the hard fighting—his men chopping with swords, hurling and jabbing with spears crashing their horses into the shield wall. The massive line of interlinked shields held against them. The English yielded nothing. Crowded together, fighting hand to hand and uphill, surrounded by a deafening din, the Norman duke's whole army began to waver. Then, on the left, suddenly, his men turned around and ran away, down the hill.

Wails of despair rose. The disorderly rout spread rapidly throughout the Norman army. Even William, in the center of the line under his blue banner, had to fall back, and suddenly, he was down.

In the confusion the rumor flew from mouth to mouth that the duke was dead. In a wild panic the Norman army fled away down the hill into the valley, scattering across it, and on the height above them, some of the English broke ranks and rushed after.

But William was not dead. His horse had been killed, but he commandeered another, bounded into the saddle, pulled off his helmet, and galloped along the scattered fleeing ranks of his army, shouting, "Look at me! I am alive, and I will be the victor, with God's help!"

Seeing him, the panicking men began to slow, to hold their ground. William gathered them swiftly and brought them around into a counterattack on the English streaming after them down the hill. All across the field, the faltering Normans saw their duke leading this new charge and swung to join it. The Englishmen spilling down the steep slope had lost their tight formation; the Normans rode them down from either side, broke them into fragments, and wiped them out piecemeal, while Harold Godwinson and the bulk of his army stayed on the hill above.

Harold Godwinson had missed his best chance to win the battle. Had the entire English army charged when William's men fled away, they could well have swept the Normans back, prevented them from regrouping, and harried them into the sea. In fact only the untrained fyrd had charged down from the height after the fleeing Norman army. In the center of the line, the housecarls stayed put.

Possibly they did not attack because no one ordered them to. In the center, under the banner of the fighting man, where the initial fighting had been heaviest, where William and Harold had fought, Harold's two brothers now lay dead, killed in that first terrific clash. Perhaps it was the loss of this leadership that held the housecarls back. Whatever the reason, Harold remained where he was, and now William brought his men under control and turned toward the shield wall again.

"Then an unusual kind of combat ensued," says William of Poitiers, "one side attacking in bursts and in a variety of movements, and the other rooted in the ground, putting up with the assault."

For the rest of the day, the Norman duke poked and probed at Harold's shield wall. Since the disorderly flight of the first attack had come to such a good conclusion, he staged another such retreat, perhaps two, luring the English down the hill each time to be hacked up when the Normans turned on them. The day wore grimly on. The ground was scattered with the bodies of men and horses; the carcasses began to get in the way of the fighting men. The fight looked like a standoff. The English were bleeding steadily, but so were the Normans, and Harold's housecarls stayed solid in the cen-

HASTINGS: FUTURES IN THE BALANCE

*The Bayeux Tapestry depicts the events surrounding the Battle of Hastings in 1066, which earned*
*William, the duke of Normandy, the name "the Conqueror." In the section shown here, one of*
*William's commanders (left) wields a club to prevent the flight of Norman cavalrymen, after a ru-*
*mor has circulated that William has been killed in the battle against King Harold's English troops.*

(Section of the Bayeux Tapestry, ca. 1080. Musée de la Tapisserie, Bayeux, France. Giraudon/Art Resource, NY)

ter behind their interlocked shields and held the hill and the road to London. One of the longest battles in medieval history was still grinding
on with no resolution. Night was coming. One way or another, it had to
end soon.

Hastings was more than a struggle between two determined men. At that
battlefield in October 1066, two rival worlds collided, and, going in, the
momentum actually favored not William of Normandy but Harold Godwinson.

England in 1066 was part of the great northern community that included Norway and Sweden, Novgorod and Kiev in Russia, Denmark, Iceland, the Faeroes, Scotland and the Orkneys, Greenland, Vinland the Good,
and even Spitsbergen, above the Arctic Circle. Northern kings and adven-

turers had been taking England apart for centuries, and the English resistance had shaped the kingdom of Alfred the Great into a realm facing north. This northern attachment was deep and strong. Norse kings had ruled York for generations; and some fifty years before the Battle of Hastings, Canute the Great, king of Denmark, overran the whole of England, was crowned its king, and ruled it successfully for twenty years as the centerpiece of an empire stretching all around the North Sea.

England was saturated with Danish culture. A good deal of England still lived under Danish law. Many people spoke the Danish tongue as much as they spoke English. Harold Godwinson himself was a symbol incarnate of this wedding of Northerner and English. Godwine, his father, had risen to prominence under Canute, in the power vacuum left by the death and exile of the English royal house, and had married a Danish woman, so Harold was half Dane. In many ways Harold's brief rule was a continuation of Canute's as much as the Saxon kingship. The housecarls who held the ridge against William of Normandy were an innovation of Canute's, a war band formed on the Danish model.

The bonds between England and the Northern sphere of influence went far beyond the political. Anglo-Saxon weekdays were Tir's day and Woden's day and Thor's day, not Mercury's day and Mars' day as it was in neighboring France, a country under a long and heavy Roman influence. *Beowulf,* the great classic of old English, written in Northumbria, portrays a world straight out of the Eddas, the traditional Norse poetry telling of warriors and darkness and grief. The English church, while Christian, paid little attention to the pope; Harold Godwinson had been crowned by an archbishop who was under an anathema from Rome. The English economy was tied to the vital North Sea trade routes: English goods went in Norse and Danish hulls across the North Sea to Danish and Swedish trading cities. The English spoke a Germanic language, heavily salted now with Danish words, not the Latin-based language of France, Italy, and Spain. From the perspective of 1066, England belonged more to Scandinavia than to the southern, Franco-Roman world across the stormy Channel.

This Scandinavian-centered northern economic empire reached the apex of its energy and power around this time. At mid–eleventh century the long ships were still visiting Vinland, even if the Norse and Danes had not been able to establish a permanent colony there, and their trade routes to the east, through Sweden, reached all the way to Constantinople.

In 862, the Viking Rurik built the Baltic stronghold of Novgorod; his successor Oleg conquered Kiev; and in the tenth century great fleets of dragon ships sailed the Black Sea, headed for Constantinople. The tremendous natural defenses of the World City daunted them, but they came back, to trade and to hire their swords out to the Byzantine army. Harald Hardraada himself fought Saracens in Sicily under the legendary Byzantine general George Maniakes. Thus Viking trading outposts at Novgorod and Kiev gave Greater Scandinavia access to the East, to the Silk Road, and thus to the whole of Asia.

No one man ever ruled this vast complex, although many tried. The first fierce boom of the north, with its individualism, its legalistic mind-set, its practical ingenuity, was in many ways an equal opportunity employment, a rapidly expanding mosaic of free farms and independent earldoms and petty kingdoms, a few cities. The century before Hastings had produced a handful of ambitious kings, who in 1066 were still struggling to get it all under one crown. For a few decades Canute had ruled the core of this empire, Denmark and Norway—from England. Harald Hardraada, with his connections back through Sweden to the Russian cities, clearly had the same project in mind.

But in the next few centuries the Northern empire retreated. The physical circumstances changed: After a warm spell around 1000 A.D., the climate in the North Sea grew steadily worse. Drift ice floated remorselessly down across the sea-lanes linking the Northern land posts. Where once Viking settlers had grazed cattle in Greenland, now the snow lay on the ground all year round. The Northerners gave up the effort to colonize Vinland, eventually lost Greenland, and even nearly Iceland, as the huge burst of energy that had flung itself out of every fjord and every vik for 300 years subsided and shrank back to its homeland. Novgorod and Kiev became more steadily Slavic than Scandinavian; even the Varangian guard of the Byzantine emperors, named for the Russian Vikings who had first filled its ranks, became mostly made up of Englishmen.

If the North had kept its grip on England, with its growing population, its grain, and its southern, open harbors, might they not have been able to sustain the effort? Then the changing climate might have driven them to expand, not contract. Searching for better land, better lives, they might have built homes in Vinland, spread their colonies down that coast, and linked the whole, Vinland, Greenland, with sea-lanes south of the danger of ice. Following the coast of Vinland southward they would have come on good harbors, better farmland, the best fishing in the Atlantic—prizes worth confronting the native peoples—or, better, since they had no such huge technological edge as the later Spanish and English—coming to terms with them.

Thus, with England as the cornerstone of a sprawling Northern empire, the European migration to the Continent on the western edge of the Atlantic could have begun much earlier than it actually did. What kind of society would the Northerners have built there? Not, surely, a kingdom. Much of the colonization of the North Atlantic Rim was done by Danes and Norse fleeing from the oppressions of greedy brutal kings. The Northern colonies in Vinland and beyond would most likely have been, at least at first, republics, like Iceland, ruled through an Althing, or general assembly. If Harold Godwinson had won the Battle of Hastings, a republic of Europeans could have appeared on the western continent 500 years before 1776—without a revolution.

And without the destruction of the native peoples. The Norse and Danes enjoyed a slight technological edge over the native tribes they encountered, but hardly a decisive one. They would have had to work out some modus vivendi with the tribes they found in the New World, and in one nation, perhaps, the Mohawk, they would have met a people much like themselves—enterprising, agressive, with a certain inclination to popular government. Perhaps a blended culture might have arisen in the dark forests and lakes of the New World—a Viking-Mohawk republic, the westernmost edge of the Empire of the North.

Perhaps at some point one dynasty would have taken all this broad Northern community under a single crown. More likely the great sprawling quiltwork of settlements, farms, jarls, and little kings and republics would have formed a commonwealth, allowing for the Northerners' practical creativity at law and government. The whole community would be bound together by the vital energy of trade, and everywhere the Norse and Danes would encounter other peoples, challenges, ideas to fertilize their continued growth. Snorri Sturlusson could write sagas about the wars with the Mohawk. Buffalo robes and tobacco might sell briskly in Constantinople, and Chinese tea might find its way to the Mississippi. Dragon ships might sail on the Great Lakes, seeking a passage west, carrying crews half native, half Norse. What they charted might have found its way eventually into a Chinese map.

Such a power, connecting the North Atlantic and Baltic Sea and reaching down through Russia to the eastern Mediterranean itself, would have presented a formidable challenge to the rest of Europe. Compared with this Greater Scandinavia, this Northern empire, fueled by a huge trading community stretching across half the world and tied at Constantinople into the whole hub of Asian trade, Latin Europe in 1066 had little to offer.

Latin Europe, in fact, was at its nadir. Centuries of ruinous wars and invasions had battered the little continent into shocked fragments. The popes were struggling to assert some kind of political control over the Western emperor and the rash of little kings; but the territory was lawless and the ox-cart economy slow. England was in fact the richest kingdom of Europe, France a minor power. So in mid–eleventh century, Latin Europe did not look like it was maturing into much of anything. The great Crusades, the counterassault on the Moslem world, were thirty years away; farther still in the future lay the magnificent creative outpouring of the twelfth century, the Gothic bloom of the High Middle Ages.

That splendid future might have never happened. The talent that raised Chartres and founded the University of Paris could very well have gone to embellish courts in Oslo and London and Kiev, draining France and Italy of their creative juices. The German states already shared culture and language with the Scandinavians, and their connection with the Latin world was always uneasy, always complicated by the illusion of the empire. Their interest would easily swing north, toward that great lifeline of trade, that familiar way of life, away from Rome. The pieces of the old Mediterranean world could have become mere satellites of the Empire of the North. If Harold Godwinson had won that October day in 1066, England might have been the keystone of another civilization entirely.

But Harold Godwinson was up against a different breed of Viking.

William of Normandy was descended from Rollo, or Rolf, or Rou, a Norse adventurer who in the tenth century seized the broad rolling lands around the mouth of the River Seine. The king of France, making a virtue of reality, granted him the title of duke and gave him a French princess for his wife. In return, Rollo kept other marauders out of the Seine and away from Paris. The duchy came to be called Normandy, the Northman's country. Rolf's men married local women and produced a hybrid strain, the Normans.

These Normans were tough, hardy, good fighters, and above all, cunning politicians. They fought all over Europe, in Anatolia, in the Holy Land, and everywhere they built states. Norman freebooters, drifting down to Italy in the eleventh century, conquered Sicily, and turned it into the most efficient kingdom in Europe. Norman Crusaders built the principalities of Antioch and Edessa. After the Battle of Manzikert, a Norman mercenary tried to build a country of his own in eastern Turkey. Normandy itself throve, with courts and laws and active dukes who did justice and kept the peace.

In 1026 or close to it the then duke's teenage brother Robert saw a girl wading in a stream and fell in love. Being of noble blood he could command this peasant girl to him, and he did. Their son was born in 1027 or 1028, in his father's castle, but grew up in the house of his mother's father, the tanner Fulbert, in Falaise, where perhaps he acquired the earthy manner that distinguished him all his life. Soon after William was born, Robert, still barely twenty, succeeded his brother as duke of Normandy.

He became known as Robert the Magnificent, and Robert the Devil. He never married, and when, seven or eight years after becoming duke of Normandy, he abruptly decided to go on crusade as penance for his sins, he presented his court with William as his heir.

"He is little, but he will grow," Robert is alleged to have said, and he made his nobles swear homage and accept him. The boy was seven years old. Then Robert rode away on crusade and never came back.

The duchy fell into anarchy. A boy duke could do no justice and command no peace. Every castle was an armed fort, most of them hostile to the boy duke. He grew up under a succession of guardians, men as rough and violent as his enemies. Four of these guardians in succession were murdered, one before young William's eyes; a courtier grabbed the child and hustled him off to hide in the wretched hovels of the village while his enemies hunted him through the castle with swords in their hands.

Yet the boy throve. He grew up strong, blunt, wily, and sober, gifted with the two chief medieval virtues: iron piety and a strong arm. When he was nineteen, half his vassals rose against him in favor of another claimant to the duchy. William made this revolt into the fulcrum of his career; he put down the rising by force of arms, killed or drove out the worst of the nobles, subdued the others, and had the whole country firmly under his control by the time he was twenty-two. Almost immediately, he cast his eyes on England, where his cousin Edward the Confessor was king.

Edward favored Normans. And he was childless. The only heir left to the great line of Alfred was living in Hungary. William began laying the groundwork for a claim to the English crown.

He visited England. He got Edward to make him a vague promise of the throne. When Harold Godwinson was shipwrecked off the coast of Brittany, William went in person to rescue him from the predatory locals and bullied him into taking an oath of allegiance. After Harold had sworn what he assumed was a personal oath, standing before what seemed a plain altar, William whipped back the cloth to reveal a huge collection of relics, making the oath, at least in William's eyes, inviolate.

At last the old king died, giving him his chance. When Harold Godwinson was elected king, William got the pope to consecrate his cause and bless his banner, and then he sent out a general call for fighting men, promising them land in England—if they won. His reputation, and their own greed, brought thousands to assemble on the Channel coast.

There they stayed, idle. William spent the months after Edward's death feverishly building and commandeering boats, gathering over 600, enough to transport his army. But the wind blew foul all that summer, preventing them even from leaving harbor, much less making the treacherous Channel crossing. William fumed and prayed, his army grumbled, the summer wore on into autumn. What would later come to be known as Halley's Comet blazed enigmatically across the sky. Everybody knew that portended some great deed to be done, the rise and fall of kings. But the wind augured otherwise.

William resolved to move his fleet and his army up the coast, to a point where he could catch a west wind for England. This little voyage along the coast was hazardous enough; several boats were wrecked, and a few men drowned. Still the wind blew from the south. William ordered prayers and fasts. He had all the relics he could find paraded along the seashore. At last the wind relented, swung around, filled his sails. The duke of Normandy and his little fleet bobbed away over the Channel. He had only been there a few days when word reached him of Harold Godwinson's approach.

Now, on the battlefield, William was looking failure square in the face. The daylight was fading. He was running out of time. Above the long slope, littered with bodies of men and horses, Harold Godwinson and his shield wall still held the height, his great gaudy banner furling and unfurling above him. Everything, all the scheming and plotting and politics and blood, came down to one final charge.

William had been resting and saving his archers since their first useless round of fighting. He brought them up again and ordered them to shoot in volleys, lifting their bows high so that the arrows would fall straight down on the shield wall. Under the cover of these arrows, William flung his whole army up the hill one last time.

Floods of arrows rained down on the English. Suddenly Harold Godwinson staggered back, clutching at an arrow in his eye. The shield wall gave way, and Norman horsemen poured through, hacking and hewing at the English as they went. Harold went down, and the English broke. Their lord was dead, the day was lost, and they began to flee into the forest. William pursued them into the night, but except for a few pockets of defiance, En-

glish resistance to him was over. The road to London was open. On Christmas Day 1066, William of Normandy was crowned king of England in
Westminster.

Few battles in all of history have been as decisive as Hastings. The outcome of those bloody hours on October 14, 1066, was to wrench England
from the northern axis of Scandinavia and the North Sea around to a profound involvement with the Southern, Latin world. Henceforth the
Northern world waned, and the Latin world blossomed into the glory of the
High Middle Ages and the Renaissance. Hastings deserves its reputation as
the greatest battle in English history, and a major turning point in the history of the world.

THEODORE F. COOK, JR.

# THE CHINESE DISCOVERY OF THE NEW WORLD, 15TH CENTURY

*What the expeditions of a eunuch admiral might have led to*

We do not think of China as a nation of seamen explorers, adventurers who probed distant oceans, and for the most part that assumption is correct. There was, however, one brief interval in its history, early in the Ming dynasty at the beginning of the fifteenth century, when China was the preeminent maritime power in the world. These were the years when the Ming emperor Zhu Di—the emperor of the reign known as Yongle, or "Perpetual Happiness"—dispatched armadas of several hundred vessels that carried as many as 37,000 men: His giant "treasure ships," which were up to 400 feet long and over 150 wide, may have been the largest wooden ships ever built. (By comparison, Christopher Columbus's flagship, the Santa Maria, was one-fifth as long, a mere eighty-five feet.) The principal Ming naval commander was a shadowy figure named Zheng He, a man of imposing size, strength, and personal magnetism, whose most enduring characteristic was his lack of manhood. A confidante of the emperor, the eunuch admiral had first served as a soldier in the civil war that brought Zhu Di to the throne. Between 1405 and 1433, Zheng He led seven expeditions into the Indian Ocean basin, reaching Madagascar and the eastern coast of Africa and venturing into the Persian Gulf and the Red Sea; some of his ships may have visited Australia. As Theodore F. Cook, Jr., writes, he "must rate as one of the monumental figures in any Age of Exploration."

The first emperors of the dynasty that would rule China for almost three cen-

*turies (1368–1644) were activists, rough-hewn warriors, and builders eager to establish a Chinese presence (and their claim to legitimacy) far beyond its borders. But increasingly the Ming rulers retreated into the Forbidden City, the imperial palace built by Zhu Di in Beijing; some hardly ventured outside its high walls during their entire lifetimes. The real power fell to a retinue of palace-bound civil administrators, many of them eunuchs, who did their utmost to restrict contact with the rest of the world. First the expeditions were called off; later, shipbuilding itself was banned. Enemies of Zheng He even burned his accounts of his voyages.*

*But how much would history have changed if the Ming emperors had not turned inward—if they had decided instead to continue the great effort that Zheng He had initiated? China had the ships, the navigational technology, and the experience to bring its influence and its civilization to parts of the world that the West would soon dominate. That domination did not have to happen. It is not inconceivable that the Americas—which would not have been known as such—might have been discovered by a Chinese admiral, a successor to Zheng He, decades before Columbus. Would historians talk about the Rise of the East?*

THEODORE F. COOK, JR., is professor of history at William Paterson University of New Jersey and an authority on the history of Asia. He is, with Haruko Taya Cook, the author of *Japan at War: An Oral History.*

T HE "AGE OF DISCOVERY," the "Era of Exploration," the "epoch of
European Expansion and Colonialism," have introduced generations
of students to the seafaring exploits of navigators, who, from about 1450 to
1600, first set out onto the Western Sea—the great Atlantic Ocean—and
then traversed all the oceans of the world. Yet in the previous half-century,
nearly fifty years before the Portuguese caravels sent out by Henry the Navigator crossed the equator on the Atlantic coast of Africa going south, and
three-quarters of a century before Vasco da Gama finally reached Calicut in
India in 1498, Chinese fleets were poised at the edge of their own explored
seas on the other side of Africa. Ready to spread Chinese civilization—
economic, cultural, political, and moral values bound together—into what
Europeans seemed to regard as their realm of exploitation, Chinese naval
forces, sent forth by the Ming emperor himself, had the capability of thrust-
ing themselves into the maelstrom of the history of Western European history as never before.

In the former port of Changle in Fujian Province, on China's southeastern coast, a tablet was erected in 1432 by Zheng He, China's "Admiral of
the Western Sea" that evoked a view of the wider world seldom associated
with the Middle Kingdom:

We have traversed more than one hundred thousand *li* of immense
waterscapes and have beheld in the ocean huge waves like mountains
rising sky high, and we have set eyes on barbarian regions far away
hidden in a blue transparency of light vapors, while our sails, loftily
unfurled like clouds day and night, continued their course [as rapidly
as] a star, traversing those savage waves as if we were treading a public thoroughfare.

. . .

Raised to commemorate the seven great expeditions the admiral had organized and led out to the edges of the Indian Ocean Basin beginning in 1405, the tablet is as much a monument to the spirit of adventure, the thrill of ocean sailing, and the experience of a generation of Chinese seamen who shared their admiral's thrill at visiting lands far from their Chinese home as it was a personal proclamation. In many ways, it was to serve as an epitaph both to the admiral himself and to China's great age of sail. Even before the admiral himself died, the dynasty that had sent him forth was implementing a policy that would call back his fleets, undo the web of diplomatic, trade, and cultural relations he had woven over almost three decades, and, by the time of the arrival of Europeans in numbers in the waters of the Indian Ocean, literally reduce his magnificent sea charts and shipbuilding techniques to ashes.

Yet need it have been so? What if China had discovered Europe?

Zheng He (1371–1433) must rate as one of the monumental figures in any Age of Exploration. His origins and personal history were surely as convoluted and exceptional as the biographies of a Bartholomeu Dias, Vasco da Gama, Christopher Columbus, or Ferdinand Magellan. Moreover, his career was tightly intertwined with the rise to power of the third Ming emperor, Zhu Di, the "Yongle" (or "Perpetual Happiness") Emperor, who ruled China from 1402 to 1424. The emperor entrusted to Zheng He the critical mission of leading what became seven stupendous maritime expeditions between 1405 and 1433. These voyages took him and the name of China into what is today called the South China Sea, through the Strait of Malacca, and past the kingdoms that sought to trade on their geographical control what they saw as "the navel of the world." He was to sail beyond into the Bay of Bengal, to Ceylon, up the Malibar Coast of India to the fabled cities of Cochin and Calicut, to the aptly named Arabian Sea—with its ancient sea route linking India to Mesopotamia and Arabia—into the Red Sea, and by land even unto Mecca. Elements of the fleets sailed down the coast of East Africa, past Zanzibar, perhaps as far as Mozambique and Madagascar. There is some evidence that elements of Chinese fleets may even have touched the northern coasts of Australia after calling at the eastern extremes of the Spice Islands.

The future admiral's origins could hardly have been less auspicious or more difficult. Stories of his youth all agree on the essentials of what was to be an extraordinary rise to power. Born in the land-bound province of Yunnan in southwest China to Muslim parents in this region conquered by Kublai Khan in 1253 to '54, and ruled as a Yuan dynasty province under a Mongol prince until the fall of that dynasty, Zheng He was ten years old when General Fu Youde, sent to subjugate the region for China by the first Ming emperor, completed another of his tasks by gathering a number of boys to be sent to the court for service as eunuchs, a class of public servant most highly prized by the Chinese court. Selected for his alertness and courage by the general himself and marked a "candidate of exceptional qualities," after enduring the excruciating agony of castration by knife (which traditionally removed both penis and testicles), the boy was assigned to the retinue of one of the emperor's sons, the Prince of Yan (Zhu Di's title during his father's reign), at the capital of Nanjing. Trained for military service, largely because of his height, powerful build, and imposing presence, Zheng He served on maneuvers along the northern frontier of China and later in battles of the civil war that culminated with his patron, Zhu Di, deposing his nephew and making himself emperor in 1402.

As one of the most trusted associates of the new Son of Heaven, the eunuch was chosen to create and lead a Ming fleet, augmenting already formidable naval forces engaged in the southern seas. It likely seemed a wise diplomatic gesture to dispatch a Muslim Believer rather than an Infidel as plenipotentiary in sea-lanes then dominated by Arab merchant sailors and to the many countries that were Muslim-ruled. Naval experience was apparently less important than loyalty, although Zheng He soon demonstrated organizational skills and leadership abilities; what was described as an "awesome physical presence," must also have justified the emperor's choice. For a eunuch to command a fleet, or army for that matter, was not unusual in Ming times. Indeed major commands were often entrusted to such men. Yet both Zheng He's success and his closeness to his sovereign were eventually to provoke great jealousy and resentment.

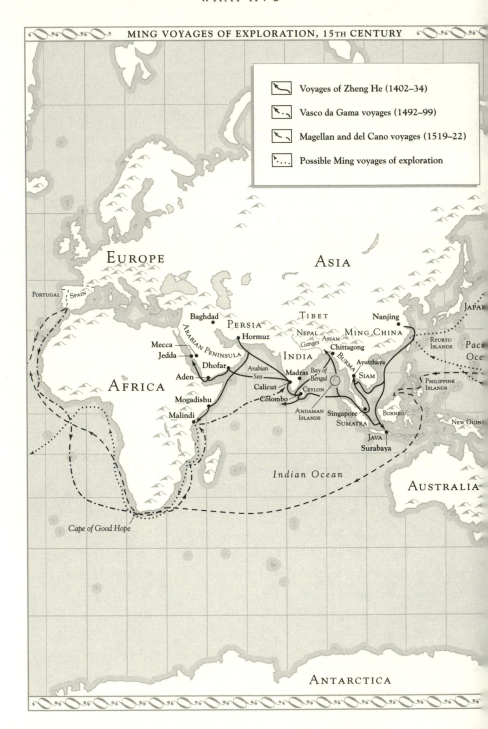

MING VOYAGES OF EXPLORATION, 15TH CENTURY

Voyages of Zheng He (1402–34)

Vasco da Gama voyages (1492–99)

Magellan and del Cano voyages (1519–22)

Possible Ming voyages of exploration

EUROPE

ASIA

PORTUGAL  SPAIN

Baghdad

PERSIA

TIBET

Nanjing

Hormuz

MING CHINA

Nepal  Assam

JAPAN

RYUKYU
ISLANDS

Mecca

ARABIAN PENINSULA

Ganges

Chittagong

Pacific
Ocean

Jedda

Dhofar

INDIA

BURMA

Ayutthaya

Arabian
Sea

Madras

SIAM

Aden

AFRICA

Calicut

Bay of
Bengal

PHILIPPINE
ISLANDS

CEYLON

Mogadishu

Colombo

Borneo

Malindi

ANDAMAN
ISLANDS

Singapore

NEW GUINEA

SUMATRA

JAVA

Surabaya

Indian Ocean

AUSTRALIA

Cape of Good Hope

ANTARCTICA

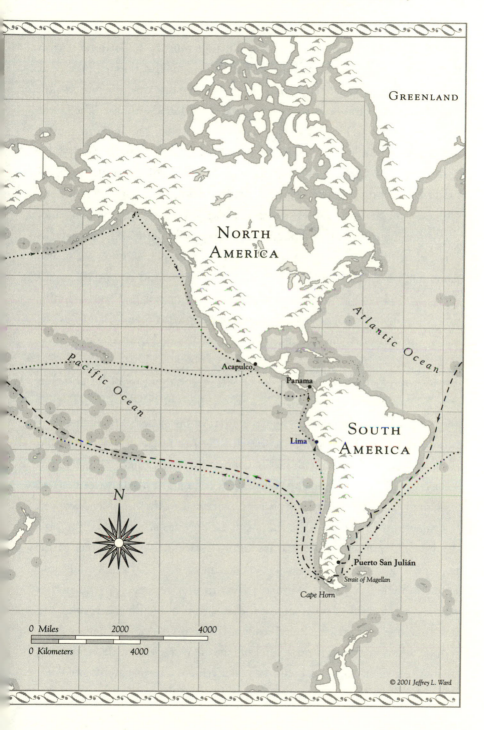

GREENLAND

NORTH
AMERICA

*Atlantic Ocean*

*Pacific Ocean*

Acapulco

Panama

SOUTH
AMERICA

Lima

N

Puerto San Julián
*Strait of Magellan*
Cape Horn

| 0 Miles | 2000 | 4000 |
|---|---|---|

| 0 Kilometers | 4000 |
|---|---|

© 2001 Jeffrey L. Ward

Why the expeditions were ordered is less immediately obvious than the choice of their commander. Their significance must be understood within the broader context of Ming history. Zhu Di became the Yongle Emperor at age forty-two, taking over leadership of the dynasty that his father, Zhu Yuanzhang, the Hongwu Emperor (r. 1368–1398), had founded. The Great Progenitor of the Dynasty, as the founder was styled, had led a successful military rebellion and then military overthrow of the Yuan, or Mongol dynasty, in 1368. A poor peasant who restored native Chinese to the imperial palace by ousting the Mongols and their entourage of Central Asian non-Chinese officials and Chinese sycophants willing to serve at the bottom of the Mongol bureaucratic hierarchy, the Hongwu Emperor's official portrait, now held in the National Museum of China in Taipei, captures his coarse features with his jutting chin, his explosive energy, and potential for violence. The long and bitter battles against the Mongols had entailed military campaigns throughout China and its peripheral regions, and Zhu Di was at the center of these campaigns once he attained his majority.

Zhu Di's usurpation of power from his nephew, and his Shakespearean ambition and simultaneous self-doubts about the morality of his acts, has long fascinated students of what has been called the "Second Founding of the Ming." Using as pretext "the defilement of his father's inviolable institutions" and proclaiming that it was "his duty to rescue the dynasty from the evil ministers exerting undue influence on a young ruler," Zhu Di seems to have sought to equal or surpass the achievements of his illustrious father. Although the former emperor probably perished in the fire that destroyed his palace on July 13, 1402, when Zhu Di's armies stormed Nanjing, his death could not be confirmed absolutely. Fearing that supporters of his nephew might find allies in areas outside the control of the Imperial Government, whether among Mongols yearning for revenge, in the nether reaches to the south, or even across the seas, the Yongle Emperor appears to have decided to make his reign known throughout Asia, to demonstrate that he was now the legitimate ruler of China. Moreover, he determined to invite their rulers to visit his court to offer tribute. His dispatching of fleets under Admiral Zheng He was an essential part of this mission.

. . .

What did these "fleets" sent out by Ming China look like? Was it really possible that China could have threatened the coming European domination of the Age of Sail? Indeed, judging from the way China seems to be perceived even today, casual historians of the era may be surprised to learn that China in the first years of the fifteenth century was arguably the world's preeminent maritime power. At the command of the Ming emperors were among the largest and best-equipped fleets the world had yet known.

No more comprehensive description of the expeditions lead by Zheng He exists in English than Louise Levathes's *When China Ruled the Seas: The Treasure Fleet of the Dragon Throne, 1405–1433*. Not only did her book bring this extraordinary period in Chinese history to the attention of the wider scholarly and popular world, but her peerless description of the eunuch admiral's world helped rescue from obscurity the grand maritime tradition of China.

China's fleets would have seemed to the Europeans of their day to be gigantic armadas, composed of myriad vessels of undreamt-of size and sophistication. The hardy caravels of the Portuguese or Spanish that made the epic voyages of the last years of the fifteenth century would have been dwarfed by the great "treasure ships" at the heart of the Ming fleet, and surpassed in size and capabilities by many of the other ships in the fleets. Zheng He sailed with an array of vessels specializing in all the needs of expeditions that would sometimes number as many as 37,000 men. He had horse ships, capable of carrying horses both from China for his forces or back in the tribute trade. He had supply and provision vessels, freshwater transport ships especially designed for missions in little-known seas near arid lands. He also had at his command a formidable fleet of combat ships including "floating fortresses," armed with cannon and other weapons well suited for bombardment of recalcitrant enemies, troop transports for his substantial land army, and smaller, faster vessels capable of warding off and running down pirates. They were coordinated at sea by a complex system of flags, drums, gongs, and lanterns, intended to allow the ships to remain in communication with one another, and to relay vital information about navigational or other dangers easily and reliably.

In 1402, the Yongle Emperor ordered his admiral to begin assembling a fleet to dominate the Indian Ocean. By 1420 it had become an imperial armada consisting of about 3,800 ships, 1,350 of which were major vessels capable of combat. Of the combat ships, some 400 were large oceangoing floating fortresses and perhaps as many as 250 were giant "treasure ships." The precise size and shape, as well as rigging and alignment of sails of these ships, which seem to have had as many as nine masts, has long been a topic for debate among students of naval architecture. Not only did the Ming fleets contain vessels larger in size than any wooden ships ever built, but they were extraordinarily seaworthy. They were equipped with the latest technology available, including magnetic compasses, sternpost rudders, detailed maps and charts, compartmentation belowdecks, and staggered masts, so placed as to better capture the wind, with sails of the strongest cloth available. In size, the ships dwarfed their European counterparts. Some displaced 1,500 tons, five times the displacement of the ships Vasco da Gama sailed to India.

Whole provinces were mobilized to build these ships. The effort engaged the minds and skills of the technological cream of the state. More than 400 households of carpenters, sail-makers, and shipwrights were transferred from the maritime regions to the shipyard at Longjiang, and thus perhaps between 20,000 and 30,000 specialists were brought together in one great nexus of shipbuilding expertise. Two shipyards were run at Nanjing—one for the normal boats and one for the huge "treasure ships." The dockyards at Longjiang included seven dry docks, most capable of handling ships 90 to 120 feet in width, with two extra-large ones, 210 feet wide, that could accommodate hulls the size of the treasure ships at the heart of the fleet.

While Western historians often claim that knowledge of wind and sea currents in the fifteenth century was considerably more advanced in the West, thanks to the Portuguese and Dutch, the great caveat must be to add "in the waters they knew." For the Chinese, the regular monsoons of the Indian and Southeast Asian waters, the extensive experience of their own countrymen, and the myriad merchants calling in Chinese ports helped make the charts used by Zheng He marvels of simplicity and practical application. Few have survived to the present day, of course, but they reportedly allowed the admiral to calculate a course accounting for wind, tide, currents, and expected weather, from any major port to any objective, reliable to within hours.

The voyages themselves spanned the period from 1405 to 1433. Zheng He began by making a base at Malacca, from which he could operate into the Indian Ocean. From there he traveled to Ceylon, Siam, Bengal, on to Hormuz and down the east coast of Africa. He forged alliances and used force where necessary. The treasures brought back to China included *quilin*, supposedly sacred animals we would call giraffes, zebras, and other exotic African beasts. These were precisely the kind of signs from nature, the "auspicious animals," that the tradition of Chinese dynastic cycles forecast would appear to indicate Heaven's sanction of a ruler's virtue.

On the first voyage, from 1405 to 1407, for example, Zheng He's fleet consisted of 317 ships accompanied by almost 28,000 armed troops. Many of these vessels were mammoth, nine-masted treasure ships with four decks capable of accommodating 500 or more passengers, as well as massive stores of cargo. Measuring up to 124 meters (408 feet) long and 51 meters (166 feet) wide, these treasure ships were by far the largest marine craft the world had ever seen. On the first three voyages (1405–1407, 1407–1409, and 1409–1411), Zheng He took his fleet to Southeast Asia, India, and Ceylon. The fourth expedition (1413–1415), went to the Persian Gulf and Arabia, and later expeditions ventured down the east African coast, calling at ports as far south as Malindi in modern Kenya. Throughout his travels, Zheng He liberally dispensed gifts of Chinese silk, porcelain, and other goods. In return he received rich and unusual presents from his hosts, including the animals that ended their days in the Ming imperial zoo. Zheng He and his companions paid respect to the local deities and customs they encountered, and in Ceylon they erected a monument honoring Buddha, Allah, and Vishnu, a kind of interfaith Rosetta Stone. Zheng He generally sought to attain his goals through diplomacy. But a contemporary reported that Zheng He walked like a tiger and did not shrink from violence when he considered it necessary to impress foreign peoples with China's military might. He ruthlessly suppressed pirates who had long plagued Chinese and Southeast Asian waters, intervened in a civil disturbance to establish his authority in Ceylon, and made displays of military force when local officials threatened his fleet in Arabia and East Africa. These seven expeditions established a Chinese presence and reputation throughout the Indian Ocean basin. Returning from his fourth voyage, Zheng He brought envoys from thirty states who traveled to China and paid their respect at the Ming court. Thereafter, however, the voyages began to lose central support, and hence the momentum and scale of the next two were substantially curtailed.

At just the moment when Zheng He's fleets seem to have achieved their initial assignment, when China's culture was drawing the attention and respect of rulers and traders throughout the Indian Ocean basin, the expeditions suddenly came to an end. As Emily Mahon has pointed out, many historians have expressed the idea that with the shipbuilding and navigational technology evident in the treasure ships, the Chinese could have met Henry the Navigator in his Portuguese home port. Instead, they apparently turned away from exploration, resuming what Michael Wood has called "their traditional inward focus." The analytical methodology used by most Western scholars has been a negative historical comparison, a "why not?" approach. They ask why *didn't* China develop as the West did? Implicit in such investigations is the assumption that something went "wrong," that the decision made by China's leaders could not have been a reasoned choice made by open-minded men, but was instead one rooted in a cultural uniqueness, reflecting a lack of some vital emotional or economic ingredient that subsequent "Western" success in the first age of imperialism would demonstrate. These arguments will not be refought here, but instead some of the main reasons advanced for them need to be touched on before we look beyond to ask what might have been.

As Zhu Di settled into his imperial role, the need for expensive overseas prestige-building missions seemed to diminish; their fabulous expense was seen increasingly to be drawing off resources needed to meet challenges to security closer to home. When challenges on the northern border from the Mongols became more serious, Zhu Di ordered a reduction in the sea service after the fifth expedition, from 1416 to 1419. There was a single, much smaller sixth expedition in 1421, but Zheng He came back early for the dedication of the new Forbidden City in Peking, the Yongle Emperor's reconstructed northern capital. The admiral presided over a parade of auspicious *quilin*. Disaster struck soon after the dedication, however, when lightning caused a great fire, which severely damaged the new palace. The emperor interpreted it as an ill omen: Had his policies put the world out of balance? He manumitted a substantial number of taxes to reduce the financial burden on the people and temporarily suspended future voyages of the Treasure Fleet. Now old and sick, Zhu Di died in 1424 at the age of sixty-four while on campaign.

His successor was his studious elder son Zhu Gaozhi. No warrior, the new emperor began plans to reverse many of his father's policies including the heavy taxation for military campaigns and public projects. However, Zhu Gaozhi died (perhaps of heart failure, perhaps from poison) after only nine months as emperor, and was succeeded in turn by Zhu Zhanji (age twenty-six) in 1426. The fifth Ming emperor was a combination of his warrior, spendthrift grandfather and his scholarly, fiscally conservative father; his reign was a time of peace, prosperity, and good government. He commissioned Zheng He to accomplish a seventh and final treasure ship expedition in 1430, for increased prestige and restoration of the tribute trade. This was perhaps the largest expedition, with 27,500 men and perhaps 300 ships.

Yet in the mid-1430s, the Ming emperors decided to end the expeditions altogether. Confucian ministers, who mistrusted Zheng He and the eunuchs who supported the voyages, argued that resources committed to the expensive expeditions would go to better use if devoted to agriculture. Moreover, during the 1420s and '30s the Mongols mounted a new military threat from the northwest, and land forces urgently needed financial support. Scholars have blamed the introspective culture of the later Ming period for a decline in many branches of science and technology. Launched on command, China's awesome maritime effort was also shut down from the center. In 1436 an imperial decree forbade the construction of new seagoing ships; the large shipyards consequently deteriorated and naval personnel were reassigned. The ability to maintain the oceangoing ships disintegrated and zealous officials seeking to assure that the expeditions would never be repeated destroyed even the records of the fabulous journeys. Zheng He himself died in 1433, apparently during his last voyage.

By 1474 the fleet was down to one-third of its size in early Ming times; by 1503 just a tenth of its peak size remained. In 1500, it became a capital offense for a Chinese to go to sea in a ship with more than two masts without special permission. Later, officials were authorized to destroy the larger classes of ships. Private merchants and shipwrights fled the maritime provinces and the harsh punishments for engaging in international trade, some finding work along the Grand Canal, and many others establishing themselves in the overseas Chinese communities throughout Southeast Asia that had first become a major feature of the region in the early years of the Ming. Moreover, a suspicion that those engaged in the coastal trade were in contact with non-Chinese beyond the reach of central authority and had a penchant for smuggling led them to forbid coastal people from plying their trades legally. This led in turn to an explosion of piracy along the China coasts, with Taiwan as a major center of activity. This development, often blamed on "Japanese pirates" (who were mostly of Chinese origin) resulted in the population of whole districts being relocated away from the coast both to "starve the pirates" and to shut down smuggling, as well as to destroy the nautical skills needed to engage in it.

What had once been a great fleet operating in response to the Imperial Will had disappeared and become such a minor factor in regional affairs that in 1515 a Portuguese envoy archly remarked that "With ten ships the [Portuguese] Governor of India . . . could take the whole of the China coast." Quite a condemnation!

Need it have been so?

What if, instead of curtailing the great overseas expeditions as it did upon the return of the last of Zheng He's missions in 1433, China's rulers had instead rededicated themselves to bringing to the world beyond eastern and southern Asia the news of China's glorious civilization and extending to yet-unvisited places the benefits of association with the Ming Imperial Court and the Chinese World Order? What if the Chinese emperor, instead of following the advice of his Confucian counselors and fiscal conservatives to abandon what they saw as reckless and unprecedented maritime activity had instead allowed it to continue, or even expanded the effort? What if, rather than yielding to a call to return to the "natural course" of Chinese history through a xenophobic looking inward, China's rulers had run the risk of inviting universal acceptance with its potential rewards as well as its hazards? What kind of world might have resulted had the Ming fleets not been reined in?

Imagine a Chinese fleet, substantially smaller perhaps than Zheng He's last East Africa expeditions, but still dwarfing those of the Portuguese, making a reconnaissance down the coasts of South Africa below Mozambique, around the Cape of Good Hope, into the Atlantic—what would surely have been seen from China's perspective as a second "Great Western Sea." Certainly, there was little to hold their attention in this barren stretch of coast, though the ostrich and other animals that hailed from the area would surely have been welcome additions to the imperial menagerie. But, was there enough to provide incentive for an expedition of discovery, taking a Chinese squadron up the western coast of Africa to Guinea or the Portuguese Atlantic islands before the Portuguese arrived in force? Perhaps there would have been just enough to carry them into contact. Confronted with a Chinese fleet—even a smallish one—that had allies and clients along the Angolan, Congolese, and West African coasts, would the Portuguese have continued to see this route to the East as desirable?

It is of course hard to envision the Roman Catholic Church accepting Chinese fleets as anything but one more instrument of the Devil sent to torment Christendom. With the Turks ascendant in the Eastern Mediterranean, the Arabs still powerful in North Africa (though no longer dominant in Iberia), a significant, sustained pressure from the south by yet another alien force could hardly have seemed anything more than another test by God of the Catholic faith. Yet what could the Portuguese have done to prevent it in the middle of the 1400s? Historically, Portugal only fortified Fort Elmina on the Gold Coast of West Africa in 1482. One almost certain outcome of a Chinese appearance on the Cape of Good Hope or the waters of the Atlantic would have been a greatly solidified Chinese position within the Indian Ocean basin and a consequent sharp check on Portuguese expansion. Might not the worst horrors of the Atlantic slave trade been aborted by a halt to Portuguese expansion along the African coast at this early date?

The Iberian princes, still somewhat unsteady on their own thrones, may well have been even less inclined to back "mad adventures" than they were historically. Instead of an East Africa ruthlessly exploited by the Portuguese as they established their first footholds in Angola on the western coast and then in Mozambique on the eastern coast of Africa, Chinese-influenced African kingdoms, perhaps buoyed up in their ability to resist, might have been able to face the Portuguese down or call on their "overlord" for assistance. Rather than European exploitation of many areas in the East from bases in Goa, Malaya, and Singapore, and the East Indies, Chinese control of the Strait of Malacca, even indirectly via a system tributary states rewarded for their obligations to the Dragon Throne, would have been a tremendous asset to any Ming emperor, and a formidable obstacle to interloping European adventurers in the late fifteenth and early sixteenth centuries. A Chinese presence in Ceylon and the Indian coasts, besides further enriching the remarkable cultural diversity of those lands, could well have made local rulers less easily intimidated and less willing to accept the fortified outposts and depots the Portuguese established as a means of asserting their control over routes of trade. Simultaneously, there exists a distinct possibility that the course of Middle Eastern history might have been altered by a continued Chinese presence in the Red Sea near Egypt and in the Persian Gulf.

The westward explorations could have had a reverse effect. If Chinese and client merchants had been able to trade and sell goods in Africa and the West, that Iberian navigators would one day acquire only by sailing halfway around the world, China itself might have been transformed. Had the constraints and controls of state enterprise been loosened, the dividends could have been enormous. The revenue potential of trade with a world seeking the products of Chinese industry and creativity might have brought about something like a mercantile revolution.

Anyone contemplating the might-have-beens of this scenario must engage in the delightful fantasy of a Chinese discovery of America and a pre-

Columbian contact with its peoples. How far-fetched was such a possibility? Certainly it could not have happened until the Chinese had firmly established themselves along the western coast of Africa. Lacking concrete knowledge of a land mass to the west, they would not have had the incentive to brave the devilish currents of the South Atlantic. Moreover, the extensive logistical train that China's approach to naval expeditions had thus far required would not have been suited to a perilous jump into the unknown. But once the entire bulge of West Africa had been incorporated into a Chinese system, probes in the direction of the South American continent would have been more likely. One might imagine a European world in close contact with Chinese fleets along the maritime frontier of Africa forced into a grand strategic defensive in these waters just as it was in the eastern Mediterranean against the Turks, Europe would have had to leave exploration to the Chinese intruders.

An intriguing alternative to the western Africa-to-Brazil route of Chinese maritime expansion might have been a grand trans-Pacific expedition. This would most likely have utilized the northern route, sailing past the Ryukyus, calling at a now still hospitable Japan, and then setting out across the North Pacific to the Aleutians and Alaska. From there, an expedition would have continued down what Europeans would come to call the Canadian shore to California—and beyond. The Chinese could surely have used the trans-Pacific route at lower latitudes, the same one that Magellan's expedition would first exploit in 1521; but, as the Spanish found, while the cross-Pacific route from Mexico to the Philippines was reliable, the reverse direction was much more problematic due to the unreliable currents and vast expanses of empty ocean.

Either route to what would become known as the Americas might have brought peoples of all races of the world under Chinese influence, with local chieftains offering to accept the Ming Son of Heaven as distant overlord in exchange for the wonders of Chinese goods and Chinese recognition. Radically altered diplomatic, cultural, and military exchanges profoundly altering the history of conquest and exploitation that was the fate of the Americas, all raise intriguing possibilities for "Latin" America's course of development. Would the "pre-Columbian" [pre–Zheng He] kingdoms have been wiped out by the diseases of the Old World with the same relentlessness had Chinese been the visitors? Would the Chinese have introduced the horses, guns, and metallurgy, all of which, in the first third of the sixteenth century, might have helped the Aztecs and the Incas keep the Spanish at bay? Or would the Spanish and their militant Catholicism have prevailed, only later in the century? Would smallpox still have tipped the historical balance?

We can be relatively sure that whatever the possibilities for the Chinese beyond Africa, the continuation of maritime and diplomatic efforts in the Indian Ocean basin could have had a great impact on the development of the world along very different lines than the European Age of Discovery we have come to accept as the natural course of world history in the sixteenth century. The Chinese attitude toward the outside world was hardly open-minded, to be sure. Since ancient times, China's imperial rulers had not conceived of their state as a small part of a larger whole—one nation among many others—but as the core of world civilization, and their own place as the "Middle Kingdom," the natural order of Heaven. Chinese rule, when it occurred in such bordering lands as Korea or Vietnam, or even Tibet, could never be described as benign.

Nevertheless, the purveyors of Confucian civilization on the world stage were likely to be less inclined to enslavement of entire peoples than their Iberian brethren and Chinese were not as likely to attempt to cleanse ancient, but newly discovered, civilizations of their essential features and force on them alternative gods as they installed foreign conquerors as their direct rulers. How different the world might have been had the Chinese brought the Old World to the New for the first time.

## A VISION AT THE GOLDEN GATE

*As the envoy passes through the Grand Portal of the Outer Palace that dominates the heart of the great coastal city of Tongjing (Eastern Capital), a splendid square suddenly stretches before him, broken in the distance only by a mountain of gilded steps rising up beneath a canopy roof of brilliant crimson that seems to float above the earth. That, he has been informed, is where the carpeted path he now treads will take him. It is the Hall of Reception where he is to present himself to the representative of the Celestial Government assigned to receive him this day. Looming off to his right, astride the rocky isle that rises from the bay, is the Temple of the Eastern Heavens, reserved for prayers by the emperor himself should he ever visit this part of his world-spanning realm. Just visible beyond are brown hills, crowned by billows of fog that appear poised to pour down and close the mouth of the bay. The envoy can see the grand harbor below, its waters covered with a forest of many-masted ships riding at anchor, sails furled, their brilliant banners flapping in the wind.*

*The escorting official assigned to the envoy boasts that Tongjing's Square of Eastern Peace, with its high walls, rivals even the mighty Forbidden City compound of the Son of Heaven in Beijing itself, but his own eyes widen as he sees how it swallows up the thousands of attendants in their silks of myriad colors who cannot begin to fill its vastness. Ranks of soldiers stand arrayed in polished armor. They are armed with weapons of all description, strange knives at their belts, shining as they catch the sun, while a special cadre of uniformed men touch fire to gleaming barrels and flame and deafening noise belch forth in salute as each delegation arrives—no matter whether large in size like the bejeweled and jingling procession that has proceeded the envoy, said to have come from the far south, or few in number, humbly clad amongst all this grandeur as is the envoy's party. Huge beasts with godlike riders high above the ground seem either impervious to the booming, or are held in check by firm hands and gentle words. Behind the soldiers who line the entire path to the distant pavilion draped in imperial yellow stand blocks of scholarly civil servants in their academic robes, formed into regular lines, a mark both of the order and the grandeur of the occasion.*

*This is, after all, the first time that the newly arrived governor of the East, an Imperial prince, fourth son of His Majesty, will be receiving visitors from the many lands and peoples that span this continent. He will allow them to make their ritual supplication and bows of submission before he issues, in his father's name, the symbols of investiture to their chieftains, lords, and kings. A numbing drone, emitted by reed instruments, punctuated by the screech made by bows pulled across little boxes by a virtual army of musicians and the clash of metal disks, seems to delight the Chinese as much as it causes the envoy's teeth to clinch. And then, at last, as the envoy makes his way along the appointed path, he finds himself quite near to small clusters of strange men whose faces are of colors not common in this land: They must be the ambassadors from far reaches of the world—even further away than his home—here to witness the ceremonies now under way.*

*It is a life-changing moment for the envoy. In addition to the symbols of office he will receive, he knows he will be entrusted with the bejeweled badges of honor and the keys to the chests of the treasure that will be bestowed upon his people by the magnanimous Chinese throne. He is well pleased that he has been able to complete this part of his role as emissary, yet remains anxious about the long journey that lies ahead on his return. Starting out at the Golden Gate on the Great Bay that offers shelter from the Eastern Ocean, called "Pacific" only by those who have never known its furies, he will have to return across the broad desert, mighty mountains, and buffalo-filled plains to his forest home in the Iroquois Confederacy. His people have finally agreed to bond themselves to the wider Ming world, now counting among its friends, allies, and subjects, all the nations and communities from the Incas in far-off Peru, to the Mexican kingdoms of the Aztecs and their former rivals, since reconciled by the benevolent influence of the Great Son of Heaven.*

GEOFFREY PARKER

# MARTIN LUTHER BURNS
# AT THE STAKE, 1521

*"O God, is Luther dead?"*

*The event that has long signaled the birth of Protestantism is Martin Luther's nailing of his Ninety-five Theses to a door of the Wittenberg castle church on October 31, 1517, All Hallow's Eve. The theses themselves were hardly revolutionary documents. The thirty-four-year-old professor of theology, an Augustinian monk, argued that indulgences, paper certificates guaranteeing in the name of the pope that sinners would not have to spend Eternity in Purgatory, should not be given to those who simply made a pious donation. "Nailed" may be a bit over-dramatic, though it has long been invested with the pound and rap of tradition; we are dealing with a powerful symbol here. "Posted" is probably more in the spirit of Luther's act, which was, as Geoffrey Parker notes, "the normal way of requesting a public debate." Luther at this point had not the least intention of breaking with the Church. Once copies of the theses were printed up and circulated, however, a controversy whose repercussions might have remained merely local became widespread and their author a figure of sudden notoriety. The printing press made Luther a celebrity, one of the first that media created. Indeed, if there had been no such invention, could there have been a Luther? By the same token, without a mass-produced Bible available to ordinary individuals, could Protestantism itself have existed? As he put it, every man could now become his own priest.*

*Martin Luther was always blessed by good luck. He died in bed, not standing upright on a pile of burning fagots, bound to a stake. What if death by fire had*

505

*been his fate when he was hauled before the Diet of Worms in 1521 and asked to recant views that had already led to his excommunication? What forms would Protestantism have taken if it had lacked the magnetizing force of a Luther? Could Protestantism, except as a scattering of dissenters, have even existed? Would his death, and the leadership vacuum created by it, have given the Catholic Church the breathing space that Rome needed? And what different directions might the history of sixteenth-century Western Europe have taken without the great schism of religion? The development of the New World might have been affected as well. To understand the stature of this rude, arrogant, yet frequently charming man, we need simply to contemplate his absence.*

GEOFFREY PARKER is the Andreas Dorpalen Professor of History at Ohio State University and the author of such works as *The Dutch Revolt, Philip II, The Military Revolution, The Spanish Armada* (with Colin Martin), and most recently *The Grand Strategy of Philip II*. He is (with Robert Cowley) editor of *The Reader's Companion to Military History*.

Aｂｏｕｔ ｆｏｕｒ ｏ'ｃｌｏｃｋ on the afternoon of April 17, 1521, the ush-
ers led Martin Luther, looking drawn and pale, before Emperor
Charles V and the German Diet, meeting in the city of Worms on the
Rhine. On a table in the center of the episcopal hall, next to the great Ro-
manesque cathedral, stood a pile of Luther's books and pamphlets. A
spokesman asked him two questions: Would he acknowledge the author-
ship of these books? And, would he recant all or parts of them? Luther, realizing that he would have no chance to state his views, requested
twenty-four hours for reflection. The next day at about six in the evening
he again entered the crowded episcopal hall, now illuminated by hundreds
of candles. Facing the emperor, the princes, and the prelates, Luther delivered in a high clear voice a ten-minute speech in German, which he later
repeated in Latin. When he had finished, the spokesman objected that he
had still not given a simple answer as to whether he would recant or not.
Luther paused and then replied defiantly:

> Since then Your Serene Majesty and Your Lordships seek a simple an-
> swer, I will give it in this manner, neither horned nor toothed. Unless
> I am convinced by the testimony of the Scriptures or by clear reason
> (for I do not trust either in the pope or in councils alone, since it is
> well known that they have often erred and contradicted themselves),
> I am bound by the Scriptures I have quoted and my conscience. I can-
> not do otherwise. Here I stand, may God help me, amen.

Pandemonium now broke loose in the hall. The emperor, angry and excited, rose to his feet and declared that he had had enough of such talk. The
meeting broke up in chaos.

For a moment, Luther's fate hung in the balance: some Catholic zealots wanted to seize him and shouted "into the fire"—the traditional fate of heretics. Nevertheless, Charles V respected the safe conduct he had given Luther to attend the diet and even allowed him a few days of further discussion with theologians. Luther left Worms a free man on April 26. No sooner was he outside the city, however, than a group of masked men ambushed him and he abruptly disappeared. On hearing the news, the German artist Albrecht Dürer wrote in his diary: "O God, is Luther dead? Who will now explain the Gospel to us as clearly as he used to do?"

We now know (as Dürer did not) that the "kidnappers" were the soldiers of Luther's patron, Elector Frederick of Saxony, and that they took him in secret to one of Frederick's castles. There he grew a beard and spent one year disguised as a knight, "Sir George," while he worked on the greatest of his literary labors: a German translation of the New Testament. By the time Luther died in 1546, his vigorous, melodious version had appeared in 253 editions and formed the basis for several other vernacular translations. Thus William Tyndale's English Bible (and therefore the Authorized Version, into which much of it passed) stems directly from Luther's version. The reformer returned to Wittenberg in 1522 where, until his death twenty-four years later, his preaching, teaching, and writing shaped a Lutheran church with some five million members around the world today.

But what if, in April 1521, Charles V had listened to those who urged him to disregard Luther's safe conduct, on the grounds that "One does not keep faith with heretics"? A century before, another critic of the papacy, Jan Hus from Bohemia, had also received an Imperial promise of safety to come from Prague to Germany and defend his views, but it had been dishonored. The emperor who issued it watched him burn at the stake and then led a series of military campaigns to exterminate his followers in Bohemia.

Martin Luther, born in Saxony to a mining family, attended primary and grammar schools away from home. He took his bachelor's degree at the University of Erfurt in 1501 and his master's the following year, at age nineteen. In 1505, after a bolt of lightning almost killed him, he became an Au-

PORTRAIT OF A SURVIVOR

*A rebel in middle age: Strong will and intelligence are captured on the face of Martin Luther in this contemporary etching.*

(Lucas Cranach the Elder, 1472–1553, *Martin Luther*. SEF/Art Resource, NY)

gustinian monk, in gratitude for his survival. But he continued to study theology in his monk's cell and obtained his doctorate in 1512. Then he moved to Wittenberg, where he began to lecture on the Bible to students at the new university, founded by Frederick of Saxony, and to deliver sermons to the citizens as preacher in the town church.

Luther always saw teaching and preaching as crucial, and he continued to do both throughout his life. He also wrote to be heard as well as to be read, always addressing himself to "my readers and hearers." "The voice should be the soul of the word," he wrote. "Letters are dead words, speech is living words." He devoted great attention to finding the right words and, as he wrote, spoke the sentences aloud to himself until the stresses, pauses, cadences, and the sequence of vowels and consonants sounded just right. One of the mourners at the reformer's funeral paid tribute to his great linguistic gifts when he claimed that "Luther taught us to speak."

These communication skills would have made Luther a formidable authority on any subject, but gradually he focused on a particularly important issue for Christians: sin and salvation. How can the sinner be saved? His close reading of the Bible suggested that good works and insincere penance would not suffice: only complete faith in Christ could assure salvation. In 1517, Luther became concerned that a practice by some of his fellow priests, members of the Dominican Order, was leading Christians astray, offering them a false security. They toured Christendom distributing indulgences that promised the living and the dead, in the pope's name, remission of ecclesiastical penalties, and of time in purgatory, in return for a contribution toward the cost of rebuilding the basilica of St. Peter's in Rome. Although the local authorities forbade the Dominicans to offer indulgences in Wittenberg, they did so nearby, and members of Luther's congregation left town to acquire them.

When his sermons failed to halt the exodus, on October 31, 1517, Luther presented a set of ninety-five objections to the practice. His criticisms fell under three heads. Most attacked the Dominicans' failure to require any penance or inner contrition before issuing their indulgences; others argued that the Gospels provided everything a Christian needed to know for salvation; a few claimed that those who stifled the Word of God to make room for indulgences—even if granted by the pope—were the enemies of Christ. Luther posted his Ninety-five Theses on the door of a local church, the normal way of requesting a public debate at the time. He also sent them with a cover note to his ecclesiastical superior, who forwarded them to Rome, and he mailed copies to some friends, who published them all over Germany.

This provided Luther's first taste of widespread popularity, and he relished it—all the while professing that he had nothing to do with it. "It is a mystery to me," he noted (with a trace of smugness), "how my Theses, more so than my other writings—or indeed those of other professors—spread to so many places." The theses also provoked envy and enmity. The Dominicans who distributed the indulgences noted a fall in revenues and complained to the pope about Luther's criticisms; so in the summer of 1518 he received a summons to Rome to explain his objections.

Political calculations now rescued Luther, for the first but not the last time. When the papal summons arrived in Germany, its ruler, Emperor Maximilian of Habsburg, urgently desired to have his grandson Charles recognized as his successor. He therefore met at the city of Augsburg with those who would make the choice: seven Imperial Electors, including Frederick of Saxony, Luther's suzerain. Frederick, who had advanced large sums of money to the emperor in the past, asked Maximilian to allow Luther to address the pope's concerns in Augsburg instead of Rome. Grateful and anxious for Frederick's vote, Maximilian agreed.

Why did Frederick care? He met Luther face-to-face only once—at the Diet of Worms—and the two men never exchanged a spoken word. The elector, however, possessed unusual piety. In his youth he had undertaken a pilgrimage to Jerusalem and afterward began to collect relics. Some he purchased, others he exchanged for pictures by Lucas Cranach (his Court painter), and a few his agents stole. By 1520, his collection exceeded 19,000 items, ranging from some milk from the Virgin Mary's breast, some straw from the stable at Bethlehem, a piece of the burning bush, and some soot from the fiery furnace, to articles of merely local appeal like the beaker used by St. Elizabeth of Marburg, a medieval German saint. When the entire collection came out on display, the total time remitted from purgatory in return for pious prayers approached two million years. Frederick kept his collection, the largest in the world, in the castle church at Wittenberg—the very spot where Luther had posted his Ninety-five Theses—and he paid eighty-three resident priests to celebrate almost 10,000 masses annually on his behalf. These were precisely the sort of "false" religious practices that Luther abhorred and against which he would preach. In 1518, however, these differences lay in the future and Frederick sought to protect Luther, apparently out of a sense of "fair play" and, perhaps, because he did not wish to see one of his own "star professors" disgraced. He therefore not only provided overt protection against those who sought Luther's destruction, but also gave him covert advice through his legal experts.

Unfortunately for Luther, the senior papal representative at Augsburg was Cardinal Cajetan, general of the Dominican Order—a man unlikely to give way on the issue of indulgences. For four days in October 1518 the two men debated. The cardinal pointed out that several popes had proclaimed the efficacy of indulgences, forcing Luther to reply that "the pope is not above, but under the word of God" and could therefore err. The following month, at Cajetan's direction, the pope issued a decree ordering that everyone should obey his teaching on indulgences. This pushed Luther one step further toward an open confrontation with Rome. He read the document and announced in January 1519 that, since it offered no biblical support for its assertions, "although I will not reject it, I will not bow down before it." That same month, Maximilian died and Germany lacked any secular authority capable of keeping the "monk's quarrel" (as many considered it) within bounds.

Luther had intended his Ninety-five Theses to provoke a scholarly debate, and a prominent German theologian, John Eck, duly challenged him. In July 1519, the two met in an open forum at Leipzig in Saxony. Luther cited the teaching of the Greek Orthodox Church, which also condemned indulgences; Eck pointed out that Jan Hus had done the same. This horrified Luther, who had previously accepted that Hus died a heretic. Now he started to read the writings of the Bohemian reformer and was amazed at what he found. "Up to now I have held and espoused all the teachings of Jan Hus without knowing it," he told a friend. "We are all Hussites without realizing it." But Hus had criticized far more than indulgences: he had denied the power of the popes and exalted the authority of the Bible. Luther realized that he would have to do the same and wrote, early in 1520:

I am in deep turmoil since I can hardly doubt that the pope is the true Antichrist whom everyone has been expecting. Everything fits together too well—his life, his deeds, what he says and what he demands.

This proved too much for some of Luther's supporters and they now abandoned him. For many Germans, "Hussite" was equivalent to "rebel" or "priest-hater." In England, one of the few countries outside Bohemia where Hussite views had gained a following, King Henry VIII wrote a tract condemning Luther and his Hussite leanings (which led the pope to confer on Henry the accolade "Defender of the Faith," a title still treasured by English monarchs). More ominous, John Eck sent a detailed list to Rome of heretical views uttered by Luther during the Leipzig debate.

Luther now published tracts that set out his beliefs in detail and, by the end of 1520, he had published over thirty of them, printed in 400 editions, with combined sales of 300,000 copies. One of them, *Address to the Christian Nobility of Germany Regarding the Improvement of Christendom*, which called on princes and magistrates to reform the Church (since the pope clearly did not intend to do so), sold 2,000 copies in five days. His style became instantly recognized—when he authored an anonymous tract he had no doubt that "anyone who reads it, if he has seen my pen and my thoughts, must say: 'This is Luther'"—and his books flooded the market. The other outstanding writer of the day, Erasmus of Rotterdam, complained huffily that one could hardly find a book in Germany that was not either written by Luther or about Luther.

The tone of the debate also became sharper. In his *Address*, Luther claimed that, whether Hus was a heretic or not, he had been unjustly executed because heretics should be refuted with arguments and not with fire. He also argued that "the prime concern" of Christians

should be to live sincerely in faith and in accordance with Holy Scripture. For Christian faith and life can easily exist without the intolerable laws of the pope. In fact, faith cannot properly exist unless there are fewer of these Romanist laws, or unless they are abolished all together.

Luther's tracts stressed that the Bible could be read and understood by any-one without any need for a church hierarchy—or, in his memorable phrase, "Every man is his own priest." Eck, for his part, secured a papal decree in June 1520 that attributed forty-one separate doctrinal "errors" to Luther, ordered him to recant, and threatened him with excommunication if he did not. Six months later, Luther responded with a theatrical gesture: he cere-monially burnt a copy of the decree and, for good measure, threw a copy of the canon law into the flames as well. "As they would do to me, so I do to them," he wrote. The following month, the pope excommunicated Luther and called on Charles V, now emperor, to outlaw him.

Charles could not oblige. In July 1519, just as Luther and Eck began their debate, the electors met to choose a successor to Maximilian. They considered three candidates: Maximilian's grandson Charles of Habsburg, King Francis I of France, and Frederick of Saxony. Frederick refused to stand and threw his weight behind Charles, who was elected unanimously. In return, however, the new emperor promised not to outlaw anyone with-out a legal hearing. At Frederick's insistence, he therefore agreed to allow Luther to attend the Diet of Worms, scheduled to meet early in 1521, albeit in the expectation that the excommunicate would simply recant.

By then, however, the execution of Luther could no longer have si-lenced the growing chorus of open critics of the Catholic Church. Luther's prolific writings and his dramatic personal appearances all over Germany to defend his views had won numerous followers and, by 1521, Albrecht Dürer was not alone in regarding Luther as the most gifted exponent of a new kind of Christianity. But he was no longer the only one. Wittenberg experienced a religious revolution even without Luther. Under the leader-ship of another university professor and priest, Andreas Bodenstein von Karlstadt, radical preachers dispensed communion in both kinds, bread and wine, to the laity (the Roman Church allowed only bread), crowds smashed church images, monks left their monasteries, and priests began to marry. Radical prophets warned that the end of the world approached and called for social justice. Far to the south, the chief preacher of the city of Zurich in Switzerland, Huldrych Zwingli, noted with approval in his diary Luther's defiance of Rome and, in 1519, persuaded the city magistrates to ban indulgences. The next year, he received permission to preach "the gospel" as he wished, and all other clergy in Zurich followed his lead. While Luther hid in Frederick's castle, others advanced his cause.

What, then, if Charles V had tried to burn *all* these critics of the Roman Church? Once again, by 1521 it was probably too late for effective persecution. On the one hand, Luther's ideas had become too popular to suppress. Even Hus's teachings—spread only by word of mouth and in manuscripts until the invention of printing with movable type in the 1450s—survived his martyrdom. Repeated attempts to invade his native Bohemia and eradicate his followers failed ignominiously: The Hussites fought back and won. Printing, which Luther regarded as "God's highest and ultimate gift of grace, by which He would have his gospel carried forward," made it impossible for any German government to destroy all copies of all of Luther's works. Moreover, they had by then spread beyond Germany. By 1530, some thirty Lutheran tracts had appeared in Dutch translation, and three in English. On the other hand, experience would show that killing Protestants did not eradicate their beliefs. In 1523, Charles ordered two Netherlands monks to be burnt because they upheld Luther's teaching and refused to abjure—the first Lutheran martyrs anywhere—and in the course of his reign at least 2,000 more Netherlanders perished for their beliefs.

Nevertheless, Lutheranism (as well as the other persecuted Protestant creeds) continued to thrive in the Low Countries. In Switzerland, an armed attack on Zurich by her Catholic neighbors in 1531 resulted in the death of Zwingli in battle, but his faith lived on and even spread to other cantons. Finally, in Germany, the relentless persecution of the Anabaptists, groups of believers who separated from both the Lutheran and Zwinglian camps in 1522–23, failed to extinguish them. Their faith survived and their descendants (Mennonites and others) today number more than one million members in some sixty countries worldwide. There is no reason to suppose that even intense and protracted persecution would have extinguished Lutheranism either.

In any case, three political considerations precluded effective enforcement of Charles's decree of outlawry. First, the king of France, rankled by his failure to secure the Imperial title, concluded a series of alliances with

Charles's enemies and prepared to declare war. Rumors of a hostile coalition reached the emperor in Worms, and he begged the Imperial Diet to vote him funds with which to organize a coherent defense. It made no sense to antagonize Frederick of Saxony, one of the richest rulers, by outlawing Luther before approval of the taxes. Charles therefore issued his edict of outlawry in May 1521—a month after Luther's defiance—only when Frederick had left Worms. Second, on the empire's eastern flank, a new Ottoman sultan, Suleiman, advanced up the Danube and captured Belgrade after only three weeks' siege. This opened the plain of Hungary and, beyond, the Habsburgs' patrimonial lands, to Turkish raids. In 1529, Suleiman and his army laid siege to Vienna. Time after time, a Turkish offensive up the Danube (or the fear of one) led Charles to agree to tolerate Lutheranism in the Empire in return for Lutheran taxes and troops to defend Austria. In 1529, Luther composed his most famous hymn, "A Mighty Fortress is our God," for the Saxon troops who marched to save Vienna after Charles had granted a further period of toleration. Third, and finally, the emperor spent little of his reign in Germany. After the Diet of Worms, he decided to go to Spain in order to supervise the suppression of a major popular rebellion (the *comuneros*), and the enmity of France kept him there for the next seven years. He was in no position to enforce his decree of outlawry (or any other measure) in Germany.

Would Luther's death in 1521 have changed anything? Undoubtedly. To begin with, we would lack his powerful translation of the Bible, as well as most of his 3,100 other publications, which take up over 60,000 printed pages in the standard edition of his works. This would have weakened the Reformation in two distinct ways. First, the very popularity of Luther's works helped to harmonize the different dialects spoken in Germany. The first Basel edition of his German New Testament included a glossary of unusual Saxon terms for the benefit of southern German readers. Without later works to popularize Luther's style, the need for such aids might have continued, complicating the spread of anti-Catholic ideas. Second, and more obviously, without Luther's commanding authority, the various centers of anti-Catholic sentiment would have developed in isolation. Instead of a relatively unified Lutheran bloc in northern Germany and Scandinavia, there would have been a patchwork of states, each with their own creed. Perhaps a divided (or, rather, a more divided) Reformation would have proved unable to withstand a Catholic counteroffensive once Charles eventually made peace with the French and the Turks.

The impact of the Peasants' War of 1524–25, the greatest popular uprising in Europe between the rebellions of the 1350s and the French revolution, would certainly have been different. As it was, the peasants of southern Germany took many of their grievances straight from the teachings of Luther and Zwingli, and several of their leaders had been (and a few still were) his followers. Luther used his enormous authority both to distance the Reformation cause from the rebellion and to legitimize the brutal repression of the peasants. His most influential tract on the subject, with the bloodthirsty title *Against the Murdering and Thieving Hordes of Peasants*, commanded "everyone who can, to smite, slay and stab them, secretly or openly, remembering that nothing can be more poisonous, hurtful or devilish than a rebel." Without his firm, shrill voice, the peasant movement would have become more radical—and perhaps more popular—discrediting the cause of reform irreparably.

Predicting the impact of Luther's martyrdom at Worms beyond the 1520s becomes more hazardous. Let us consider, for example, the impact of a weaker Reformation camp on the Catholic Church. Perhaps burning Luther, and intimidating (though not eliminating) his supporters, would have lulled the papacy back into complacency, leading it to write off the few isolated Protestant enclaves just as it had written off Hussite Bohemia. Probably, then, later reformers (such as John Calvin) would still have divided Europe with new calls for reform. Conversely, however, a weaker and less abrasive Reformed movement might have proved easier for the Catholic Church to accommodate. Many sincere Christians, including Charles V, wished to end the schism and compelled Catholic and Protestant leaders to attend several meetings to resolve their differences. All of them failed, in part because of Luther's intransigence. Without him, perhaps papal negotiators could have reached an agreement with at least some of the Protestant leaders, healing the schism and reuniting all Western Christians under papal authority.

Without the great divide between Protestant and Catholic, certainly the history of sixteenth-century Western Europe would have been very different: no religious wars, no Dutch Revolt, no Thirty Years' War. The forces of a united Christendom might have held back the Turks at Belgrade or Budapest; the united forces of Charles V's subjects might have established Habsburg hegemony in Europe, precluding all settlements in the Americas by other Europeans. So just possibly: No Luther, no United States as we know it.

Luther might well have relished that extreme connection. As with the thunderbolt that narrowly missed him, he believed that the fate of his cause as well as his personal future rested solely in God's hands. In April 1521, he jauntily told the Diet of Worms, quoting the Acts of the Apostles:

> "If this is the counsel of men, this work will be overthrown; if it is of God, you will not be able to overthrow it." The emperor and the imperial estates are welcome to write that to the pope in Rome! I know that if my work is not from God, within three years, or even two, it will perish of its own accord.

A year later, as he rode back to Wittenberg to resume his duties as teacher and preacher, he felt vindicated and empowered. At Worms, Elector Frederick had found Luther "much too bold," but he had seen nothing yet. In 1522, his persistent carping persuaded Frederick to pack up his collection of relics, and later that year the elector and his entourage appeared at the Imperial Diet wearing a Lutheran slogan ("The word of God endures forever") on their clothes. In 1524, the emperor's sister Isabel went to Wittenberg to hear Luther preach and publicly took communion in both kinds. Before he died in 1525, Frederick also received both wine and bread at communion, a clear sign of his personal break with Rome.

That same year, Luther abandoned his monastic habit and married a nun, and shortly afterward he began to celebrate October 31, the day he had published his Ninety-five Theses, with a special toast. In his last years, he drank the toast out of one of the few surviving relics from Elector Frederick's collection—the beaker of St. Elizabeth of Marburg—symbolizing his victory not only over the pope but also over the emperor, the princes, and the prelates who had once sat in judgment upon him at the Diet of Worms. In 1546, he died serenely in his bed in the town where he was born sixty-two years before. His career offers one of the best defenses of the "Great Man" theory of history: that a single individual can decisively influence the course of human affairs. There might still have been a Reformation without Luther, but it would have taken a totally different form.

THEODORE K. RABB

# IF CHARLES I HAD NOT LEFT WHITEHALL, AUGUST 1641

*As a starter, no English civil war*

*"Charles I," Theodore K. Rabb remarks, "is the perfect exemplar of the truism that the personality and actions of a major historical figure can alter the course of events." Without Charles (who reigned from 1625 until he was beheaded in 1649), the English civil war probably never would have happened and Oliver Cromwell would have remained at home singing hymns and breeding horses. It was a war that changed nothing and everything. Cromwell's short-lived republican experiment died with him and the monarchy was restored, its powers apparently intact. But this was not the authoritarian monarchy of Charles, and would never be again. His son Charles II was a king who liked to rub shoulders with his subjects (and to take some of the fairer ones to bed). When his successor, James II, tried to revert to the old ways (and to the Catholic Church), he was sent packing.*

*But more than the monarchy had changed. An elected Parliament was now supreme, and rudimentary political parties were beginning to take form. Governments could actually be voted out of office. "The basic elements of electoral democracy as we know them," Rabb writes, "gathered inexorable force in England." By the end of the next century, a truer democracy, embodying the ideal of universal suffrage—not just the rule of the landed classes—would emerge in the rebellious British colonies across the Atlantic.*

*None of this might have happened had it not been for the devious obstinacy of Charles I. Since it was against his beliefs to compromise with Parliament, a confrontation was inevitable. But as Rabb observes, there was one scenario, not at all improbable, that might have changed everything. It hinged on the recurring scourge of seventeenth-century Europe—the plague. In August 1641, Charles I headed north to deal with rebellious subjects in Scotland. Six days later, in a house just one hundred yards from his Whitehall Palace, the inhabitants came down with the usually fatal disease. What if Charles had delayed his trip by just a week—and had become a victim himself? The future, our past, might have assumed a considerably different shape, and not necessarily a democratic one.*

THEODORE K. RABB is a professor of history at Princeton University and the author or editor of such notable works as *The New History, The Struggle for Stability in Early Modern Europe, Climate and History, Renaissance Lives*, and *Jacobean Gentlemen*. He was the principal historical adviser for the acclaimed and Emmy-nominated PBS television series *Renaissance*.

A MONG THE WARS, military campaigns, and individual battles that can change the face of a continent, civil wars are often the most agonizing. Though the landscapes they alter tend to be only within specific countries, the intensity of the conflicts and the transformations that they bring about can have long-term consequences that extend far beyond national borders. In the twentieth century, for instance, the effects of internal strife were not restricted to Russia, Spain, China, or Vietnam, to name but four of the most brutal instances. And the same can be said, in earlier centuries, of America in the 1770s or France in the 1790s.

The importance of these struggles is only enhanced if one considers how easily they could have come out otherwise. What kind of world would we have inherited had Lenin, Franco, Mao, Ho Chi Minh, Washington, or the Third Estate lost their assaults on the existing order? Each had more than one moment when their movements could have collapsed, sending history into very different directions. And the argument holds even when a civil war seems not to have shifted many landmarks, as appears to have been the case with the upheavals that shook England in the 1640s and '50s.

Although armies were either on the march or trying to dissuade resistance for most of the period from 1640 to 1660 in England, they seemed to leave little mark. The persistence of political structures had been notable in the wake of previous English civil wars, such as the Wars of the Roses that had raged some 150 years earlier, and at first sight the events of the 1640s and '50s appeared to follow the same pattern. The monarchy, which for a few years had ceased to exist, returned in 1660 with just about all of its powers intact. Both the House of Lords and the Anglican Church, which had been abolished, were restored; traditional powers in the counties were resumed by the landed country gentry; and Parliament once again was both summoned and dissolved at the command of the king. A few legal rights and practices had been reformed, but common law and the power of precedent were not significantly more authoritative than before. Nor were religious dissenters, on the whole, much more comfortable than they had been in the 1630s. And the many unprecedented ideas that had bubbled to the surface as the established order dissolved—from a belief in equal political rights for all men to the wish for complete freedom of the press—seemed to evaporate after 1660, their later influence impossible to predict. Behind the outward show, however, there had been a fundamental shift in political culture, reversing the drift toward authoritarianism that Charles I had represented.

During the civil wars that outcome could not have been predicted, because the voices of hope for a new future, represented notably by the poet John Milton, were often drowned out by the despair of those who regarded the disintegration of England's traditional institutions as a prelude to anarchy, redeemable only by a determined sovereign. Among the latter, the most acute observer was probably Thomas Hobbes, whose *Leviathan* may well be the most powerful response to civil war ever written. Deeply disturbed by the chaos that had forced him into exile, he published his masterpiece in 1651, just two years after the execution of King Charles I. Writing in the context of profound and unprecedented social uncertainty, Hobbes sought to define a political system that would have as its prime purpose the assurance of stability for all its citizens. The only logical possibility, he concluded, was an all-powerful sovereign, dedicated to the maintenance of order and capable of imposing his will without restraint.

Given the spread of absolutist doctrines and practices through much of the Europe in which Hobbes wrote—certainly in the France of Louis XIV, where his exile had taken him—his conclusions seemed to capture the spirit of his times. There was a relentless single-mindedness and a devastating finality in his dismissal of alternatives, which made his views less than popular (though hugely influential) in his own lifetime, but there could be no doubt that most of his contemporaries would have taken his side if faced with a choice between the might of centralized authority and the chaos of resistance to that authority. Hobbes may have written amid crisis, but his rethinking of the purpose of government has remained fundamental to political theory ever since.

Yet it was not a Leviathan-like king who returned to power in 1660. The Stuart dynasty had learned how dire could be the effects of arbitrary rule, and Charles I's son Charles II was determined to retain the affections of his subjects. Where his father had been remote and aloof, he mingled enthusiastically with the people of London. He went riding in Hyde Park; he frequented the theater; and the most famous diarist of the age, Samuel Pepys, reported that he was swept along so far by the crowd that gathered when the king was opening a new session of Parliament that he eventually found himself at Charles's elbow, reading along as the royal speech was delivered. Such mingling, and the political relationships it implied, would have been inconceivable under the autocratic Charles I or across the Channel in Louis XIV's France.

What this changed atmosphere reflected, however, was something more profound than clever public relations or a warm personality. It was the realization that, for all the apparent continuities, the country's political culture had been fundamentally altered by the experience of civil war. Thus, it is true that disabilities were again imposed on dissenters from the official Anglican Church. They were excluded from the universities and public office; forbidden to come too close to the capital, London; and made sufficiently uncomfortable that, as in the 1630s, a nonconformist like William Penn sought better prospects in the New World. But they were not hounded, directly persecuted, or prevented from observing their own forms of worship. A de facto tolerance was extended, and it embraced even a growing community of Jews, who had been forbidden to settle in England for centuries, but who now began to return in some numbers even though the formal legal prohibition had not been repealed.

This unwritten acceptance of new conditions also transformed the political system. So deep was the reaction to the bloodshed and upheaval of the midcentury that the English were determined to avoid such confrontation again. The troubles had wracked the Continent, too, where the Thirty

Years' War had devastated Germany, and where rebellions and open conflict had broken out from Portugal to Russia. The reaction of another acute observer, John Locke, was typical, if exaggerated, in that he hoped all means could be found to avoid repeating the "perpetual foundation of war and contention, all those flames that have made such havoc and desolation in Europe, and have not been quenched but with the blood of so many millions."

When, therefore, Charles II's brother and successor, James II, a committed Catholic, sought to reintroduce that hated and feared religion into his realm in the 1680s, he was removed from the throne in a bloodless coup, engineered by the leaders of English society, and known ever since as the Glorious Revolution. There was no need for battle or civil war, though it is possible that, had James decided to stand and fight rather than flee to France, his legitimacy might have enabled him, perhaps with compromise, to retain his crown. That, however, is another "what if?," and one whose main casualty would have been the disappearance from the romance of history of the valiant and hopeless Jacobite movement, which sought for decades to restore James and his descendants to the throne. In the event, James did flee, and his very surrender was an indication of how completely the English polity had changed since the 1630s: Parliament was now unmistakably supreme, and no monarch could flout its wishes or those of the landed classes it represented.

This new outlook found its champion and its most influential exponent in John Locke himself. In his *Second Treatise of Civil Government*, written before the Glorious Revolution, but not published until the new king, William III, was safely on the throne, Locke defined the political outlook that, as developed by his followers, has come to be known as liberalism. He was deeply influenced by Hobbes's theories, but he softened their implications so as to justify the establishment of a regime that, rather than exercising total control, took care (as did the English government of his day) not to ignore the concerns of its leading citizens. Where Hobbes had described the State of Nature before the invention of government—a brilliant and original intellectual construct—as hellish, shaped by the greed and cruelty of man into a war of all against all, leaving life "nasty, poor, brutish, and short," Locke argued that human reason was already operating in the State of Nature. When government was created, therefore, it was willingly set up so as to meet peoples' needs, not established in fear so as to protect its subjects from one another. Hobbes, determined to minimize resistance to authority, reserved just one right to the individual: protection of life. Locke, speaking for the self-assured landed gentry, expanded those rights to include not only life but also liberty and property.

From then on, the basic elements of electoral democracy as we know them gathered inexorable force in England. By 1700, nationwide political parties with distinct agendas were beginning to organize; there were contested elections that forced governments out of office; and a significant segment of the population felt itself entitled to influence the direction of events in the capital. The electorate was still small, but the assumptions about the nature of politics had changed dramatically in little more than half a century. And the momentum continued as the mother of Parliaments spawned countless imitators over the next 300 years.

This is a central story of modern history, and it is one of the crucial reasons that the West has had so powerful an influence on the rest of the world. But it could so easily have turned out differently. It may be that the democratic idea, which has its roots in ancient Greece, would eventually have flowered anyway. Other theorists, practices, and traditions could well have appeared. But this was the particular road that opened up, and one needs only a modicum of imagination to see how, in its earliest days, it could have turned into a dead end. For civil wars are times of such rapid change that even a slight shift in circumstances can have momentous results.

Charles I is the perfect exemplar of the truism that the personality and actions of a major historical figure can alter the course of events. Possibly because, as a young man, he had stayed at the Spanish court for a number of months, and had been able to watch an absolute monarch exercise total command of people and policy, Charles as king developed a haughty and dismissive view of the rights of his subjects. His reign began with four years of struggle with Parliament, at the end of which the House of Commons

CHARLES I: A STUDY IN STUBBORNNESS

*Charles I of England, the foremost art collector of the seventeenth century, posed on horseback for this portrait by one of his favorite painters, Anthony Van Dyck. For Charles, compromise was never an option, and he would lose the English civil war (and his head). But what if he had been out of the picture?*

(Anthony Van Dyck, 1599–1641, *Portrait of Charles I*. Louvre, Paris. Alinari/Art Resource, NY)

even sought to challenge his ancient right to dissolve the session. At that point, in 1629, he decided he had had enough, and for the next eleven years he ruled without Parliament. Distant and disdainful, he became a deeply unpopular figure, and when his authoritarian policies drove his Scottish subjects to revolt, the carefully constructed facade of imperturbable majesty collapsed around him.

Unable to finance an army to repel the Scots without parliamentary taxation, Charles was forced to recall the assembly in 1640, but the Commons, organized by a determined member of the landed gentry, John Pym, made demands Charles could not countenance, and he quickly dissolved what came to be known as the Short Parliament. As the crisis deepened, though, he was forced to give way again and to summon the so-called Long Parliament, which gained the right not to be dismissed without its own approval and was to sit until 1653. It was this assembly that led the revolution.

Most of the radical changes in the law, in political structures, and in the Church that the members of the Long Parliament decreed did not long survive the revolution. But the shock they delivered to the country's system of government was never forgotten, especially since the climax was an assault on the monarchy itself. Constantly deceived by a king who, despite defeat on the battlefield, regarded himself as bound by no promises or agreements, the parliamentarians finally lost all patience. The commander of their army, Oliver Cromwell, called Charles "a man of blood" for the deviousness and the plots that scuttled every compromise and repeatedly forced a renewal of the fighting. Finally, in January 1649, the king was executed after a trial whose legality he refused to recognize, and England became a republic.

By this time, many of the revolutionary ideas for which the period is remembered had come to the surface, most notably a demand for virtually universal male suffrage—a proposal that was not to be implemented for more than two centuries, but which has come to be seen as a pillar of modern democratic practice. And the execution also inspired the counter-theory of Hobbes's *Leviathan*. As for the structure of government itself, the major assault on tradition (the destruction of the authority of the Church of England, the aristocracy, and the monarchy itself) had taken place, and none of the many experiments tried over the next decade left a mark on England's polity. But might the intensifying conflict of the 1640s have been avoided? Could things have turned out otherwise, and if so, what would the consequences have been?

* * *

One scenario requires no more than a slight adjustment in the incidence of the great scourge of seventeenth-century Europe, the plague. Nobody was immune to its dread assault. The only recourse was to flee from an outbreak and to hope that one escaped before the contagion spread to one's own home. That is indeed what happened, for example, in August of 1641, when Charles's relations with his subjects had reached a perilous moment.

With the armed threat from Scotland intensifying, the king left London for the north to face his rebellious subjects on August 10. Just six days later plague was discovered in a house in Westminster, near parliament. As Charles's adviser, soon to be secretary of state, Edward Nicholas, reported in October, the more hotheaded members of the Commons "wished rather that they should sit here at Westminster and die here together, but I believe Mr. Pym will find few (besides those of his juncto [faction]) of that opinion." The caution was only natural, but the proximity of the outbreak to the person of the king himself bears emphasizing.

Charles's splendid Whitehall palace was but a few yards from where parliament sat in Westminster. Tourists today flock to the palace's one remaining building, Inigo Jones's magnificent Banqueting House in Whitehall. Its ceiling, painted by Rubens, was commissioned by Charles to glorify his father, and in a supreme irony it was to be outside this house that the royal scaffold was to be erected in January of 1649. For most tourists these days, the site is a convenient stop, because at the end of Whitehall, perhaps a hundred yards away to the south, is Parliament Square. That was the trivial distance that would have separated Charles from the plague had he left for Scotland just one week later.

It happened that the plague of 1641 was a minor outbreak. In 1636 it had been quite serious, and the worst casualties of the century were to come in 1665. But the pestilence of 1641 could easily have been far worse; it was merely luck, and perhaps the weather, that restrained its virulence. And we know what its effects could have been. One has but to read Samuel Pepys's diary for 1665 to get a sense of its ravages. Many who were close to Pepys died, and as he traveled the streets of London, he encountered regularly the

stricken, covered in sores, and corpses. He was alternately fearful and resigned as he recorded what was "every day sadder and sadder news." He calculated that in one week some 10,000 had died of the plague, and in the
midst of it all he decided to draw up his will, "the town growing so un-
healthy that a man cannot depend upon living two days to an end." That
he made it through—on one occasion finding that he could escape the
stench of death only by chewing tobacco—was, he admitted, pure luck. His
terror at every report of illness or at any hint of a symptom, such as a
headache, was well-founded; only the stoicism he managed to muster in the
face of this most dreadful of the seventeenth century's scourges was unusual.

It is clear that, had the king succumbed in the summer of 1641, his children would probably have died as well, because the young were especially
susceptible to plague once it had entered a home. And the eradication of
the immediate Stuart dynasty would have had incalculable consequences.
For the heir would have been Charles's sister, Elizabeth, now in her mid-
forties, who in 1613 had married Frederick, the elector of the Palatinate, a
rich principality on the banks of the Rhine. This unfortunate couple had
become one of the saddest spectacles in the Europe of the day. When, just
six years after Elizabeth's wedding, the kingdom of Bohemia, which was
heavily Protestant, had revolted against its staunchly Catholic Habsburg
rulers, the rebels had turned to her husband, the leading Calvinist prince in
Germany, to take over the throne. Despite warnings from all his friends
that it was foolhardy to make common cause with rebels, the impulsive
Frederick, excited at the prospect of a royal crown, had accepted the offer.

The result had been total disaster. Before he had enjoyed even a year in
his new rank, Frederick and his supporters had been crushed by the Habsburgs and their ally, Catholic Bavaria, at the Battle of the White Mountain, just outside Prague. For the Czechs, this may have been merely one
in a series of subjugations that have dotted their history, but the defeat
loomed especially large because it signaled the final suppression of their religious unorthodoxy and placed them under Habsburg domination for 300
more years. And for Frederick and his family it was a catastrophe. Mock-
ingly referred to as the "Winter" king and queen thereafter, he and his wife

had to flee Prague ignominiously. Moreover, as punishment for his treason, the Habsburg Holy Roman emperor, who was his overlord, stripped him of the Palatinate; transferred his title as one of the seven electors of the empire (who elected each new emperor) to Bavaria; allowed Spain's Catholic army to occupy his lands; and forced him into exile.

The years that followed were utterly miserable. From his refuge in the Netherlands, Frederick became a rallying point for the Protestant resistance to the Habsburgs, but to no practical effect. Indeed, it became possible to end the Thirty Years' War in the 1640s only when a compromise was finally reached, allowing his family to return to the Palatinate and their electorate, while at the same time allowing Bavaria to keep a newly created eighth electorate. By then the Winter king was long gone: he had died during a surreptitious visit to the Palatinate in 1632, and his grave site has been unknown ever since. His widow, Elizabeth, was left to bring up in exile the survivors of the twenty children the couple had produced in just under twenty years of marriage.

That she had come through twenty childbirths, and was to live another thirty years, made Elizabeth an extraordinary figure in the Europe of her day. Pregnancies were highly dangerous in an age of easy infection and ineffective medicine, and it was almost unheard of to bring twenty of them to a successful conclusion. That, in addition, she was able to shoulder the huge burden of a fatherless family makes her one of the more remarkable women of the century. She had assistance for a few years from her brother, Charles I. And the sympathetic Dutch who were her hosts ensured that her exile was comfortable. Most important, she became a symbol for all Protestants, especially her English countrymen, of persecution by the Catholic leaders of Europe. Indeed, one of the accusations leveled at her father and brother by their more strident subjects was that they had betrayed not only the Protestant cause, but family duty, by doing nothing to restore Elizabeth to her lands and titles.

This was the woman who would have inherited the English throne in 1641 if that August plague had erupted just a week earlier, spread one hundred yards to Whitehall Palace, and carried off Charles I and his family. She would have reigned for twenty-one more years, and her oldest son, Karl Ludwig, who was to regain the Palatinate electorate in 1648, would have brought a German line on to the English throne half a century earlier than it actually arrived (with George I and the Hanoverians, whose title was to descend from Elizabeth's youngest daughter, Sophia). Elizabeth's most famous child, her third son, Rupert, a soldier who fought in the Thirty Years' War and later in Charles I's army, would doubtless have been a major figure in English society. But her most unusual daughter, also Elizabeth, who was a friend of Descartes and the abbess of a community of pious Lutheran women in Germany, would probably have led much the same life.

How might things have been different, however, for Elizabeth and for England? That there would have been no civil war seems almost certain. Parliament's power was secured by the summer of 1641, and the new queen would have been a heroine to the very rebels who were so suspicious of Charles I. There is little in her life to suggest that she would have encouraged the schemes and the confrontations that drew her brother into the fatal war with his subjects. The compromises that required so much shedding of blood might well have been achieved in peace. In particular, because of her Calvinist background, and her many years in the tolerant Netherlands—that "staple of sects and mint of schism . . . where not one so strange/Opinion but finds credit and exchange," in the words of the poet Andrew Marvell—Elizabeth would almost certainly have supported a more open and expansive religious settlement than the one that was reached in the 1660s.

It is possible that the more conservative elements in English society would have remained opposed even to the moderate settlement that could have been reached in the last months of 1641. They resented Pym deeply, as Nicholas's letter to Charles that autumn made clear. But Pym was not to live long, and in the absence of warfare it is implausible that Cromwell would have filled his shoes as a political leader. It is far more likely that he would have remained, as he had been until 1640, a retiring country gentleman, happy on his estates and in the practice of his Puritan beliefs.

Other radicals in Parliament might still have caused trouble, but without a civil war their influence would have been minimized. The voices of the dispossessed would have remained unheard, and the heritage of such ideas as universal male suffrage or freedom of the press (which Milton was soon to advocate) would have had to await their first champions, perhaps for more than a century. That neither Hobbes nor Locke would have felt the need to write about politics is perhaps the most dramatic change of all. The concept of the state, the definition of authority, and the quest for freedom as we know them today would have developed more slowly and possibly in entirely different forms. One hundred fifty years later, the absence of the precedent of a people trying and executing their king might also have affected the course of the French Revolution, not to mention the entire revolutionary tradition of modern Europe. The fact that England had not gone through the trauma, though, might have removed the restraint that helped make her a mere spectator during subsequent revolutionary upheavals.

Sometimes, however, it is the small detail that is especially telling about the contingencies that shape our ends. With Elizabeth on the throne, and dissenting faiths quietly accepted, there would have been no need for William Penn to emigrate to America. There might still have been a United States, but there would certainly have been no state named Pennsylvania. Move a plague just one week earlier, and have it travel no more than a hundred yards northward, and you shift the contours of both the little hillocks and the large ranges that determine history's wayward path.

THOMAS FLEMING

# NAPOLÉON'S INVASION
# OF NORTH AMERICA

Aedes aegypti *takes a holiday, 1802*

*As we have seen in Theodore K. Rabb's essay about Charles I, disease can be history's great leveler, literally, and epidemics, those accidental force multipliers, have been responsible for more than their share of turning points—and might-have-beens as well. You think of the mysterious plague that decimated an all-conquering Assyrian army in front of Jerusalem in 721* B.C., *a decisive moment in the religious history of the world; the flulike illness that ravaged Periclean Athens (and killed Pericles himself), helping to destroy Athenian power; or the smallpox that wasted Native American tribes and brought down two empires, the Aztec and the Inca. The list could go on. What if these epidemics had never happened, had broken out at a slightly different time or in a form less severe?*

*There may be no better example of the effect of disease on history than the yellow fever epidemic that largely wiped out a French army in Haiti in 1802 and presented the young United States, just twenty years after the Revolutionary War, with a matchless opening to the West. That was of course the Louisiana Purchase, the 868,000 square miles of the lands west of the Mississippi that Thomas Jefferson's representatives in France picked up for a bargain price of $15 million, or approximately four cents an acre. No longer would the United States be hemmed in by the Mississippi River and British Canada. New Orleans, the key trading city for the trans-Appalachian states and territories, would be ours. The westward movement (and with it, a half century of rancorous dispute over the spread of slavery) could begin.*

534

*But Thomas Fleming asks us to consider some of the alternatives, and ones that would have been altogether impossible without Aedes aegypti, the mosquito that carries yellow fever. Would a French-led Caribbean-American empire, a second New France, have taken shape? How would a Louisiana Territory in which slavery was banned have affected the United States? Might Napoléon himself have sought refuge in New Orleans—with a Waterloo in the bayous as the result?*

THOMAS FLEMING is a historian whose many books include biographies of Thomas Jefferson and Benjamin Franklin; an account of the American Revolution, *Liberty!*; *Duel: Alexander Hamilton, Aaron Burr, and the Future of America*; and most recently, *The New Dealer's War: Franklin D. Roosevelt and the War Within World War II*.

E VERYONE AGREES THAT the 1803 Louisiana Purchase was the great triumph of President Thomas Jefferson's administration. In one stroke, the man from Monticello doubled the size of the United States. Few realize the so-called "greatest real estate deal in history" also solved one of the president's most unnerving problems: the possibility of a biracial Revolutionary French army in New Orleans—a presence that would almost certainly have changed the course of American history.

Even fewer know that the solution to this nightmare—and the origin of Jefferson's triumph—was largely the product not of clever diplomacy or glorious feats of arms, but of the existence of a tiny female creature known to scientists as *Aedes aegypti*—the mosquito that produces yellow fever. Breeding in pools of stagnant water in cities, towns, and army camps, *Aedes* triggered devastating epidemics in the Caribbean, South America, and tropical Africa, with death rates as high as 85 percent. At the turn of the nineteenth century, no one had any idea that this seemingly harmless insect was the source of such woe.

When Jefferson became president in 1800, he was still in the throes of his long love affair with the French Revolution—a romance so intense, he once declared he would have gladly seen the entire world depopulated rather than permit "that cause" to fail. This ideological fervor enabled Jefferson to dismiss the blood-soaked orgy of violence into which the historic upheaval collapsed—and its evolution into a virtual tyranny under the leadership of Napoléon Bonaparte. The new president was equally blithe about the nasty undeclared war the United States had fought with France during the last two years of President John Adams's administration, in which French warships and privateers had destroyed $12 million worth of American shipping—the equivalent of $600 million in modern money.

Also ready for diplomatic revision in Jefferson's White House was America's relationship with the republic that had been established on the island known variously as Hispaniola and Saint Domingue. Then as now it was divided into a French-speaking western third (the future republic of Haiti) and a Spanish-speaking eastern two-thirds (the future Dominican Republic), with a range of mountains as a geographical barrier between them. Spain had ceded the Spanish part of the island to France in 1795. For American merchants, Saint Domingue's wealthy upper class were prime customers. In 1790, before the French Revolution exploded, U.S. exports to the island, mostly food and lumber, amounted to $3 million, second only to the $6.9 million that the United States shipped to England. Small wonder that the island was considered the ultimate prize in the numerous wars the great powers fought in the Caribbean.

The French Revolution's cry of liberty, equality, and fraternity had reached Saint Domingue early in the 1790s. The precarious social mixture of royal officials, rich creole planters, middle-class storekeepers, and craftsmen and free mulattoes was sitting on a potential volcano of 400,000 black slaves, whose toil on the sugar plantations made the island France's most lucrative overseas possession. In 1793, war erupted between England and Revolutionary France—a conflict that roiled the politics of the United States for a decade. The two embryo parties, the Jeffersonian Republicans, forerunners of today's Democrats, and Alexander Hamilton's Federalists, forerunners of the Republicans, took opposite sides.

The British and their allies made very little headway against the French Revolutionary armies on land. But overseas, the British fleet proved a major advantage. Island after island of France's Caribbean empire fell to British amphibious assaults, an art they had mastered during the Seven Years' War (1754–61). In Paris, meanwhile, the radical Jacobins seized control of the French National Assembly. In 1794 they issued a declaration freeing all the slaves in France's overseas dominions. The move was motivated only partly by a belief in universal liberty. The French also hoped to trigger massive slave revolts in Jamaica and other English colonies and in the United States. By that time President George Washington had declared America neutral in the global war—with a distinct Hamiltonian tilt toward England.

When news of the Jacobin decree reached Saint Domingue, a civil war of unbelievable ferocity exploded, with massacres of whites by blacks and vice versa, compounded by the invasion of a British army. Out of the turmoil emerged a charismatic black leader, Toussaint L'Ouverture, a figure who terrified slave owners in the American South. The Federalists in control of the American government took a different view. President John Adams and his secretary of state, Timothy Pickering, saw L'Ouverture as an opportunity to frustrate British and French imperialism in the Caribbean and maintain America's lucrative trade with Saint Domingue. They shipped L'Ouverture's army supplies and ammunition and at Alexander Hamilton's suggestion, sent his boyhood friend Edward Stevens, born on St. Croix, to the island's major port, Cap François, where he became L'Ouverture's trusted friend and adviser. The Adams administration even ordered the American fleet in the Caribbean to show the flag at Cap François. Without quite saying it, they urged L'Ouverture to declare independence.

Secretary of State Pickering performed masterfully in this delicate diplomacy, persuading jittery South Carolina Federalist slave owners to back him in Congress by producing evidence that the French government's representative in Saint Domingue, a demagogic Jacobin named Theodore Hedouville, had urged L'Ouverture to invade British Jamaica and the American South to foment slave uprisings there. But the black leader had refused to pursue this racist foreign policy.

Backed by American diplomacy and firepower, L'Ouverture routed the British army and became the de facto ruler of Saint Domingue. His troops quickly conquered the Spanish part of the island as well. Through Edward Stevens and Timothy Pickering, Alexander Hamilton was invited to advise the black leader on a constitution. True to his authoritarian instincts, Hamilton told L'Ouverture to appoint himself governor general for life—and enroll every able-bodied man in the militia. An assembly was also added to the government's structure, but it had no power to initiate legislation.

With driving energy, L'Ouverture invited whites and mulattoes to join him in restoring a semblance of prosperity to Saint Domingue. He banned slavery forever but persuaded the former slaves to return to the sugarcane fields to work as draftees in the service of the state. Unfortunately, he never trusted the slave-owning British and Americans enough to declare independence. He retained a frequently expressed loyalty to Revolutionary France, which had given his race their freedom.

When Napoléon Bonaparte seized power in Paris, followed within a few months by Thomas Jefferson's electoral triumph in 1800, Toussaint L'Ouverture was doomed. In Washington, D.C., the new American president urged the French chargé d'affaires, Louis Pichon, to tell his government that America was eager to help restore French rule in Saint Domingue. He advised France to make peace with England and send an army to crush the black rebels; "Nothing would be easier than to furnish your army and fleet with everything and to reduce Toussaint to starvation," Jefferson said.

Historians debate whether this ruthless reversal of American policy was rooted in Jefferson's eagerness to show his friendship for the new ruler of France or in his fear of a slave republic that would communicate dangerous ideas about freedom and equality to the restless blacks of the American South. It was probably a mixture of both motives. Napoléon had not yet made himself France's ruler for life. Jefferson was still able to view him as a legitimate heir of the Revolution. In September 1800, Virginia had been badly shaken by the aborted rebellion of Gabriel Prosser, a Richmond blacksmith, and his brother Martin, an itinerant preacher.

The Prossers, both free blacks, had organized slaves at funerals and secret religious meetings, using the language of the American Declaration of Independence and the French Declaration of the Rights of Man. The plan called for a march on Richmond from nearby plantations, a seizure of the state arsenal to equip a black army, and the massacre of all the white inhabitants except Methodists and Quakers, who opposed slavery. On the night of the rebellion, a storm washed out the roads to Richmond and the would-be rebels scattered. Before they could reorganize, the secret leaked and the Prossers and other leaders were promptly executed. But sporadic smaller slave revolts had continued to disturb the state for the next two years.

In Europe, Jefferson's election as president coincided with the exhaustion of the two superpowers, after eight years of global warfare. As peace negotiations began, Napoléon acted on Jefferson's invitation. In November 1801, the First Consul shipped a 20,000 man army to Saint Domingue, commanded by his brother-in-law, General Charles Leclerc. Unknown to Jefferson or anyone else, this expedition had another purpose. In March 1801, the Man of Destiny, as Napoléon liked to be called, had browbeaten his reluctant Spanish ally into retroceding the immense territory of Louisiana to France. It had been given to Spain as compensation for her losses in the Seven Years' War.

In secret orders, Bonaparte told Leclerc to transfer the bulk of the army to New Orleans as soon as he restored French supremacy in Saint Domingue, a task that Bonaparte estimated would take only six weeks. As for slavery, Napoléon thought it ought to be reimposed along with French rule, but he withheld judgment on that decision for the time being. The goal was the creation of a self-sufficient overseas empire. Louisiana would supply Saint Domingue and the other French islands with food at cut-rate prices, eliminating the need to buy from the Americans. The islands would produce sugar, coffee, and cotton to swell France's depleted exchequer. Ships of other nations would be excluded from this lucrative business.

A confident Leclerc arrived in Cap François in February 1802, and promptly went to work on "the gilded Africans," as Napoléon contemptuously called them. The size of the French fleet and army made L'Ouverture and his allies more than a little suspicious. It was much too large to be the mere escort of a delegation from Paris, reaffirming France's theoretical sovereignty. When Leclerc called on Henri Christophe, one of L'Ouverture's generals, to surrender the port city, he declined. Leclerc promptly attacked from land and sea. Christophe responded by burning Cap François and retreating into the country.

All-out war erupted throughout Saint Domingue. At first it seemed to go well for the French. The Spanish section of the island was quickly occupied with the help of the local population. Some black garrisons surrendered to oncoming French brigades. In ten days Leclerc had captured all the key coastal ports and forts and was preparing an offensive into the interior. But

L'Ouverture remained beyond his grasp, and another black general, Jean-Jacques Dessalines, rampaged through the countryside, slaughtering every white person he found—and any black who tried to help them.

An attempt at negotiations failed and on February 18, 1802, Leclerc launched an offensive against L'Ouverture's interior stronghold, Gonaïves. Advancing in four columns, the French discovered they had to wade through "fire and bayonets" for every foot of ground. Losses were heavy on both sides but the aggressive attack paid off when several black generals switched sides and supported Leclerc. The French commander combined force with lavish promises of money and power to those who joined him in a pacified Saint Domingue.

On February 23, L'Ouverture ambushed a French force of 5,000 men a few miles from Gonaïves. For a while the French teetered on rout. But their commander, General Donatien de Rochambeau (son of the general who was George Washington's partner at Yorktown) rescued the situation with a moment of bravado. Tossing his hat into the ranks of the oncoming blacks, he shouted: "My comrades, you will not leave your general's hat behind!" The French infantry wheeled and soon had L'Ouverture's men on the run. The next day Gonaïves went up in flames.

Leclerc was losing men—as many as two thousand in a single battle. Also, for the first time he noticed a strange illness creeping through his army. Soldiers weakened without warning; in a day they were too sick to walk. Then came black vomit, yellowing skin, convulsions, and death. But the French commander, as determined and as ruthless as his imperious brother-in-law, pressed his offensive, and soon other black generals—notably Henri Christophe—switched sides.

On May 1, L'Ouverture agreed to peace terms. He would give up power and retire with a respectable bodyguard to a plantation in the interior. His generals and officers would receive equivalent ranks in the French army, which soon became 50 percent black.

Why did Toussaint surrender? Probably because he learned that Napoleon had signed what seemed a definitive treaty of peace with the British at Amiens. This left him and his black army at the mercy of Bonaparte's vastly superior numbers and weaponry. The black leader capitulated, hoping to get the best possible deal from Leclerc. L'Ouverture's second in command, Dessalines, sullenly accepted similar terms on May 6.

But the war was far from over. Guerrilla resistance continued to flare throughout the interior of the island. Moreover, Leclerc was confronting other problems beyond Saint Domingue's horizon.

In the same first months of 1802, Jefferson and his secretary of state, James Madison, learned that the French now owned Louisiana. Next, the American ambassador in London warned them of Napoleon's plan to make Saint Domingue a mere way station on Leclerc's voyage to New Orleans. Jefferson's love affair with the French Revolution came to an abrupt end, under the influence of the cooler, more suspicious Madison and other advisers. Tench Coxe, a Philadelphia merchant who was heavily involved in the cotton business, warned that the United States could not "be too much on our guard against the consequences" of a French army in Louisiana.

When General Leclerc proclaimed a blockade of the Saint Domingue's rebel-held ports and asked Charge Louis Pichon to obtain American cooperation, the dismayed Frenchman encountered an American about-face that left him speechless. Jefferson and Madison informed him, presumably with straight faces, that they would not be able to starve Toussaint's army after all. The United States did not have the power to enforce an embargo against American merchants, who were making millions trading with the blacks. An agitated Pichon reported that he found Jefferson "very reserved and cold."

Secretary of State Madison told Pichon the United States would adopt a posture of "neutrality" if war broke out between the French army and the black rebels. That meant the French could seize American ships if they could catch them. But it also meant that the American government would not give Leclerc's army loans or credits to buy food and ammunition for his men. The French did not have enough warships to clamp a meaningful blockade on the island's thirteen ports and France was too far away to supply them with food.

A testy Leclerc tried to force American merchants trading with Saint Domingue to accept lower prices or promissory notes for their cargoes. They refused the notes, knowing that France was more or less bankrupt, and preferred to sell their goods to the rebels. Most merchants had deduced or otherwise learned Napoléon's plan to make trade with Saint Domingue an exclusively French affair. Profits, present and future, accentuated the American tilt to the rebels.

Next came an uproar from New Orleans that had a huge impact on Jefferson's attitude toward Leclerc's expedition. The Spanish, still in control of the port city, suddenly announced they were revoking the "right of deposit," which George Washington's administration had negotiated in 1795. Under this agreement, Americans were entitled to export cotton, farm produce, and other items of trade through New Orleans. When the right was revoked, an instant shout for war rose from the Western states, led by warrior politicians such as Andrew Jackson of Tennessee. Kentucky alone had a half million dollars in goods and crops on the Mississippi when the news of the revocation arrived.

General Hamilton warmly seconded this call for war in the pages of the New York *Evening Post*. In private letters he gloated over the dilemma Jefferson confronted. He had been elected deploring the large army and navy the Federalists had raised for the undeclared war with France and the taxes that supported the new military establishment. He had repealed the taxes and reduced the armed forces to a shadow. Now he was faced with "the great embarrassment of how to carry on a war without taxes."

When Jefferson tried to defuse the situation by sending James Monroe to France as an envoy extraordinary, Hamilton, writing in the *Evening Post* under the pseudonym Pericles, ferociously attacked the move. Hamilton recommended going to war immediately, before the French had time to ship an army to New Orleans. He called on Jefferson to triple the size of the pathetic 3,000-man regular army and muster a 40,000-man standby force of militia. The Navy should be strengthened and negotiations opened with England to "cooperate with us at a moment's warning."

Now the whole country, instead of a few administration insiders, knew the threat President Jefferson was confronting—and Hamilton had used it to portray the president in the worst possible light. Unfortunately, the details were essentially true. Jefferson had reduced the army and navy to a shadow. Worse, we now know, thanks to a chance to explore French and Spanish archives, Napoléon had on his secret service payroll men who could have made his conquest of the Mississippi valley a simple matter.

Brigadier General James Wilkinson, the commander in chief of the American army, received a secret annual stipend from Madrid (currently allied with France). Known to his Spanish handlers as Agent 13, Wilkinson had taken an oath swearing allegiance to Spain back in 1787. George Rogers Clark, conqueror of the Northwest Territory in the Revolution, was among the distinguished names on the French secret service payroll. Such allies might well have enabled Napoléon to add the United States to Holland and other nations of Europe that had become French satellites, with governments that obeyed orders from Paris.

By now President Jefferson was a very troubled man. Doing a hitherto unthinkable foreign policy somersault, he talked of "marrying ourselves to the British fleet and nation" to keep Napoléon out of Louisiana. It is unlikely that the British would have been eager to do business with a man who had vilified them for the previous decade.

Fortunately for the disturbed president, that aforementioned character, *Aedes aegypti*, was hard at work, decimating the French regiments. Noting Leclerc's growing weakness, a watchful L'Ouverture began intriguing for a comeback. But Leclerc was watching him too. Lured to a nearby plantation without his usual escort, the black leader was seized, thrown on a ship, and deported to France as a common criminal. There, Napoléon deposited him in a freezing fortress in the Jura Mountains, where L'Ouverture died a year later.

At this point Bonaparte made a truly egregious blunder. Pressured by refugee planters from Saint Domingue and by numerous merchants in Le Havre and other French ports who had grown rich on the slave trade, he decided to reimpose slavery. When word of this decision reached Saint Domingue in June 1802, the black masses rose in fury against the French and the black soldiers allied with them, triggering a new cycle of massacre and countermassacre. General Leclerc was stunned by the ferocity of the blacks' resistance. "They die with incredible fanaticism—they laugh at death; it is the same with the women," he said. The astonished French commander concluded he would have to kill everyone above the age of twelve, a policy he proceeded to put into brutal practice.

Weakened by a growing food shortage and a lack of water bottles and medical supplies, the French also found themselves fighting a losing battle with *Aedes aegypti*. Whole regiments died virtually en masse. Soon an appalling 60 percent of Leclerc's staff was dead. Finally, on November 2, 1802, the French commander himself succumbed.

American merchants continued their clandestine trade with the black rebels, shipping them guns and ammunition as well as food. The enraged French threatened to send captured blacks to America, where they would make good on Hedouville's plan to spread slave revolts throughout the Western Hemisphere. A grimly determined Napoléon poured in replacements and ordered General Donatien de Rochambeau to continue the struggle.

Reinforced by 15,000 men, Rochambeau seemed on his way to restoring French control of the island. He drove black rebels from all the chief seaports, cutting off most of their supply of guns and ammunition, and began launching devastating attacks into the interior. But in Europe events were unfolding that soon turned these victories into hollow triumphs. The British decided that their experiment with a purportedly peace-loving Napoléon was not working. France was exhibiting aggressive behavior in the Mediterranean and elsewhere. It soon became obvious to Napoléon that the war for world supremacy was about to resume.

With that near certainty in mind, the Man of Destiny rethought his plans for Louisiana. Without a fleet, he would be unable to defend the territory. Pichon reported that the cancellation of the right of deposit at New Orleans had turned American public opinion strongly against both France and Spain. That aroused the specter of fighting a war with the Americans, which he was unlikely to win, especially if war with England resumed and the British fleet interdicted support from France for Rochambeau's army.

Perhaps more important, Bonaparte needed money for his war machine. When Ambassador Robert R. Livingston visited him in early 1803 seeking to buy New Orleans and Florida, Napoléon suddenly asked him how much he would be willing to pay for all of Louisiana. The amazed ambassador was soon joined by special envoy Monroe, who could speak forcefully for President Jefferson. By July of 1803, they had bought 868,000 square miles of North America for $15 million, and Jefferson was able to proclaim a tremendous political triumph over Alexander Hamilton, who had solemnly predicted Napoléon would never sell Louisiana.

Napoléon continued the struggle to subdue Saint Domingue—stirring fears that he might repudiate the Louisiana deal. But the moment news of the declaration of renewed war with England reached the Caribbean, the British West Indies fleet made Saint Domingue target number one. The royal navy bombarded the French-held seaports and smuggled guns and encouragement to the rebels. A desperate Rochambeau told French chargé Louis Pichon the situation could be rescued only if he received a million francs a month to buy food and weaponry. Jefferson declined to help and American bankers were equally cold. In November 1803, Rochambeau, his army reduced to 8,000 men, retreated for a last stand in Cap François. With yellow fever continuing to ravage his ranks, he surrendered to a British fleet cruising offshore.

On January 1, 1804, the new black ruler, General Jean-Jacques Dessalines, who had long since switched back to the rebel side, proclaimed the island independent of France and declared it would henceforth be known by its Carib-Indian name, Haiti. Taking a French tricolor, Dessalines tore the white strip from the flag, a graphic illustration of his regime's racial policy. He proceeded to massacre all the remaining whites on the French part of the island. (The Spanish part of the island regained a precarious independence with the help of the British fleet.) Under Dessalines's personal direction, white men, women, and children were hacked and shot to death. It was a blunder that sent Haiti careening into isolation for decades—and banished all thoughts of emancipating slaves in the American South.

If Napoléon had been a true son of the French Revolution, with a genuine commitment to universal human rights, instead of a Corsican military genius with only minimal moral standards, he might well have succeeded in his original vision of using Saint Domingue as a first step toward the establishment of a Caribbean-American empire. The key to his possible success was a genuine alliance with Toussaint L'Ouverture and his black legions. Philadelphia merchant Tench Coxe knew whereof he spoke when he described Toussaint's soldiers as "military" with "habits of subordination" broken forever.

A worried Coxe envisioned the possibility of a "large detachment of republican blacks [being sent] to Louisiana, accompanied by the sudden emancipation of the blacks there." The result might well have been a race war on the American continent with barbarities that more than matched the gruesome horrors of Haiti. Out of the turmoil might have arisen an American warrior whose generalship matched L'Ouverture's, and whose ferocity matched Dessalines's—Andrew Jackson. Almost certainly, Old Hickory would have meted out to the blacks the fate he inflicted on the Creek Indian nation in 1814: extermination.

If Napoléon had established a biracial colony of free blacks and whites in Louisiana and avoided war with the United States, it would have put terrific pressure on the American South to begin a policy of gradual emancipation. President Jefferson was strongly in favor of this idea. Before Gabriel's Rebellion, he had drawn up a draft constitution for Virginia that would have freed all slave children born in the state after December 31, 1800. Even after Gabriel Prosser's attempted insurrection stoked white fears, the Man from Monticello continued to insist that gradual emancipation, instead of guns and whips and patrols, was the best way to defuse black anger.

If such a policy had prevailed, the United States would have been spared the national nightmare known as the Civil War, with its 600,000 dead. A biracial nation might have emerged a hundred years earlier than the one that is still struggling to heal the spiritual wounds of involuntary abolition and slavery's incalculable humiliations.

The grisly events in Saint Domingue combined with Gabriel's Rebellion to make this biracial dream untenable in 1804. Jefferson was a politician as well as an idealist and he soon found himself under terrific pressure from fellow Southerners to make sure Haiti remained isolated from the American South. His son-in-law, John W. Eppes, rose in Congress to declare that U.S. merchants should have nothing to do with people of a race Americans needed "to depress and keep down." Congress soon concurred and passed a law prohibiting all trade with Haiti, which Jefferson signed. Former secretary of state Timothy Pickering, now a U.S. senator from Massachusetts, attacked this measure, claiming that the Haitians were only guilty of having "a skin not colored like our own." It was, thanks to Napoléon and Dessalines, much more complicated.

An even larger possibility swirls out of this historical kaleidoscope. If Napoléon had followed a wiser, more moral policy and created a biracial Caribbean-American empire, when he was defeated in Europe and exiled to Elba, he might have fled westward from that island and found refuge in the still loyal colony of Louisiana, where the blacks of the French army would have welcomed him as an apostle of emancipation. His white troops would have been equally ready to rally to his standard.

The Spanish policy of closing New Orleans would have been long since revoked, stirring warm feelings for France up and down the Mississippi Valley. Napoléon's charisma would have electrified the fighting men of the west. It is hard for us to realize the fascination with which everyone regarded this larger-than-life figure. Newspapers reported his taste in food, women, clothes, horses, in rapt detail. Combine this hypnotic effect with a call to defend the rights of man against Perfidious Albion and you have the makings of a titanic confrontation.

The British, determined to hunt down the great predator, as they viewed Bonaparte, would have dispatched a huge fleet and army in pursuit of final victory. What might have happened? One can easily envision a battle of New Orleans in which Andrew Jackson performed as one of Napoléon's brigadiers. Also in the upper ranks of this force might have been another devotee of political power—Aaron Burr.

With the French firmly in control of New Orleans and the lower Mississippi Valley, there would have been no opportunity for Burr to launch his 1806 scheme to detach the western states from the Union and conquer Mexico. That gambit depended on intimidating an enfeebled Spain. But Burr's hatred of Thomas Jefferson and James Madison would have been no less intense. With his confederate, General James Wilkinson, who almost certainly would have thrown in his lot with Bonaparte, Burr might well have convinced Napoléon to launch a war of conquest to absorb Texas and

Mexico. By the time Napoléon arrived in New Orleans, Spain would no longer have been an ally. The lure of filling his exchequer with Mexico's gold and silver would have been all but irresistible. Moreover, General Wilkinson had something very tangible to offer—a collection of rare maps of the Southwest that would have enabled the Man of Destiny to invade Mexico from a half dozen possible routes.

But first, there was the ultimate battle with the English. How fitting, the Americans (and even Bonaparte) might have thought, that this decisive clash should take place in the New World, where the idea of liberty first flowered. The British would have been driven by a variant on this idea— here was a chance to stamp out once and for all the American perversion of that noble idea, British liberty, into the license of a rabble in arms to defy their lawful sovereign.

To command their forces in this revised battle of New Orleans, the British would not have sent any old general, picked out of the government's hat, to finish off Bonaparte and the Americans. They would have chosen their best man—Arthur Wellesley, the Duke of Wellington. Napoléon, fighting on unfamiliar ground, without the massed cavalry that so often shattered his foes at a battle's crucial moments, might have found himself at a severe disadvantage. The Russian debacle would have also shaken his self-confidence.

We can be certain that the Iron Duke would not have committed the blunders perpetrated by his impulsive brother-in-law, Major General Edward Pakenham, in the confrontation with General Jackson at New Orleans in January 1815. There would have been no suicidal frontal assault against massed French and American muskets. Wellington would have had the advantage of an overwhelming British fleet—something Pakenham's puny squadron never gave him. With full control of the Mississippi in his grasp, the British commander would have enfiladed the French-American barricades from the river, forcing the defenders to fight in the open against his battle-tried veterans.

A British victory, a Waterloo of the bayous, would by no means have been impossible or even improbable. Napoléon would have ended up on St. Helena with a steady diet of British arsenic, as he did in factual history.

George III's delighted ministers would have found themselves in control of the city that dominated the American heartland—with a force majeure claim to possession of the entire province of Louisiana. Up in New England, Senator Pickering and other Yankees, disgusted by fourteen years of Jeffersonian government, were discussing secession from the Union. They would have greeted the news of Wellington's triumph with gloats of grim satisfaction.

For a decade Pickering had been talking about negotiating a New England alliance with London, which would join the descendants of the Puritans with Canada and the Maritime provinces to create a nation capable of eventually dominating the continent, reducing Jefferson and his slavocrats to a humbled minority. The destiny of North America—and the world— would have been far different, if this political realignment had come to pass on Wellington's bayonets.

Such are the amazing possibilities negated by a tiny insect with an evolutionary compulsion to feast on humans' blood—and infect them with one of the world's deadliest diseases. With blind indifference, these buzzing creatures frustrated the dirtiest schemes and the noblest ambitions. On the Fourth of July, Americans, after toasting their heroes, might well raise a glass to *Aedes aegypti* as one of the unsung heroines of the republic.

TOM WICKER

# IF LINCOLN HAD
# NOT FREED THE SLAVES

*The inevitable results of no*
*Emancipation Proclamation*

*Abraham Lincoln's Emancipation Proclamation of September 22, 1862, which
declared slaves "forever free," is the supreme moral moment of American history.
"Lincoln's political artistry," Tom Wicker writes here, "assured that the Proclamation . . . would be seen as a justified war measure, as well as a great humanitarian deed." When he proposed it to his Cabinet that July, he argued that the
taking of the moral high ground "was absolutely essential to the salvation of the
nation." Though the North had won big victories in the West, the Civil War
closer to Washington seemed that summer to be turning in favor of the Confederates. They had stopped the Union in the outskirts of their capital, Richmond, won
a heady triumph at the Second Manassas, and now Robert E. Lee's Army of
Northern Virginia was preparing to invade Maryland and Pennsylvania. It would
make a scythelike swing that, if unchecked, might very well have ended in the capture of Baltimore and the isolation of Washington. Before he could issue his
Proclamation, Lincoln badly needed a victory, any kind of victory. What he got
on September 17 at Antietam—the famous bloodiest day in American history—
was a tactically drawn battle but a strategic victory, a combination that the war
produced again and again. Lee retired to Virginia, ending the invasion threat and
buying precious time for Lincoln. Five days later the president made his announcement.*

*The Emancipation Proclamation was more than a visionary document; it was* a strategically astute move, something too often forgotten. It "made the war appear to be a Northern crusade against slavery," Wicker writes, and from that point on, the European recognition that the Confederacy so desperately sought would seem "an endorsement" of slavery. But what if the moment of victory (or the illusion of one) had not come in time? In Wicker's unhappy scenario, it is not improbable that the proclamation would have gone unissued and the war would have ended in a negotiated peace brokered by England and France. "Neither the moral question of slavery nor the political question of secession would have been resolved." Slavery might have survived for decades more. But beyond slavery, the consequences of an unresolved Civil War might have persisted into our own time. The counterfactual stakes of the Emancipation Proclamation could not have been more potentially damaging.

TOM WICKER is a former *New York Times* Washington bureau chief and a columnist for the newspaper. Among his many writings on the Civil War is the novel *Unto This Hour.*

Political analysts, sociologists, journalists, and historians agree that the "race problem" remains a virulent, underlying issue in American politics, local and national. How could it be otherwise? When black citizens retain a virtually genetic memory of centuries of enslavement, and when the fight against racial segregation, share-crop peonage, and voteless second-class status barely triumphed less than a half-century ago. When the "black ghetto" with its crime, poverty, unemployment, and hopelessness has become a permanent feature of urban life. When even middle-class blacks still suffer blatant discrimination in housing, health care, school and professional admissions, and a criminal justice system in which a black man is more than seven times as likely as a white to go to prison.

If black-white relations in America remain so largely tense and unsympathetic 137 years after Abraham Lincoln declared former slaves "forever free" and 135 years after Robert E. Lee surrendered the main Confederate army at Appomattox, who can say how hostile those relations might be had there been no Emancipation Proclamation, no "Great Emancipator," no successful war to end slavery, no constitutional amendments to give at least legal validity to the equality of all Americans of whatever skin color?

It seems altogether likely, if such were the case, that the "civil rights movement" of the fifties and sixties, coming earlier or later, would have been more violent and more violently resisted, that the "long hot summers" of black uprising that followed in the greatest American cities would have been even more destructive of life and property, and that our vast fortress prisons, in addition to giving "the impression of institutions for segregating the young black and Hispanic male underclass from society" (as the criminologist Norval Morris put it) would long ago have erupted in rage and resistance even more furious, on both sides, than was demonstrated at New York's Attica Correctional Facility in 1971.

## If Lincoln Had Not Freed the Slaves

As for other vital developments in the nation's chronic racial problem—the desegregation of the armed forces in 1949, the Supreme Court's school desegregation ruling in 1954, or the monumental post–World War II migration of blacks out of the South and into cities whose faces and futures were changed forever—of these and other events it can only be said with any certainty that they would not have happened as they did, or when they did, or under the circumstances that actually prevailed, had not a savage and terrible war forced our greatest president to the most important act in American history.

Abraham Lincoln did not set out, however, to free the slaves by proclamation. Not that he favored human bondage: "As I would not be a slave," he said, in one of his precise formulations, "so I would not be a master. This is my idea of democracy." Nor did Lincoln lack human sympathy and understanding. "He treated me like a man," said the former slave Frederick Douglass, after a White House visit in 1863. "He did not let me feel for a moment that there was any difference in the color of our skins."

That was in keeping with Lincoln's deep sense of human brotherhood. But his attitude toward Douglass, an educated and accomplished black man, did not connote a belief in the genuine equality of what Lincoln often called "separate races." Blacks, "suffering the greatest wrong inflicted on any people," he told an audience of free black leaders, yet were "far removed from being placed on an equality" with whites. Not only had they been ill-treated but a broader difference than exists between almost any other two races" would always cause "a ban" even upon blacks freed from slavery and treated well by white people.

When he became president of the United States in 1861, Lincoln *did* favor emancipation—but gradual and compensated. In his Cooper Union speech of February 27, 1860, which greatly aided his presidential campaign, he had quoted Thomas Jefferson as having said:

It is still in our power to direct the process of emancipation and deportation, peaceably, and in such slow degrees, as that the evil will wear off insensibly; and their places be, *pari passu,* filled up by free

A CAUSE NOT LOST

*This elaborately decorated version of Abraham Lincoln's Emancipation Proclamation appeared not long after the Union president's order became official on January 1, 1863. Many regard the Proclamation as the supreme moral moment of U.S. history. Had it not been for a drawn battle, which Lincoln treated as the victory he sought, the opportunity might have been missed.*

(Library of Congress)

white laborers. If, on the contrary, it [slavery] is left to force itself on, human nature must shudder at the prospect.

But slavery was "forcing itself on," even as Lincoln won the presidency, the Civil War began, and in his first years in office he seemed to be presiding over a losing military effort. As late as his annual message to Congress of December 1862 (*after* the "preliminary" Emancipation Proclamation had been issued in September), the president proposed a constitutional amendment providing that states abolishing slavery *before the year 1900* would be compensated in U.S. bonds; that any slave earlier freed by presidential proclamation should be permanently free and his or her former owners compensated; and that Congress should have power to spend money for the colonization of blacks in a foreign land.

This proposal, subsumed in the freedom that followed Emancipation's effective date of January 1, 1863, obviously came to naught. It nevertheless reflected Lincoln's oft-stated conviction that the Constitution gave neither the president nor Congress the power to seize citizens' property, including slaveholders' bondmen; as well as his belief that whites and blacks could not live together amicably. Blacks, therefore, should be sent to Africa or elsewhere to rule themselves. (Neither Lincoln nor anyone else proposed that *whites* should emigrate and leave the territory of the United States to blacks.) This attitude toward black-white social and economic relations was shared by most nineteenth-century white Americans (and a century and a half later still influences admissions, housing, and criminal justice practices in a supposedly integrated nation).

Presidents are not kings, however, and events through the first seventeen months of Lincoln's presidency were driving him toward emancipation. ("I claim not to have controlled events but confess plainly that events have controlled me," he later wrote in a wartime letter to Albert G. Hodges of Kentucky.) Not only were aggressive abolitionists, many of them influential Republican members of Congress, urging him to take action; the threat of European intervention on the side of the Confederacy was ever-present. The war itself was going badly enough that the president came to believe that he had to seek some more dramatic means of waging it, while still maintaining unity in the war effort.

On the other hand, an army faction around General George B. McClellan, and a substantial portion of Northern political opinion, resisted the idea of "revolutionary" warfare, as well as punitive measures against the "erring sisters" of the South. Emancipation, Lincoln himself feared, might shatter the tenuous federal unity in waging the war. (The four vital "border states"—Missouri, Kentucky, Maryland, and Delaware—that remained loyal to the Union themselves sanctioned slavery, as did the District of Columbia. Abolition was a loud but not necessarily a majority sentiment in the Union of the 1860s.)

By July 13, 1862, with McClellan's Army of the Potomac newly turned back from the gates of Richmond, Lincoln told members of his Cabinet that he had "about come to the conclusion that it was a military necessity, absolutely essential to the salvation of the nation, that we must free the slaves or be ourselves subdued."

In the 1864 letter to Hodges, he elaborated on his view in 1862:

When [early in that year] I made earnest, and successive appeals to the border states to favor compensated emancipation, I believed the indispensable necessity for military emancipation, and arming the blacks would come, unless averted by that measure. They declined the proposition; and I was, in my best judgment, driven to the alternative of either surrendering the Union, and with it, the Constitution, or of laying strong hand upon the colored element. I chose the latter.

On July 22, 1862, Lincoln acted on that choice and read to the Cabinet a first draft of the preliminary Emancipation Proclamation. His mind was substantially made up, he said, but he delayed publication on Secretary of State William Seward's advice that the proclamation might seem a "cry of distress" if issued on top of federal military defeat in Virginia.

Even then, with the proclamation already drafted, but while Lincoln waited for a Union military victory to make it public, he told the nation in a masterfully phrased open letter to Horace Greeley, the editor of the *New York Tribune*:

My paramount object in this struggle is to save the Union and is *not* either to save or to destroy slavery. If I could save the Union without freeing any slave I would do it; and if I could save it by freeing all the slaves I would do it; and if I could save it by freeing some and leaving others alone, I would also do that. What I do about slavery, and the colored race, I do because I believe it helps to save the union, and what I forbear, I forbear because I do *not* believe it would help to save the Union. I shall do less whenever I shall believe what I am doing hurts the cause, and I shall do more whenever I shall believe doing more will help the cause.

Within days, still another Union defeat, this time virtually on the outskirts of Washington—the second battle of Bull Run—again delayed the proclamation. "The bottom is out of the tub!" Lincoln lamented, when he heard the news. But he had been persuaded by Seward to wait until Union war progress made the Emancipation Proclamation seem more effective, and the president more in command.

If such a moment had never come, it's at least conceivable that Lincoln might never have issued the great document—and in the autumn of 1862, with Lee and the Army of Northern Virginia moving into Maryland in their first invasion of the North, and another powerful Confederate army marching into Kentucky toward the Ohio River, many in both North and South doubted, with reason, that such a moment ever would arrive.

If it had not, owing to a continuing Confederate victory trend, the war might well have ended in a negotiated peace. That would have been, in effect, a Southern success, with slavery surviving much as it was before Fort Sumter. Something like Lincoln's proposed Constitutional Amendment of December 1862 eventually might have been adopted; as wartime animosities in the states of the former Confederacy gave way to peacetime calculations of interest. History and economics ultimately would have argued for compensated emancipation.

The subsequent history of the nation, of course, would have been quite different—disastrously so.

We can only speculate about that, however; because, in fact, the moment *did* come—a moment, at least, that Lincoln could treat as if it were the longed-for victory. On September 17, 1862, within weeks of the Greeley letter, McClellan—briefly and reluctantly restored to command—fought the Battle of Antietam (called Sharpsburg in the South) just well enough to stop Lee and his invading army. McClellan was fatally afflicted, however, with what Lincoln in a cutting phrase called a case of "the slows"; so, unfortunately, the general and his army let the mauled and ragged Confederates escape back to Virginia.

Ever the adept politician, Lincoln nevertheless seized even this flawed moment. Five days after Antietam, the president called his Cabinet together again, read them a humorous passage from Artemus Ward, reminded them of the draft proclamation he had read aloud a few weeks earlier, and told them he did not wish their advice about "the main matter—for that I have determined for myself." Then he read the proclamation again, this time intending it for publication.

So the deed was done and after the long months of hesitation, emancipation was proclaimed—hardly a moment too soon. In December at Fredericksburg, Virginia, federal forces, then under Ambrose Burnside, suffered probably the most devastating defeat of the war. Simultaneously, perhaps the most propitious *military* moment for British recognition of the Confederacy was at hand.

Such a perhaps fatal (for the Union) diplomatic act was prevented by Lincoln's proclamation of September 22, 1862, to take effect on January 1, 1863. The Emancipation Proclamation precluded the possibility of European intervention because it made the war appear to be a Northern crusade against slavery (however tardily and reluctantly conducted). If a foreign nation had recognized and supported the Confederacy after emancipation, that nation's action would have been seen throughout the world as an endorsement of chattel slavery.

Despite his earlier doubts about the constitutionality of compelled abolition, Lincoln justified his proclamation as a war measure falling within the emergency powers of the president—and a powerful war measure it turned out to be. Not only did emancipation prevent foreign intervention by proclaiming a crusade for human freedom; it undermined the Confederate home and military fronts with slave unrest, labor depletion, and military desertion, causing many rebel soldiers to recognize that they were risking their lives and their families' well-being in "a rich man's war but a poor man's fight."

On the federal side, emancipation provided spiritual support for the cause of "Father Abraham," who was beginning to be seen as a symbolic moral leader. It also tapped a new and welcome source of manpower—180,000 black troops serving in federal ranks by the end of the war in 1865. The document made Lincoln "the Great Emancipator" and ensured that his death would bring him the martyrdom and reverence he is accorded today, everywhere in the world—including the states of the old Confederacy.

Rightly so; for not only was the concept of emancipation morally and strategically powerful; but Lincoln's political artistry assured that the proclamation really would be seen as a justified war measure, as well as a great humanitarian deed. His timing, in the wake of Antietam, gave the document plausibility. It signaled the end of slavery everywhere in the nation, though legally it freed slaves only in states and parts of states then in rebellion against the Union—not in any place (the District of Columbia, for instance) where Lincoln had the immediate power to strike off their bonds.

Thus, whatever divisive effect a less considered, less well-timed proclamation might have had in the North was minimized. Even so, in the congressional elections of 1862, the Democrats made substantial gains.

The excess of the North's manpower, industrial strength, and military might over those of the Confederacy, together with stronger Northern political institutions and Southern dissension, might well have brought *eventual* Union victory, even without emancipation, even after European intervention.

That argument, however, overlooks the real possibility that continued Confederate military success, even in defense, might have sapped Northern morale, destroyed Lincoln's political support, and brought about his defeat in 1864 (when George B. McClellan was his Democratic opponent). In the long hindsight of history, it seems likely that the Northern public, tiring of an apparently unwinnable war, would have forced a negotiated peace at some point *before* those underlying Northern advantages could have had their likely effect.

Aside from what would have happened in the war itself had not Lincoln

freed the slaves as and when he did, the postwar and contemporary consequences are almost incalculable. What *would* have happened had the nation failed even in a great war to win the freedom of the black bondmen
and women of the wartime and antebellum South? And had a compromise
peace left the "peculiar institution" in place and its masters in their former
seats of power?

A few likelihoods, approaching certainties, can be suggested: Slavery
would have continued for a time in the old Confederate and border states,
though the increasing pressures of world opinion and of an inefficient and
wasteful labor system eventually would have brought about its end—probably gradually, and with compensation, as Lincoln and many other leaders
of goodwill once had envisioned, but to which the South had preferred war.

Had eleven undefeated Southern states returned to the Union, to Congress, and to American politics, neither the thirteenth Amendment, abolishing slavery, the fourteenth, guaranteeing equal protection of the laws,
nor the fifteenth, establishing the right to vote to persons of color and to
former slaves, would have been added to the Constitution—at least not for
decades, perhaps never.

The so-called "reconstruction" of the Southern states that actually did
take place after the historical Confederate defeat would not have been necessary or tolerated by an undefeated (counterhistorical) South. Freed
Southern blacks would not have enjoyed the temporary political and other
forms of power some gained in the "reconstruction" years after the war. Resentful Southern whites therefore would not have felt it necessary to form
the original, terrorist Ku Klux Klan—with its hateful echoes into the
present.

If these events, taken together, had *not* happened, the decades of hostility between Southern whites and blacks (repressed but real, on both sides)
that had its origins in the post–Civil War years, and the racial repression
and segregation to which whites soon resorted, might have been avoided,
or at least softened. So might the long years in which a "solid South" voted
religiously Democratic, dominated Congress, and controlled—with the so-
called "two-thirds rule"—party presidential nominations.

These would have been paltry gains compared to other, inevitable developments. Had gradual and compensated emancipation ultimately prevailed—perhaps by the end of the nineteenth-century, as Lincoln had proposed in December 1862—the system of "sharecropping" by which the white South maintained virtual peonage, and the "separate but equal" rule of law that enforced racial segregation, no doubt would have evolved anyway—later, perhaps, but otherwise about as it actually did.

These were responses not so much to the end of the Civil War as to the end of slavery. They also were effective Southern efforts—mostly winked at by the rest of the nation—to maintain white supremacy even after defeat in war and military emancipation. There's no reason to suppose that the white South would not have devised the same or equally clever means, or worse, to continue white supremacy, even after having consented—under economic pressure—to gradual and compensated emancipation.

The *fact* of black political, economic, and social freedom—no matter how achieved—would have been resented and feared by whites (as in many ways it is today), and would have demanded perhaps even more forceful responses from the fearful. Even as it was, between 1882 and 1900 there were at least 100 lynchings of blacks a year, and by 1968 more than 3,500 African-Americans had been lynched. And there's certainly no reason to suppose that other Americans would have protested anymore strongly than, historically, they did—at least until prompted by resisting blacks themselves, as in the actual civil rights movement.

No Emancipation Proclamation? A compromise peace with slavery surviving the Civil War? The nation would have been tenuously and unhappily reunited in those circumstances, but not on the basis of victor and vanquished—only in an apparent stalemate in which both sides had achieved their essential war aims: continued slavery for the Confederacy, a restored Union for the government at Washington.

Neither the moral question of slavery nor the political question of secession would have been resolved. Gradual and compensated emancipation might have drained some of the urgency from the former, but the strained theory of a right of secession might well have remained troublesome even today—far more so than in actual contemporary circumstances, when occasional secession threats sound more than a little empty (owing precisely to that Union victory in 1865 to which the Emancipation Proclamation contributed so heavily).

Of all the consequences of a less salutary course of events in the 1860s—no compelled emancipation, no Union victory—the worst might well be the knowledge of the 12 percent of Americans who are black that their forebears were *not* freed from bondage by crusade, by the willingness of a generation "touched by fire" to sacrifice its lives and futures, by the greatness of a leader martyred not least for his proclamation of brotherhood. Instead they would live with the knowledge that the forces of bondage and oppression had prevailed—perhaps far into the twentieth century, if not permanently.

If black Americans could not take at least small satisfaction in what, in historical fact, *did* happen more than a century ago, what faith could they have in a nation to which their race was borne in chains? In a "democracy" that had failed, in its most fundamental test, to strike off those chains? In freedom itself, so long denied their ancestors, so boldly and belatedly won for themselves, from a reluctant and grudging majority?

In winning freedom for slaves more than a century ago, however, the nation finally accepted freedom for itself—though not without protest. In issuing the great proclamation, Lincoln responded not just to the pressures of his era but—as if to a vision—to the needs of later times, into the present and on into the future. His "justified war measure," taken for reasons so compelling in 1862, is even more vital to Americans today. It strengthened the Union war effort as desired—but, more importantly, it began the "unfinished work" that Lincoln was to define at Gettysburg: a "new birth of freedom" in a nation "conceived in liberty" but not yet devoted to it.

For white and black alike, that is still what he termed it—"the great task remaining before us."

ALISTAIR HORNE

# FRANCE TURNS THE OTHER CHEEK, JULY 1870

## The needless war with Prussia

The unification of Germany in January 1871, at the end of the Franco-Prussian War, was a central event of the nineteenth century; it would be the defining one of the twentieth. Its poisoned fruit produced three world conflicts (if you count the Cold War), and all manner of attending horrors, from the Stalinist purges to the Holocaust. Unification may have been bound to happen—and could have occurred without especially dire consequences—but was achieved prematurely through the unexpected humiliation of France, which left a spreading taint of bitterness, a kind of historical oil spill. The French ambassador's July visit to the Prussian king William, taking the waters at Bad Ems, and the king's refusal to give in to his provocative demands, was the inconspicuous beginning of a crisis. The somewhat doctored account of the meeting, known as the Ems telegram, that Otto von Bismarck, the Prussian chancellor, sent out hardly seemed a pretext for armed confrontation. But it was a perceived affront that Napoléon III, the French emperor, could not afford to ignore: two days later, on July 15, France was at war with Prussia and its client states.

The cause of the Franco-Prussian War may have been feckless and French preparation to fight chaotic, their strategy inviting disaster; yet the odds were not totally against France. Its army, though outnumbered, was based on a solid core of professional soldiers, who relied on weapons—notably a breech-loading rifle and a primitive but effective hand-cranked machine gun—that were superior to those of the Prussians. The early battles were close (in one, the French inflicted

565

*8,000 casualties in less than twenty minutes). But the ailing French emperor allowed his army to be trapped at Sedan and was forced to surrender. In one of the most brilliant campaigns ever waged in Europe, one Napoléon I would have been proud of, the encirclement of Metz and Paris soon followed Sedan. For Prussia, 1870 was the year of the trap, not once but three times, something of a military tour de force. By the time the capital fell in January 1871, its population had been reduced to eating zoo animals and rats: starvation and not Prussian artillery led to its surrender. But for France and the rest of the world, the most potentially lethal trap of all, though one that would not be sprung for another generation, was a unified Germany, with its military growing in overconfidence.*

*The lamentable record of what did happen brings us inevitably to what might have happened. What if the French had won those early battles, as they nearly did, and had forced a stalemate? Would the various German principalities have held together without the quick-drying cement of victory? (Some, remember, had fought Prussia a few years earlier.) What if France had acquiesced to unification as a quid pro quo for German concessions and a peace in which neither side was a victor—a peace in which Alsace and Lorraine would have remained French? How different would Germany have been without a fatal dependency on the myth of an all-conquering military? How different, too, would the world have been without a century of antagonism between France and Germany?*

*There is, of course, another, simpler scenario, the simplest of all, which Alistair Horne suggests in the chapter that follows—namely, that Napoléon could have done nothing, that he might have ignored the bait of the Ems telegram. In which case, the predominant cause for World War I—the loss of Alsace-Lorraine—would have been removed; and no World War I would have meant no Hitler, and no World War II. Horne's counterfactual may take a fanciful turn but the facts are closely and logically reasoned. A hint: In this case, the medium really was the message.*

ALISTAIR HORNE, a Cambridge University Litt D., is the author of seventeen books. He has been awarded the British CBE, and has been made a Chevalier of the French Légion d'Honneur for his historical writings, which include *The Price of Glory: Verdun 1916; The Fall of Paris: The Siege and the Commune, 1870–1; and How Far from Austerlitz? Napoléon 1805–1815*. He is currently completing *Seven Ages of Paris.*

I N JUNE 1870, the newly appointed British Foreign Secretary, Lord
Granville, gazed out with satisfaction on the world scene and claimed—
with reason—that he could not discern "a cloud in the sky." In all his experience he had never known "so great a lull in foreign affairs." In Paris,
Emperor Napoléon III's prime minister, Emile Ollivier, echoed Granville
by declaring that "at no period has the maintenance of peace seemed better assured." Indeed, peace seemed to be in the air everywhere. Over Europe as a whole such a spring of content had not been seen for many years.
As summer developed, however, it became a particularly trying one; in fact
one of the hottest in memory. From several parts of France there were reports of drought, with the peasants praying for rain and the army selling
horses because of the shortage of fodder; but then, what urgent need was
there for cavalry when there was absolutely no threat of war on the horizon? Nevertheless, it was the kind of summer, not unlike those fateful summers of 1914 and 1939, when tempers frayed.

Even so, who in July 1870 could have predicted that within a matter of
weeks the emperor of France, Napoléon III, would be deposed and seeking
refuge in England; that Paris would be besieged and within a few months
starved into surrender, while proud France herself lay prostrate and suing
for peace with Bismarck's Prussians; and that the whole balance of power
that had regulated Europe so meticulously since Waterloo in 1815 would be
fundamentally altered?

At the beginning of July 1870, a small cloud passed across the sun—but
it seemed only a very small cloud. For the past two years the throne of
Spain had been vacant, following the deposing of the unsatisfactory Queen
Isabella. One of the possible candidates was a German princeling, Leopold
of Hohenzollern-Sigmaringen. He was a good Catholic, father of a family,
and his brother Charles had recently accepted the crown of Romania with-

out anyone objecting. The idea of the Hohenzollern Candidacy had originated in Spain; Leopold's kinsman, King William I of Prussia, had agreed to it—but only with considerable reluctance—but regarded it as purely a family matter. When his bombastic chancellor, Otto von Bismarck, however, picked up the ball and ran with it, Paris rose up in alarm. It was the thought of having German princes on the Pyrenees frontier as well as the Rhine; though historians could have reminded French statesmen that, by filling the Spanish throne with a Bourbon prince less than two centuries previously, this kind of hegemony was almost exactly what Louis XIV had sought to impose on Europe.

So violent was the storm in France, egged on by inflammatory articles in the Paris press, that the Hohenzollern Candidacy was promptly withdrawn. Relieved, Lord Granville chided the French government for resorting to such strong language, and the British press returned to themes of Queen Victoria dispensing prizes in Windsor Park. But the furor in Paris continued to mount dangerously. Napoléon III was a tired and sick man, with a large stone growing in his bladder, and certainly not the match of his illustrious uncle. His foreign policies had been thwarted at every turn, coming up against two of the most adroit and dangerous statesmen of the nineteenth century: Bismarck in Prussia, and Cavour in Italy.

In nearly two decades of absolute rule, as one way of diverting French minds from the loss of their essential liberties, Napoléon had brought huge prosperity to France. This had become an acceptable substitute for the majority of Frenchmen—though only temporarily. Under his famous Prefect, Baron Haussmann, he had remodeled Paris. The railway network increased from 3,685 kilometres to 17,924, so that all of a sudden the Riviera—formerly the haunt of only a few eccentric English at Cannes—became a Parisian resort. Telegraph lines radiated out all over the country, and shipbuilding expanded as never before. Mighty banking concerns like the Crédit Lyonnais and the Crédit Foncier were established, the latter especially designed to stimulate the vast new building programme. "*Enrichissez-vous*" (Get rich) was the slogan of the era, and a new wealthy bourgeoisie had arisen. Yet at the same time the gap between rich and urban poor had widened drastically. In Paris there was menacing discontent, at times with echoes of 1789; worse still, and more dangerously, despite (or perhaps because of) his attempts at liberalization, France was bored with Napoléon III— *la France s'ennuyait.*

As at many other times in French history, hotheads clamored for the distraction of a successful adventure abroad. If the emperor needed such a success, no one was pushing him harder than his Spanish-born empress, Eugénie, who took the opportunity to remind her husband of Prussia's lightning victory over Austria in 1868, which was widely regarded as a humiliation to French foreign policy. Pointing to their heir, the Prince Impérial, she declared dramatically: "This child will never reign unless we repair the misfortunes of Sadowa."

Meanwhile, France's heavy-handed foreign secretary, the Duc de Gramont, held a personal grudge against Bismarck for having once described him (not unreasonably) as "the stupidest man in Europe," and he now began to adopt a plaintive, hectoring tone toward Prussia. It was not enough that the Hohenzollern Candidacy had been retracted, Prussia had to be humbled for her presumption. Accordingly, Gramont sent the French ambassador in Berlin, Count Vincent Benedetti, to badger the king at Bad Ems, where he was taking the waters. Benedetti was received with the greatest courtesy by King William, who had no desire (any more than his fellow German rulers) for war, observing that the unification of Germany would be "the task of my grandson," not his. (That grandson would be Kaiser Wilhelm II, who would lead a united Germany into World War I.)

This was, however, not the view of Bismarck, who was in no way determined to wait two generations, and who calculated that a war with France would provide the essential mortar required to cement together the existing, rather loose structure of the German federation into a unified nation— dominated, of course, by his native Prussia. But the *casus belli* would have to be most carefully selected, so as to cast France in an unfavorable light among the other nations of Europe—but also with Prussia's own German allies. As he once remarked, "A statesman has not to make history, but if ever in the events around him he hears the sweep of the mantle of God, then he must jump up and catch at its hem."

With the French now bent on pressing for diplomatic victories, Bismarck, twisting the knife in the wound, saw his chance. Irritated by Bene-detti's importuning at Bad Ems, the benign old king refused to give a guar-antee that the Hohenzollern Candidacy would never arise again, and declined a request for a further audience. A telegram giving an account of the interview was duly dispatched to Bismarck in Berlin. Bismarck saw "the mantle of God"; without actually fudging the text, as he has often been ac-cused of doing, he sharpened the tone of the dispatch before passing it to the Berlin press—and the world.

As edited by Bismarck, it stated that the king had "decided not to re-ceive the French Ambassador again, and sent to tell him through the aide-de-camp that his Majesty had nothing further to communicate to the Ambassador."

Even with Bismarck's editing, certainly when compared with the diplo-matic language that was to prevail during the Cold War in the second half of the twentieth century, the famous Ems Telegram hardly seems to have constituted a *casus belli*. But Bismarck had his ear well tuned to the pre-vailing tone in Paris. Frenzied crowds surged through the streets shouting "*À Berlin!*" In one of the rashest claims in all military history, the French commander in chief, Marshal Leboeuf, encouraged the hawks with his fool-ish declaration that the army was "ready down to the last gaiter-button." (Wits remarked that this was largely true, as there were no gaiters in stock anyway.) Now, on receipt of Bismarck's telegram, urged on by his empress and Gramont, fired by the ever shriller Paris press, Napoléon III took the plunge.

On July 15, France declared war—in a state of exhilaration, recalling Napoleon I's repeated successes beyond the Rhine, and expecting a repeat performance. But, through Bismarck's cunning, she found herself at once branded as a frivolous aggressor. As the *Illustrated London News* declared, "The Liberal Empire goes to war on a mere point of etiquette," and this was precisely how opinion, in America as in Europe, saw the new conflict. In the severe judgment of a leading British expert on the Franco-Prussian War, Sir Michael Howard: "Thus by a tragic combination of ill-luck, stu-pidity, and ignorance France blundered into war with the greatest military

UNNECESSARY ADVERSARIES

*The Franco-Prussian War may have been an avoidable confrontation, but it was one that would shape the history of the world. Here, a dejected Napoléon III of France (left), captured with his entire army at the battle of Sedan on September 2, 1870, meets with the victorious Prussian chancellor, Leopold von Bismarck.*

(Hulton/Archive)

power that Europe had yet seen, in a bad cause, with her army unready and without allies."

In sharp contrast, the Prussian military machine was superbly ready, superbly equipped and led, and well tested in battle. Within eighteen days of mobilization, Bismarck and his German allies were able to field an unheard of force of 1,183,000 men. For France, military disaster followed on military incompetence. On September 1, a sick and defeated Napoléon III surrendered to King William of Prussia at the head of his army in Sedan. On the fourth, a stunned Paris greeted the news first with horror, then with a mixture of delight. As the empress fled to England, the mob invaded the Tuileries Palace where they found all the pathetic signs of an unintended departure; a toy sword half-drawn on a bed, empty jewel cases strewn on the floor, and on a table some bits of bread and a half-eaten egg. The end of the empire was proclaimed, and a new republic formed in the Hotel de Ville. Momentarily there reigned an atmosphere of unrestrained carnival; it was a sparkingly sunny day, no blood had been shed, and all Paris now turned out in its Sunday best to celebrate the most joyous revolution it had ever had. Automatically it was assumed on the street that—now that the emperor and his bellicose regime were gone—the victorious Prussians would return home and leave France alone.

Not so. A bitter four-month siege lay ahead, followed by an even more savage civil war as the Commune de Paris took over. By the summer of 1871 peace returned. But France was in financial ruins; much of proud Paris in physical ruin. Under Bismarck's harsh terms, France lost two of its fairest and richest provinces, Alsace and Lorraine. The nation would never forget. Forty-four years after the Ems Telegram, France would go to war to regain them, bringing the whole world with her into a new catastrophe. The whole world equilibrium would be fundamentally altered, and a second, even more terrible world war would be fought before some semblance of the pre-1870 Europe could be rediscovered. From the moment at Ems in the torrid July of 1870 was born all the evils of our twentieth century, which would scourge our planet with two terrible, and—worse than terrible—unnecessary world wars. Unnecessary, that is, if somehow war between Prussia and France could have been avoided that summer; if the Ems Telegram had never been sent—or, better, conveniently overlooked in Paris.

Could it have been otherwise? Well, yes it could, and this is one way a peaceful outcome might have happened.

In June 1870, Napoléon III is miraculously cured of the enormous—and debilitating—stone in his bladder by a brilliant young English doctor, passing it out of his system. He is still only sixty-two, and suddenly seems quite rejuvenated. Apart from his trust in medicine, at various times in his career he had sought advice from a greatly acclaimed Parisian *occultiste*, or medium, Allan Kardec—his real name, Hippolyte Léon Denizard Rivail. (To this day you can find Kardec's Stonehenge-like grave in famous Père

Lachaise cemetery [section 44], still kept heaped with the flowers of fans—apparently hoping to transfer to themselves his psychic powers. Supposedly his darkened bronze effigy also exudes a special appeal for the sexual fetishist; as the guidebook will tell you, a certain part of the body shines brightly, thanks to the caresses of sterile women. Kardec died in 1869, the year before the Ems Telegram—but for our purposes we will give him a few more years of life. And if it wasn't Kardec, it could have been another medium like him.)

So, cured of his disabling physical malady, Napoléon III goes off secretly to Kardec's Paris apartment to seek his help in the crisis that was brewing with Prussia. Could he, for instance, summon up the spirit of his illustrious uncle, Napoléon the Great, and ask him what he would do under the circumstances? Accordingly, in a darkened room, the medium's table begins to heave and levitate. All of a sudden the air is filled with an imposing presence; then a violent *coup de pied dans le derrière* [kick in the rear] suddenly propels the emperor across the room, throwing him flat on his face. (This seemed to confirm a popular joke much realized by Parisian wits and opponents of Bonapartism.) A voice out of the ether, with a strongly Corsican accent, fulminates:

"You fool, *tus es imbecile!* You're getting everything wrong. Even worse than I did. Why don't you call up that slimy old Talleyrand? He's a horrible old rascal, 'shit in a silk-stocking,' I once called him—but if only I had listened to him and gone for peace, instead of war, after the Treaty of Tilsit in 1807, I would never have had to face Wellington at Waterloo."

The bruised nephew goes away and thinks about it, then returns to Kardec the following day. "Get Talleyrand, *et tout de suite!*" A smooth, oily voice comes across the firmament:

"Yes, *Sa Majesté*, your uncle is absolutely correct. Alas, if only he had listened to me, you wouldn't be in this kind of mess now—but he forced me to resign after Tilsit."

"So, what should I do with that tiresome bully, Bismarck?"

"First of all, sack Garmont. Bismarck was being too kind when he called him 'the stupidest man in Europe.' You and I can run French foreign policy by ourselves. Then replace Benedetti in Berlin."

"By whom?"

"Well, what about that annoying hack, the opposition leader Adolphe Thiers? I know he's caused you a lot of trouble—but I always used to say, bring the troublemakers in, don't let them fester outside. He's quite sympathetic to the Prussians, at least they think so. He's a canny politician, he'd be able to tie Bismarck in knots, wrong foot him. After all, what is Bismarck but an overweight Kraut bully? And he's got plenty of other problems at home on his agenda. But, first, you must get rid of the hard-liners."

"What about the empress?"

"Well, *Majesté*, really she's your problem."

The emperor, always keen on the ladies and still with a hankering after the beautiful Italian countess of Castiglione (to whom he once gave a 422,000-pearl necklace, plus Fr 50,000 a month pin money), has an inspiration. Eugénie is frigid, but there were rumors that her virtue had once lapsed when opening the Suez Canal in 1869, just the previous year, when she had fallen for the sexy khedive of Egypt. He, Louis-Napoleon, could speak to his lawyers in the morning. After all, his uncle had divorced the magical Josephine and gotten away with it.

Talleyrand continues:

"Above all, *bin* that telegram of Bismarck's. Ignore it—it doesn't mean a thing, or at least don't let it. Remember what I used to say in your uncle's time—*surtout point de zèle* ['not too much zeal']."

"I know," says the emperor, ruefully, "and my favorite motto was always *Il ne faut rien brusquer* ['never rush things'], but the Impératrice would never listen to me . . . So, what next?"

"Reconvene my Congress of Vienna, which I put together in 1814 to save France—and Europe—when your uncle was sent to Elba. I don't want to boast, but it did give Europe fifty-five years of peace—and, with all those balls, the delegates had a devilish good time in Vienna while it lasted. As I say, Bismarck's got a lot of other things on his agenda, all sorts of problems at home to distract him—keep him talking, for months, if possible; then he'll lose momentum—and that'll be the end of him.

"Remember what Wellington used to say about you, *Sa Majesté, votre oncle*—a conqueror is like a cannonball, it has to go on; once it comes to rest, that's the end of it. That nice, cozy old king of Prussia, William, hates and fears Bismarck and his policies and would love to get rid of him. So wrong foot Bismarck."

"That's all wonderful advice, Monsieur Talleyrand; as a man of peace, you really should have been a bishop."

"But I was, *Majesté*, I was. . . ."

Talleyrand disappears, leaving behind an aroma of snuff, incense, and expensive perfume. Emperor Napoléon III returns to the Tuileries Palace, determined to take Talleyrand's helpful advice. It is July 14. His hand is greatly strengthened by an urgent dispatch just arrived from Granville in London, pressing France to do nothing drastic. This has a considerable effect when read out to the imperial ministers meeting in Council. Precariously the "doves" in the government seem to have gained the ascendancy. Under Louis-Napoléon's pressure rash thoughts about mobilization are shelved. That evening he summons to the Tuileries first Thiers, the opposition leader (and his principal political opponent), together with Thiers's leading left-wing followers. He urges them to take a bipartisan line and support his new drive for peace. Remember Talleyrand, he exhorts them! Thiers and his team agree—provided Louis-Napoléon's prime minister, Emile Ollivier, will tow the line. Next the emperor calls in Ollivier. Ollivier, a forty-five-year-old lawyer with a Republican background, had only been brought in that January to herald a new "Liberal Empire," and one of his first acts, as a man of peace and moderation, had been to cut France's excessive burden of arms expenditure. Over the past weeks he had been sitting on the fence, uncomfortably, as regards the Hohenzollern crisis, inclined toward conciliation but buffeted by the hawkish head of the army, Marshal Leboeuf, and Louis-Napoléon's sabre-rattling empress. Now, with the emperor's new—and surprising—change of heart, together with the promised support of Thiers, his former Republican ally, he is happy to climb off the fence and join the "Peace Party."

That night in the Tuileries, Louis-Napoléon has a furious row with the bellicose Impératrice. Recalling their passionate tryst in a grotto of Cairo's Gezira Palace of the previous fall, she reckons that there, in Egypt, at least, was a monarch who would obey her whims; and richer than Napo, too. She makes her plans, while Louis-Napoléon makes his.

The next day, July 15, in the Corps Législatif, Thiers—as good as his word—rises to denounce war. "Do you want all Europe," he challenges the hawks with forceful eloquence, "to say that although the substance of the quarrel was settled, you have decided to pour out torrents of blood over a mere matter of form?"

Thiers is followed by Ollivier, who—declaring that he cannot accept the responsibility of war "*d'un coeur léger*" ("with a confident heart")—wins over the Assembly with his proposal to launch an international appeal to a Congress of Powers.

The crisis of 1870 is over. Empress Eugénie takes the next available boat from Marseilles. Napoléon III heaves a sigh of relief, and—in his newly rejuvenated vigor—sends a note to his old love.

Paris remains tense for a few days. There are anti-Prussian demonstrations, but after a few troublemakers shouting "*À Berlin*" have been shot or sent to Devil's Island, calm is restored. Prime Minister Ollivier and his liberally inclined supporters are triumphant. Gramont retires to his estates in the provinces, in voluntary exile. Benedetti, by now the former ambassador to Berlin, is given the Latin American desk in the Quai d'Orsay, where he writes minutes (which no one reads) on conflict between Bolivia and Peru. Napoléon III persuades the Great Powers to convene a new Congress of Vienna, which he leads with distinction. In London, Foreign Secretary Granville heads for Scotland and the grouse, delighted that once more the skies are truly cloudless.

Henceforth Britain, and Queen Victoria, will do anything for Louis-Napoléon's new, prudent France (she, anyway, remembered how, on a visit to Paris in the '50s, she had found the emperor more attractive than any man since poor Albert). The whole world is impressed by France's cool-headed statesmanship; leaders suddenly recall the aggressiveness of Frederick the Great, rather than the successive ravaging of Germany by Louis XIV and Napoléon I. Bismarck is no longer the flavor of the month anywhere.

There is no war.

As clever old Talleyrand predicted, the new Congress of Vienna drags on into 1872. Bismarck has been humiliated, if not routed—totally wrong footed and made to appear before the world as a blustering bully, and a threat to the concert of nations. In Berlin the doves prevail; the king, who had certainly never wanted to be promoted to kaiser of a united Germany, returns to a quiet life at Potsdam, growing grapes in the conservatories built in a rare moment between wars by his ancestor, Frederick the Great. Moltke's huge army is progressively stood down, so that more money can be spent on education and roads. The 50 percent of Germans who are Roman Catholic rejoice that the march toward domination by Protestant Prussia, which once seemingly inexorable, is now halted. Once Bismarck had his impetus over the Hohenzollern Candidacy removed, like Wellington's cannonball, he and his policies are rendered pointless. Again, as Talleyrand predicted, he had plenty on his agenda—and problems—at home to occupy his mind. Like all bullies, once resisted, he collapses.

As soon as he decently can, good King William "drops the pilot"; full of unheeded resentment, the "Iron Chancellor" retires to his estates at Varzin, resuming his voracious diet of eleven hard-boiled eggs for breakfast, plus plates loaded with Reinfeld ham, goose with olives, and Varzin wild boar. A forgotten man, Bismarck dies in 1898 of gluttony (exacerbated by acute constipation) and disappointment.

In the meantime, Catholic Bavaria has formed a customs union with its neighbor, Catholic Austria, thereby providing a powerful counterweight to Prussia in the German-speaking world. In the west, the discovery of vast deposits of iron in Alsace-Lorraine (which, of course, continue to belong to

France) and coal in the neighboring Rhineland Ruhr led to a transfrontier coal-and-steel pool, the beginnings of a European Common Market. This is strongly backed by U.S. commercial interests, and contributing massively to overall European prosperity, thereby eradicating one of the main causes of war.

And what of America in all this? General Ulysses S. Grant comes to power in 1868 for two terms, on a campaign slogan of "Let us have peace." Having on his conscience the deaths of more men in the recent War between the States than any other general, he is so appalled by the prospects of a similar carnage in Europe that, renouncing the strictures of the Founding Father, George Washington, he commits the United States to playing a far-reaching role in European affairs. The brilliant U.S. ambassador in Paris in 1870, Elihu B. Washburne, is appointed secretary of state, and under his guidance the United States assumes a leading influence in the new Congress of Vienna. Under the Washburne Plan, there is widespread economic cooperation between the United States and Europe, with Washington offering troops in case of an outside threat—for instance, from an expansive, czarist Russia.

U.S. forces and mediation are indeed very nearly needed in 1898, when a serious conflict breaks out in Africa between Britain and a new, powerful France, called by historians the Fashoda Incident—Europe's ugliest moment since 1870. Pushing the claims of their rival empires, French troops under General Marchand, marching all the way across Africa, running up against the British forces on the Nile at Fashoda. Thanks to U.S. intervention, however, war is once more averted.

At the same time, Britain finds a new ally in the shape of King Frederick III's Prussia, now feeling distinctly inferior to the new France. Married to Queen Victoria's daughter, "Dear Vicky," Frederick had always been pro-British. He inherited the throne from his father, William I in 1888, and (instead of dying after a few months from cancer of the throat, possibly caused by all the stress of the Franco-Prussian War), lives to a ripe and fulfilling old age of eighty-three. Casting aside Bismarck's silly (and dangerous) notion that his map of Africa lay in Europe, under the Gute Fritz [b. 1831] as he was nicknamed, Prussia is now happy to accept, in return for her support, some tidbits of the British Empire south of the Sahara. As contemporary historians note, enlightened and benevolent colonialism in Africa continues into the twenty-first century—much to the benefit of the residents.

To gain him administrative experience, and quiet the aggressive impulses of a troubled heir born sadly with a withered arm, Frederick sends the prospective Wilhelm II to German South-West Africa—where tragically he succumbs to malaria. Frederick's fun-loving grandson, nicknamed "Little Willie" by the English, takes over in Berlin as Wilhelm II—instead of commanding an army at Verdun in 1916. Under him, emulating his uncle, Edward VII, Berlin becomes the *gai Paris* of Eastern Europe.

In France, the heir of Napoléon III, the beloved "Prince Impérial," having no need to seek refuge in England, does not join the British army to get killed by Zulu spears; instead he becomes a studious young man at the Polytéchnique, dim but peace-loving and succeeding his father in the Tuileries in 1875, but with most of his hereditary powers shorn by Republican politicians.

Meanwhile, in 1889, a boy, called Adolf, is born in the small Austrian town of Braunau, to the lower-middle-class Hitler family. He takes up painting, but nobody buys his pictures; called up into the Austro-Bavarian army, he manages to avoid the inconclusive border skirmishes that ensue after the assassination of an archduke in Sarajevo. In Berlin, the Prussians view with some pleasure the discomfort of their rivals to the south; in St. Petersburg, the czar rattles his sword, but a few brisk dispatches from President Teddy Roosevelt (reelected in 1912, he defeats an ineffectual Princeton professor named Wilson), and the newly formed North Atlantic Treaty Organization (NATO)—nothing quite as rude as the Ems Telegram—suffice to keep the lid on the kettle. Returning to Braunau, young Adolf gets involved in local politics, isn't elected as he is too far-out right wing and anti-Semitic; prosperous Austro-Bavaria has no time for that kind of nonsense. He dies, unknown and unmourned, in the arms of his mistress, Eva, of apoplexy while on a trip to Berlin in the spring of 1945. His dreadful paintings are eventually bought up by London's Tate Modern—along with a lot of other junk; which is why we remember the name of Hitler.

. . .

So there is no Great War, no Second World War—and no Holocaust. Such notional events were indeed utilized in a far-fetched, prophetic novel from the imagination of a little-known English science-fiction writer called H. G. Wells. But the critics panned the excessive fantasy that the peace-loving Americans could conceivably wipe out two cities in smiling Japan with bombs made from a handful of atoms. It was recalled that Wells, with his fevered imagination, had also previously written a book that was equally way-out—about the world being invaded by men from Mars; hence his novel, *1945 and All That*, was dismissed as just too fantastical by a tranquil twentieth century, which had come to regard itself evolving as an extension of the "perfectible" eighteenth.

A lovely, Arcadian dream perhaps; and possibly it takes too little into account the inbuilt aggressiveness and greed of the human race, which will one day wreck our planet. But impossible? No! All this from France's refusal to get overexcited about the Ems Telegram? Why not? Great events so often have tiny beginnings; and think of Ulysses' famous speech in *Troilus and Cressida*:

. . . untune one string,
And, hark! what discord follows; each new thing meets
In mere oppugnancy. . . .

JOHN LUKACS

# THE ELECTION OF THEODORE ROOSEVELT, 1912

*Brokering an earlier end*
*to World War I*

*That Theodore Roosevelt could have recaptured the Republican nomination for president in 1912—and with it certain victory in the November election—is not fantasy. Even the unseating of a president in his own party, William Howard Taft, was possible, and Roosevelt almost brought it off. TR, who had spent his first four years out of office writing books and hunting big game in Africa, had become increasingly disenchanted with his handpicked successor: He described Taft as "a flubdub with a streak of the second-rate and the common in him." (The final break came over the Taft administration's prosecution of U.S. Steel, a trust whose formation Roosevelt had previously consented to. The antitrust suit seemed to imply that TR had countenanced an illegal monopoly.) Making the famous statement that his "hat was in the ring," he took the primary route against Taft. (Nationwide presidential primaries were one of the central planks of a program he called a "New Nationalism.") TR won ten out of twelve contests—he even took Taft's home state, Ohio—and beat the president by more than a million votes; he came to the August Republican convention in Chicago with 278 delegates. Though TR was clearly the choice of the party's rank and file, Taft was backed by the powerful GOP regulars. The outcome was practically settled before the convention, in a battle over the seating of pro-Roosevelt delegates, who might have given their leader the fighting chance he needed. As we know, the regulars won, but it was a Pyrrhic victory.*

*In John Lukacs's scenario, TR shows up at the convention to spellbind it. In*

581

*actuality he was prevented from doing so, but he did go on to preside over the formation of his new Progressive Party—which, in the election, would capture more votes than the Republicans, though two million less than those of the victorious Democratic candidate, Woodrow Wilson.*

*What would have happened, Lukacs asks, if TR had been elected for a third term? As far as his domestic policies were concerned, they may not have been radically different from those of Wilson. But Roosevelt would have asserted America's role in the First World War much earlier, intervening on the side of the Allies as early as 1916. (By that time, TR, a champion of universal military training, would have had an army ready to fight—"the military tent where they [men of different backgrounds] sleep side by side," he once said, "will rank next to the public school among the great agents of democratization.") It was Roosevelt, after all, who had brokered the end of the Russo-Japanese War with the Treaty of Portsmouth in 1905 and who, the following year, had supported the Algeciras Conference, at which the statesmen of the great European powers had settled the crisis over Morocco. He would not have acted less positively in the world crisis after 1914.*

*This chapter and the next present two scenarios, both plausible, that might have led to variant outcomes for the First World War. (Lukacs gives us what academics call a "second-order counterfactual"—which is to say that after big changes a familiar pattern of history would reassert itself.) Both scenarios turn on the personalities of two individuals, in the first case Roosevelt, and in the second, the German chancellor in the early years of the war, Theobold von Bethmann-Hollweg. They are counterfactual case studies in the active and passive uses of power.*

*But let us start with Lukacs's proposition: that TR had been able to gain the Republican nomination.*

JOHN LUKACS, an emeritus professor of history at Chestnut Hill College, Philadelphia, is the author of many books, among them *The Duel, The Hitler of History, The Thread of Years,* and *Five Days in London, May 1940.* He lives in Pennsylvania.

HISTORIANS HAVE PAID insufficient attention to Theodore Roosevelt's triumphant third-term campaign in 1912. His landslide victory in November overshadowed the complicated story of his nomination at the Republican National Convention in Chicago four months earlier. They also ought to have at least asked the question: What if not Roosevelt but Wilson had been the president of the United States at the time of World War I in Europe?

The Roosevelt nomination in Chicago in August 1912 was by no means a foregone conclusion. Most of the leading Republican politicians and, perhaps more importantly, the managers of the convention, wanted President Taft for a second term for many reasons, the prime one having been their distrust of Theodore Roosevelt and their dislike of his Progressive ideas. (This counted more against TR than the accusation of his departure from George Washington's traditional reluctance to seek the presidency for the third time; after all, TR had not chosen to run for a third term in 1908, and there was the recent example of Grover Cleveland, who had sought, and won, the presidency after a four-year interruption.) Well before the convention met in Chicago the Credential Committees of the Republican National Committee succeeded to "contest" pro-Roosevelt delegates in various states. Intimates also had a general impression that TR was no longer his old self. Henry Adams had met him on a Washington street in December 1911 and wrote that Theodore "looked bigger and more tumbled-to-pieces," that his manners were "more slovenly," that he showed some "mental enfeeblement." However, that was not the impression the nation had, especially when reading TR's statement to the press even before his declaration in Columbus, Ohio: "My hat's in the ring! The fight is on and I'm stripped to the buff!"

And when Roosevelt appeared on the floor in Chicago, breaking the unwritten custom of presidential candidates keeping away from the convention until they are nominated, the roar of his supporters drowned out much of the opposition—as well as the careful preparations of the managers, which included the presence of 1,000 Chicago policemen and strands of barbed wire hidden beneath the bunting of the platform, to prevent Roosevelt enthusiasts from rushing up there to claim it. Breaking with yet another unwritten custom, on the third day of the convention, during a hot and, for once, milling rather than roiling crowd, Roosevelt suddenly rose and began speaking from the floor. There was an unaccustomed tide of silence; and his high-pitched voice soothed and inspired, rather than fired up the mass. "Now I am but a voice in a crowd," he said, "but allow me to think out loud. What I am going to say may represent the inner convictions and the patriotic inspirations not only of Republicans but of the great majority of my countrymen." What he said and how he said it impressed hundreds of delegates, and even some of his opponents. This was not a speech from a bully pulpit; it breathed the music of a realistic idealism. It was the psychic turning point of the convention. His once friend and ally, and his former secretary of state, Elihu Root, had deserted him, being the august chairman of the convention and siding with the orthodox party; but now Root, too, had to turn around or, rather, adjust the timings of his gavel. He thought that he had to allow giving the platform to at least two speakers nominating Roosevelt—who was then nominated by a majority.

The rest we know. He triumphed over Woodrow Wilson with more than two million majority. He carried nearly every state in the North and West, and even two states in the South. He picked the Pennsylvania conservationist Gifford Pinchot for his vice president (a favorite of his who had been dismissed by Taft) and Albert Beveridge for his secretary of state. Elihu Root wanted that job and would have been a natural for it; but TR, though not an especially vindictive man, could not forget Root's association with the Taftite financiers of the Republican party.

The Roosevelt who rode to his inauguration with Taft next to him in the largest motor car Americans had yet seen in March 1913 was more corpulent and less physically fit than before. This was visible in some of the photographs and in the flickering newsreels in the movie houses, but it did not

THE BULL MOOSE CANDIDATE

*When ex-President Theodore Roosevelt was denied the Republican nomination in 1912—after handily carrying the primaries—he ran as the presidential candidate of the Progressive Party; its adopted symbol was the fierce, proud bull moose. Above, TR hitches a ride on a temporarily co-operative animal.*

(Underwood & Underwood/CORBIS)

seem to matter. He had a popular mandate as great as he had in 1904. There was another difference. There was a considerable similarity in the propositions that he and his opponent Wilson represented; in one way or another, both of them were Progressives. Roosevelt—and the nation, and the world—believed that his main agenda, indeed, that perhaps his only important immediate agenda, was domestic. He ran it through Congress and the various state legislatures with remarkably little trouble. They consisted of four pieces of legislation: the establishment of a national income tax; of the direct selection of senators; of the admission of one very large south-western state, "Arizona," uniting the Arizona and New Mexico territories (against the wishes of most of the latter's inhabitants); and of the preparation of a new immigration law, establishing more stringent measures than heretofore, and a yearly maximum quota (though not a national quota system) of allowable immigrants. Except for the second, these laws, including the income tax law, came to fruition without the need for a constitutional amendment. Only the new immigration legislation (which Roosevelt insisted was essentially a regulation, not necessarily in need of detailed congressional approval) was still pending when World War I erupted in Europe in 1914.

On June 15, 1914, two weeks before the assassination of the Archduke Franz Ferdinand in Sarajevo (which Roosevelt immediately denounced as "a heinous crime committed by terrorists"), Roosevelt stood in a cloud of steamy heat at the Gatun Locks, opening the Panama Canal, of which he was both godfather and father. That was a moment of apotheosis, a monument to him and to the America he represented, the Big Brother of the entire Western Hemisphere. (The pejorative sense of those two words would not appear until George Orwell's *1984*, more than a generation later.) TR—sometimes having had to face down his often cantankerous and imperialist secretary of state, Beveridge—had already demonstrated his ability in conducting foreign affairs, together with his strong and measured espousal of American national interests. Thus during the Mexican civil war of 1913 his stern warning from the White House was enough to bring about a sudden (though temporary) halt of the anarchy in Mexico City and Vera Cruz, establishing thereby a guaranteed protection of American and British interests. Contemplating another murderous anarchy in Haiti in early 1914, he intervened and sent the marines to maintain law and order in Port-au-Prince, after which he negotiated the permanent establishment of a U.S. Navy base at Petit Goave, similar to that at Guantánamo in Cuba, against the wishes of Beveridge, who preferred putting all of Haiti under American jurisdiction, somewhat like Hawaii or the Philippines. But Beveridge was not only cantankerous and an alcoholic; he was also getting old. In June 1914, Roosevelt replaced him with Bainbridge Colby. Colby was a decent minor statesman but not a particularly willful one. As is the case with so many powerful leaders, TR would often act as if he were his own secretary of state. That Beveridge's final letter of resignation had reached TR at his breakfast table on June 28—in the same hour when 4,000 miles away the fatal shots rang out in Sarajevo—was proof of what Chesterton once said, that "coincidences are spiritual puns."

There was a duality in Theodore Roosevelt's first reactions to the European War. (The phrase "World War" became current only a year later, mostly employed by American newspapers and Germans.) He was appalled by the German invasion of neutral Belgium, and said so to his circle; at the same time he assured his friend, the German ambassador to Washington, that the United States was neutral. He made a few public statements extolling the differences of the New from the Old World; but privately he was disgusted with the behavior of many Americans in Europe, who were scurrying homeward in a panic and demanding the protection of every possible American authority. But soon Roosevelt's duality began to melt away. "They all miscalculated," he said to his friends, meaning the various European governments and General Staffs; this will be a long war. And therefore the United States must ready itself for all emergencies. In addition to its superb navy, TR ordered the rapid building up of the army, calling in ringing voices for Patriotic Volunteers. First to Plattsburgh, New York, then to 125 other training camps across the nation flowed two million young American men, ready to be drilled at arms. Roosevelt's recent opponent, Woodrow Wilson, said that he was "proud to speak out against educating our youth for Armageddon." Roosevelt privately (and not so privately) said that Wilson was "an abject coward." Then, in a famous speech, he spoke against "the craven fear of being great." (A phrase that Winston Churchill would employ thirty years later, warning the British people of new dangers on the morrow of VE Day in 1945). Incidentally, TR appreciated the young Churchill, with whom he had entered into a confidential correspondence already in 1914; and he expressed his regret when Churchill's imaginative thrust into the Dardanelles had failed and when Churchill had to resign as First Lord of the Admiralty.) In April 1915 a German submarine sank the *Lusitania*. TR did not mince words: "Murder on the high seas!" he exclaimed. When Henry Ford hired and sent his Peace Ship packed with pacifists and all kinds of odd people into the North Sea later that summer, TR dismissed Ford as "an ignorant mechanic." Less than one year after the outbreak of World War I, Roosevelt seemed to have concluded that the prestige of the United States was great enough to make its voice heard, and that its power was great enough for the European Powers to weigh its effects at once. In an important speech in Boston in November 1915, he said that "the United States cannot be indifferent to the firestorm ravaging Europe, and *especially* not to what happens in the Atlantic Ocean and on its Western European shores."

This was the first definite indication that Roosevelt would not accept an eventual German domination of Western Europe or an eventual German preponderance in the North Sea. He knew that such an American policy, including its prospect of drawing closer and closer to the European War on the side of Britain (and of France) against Germany had many opponents besides Ford's pacifists: German Americans, Scandinavian Americans, Irish Americans, Jewish Americans (the latter mostly emigrants from the Czarist Russian empire whose numbers were considerable, and perhaps growing). In Milwaukee a man tried to shoot him; the bullet fortunately only grazed his neck. "Don't touch him!" TR shouted. The potential assassin was a German American; Roosevelt thought it best to call him an anarchist. The episode redounded in his credit. Still, aware of the rising tide of anti-Roosevelt opposition in the approaching presidential election, he weighed the alternatives. Should American intervention come before or after November? By the spring of 1916, he chose the first option. "The people will not want to change horses [he meant *this* horse and *this* horseman] in midstream." He was right; he was renominated, easily, for a fourth term. ("My last!" he exclaimed.) He won the presidency, defeating Wilson again—though with a lesser majority than four years before. Illinois, Wisconsin, Michigan, and California went to Wilson—in the latter Roosevelt's earlier ally, Hiram Johnson, had turned bitterly against him.

But all of this happened after Verdun, and after the Somme, and—more important—after Presidential Order Number One, issued by Roosevelt in March 1916, ordering the navy to enter the Eastern Atlantic and the

North Sea, protecting and escorting merchant ships sailing those waters (including ships not only from the United States but from the entire Western Hemisphere, and merchantmen carrying arms and munitions to Britain and France); and ordering the establishment of an American navy base in Rotterdam (after the German government had threatened the Netherlands government for having allowed the transfer of transatlantic goods to Britain). At the end of May, the German Naval High Command thought it best not to interfere with a chain of American destroyers patrolling the Dutch coast and the North Sea—which contributed to the strategy of the British victory over the German High Sea Fleet off Jutland at the end of May. Immediately after his reelection in November 1916, Roosevelt sent a three-point note to each of the warring powers in Europe. (When its contents became known, his enemies—and, of course, some German newspapers—called it not the Roosevelt Corollary but the Roosevelt Effrontery, but no matter.) It was a state paper of the greatest importance. The government of the United States, Roosevelt declared, proposes one, the cessation of all hostilities in Europe and on the high seas within a month; two, the return of all armies and Powers to their state frontiers of July 1914; three, the convocation of a Peace Congress in The Hague three months after the armistice, with the United States represented together with all other Powers. None of the governments of Europe had expected such a definite proposal, not even the British. The world was stunned and startled. The cartoonist of a Hearst paper in New York drew TR, with the sun behind him, rising as Augustus Caesar over the tribes of the world.

Cautiously and slowly the British, and very reluctantly the French (and the Russian and the Italian) governments expressed their inclination not to reject the proposal; surprisingly so did the Austrian government, to the distaste of Germany, which did reject it. Indeed, on January 31, 1917, Berlin announced the resumption of unrestricted submarine warfare; within three days, five American merchant ships were sunk in the Western Approaches to the British Isles. Immediately, Theodore Roosevelt went to Congress and asked for a declaration of war against Germany. After a very brief debate he got it. By that time much of the new American army—armed, trained, drilled by the two million Plattsburgh-type graduates who were now second lieutenants and sergeants, suitable leaders of a four-million-man draft army that Roosevelt had organized after shoving a draft bill through Congress the previous year—were crowding and milling in the Eastern ports, ready to sail for France. The swiftness and the size of this unprecedented movement from the New World to the Old—a reversal of the movement of peoples across the Atlantic during the four previous centuries—was such that the German government announced the temporary suspension of submarine warfare against American vessels. That was the first crack of the German resolve. The second came in April 1917, when a brief advance of the American First Division lodged along the Argonne-Meuse line was sufficient for the Germans to attempt a cautious withdrawal of about six miles in front of the British in Flanders and of the French on both sides of Verdun. On the first of May the German Catholic Center party and the new German Democratic party joined the Social Democrats in the Reichstag to request that the imperial government consider the Roosevelt Three-Point Declaration—provided that it was still valid. Late that night Roosevelt—who was not in the best physical state—received this news from a telegram brought to the White House. "I had a very good sleep," he declared to his family the next morning. "I will tell that, yes, it *is* still valid; but they'd better pull up their pants and get moving at once."

They did. The British and the French were abashed—a little: they hoped that with more and more American troops on the way the Germans would collapse sooner rather than later. But they had to go along, and so did the Germans. In the highest war councils General Ludendorff and Admiral Tirpitz were voted down; and as soon as the Social Democrats declared that they did not insist on the proclamation of a German republic, William II was advised to abdicate in favor of his son. A German constitutional monarchy came thus into being. The armistice was signed on May 15 and the fighting came to an end. The Hague Peace Congress met on August 4, 1917, three years to the day after Britain had declared war on Germany. Theodore Roosevelt had sailed to Rotterdam aboard the USS *New York*, diplomatically avoiding a landing in Britain en route. Despite the objurgations and insistences of minor Powers, the 1914 frontiers were restored everywhere (except for Alsace and Lorraine, which reverted to France), with the provision that The Hague International Court of Justice (an old project of Roosevelt's) examine all requests for indemnities and frontier problems within five years, through a series of international commissions, in each of which Americans would be represented. TR's presence—and influence—towered over all others during the Peace Conference. Yet domestic opposition to his policies (especially among many Republicans) went on to prevail.

Before that, in March 1917, a revolution had broken out in St. Petersburg. The czar abdicated. Roosevelt who, as we have seen, had plenty on his plate at that moment, still deemed it necessary to pay considerable attention to the developing events in that vast country. Less than a week after the abdication of the czar, Roosevelt declared that "it is in the interests of the United States and of the entire civilized world that law and order should prevail within the Russian Empire." The Russian military then—encouraged by the Three-Point Declaration, allowing them to reoccupy the territories they had lost to the Germans during three years of war—was instrumental in installing a new monarch, the former Archduke Michael I, as czar of the Russians, under the conditions of a constitutional monarchy that was then affirmed by a transnational referendum. TR and the Secret Service were aware of revolutionary movements in Russia, including agitators and agents abroad. They took a few measures against them. Thus Lev Bronstein (alias "Trotsky"), an agitator and former movie extra on Long Island, attempting to return to Russia, was nabbed by Canadian agents in Halifax and brought back to Brooklyn, while the Swiss federal police in Zurich made sure that V. I. Ulyanov (alias "Lenin") and his friends would not be allowed to cross the frontiers of Switzerland. The third leading "Bolshevik," a mustachioed Caucasian by the name of I. V. Dzhugashvili (alias "Stalin") chose to abandon his subversive affiliations and became a highly efficient agent of the newly formed Russian State Police.

Of course The Hague Tribunal was not able to bank the fires of nationalist and revolutionary agitation everywhere. Bloody skirmishes and wars broke out in Transylvania, Bohemia, South Tirol, Trieste, along the Italian–Austrian, Austrian–Czech, Hungarian–Romanian, Bulgarian–Turkish, and Turkish–Arab frontiers. Some of these were settled, others were not, and flared and festered for a long time. The authority of The Hague Tribunal was considerable, but its powers were, after all, limited—especially when its American representation was gradually withdrawn after 1920, during the Hoover and Coolidge administrations. In 1918, a stern Rooseveltian warning stopped Japan from resuming its war and conquest of China; in the same year, agitation in Ireland against British rule was gathering speed; and the hottest place in Europe was Poland, whose people rose against both German and Russian occupation—that is, for the restoration of the frontiers of 1914—with creditable success. Roosevelt was unwilling to assert American intervention in some of these conflicts—for which he was more and more frequently criticized by his domestic opponents. The Democrats made considerable advances in the November 1918 congressional elections.

Roosevelt had not begun to weigh the question of his eventual successor when—suddenly and tragically—in January 1919 he died. That he was one of the greatest—and perhaps *the* most influential—of American presidents few people doubted, including his adversaries. His task was not finished; as we have seen, agitation and disturbances went on in Europe and in the Near East, but also in the cities and industries of the United States. But his greatest achievement was his establishment of a philosophy of American world relations, of a foreign policy that rested on geographical and national realities rather than on "international" illusions; on the recognition that the freedom of the entire Atlantic region, including that of Western Europe, was in the prime interest of the United States (as it had been of Britain). This was in profound contrast to the ideological vision of his former opponent Wilson, another Progressive, with his Fourteen Points and the War to End All Wars. For Roosevelt three points were enough; and he also knew that wars cannot be abolished by legislation or by the nonexistent powers of an illusory League of Nations (about which he was less sanguine than about the International Court of Justice).

And yet, as the wise (and melancholy) proverb says, God Writes Straight With Crooked Lines. In 1920, the anti-Roosevelt Republicans swept back into power. Their presidential candidate, Herbert Hoover, made sure it was known that he was a Progressive; indeed, he was (and felt) much closer to Wilson than to the Theodorian tradition. Slowly, gradually, the Wilsonian ideology of international relations grew more attuned to American intellects than the Rooseveltian vision of the Western world (which his intellectual critics called "The Theodorian *Realpolitik*": a shorthand and inaccurate summary phrase). There was also the isolationism of "America First," the future leader of which was to be Taft's son, a Republican senator from Ohio. The Republicans governed the country for another twelve years, until the bankruptcy of their financial and social policies became increasingly evident. In 1932, the American people gave their overwhelming support to Franklin Delano Roosevelt, Theodore's young cousin. He was a Democrat.

By that time it had begun to appear that the thunderous success of the 1917 Roosevelt Declaration notwithstanding, Europe—and the world—could not be turned back to 1914. In the 1920s, a former Italian Socialist who had turned nationalist, Benito Mussolini, became the dictator of Italy, reducing the king to the role of a figurehead. Ten years later a former German soldier and artist, Adolf Hitler, became the leader of a German popular movement, rejecting the conditions of The Hague settlement, and especially the reluctant German acquiescence in the existence of an independent Polish state. The War to End All Wars was a mirage, the League of Nations was an illusion; Germany was rising and arming again, and a second world war was in the wings. Few men saw this clearer than Theodore Roosevelt's erstwhile correspondent, Winston Churchill; but these were events we need not recount, as they are only too well known to us.

We know that in another sense, too, the world of (or before) 1914 could not be restored. The symptoms of the breakup of the old and largely bourgeois order of the Hundred Years' Peace before 1914, were there well before that year—in letters and art and fashions and music and mores and manners and social unrest, signs and clouds and antennae registering then. James Joyce and Ezra Pound had succeeded William Dean Howells and Edward Arlington Robinson (who had been TR's favorite contemporary novelist and favorite contemporary poet, respectively); ragtime and the tango were already raging in 1914, to be followed by jazz and the Charleston; the women's suffrage movement was rising almost as fast as the hems of women's skirts; "socialist" and "radical" had become positive words among the intelligentsia, even more exciting than "progressive." In 1913, TR was among those who denounced the "art" displayed at the New York Armory Show; he was acclaimed by the New York bourgeoisie, many of whom were howling outside. Fifty years later, at the anniversary of the same Armory Show, the descendants of these philistines were inside the Armory, mumbling their approval of "nonrepresentative art." *Toujours ça change, toujours c'est la même chose*. The more things change, the more they remain the same. Do they? Yes; and no.

ROBERT L. O'CONNELL

# THE GREAT WAR TORPEDOED

*The weapon that could have won
the war for Germany in 1915*

*Few events lend themselves as poignantly to counterfactual scenarios as the First
World War. A certain amount of wishful thinking is involved, the understandable
urge to wipe out the multiple catastrophes, traumas, and political disasters that the
conflict spawned. But more than just historical wishful thinking confronts us. It is
conceivable that, with a small number of slightly changed, yet altogether plausible, tips of the dice, some of the nastiest sequels of the late century might have
been avoided, or at least rendered less extreme. The most familiar turning points,
as Robert L. O'Connell observes, focus on the early months, and the majority arrive at the same conclusion: Germany could have won—no, should have won—
a war that was still a continental power struggle and not yet a worldwide one.
Once the trench stalemate set in, most historians agree, the might-have-beens diminished, with odds on a German triumph lengthening as the years went on.
O'Connell, who has written extensively on the history of armaments, does not
share that view. He maintains that we have overlooked the one weapon that could
have genuinely altered the strategic balance in Germany's favor, sooner rather
than later. That weapon was the submarine.*

*What if the submarine had not been held hostage to the German government's
fear of United States involvement, at least early on, when the Great Neutral was
not even prepared to be prepared? Berlin did announce a campaign of unrestricted
submarine warfare at the beginning of 1915, but as yet it did not have a U-boat
fleet large enough to make that campaign truly effective. Had an all-out U-boat*

*construction program been initiated at that time, O'Connell argues, and had the effort to isolate the British Isles not been abandoned as a result of the furor over the May sinking of the Lusitania and the loss of 128 American lives, Germany might well have been able to bring the Allies to the peace table within a year. The Battle of the Somme would not have been for Germany the beginning of an attritional mudslide downward but the ending of the Western Front bloodbath, in which the Allied fighting spirit would be broken once and for all.*

*One person stood in the way—and counterfactual history has a way of etching in relief otherwise inconspicuous figures. The blandly malign presence who emerges in the pivotal months after the wasted opportunities of 1914 is that ultimate bureaucrat, the German chancellor Theobald Bethmann-Hollweg. He, as much as anyone, was responsible for Germany's defeat. When the chief of staff, Erich von Falkenhayn, informed him in December 1914 that the war was no longer winnable, Bethmann-Hollweg answered that the people (by which he probably meant the kaiser) would not stand for a negotiated settlement—thereby sentencing a generation of Europeans to death. In the months that followed, it was Bethmann-Hollweg who also lobbied against unrestricted submarine warfare— but at what price? Without him, O'Connell writes, "everything might have been different."*

*In the event, Germany did turn again to unrestricted submarine warfare at the beginning of 1917. The results were, for a time, spectacular, but it was already too late. The main effect was to bring a more energized United States into the war, with the promise of fresh and practically limitless cannon fodder. That was an offer the Allied warlords would never refuse.*

ROBERT L. O'CONNELL is the author of *Of Arms and Men: A History of War, Weapons, and Aggression; The Ride of the Second Horseman: The Birth and Death of War; Sacred Vessels: The Cult of the Battleship and the Rise of the U.S. Navy;* and the forthcoming *Soul of the Sword,* an illustrated history of weapons. He has also written the novel *Fast Eddie,* based on the life of Captain Edward Vernon Rickenbacker. O'Connell lives in Charlottesville, Virginia.

I T MAY BE COINCIDENTAL, but it is suggestive nonetheless that the interest among serious historians in counterfactual analysis basically corresponds with the rise of a dramatically new way of looking at the physics of complex systems, known popularly as chaos theory. In both pursuits a key operative principle is the sensitivity of any complicated chain of events to small changes in initial conditions, symbolized by the whimsical notion of a butterfly flapping its wings in Tokyo changing the weather over Washington two weeks later.

Since there are few areas of human endeavor more chaotic and more subject to chance occurrence than warfare, it has become a logical focal point in the counterfactual analysis of history, the venue of greatest leverage, where the smallest changes can plausibly bring the biggest results. But there are broader issues involved. However tragic or ridiculous or outmoded our propensity for organized violence, wars matter; like few other events, they have the capacity to change things fundamentally for good or ill. Plus, the science of complex systems informs us in a very convincing way that nothing is inevitable, or even necessarily probable. On the surface of events, history simply happens, a roll of the dice or rather an accumulation of rolls. So it is far from trivial to examine the alternatives. What might have been not only *really* might have been; but also could have been profoundly important.

World War I was arguably the pivotal event of the twentieth century, the historical train wreck responsible for the Bolshevik revolution and world Communism, the Second World War, the Cold War, and all the cataclysm surrounding these phenomena. As such it has exerted a magnetic attraction on counterfactualists. Intuitively they have been drawn to the earliest stages of the conflict, exploring initial conditions on the political front (What if the Russians had not mobilized first; or the British had declared their neutrality?) and the first key operational decisions (What if Moltke had not weakened the German right flank?).

Nevertheless, a case can be made that the tragic consequences of the Great War actually flowed primarily from the unintended effects of weapons technology. More than anything it was the characteristics of available armaments that enforced the stalemate that slaughtered ten million soldiers and made a mockery of rational political and military calculations, along with the leadership responsible for them. Yet 1914's card deck of death machinery does not seem, on the face of it, a promising playground for counterfactualists, being packed with high-powered artillery, machine guns, and barbed wire, which only served to bog down the action; aircraft so underdeveloped that they amounted to little more than a diversion for the suffering entrenched masses, and vast fleets of surface ships enthralled to giant dreadnought battleships so specialized and vulnerable that they were inherently indecisive. In the entire stack there was but one wild card, a joker so misplayed that historians have largely dismissed its influence, except in the negative sense of being responsible for American belligerency and Germany's ruin. Yet it could have been otherwise. The kaiser's submarines, had they been used relentlessly against Britain's commerce, could have changed everything.

Few expected much, but unlike other warships, the submarine proved surprisingly effective right from the earliest stages of hostilities. Barely a month passed before a German submarine managed to sink its first man-of-war, the light cruiser HMS *Pathfinder*. Just two weeks later, on September 23, U-9 torpedoed and sank in rapid succession three British armored cruisers, *Cressy*, *Hogue*, and *Aboukir*. The ships were old and obsolescent, but they were large (12,000 tons each) and filled with sailors, most of whom died. The 1,459 fatalities were greater than the cost of Trafalgar, and constituted the worst wartime disaster the Royal Navy had suffered in nearly 300 years. As if this was not enough, the main body of the British fleet at Scapa Flow was so harassed by submarine sightings, both real and imagined, that in October it was forced to withdraw to the north coast of Ireland until a complex of booms and obstructions could be installed at its main base.

This may have bought some safety for the dreadnoughts of the Grand Fleet. But there were far easier targets available.

Eighteen months before the war began, Arthur Conan Doyle, the opium-smoking creator of Sherlock Holmes, published a novel called *Danger*, a prescient war fantasy describing an imbroglio between England and Nordland, a small imaginary European state. Lacking an effective fleet, Nordland's monarch is about to submit, when he is reminded of his eight submarines by John Serious, a resourceful naval officer. "Ah, you would attack the English battleships with submarines?" inquires the king. "Sire, I would never go near an English battleship."

Instead, he proposes to wage a merciless campaign against merchant shipping, striking at the island kingdom's greatest weakness, utter dependence on seaborne foodstuffs. Transports are attacked wherever they are found and without warning. "What do I care for the three mile limit, or international law?" growls Serious. In short order, England is pushed to the edge of starvation and forced to accept a humiliating peace.

Not surprisingly, *Danger* was basically dismissed by the English, especially those acting in an official capacity. The Germans found it intriguing, however, and it was brought to the attention of the naval staff and Grand Admiral Alfred Peter von Tirpitz, the patriarch of the fleet. Since Tirpitz and his colleagues were battleship advocates, and the only prewar intelligence estimate of what it would take to enforce a blockade against England called for 221 submarines (Germany entered the hostilities with only nine), it can be assumed that the scheme was still buried far back in their collective naval minds when the guns of August first roared.

Soon, however, everything changed. The great pendulum that was the Schlieffen Plan slowed to a halt, the fighting degenerated into trench warfare, and Germany accumulated in excess of half a million casualties in the first three months. At the same time, the oxymoronic High Seas Fleet barely ever ventured out of sight of land, utterly thwarted by the specter of England's dreadnoughts. Against this grim backdrop the submarine's early successes, though limited, were riveting to a high command looking for a quick way out. The public also liked the submarine, due in part to a carefully mapped propaganda campaign. More to the point, newspaper accounts indicate that a majority wanted the new and powerful weapon set against Britain's merchant shipping without restraint.

For the first months of the Great War, Germany held its submariners strictly to the time-honored prize rules of "detention and search" when they came upon merchant vessels at sea. The relevant international laws, formulated with surface vessels in mind, demanded that transports first be searched for contraband and only sunk after the passengers and crew had been safely put off into boats. In effect, this robbed the submarine of its key advantages of stealth and surprise, while forcing it to surface and operate under conditions that exposed the slow and vulnerable craft to greatly increased levels of danger. The chief reason for adhering to this self-defeating guidance was the Germans' fear of turning neutrals against them. And, although the already pro-British giant far to the West, the United States of America, was hardly foremost in their minds, it would soon loom large.

By the late fall of 1914 the scales of Teutonic policy were plainly tilting in a new direction. In early November the chief of the Naval Staff had decided to urge a program of unrestricted submarine warfare upon the chancellor and the emperor. On December 14, Admiral Tirpitz weighed in with a surprise interview given to the Berlin correspondent for the United Press in which he publicly questioned Germany's submarine policy. "What will America say if we open U-boat warfare against all ships sailing to England and starve it out?" It seemed less like a question than a taunt.

The German press and public were jubilant, but the chancellor, Theobald Bethmann-Hollweg, was appalled, believing the interview was entirely premature and inflammatory. Bethmann-Hollweg was a true insider. His career had been spent in the Prussian civil service and his skills were those of a bureaucrat—parochial manipulation and extreme persuasiveness in small groups. He had no particular grasp of military-technical issues, and his understanding of the submarine was purely that of a generalist. But on these grounds he could certainly see that the momentum for unleashing it was growing irresistible, and therefore avoided open opposition, at least initially.

The die was cast during the first days of February 1915, when Admiral

Friedrich von Ingenohl, the timid commander of the High Seas Fleet, was replaced by the more aggressive Hugo von Pohl. Although the new admiralissimo saw little prospect of going head to head with the Grand Fleet, he was utterly convinced that an underwater assault on British seaborne trade was the key to victory. Consequently, when the kaiser came to Wilhelmshaven on February 4 to review the fleet, Pohl demanded and got approval for declaring the waters around the British Isles a war zone. After February 18 any ship found there, including neutrals, would be sunk. (The inclusion of nonbelligerent vessels arose from the fact that the British Cunard liner *Lusitania* was spotted flying the stars and stripes in the Irish Sea on January 31.) For better or worse, the unrestricted submarine campaign was on.

Was it a good decision? Could it have won the war for Germany? The votes of historians have been decisively cast in the negative, based largely on what they perceive as the capabilities of the available submarines, and the political ramifications of the campaign itself. Both deserve closer examination.

Critical here was the belief that the Germans simply did not have enough undersea craft to do the job. The raw numbers do seem daunting. Whereas Great Britain entered the war with over twelve million tons of merchant shipping, Germany commenced unrestricted submarine warfare with but twenty-one boats, only nine of which were the superior diesel type. To make matters worse, so much time was taken in transit and repair, that only about a third of the total was available to sink ships at any one time.

Like the submarine itself, however, much was concealed beneath the surface of these statistics. Individually, German submarines were proven killers—their torpedoes ran true and were devastatingly powerful; they could lay minefields practically anywhere and remain undetected; the diesel boats had ranges in the thousands of miles and endurance limited only by the staying power of their crews. Technically, U-boats were extraordinarily lethal weapons.

But accumulating enough of them was plainly a problem, though not necessarily an insurmountable one. Initial production was ragged; there were problems with diesel design and fabrication, and inexperienced ship-yards were continually behind schedule. Only eleven boats were delivered in 1914. But, from this point, production began to ramp up until it had at-tained considerable momentum. In 1915 a total of fifty-two new sub-marines were added, and between January and August 1916 a further sixty-one were commissioned. Meanwhile attrition remained very low, since the Royal Navy had little in the way of defenses.

The initial English efforts against the submarine bordered on the laugh-able. Picketboats armed with blacksmiths' hammers were sent out to smash periscopes; attempts were made to catch submarines with nets like cod; sea lions were even trained to seek out unwanted submerged intruders—none of which met more than the slightest degree of success. It took until July 1915 and the formation of the Board on Invention and Research before the English made a wholesale effort to generate effective countermeasures. Even then progress was slow. Only in June 1917 were sufficient quantities of hydrophones (the first workable acoustical detection system) and depth charges available for surface ships to menace submarines consistently. Be-fore that, success against them remained highly problematic. From the be-ginning of the unrestricted campaign to August 1916, Germany lost thirty-three boats, only eighteen of which were confirmed kills. For the fifty-one months of the First World War (including the later stages when defenses were better) the exchange rate was 29.67 merchant ships, or 69,015 tons sunk per U-boat lost. This amounted to a very substantial ad-vantage, which allowed the German Navy to build up U-boats quite rap-idly, until their total in August 1916 stood at 111, with an average of 68 submarines available for the nineteen months beginning in February 1915—probably enough to do the job. But they were not allowed to, and this was a matter of politics.

Unrestricted submarine warfare was undertaken by the German leader-ship with barely any consideration of what the American response might be. They were in for an unpleasant surprise. Woodrow Wilson immediately denounced the decree, threatening to hold the German government "strictly accountable" for the loss of American lives. Nothing of great sig-nificance happened until early May, when the *Lusitania* (no longer flying an

American flag) was sunk by a U-20, killing 1,198, including 128 Americans. Wilson responded with a series of increasingly truculent notes, which culminated in an implied threat of war if the unrestricted submarine campaign persisted. This led directly to the suspension of the program in September 1915. Most historians have judged the Germans prudent and Wilson to have been on firm ground in making the threat—especially considering the decisiveness of America's ultimate intervention.

Yet the state of the United States as a potential belligerent in the summer of 1915 argues strenuously in the opposite direction. While the influence of domestic political disunity and pacifism easily can be exaggerated, it is hard to overestimate the military unpreparedness of the United States at this point. The army was tiny and ill-equipped; the navy focused on relatively useless dreadnoughts; realistic battle plans were lacking; and the arms industry was incapable of producing modern heavy weapons. All of this could be righted, but it would have been time consuming. Even with the benefit of a gradual but significant Preparedness campaign, it required more than a year after the United States' declaration of war in April 1917 before American troops began making a significant difference on the Western Front. In 1915 it would have taken considerably longer. So Wilson's threat was without real substance. America could very well have declared war; but all it had to offer the Allies was a vast pool of untrained bodies. And the Germans should have known as much. The future chancellor, Franz von Papen, an energetic military attaché in Washington at the time—he was soon to be expelled for his espionage activities—was disdainful of America and the threat it posed. While he plainly overestimated the degree of pro-German sentiment, he had access to a network of informants and must have been aware of the true state of American military weakness. It was obvious.

Yet on the other side of the Atlantic, German decision-making was hermetically sealed, far more subject to influence than information. The key was the kaiser, who retained ultimate authority over all decisions relating to foreign and military policy. But Wilhelm was at this point a pathetic figure, still pompous, but terrified of losing his throne and ready to jump at the advice of the last courtier who caught his ear. Bethmann-Hollweg, on the other hand, knew exactly what he wanted and was a master of isolating his prey and enforcing his opinions. Not only was he convinced that the submarine campaign could not prove decisive against England; but he was certain that it would draw the United States into the war, with inevitably disastrous consequences for Germany. He may well have been correct on the issue of America going to war; but there is good reason to believe his judgment was seriously flawed on the technical matters of the submarine's capabilities and the potential U.S. impact on the battlefield. Meanwhile, he was virtually without allies. The press, the public, and the Reichstag were solidly behind unrestricted submarine warfare. And among the inner circle, where it really mattered, his only support came from Admiral Georg Alexander von Muller, the chief of the Naval Cabinet, a secondary figure at best. Nonetheless, Bethmann-Hollweg, through sheer force of personality, managed to win over Erich von Falkenhayn, the all-important chief of staff of the army, and then use him in a successful assault on the pliant kaiser. It was a virtuoso performance, and also an unlikely one. Germany, already up to its neck in blood and desperation, allowed itself to be shorn of its most valuable weapon—which, after all, killed only in the thousands rather than the millions already lost on the Western Front—all because of the persuasiveness of a single individual who took advantage of a closed decision-making process, a weak monarch, and arguing on the basis of questionable information. Without Bethmann-Hollweg, everything might have been different.

So, as the basis of our counterfactual analysis, Bethmann-Hollweg will be removed from the scene on May 10, 1915—a victim at age fifty-nine (he actually died only six years later in 1921) of a fatal heart attack brought on by overwork and, suitably enough, concern over the *Lusitania* sinking. Among the inner circle, only Muller's dissenting voice is left, Falkenhayn and the kaiser remain on board, and the campaign rolls on with no apparent source of opposition.

Success follows in its wake. Backed by unwavering support, monthly scores could be expected to have accelerated from 127,000 tons in May (actual) to around 250,000 tons in August (183,000 actual). At this point the total of boats stabilized at around 58 until the first part of 1916, so it makes sense to keep the scores steady at a quarter million ton per month for the remainder of 1915. Since the next eight months roughly doubled the flotilla to 111, a steady increase in kills up to 550,000 tons seems reasonable. (If these figures seem high, it should be remembered that actual U-boat sinkings peaked in April 1917 at 860,000 tons, achieved with a flotilla of 156 submarines.) The net result from this nineteen-month campaign would have been roughly 5.3 million tons sunk.

Yet based on the actual facts, the British reaction can be projected to have been fatally sluggish. The admiralty had only a vague idea of the shipping situation, since it failed to keep the necessary statistics. Hence, it remained blissfully unaware of both the precipitous drop in replacement merchant ship construction during the 1915–16 period and the submarine-induced congestion in ports, which was estimated to have reduced the annual carrying capacity of the ships affected by as much as 20 percent. (The submarines never posed an effective challenge to the transport of troops to the Continent, since the English Channel was well patrolled, heavily mined, and blocked by obstacles such as nets.) The added pressure of a truly unrestricted submarine campaign might have added to an intuitive sense of a brewing crisis; but, without access to the necessary figures, the admiralty would have had little way of understanding how truly desperate their situation was becoming. To further compound matters, British naval authorities could be depended on to have refused to take the critical step necessary to save themselves, the introduction of merchant convoys. Prior to the Battle of Jutland on the last day of May 1916, the combat readiness of the battleships of the Grand Fleet at Scapa was universally considered vital. Therefore, any request to detach even some of its seventy to eighty destroyers for convoy escort duty would have been summarily rejected. (Even after the disastrous month of April 1917, the admiralty only reluctantly acceded to convoys on the insistence of Prime Minister David Lloyd George.) So the noose would have tightened silently and rapidly around the condemned, with little prospect of the rope being broken.

Meanwhile, the sheer futility of the war's major events during the first six months of 1916 take on added significance, hammer blows to the morale of all participants. Although the United States declares war against

Germany at the beginning of January, it refuses to send troops immediately and has virtually no impact on the conflict during the months that follow. The horrific stalemate at Verdun softens up not only the French but the Germans, who are led to believe victory is imminent. For the British population the news of the disappointment of July 1, 1916, at the Somme, coming on top of the letdown of Jutland, is just too much. The combination of a diminished food supply and widespread hoarding results in a sudden perception of mass starvation. On July 6, food riots break out in Liverpool and spread quickly to every major urban center. Looting follows; martial law is declared, and 350 are shot by the Home Guard on the night of July 7. Two days later a general strike paralyzes the country and then spreads to the troops on the Somme, who stage a passive mutiny; plans for a renewal of the offensive are cancelled. On July 14 Prime Minister Herbert Asquith informs the king and the Russian and French ambassadors that Britain can no longer continue the war, upon which the Cabinet resigns. The king promptly asks David Lloyd George to form a government and then charges him with negotiating a peace settlement. Reluctant to give up the ghost on Bastille Day, the French hang on one day longer, declaring a unilateral cease-fire beginning on July 15. The Russians follow suit on July 17, and the czar abdicates. One week later progressive forces in the Duma form a provisional government dedicated to democratic principles under liberal Prince Georgi Lvov. Aleksandr Kerensky is appointed chief of the peace commission. In Washington, Woodrow Wilson declares the Great War "effectively over," and offers his services to preside over the formation of a "just and lasting peace"—a proposal for which there is little enthusiasm elsewhere.

Germany stands victorious on all fronts; yet events prove it to be in no mood to ratify its peace plans. On July 19 the kaiser and the high command outline their terms, which include the annexation of Belgium, painful territorial concessions by France and Russia, the partition of the British Empire, and in particular, a German mandate over Canada—this last thrown in by the kaiser. To ensure their acceptance, German troops are ordered to ignore the cease-fire and ready themselves for a "crushing offensive." Instead, they are swept by a sit-down strike, which the officer corps proves unable to quell. Fraternization between German and Allied troops becomes general, and within a week the various fronts cease to exist. A general strike sweeps Germany, and on July 25 the Social Democrats publish their own peace terms based on status quo antebellum and an immediate national referendum. The kaiser orders Philipp Scheidemann and the Socialist leadership arrested, but instead is himself forced to flee the country.

With progressive elements in power among all the major belligerents, the so-called Third Hague Conference proves remarkably free of recriminations. Although it is later seen as postponing the inevitable, the general principle of "no territorial gains" prevails. Initially, there is strong sentiment for arms limitation, but only chemical warfare is banned. Overall limitations on the size of armies and navies are stipulated, but these are so generous that no European power ever actually exceeds them. American president Woodrow Wilson comes to the conference with high hopes and proposals for an international governing body and diplomatic negotiations open to public scrutiny. But the United States' marginal role in the fighting ensures he will be roundly ignored. To compound Wilson's humiliation, in the midst of the conference he is voted out of office and returns home a bitter and defeated man. His replacement, jurist Charles Evans Hughes, divorces himself from the proceedings and the United States never signs the treaty.

On the basis of such a denouement, the subsequent course of the twentieth century might well have looked a good deal different—still turbulent but not nearly so cataclysmic. Arguably, the net effect of the Great War would have been not simply the deromanticizing of militarism, but the spread of democratic regimes robust enough to resist its siren song. Very likely the process in Russia would not have been smooth, especially given the probability that major parts of the former czarist empire, such as Poland and the Ukraine, would strike for independence. Nevertheless, the Bolshevik revolution almost certainly would not have happened, effectively aborting international Communism as a philosophy of the underdog. In the Middle East the survival under the secular Ataturk of a greater Turkey that would still encompass much of the old Ottoman empire might have more effectively spread modernization, representative government, and, down the line, headed off Islamic fundamentalism. Further west, it becomes possible to draw the rapprochement of a politically and economically stable France and Germany back from the 1950s and '60s to the '20s and '30s. The breeding ground for general war is transformed into a pillar against it, and Adolf Hitler, World War II, the Holocaust, and even nuclear weapons fade from the pages of history. Meanwhile Britain, the Great War's biggest loser, very probably would have been forced to face up to the incongruities of its imperial system and begun the process of decolonialization much sooner, forcing the other European powers to follow suit. Without these burdens, the English might have avoided or, at least, mitigated the half-century economic funk from which they have only recently emerged. Certainly, not having to fight World War II would have helped.

Of course not everything would necessarily have turned out for the better. America, thwarted by its experience with European politics, likely would not simply have turned inward. Rather, it might have looked southward and laid a heavier and not necessarily more beneficial hand on Latin American developments. Almost certainly its gaze would have been focused on the Far East and Japanese military expansion. Given domestic attitudes and the aggressiveness of Japan, a major military confrontation seems almost inevitable—perhaps as soon as the 1930s. The United States would have won, but also found itself thrust in the midst of turmoil, as anticolonialism and nationalism worked its way across the Asian rim. Under the circumstances, it follows that Americans would have been perceived as imperialists and suffered consequences not so different from what actually happened in Korea and Vietnam. Yet Americans would not have been alone.

Overall, it is logical that a different end to the Great War only would have hastened a fundamental North-South split, instead of an East-West one. The absence of a Second World War and more uninterrupted economic growth in the North, along with hastened decolonialization and nationalism in the South would have fostered and intensified perceptions of exploitation and racial tension. In the absence of Marxism-Leninism, leaders of the South would have had to look to another source for a unifying developmental philosophy. Were we all to have been very lucky, it might have been Gandhi—but the alternatives are mostly far less benign. Meanwhile, all of us would still be faced with the underlying problems of the North-South relationship: overpopulation, gross inequality, and ecological degradation. A better end to the Great War might have taken the edge off the rest of the twentieth century, but we would not have escaped its most profound contradictions.

GEORGE FEIFER

# NO FINLAND STATION

*A Russian Revolution without Lenin?*

Vladimir Lenin's domination of the Bolsheviks he led to power—"willed" might be a better word—was total, and in a way that had never been known before. "No other political party," the historian Orlando Figes writes, "had been so closely tied to the personality of one man." Impatient and acerbic, perpetually angry, Lenin did not tolerate dissent: There was no way but his. Moral choice (or immoral, as the case might be) was resolved by force of character—his. He was never one to mix personal feelings with impersonal fact. "I can't listen to music too often," he once commented mirthlessly after he had been forced to sit through a concert. "It makes me want to say kind, stupid things, and pat the heads of people. But now you have to beat them on the head, beat them without mercy." He trafficked in abstractions and treated human beings, indeed entire populations, as if they were boxcars in a switching yard. And yet this man of few contradictions was a natural leader, whose obsession would sweep along hundreds at first and, eventually, millions. Lenin's single-minded inflexibility would influence the future of most of the world, now almost entirely to its regret. Can history demonstrate a better example of winning through intimidation?

Had there been no Lenin, or a Lenin who showed up in St. Petersburg late, there might have been no Bolshevik revolution of October 1917, and perhaps no revolution ever. Whenever events center on a single individual, the counterfactual scenarios multiply. In Lenin's case, most center on timing, both before his arrival and after. Once the czar abdicated in February, to be replaced by a democratic *provisional government, Lenin's dilemma was how to get from his base in Zurich to the Russian capital: Hundreds of miles of Germany and Austria-Hungary, Russia's enemies, intervened. The professional revolutionary, who had spent more than a third of his life in exile and had not been in Russia for eleven years, considered his options, none of them satisfactory. Should he attempt to go via England? That scenario he ruled out because the British had a record of detaining Russian Marxists. He even considered hiring a plane to fly him to the homeland he barely knew any longer. He abandoned the idea as being too impractical and dangerous. Lenin, who thought nothing of condemning others to death and who would soon institute a system of state terror, was something of a coward—as one associate put it, he had "an anxiety for self-preservation." Here the Germans came to the rescue with their famous "sealed train." What if they had not done so? Or if the Provisional Government had rejected its notorious passenger before he reached St. Petersburg's Finland Station? What would Russia (and by extension, the whole world) have been like if Lenin had been delayed until the time was no longer ripe for his messianic vision?*

GEORGE FEIFER is the author of eight books on Russia, including *Justice in Moscow, Moscow Farewell,* and *Red Files*. Since his first visit in 1959, he has lived there extensively; he spent a year as a graduate student at Moscow University. His most recent book is *The Battle of Okinawa*.

*The comrades all groped about in darkness until Lenin's arrival.*

—Bolshevik Ludmilla Stal, 1917

*The uprising's object is to seize power. Its political task will be clarified after the seizure. . . . The people have the right and duty to solve such questions not by voting but by force.*

—Lenin, shortly after returning to Russia in 1917

VLADIMIR LENIN may be said to have lived his forty-seven years for his return to Russia in 1917. A week before departing, the reckless extremist, as most of the few Russians who knew of his existence regarded him, had been stewing in frustration some 1,500 miles from St. Petersburg, with a huge obstacle in between. Stuck in Zurich, the Bolshevik party's founder and guiding spirit had every reason to bite his nails in fear of missing an opportunity of which not even he, the supreme political fantasist, had dreamed mere years before. The route devised for slipping him through the mighty obstacle and into the Russian capital's ferment was a highly risky gamble—and even if it paid off, his further plans hung on extremely doubtful chance.

His last visit to St. Petersburg had been during the 1905 Revolution. Slinking back to Western Europe in its embers, the master of splinter-group polemics spent the intervening dozen years dispatching fierce but insignificant denunciations to less relentless Continental revolutionaries. (He was utterly alone in visualizing backward Russia, rather than the most advanced European powers specified by Marxism, serving as the spearhead of the world's proletariat.) Unable to handpick all his lieutenants from his refugees in exile, the lover of absolutes and controller of his fringe movement's every possible aspect greeted those who had managed to make their way out of Russia with bullying attacks on any deviation from his views. *Renegades! Traitors!*

What if he'd lived amid the give and take of Russia's rapidly changing political and social realities instead of watching from a distance that inevitably simplified them? Actually, his brief Russian stay from 1905 to 1906 was his single break in seventeen years of foreign exile, beginning in 1900. For years before the outbreak of World War I, the dogged political Quixote wondered whether he'd ever again set foot on Russian soil. His chances of doing that seemed as slight as his ideas were cosmic. But now, after three years of that calamitous war and the revolution they triggered—the one that toppled the czar and his government in February 1917—the prophet tasted validation and power. His primary instinct—to snatch the latter as quickly as possible, *then* carry out his program—would astonish even his closest collaborators. It set him apart from all other revolutionary thinkers, especially after taking him from scholarly/journalistic disputation to chiefly *doing*, and in the most opportunistic ways.

The gaping obstacle on his return route was the Germany that couldn't be fully trusted even in her exhausting third year of war with his Russia. Imperial Germany's military and civil burdens had become enormous. The kaiser, his ministers, and the General Staff had ever more reason to see the fighting on two fronts—in this case, both hugely draining—as the long-predicted national disaster.

Yes, good things were happening on the Eastern one. The Romanov dynasty had collapsed, and the Russian army, whose 1916 "Brusilov offensive" had at last threatened, albeit momentarily, to become the feared "steamroller," was disintegrating. That was what had delivered the final blow to the disastrously inflexible Nicholas II, who abdicated when popular opposition to him gained an unstoppable momentum. But the Reichswehr, well aware of Russians' ability to endure and prevail even after ghastly losses, remained apprehensive, all the more because the new St. Petersburg government was sworn to continue fighting. Thus the obvious motive for permitting and facilitating an enemy national's travel through the German heartland: Lenin, who called himself a "professional revolutionary," might serve a subversive purpose.

THE GOD THAT ALMOST FAILED

*Vladimir Lenin addresses a crowd, in a painting that has less to do with reality than iconography. Luck had been on his side, in the form of the German government's decision in the spring of 1917 to whisk him on the famous "sealed train" from his Swiss exile to Petrograd.*

(Alexander Gerasimov, 1881–1963, *Lenin at the Tribune*. Tretyakov Gallery, Moscow. Scala/Art Resource, NY)

But what if Berlin had made a more enlightened decision? What if the government there *hadn't* permitted his return to St. Petersburg in the celebrated "sealed train" because it had thought more carefully about Germany's future? World War II's devastation and the Cold War's rending would remind succeeding generations of suffering Germans that subversion, like poison gas, tends to spread beyond its intended limits. The ultimate goal for Russia of a German government that took that menace into account would have been nearly opposite: a *stable* state with which to negotiate and settle conflicts peacefully and efficiently. But wartime Germany had neither the luxury nor the foresight to act in its long-term national interests. Instead, it opened a switch to Lenin that otherwise would have been carefully closed: a gift of chance in what would become an implausible series of them.

In the late winter of 1916 to 1917, secret exchanges between Wilhelmstrasse, its ambassadors in Bern and elsewhere, and the General Staff confirmed, as one put it, that "We must now definitely try to create the utmost chaos in Russia. . . . Our support of the extreme [Russian] elements is preferable, because that way the work is done more thoroughly. . . . According to all forecasts, we count on the disintegration being so far advanced in three months or so that our military intervention will guarantee the collapse of Russian power." An official deal was therefore struck with St. Petersburg to exchange German nationals interned in Russia for Marxist exiles in Switzerland, who were given the permission and means for transit.

But there are of course two sides to every bargain, and this one was clearly unappealing to Russia. What if her new government hadn't entered into it? More experienced leaders probably wouldn't have. Nor less idealistic ones. A tad more caution might have kept them from authorizing the return of the exile whose intentions they knew far better than any German did, thanks to czarist police reports. Nevertheless, they threw open another switch for Lenin's revolutionary fervor, thanks not only to the paralysis that often overcomes democratic politicians who are faced by the old and enduring dilemma of what to do with people who advocate nondemocratic methods. That was stiffened by the lifetime of repression by czarist officials that made their replacements particularly loath to limit Russia's new freedoms of travel and speech. Another circumstance, another chance. Besides, the new government believed it had little to fear from the impossible zealot, especially because his enemy-assisted journey would surely put him in disgrace with a population whose wartime suffering had intensified its enmity toward Germany. And in addition to everything else, the government's authority and power were challenged by a rival Russian body, as we're about to see.

None of that, however, spared Ilich, as hundreds of millions would soon call him in reverent tenderness, from apprehension that the switches were being opened to a trap and imprisonment rather than to the political battleground he yearned to enter. His rail journey in a single-carriage train— its "sealed" label applied because the German authorities accepted his demand that no outsider enter for any reason—would take him from Gottmadingen near the Swiss border almost due north to Frankfurt, then northeast to Berlin, and further up to the Baltic coast. The "bald, stocky, sturdy" man whose forehead reminded Maxim Gorky of Socrates wore a three-piece suit and bowler hat that spoke of the comfortable birth he shared with many other revolutionaries. Leaving Bern on April 13 [April 1 according to the Russian calendar then in use], he remained on guard throughout the two-day trip, and not only against external enemies, for his personal habits were worthy of the keenest missionary. Detesting the corridor drinking and singing of some of his thirty-odd fellow exiles, he permitted his small entourage to smoke only in the lavatory, use of which he gave priority to the nonsmokers. Such dictates, a fellow Bolshevik would quip, prepared him to assume the leadership of the Russian government.

But the exiles went unchallenged during their uneventful trip across much of Germany's north-south axis. (To keep it smooth, a train of the crown prince was delayed some two hours near Berlin.) Continuing over water by ferry, they proceeded up to neutral Sweden for their route's final leg, which was again northeast, via Finland. An advance welcoming party met the new train at the Finnish border. It included Lev Kamenev, who would become deputy chairman of the USSR Council of People's Commissars before Stalin had him executed in 1936. Now Kamenev was high on the editorial board of the formerly underground *Pravda*, the ban on which had been lifted a month after the February Revolution and a month before now, as Lenin's return neared completion. The star passenger hardly resumed his seat in the carriage before chiding Kamenev for his insufficiently revolutionary line. The party newspaper, operating beyond Lenin's control, had been cautious. With the Bolsheviks so outnumbered—no more than 40,000 adherents nationwide—Kamenev, like all other party leaders to one degree or another, advocated cooperation with other Socialist parties while revolutionary prospects ripened, as they were expected to do. Ilich, however, saw that as heresy. Cordial as he was to the comrades who'd come to greet him, he seethed internally. For it was time, as he'd written just before embarking on this unlikely trip, for the Russian proletariat to seize power, "with the people armed to a man."

If that daring now sounds unremarkable, even expected as a core assumption of Marxism-Leninism, it is thanks only to the inevitability that historical events acquire when viewed in retrospect. To those who read it then and there, the call to armed action was outlandish, even in that day when street orators touted all manner of weird delivery from Russia's troubles. Her other political activists, somber and discordant as many were, believed in an entirely different approach. Apart from the extreme right that aspired to restore the monarchy, they were struggling, among other things, to become practicing democrats by *sharing* power.

Whether they'd have succeeded if not for Lenin will of course never be known. But if they had, the rewards would have been huge. Alexis de Tocqueville, the author of the justly acclaimed *Democracy in America*, had reasons to predict that a second country, although started from a very different place, seemed headed toward great prominence among nations. While free-wheeling America was tackling the frontier, slovenly Russia was bogged down in autocracy—yet she too showed immense promise during the late nineteenth and early twentieth centuries. Compared with Western Europe, the Empire remained retarded in many ways, especially in its political social development, which the benighted czar was sworn to thwart. But it's not too much to speak of an explosion of energy in other areas. Literacy was soaring, along with education in general and commercial development, particularly industrial. With no help from the throne, the judicial system operated independently and reasonably well. Russia had surged to the fore-front—or was making her way in that direction—in literature, the visual arts, music, theater, film, and ballet. Her resources were vast and creative talents remarkable; her scientific, technological, and industrial capacities revealed ever more potential as they raced ahead. Full of excitement despite the proverbial Russian passiveness and restraints—or because of them, thanks to the zest that can follow awakening—the country had taken off toward almost certain realization of de Tocqueville's vision.

It "only" remained to establish and secure a suitable political structure and civil society—the chances of which were fair to good, despite the hugely divisive pressures generated by the staggeringly costly Great War. So suggested the course of Russian history until now, especially after the lifting of the Romanov burden, because it resembled Western Europe's, however much delayed, in certain critical ways. The rooting of the education, training, and ideals of the great majority of Russian leaders and opinion-makers in European patterns and standards also justified guarded optimism. Enormous social and economic rewards beckoned if the country could keep to its present road, curvy and unfamiliar as it was. That road not taken remains among the great might-have-beens of the century just ended.

It also explains a good part of the bewilderment prompted by Lenin's summons now, in 1917. Didn't he understand, for a start, from *whom* he proposed seizing power? Not from the wholly discredited Nicholas II or his ancien régime, because those old oppressors had been gone since February. Free of the autocracy at last, the new Russia was enjoying elements of the democracy of which all progressive and radical parties had dreamed seemingly forever. That was why the infant republic, wobbly as it was in its attempts to establish a better new order, emanated more promise than foreboding. Leon Trotsky, the brilliant writer and orator who had played a larger role in the 1905 Revolution than Lenin (whose dictatorial qualities he criticized at the time, before he himself became a ruthless Leninist) called her the freest country in the world.

That freedom was much enhanced by governmental omission and contradiction, for this was the curious "dual power" interval, when its two fragile sources lived in a kind of uneasy truce, now competing, now cooperating. One of them, the Provisional Government that had "graduated" from the Duma (parliament) witlessly hobbled by the fatally obscurantist Nicholas, met in the Marinsky Palace. To the degree that anything was strictly legal in the transition to undetermined permanent arrangements, that generally centrist coalition was the czarist government's legitimate successor. The second source, the predominantly Socialist Soviet of Workers' and Soldiers' Deputies, was a more self-assertive rebirth of the assembly that had constituted itself, of course without the czar's authorization, during the 1905 revolution, after which it was repressed. Its members were elected by spontaneously formed local councils—"soviets"—that more or less represented "the masses." The Petrograd Soviet, as it was also called, met in the Tauride Palace, less than an hour's walk from the Provisional Government.

Although two sets of rival authorities governing a country so much in flux was confusing, everyone knew the Provisional Government, led largely by liberal Duma veterans, was well to the right of the looser congregation of "the people's" representatives. Therefore, it's no surprise that Lenin's revolutionary presumption was anathema to the former body—but it also shocked its much more radical sibling. Virtually everyone in the latter, even the Marxists—including the Bolshevik Marxists who'd been working in Russia, beyond the influence of his personal prodding—considered seizing power a foolish daydream. But that left him the passenger in the curious train as undaunted as did the complexities of the maelstrom he was about to enter and long odds against his ambition.

Reports reaching Zurich of prominent Bolsheviks compromising for the sake of Socialist unity had made him squirm. Lenin's long history of excoriating opponents and manipulating followers convinced Georgy Plekhanov, one of the fathers of (nonviolent) Russian Marxism, that he saw all unity as a piece of bread he was swallowing. Now Lenin considered collaboration with anyone not prepared to support immediate revolution fraudulent and impossible. The Volga-born sage had the answer to the old question of "What's to Be Done?" about Russia's backwardness and malaise. His "scientific" vision and unshakable willpower would set the country straight—if, that is, he wouldn't be arrested upon arrival and delivered to the Russian capital's grim Peter and Paul Fortress. That was where his revered elder brother Alexander had been imprisoned thirty years earlier, before being hung for an attempt on the czar's life. (That trauma advanced Vladimir, then seventeen years old, from a dissident to a revolutionary.

What if Alexander's life had been spared and Vladimir didn't swear to take revenge?)

To his relief, nothing of the kind awaited the surviving younger brother now. The Provisional Government had no plans to curtail his freedom, even though it knew he'd accepted German financial aid for his trip (which is not to say, as many historians still do, that he was a German agent).

Lenin's new train pulled into the Finland Station in Petrograd, as the capital had been rechristened in the war-beset Motherland's purging of its German names, in the late evening of April 16 (April 3, old style). The eternal belligerent who had come to preach force was apparently embarrassed by a bouquet of flowers handed him by Alexandra Kollontai, a follower soon to become notorious for championing "free love," as if that were the sum of her political activity. Apart from that, he had utterly no doubt about the country's need—nor, for that matter, the world's. That supreme confidence alone was unique, even—this merits repetition—to his narrow group of relatively disorganized fellow radicals. In fact, that confidence had never been greater. For the relatively inconsequential Marxist theorist was about to metamorphose into a preeminent fighter in the political combat of the here and now. He was ready to "bring down Marxism's ten commandments from Mount Sinai," as an early follower would put it, and hand them to Russia's young. *Action at last!*

Just after 11 P.M., the exhilarated traveler rushed from the train into the station, where Nikolai Chkheidze, the chairman of the Petrograd Soviet—the Provisional government's rival on the left—welcomed his "comrade" on behalf of "the entire revolution." Chkheidze also cautioned, however, that the revolution's chief tasks at the moment were to make common cause to strengthen itself and defend against "every kind of attack, both from within and from without."

Although Chkheidze's work exposing and opposing the woeful czarist government had earned him the title of the "papa" of the February Revolution, it was enough for him to be a Menshevik for Ilich to despise him. The Mensheviks were the Bolsheviks' more moderate and numerous Marxist rivals, although Lenin, with his genius for propaganda, had branded them with their name, which derived from the Russian for "minority." Even worse than being a Menshevik, Chkheidze had been appealing for a closing ranks in defense of "our revolution"—meaning the essentially democratic one embracing all the reformist parties—instead of igniting what Lenin saw as the second one needed to overthrow it. (Alternatively, he sometimes called the February upheaval the "first stage" of the full revolution.) Ignoring the chairman's judicious greeting, he hurried outside to the station square, where Bolshevik colleagues had organized a demonstration of several thousand sympathizers, many waving red flags. A band struck up the Marseillaise when he appeared, then went quiet, the better for a call for the class war on which Lenin had raised himself to resound. Saluting his "dear comrades, soldiers, sailors, and workers," his confident, upper-class stridency leaped to attack "the robbers' imperialist war." "Any day . . . the crash of all European imperialism may come. . . . The Russian revolution you made has begun that and opened a new epoch. Hail the worldwide socialist revolution!"

The worldwide socialist revolution? No participant in the February one saw that as even faintly imminent. A scattering of fellow Bolsheviks did occasionally evoke it as a never-quite-believable goal, but it was always that remote. Still, Lenin pounded his message into his captivated audience. Fight. Fight for the ultimate good, for the great second revolution that would bring the highest human happiness. Ridicule and destroy every less radical approach. Consign even the non-Bolshevik majority in the predominately Socialist Soviet to the class enemy's camp, as if they were no better than czarist minions. Gorky would later write that the deskbound, print-fixated crusader's limitless ignorance of daily existence and sufferings gave him a "pitiless contempt, worthy of a nobleman, for the lives of the ordinary people." Of course the contrary can still be argued: that Lenin's every act, however mistaken or ugly, was motivated by a desire to improve precisely those lives. But Gorky's further observation that "life in all its complexity" was unknown to him is hard to dispute.

The city's Bolshevik leadership had been driven to the square in armored cars decked with red banners. Their crews helped Lenin mount one of them. When its projector threw a beam into the dark night, a witness in whose ears his proclamation of a worldwide Socialist revolution still rang saw the effect as brilliantly symbolic of the arming for which Ilich had called, together with changing the party's name to "Communist."

The Bolshevik party had installed its headquarters in the mansion of a former mistress of the still-uncomprehending Nicholas II, who was now under a kind of house arrest in Tsarskoye Selo, the "Tsar's Village," outside Petrograd. She was Mathilde Ksheinskaya, the glorious dancer. When the same armored car rushed Lenin from the station square to that "satin nest of a court ballerina," to use Trotsky's image of the unlikely site, a national party conference was still in session, having just approved a policy of making common cause with other Socialist parties. From the train to the tussle, to adopt an old Russian saying about newcomers to a crucial scene. Lenin's single-mindedness had never been sharper or more stunning. He rose to denounce the agreed strategy. Bolsheviks should work not for a parliamentary system but for "a republic of soviets of workers', soldiers' and peasants' deputies throughout the land."

A member of another Marxist party, whose invitation that evening represented the kind of discipline breach Lenin detested, was stupefied. The speech "shook and astonished not only me, a heretic accidentally thrown into the delirium, but also the faithful, all of them." It seemed as if a "spirit of universal destruction, knowing no obstacles, doubts, human difficulties, or human considerations" had risen from its lairs. Another distinguished observer felt he'd been "flogged over the head with a flail. Only one thing was clear: there was no place for me, a nonparty man, beside Lenin."

But there was also no place then for most fellow party members. The following day, a conference of Bolsheviks, Mensheviks, and representatives of radical splinter parties convened to consider unifying their actions. When Lenin more or less repeated to the mixed members his summons of the previous evening, an old Bolshevik who'd long supported his hard lines expressed a general outrage by piercingly denouncing "the delirium of a madman." E. H. Carr, historian of the revolution, would call Lenin "completely isolated" at this juncture. Once again, solid Bolshevik opinion opposed what *Pravda* called his "unacceptable" ideas. After discussion, his own party's Petrograd committee rejected them by a vote of 13 to 2. What

if that overwhelming majority included someone with enough skill and de‐
termination to control Lenin's obsessiveness?

But chance was still favoring him in unpredictable ways. The disap‐
proval by even his own fellow Bolsheviks further dimmed the perception of
the danger he posed. It wouldn't have been too late to counter that by ex‐
pelling or otherwise silencing him. On the contrary, now may have been
the best time for that, after his full and blatant profession of outlandish dis‐
dain for any kind of accommodation, all forms of the overwhelmingly de‐
sired democracy. Besides, his own party's rejection of that might have, at
that point, inoculated it against that ultimate, irreversible extremism. But
the Provisional Government made no effort to defend itself. Another un‐
predictable circumstance; another opportunity bestowed on him, this one
by default of the opposition—which remained inert in the face of ever‐
increasing provocation during the following days. For Lenin's answer to
*Pravda*'s admonition was to attack the newspaper for failing to understand
that the Provisional Government *must be taken down* because it was capi‐
talist.

He kept to his habit of putting his views on paper. Much of the "April
Theses," as his "On the Proletariat's Tasks in the Present Revolution"
would become known when codified by Soviet rule, was devoted to con‐
demning Russia's "predatory imperialist war," for which no effort and "not
the slightest concession" should be made. That went with reiteration of his
larger arguments against "the government of capitalists, the worst enemies
of peace and Socialism." "The specific feature of Russia's present situation
is that it represents a *transition* from the first stage of the revolution . . . *to
the second stage*, which must place power in the hands of the proletariat and
the poorest strata of the peasantry." Thus "no support for the Provisional
government; the utter falsity of all its promises should be explained. . . . Ex‐
posure in place of the impermissible, illusion‐breeding 'demand' that *this*
government, a government of capitalists, should *cease* to be imperialist."

Since Russia's future turned almost entirely on whether she could manage
to construct a political order the majority would accept and respect, further
examination of why other radicals considered such talk utterly wrong seems

merited. Writing in exile fifteen years later—and eight before his murder by an agent of Stalin—Trotsky gave the broad answer: "For the others at that time, the revolution's development was identical with a strengthening of the democracy," meaning the fruit of the February Revolution. That went without saying for the conservatives, liberals, and nonrevolutionary Socialists. But the Marxists' reasons for opposing the use of force to overthrow the government of a country so relatively backward in economic development were even more absolute. For no nation was supposed to have—no, *couldn't* have—a Socialist revolution until capitalism had incubated the conditions for it. That came from Marx himself, after all. It followed from his dictums that every society's "economic structure . . . independent of human will . . . determines the general character of the social, political and spiritual processes" and that "no social order ever disappears before all the productive forces for which it has room have been developed." Of course the Provisional Government was "capitalist." Every political system *had* to reflect its economic foundation, just as real life, here meaning the ownership and workings of the means of production, determined political attitudes. Mass allegiance to socialism would surely—but only—be generated by capitalism's full flowering.

That was central to Marxism's foundation. It was what made the axioms "scientific," the observations and predictions being based not on subjective opinion or wishful thinking but on the undeniable, always-formative reality of economic workings and appetites. That wasn't a mere theory, like those that had been advanced and disproved during all of human history before Marx divined the ultimate pattern of its development, but bedrock reality. It was an essential canon of *The Answer* that comforted and inspired Marxists with conviction that socialism was historically inevitable, since "state forms are rooted in the material conditions of life" and the progression to higher and higher stages—from prefeudalism to socialism—was inexorable just because it was driven by iron *economic* imperatives. But Russia's conditions were far from ready for the final (supposedly easy) shift to socialism, nor had anything remotely approaching a revolutionary majority been massed. That was precisely what Lenin himself had been instructing—years earlier, of course, when all such rumination was profoundly abstract; when a Bolshevik seizure of power in czarist Russia was as likely as a speech from one of the angels who danced on pin heads. And it was hardly more likely now, except to Lenin alone, since more or less liberated capitalism and the "bourgeois-liberal" state that Marxist dogma decreed it must serve had been achieved only two months ago, with the February Revolution.

The April Theses were unacceptable, *Pravda*'s April 21 issue declared, because they "start[ed] from the view that the bourgeois-democratic revolution has ended." That was the argument not of effete liberals but of the stalwarts of Lenin's own grouping. But he didn't care. Infant bourgeois democracy *would* soon be ended—by him. For much as he too believed in "scientific Marxism," he tossed it overboard when he—at that point still alone—glimpsed an opportunity for a shortcut. His impatience to reach "history's highest goal," to put the best light on his deepest intention, or his evangelical arrogance and intolerance, which may have had more to do with it, took over. Or his unconscious yearning for revenge, if that applied.

His replies to the charge of betraying Marx might seem laughable if so much pain hadn't been coming. The sophistry of his justification would matter enormously to the world because it mattered so little to him.

But it didn't yet matter much because his was still a very much minority opinion in a minority party on the periphery of Russian political thought and activity. What if a series of unlikely boosts didn't now advance that still-outrageous opinion? Lenin's attempt to rework Marxism would have never advanced more than it already was from the Finland Station: a matter of inches or feet, metaphorically speaking, in Russia's immense landmass.

As it happened, the seven-month zigzag to the second Bolshevik revolution went far less smoothly than the journey in the sealed train. At first, Ilich pulled a number of people his way, if slowly. He was a mediocre speaker but a bruising debater. His incessant castigation of the Provisional Government—which he called a "stinking corpse," borrowing an admirer's characterization of nonrevolutionary German Social Democracy—began to work on the Petrograd Soviet, especially as resentment grew of the still-sacrificial war against the Central Powers. At the same time, his exhortations and reproaches began drawing Bolsheviks away from the fragmentary Socialist unity the Soviet had so far prided itself on for maintaining.

The first Congress of Soviets—a gathering of representatives of similar councils in various regions—was convened in June, two months after his arrival. During the course of an address, one of its democratically inclined speakers implied that no single party was prepared to assume sole responsibility for governing—to which eager Lenin famously replied "There *is* such a party!" But that too represented his chutzpah more than any reality: The Bolsheviks were still a small minority in that Congress, and even smaller in the country as a whole. Despite their growing popularity, they'd won no election in any city. Much worse for them, Lenin had cause to fear for his life by late the following month.

In July, workers and soldiers, some partially organized by low-level Bolshevik organizations, instigated mass demonstrations. Above all, the so-called "July Days" of feverish protest and violence on the streets were a reaction against the disastrous pursuit of the war. Now Lenin's prospects plummeted. The participation of military units in the disorder boosted ministerial fear of fatal insurrection, while press and popular censure of the Bolsheviks much diminished their appeal. Finally acknowledging the danger Lenin posed to it, the Provisional Government cracked down on his party and ordered his arrest.

What if a more alert police had performed that arrest quickly instead of setting out, or failing to, with hardly uncommon Russian inefficiency? Would the October Revolution have been launched if Lenin were now taken into custody, as lesser Bolshevik leaders were? Very doubtfully, to put it mildly; doubtful even that the party would have continued to consider the "second" revolution. But Lenin slipped the noose, thanks not only to police delay but also a last-minute warning by a sympathizer in the Ministry of Justice. That added a car-chase element to his sequence of "what ifs?": His escape turned on a lost or gained hour, depending on one's view of him.

Disguising himself as a workman, he slipped back into Finland for refuge. Despite his political daring that took people's breath away, the great polemicist wasn't blessed with physical courage. From his new hiding place, he wrote Lev Kamenev to be certain to publish his notebook if he were "bumped off." But although Finland was still part of the Russian Empire, his fear of being hunted down turned out to be exaggerated.

How the Bolsheviks managed to recover enough to accomplish their actual seizure of power three months later is another story, this one full of yet more unforeseeable openings, most provided by disastrous right-wing fumbles. In August, it managed to outdo the left wing's blunder of July. Its purpose was to stem popular hostility to the army and bolster the Provisional Government's crumbling authority. Its method was an attempt to reestablish public order and discipline by General Lavr Kornilov, the army commander in chief. That convinced much of the population, not entirely without reason, that reactionary czarist generals were intent on establishing a military dictatorship and/or restoring Nicholas to power. The Bolsheviks were seen as the best defense against that, just as many would see them as the best resistors to Nazism twenty-five years later.

Although Lenin made no public appearances from July through the October Revolution, he remained the party's unrivaled leader even from his hiding places. Writing furiously, he prodded and browbeat other Bolsheviks toward insurrection, rebuking those who clung to despised "parliamentary tactics." Such people were "miserable traitors to the proletarian cause," especially after the party's popular support grew in reaction to the failed military coup. "We're on the eve of a world revolution!" To wait for action or approval by the Second Congress of Soviets, which would convene in October—and might vote to continue the policies of democratic rule and substantial cooperation with other bodies—would be "utter idiocy or sheer treachery." Missing this perfect moment for armed action would "*ruin* the revolution."

The world would have been incalculably different if the moment for which Lenin had called from his homecoming exhortation at the Finland Station had indeed been missed. To say his role in creating it was utterly critical is not, of course, to prove that a later moment wouldn't have been seized without him; but all the most reliable observers of the time are convinced of that. His greatest contribution to Russian and world history was a sense of destination *now*—and the "hypnotic power," as described by an early collaborator who was soon repelled by his methods, of the sort exercised by many who assume command. "Only Lenin was followed unquestioningly as the indisputable leader, as it was only Lenin who was that rare phenomenon particularly in Russia—a man of iron will and indomitable energy, capable of instilling fanatical faith in the movement and the cause."

Would the country have taken his path without his leadership, imagination, and compulsion? Would other croupiers have appeared to spin the roulette wheel, as a history professor recently asked? Although anything's possible in Kierkegaard's "game of world-history," it's hard to imagine a less likely crucial happening than a Bolshevik revolution without Lenin's "supreme genius of revolutionary leadership," as the historian Henry Chamberlin called it, supporting Gorky's further description of him as "a man who prevented people from leading their accustomed lives as no one before him was able to do." Eager-to-please Stalin—who was nine years younger than Lenin and had considerable underground experience but none of the founder's ability to conceptualize and inspire—originally opposed the "go for broke" gamble. The dutiful executor of assigned tasks was also a member of *Pravda*'s editorial board, having returned from banishment after the February Revolution. Although he quite soon converted to Lenin's side, and later actually admitted the mistake in vision he'd "shared with the majority of the party," he remained too narrow to conceive grand concepts, too cautious for bold action on a sweeping scale, too intellectually limited to bully his fellows with argument, and too uncharismatic to rouse audiences.

Even Trotsky's splendid oratorical, literary, and organizing skills were no substitute for Ilich's obsessiveness and daring. His theory of Permanent Revolution may have helped prompt Lenin's crotchet that Russia *was* ready for Bolshevik rule, since her special case required combining the capitalist and socialist revolutions. Trotsky, however, who had long preached a need for unity among all Social Democrats when Lenin was preaching and practicing the opposite, changed his mind only after his own return from abroad, a month after Lenin's. Even then, he remained quiet about it until

July, following General Kornilov's attempted military coup that sparked the Bolshevik resurgence. After that, and until Lenin considered it safe enough to return from Finland in early October, Trotsky's work was essential, especially in organizing the actual coup as a kind of operations commander and symbolically linking it to Congress of Soviets because its Bolshevik contingent was still small. Nevertheless, he would bow to Ilich, and not only for convening the Central Committee's secret October meeting but also for taking the party's most important decision ever: to prepare for the armed insurrection. According to *The People's Tragedy*, Orlando Figes's authoritative history, Lenin "once again . . . managed to impose his will on the rest of its leaders." It was fitting that the party's inspiration and commander in chief returned to public view on November 7 [October 25 in the Russian calendar that was still in use there], to announce his momentous news to the Petrograd Soviet. "Comrades, the workers' and peasants' revolution, which we Bolsheviks always said must come, has been achieved." But Trotsky's greater praise of Lenin was for having made that possible by "shifting the whole question" from the moment he returned in April.

From the very first, he'd accused the party for not having taken power earlier, and only because it hadn't sufficiently educated and organized the proletariat. (The visionary who *knew* had only contempt for the wishes of other Russians, the overwhelming majority.) The "boldness of his revolutionary grasp, his determination to break even with his longtime colleagues and comrades in arms if they proved unable to march with the revolution . . . [and] his infallible feeling for the masses" were, Trotsky acknowledged, indispensable. He quoted a prominent provincial leader on Lenin's arrival in April. "His agitation, at first not wholly intelligible to us Bolsheviks but seen as utopianism deriving from his long absence from Russian life, was gradually absorbed by us. You might say it entered our flesh and blood."

It hardly needs saying that Ilich wasn't solely responsible for Russia's intensifying disgust with the war and waxing revolutionary mood among the Bolsheviks, let alone the country at large. The Western Allies—Britain, France, the United States—helped with their pressure to keep fighting their nemesis Germany, although the Provisional Government should have withdrawn from the war as quickly as possible. What if it had done so? What if it had taken the disagreeable but utterly necessary step even as late as July, even after its ill-advised, ill-executed, grievously costly attempt at yet another offensive (the Galician fiasco) then launched in aid of the common Allied effort? The democratically inclined parties and personalities would probably have been strong enough to resist the bacillus of Bolshevism, as its enemies were already calling it—even after Lenin had made his escape from arrest. Just as the war did more than anything else to bring down the monarchy—or, more precisely, the revelations of the appalling failures of Nicholas and his servile ministers in prosecuting it—it did the same to the Provisional Government, despite the time its members had had to know better. Having suffered catastrophically, the justifiably demoralized Russian rank and file could not understand why it should continue fighting, and turned against the officers and "statesmen" who urged them to do so.

If only the Allied leaders, Russian *or* Western, had been as astute as Lenin in recognizing that Russia must immediately abandon the war! Still, he saw the withdrawal itself as secondary to using that richest opportunity for, without punning, capitalizing on the discontent. With his singular drive and his intellectual superiority over his opponents, the magnetic man channeled it to *his* revolution, the supposedly proletarian one. A mind "capable at any moment of providing a centralized organization with decisions [and] each individual with detailed instructions" was among his critical assets, Aleksandr Solzhenitsyn would conclude. But his ability to furnish the masses with stirring slogans was equally important.

He of the iron will was also the master of taking uncompromising stances and pushing them upon others, despite everything. Later, he'd permit an occasional slight relaxation, most notably when reviving the economy ravaged by the Civil War. During the struggle for power, however, he hated nothing more than concession and conciliation. If a healthy person hates, an admirer quoted him, "then he really hates." His entire life was animated by a need to lead, not just nourish, the class struggle. Although his sympathy for the downtrodden was no doubt genuine, his animus against the system that had cost him his brother submerged it. ("I'll make them pay for that, I swear I will," he is said to have reacted to the news of the execution.) That, of course, wasn't the *cause* of the October Revolution—but his *sui generis* leadership was its catalyst.

The Provisional Government's stated reasons for ordering Lenin's arrest in July included a charge—supposedly proved by a packet of documents released by the Ministry of Justice—that he was a German spy. Having made the desired injury to his prestige, those dubious materials went on to enjoy a long life among his haters. The weight of the evidence accumulated since, however, strongly suggests that while he indeed took some travel money, as mentioned, he never served as a German agent. In fact, he used Germany more than the other way around, even, in the end, catastrophically damaging her. The kaiser's government helped him return in order to—again quoting a cable to the Foreign Ministry in Wilhelmstrasse—"exacerbate the differences between the moderate and extremist parties because we have the greatest interest in the latter gaining the upper hand, since the Revolution will then . . . shatter the stability of the Russian state." Few diplomatic maneuvers worked better—or worse. Worse because it helped cause Germany's ruin, starting in 1933. Although the factors explaining that progressive, cultured country's descent into Nazism have never been definitively categorized by importance, popular fear of Communism is high on every list. Hitler's revolution surely wouldn't have succeeded without a Bolshevist monster for panicking his audiences.

Then what if Germany *hadn't* permitted Lenin to pass? He might have devised another route, through England, France, or Norway, for example. But he and his agents considered those options at the time and rejected them as impractical or impossible. (A plot to sneak him through Germany disguised as blind, deaf, and mute—Swedish for some reason—was also discarded, his wife joking he'd give himself away by abusing his nonrevolutionary adversaries in his sleep.) The Western Allies, whose chief interest in Russia, as we've seen, was as a second front against the Reichswehr, would have been very reluctant to aid his travel because they had no reason to share Germany's liking for his potentially corrosive opposition to continued pursuit of the war. Besides, other arrangements would surely have taken a month to coordinate—or more, as with England's detention of Trotsky on *his* return to Russia at about the same time. During that critical waiting, the Provisional Government and the Petrograd Soviet might have solidified their positions and status by achieving more cooperation, as members of both bodies were already urging. Ilich, who was uncannily perceptive about many such tactical issues, felt at the time that he had to undermine their foundations before they hardened, leaving the sealed train as *the* hope in his impatient eyes.

If Germany had indeed rejected the scheme, the consequences would have been measureless, and no doubt happily so. Russia's long-planned Constituent Assembly for hammering out a democratic structure for the nation convened in Petrograd in January 1918. Its members had been chosen in remarkably fair national elections—but too late. That the first free, popular referendum in Russian history was held under Soviet rule was tragic as well as ironic. For Lenin, who had previously claimed only the Bolsheviks could be trusted to convene such an assembly, dispersed it after a single session, although, or because, the Bolshevik share of the vote was only 25 percent.

What if it hadn't been dismissed? What if the Bolsheviks didn't have the guns to do that? It's worth repeating that the assembly might not have achieved enough compromise to establish a working system of government that would have commanded popular allegiance, just as the country as a whole wouldn't necessarily have fashioned a functioning democratic civil society. "If Lenin had never boarded that train," a longtime resident of dismal, post-Communist Russia recently mused, "this place would still be a mess." But not the same kind of mess. Pre-Bolshevik Russia wasn't the haunted land of the Marquis de Custine, whose nineteenth-century images of backwardness, suspiciousness, and duplicity still rivet many Western eyes. Despite everything, it had a fighting chance for recovery, prosperity, and respect for civil rights under a parliamentary system Europeans would recognize as more or less "normal." The elections for that Constituent Assembly served as a national poll. The Bolshevik capture of no more than a clear minority, although the party was already in power and manipulating hard, spoke of the strength of the other groups, all of which had more or less democratic instincts. Their leaders' declarations during the single assembly session testified—as had the exchanges and arguments throughout the time of the dual power, even in the Petrograd Soviet—to a general acceptance of parliamentary norms and aspirations. Only Lenin would have scattered that very promising congregation of idealists and reformers, just as only he could have galvanized the Bolsheviks to his goal of seizing power.

If not for his extremism, a Russia still full of creative, productive, rational, and even moderate forces may well have been governed by Socialists for a time, but nothing like the kind who proclaimed a dictatorship of the proletariat, viewed the state as "an organ of class *domination*" (Lenin again, with his italics), and rushed to construct apparata of repression. (Having ignored Marx's prophecy that the proletarian revolution would take place in advanced countries whose workers constituted the great majority, Ilich had to alter the dictum that the state would wither away. On the contrary, a very powerful state was now needed for remorselessly countering socialism's inevitable enemies.) Surely she'd have been spared the concentration of immense power in a militarized party whose world-encompassing ideology was entrenched by a terrorizing secret police.

Whether or not it was inevitable, the house Ilich built was open for Stalin to move in. Although the extent to which he was the rightful heir remains debatable, the latter would surely have remained a very peripheral figure without the former. To put it more simply, no Lenin, no Stalin. That is to say, no Stalin of whom anyone but historians would have heard: a dedicated revolutionary who, however, would have died in relative obscurity.

And also no Russian Civil War? No famines, including the half-intentional ones for forcing the peasantry into collectivized agriculture? And no murderous purges and boundless other misery to fill the vast landmass? Almost certainly not. Almost as certainly, an essentially European civilization would have flowered richly, its blooms not seriously blighted, and in some ways actually fertilized, by elements of Russian mess. The purges and the Great Patriotic War, as Moscow called its death struggle with Nazi Germany, claimed some 40 million Soviet lives. It's hard to imagine a fraction of that loss without Lenin's obsession and legacy.

It's also hard to imagine all-embracing conflict with the West. Twentieth-century Russia would have become very powerful under any system, probably enough to rival America in economic and political influence, and possibly discomfort Western Europe in the process. Statistical evidence indicates that her growth, which had surged before 1917 despite all the impediments and restraints, would have been substantially *greater* if she hadn't fallen to Soviet rule. Without that, however, there would almost as certainly have been no Cold War either.

Only the Communists, as the Bolsheviks indeed renamed themselves, could have provoked such Western reaction to threats from the East. Washington's intentional exaggeration of them and its stooping to the Soviet level brought more responsibility for the Cold War than most Americans like to think. Still, its ultimate cause was the same arrogance that Lenin, convinced he'd attained supreme wisdom and held the keys to human history and happiness, displayed in forcing his revolution on his unwilling country. Taunting and deriding foreign "bourgeois-democratic" governments as well as the Russian one, he challenged not only Western capitalism but also the increasingly liberal democracy in which it functioned. *We know what's good for everyone. We'll do you a favor by helping tear down your rotten, doomed institutions.* Without that ideology, which Lenin advanced from theoretical rumination to actual provocation, Russia and the other countries of Europe and North America may well have engaged in very serious competition. But surely even the most intense rivalry wouldn't have come close to Cold War proportions. On the contrary, Russia would probably have been integrated, if slowly and at times painfully, into what came to be known as the free world.

No Cold War, no girding for outbreak of a shooting one. No draining of measureless effort, money, and resources by "defense" on virtually every continent. And no hideous inquisitions, monstrous imprisonments, grotesque espionage "games." (No bullets in the back of the heads of perhaps 12,000 Polish officers, to take just the single example of the Katyn Forest massacre among a numbing surfeit of them.) No censorship, twisted information, and big and little lies employed for and against Communism, served up by the one side as paradise and the other as hell, with all the religiouslike righteousness of both sides' leaders. In short, no sundered planet stumbling in hostility. Of course, Russia herself squandered and distorted more than any other country, but America, whose national purpose largely shrunk to fighting Communism for forty-five years, ran a good second. It's not too much to say that the struggle diminished human life everywhere in the second half of the twentieth century.

In that sense, the hoary Communist slogan that "Lenin Is More Alive Than the Living" is true even now. The burden has lifted but the deformity and impoverishment endure, again most cripplingly in the Russia to which the forty-seven-year-old Ilich returned in his curious way—Germany having actually given his train extra-territoriality—in order to take her down his singular garden path, with its collection of lucky turns for him that proved so unlucky for the world.

GEOFFREY C. WARD

# THE LUCK OF FRANKLIN
# DELANO ROOSEVELT

*Seven might-not-have-beens on*
*the road to the presidency*

*Franklin D. Roosevelt, his biographer Geoffrey C. Ward writes, was an extraordinarily lucky man. You might say that he was a case study in might-have-beens that all seemed to go his way. For FDR, the roads not taken mostly turned out to be the ones he should have avoided. Decisions that others made, not always favorable, turned out to help rather than hinder. Early on, for example, the woman who had been the "loveliest" debutante rejected him: she would have been the wrong person for his career, and besides, she was a Republican.*

*Political opponents underestimated him and refrained from all-out attacks: They lived to regret it. Luck, in the form of a press too discreet to delve into personal follies, saved him from the broadcasting of an infidelity scandal that easily could have terminated a promising future in politics. Sickness resulted in options, not endings. What proved to be a timely bout of typhoid fever when he was an obscure state senator from upstate New York linked FDR with the one man who believed all along that he had the potential to be president. Even his greatest misfortune, polio, turned out to be a stroke of luck in political terms (and also forestalled the certain tarnish of another scandal). But after FDR's election as president, luck of another sort, his refusal to give in to the importuning of Miami newsreel cameramen, may have saved his life in February 1933—and spared the nation the leadership of a man totally unequipped by desire or ability to guide the United States through its worst crisis since the Civil War.*

*You have to think of another close call in Manhattan less than two years ear-lier, when a visitor from England, looking the wrong way as he crossed Fifth Av-enue, was hit by an automobile; he almost died. "Those who believe that personalities make no difference to history," Arthur M. Schlesinger, Jr., has writ-ten, "might do well to ponder whether the world would have been the same in the next two decades" if a car had killed Winston Churchill, or an assassin's bullet Franklin D. Roosevelt.*

GEOFFREY C. WARD is the author of twelve books, including A *First-Class Temperament*, his account of FDR's early career, which won the 1989 National Books Critics Circle Award and the 1990 Francis Parkman Prize of the Society of American Historians. In collaboration with the filmmaker Ken Burns, he has written *The Civil War*, *Baseball*, and most recently *Jazz: A History of America's Music*.

I⊤ IS ALWAYS risky for a biographer to speculate what might have
been—biography is, after all a record of choices made, paths taken, options closed—and it seems especially perilous for a biographer of Franklin
Roosevelt to do so since FDR himself always refused to answer what he
called "iffy" questions. Still, Roosevelt *mattered*—I wouldn't be interested
in writing (and few would be interested in reading) an essay on what might
have happened if, say, Franklin Pierce or Benjamin Harrison, had been
kept from the White House—and looking back over Roosevelt's life before
the presidency, it is hard not to be impressed by the number of moments
when fortune seemed to smile upon him with unusual brightness, when
things might just as easily have gone the other way and left him more or less
what his father had been; an amiable well-respected country gentleman,
little known beyond the borders of Dutchess County, New York, and the
paneled confines of his Manhattan clubs.

*What kind of politician might Roosevelt have become, for example, had his pro-
posal of marriage to a dazzling but conventional heiress been accepted, not
spurned?*

Roosevelt was an eighteen-year-old Harvard freshman in the autumn of
1900 when he was smitten by Alice Sohier, the tall, slender, high-spirited
fifteen-year-old daughter of an old North Shore, Massachusetts, family. Hers
was just the sort of patrician clan his mother, Sara Delano Roosevelt, might
have picked for him to marry into; Alice's mother was a collateral descendant of John Alden; her father an ardent yachtsman with three elegantly
appointed summer homes. And Alice herself was a great beauty—"of all the
debutantes [of the year]," FDR recalled long after, "she was the loveliest."

The young Roosevelt pursued her avidly for more than a year, noting his time with her in his Line-A-Day journal: "To see Alice Sohier"; "dance with Alice Sohier"; "A.S. for supper"; "To Sohiers in the evening." And at some point during the spring of 1902, he evidently made an impetuous of-fer of marriage. He and Alice were still very young. She already had other suitors. And the young Roosevelt's raw ambition had struck her parents as bumptious, even unseemly; when he told the Sohiers one evening at din-ner that he was planning a political career and thought that he, like his hero and distant cousin, Theodore, might even become president one day, an older cousin of Alice's had asked "Who *else* thinks so?" and the whole family had burst into laughter. But beyond that, he confided to Alice, he had ambitions for his future wife, as well: He'd felt isolated as an only child, he explained, and wanted six children, the same number that tumbled across TR's lawn at Oyster Bay. Alice Sohier was flattered by FDR's atten-tion but appalled by his plans for her: in the end, she told a confidante many years later, she had rejected Franklin Roosevelt's suit because "I did not wish to be a cow." (She would later marry an insurance executive, re-main a lifelong Republican, and profess always to be grateful that she'd never become "the president's lady.")

A mournful FDR saw her off on a trip to Europe in October of 1903. Just five weeks later he found himself a fellow-guest at the New York Horse Show at Madison Square Garden with his shy cousin Eleanor and began to turn the full blaze of his charm on her.

Alice Sohier had largely been satisfied with the world as it was. Eleanor Roosevelt never was—and set out to see to it that her future husband should not be either. In later years, she loved to tell of how, during their courtship, she deliberately arranged for him to pick her up in the evenings at the Lower East Side settlement house where she served as a volunteer. Once, after helping to carry a sick child up several flights of tenement stairs to the fetid one-room flat that housed his whole family, FDR emerged pale and shaken. "My God," he said. "I didn't know anyone lived like that."

"I wanted him to see *how people lived*," Eleanor Roosevelt would say, smiling at the memory. "And it worked. He saw how people lived, and he *never* forgot."

It seems likely that Franklin Roosevelt would have succeeded in politics no matter whom he married. He entered his very first race—for the New York State Senate in 1910—already armed with gifts that would be the envy of everyone who ever ran against him: good looks and boundless charm, genuine interest in people, almost manic energy, plus personal wealth and a celebrated name. But it is hard to see how, without Eleanor Roosevelt's consistent, if sometimes tactless goading, her relentless appeals to his better nature, he would ever have moved far enough beyond the benign insularity of his parents and the other river families among whom he had grown up to have become the sort of president who could say to his secretary of labor, Frances Perkins, "What we are doing, Frances, is trying to build an America in which no one is left out."

*How might Roosevelt have fared in politics had a long-forgotten New York reformer named Thomas Mott Osborne been more successful? Or if he had himself not fallen victim to typhoid fever in the midst of his first campaign for reelection?*

The young state senator brought political weaknesses as well as strengths with him to Albany. He still often seemed disdainful of people whose upbringing was less patrician than his own. (A good many of his fellow Democratic legislators saw him simply as a snob.) And he was altogether too eager to wage noisy battles against Tammany Hall that produced plenty of headlines but precious few results. And, while he was blessed from the beginning with an uncanny ability to absorb and marshal disconnected bits of information, he also had a short attention span and intensely disliked detail work.

It was Louis Howe, the seasoned but threadbare Albany newspaperman with progressive tendencies and a fierce desire to wield political power behind the scenes, who famously did the most to set him straight, but it has largely been forgotten that Roosevelt was not the first charismatic New York reformer whose career Howe attempted to shape.

In 1906, Howe had attached himself to the magnetic former mayor of Auburn, Thomas Mott Osborne, then engaged in a struggle to deny the Democratic nomination for governor to William Randolph Hearst. Osborne was handsome, eloquent, and high-minded (he would become the best-known prison reformer of his day), but he was also vain, bombastic, and gratuitously insulting—he refused even to parley with the "dogs" and "curs" who he said ran the Democratic machine—and he was badly beaten. Howe believed Osborne had a great future in politics, nonetheless, and clung to him for six more years, acting as a secret operative and using his credentials as a supposedly objective journalist to garner information about party regulars for his boss. In 1912, he quit his newspaper job to work for Osborne full time, confident that his employer would one day ascend at least as far as the governorship and that he himself would rise with him.

Then, without any warning, Osborne withdrew from politics altogether. Howe was out of work and desperate that fall when Eleanor Roosevelt telephoned him. Her husband was in bed with typhoid fever, she said, far too ill to run personally for reelection to the state senate. Would Howe be willing to take over his stalled campaign? Howe gratefully signed on, began addressing Roosevelt privately as "Beloved and Revered Future President," and remained at his new boss's side until his own death in 1936. It is hard to see how FDR could have risen as far as he did without Howe's inbred caution and unswerving loyalty, his insider's perspective—and his willingness to see to all the burdensome details.

*What would have happened to Roosevelt had he worked during his years at the Navy Department for a superior less forbearing than Josephus Daniels?*

FDR brought enormous vitality and remarkable administrative ability to the job of assistant secretary of the navy before, during, and after World War I, and he was almost always courteous when in the presence of the avuncular North Carolina newspaper editor who had invited him to Washington at thirty-one despite the prescient warning of an old friend that "Whenever a Roosevelt rides, he wants to ride in front."

Daniels's affection for the youthful Roosevelt had been "love at first sight," he liked to say. FDR's feelings about his boss were more complex: There were genuine differences of both substance and style between them. Roosevelt had yearned to be part of the navy since boyhood; Daniels was wary of the military and suspicious of admirals. FDR believed America was sure to be drawn into World War I; Daniels did not. Daniels was slow-moving, courtly, and cautious; Roosevelt was impatient, brash, eager for action.

FDR was given the freest possible rein; no assistant secretary of the navy had ever been given more responsibility. It was never enough for Roosevelt. He had been taught since birth that no man should be his chief, that he and no one else was supposed to be in charge. "I am *running* the real work," he claimed in a letter to his wife in 1914, "though Josephus is here! He is bewildered by it all, very sweet but very sad!" He portrayed his boss and benefactor as a countrified naif so frequently at Washington dinner tables that a close friend took him aside and told him he should be ashamed of himself. He kept right on doing it, anyway. He also leaked damaging information about Daniels to hostile newspapermen, lobbied to replace him at the top, and conspired with several of his chief's enemies—including the archenemy of the Wilson administration in which he served, Theodore Roosevelt. That Daniels seems not merely to have liked but actually to have *loved* Franklin Roosevelt, in spite of all this, is one of the enduring puzzles of American political history. Anyone but Daniels, it seems to me, would have delighted in sending Roosevelt back home to Hyde Park before he'd been on the job six months.

*Would FDR ever have had a national political career had Theodore Roosevelt still been alive in 1920?*

In later years, FDR liked to say that it had been his vigorous record as assistant secretary of the navy that had won him the Democratic nomination for vice president in 1920: "They chose me," he told one early biographer, "because my name had become known during the war." In fact, he was chosen in large part simply because he bore the same last name as the late Theodore Roosevelt.

It would be hard to exaggerate the importance of TR's example in FDR's life. It was he who had first demonstrated, in Sara Delano Roosevelt's words, that a member of the family "might go into politics but not *be* a politician." At Groton, fourteen-year-old Franklin adopted pince-nez because his fifth cousin had worn them when he charged up Kettle Hill in Cuba. At Harvard, FDR joined the Republican club and marched through the rain in support of his hero. His love for Eleanor Roosevelt was genuine but the entrée she provided to her uncle's circle at Oyster Bay was a considerable part of her dowry, nonetheless. The fact that TR had four sons, any one of whom then seemed more likely than he to inherit the Roosevelt political mantle, may have helped persuade FDR to enter politics as a Democrat in 1910; there seemed to be no future for him as a Republican, and his unexpected victory for the state senate that same year was largely a result of the split in GOP ranks engineered by TR's progressive followers. Theodore Roosevelt hoped to wrest power back from the Republican bosses and make himself the party's presidential nominee in 1920; hundreds of thousands of his admirers were awaiting word from him to enlist once again in his cause when he died suddenly in January of 1919.

Franklin Roosevelt was only thirty-eight and looked still younger when he traveled west with the New York delegation to attend the Democratic National Convention in San Francisco the following summer. Once he had made a good impression on the crowd by seconding Al Smith's nomination for president, all the excitement seemed to be over for him. But it took forty-four ballots before the exhausted delegates picked the third-term governor of Ohio, James Cox, as their presidential nominee and when it was over, the governor turned to the young Roosevelt as his running mate. As an eager young supporter of Al Smith, Cox told his startled aides, Roosevelt might help carry New York without which victory in November would be impossible. But above all, he said "his name is good," by which he meant that it would appeal to progressive Republicans sickened by the nomination of Warren G. Harding and still mourning Theodore Roosevelt. The newspaper headlines that appeared the following morning echoed Cox's thinking: Franklin Roosevelt's Career Parallels Cousin Teddy's . . . Liken Career of Roosevelt to Cousin's . . . Cousin of TR Is Picked for Second Place . . . The Democrats Hope Name of Roosevelt Will Draw Votes . . . All the World Loves a Roosevelt.

The Cox-Roosevelt ticket was crushed by Harding and Coolidge that fall and the Roosevelt name was not enough to carry a single New York county. But party professionals did not blame Franklin Roosevelt. Millions of voters now considered him not merely a pale reflection of his late cousin but a vigorous, attractive personality in his own right.

*Would FDR ever have reached the White House if the press of his era had approached candidates with the intractable cynicism and obsession with personal scandal that seems so pervasive in ours?*

There is no clearer evidence of how different the age of Roosevelt was from our own than the ease with which the complexities of Roosevelt's private life were concealed. To begin with, there was FDR's early romance with Lucy Mercer, widely known among his contemporaries in Washington but never so much as hinted at in print during his lifetime. Once Eleanor Roosevelt discovered it in 1917, her cousin Corinne Alsop remembered, "everybody behaved well and exactly as one would expect each of the protagonists . . . to behave." Eleanor offered Franklin a divorce. His mother said that if her son chose divorce he could expect to be overlooked in her will. Lucy Mercer, a practicing Catholic, agonized over whether or not she could marry a divorced man. And Louis Howe counseled that if FDR allowed his heart to rule his head he could say good-bye to politics. Divorce would be political suicide.

In the end, Howe's view prevailed. It is impossible to know what would have happened to the presidency, to the country, or to the cause of freedom itself had Franklin Roosevelt divorced his wife, married Lucy Mercer, and thereby ended his political career. But the late Murray Kempton once offered a memorable "fugitive fantasy" about Roosevelt and his second wife. The two would have retreated to the Hudson Valley, he suggested, and there "endure in the imagination, growing old together, say near Newburgh, he languidly farming and drawing wills and litigating country quarrels and she stealing now and then into the dreary little church to grieve a while for the spiritual loss that had brought their happiness. The Depression is hard on him; but when he dies he has managed to recoup by selling his remaining acres for a postwar housing development. His obituary is exactly the size the *Times* metes out for former assistant secretaries of the navy who had been nominated for vice president of the United States in a bad year for their party."

Roosevelt had other closely guarded secrets that responsible newspapermen and women of his time simply considered none of the public's business, including his closeness to his unmarried secretary, Marguerite Le Hand, and the fact that once their children were grown, he and his wife lived apart for all but ceremonial purposes, maintaining separate residences when away from the White House, surrounding themselves with separate circles of friends, rarely even dining together unless guests were present.

The fact that Roosevelt was a paraplegic after polio—and not merely "lame" as *Time* magazine reported and most Americans believed—was also tactfully concealed by mutual agreement between him and those who covered him. If there had not been such an unspoken pact—had photographers and newsreel cameramen routinely shown him being carried from place to place, unable to take a step unaided or even rise from his chair—it is hard to see how a country already grievously disabled by Depression would ever have elected such a man to lead it. (Nor do I think things have changed much over the intervening years: Were some other candidate, equally well qualified but no less physically impaired, to try to win the nation's highest office today, television's unblinking, unforgiving omnipresent eye would make his or her election impossible.)

*What would have happened to Franklin Roosevelt had he not contracted infantile paralysis in 1921?*

As late as the 1920 vice presidential campaign, his loyal press secretary, Steve Early, once confided, FDR was "just a playboy" who "failed to take life seriously enough . . . [and] couldn't be made to prepare his speeches in advance, preferring to play cards, instead." The late Franklin Roosevelt, Jr., once told me more or less the same thing: his father had been "a playboy in politics" before the onset of his illness, he said, "living off his cousin's name and his mother's money." And FDR Jr. further believed that his father's illness, ghastly as its physical impact was, had also turned out to be still another "stroke of luck" in political terms. It taught him patience, he said, and, more important, it kept him from "making a fool of himself" by running for the presidency in the hopelessly Republican twenties, before he was ready for the job or the country was ready for him. FDR Jr. overstated his case—Al Smith would likely have remained New York's favorite son in 1924 and 1928 whether or not FDR had remained able-bodied—and the son's harsh portrait of his youthful father may have been colored in part by raw memories of his own repeated disappointments in political life.

Still, polio did indirectly save FDR from the one threat that really might have cut short to his career—the controversial part he had played in what came to be called the Newport scandal. In the spring of 1919, Secretary Daniels had sailed for Europe to attend an Allied naval conference, somewhat nervously leaving the Navy Department in the hands of his eager young assistant secretary, with instructions not to sign anything really important until he got back and they could talk it over. As always, Roosevelt reveled in being in charge: "You ought to see the change in the carrying on of the department work," he boasted to a friend who had worked there with him. "I see civilians in the old building from 9 A.M. to 10:30, then I see the press, and then dash down to the new building in a high-powered car, and from that time on—11 A.M.—see no outsiders, congressmen, senators, or anybody else. The department mail is signed at regular hours and absolutely cleaned up everyday, with the result that nothing is taken home, mislaid, lost, et cetera, et cetera." Among the documents to which both he and his chief would later wish he had never affixed his bold blue signature that spring were several orders setting up a top-secret intelligence unit, to be attached to his own office, whose purpose was to end homosexuality on and off the naval base at Newport, Rhode Island. In that time there was nothing especially remarkable in working toward that goal: Both military and civilian law then held homosexual acts to be criminal.

It was the *methods* employed that came close to derailing Roosevelt. For under his at least tacit approval, young sailors were recruited with instructions to become sexually involved with homosexuals "to the limit," in order to obtain evidence against them. Among those arrested was a prominent Episcopal clergyman whose arrest made national headlines and whose lawyers, understandably enough, charged entrapment.

There were two separate investigations of the incident, one by the navy, the other by a Senate subcommittee. FDR angrily denied everything. He couldn't recall even *reading* the letter he'd signed setting up the secret squad, he claimed, had never been told how it gathered its evidence, and had never asked.

Hadn't it been his duty to do so? No it had not, he answered under oath. He was a busy man. Only results had mattered to him.

The navy court of inquiry eventually let him off with a gentle reprimand. But the Republican majority on the Senate subcommittee dismissed Roosevelt's testimony as "unbelievable" and "incredible." They had him coming and going: If he *hadn't* made it his business to know what sort of dirty work was being directed from his own office then "he was most derelict in the performance of his duty," they said; and if he *had* ordered "the use of enlisted personnel for the purpose of investigating perversion"—and the Republican senators were convinced he had—then that decision should be "thoroughly condemned as immoral and an abuse of the authority of his high office."

The degree of Roosevelt's actual culpability in this sordid business is impossible to assess all these years later, but he seems to have been less complicitous than oblivious, signing the orders in his superior's absence without much thought, probably relishing the air of importance that surrounded a clandestine investigation but too busy or too distracted to learn the day-to-day details. In any case, it certainly *looked* bad, and some newspapermen—with encouragement from Republicans eager to write an end to the young Roosevelt's promising political career—looked forward to probing the part he'd played still further.

Here, Roosevelt's illness turned out to be an unlikely boon. The Senate subcommittee's charges had just surfaced on the front page of the *New York Times*—which had headlined its story "Lay Navy Scandal to F. D. Roosevelt" and then made things look even worse than they were by declaring its details "Unprintable"—when he sailed for Campobello and his rendezvous with infantile paralysis in the summer of 1921.

After Roosevelt was stricken, even his most implacable opponents saw nothing to be gained in doing further damage to a now-helpless man whose political race had so obviously been run. The story was allowed to die away. Still, back in politics and running for president eleven years later, Roosevelt remained so worried about its potential for political damage that he and Howe insisted that Earle Looker, his first campaign biographer, include in his book the complete text of the lengthy press release FDR had issued in his own defense in 1921; in the finished volume, it took up eight of the eighteen pages devoted to his years at the Navy Department.

The Republicans who dropped the Newport scandal because they believed FDR no longer a threat to them were joining a long line of people who lived to regret having underestimated Franklin Roosevelt. That line began forming early, with his classmates at Groton and Harvard, who could never quite understand how the glossy youth they remembered as altogether too easy to please could possibly succeed in the sweaty world of politics. And it stretched on to include the Roosevelts of Oyster Bay, who thought that in marrying him, Eleanor Roosevelt had married beneath herself; the Dutchess County Democratic bosses who picked him to run for the State Senate in what had been a hopelessly Republican district mostly in hopes of tapping into his mother's fortune; the Tammany bosses who thought they had permanently put him out of business when they trounced his candidacy for the United States Senate nomination in 1911; and finally Al Smith, who in 1928 thought Roosevelt a lightweight in frail health and therefore believed it safe to ask him to return to politics and run for governor.

Wasn't he raising up a dangerous rival? an old ally named Dan Finn asked Smith.

"No, Dan," the governor replied confidently. "He won't live a year."

He lived another seventeen years, of course, and would spend the last twelve of them in the White House. But before he could move in, he would be favored by fortune one more time.

*What if Giuseppe Zangara's bullets hadn't missed?*

At seven in the evening on February 15, 1933, Vincent Astor's yacht, the *Nourmahal*, docked at Miami, Florida. Among the passengers on deck was the president-elect, FDR, tanned and rested after a Caribbean fishing trip.

His inauguration was only seventeen days away. The mayor had organized a welcome-home rally at the Bayfront Park amphitheater, and thousands of people had already gathered there to see and hear him. Among them—in the second row, just thirty feet from the spot where the president-elect's open car was to stop so that he could speak to the crowd—was a delusional Italian immigrant named Giuseppe Zangara, wracked with pain from peptic ulcers and consumed with rage at all the "people who run the government . . . [and] suck the blood out of the poor." He had a .32 revolver in his pocket. He had once hoped to kill Herbert Hoover. Now, Roosevelt was his intended target; if he didn't get a clear shot at him here he planned to travel to Washington and shoot him during the inaugural parade.

The president-elect's car nosed its way through the cheering crowd and pulled to a stop at about seven-thirty. As well-wishers closed in around it, FDR hoisted himself up onto the back of the car seat so that people could see him while making a few cheery, inconsequential remarks into a microphone—so few remarks that by the time a newsreel crew got ready to start filming, the president-elect had already slid back down into his seat. The cameraman begged him to climb back up again and repeat his words for the newsreels. Roosevelt gently demurred. "I'm sorry," he said. "I just can't do it." At that moment, Zangara, frustrated that his target had dropped from sight before he could get a clear shot at him, clambered onto a metal chair and started firing. He managed to get off five shots, hitting five people— including Mayor Anton Cermak of Chicago, who subsequently died of his wound—before members of the crowd hurled him to the ground.

Somehow, FDR remained untouched. Had Zangara reached Bayfront Park early enough to find a place in the front row of the crowd instead of the second, or had FDR given in to the importuning of the newsreel crew, things might have been very different. It is impossible to know what would have happened next, except for one thing: under the new twentieth amendment, the presidency would have passed to the vice president–elect. John Nance Garner of Texas would have found himself faced with the gravest crisis since the Civil War—the Depression.

There was precious little to suggest that he was interested in breaking "foolish tradition," as Roosevelt had promised *he* would do, no hint that

Garner came to the job equipped with the kind of fresh ideas needed for what FDR had called "unprecedented and unusual times." Born in 1868 in a log cabin at Blossom Prairie, Texas, he was the son of an ex-Confederate cavalryman and a mother whose earliest memories were of fortifying the family cabin against Comanches. He had walked three miles each day to a one-room schoolhouse, first won local fame as the star shortstop for the combined Blossom Prairie–Coon Soup Hollow baseball nine in its annual battles with a team fielded by neighboring Possum Trot, and he learned his law, just as Abraham Lincoln had learned his, in a small-town law office. He passed the bar at twenty-one and in 1893, after a doctor suggested he might be developing tuberculosis, he set up shop in Uvalde in the dry-ranch country west of San Antonio. There, he rode the circuit over nine counties, sometimes accepting cattle and mohair goats for his services instead of cash, married a rancher's daughter whose considerable inheritance helped him build a fortune as a rancher, pecan-grower, and small-town banker, and got himself elected to the state legislature where, as chairman of the committee on redistricting, he saw to it that the map of Texas was redrawn to ensure him a safe seat in Congress. He went to Washington in 1903 and, through persistence, seniority, and shrewd parliamentary astuteness, rose steadily to the Democratic leadership. When the Democrats took over the House in 1931, he became Speaker. He remained an unreconstructed Jeffersonian: "The great trouble today," he said in the third year of the Depression, "is that we have too many laws. I believe that primarily a government has but two functions—to protect the lives and property rights of citizens. When it goes further than that, it becomes a burden." (As late as April of 1937 he would argue in Cabinet meetings that many of the nation's problems could be solved if city dwellers could only be persuaded to move en masse back into the countryside.)

His presence on the 1932 ticket had been the price Roosevelt had to pay for Texas support at the convention. Garner would have much preferred to remain Speaker. "The vice presidency," he once told a reporter, "isn't worth a pitcher of warm piss"—and when the newsman changed it to "a pitcher of warm spit" for public consumption, Garner privately called him a "panty-waist." Only lifelong devotion to party unity persuaded him to run.

A RELUCTANT LEADER?

*FDR's first vice president, John Nance Garner of Texas—"Cactus Jack"—posed for a formal portrait in 1934. A year earlier, only a would-be assassin's wild shot kept this profoundly negative man from becoming president during one of the greatest crises the United States ever faced.*

(Culver Pictures)

He barely knew FDR and made only a single campaign speech before hurrying home to Uvalde to await the results. It was probably just as well. He was an unprepossessing figure: short—just five-foot-one—red-faced, and faintly redolent of bourbon, with close-cropped white hair and formidable eyebrows ("like two caterpillars rasslin'," he himself once said) and a dead cigar perpetually stuck in the corner of his tiny mouth. He was also a dreadful speaker. In his safe, Democratic district there had been no need for speechifying and he had seen little need for it in the House, either. His standard counsel to new congressmen was to keep quiet and get things done behind the scenes. "It was a good many years before any remarks of mine got into the [*Congressional*] *Record*," he told his successor in Congress, "and I hope you won't make a damn fool of yourself either." An America desperate for reassurance on inauguration day in 1933 was unlikely to have gotten much from the taciturn Texas politician who had once been pleased when the press called him "the Texas Coolidge."

Garner opposed none of the bills proposed by the president in his first one hundred days, granting Roosevelt more power than any chief executive in history—though he privately thought the NRA "a moony adventure." Even he believed that desperate times demanded desperate measures and he used his position as presiding officer of the Senate to slam them through. "After a bill was read," his friend and chronicler, the veteran newspaperman Bascom Timmins, remembered, "and before a senator had time to clear his throat, adjust his papers and call for recognition, Garner in rapidly tumbling words would say: 'The question is: Shall the bill be engrossed, read the third time and passed? There being no objection the bill is passed.'" Senators too slow to react were out of luck. Still, as early as 1934, the journalist John Carter Vincent would suggest that the Texan was "as out of place in the New Deal as a dead mouse in a mince pie. . . . The epitome of the Western middle class: a big farmer, a banker, and a businessman, the individual entrepreneur who has made a conspicuous success under the old rules of the old game. He is against Big Business, but only because it interferes with small business, and if the New Deal should ever fall into his hands, God save the New Deal and Heaven help the country."

Garner remained adamantly opposed to deficit spending of any kind: Mrs. Garner had never had a "charge account," he once said, and he saw no need for the country to have one, either. His views on labor were out of sync with his times, as well. His own fortune was built in part on cheap labor: while union carpenters in Texas got a dollar and a quarter a day, those who worked for Garner got only the quarter; the Mexican-Americans who gathered and shelled him pecans for a penny a pound "are not troublesome people unless they become Americanized," he unwisely confided to a visiting reporter from Philadelphia. "The sheriff can make them do anything." Sit-down strikes, he told the Cabinet, constituted simple thievery.

He was also utterly uninterested in foreign affairs. It had been his hostility to the League of Nations and his interest in his "own people" and "his own country" that had made him William Randolph Hearst's first candidate for the Democratic nomination in 1932. He opposed FDR's recognition of the Soviet Union in 1933 and was at home in Uvalde feeding his chickens later that same year when, after five Cuban presidents in a row had been overthrown by coups, the president called to consult him on whether the United States might have to intervene to protect U.S. interests on the island.

"What do you think we ought to do, Jack?" FDR asked.

"I'd keep out of Cuba."

"But suppose an American is shot?"

"I'd wait," Garner answered, "and see which American it was . . ."

The Nazis didn't worry him much, either. When someone at an early Cabinet meeting worried aloud that the new Hitler regime seemed serious about persecuting the Jews, according to John Carter Vincent, "Garner—perhaps remembering the effect of fifty years of Northern moral indignation with the Southern treatment of Negroes—tartly reminded his colleagues that the internal politics of Germany were none of the business of the American government, and hopefully suggested that the hotter the Nazi excesses, the sooner they would burn out." In 1938, he told the Cabinet he hoped Britain never paid its war debt because then it could borrow no more money. As late as midsummer of 1939, he refused to believe a European war inevitable, let alone concede that America might become involved if one started. Secretary of State Cordell Hull, who detested him, told Interior Secretary Harold Ickes that Garner saw all international relationships in the light of Uvalde, Texas. That evidently went for some domestic issues, as well: when Marion Anderson sang at the White House for the visiting king and queen of England in 1939, the vice president alone among the guests assembled in the East Room refused to applaud.

No one can tell how much of the New Deal might have been enacted without FDR or how close we would have come to revolution from the right or left had his unshakable, contagious confidence in America's ability to solve even its most serious problems not spread among its people. Nor can we know whether without him Americans would have awakened in time to meet the Axis threat. But it seems clear that the thirties would have been a far grimmer time for America and the world a far more frightening place had Franklin D. Roosevelt's extraordinary run of luck ended on that warm winter evening in Miami.

## WILLIAMSON MURRAY

# THE WAR OF 1938

### Chamberlain fails to sway
### Hitler at Munich

If there is a single enduring image of the Munich Pact of September 1938, it is of the British prime minister Neville Chamberlain emerging from a plane and waving a clutch of papers that, he said, assured "peace in our time." The British and French had just allowed Hitler to annex the Sudetenland, those large portions of Czechoslovakia with a predominately German population (as well as the Czech version of the Maginot Line). Hitler claimed that this would be his last demand: Six months later he swallowed up the rest of Czechoslovakia. Munich, the historian Norman Davies has written, "must qualify as one of the most degrading capitulations in history."

Chamberlain's defenders have long claimed that the unfortunate pact gave Great Britain needed breathing space, in which it had time to build up its defenses, the RAF especially. In Williamson Murray's view, that is nonsense: Not England but Germany benefited most from the remission. Hitler almost threw that advantage away. He was determined to go to war against Czechoslovakia and would have done so within days of the last-ditch Munich meeting of September 29 and 30, when Chamberlain unexpectedly caved in. Even as the talks went on, troops were moving up to the Czech border. "Until his dying days," Murray writes, Hitler "remained bitterly disappointed that the British had deprived him of the opportunity of launching the Wehrmacht against the Czechs."

What would have happened if a major European war had broken out in the autumn of 1938? Its results, in Murray's view, would have been very different from *what actually happened. Germany in 1938 was simply not prepared for a conflict of any duration. The problem for Hitler was not taking Czechoslovakia: Though his armies and air force would have been roughed up, the entire campaign would have lasted no more than a month, about the time needed to roll over Poland the following year. More to the point, what would have happened afterward, when Hitler's armies would inevitably have been forced to turn westward? To consider that prospect, Murray argues, is to understand how unfortunate was the respite that Neville Chamberlain bought.*

WILLIAMSON MURRAY, a senior fellow at the Institute for Defense Analyses, is a professor of history emeritus at Ohio State University and, with Allen R. Millett, the author of *A War to Be Won: Fighting the Second World War.*

O N SEPTEMBER 29, 1938, Adolf Hitler, führer of Nazi Germany, Benito Mussolini, duce of Fascist Italy, Edouard Daladier, premier of France, and Neville Chamberlain, prime minister of Great Britain, met in the Bavarian capital of Munich and agreed to a peaceful settlement of the Czech crisis that the Nazis had manufactured over the course of that summer. That agreement sealed the fate of Czechoslovakia. Yet only the day before the conference convened, German troops had been rolling up into their jump-off positions against a mobilized and deployed Czech Army, while the Luftwaffe was completing deployment of its aircraft onto bases in the immediate vicinity of the Czech Republic. Determined to crush the Czechs by war, Hitler had created a crisis that seemed headed toward war. Only at the last moment, for reasons that still remain inexplicable, had the führer backed off.

The Munich conference resulted from the course of German military and diplomatic policy throughout 1938. Nazi strategy had in turn resulted from a number of factors, the clearest being Hitler's implacable long-term aim to destroy the European balance of power and replace it with a German hegemony that would stretch from the Urals to the Atlantic. Coming to power in January 1933, the führer had immediately launched a massive program of rearmament for the war he saw as inevitable. But by late 1937 the Reich's rearmament remained incomplete, while the German economy appeared headed toward bankruptcy, pressures of a serious economic situation, combined with Hitler's unwillingness to abandon his goals, led the führer to determine on a riskier approach in 1938.

The Austrians were the first to feel the pressures of Nazi expansionism in early 1938. Confronting the severe economic problems occasioned by his massive rearmament program and a political crisis occasioned by his firing of the army's commander in chief, Werner von Fritsch, on trumped-up charges of homosexuality, Hitler moved against the Austrians. While Hitler browbeat the Austrians into submission, the major European powers backed away from the crisis and abandoned Vienna to its fate. In mid-March 1938 the Nazis overthrew the Austrian government, and the Wehrmacht occupied Hitler's native land.

If the Europeans thought that the *Anschluss* (the union of Germany and Austria) would relieve international tensions, they were quickly disabused of that notion. In May 1938 the Czechs, alarmed at German propaganda in their borderlands—the Sudetenland, largely inhabited by Germans—mobilized and placed their frontier districts under martial law. Outraged that the Czechs had taken matters into their own hands, Hitler ordered his military planners to begin immediately drawing up plans for an invasion of Czechoslovakia on October 1, 1938. At the same time he had his propaganda minister, Joseph Goebbels, unleash a massive propaganda campaign to justify such an invasion. As storm clouds gathered in the summer of 1938, the French and British desperately attempted to divert Hitler from an attack on Czechoslovakia. They had reason to do so; the Franco-Czech alliance directly committed the French to intervene on the side of the Czechs, were they attacked by the Germans. But the British, with close ties to the French, were also desperately afraid that in the case of a major European war, unleashed without justification by the Nazis, they too would inevitably be drawn in at the side of the French. Thus, throughout the summer, Chamberlain made desperate efforts to appease the Germans. In September, having never flown before, he undertook two journeys by air to Germany. Only at the last minute did the führer back down and agree to a conference at Munich, where he obtained all of his demands. But Europe had perched on the edge of a major war—one that would have occurred under very different circumstances from those surrounding the one that began in September 1939.

Almost from the moment of the signing of the Munich Agreement, the arguments of contemporaries and then historians have swirled around the issue of whether the military weaknesses of the Western Powers justified the surrender or whether war in 1938 would have more readily and quickly resulted in Nazi Germany's demise than the war that broke out a year later.

HITLER'S INVASION OF CZECHOSLOVAKIA, OCTOBER 1938

ARMY DESIGNATIONS

Army

Divisions:
Infantry
Mountain
Motorized Infantry
Armored
Light

HUNGARY

0 Miles    60    100
0 Kilometers    100

POLAND

Kraków

Breslau
(Wroclaw)

SILESIA

CZECHOSLOVAKIA

Brünn (Brno)

Bratislava

Danube River

Vienna

Prague

Pilsen

Dresden

Danube River

GERMANY

N

© 2001 Jeffrey L. Ward

On one side, Winston Churchill, speaking before a hostile House of Commons in 1938, warned that the British people had "sustained a defeat without a war, the consequences of which will travel far with us along our road; they should know that we have passed an awful milestone in our history, when the whole equilibrium of Europe has been deranged, and that the terrible words have for the time being been pronounced against the Western Democracies: 'Thou art weighed in the balance and found wanting.'" On the other hand, the British chiefs of staff, just a few weeks before Munich, had warned that the military situation heavily favored Nazi Germany. The argument has continued unabated since.

What matters in thinking about war in 1938 is the actual balance of military, economic, and political forces in the fall of that year and the possible outcome of a major war. As was not the case in the other crises of the 1930s, Hitler had every intention of fighting; he had created a situation that would have forced the Western Powers to intervene, if the Wehrmacht had attacked Czechoslovakia. The brutal, aggressive behavior of Nazi Germany in the face of Neville Chamberlain's extraordinary peacekeeping efforts had finally resulted in a fundamental shift in British and French public opinion in favor of standing against Hitler's unreasonable demands. Until his dying days he remained bitterly disappointed that the British had deprived him of the opportunity of launching the Wehrmacht against the Czechs.

In thinking about a war in 1938, one simply cannot point to a replay of the Battle of Britain. First, the Germans were not yet in a position to achieve the kind victory that would have destroyed the French Army on the Continent and secured the air bases on the Channel coast that made the Battle of Britain possible. Second, in 1938 the Luftwaffe possessed none of the prerequisites for such a battle. In fact, a war in 1938 would have looked nothing like the war that actually occurred in 1939 and 1940.

In considering the German Army's development in the 1930s, it is difficult to avoid considering the impression created by its later victories. In 1938 its forces still possessed considerable weaknesses. Re-armament had built the army up to forty-eight regular divisions, only three of which were panzer, four motorized infantry, and four light divisions (which consisted of a mixed bag of motorized, mechanized, and cavalry units), while the remainder were World War I–style infantry units, their equipment largely drawn by horses, and most with considerable shortages in artillery and other weapons.

Moreover, German rearmament had yet to establish any depth; there were few reserves except for Landwehr divisions consisting of overage and out-of-shape World War I veterans. Even the three panzer divisions had considerable weaknesses; their equipment consisted entirely of six-ton PzKw Is and ten-ton PzKw IIs, the former a glorified tin can. The result was that the existing armored forces possessed little hitting or staying power.

But the real weakness in the army lay in the quality, training, and skills of its junior officers and NCOs. The army's growth from the minuscule Reichswehr of 1933 had resulted in an officer corps that had expanded far too rapidly. Consequently, the Germans still confronted two crucial problems in 1938: Not only did the army's combat potential suffer from real deficiencies in training and leadership, but the reserve forces on which Germany depended to defend its western frontier and take part in any sustained combat, did not yet exist.

Thus, the strategic demands of a war in 1938 would have been beyond the army's manpower, equipment, and resources. Because the Germans could not trust the Poles, three divisions had to remain in East Prussia (separated from the rest of the Reich by the Polish Corridor), whatever the strategic situation. Five of the army's regular divisions had come directly into the army as a result of the *Anschluss* and fully reflected their heritage in the Austrian Army. By the fall of 1939 the Wehrmacht managed to correct those deficiencies, but in 1938 they remained quite apparent. As one senior general noted, the difference between Austrian and German units was the difference between night and day.

In planning *Fall Grün* (Case Green, the attack on Czechoslovakia) the OKM, or Oberkommando des Heeres, the army high command, allocated thirty-seven divisions for the campaign. After the subtraction of three divisions in East Prussia, there remained only eight for the defense of the west, Pomerania, and Silesia against the French and Poles. Backing up this scanty operational reserve were fourteen Landwehr divisions, all under-trained, underequipped, and unprepared for combat. In nearly every respect, the army was not ready.

There was also considerable political dissatisfaction among senior officers over Hitler's handling of the Fritsch/Blomberg crisis during the winter of 1938. Even pro-Nazi officers like Heinz Guderian were angered by the phony charges of homosexuality that the SS had manufactured against General Werner von Fritsch, the army's commander in chief. Only the stunning success of the *Anschluss* that March prevented a simmering crisis in civil-military relations from becoming a full-blown eruption. In addition, Hitler's war policy toward Czechoslovakia occasioned deep worries among senior generals. The chief of the general staff, Ludwig Beck, had resigned as a result of his disagreement with Hitler's drive toward war. The disquiet with Hitler's policies even led a number of senior generals to plot against the Nazi regime as the crisis reached its height in September. Thus, the army was hardly the unified, ideologically committed organization it would be in the early 1940s.

If the mid- and long-term prospects of the German Army in war in 1938 did not look bright, the Czechs also confronted serious problems. They had begun work in the mid-1930s on a complex series of fortifications to defend against a German attack from Silesia. While considerable work had gone forward in creating field fortifications, their defensive works still had serious deficiencies. The old frontier with Austria was particularly vulnerable. While the mountains and forest ringing the Bohemian/Moravian plateau offered considerable challenges to an invader, the Germans had the opportunity in the area between Silesia and Austria to cut the Czech Republic in half—particularly given the lack of fortifications along the Austro-Czech frontier.

The Czech Army's potential is, of course, difficult to evaluate, since it would never fight. Its equipment was excellent, a reflection of the up-to-date, highly efficient armament complexes in Czechoslovakia, the Skoda works being the most famous. Ironically, those works would turn out high-quality weapons for the Wehrmacht right through 1945. But the quality of the army is another matter. The human material from the Czech regions was motivated and well-educated, but the Czechs only made up approximately 50 percent of the republic's population. The fighting qualities of even the Slovaks were problematic, while those of the republic's smaller nationalities such as Ruthenians, Hungarians, and Sudeten Germans was almost nonexistent. Generally the officer corps was competent, but senior officers were not a distinguished lot. The operational planning for *Fall Grün* suggests the risks Hitler was running. In the west General Walther von Reichenau's Tenth Army was to break into Bohemia with a blow aimed at Prague. But Franz Halder, Beck's replacement as chief of the general staff, placed the emphasis on General Gerd von Rundstedt's Second Army, which was to attack from Silesia to meet General Wilhelm List's Fourteenth Army attacking from Austria. The aim was to cut Czechoslovakia in half and isolate the Czechs from receiving outside aid.

At the first briefing of invasion plans by Halder, Hitler objected to the OKH's operational conception. He suggested that Rundstedt's attack from Silesia would result in heavy casualties in fighting through the strong Czech defenses in the region; he worried that the fighting might turn into another Verdun. Hitler also demanded that Halder reinforce Reichenau's Tenth Army with panzer and motorized divisions so that German forces could capture Prague early in the campaign and thus deter the French and British from intervening. As Hitler suggested:

There is no doubt that the planned pincer operation is the most desirable solution [from the military point of view] and should take place. Its success, nevertheless, is too uncertain to depend on, especially as, politically, a rapid success is necessary. The first eight days are politically decisive, in which period of time we must achieve far-reaching territorial gains.

In the end the final plans represented a compromise between Hitler and Halder. Reichenau's Tenth Army received additional divisions, but nothing on the order of what Hitler had initially demanded, while Rundstedt's offensive was to go forward into the teeth of the Czech fortifications. In political terms, Hitler's conception was both daring and offered better prospects for deterring the Western powers. However, the compromise weakened the blow from Silesia without significantly increasing the chances for a successful capture of Prague in the invasion's first days. As he was to do for the remainder of his career, Hitler was ready to take great risks.

The balance in air power between the Czechs and the Germans was relatively straightforward. While the Luftwaffe enjoyed great superiority, it would have confronted some significant problems. Eight of the days between October 1 and October 11 (the first days of the scheduled invasion) had bad weather—the kind of conditions that would have presented an inexperienced air force with considerable difficulties. In retrospect, the Luftwaffe would undoubtedly have played a major role in the conquest of Czechoslovakia, but because of bad weather and its own weaknesses, it would have suffered heavy losses that would have hampered its ability to execute further operations.

The ground capabilities of the other European armies are relatively easy to lay out; in contrast to 1914 virtually everyone was unprepared for another great war. At best the British could have sent two unprepared and ill-equipped divisions to support the French. The Soviets possessed great masses of equipment and huge numbers of soldiers, but Stalin had shot most of the Red Army's senior leadership in the purges that had begun in May 1937. The year 1938 represented the nadir of Soviet preparations for war, as an imaginative and innovative military leadership had given way to the worst sort of sycophants—few of whom knew the slightest thing about the conduct of military operations. The great wild card in the 1938 situation remains the question of what the Soviets, who had little real interest in helping the Czechs, would have done. The Poles represented a more serious military factor, since their army was not nearly as bad as the campaign in 1939 would suggest. In a war in 1938 they could have picked the time and place for military operations against the Germans. German forces in Silesia, tied down as they would have been in attacking Moravia, would have been particularly vulnerable to Polish attack.

In the west the French possessed strong military forces. If confronted with a German invasion, they would have fought well in defense of their homeland. As we now know, French soldiers would fight hard in 1940;

123,000 would die in defense of the republic in that campaign, betrayed by abysmal generalship. The generalship would have been no better the year before, but the German Army would not have been in a position to take advantage of those weaknesses. It is doubtful whether the French would have launched a serious offensive against the Rhineland. But, if presented the opportunity, they would have acted against the Italians, whom they regarded with reason as ill-trained and ill-prepared. Of all the armies in Europe, Italian ground forces were the least effective. The cause of this state of affairs had nothing to do with the bravery of Italians—over 600,000 had died in the Alps in some of the worst battles of World War I—but because of a general staff and leadership that displayed not a hint of serious military professionalism. The megalomaniacal tendencies of Mussolini's regime only served to exacerbate the incompetencies of generals like Marshal Rudolfo Graziani, who commented at the last crown council immediately before the war that "when the cannon sound, everything will fall into place."

The European naval and air balances underline how much weaker the Germans were in 1938 than they would be the next year. On the naval side, the Kriegsmarine was categorically not ready for war. It had yet to complete any of the major fleet units laid down under the Nazi construction programs. Neither *Scharnhorst* nor *Gneisenau,* the first battle cruisers, had yet to complete fitting out or working up. There were no heavy cruisers, no aircraft carriers, only seven destroyers and three "pocket" battleships (glorified heavy cruisers). Even more glaringly there were only seven oceangoing U-boats available for service in the Atlantic. Consequently, the Germans were hardly in a position to protect their own coasts, much less execute a war on Allied commerce in the North Atlantic. As a result, the Western Powers could have concentrated their naval resources in the Mediterranean, where the Italians were even more vulnerable.

The air balance was, of course, one of the crucial elements in the strategic equation of 1938. One of the most persistent myths in the post-Munich literature has argued that Chamberlain saved Britain at Munich from defeat at the hands of the Luftwaffe and won time for the RAF's Fighter Command to win the "Battle of Britain." Supposedly, the year's grace provided by the Munich surrender allowed the RAF to equip its fighter squadrons with Spitfires and Hurricanes and extend the radar system and sector stations to cover the whole of the British Isles. In fact, the Luftwaffe was completely unprepared to launch a strategic bombing campaign against the British Isles.

The persistent belief in the possibility of a German air campaign against Britain in 1938 is the direct result of the massive disinformation campaign the Germans waged in 1938 to persuade their potential enemies of the Luftwaffe's terrifying capabilities. Charles Lindbergh was to mar his reputation for the rest of his life by the gullibility with which he swallowed the propaganda line that Hermann Göring and other Luftwaffe leaders fed him during his visits to Germany. But the chief of staff of the French Air Force, General Joseph Vuillemin, was no more perceptive during a visit to Germany in August 1938. He returned to France to fill the highest councils of the French government with reports about the terrifying capabilities the Luftwaffe possessed. Astonishingly, a number of historians, without the slightest reference to German records, have projected German capabilities from such disinformation.

By September 1938 the RAF's rearmament program had made little progress. Reequipment of fighter squadrons was only beginning, while Bomber Command had no modern aircraft in production. Instead of the fifty fighter squadrons considered the minimum for Britain's air defense, only twenty-nine existed. Of these only five possessed Hurricanes and none Spitfires. Even the Hurricanes could not operate at altitudes above 15,000 in combat, since they had no gun warmers. The remaining squadrons possessed obsolete Gladiators, Furys, Gauntlets, and Demons, none of which could catch the newest German bombers.

But the Germans were no better off. For most of 1938 the Luftwaffe was exchanging its first generation of aircraft for newer models with which it would eventually fight much of World War II. Fighter squadrons were receiving Bf 109s in place of obsolete biplanes, but in fall 1938 there were no more than 500 Bf 109s in front-line squadrons. Virtually all the fighter squadrons transitioning to Bf 109s ran high accident rates, as inexperienced pilots struggled to handle the aircraft's high performance and narrow undercarriage. In the bomber squadrons, neither of the models in production, the Do 17 and He 111, possessed the range or load-carrying capacity to act as "strategic" bombers. The Luftwaffe was waiting for the introduction of the so-called *Schnell* (swift) bomber, the Ju 88, which would not arrive for another year. From bases in Germany the available bombers could have only carried minimal bomb loads against targets in Britain. The *Knickebein* blind-bombing system that used radio beams to guide bombers to their target was not yet deployed. In effect the Germans could have done little against British targets in 1938 and 1939. As it was, introduction of technologically complex, high-performance aircraft occasioned serious problems in the Luftwaffe's maintenance and supply organizations. The chief of the Luftwaffe's supply branch characterized the Luftwaffe's state in the fall of 1938 in the following terms: "The consequences of these circumstances [the Czech crisis] was a) a constant and, for first-line aircraft, complete lack of reserves both as accident replacements and for mobilization; b) a weakening of the aircraft inventory in the training schools in favor of the regular units; c) lack of . . . reserve engines, supplies for the timely equipment of airfields, supply services, and depots both for peacetime needs as well as for mobilization."

Thus, there was no possibility of conducting a successful strategic bombing campaign in 1938 due to the state of the Luftwaffe's armament and support structure. Moreover, Luftwaffe planning staffs had only recently begun thinking about such a possibility. In August 1938, the Luftflotte 2. (Second Air Force), which had responsibility for operations over the North Sea and Britain, characterized its combat capabilities as no more than the capacity to launch pinprick attacks against the British Isles. The command emphasized that German ground forces would have to seize Belgium and Holland before the Luftwaffe could attack targets in Britain. General Helmuth Felmy, commander of the Luftflotte 2., warned the Luftwaffe's high command in late September 1938 that "given the means at his disposal a war of destruction against England seemed to be excluded."

The basic strategic problem for Germany was that an attack on Czechoslovakia would not have remained a limited war, and the more the war spread, the more critical Germany's strategic situation would have become.

In Eastern Europe the attitude of the Soviet Union and of Poland would have been crucial in determining the course of a Czech-German war. Yet Stalin's purge of most of his officer corps and Soviet actions in late September, which aimed at paying the Poles back for their invasion of the Ukraine in 1920, suggest the Soviet Union would have been a doubtful participant, at least in providing significant help to the Czechs. Significantly, the Soviet Union had no frontier with either Germany or Czechoslovakia, so that it is difficult to visualize exactly what help the Soviets might have provided.

The Poles would have been a more important strategic player in a 1938 war. Józef Beck, their foreign minister, believed the Czechs would not fight, the West would refuse to take a stand, and Poland must remain implacably hostile to the Soviet Union. Still, he indicated that if the British and French intervened on behalf of the Czechs, Poland would support the Czech Republic. The great question in the 1938 confrontation, however, was whether the Poles could have intervened against the Germans or whether a Soviet attack on Poland under the guise of forcing the Poles to allow the Red Army to cross Polish territory to aid the Czechs would have forced the Poles to look east.

The most important difference between 1938 and 1939 was the fact that the overall strategic situation in the Balkans and Eastern Europe was far more favorable to the West. In 1938, whatever the Red Army's military capabilities, the Soviets would not have been the willing allies of Nazi Germany. Thus, the Germans would not have received the flood of goods they received from the Soviets after the signing of the Nazi–Soviet Non-Aggression Pact the following year. Equally important, the Germans in 1938 had not yet succeeded in overawing the Eastern European nations. The Yugoslavs and the Romanians gave tacit support to the Czechs during the crisis, while the Romanians went so far as to warn the Germans in late September 1938 that they were about to cut off petroleum exports to the Reich. Such an action would have had enormous implications for the effective functioning of the German war machine, not to mention the Reich's economy.

While the Germans confronted serious difficulties in the east, things were not much better in the west. With only eight regular divisions and a number of weak Landwehr divisions in that theater, the Germans were in a weak position. Only in March 1938 had the Germans begun major work on the Westwall—a chain of fortified bunkers along the Reich's frontier with France. The Czech crisis, which began to heat up in May 1938, then led Hitler to undertake a massive program of construction. But most of this effort was eyewash, because there was not sufficient time for concrete to set, while many of the fortifications were badly sited. The Westwall's weaknesses and the few troops available led the chief of staff of the armies in the west to declare to Hitler that the French would penetrate deep into the Rhineland within three weeks of the start of hostilities. With typical aplomb, Hitler declared that the fortifications could be held not for three weeks, but for three years.

The difficulty was that the French had no intention of taking advantage of German weaknesses. As Charles de Gaulle, still a relatively junior officer, put it to Leon Blum: "It's quite simple. . . . Depending on actual circumstances, we will recall the . . . reserves. Then looking through the loopholes of our fortifications, we will passively witness the enslavement of Eastern Europe." The visit of Maurice Gamelin, the French commander in chief, to London on September 26, 1938, underlines the accuracy of de Gaulle's appraisal. Gamelin indicated to his British hosts that after mobilization, the French Army would attack. But what he meant by attack was not exactly what the Germans meant by that word. He suggested that while there were advantages to an offensive, it might be more prudent to allow the evacuation of Paris. He then wondered how soon the Germans might begin transferring troops from east to west. When the Germans began that transfer, he admitted, his plan was for the French Army to "retreat strategically in the manner of Hindenburg in 1917 to their fortifications in the Maginot Line, devastating the territory as they went." This was surely a recipe for doing nothing, which was exactly what Gamelin did in 1939 and 1940.

Serious problems for the Germans in a war in 1938 would also have risen in the Mediterranean. No one in Italy yet understood the extent of German irresponsibility. Thus, throughout September Mussolini made a num-

ber of strong speeches declaring his intention to stand by his fellow dictator. It would have been difficult for the duce to disavow such statements,
had a war over Czechoslovakia broken out. An Italian declaration of war
would have been a disaster for the Germans. Italy's participation in the war
would have harmed the Reich in a number of important respects. It would
have increased the effectiveness of the Allied blockade. The burden of supplying Italy as well as the German war economy with raw materials from
the limited resources available might have strained the German economy
to the breaking point. Considering British and French naval superiority in
the Mediterranean, there is no doubt that Allied navies would have quickly
cut supply lines to Libya and bombarded the Italian coasts. With reason,
the French were optimistic about prospects both in the Alps and in Libya.
As one French staff officer commented, the Allies could have scored major
successes against Italy in the Mediterranean within the first two months of
the opening of hostilities.

Bur of all the adverse factors confronting the Germans in a fall 1938 war,
the most serious lay in the economic sphere. Although the *Anschluss* and
the seizure of Austria's gold and foreign exchange reserves had temporarily
improved Germany's economic situation, these gains had proved to be
wasting assets. Over the summer of 1938 a combination of the massive rearmament program, construction on the Westwall, the initiation of a drastic
program to increase production of synthetic fuels (from coal) and munitions, and the mobilization of hundreds of thousands of soldiers created a
serious economic crisis. Four-year-plan experts admitted among themselves
that in the last half of 1938 the German economy had faced "undreamed-
of difficulties. The strongbox was empty, industrial capacity was committed
for years to come." Construction on the Westwall compounded all these
problems.

Signs of an economic crisis appeared throughout the fall of 1938 in the
German economy. The economic strain was so bad in October 1938 that
the Reich's Defense Committee reported that "in consequence of Wehrmacht demands [occupation of the Sudetenland] and unlimited construction of the Westwall, so tense a situation in the economic sector occurred . . .

that continuation of the tension past October 10 would have made an [economic] catastrophe inevitable." One month later at a sitting of the same committee, Göring admitted that the strain on the economy had reached the point where no more workers were available, factories were at full capacity, foreign exchange was completely exhausted, and Germany's economic situation was desperate.

The German economy in 1938 did not possess the strength to support a breakout from the Reich's constrained economic base, as occurred in spring 1940. Not only was the production of synthetic fuels, synthetic rubber, and munitions substantially lower than in 1939, but the Germans could expect no help from the Soviet Union and little from the Balkan states. The crucial problems in 1938 were the consistent and endemic shortages of raw materials and the lack of foreign exchange to increase imports, all of which disappeared when the Germans conquered Western Europe and opened the floodgates of Soviet support. Most probably the German economy would not have suffered a catastrophic collapse had war broken out in the fall of 1938. Instead, the situation would have resembled Germany's situation in 1917 in the midst of World War I, after which a slow, steady economic disintegration took place. In a war starting in 1938, the Germans would have had to resort to a series of expedients to meet present demands, and then only at the expense of future requirements. As production decreased and raw materials became in shorter supply, the Wehrmacht's fighting capabilities would have suffered a corresponding decline. Once this vicious cycle began, there would have been little chance that Germany could have escaped the inevitable consequences: defeat.

The German invasion of Czechoslovakia was scheduled to begin on October 1. How might it have unfolded? As was to be the case the next year against Poland and then against France and the Low Countries, the Luftwaffe would have begun operations with a massive strike at Czech air bases and transportation centers. However, the bad weather would have severely limited the impact of the first attacks, particularly on the Czech ground defenses. It is also clear that the Germans would have lost heavily in the opening attacks, as they did in France in 1940. Thereafter, the Luftwaffe would have gained a measure of air superiority, but given its inexperience at a heavy cost in terms of pilots and air crews.

The most important drive would have come from the Tenth Army. Most probably, it would have broken through the Czech defenses confronting Bavaria and onto the Bohemian plain. But it is unlikely that Reichenau's troops would have captured Prague in their first rush. The Czechs had a second line of field fortifications in front of their capital and substantial reserve forces available to support the fight to protect Prague from an attack from the west. Moreover, Reichenau possessed only one panzer division and one light division; the bulk of his motorized strength was concentrated in three motorized infantry divisions. In effect the Germans were not yet able to put a single panzer corps into the field. Thus, even if the Germans had achieved a breakthrough of the Sudeten frontier, Tenth Army did not possess the armored strength to exploit that opening.

The OKH divided the other two panzer divisions between List's Fourteenth Army and Rundstedt's Second Army. Rundstedt's forces confronted the daunting task of fighting their way through the strongest Czech fortifications. To help in the effort the Germans planned to drop what airborne forces existed behind Czech defenses at Bruntal, south of Silesia. (After the Czechs evacuated the area in early October, the Germans actually did execute the planned drop in a major exercise. The test was a shambles; transport aircraft dropped the paratroopers all over the landscape including many too close to the main fortifications; engineers failed to clear landing fields for follow-up troops; and much of the heavy equipment failed to arrive on schedule. The exercise suggested the attack would have been a catastrophe, had it taken place under combat conditions.)

Thus, Rundstedt would have received little help from the paratroopers, and Second Army would have fought its way through heavily fortified positions held by strong Czech forces. The Czechs also had powerful reserves of one mechanized division and two reserve divisions immediately behind the front line, facing Silesia. In the south, the German Fourteenth Army, advancing from Austria, would have confronted a less formidable defensive system. But again the Czechs held strong reserves near the frontier—three regular divisions, two reserve divisions, and a mechanized division. Here the Germans would have run into substantial opposition that would have significantly interfered with closure between Fourteenth and Second Armies. All this suggests that on the tactical level, the Czechs could have put up sustained resistance and inflicted severe losses on the attackers. Because of the shape of their country, the Czechs would probably not have lasted much longer than the Poles did in 1939, three weeks at the maximum. But they would have inflicted heavier losses on the Germans, who had no prospect of gaining the kind of operational freedom that proved so devastating in the 1939 campaign, because Czechoslovakia's mountainous terrain was so much more defensible than the plains of Poland.

Equally important for its long-range impact on the Wehrmacht's buildup would have been the fact that a sustained campaign would have destroyed virtually all of the Czech Army's equipment. Those arms fell into German hands in undamaged condition in March 1939 and provided the equipment for four Waffen SS and eight army divisions, and tanks for three panzer divisions. Bombing attacks and deliberate sabotage by the Czechs would also have wrecked much of Czechoslovakia's armament potential—which the Germans would take advantage of throughout World War II. The most significant strategic factor is that sustained Czech resistance would have forced the British and French to declare war. However, the French would have failed to launch any kind of a serious offensive against the weak German defenses and forces in the west, whatever was happening in the east.

A Polish entry into the conflict with a limited attack on Silesia would have placed Rundstedt's forces in a dangerous position. Limited attacks on Pomerania and East Prussia would have added to the difficulties the Germans confronted. The critical element in Poland's decision would have been how quickly the Western Powers would react to the Nazi attack on the Czech Republic—the slower the Western response, the more unwilling the Poles would have been to act. However, the Soviets might well have taken advantage of a German attack on Czechoslovakia to settle scores with the Poles. Whatever the Soviets did, however, would have achieved minimal success, given the disastrous impact of the purges on the Red Army's officer corps.

But for the Germans, the Poles would have represented only one of many strategic worries. The economic situation would have been even more desperate than it was to be in the fall of 1939. And German economic difficulties a year later almost forced Hitler to move against the almost unanimous advice of his generals. Hitler would have confronted the strategic and economic problems raised by an economy starved for raw materials and by oil stocks at minimum levels. In addition, there were no obvious sources to replace those blocked off by an Allied blockade, as there would be in 1939 and 1940, when the Soviets so enthusiastically stepped in to help the Germans.

Exacerbating German difficulties might have been a coup attempt. Two senior officers, Erwin von Witzleben and Erich Hoepner, both had committed themselves to removing Hitler should he provoke a war with Czechoslovakia. Halder was also dabbling in the plots that were constituting and then dissolving according to the political situation in September 1938. Considering the inept effort that took place in July 1944, one cannot place much confidence in these efforts by a variety of plotters. In the summer of 1938 Beck had even suggested arresting Hitler's advisers, but leaving the führer in charge!

Unfortunately, most of the junior officers and enlisted men remained solidly behind the regime. But if ever there was a time when a coup might have succeeded, it would have been in the fall of 1938, when there was enormous dissatisfaction in the German population over the prospect of another great war. Nevertheless, even had a coup failed, it would have further shaken the confidence of a population dubious about the prospect of war.

Moreover, the Nazi leadership would have had to confront the problem of what next after Czechoslovakia? A Luftwaffe that had suffered heavy losses against the Czechs would not have had sufficient strength to launch a major air campaign against France, much less Britain. Even had the Germans possessed sufficient aircraft, there were two daunting problems: insufficient fuel and the bad weather that cloaks Europe from October until May. In such conditions, there was no possibility the Luftwaffe could have hit major targets on a sustained basis. Even as late as the summer of 1939, the future field marshal Albert Kesselring admitted that his bomber crews were incapable of hitting targets accurately in such conditions.

If the Luftwaffe could not solve Germany's strategic problem, Hitler would have had to turn to the army. With Germany's economy in serious difficulties, the pressure would have been to settle matters with the French before the British arrived in strength. Over the winter of 1939–1940 the Germans delayed their attack through the intervention of fortuitous (from their point of view) bad weather; in 1938 the exigencies of the situation—i.e., their desperate economic situation—would have forced them to seek a decision in the west. Here their prospects would have been most uninviting. German mechanized forces would have consisted of three badly battered panzer divisions, three light divisions in not much better shape, and four motorized infantry divisions. The rest of the attacking force would have consisted of regular infantry divisions, most of which would also have suffered heavy losses against the Czechs. The Germans would have also disposed of the fourteen Landwehr divisions, most of which would have been moved east to occupy the conquered portions of Czechoslovakia and protect the frontier with Poland.

As in October 1939, the Germans would have confronted the problem of how to defeat the French. Since we know that the OKH had no advanced planning available for a Western campaign in October 1939, we can assume that the Germans would have had no extant plan in the fall of 1938. The planning for a war in the west that did exist consisted of efforts aimed at defending the Rhineland against a combined French/Belgian offensive. Thus, the Germans would have had to cobble together a plan for a campaign against the west, one that would have looked quite similar to what Hitler and the OKH put together in October 1939: a great offensive to take Holland, Belgium, and northern France to the Somme. But unlike the situation in 1939, there would have been greater pressures, particularly considering a desperate economic situation, to attack in the winter. Thus, there would have been no time to consider the Ardennes alternative—and even if the Germans had hit upon that possibility, they did not have the armored forces to create and then exploit a breakthrough along the Meuse.

What then would a straight-out infantry offensive against the Low

Countries and Northern France have looked like? The attacking force would have resembled those it was attacking far more than in 1940. The Germans would not have had time to absorb the lessons of even the campaign against Czechoslovakia. Their opponents would clearly have been ready for such an attack, as they were in May 1940. The Dutch would probably have been the least effective in resisting a German offensive, although it is unlikely that there were sufficient German paratroopers to achieve the stunning success of May 10, 1940, nor would the Germans have had a panzer division to drive deep into Fortress Holland. Instead, they would have had to take Holland by an infantry assault on the Dutch fortifications.

The problem would have been the same in the assault of northern France and Belgium. The Germans would have been advancing into the teeth of their opponents' defensive strength. Conceivably, the Germans might have taken the Belgian fortress of Eben Emael by a *coup de main*, but thereafter, it is difficult to see much opportunity for the Germans either to achieve a breakthrough, or had they done so, to exploit such an opportunity in the fashion they were to do in the spring of 1940. The campaign then would have turned on a World War I–style infantry battle. It would not have been a battle of trench lines, but rather a war of movement that characterized the fighting after March 1918. Here the Germans would have had some advantages. Both in terms of doctrine and training, they were far in advance of their French opponents. But unlike 1940, these advantages would not have been sufficient to achieve a decisive breakthrough. And they would have involved heavy casualties: The German attacks in the spring of 1918 that returned maneuver to the battlefield also proved very costly. The German losses for the four months from March through June 1918 were double the British losses at Passchendaele—nearly one million casualties.

At best the Germans would have gotten to the Somme, but no further. The French would also have suffered heavy casualties, but as suggested above, even in 1940 under impossible circumstances, they suffered heavy casualties in defense of their homeland. A 1918-style infantry battle in the fall of 1938 would have been precisely the one that the French high command had prepared to fight; and if the French generals did not have the skill to fight that battle in a flexible fashion, at least their men would have fought the battle tenaciously.

Reaching the Somme with a burned-out army would have solved none of the Reich's difficulties. The Germans would still have confronted their problems in the east, while they might have also faced the collapse of their ally in the Mediterranean. There, a declaration of war in support of the Germans by Mussolini would have opened a Pandora's box of troubles for the Italians. With no fleet to speak of (two of Italy's four battleships were in dockyard, undergoing refit, and none of the new battleships were yet complete), the Italians would quickly have come under assault by sea. The Royal Navy and the French Navy would have had a field day, particularly since there was so little for them to do in the Atlantic. The Regia Aeronautica (the Italian Air Force) had neither aircraft nor training to support the Italian fleet, while the army was in even worse shape than two years later. Allied successes, of greater magnitude than in fall 1940, would only have encouraged the British and French to further action. And the Germans would have been in no position to provide assistance, given their own troubles.

It is difficult to carry the scenario for the war over Czechoslovakia out much further than the above discussion. But at a minimum the strategic situation for Germany's opponents would have been far more favorable than would be the results of the first nine months of the conflict that actually occurred. And the ensuing conflict would have resulted in far less destruction and fewer deaths. It would also probably not have resulted in the Holocaust, although Europe's Jews, and German Jews in particular, might well have suffered onerous persecutions, given the racist climate of the time. There are a number of imponderables that must remain unanswered: Would Hitler and Stalin have made a deal? Would Hitler have survived? How effectively would the Poles have intervened against the Czechs and Germans? Would a Soviet-Polish War have resulted from the German attack on Czechoslovakia? How effective might the German opposition have proved, had things gone badly for the Reich in the course of the war's first months? Would the British and French governments have displayed the toughness to take advantage of German troubles?

A close analysis of the military balance in the fall of 1938 suggests that the Germans would have emerged from their attack on Czechoslovakia weakened rather than strengthened, as would be the case in 1939. In that weakened condition the Germans would have had to launch the Wehrmacht west with little prospect of gaining a decisive victory, much as had been the case in March 1918. The result would have been that there would have been no Norwegian campaign, no catastrophic defeat of France, and certainly no Battle of Britain.

What the historian can suggest from the available evidence is that the strategic situation in 1938 was far more favorable to the Allies than it would prove the following year. Tragically, in mid-September the British tried and failed to grapple with the question of whether the loss of Czechoslovakia to the Germans might fundamentally alter the European balance of power in Germany's favor were war to break out in 1939. The evidence clearly indicates that it did, and that a major factor in the catastrophic German victories of the spring of 1940 resulted from the additional year and a half the Germans had to prepare. Winston Churchill quite accurately described Munich as a "defeat without a war." The tragedy of European history was the fact that the one great risk Hitler decided at the last moment not to take was the one risk that might well have ended the terrible adventure before it had begun.

ANDREW ROBERTS

# PRIME MINISTER HALIFAX

*Great Britain makes peace
with Germany, 1940*

*Six decades after Winston S. Churchill became prime minister of Great Britain in
May 1940, it is easy to forget that he was hardly a universal favorite: not quite a
choice by default but almost one. Many of his fellow Conservatives distrusted him
because Churchill had on occasion crossed party lines. His stability was questioned. And many too blamed the first lord of the admiralty in Neville Chamberlain's government for the looming disaster in Norway. Few probably saw that
Churchill possessed (as the American novelist James Gould Cozzens once put it)
"greatness's enabling provisions—the great man's inner contradictions; his mean,
inspired inconsistencies; his giddy acting on hunches; and his helpless, not mere
acceptance of, but passionate, necessary trust in, luck."*

*As it became ever more obvious that Chamberlain had lost the confidence of
the nation and his party, the choice of a replacement narrowed to Churchill and
the foreign secretary, that tall, slope-shouldered scarecrow in a derby hat, Lord
Halifax. The former viceroy of India was widely admired but deeply associated
with Chamberlain's failed appeasement policies. Think of him as a British Herbert
Hoover, a man whose credentials were impeccable but who lacked the one ingredient most needed in a crisis: the ability to inspire. "A tired man," the indefatiga-
ble diarist Harold Nicholson called Halifax. But he was plainly Chamberlain's
preference.*

*The prime minister made one final attempt to stay in power, inviting the lead-
ers of the Labour party into his government; they declined. On the afternoon of*

May 9, Chamberlain met with Churchill and Halifax. As Churchill later remembered, he wanted to know "whom he should advise the king to send for after his own resignation had been accepted." There was a long silence. "Then at length Halifax spoke. He said he felt that his position as a Peer, out of the House of Commons, would make it very difficult for him to discharge the duties of prime minister in a war like this. . . . By the time he had finished it was clear that the duty would fall on me—had in fact fallen on me." The next day, May 10, Hitler invaded the Low Countries and the king summoned Churchill to Buckingham Palace.

That is what did happen. But Andrew Roberts, one of the foremost authorities on this period, wonders how the next months and years would have played out had Halifax not taken himself out of the running. His speculation is hardly outlandish: As late as the weekend of Dunkirk—the beginning of June—some members of Churchill's cabinet, including Halifax (who had stayed on as foreign secretary) were seriously discussing the possibility of making a deal with Hitler, going through Mussolini, who was not the tragicomic figure he would presently become. Churchill, it should be noted, stood firm in his determination to resist. But Roberts here presumes that Churchill's star was already waning and that there would be no Dunkirk, no "Finest Hour."

ANDREW ROBERTS is the author of a biography of the Earl of Halifax, *The Holy Fox; Eminent Churchillians*; and a biography of the Victorian prime minister the third marquess of Salisbury, *Salisbury: Victorian Titan*, which won the Wolfson History Prize and the James Stern Silver Pen Award for nonfiction. His latest book is *Napoleon and Wellington: The Long Duel*.

H ITLER'S LIGHTNING ATTACK on Denmark and Norway on April 9, 1940, as successful as it was unexpected, severely unnerved the British people and political class. Only a few days earlier the British prime minister, Neville Chamberlain, had reassured the country that "Hitler has missed the bus." Yet by April 14, the Royal Navy had to be dispatched to the west coast of Norway, where an expeditionary force failed to take Trondheim due to lack of air power. Only two weeks later, on May 2, British forces had to evacuate Norway altogether, adding a military humiliation to the long list of diplomatic defeats the government had suffered at the hands of Adolf Hitler.

The whole northern flank of the Western alliance had collapsed in a matter of days, and a significant body of members of parliament in the British House of Commons were now in a mood to exact vengeance on Chamberlain, the man they blamed for displaying a lack of grip and determination in his conduct of the war.

The four men who met in the Cabinet room at Number 10, Downing Street on Thursday, May 9, 1940, were under no illusions as to the gravity of their deliberations. The previous night had seen the climactic conclusion of the adjournment debate in the House of Commons, which had turned into an issue of confidence in Neville Chamberlain's Conservative-dominated National Government. The government's majority had fallen from around 200 to only 80, the result of widespread abstentions and no fewer than 41 defections. The prime minister was under enormous pressure to resign and allow a coalition government to be formed, which would include the Opposition parties. Yet who would succeed him?

The only two serious candidates were Lord Halifax and Winston Churchill, and the decision could easily have gone either way. The following presupposes that it did not go Churchill's:

Present in the Cabinet room were Chamberlain himself, the foreign secretary Viscount Halifax, the Government chief whip David Margesson, and the sixty-five-year-old first lord of the admiralty Winston Churchill. The last had clashed violently with Labour MPs at the end of the debate, in which he had stoutly defended the government's record over the recent conduct of military operations in Norway, for which his own department had been largely responsible.

After a short discussion about the possibility of Chamberlain staying on, which was conclusively ended by Margesson stating that the Labour party leader, Clement Attlee, was known to be unwilling to enter a coalition government under the present prime minister, Chamberlain bluntly asked the two candidates whom they thought ought to take on the premiership? In his memoirs, Churchill records how "a very long pause ensued. It certainly seemed much longer than the two minutes which one observes in the commemorations of Armistice Day."

After Halifax had judged that Churchill had had enough time to make a statement of self-abnegation but had failed to do so, the foreign secretary pressed his claim, adamant that he was the best candidate. He pointed out that he was senior to Churchill, was trusted by the Lords and Commons, was the preferred choice of the king and queen, and enjoyed good relations with the Opposition. While Churchill had been antagonizing Labour during the General Strike in 1926, he pointedly remarked, he had been *hors de combat* as viceroy of India.

Halifax fully admitted that he was no military expert, but a German attack had yet to materialize on the Western Front. Churchill could anyway, as minister of defense, take over the day-to-day running of the war, albeit with a chiefs of staff committee to ensure that no "disastrous flanking operations were decided upon unilaterally," a clear reference to Churchill's role in the planning of the Gallipoli campaign a quarter century before. The primary task of a wartime premier, Halifax contended, was to keep national morale high, which required avoiding "histrionics" on the wireless and in Parliament. Churchill winced as each dig went home.

With Churchill still silent, Margesson then added that Halifax's undoubted moral stature would be invaluable in rallying the country, and that

PRIME MINISTERS IN WAITING

*In a 1938 photograph, Winston Churchill (left) strolls with Lord Edward Halifax, that gaunt, dapper figure in a bowler hat, who seemed destined to become prime minister. Had this consummate politician not taken himself out of contention when Neville Chamberlain resigned on May 10, 1940, Halifax and not Winston Churchill would have led Great Britain.*

(Hulton-Deutsch Collection/CORBIS)

only that very morning a letter had appeared in the *Times* written by the Labour-supporting Oxford All Souls fellow A. L. Rowse, suggesting that Churchill should be minister of defense in a Halifax Cabinet, an arrangement that the senior Labour leaders Hugh Dalton and Herbert Morrison were also known to support. Margesson added that his whips had ascertained that the vast majority of the Conservative party, which was preponderant in the Commons, wanted Halifax. Almost rubbing the matter in, Margesson added that Churchill's support was confined to a tiny minority of MPs thought to number little over thirty, a hodgepodge of politicians with no one other than Anthony Eden of any great weight. Churchill, knowing this to be true, stayed silent.

Chamberlain then spoke about the constitutional difficulty of having a peer as prime minister, debarred from sitting in the House of Commons. He revealed that the previous December he had asked the parliamentary legal adviser, Sir Granville Ram, whether "as a special ad hoc war measure" a peer could be allowed to sit—speak but not vote—in the Lower House. Ram had answered that all that was required would be a resolution in both Houses, which in emergency circumstances could be effected in an hour or two.

The prime minister then spoke of the wider implications of Halifax succeeding him. He pointed out Halifax's superior qualifications for the post, above all the trust the Conservatives placed in him and his good relations with the Opposition, who had already let it be known that they would serve under him in a coalition government. Grand strategy could be left to Churchill for the duration of the war, but as everyone who had watched his career during the Abdication Crisis, the Sidney Street Siege, the Gold Standard issue, the India Bill debates, and the General Strike attested, the cool judgment required of a prime minister was not Churchill's strong suit. Instead he was considered by many to be overly romantic, prone to bombast, and exceedingly ambitious. Yes, Chamberlain fully admitted, Churchill had been proved right about the true nature of Hitler and the inadvisability of appeasement, but now was not a time to look back to the past and, anyhow, the Munich agreement had bought the crucial year of peace with which Britain had boosted her air defenses.

"Stick to the war, Winston," seemed to be the united cry of the outgoing premier, the royal family, the majority of the Cabinet, senior Opposition figures, *The Times*, the Tories, the House of Lords, the city, and the higher reaches of society. Most importantly, though, it was emphatically Halifax's view also. Churchill knew that were he to refuse to serve in a Halifax ministry he would be accused of putting his personal ambition before his patriotic duty at a time of grave national crisis.

Churchill had been advised by Anthony Eden and the lord privy seal Sir Kingsley Wood to stay silent at the meeting and thus effectively to stage a coup, but the plan had hopelessly backfired. It was clear that the premiership was Halifax's for the taking and the best he could do was to haggle for a powerful Defense Ministry with all-pervading powers over the Admiralty, War Office, and Air Ministry. He also tried to ask for jobs for some of his supporters such as Alfred Duff Cooper, Lord Beaverbrook, and Brendan Bracken. Halifax, with a perceptible tone of relief, agreed to the Defense idea, but said he could not commit himself to finding posts for all the more outré of Churchill's friends. Churchill shrugged glumly; he had done his best.

Saturday, May 25, 1940, is undoubtedly the most controversial date in contemporary British history, being the day on which the Butler-Bastianini Pact was signed, bringing Britain's participation in the second Franco-Prussian War to an abrupt end. Depending on your viewpoint, it was the day that the Halifax government saved the British Expeditionary Force (BEF) from almost certain capture at Dunkirk and brought it safely home, or the day when a craven peace was signed that betrayed Britain's allies. Yet whichever view one takes, the facts are clear.

The story of the Wehrmacht's vast flanking attack around the Maginot Line at dawn on May 10, knocking the Allies back with its revolutionary Blitzkrieg tactics, is well-recorded. By May 24, all objective military analysis agreed on the likelihood of the BEF, then in full retreat toward the Channel ports, being doomed. It has since been suggested that Hitler was about to halt his panzers on the ridge above Dunkirk the following day, which might have allowed the BEF a temporary respite, but that was obviously not known in London at the time.

At a special Cabinet meeting at nine A.M. on Saturday May 25, the new prime minister Lord Halifax announced a surprise development. (He had been encouraged to set up a small War Cabinet but had resisted, realizing it would only have strengthened Churchill's position vis à vis his own.) Halifax, who had retained the Foreign Office portfolio for himself, handed the discussion over to his undersecretary for foreign affairs R. A. B. Butler. To general astonishment, Butler informed their colleagues that he had entered into advanced, fruitful discussions with the Italian ambassador, Giuseppe Bastianini, about an immediate armistice and that subject to Cabinet approval it would be declared effective from noon that day.

The terms negotiated by Mussolini's foreign minister and son-in-law Count Ciano in Rome, in close consultation with Ribbentrop and Hitler in Berlin, could hardly have been more favorable to Britain. In return for a complete cessation of hostilities and the signing of a ten-year nonaggression pact, Germany would allow the BEF to return to Britain unmolested, seek an armistice with France based on the occupation of Paris but not much further south, and would guarantee the British Empire against attack from any third party. In return, Britain would return those African colonies confiscated from Germany by the Versailles Treaty and would demilitarize Malta and Gibraltar.

After a brief but vitriolic exchange of views, in which the word "traitor" was leveled at the prime minister, Churchill, Eden (minister for war), Ernest Bevin (minister for Labour), A. V. Alexander (first lord of the admiralty) and Duff Cooper (minister of information) walked out of the Cabinet and wrote vituperative letters of resignation.

The Halifax Government nonetheless survived, with the Labour leader Clement Attlee and the Liberal leader Sir Archie Sinclair viewing the Pact as not particularly noble but the very best terms that could be obtained under the extraordinary circumstances. Had the BEF been captured wholesale, as seemed the most likely outcome, it was feared that any future terms from Hitler might call into question the existence of the Royal Navy or even the very independence of Britain herself.

This view was echoed by the media, especially by *The Times*, which was edited by Halifax's close friend Geoffrey Dawson and by the state-controlled

BBC, which kept anti-Pact propagandists such as the National Labour MP Harold Nicolson resolutely off the airwaves. The noisy support the Pact gained from the British Union of Fascists leader Sir Oswald Mosley was an embarrassment for Halifax, but the diaries of King George VI, Sir Alec Cadogan (permanent undersecretary at the Foreign Office), Sir Henry "Chips" Channon MP, Victor Cazalet MP, and many others testify to its grudging acceptance generally, especially once the boys in khaki began returning home safely. After a famously bitter debate in the Commons, in which Churchill made one of his best speeches claiming that "this might have been our finest hour," the Pact was approved 420 to 130.

The war over, it was incumbent on the government to hold an immediate general election, the first since 1935. Of course it turned into a virtual referendum on the Pact and was won by the National Government with a majority of 60, nothing like the landslides of 1931 and 1935 but enough for Halifax to govern comfortably.

In the wider world, the Pact had tremendous strategic implications. American support and sympathy for Britain, lukewarm in the Phoney War, had been growing in the fortnight campaign between May 10 and 24, but fell away sharply once the Pact was announced. The war in Europe over, American attention increasingly focused on the darkening situation in the Pacific.

Meanwhile Hitler was able, once Paris was occupied and the Reynaud Government signed their own peace agreement, to concentrate on the East without any fear of having to fight a war on two fronts. His new Western provinces were held with relatively few divisions, the only continental opposition to the peace being articulated by a Colonel de Gaulle, who found it impossible to raise French enthusiasm for a war of *revanche*. German factories hitherto dedicated to U-boat production were reconditioned to build the tanks and aircraft Hitler now required for a final settling of accounts with Bolshevism.

Without any British-backed provocation in Yugoslavia and Greece, Hitler felt no inclination to divert his attention toward southeast Europe before unleashing Blitzkrieg on Russia. He duly launched Operation Barbarossa on April 22, 1941, as soon as the roads across the steppes were dry and long before the Russian winter could be mobilized in Stalin's support.

The Butler-Bastianini Pact also had profound implications for the continental alliance, which Halifax had painstakingly built up during his foreign secretaryship. The French, not unnaturally, ascribed their humiliation on betrayal by "perfidious Albion." King Léopold of the Belgians even broke off diplomatic relations with Britain for their "treacherous" failure to warn him before the Pact was signed. On the other hand, most of the British Commonwealth dominions applauded the Pact, especially South Africa, which had been deeply split over the conflict, and Australia, which was looking toward her domestic defenses against an increasingly aggressive Japan.

When, in December 1941, Japan simultaneously attacked the U.S. naval base at Pearl Harbor and the British possessions in the Far East, Germany—in accordance with its undertakings to guarantee the Empire—declared war against Tokyo. This was a mere pro forma declaration but President Roosevelt nonetheless made known his appreciation of German effective neutrality in the conflict.

With no European war to mobilize American public opinion behind close Anglo-American cooperation the United States and Great Britain fought essentially separate campaigns in defense of their Indian and Pacific Ocean interests. Failing also to pool their knowledge in the field of atomic research, the war against Japan was fought out, island by island, until the final, costly victory in August 1949.

As befitted a Christian gentleman, Lord Halifax steadfastly stuck to the spirit and the letter of the Pact, whilst prudently maintaining high defense spending on all three services. The loss of the bases on Malta and Gibraltar severely stretched Britain's Mediterranean fleet, which had to use Cyprus as its main center of operations. When battle was joined between the German Fatherland and Russian Motherland, Britain and America stayed resolutely neutral, refusing to help either side even covertly in the struggle.

The result was, of course, that when the Soviet forces finally prevailed there was no Anglo-American presence in Western Europe when the triumphant Red Army marched on Berlin and beyond. Although the Wehrmacht had taken Moscow—which the Russians evacuated and burned as in 1812—and captured Stalingrad and subjected Leningrad to a grueling thousand-day siege, the final outcome was not in doubt. The combination of overlong German supply lines, appalling Russian winters, and dogged Soviet resistance, with manpower easily replaced wherever it was lost, meant that Stalin triumphed in the end, albeit at the cost of nearly 40 million Russians dead.

For all Hitler's strategic and matériel advantages in 1941–42, the sheer size of Russia and her army, and the willingness to accept any privations rather than surrender began to tell against him by 1944–45. The watershed year came in 1945, and by January 1946, the Wehrmacht was in full retreat back to Germany's borders.

Stalin felt no compunction to stop his march westward once Hitler had committed suicide in the ruins of Berlin in April 1946 and the Third Reich lay crushed beneath the Soviet heel. Indeed the lack of any help from Britain or America in his struggle, and their complete military absence from the European theater, probably goaded him on. In the spring of 1946, Stalin picked up the rest of Hitler's Western spoils. Communist-led resistance movements in Northern France, Denmark, Norway, Italy, and the Low Countries welcomed the Red Army into their countries, lynching the quislings who had administered their countries for the Nazis. Opponents of Communism, such as Colonel de Gaulle in Bordeaux, were arrested and executed; and there were several unpleasant instances of British businessmen having their heads forcibly shaved.

Stalin celebrated May Day 1946 at Versailles. Even Czar Alexander I in 1815, *Pravda* declared, had not entered Paris in such glory. Stalin was soon planning how to settle his score with General Franco on his new southern border. With 100,000 Spanish Republican refugees in southern France he could be assured of an enthusiastic campaign.

It was against this backdrop that the renegade Conservative backbencher Winston Churchill made a speech entitled "The Sinews of War" at Westminster College in the small Missouri town of Fulton. At the age of seventy-one he had been written off by most in British politics as a has-been and warmonger, but still retained an American following due to his opposition to the appeasement first of Hitler and now Stalin. In the past seventeen years since losing the chancellorship of the exchequer in 1929, Churchill had only held office for eight months between the outbreak of war in September 1939 and the coming of peace in May 1940. For a man of his undoubted talents it was a sorry record. Indeed it was considered a gracious act that Halifax had not had Churchill expelled from the Tory party despite his opposition to the central plank in the government's foreign policy.

"From Narvik in the North Sea to Toulon in the Mediterranean," thundered Churchill, "from Calais in the English Channel to the very heights of the Pyrenees an iron curtain has descended across the continent. Behind that line lie almost all the capitals of the ancient states of Europe. Warsaw, Berlin, Prague, Vienna, Helsinki, Budapest, Belgrade, Bucharest, Rome, Athens, Sofia, Paris, Brussels, Oslo, Copenhagen and The Hague, all these famous cities and the populations around them lie in what I must call the Soviet sphere."

Churchill's speech went largely unrecorded. He was known not to speak for the British government and anyhow he was only stating the obvious. Historical records show that on the day the speech was delivered, Stalin was not even informed of it. Instead that same day the Russian dictator had another, far more important file in his in-box. The debriefing of German scientists, his NKVD agents reported, had revealed that they had been working on a very interesting project to do with the military use of nuclear fission. The file was codenamed Tube Alloys and it did not take long for Stalin—by then the undisputed master of Europe with ambitions now stretching further afield—to recognize its potential significance.

JAMES BRADLEY

# THE BOYS WHO SAVED AUSTRALIA, 1942

*Small events can have large results*

*In the first months of 1942, Americans were consumed by dire "what if?" scenarios that, for the moment, were not altogether fantastic.* NOW THE U.S. MUST FIGHT FOR ITS LIFE, *read the lead headline of the March 2 issue of* Life. *Less than three months after Pearl Harbor, the world was collapsing before the twin onslaughts of the Germans and the Japanese, and the United States seemed as vulnerable to Axis attack as the Philippines or the Soviet Union. The invasion fears were well-founded. When the war began, there were only 100,000 troops to guard the entire Pacific coast and precious little ammunition to arm them with. Major General Joseph W. Stilwell, who in December 1941 was charged with defending central and southern California, noted in his diary, "If the Japs had only known, they could have landed anywhere on the coast, and after our handful of ammunition was gone, they could have shot us like pigs in a pen."*

*The same March 2 issue of* Life *served up a chilling menu of invasion schemes, and to make the peril more graphic, the magazine provided a series of artists' conceptions of how the Battle for America might unfold. Those pictures showed U.S. demolitions men blowing up the San Francisco Bay Bridge just as a Japanese troopship arrived; the city was burning in the background. Lines of Japanese troops plodded by Mount Rainier and tankmen joined in a firefight at a southern California filling station. Indeed, these scenes perfectly suited the plans Japanese strategists had for their suddenly expanding Pacific empire. Overcome by what was known in Japan as the "victory disease," they contemplated sweeping through the Indian*

Ocean to Africa, capturing Australia, New Zealand, and Hawaii, as well as invading Alaska and thrusting southward along the Pacific coast of Canada and into the U.S. Northwest. And while they were at it, they would take over all of Central America (including the Panama Canal), Colombia, Ecuador, and even extend their domain to Cuba.

If the United States was as edgy as it was unprepared, Australia faced a prospect that was even more dismal. By the end of the spring, Japanese troops had established themselves on the north coast of New Guinea, only a few hundred miles away from the island continent. Invasion seemed likely in a matter of months, and there was little that could be done to prevent it. The results of a Japanese beachhead could have drastically altered the way the Pacific war was played out. Why that invasion did not happen is one of the seldom-remembered episodes of World War II—except, of course, in Australia. The battle for the Kokoda Trail over New Guinea's Owen Stanley Range and the Japanese attempt to reach and take Port Moresby, the settlement that would be the staging base for their Australian operation, had an undeniably epic quality. Though it is generally thought that the Battle of Midway in the first days of June marked the beginning of the end for the Japanese empire, the struggle for the Kokoda Trail and the bravery of a handful of young Australians may have been equally important in the reversing of what had seemed an irreversible tide. Only a few thousand men may have been involved on both sides, but the Kokoda Trail was a perfect example of what has been called the minimal rewrite rule of counterfactual history: that small events can have great consequences.

JAMES BRADLEY, the son of one of the six flag-raisers of Iwo Jima, is the author (with Ron Powers) of the best-selling *Flags of Our Fathers*. A movie producer and motivational speaker, Bradley is currently at work on his second book, *Flyboys*, about World War II carrier pilots.

B Y THE SUMMER of 1942, Japan had conquered the largest and most populous empire in the history of modern warfare. With shocking ease, its army had overrun Hong Kong, Singapore, the Philippines, Burma, the Solomons, much of China and what is now Indochina, Malaysia, and Indonesia. Hitler's empire at its greatest extent would fit comfortably into a corner of Japan's vast new imperial map. The Chinese, Dutch, and British had been humbled. In the Philippines, the emperor's troops had handed the United States Army its most costly defeat ever. Only Australia remained to be subdued and its prospects seemed bleak.

To invade Australia, Japan needed an air base and harbor from which to launch its attack. Port Moresby on the southeast coast of New Guinea was the obvious choice. From there, it was just a short hop across the Coral Sea to the peninsula of the province of Queensland. The Japanese came close to that goal at the beginning of May 1942. They dispatched troopships with aircraft carriers to cover them: Their intention was to land at Port Moresby and capture it. But they headed into the Coral Sea, between Australia and the eastern end of New Guinea, and they ran into an American carrier force. In the Battle of the Coral Sea (May 3–8), the Japanese sunk one carrier and badly damaged another; but their own losses forced them to turn back. For the moment Port Moresby was safe.

It would be a brief respite. A little more than half a year after Pearl Harbor, elite Japanese troops landed at Gona, on the north coast of New Guinea. They prepared to trek over the Owen Stanley Range to seize Port Moresby, following a route called the Kokoda Trail. It is true that those 130 history-changing miles passed through some of the most difficult terrain any army has ever stumbled over. It is true that almost no one except the native cannibals had penetrated the darkness of this mountainous, equatorial nightmare. And it is true that the combination of heat, humidity, altitude, and tropical disease sapped a man's strength and began to eat away at his body the moment he dared to set foot on a trail that hardly qualified for the name. The Kokoda Trail is a muddy track just a few feet wide in its good spots. To traverse the Owen Stanleys involved climbing switchbacks with precipitous drops and crossing bridgeless streams.

Japanese soldiers would be swept away in those streams, which could rise nine feet in an hour. Not a few who strayed from the track were felled by blow darts of Stone Age headhunters, men who still seek human heads for trophies. Others succumbed to bizarre unnamed diseases or plummeted to their deaths because they stepped a few inches too far or slipped off the cliff-hugging trail. But what finally did them in was an unlikely force that seemed to conspire with nature—a group of young Australians, many of whom were still teenagers. On the Kokoda Trail, the Japanese Army would experience a land defeat for the first time in the Pacific War.

July 21, 1942, was a bad news day for the Bataan Bunch. That was the derisive name Australians used to refer to Douglas MacArthur and his advisers who had fled to Australia four months earlier after their defeat in the Philippines. Australia had turned over command of their paltry armed forces to MacArthur. With most of their best fighting men away in North Africa or in Japanese prison camps after the fall of Singapore, he seemed the country's last hope. Now the shocking news had reached Allied headquarters that the Japanese had landed in northern New Guinea and were on their way to invade Australia.

Australia was almost completely undefended, ripe for invasion. During the 1920s and '30s she had systematically disarmed as Great Britain, her colonial ruler, assured her that the impregnable "Rock" of Singapore and the Imperial Fleet would shield her from any attack. The fleet had lost a battleship and a battle cruiser in the opening days of the war. And thousands of British soldiers had surrendered when the Japanese surprised the Singapore defenders by not attacking from the sea as anticipated, but had come through the wide-open overland back door instead. There would be no reinforcements. The British were fighting for their own survival against Hitler.

Australia may have been a country of rugged individualists, but that was

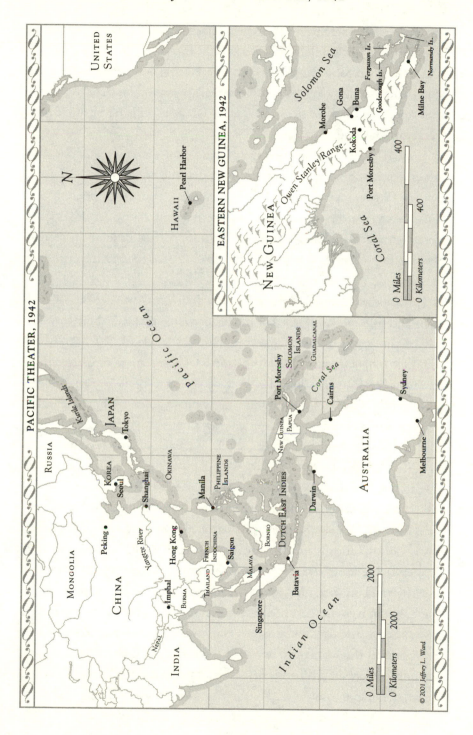

PACIFIC THEATER, 1942

EASTERN NEW GUINEA, 1942

UNITED STATES

N

Pearl Harbor

HAWAII

Pacific Ocean

RUSSIA

Kurile Islands

JAPAN

Tokyo

MONGOLIA

Peking

KOREA

Seoul

Shanghai

OKINAWA

CHINA

Yangtze River

Hong Kong

Manila

PHILIPPINE ISLANDS

FRENCH INDOCHINA

Saigon

Imphal

BURMA

THAILAND

MALAYA

BORNEO

DUTCH EAST INDIES

Darwin

NEPAL

INDIA

Singapore

Batavia

Indian Ocean

Port Moresby

NEW GUINEA

PAPUA

SOLOMON ISLANDS

GUADALCANAL

Coral Sea

Cairns

AUSTRALIA

Sydney

Melbourne

0 Miles     2000
0 Kilometers  2000

© 2001 Jeffrey L. Ward

NEW GUINEA

Owen Stanley Range

Solomon Sea

Morobe

Gona

Buna

Kokoda

Port Moresby

Ferguson Is.

Goodenough Is.

Milne Bay

Normanby Is.

Coral Sea

0 Miles     400
0 Kilometers  400

little help when there were not enough rifles to arm volunteers, not enough bullets for the few available rifles, and only enough shells to keep field artillery in action for a day and a half. The Australian Cabinet hoped that MacArthur had the clout to focus America's attention on their plight. But U.S. troops and planes were mostly still far away and the Japanese were threateningly close.

The Pacific War would be largely a battle for island airfields and Port Moresby was the airfield closest to Australia, the one piece of real estate that would guarantee Japan's ability to invade. After the Japanese Navy's failure at the Battle of the Coral Sea, the Japanese Army decided to take matters into its own hands. It would land unopposed on the north shore of New Guinea and then hurry along the Kokoda Trail to seize the prize from the land side.

The Americans had been reading coded Japanese military messages all along and in May had learned of the Japanese plan. MacArthur refused to believe the scoop his intelligence people had handed him. MacArthur's chief of Intelligence wrote, "An overland advance in strength is discounted in view of the logistical difficulties, poor communications, and the difficult terrain." The Owen Stanley Range was thought to be so impassable that the Allies didn't even bother to order a reconnaissance of the Kokoda Trail.

If you were to search for the most inhospitable territory encountered in all of World War II, New Guinea would be at the top of the list. New Guinea is the world's second largest island and had been known to Western settlers for 400 years, but few explorers had penetrated its miserable mysteries and no maps existed of its interior. There were no roads and no towns. New Guinea is geologically new, with numerous volcanic peaks. A thousand-mile-long spine of mountains reaching as high as 16,000 feet creates a barrier between north and south. Rivers with their innumerable tributaries bar movement between east and west. New Guinea lies just eleven degrees below the equator, and heat combined with moisture creates a giant sauna. In the highlands, however, travelers may shiver from frost and hail or be drenched by downpours so violent that an inch of rain has been known to fall in five minutes. The climate that allows the jungle to flourish is also home to a bewildering variety of microorganisms, many of them harmful to man.

In general, gold mining will tame any country, no matter what the climate. In the 1930s gold was discovered in New Guinea, but a road just seventy miles long was deemed impossible to build and planes had to ferry supplies in and ore out.

New Guinea was the green armor that protected Australia and MacArthur assumed it would prove an effective barrier against Japanese invasion. But Hirohito's troops had other plans.

MacArthur and his staff thought in Western terms when evaluating the needs and capabilities of an enemy. They could not imagine that they were facing an army that in all ways was composed and balanced differently than any troops Westerners had ever encountered. Western armies want their troops to survive. Japanese soldiers sought glory in death. The Japanese army fought with fewer rations than their counterparts, believing that it could live off the land. Japanese soldiers required fewer clothes and demanded less in the way of shelter, transport, and creature comforts than Westerners.

In their swift victories in Malaysia, the Netherlands East Indies, and the Philippines, the Japanese had proved themselves expert jungle fighters, the best in the world. They had learned how to operate in small, self-sufficient units. They were trained to move silently through the jungle. As one observer later wrote, "They could conceal themselves like leaf insects and move with the silence of a cat."

Although Port Moresby on the south coast of New Guinea was the obvious base from which to launch an invasion of Australia, the Japanese had telegraphed their intention to take it with the attempted naval assault, and the Allied command had intercepted Japanese army messages detailing their invasion plans, MacArthur had stationed only a ragamuffin outfit to defend it.

Militia troops, akin to the U.S. National Guard, who thought their job was to defend the homefront, were sent to New Guinea. They were called up from stores, factories, and farms and received only perfunctory training. Clad in ill-fitting khaki, they were issued weapons they hardly knew how to fire. Once they arrived, these raw troops were given almost no training in jungle fighting but were employed in Port Moresby mostly to dig trenches. A visiting Australian general on an inspection tour gave them an "F" rating and proclaimed them to be "quite the worst regiment in the Australian army."

On the other hand, Japan had sent their best. For the all-important task of securing the Australian invasion base, Major General Tomitaro Horii had assembled an elite formation of shock troops designated as the South Seas Detachment. They were hardened veterans flushed with success from victories throughout Asia.

General Horii's plan depended upon two factors: time and *Yamato Damashii* (Japanese Spirit). He landed with 6,000 troops and relatively few supplies. His hope was that his lightly provisioned troops could race across the Kokoda Trail, beat back any opposition, capture provisions, and then seize Port Moresby. His soldiers would have to achieve victory with only the food and ammunition they could carry on their backs: Food supplies had been sacrificed in the interests of mobility. The trail could not accommodate vehicles or even beasts of burden. The whole plan depended upon surprise and audacity.

A full month after the invasion, Allied intelligence still refused to believe the Japanese would attempt the Kokoda Trail. The Japanese objective, they insisted, was to only build an airfield at Buna. Finally bestirring himself, MacArthur ordered members of the militia to investigate. An Australian general assured the raw troops that all they had to do was get to a "gap" in the range and hold on. One of those Australian boys, Ken Murdoch, remembers that company commanders were told that they were to "rush forward and sit on 'the Gap.' One platoon could stop an army there. The Owen Stanleys are impassable."

The boys carried no maps or surveys. They knew only that somewhere along that jungle trail they would collide with the enemy. Worse, they were being sent into a green wilderness with khaki clothing that was fine for the Australian or North African deserts, but screamed "shoot me" against the deep green of the jungle. They wore leather boots with smooth leather soles, the worst possible footgear for climbing wet, slimy trails; moreover, the leather began to rot. They were issued only World War I vintage rifles and carried no heavy mortars. By contrast, the Japanese wore jungle boots with treads that gripped the soil, green camouflage uniforms, and steel helmets garnished with camouflage leaves that blended into the surroundings. They carried abundant supplies of ammunition, a machete for clearing the jungle, and specially designed easy-to-assemble mortars.

After a short trek from Port Moresby the Australians encountered what came to be known as the "Golden Stairs," slippery steps crudely cut into the mountain. "Don't tell me about the Golden Stairs," remembered Geoffrey Lyons. "We started in the morning and I finished about nine at night on my hands and knees. But we made it."

Ralph Honner, another veteran of the Kokoda Trail, recalls: "I saw what the country could do to raw troops. A detachment came in behind us in full marching order. Most of them were big men and were fit by normal standards. They made the last few hundred feet of the climb out of the valley in five- and ten-yard bursts. Half of them dropped where they stood when they reached the plateau. Their faces were bluish with strain, their eyes staring out. They were long beyond breathlessness. The air pumped in and out of them in great, sticky sobs. And they had a hundred miles of such traveling ahead."

The Australian boys soon learned the quality of counsel they had received from their superiors back in Port Moresby. The narrow "Gap" where they were told to head off the Japanese was a valley seven miles wide.

Neither side realized that sending men up the Kokoda Trail was like sending them into another world, a different planet with different physical rules, with changes as severe as those experienced by a deep-sea diver who plunges 100 feet below the surface. One who survived the Kokoda Trail remembered how "We slogged through continual rain, which made the trail a muddy river. Our ankles were twisted by tangled roots concealed beneath the deep mud. The feeling was eerie in that dark moss forest, with the water dripping on us." During the day the humidity-amplified heat sapped their strength and at night they shivered in the cold high-altitude damp.

And as Eric Bergurud writes in *Touched with Fire,* "Mud bothers all armies, but the rain and mud here took on a different dimension. To begin with, they were always present. There was no genuinely dry terrain in the theater. Volcanic soil, so common in the South Pacific, turns to an ugly grey slush when rained upon, creating some of the most noxious mud on the planet."

Frank Taylor, a present-day guide on the Kokoda Trail, talks about the difficulties: "The physical exertion is continuous. You're never walking on a flat surface. You can only take boot-length steps going up. Going down you have to go sideways, switching from one side to the other. It's a constant physical strain, the lactic acid builds up. You are quickly so tired you make mistakes. One foot placed not perfectly and you fall. You fall at least three times a day."

"It is difficult to describe the abysmal depression that had me in its grip," wrote Oscar White. "The rain did not vary in intensity for as much as a minute—an endless, drumming, chilling deluge. It roared and rustled and sighed on the broad leaves of the jungle top. It soaked through the green pandanus thatches of shelters and spilled clammy cascades upon the bowed backs of exhausted men. It swamped cooking fires. Creeks ran in every hollow. One's very bones seemed softened by the wetness. For long stretches the trail was precipitous—no more than a muddy cleft in a clay cliff, down which one swung on lawyer vines and supple branches made ragged and greasy by thousands of pairs of clutching hands."

Japanese tactics called for a spearhead to encounter the enemy with leading scouts running forward, sacrificing their lives so that their fellow soldiers could identify and target the Australian positions. The Japanese out-ranged the Australians with mortars, heavy machine guns, infantry support guns, and mountain guns; the Australians possessed nothing larger than Bren light machine guns.

The Australian boys may have been outclassed, but they had a motivation that the Japanese lacked: They understood that they were fighting for their homeland. "I looked around at my mates," recalled Jack Manol, twenty-one years old at the time. "They all had yellow, malarial skin, eyes back in their heads, all scruffy, and I thought to myself, 'Christ, there's no one between us and Port Moresby. If the Japanese get through us, Australia's gone.'"

Men on the other side recognized that determination. As a Japanese lieutenant named Onogawa wrote in his diary: "Although the Australians are our enemies, their bravery must be admired." At one point there were only about 480 Australians holding off over 2,000 Japanese troops, yet a report to General Horii stated: ". . . We are engaged in a battle with 1,200 Australians and have suffered unexpectedly high casualties."

The boys held out for thirty days. They were making what they assumed to be their last stand against a numerically superior force when reinforcements finally arrived. Raymond Paull describes what the replacements witnessed: "The morale of officers and men was as high as their physical appearance was low. They resembled neglected scarecrows—gaunt, unkempt, and ragged. They had lived for weeks without a change of clothing, and the musty smell of the jungle clung about them. Their boots were grotesque leathery objects of gaping holes and sagging soles. The constantly damp climate had rusted their weapons. Their food was monotonous and not always plentiful. Malaria and dysentery scourged them. Although the rain poured continuously upon them, and the nights were cold, most men had no shelters, no blankets, and many had no ground sheets."

So now there were a few more Australians on the trail, including regular army troops, but still there was no place to make a stand, not even a clearing to gain a foothold. Vastly outnumbered, all the Australians could do was hit out and withdraw, then hit out and withdraw again: Unable to defeat the Japanese, they hoped only to slow their advance. The generals in Port Moresby and back at MacArthur's headquarters could not fathom the conditions on the trail and were dismayed by the battle reports they were receiving. A visitor to MacArthur's headquarters found him beside himself at the Japanese advance over the Kokoda Trail and "obsessed by a plan he can't carry out, frustrated, dramatic to the extreme and even shell-shocked."

Assuming just the opposite of reality, that the Australians had the upper hand in numbers, MacArthur repeatedly demanded aggressive action. Safe in his Brisbane headquarters, far from the misery of the Kokoda Trail,

MacArthur radioed the beleaguered troops: "Operation reports show that progress on trail is *not* repeat satisfactory. The tactical handling of our troops in my opinion is faulty. With forces superior to the enemy we are bringing to bear in actual combat only a small fraction available strength enabling the enemy at the point of actual combat to oppose us with apparently comparable forces." Unable to face reality, MacArthur sent a wire to Washington: The Australians, he said, lacked fighting spirit.

In fact, with bad advice from their superiors, inadequate armaments, and few supplies, fighting spirit was all the Australian boys had. Charles Mc-Callum was wounded three times but still managed to cover the withdrawal of his mates. With two machine guns, he fought off scores of Japanese who fired from unseen positions in the thick foliage. At one point the enemy was so close that one of them wrenched away the utility pouches on his chest in an effort to seize him. He shot the man. It wasn't until the wounded had been carried out and his comrades called to him that they were clear that McCallum swept the area in a final defiant gesture. Witnesses claimed he killed forty Japanese in the brief action; he was later awarded the Distinguished Conduct Medal.

Keith Norrish fought on even though a pink froth covered his upper lip and chin like a moustache and beard. It was aerated blood coming up from his lungs. Keith had been shot four times in the chest and had three broken ribs. "The medic stuffed sulfaminde tablets into the holes, wrapped it and that was that," he remembered. Why didn't Norrish die? "I had no intention to. We had spirit. It never entered our heads that we would fail. Defeat was never an option."

Jim Moir was twenty-two when he got shot from behind. "I was shot in the hip. It hit the main bone and exploded out my groin. It burst out between my thigh and genitals. I was paralyzed from the waist down. I thought I was dying, such a mess in front of me. The stretcher bearers got me on the track and into the jungle. The chaps who were carrying us were getting so far behind that the CO decided that we should be left behind. I had no medication in those thirty-one days. We had to let the blowflies get to our wounds. They eat rotten flesh, which prevents gangrene. I had no pants on and half a blanket. You wanted to get away from those wriggling maggots on your body, but you had to let them eat. I spent thirty-one on the same stretcher with no medication. Just lying on that stretcher." He later completely recovered.

Charles Metson's leg was shattered by a Japanese machine gun. Offered a stretcher, he refused, explaining, "It will take eight of you chaps to carry that thing," he said. "Throw it away. I'll get along somehow." He crawled down the muddy trail, dragging his useless leg, his knees and hands wrapped in bandages to protect them from the sharp rocks that lay beneath the mud of the trail.

Chester Wilmot, an Australian journalist who later wrote a memorable history of World War II in Europe, was so appalled by the fighting on the Kokoda Trail that he wrote a secret report and presented it to the prime minister of Australia in person. For his efforts, his press credentials were withdrawn and he was prohibited from publishing his findings.

Time now became the Japanese Army's enemy. The Australian holding actions had played havoc with General Horii's plan of a rapid advance and a quick conquest. Japanese troops had indeed captured provisions abandoned by the retreating Australians, but the Australians had punctured cans and left the bags slit open to make sure they would be spoiled. Now the Japanese were dogged by hunger and dysentery. The emperor's finest made it to within thirty miles of Port Moresby; they could see the twinkling lights of their prize. But they had been fighting for too long. Three months of battling the Australian defenders had ravaged the Japanese.

And then in mid-September the order came from Tokyo. Imperial Headquarters had lost patience with General Horii's campaign in New Guinea and ordered him to retreat, using his depleted South Seas Detachment to reinforce besieged troops in Guadalcanal.

The Australian boys had worn down the best the Japanese could throw at them. Now it was the turn of the Australians and Americans to pursue and harass the Japanese as they tried to reach the safety of the northern coast. The campaign ended when the Australian 7th and American 32nd divisions overran Buna and Gona at the end of January 1943.

. . .

The Australian defense of the Kokoda Trail marked the first check on land suffered by the Japanese. Obscure events can have big consequences. A Japanese victory would have changed the entire calculus of the Pacific War. Once they had taken Port Moresby, an invasion of the almost unpopulated northeastern peninsula of Australia, just a few hundred miles away from Port Moresby, would have been impossible to stop. It would have forced the United States to divert its resources, still fairly negligible in mid-1942, to the defense of the island continent. (This was a time when more American soldiers—close to 20,000—were in Japanese POW camps than were available to fight.) Landings on islands like Guadalcanal and Bougainville would have to be postponed, as would any thought of an island-hopping strategy. Where could the Allies begin their opening thrust? Even if Japan could not conquer the entire continent, a substantial foothold would have been enough to provide a southern anchor for its empire. Imperial forces would have the Pacific battlefield bracketed by the Australian and Chinese landmass. Moreover, the securing of the Australia–New Guinea flank would have allowed the Japanese to cut off American aid to Australia and to initiate an island-hopping strategy of their own, with Hawaii as their ultimate goal.

The war may have turned on the struggle for the Kokoda Trail as much as it did on the more heralded June naval victory at Midway.

For their heroic defense the Australian boys were vilified. Australian commanders, bending to MacArthur's will, criticized them for their masterful defensive withdrawal. The officers who led the defeat of the Japanese were demoted and reassigned as punishment for not following the ruinous orders of an out-of-touch command.

But through the years the truth of Australian bravery on that wretched trail has come out. Every year Australia now celebrates Kokoda Day, August 29, as a national holiday. It's a day that recalls not generals or government ministers, but a handful of boys who fought against all odds to keep the enemy from their shores, those boys who saved Australia.

DAVID KAHN

# ENIGMA UNCRACKED

*The Allies fail to break the*
*German cipher machine*

The clandestine success of the Allies in breaking Axis codes has been called the greatest secret of World War II after the atomic bomb, but it was a secret that would remain largely unrevealed until 1974. Great Britain, it turned out, had its own version of the Manhattan Project. Bletchley Park was an ugly late Victorian mansion north of London whose gardens had been replaced by rows of wooden barracks, where code breakers worked, as many as 10,000 by the end of the war. It was a veritable factory of intelligence. The object of all this effort, directed by mathematicians and cryptographers, was the German Enigma machine. The machine was about the size of a typewriter. The cipher clerk pressed the letters of the original message on the Enigma's typewriter-like keys and noted which cipher letters lit up on an illuminable board. The machine enciphered the letters by passing them through an electrical maze that consisted of three wired codewheels. They were selected from a set of five (for the army and Luftwaffe) or eight (for the Kriegsmarine). The choice of codewheels, their starting positions, and the connections of plugs to them were changed at least daily.

The Germans believed that the Enigma codes were unbreakable. But in fact the Poles had broken the code in 1930 and given their solution in 1939 to their allies, the British and the French.

With the fall of Poland and France, England became the code-breaking center of the shrinking Allied world. British cryptographers took over and improved on the high-speed calculating machine known as the Bombe that the Poles had invented, a code-breaking aid that was a forerunner of the computer. Machines were now being used to break into and neutralize other machines, a first in history. The Germans constantly improved the Enigma, "not because," as David Kahn has written, "they thought it had been compromised but because they feared that growth in communications might produce a leak." There were periods when the Allies could not read Enigma messages. But the code breakers of Bletchley Park always managed to catch up in time. Code breaking by itself did not win the war, but it gave the Allies advantages that helped them to win.

Kahn is the world's foremost authority on the history of codes and code breaking, and in the chapter that follows he speculates on what might have happened if the Allies had not broken the Enigma codes. Had the Allies not read the U-boat messages during the Battle of the Atlantic, their efforts to return to the Continent in the Normandy invasion would have been set back. Less important but immediately more dramatic was the desert war in Africa. What would have happened, Kahn asks, if intercepted Enigma messages had not led to the sinking of tankers carrying the fuel that Field Marshal Erwin Rommel's Afrika Korps so urgently needed? Could that gas have carried his panzers to Cairo and beyond? And how far?

DAVID KAHN is the author of *The Codebreakers* and *Seizing the Enigma*.

The Allied domination of enemy secret communications is universally regarded as an important contribution to their victory in World War II. In the Pacific, American solution of the Japanese naval code JN-25b enabled the U.S. Navy to spring with surprise upon the Imperial Combined Fleet at Midway and all but destroy it, turning the tide of the war in the Pacific: Japan never again advanced, but only retreated. In Europe, the Allies' reading of German cryptosystems—code-named ULTRA—helped them win victory after victory. In the battle of the Atlantic, the most fundamental struggle of the war, their knowledge of the location of U-boat wolfpacks let convoys steer around them, avoiding crippling losses and helping bring men and material to Britain. Later, in the great invasion of Europe that conquered Hitler's Reich, solution of German messages helped the Allies to foresee and ward off counterattacks and drive more successfully through German weak points toward the Ruhr and Berlin. Soviet code breakers, too, exploited German communications intelligence to help win the war in the East.

But what if the Allies had not been able to crack enemy communications? The question cannot be answered with a single response. The Axis utilized many different communications systems. The Japanese, for instance, depended not only on its chief naval code, but also an administrative code, a flag officers' code, an army transport code, air codes, and many low-level military tactical codes, to mention only some. The Germans likewise used not only their famed Enigma cipher machine but also the tactical double-square cipher, whose key changed every twelve hours, two different on-line teletypewriter cipher machines, the naval dockyard cipher, a plenitude of constantly changing ground-to-air systems, and some local cryptosystems. Even the Enigma was used in a variety of ways. Each service gave each of its communications nets its own key for the Enigma. Every corps in the army, for example, had one. The Kriegsmarine in particular divided its Enigma settings keys between U-boats and surface vessels and between various coastal commands. Solution of messages in one key did not automatically give the Allies access to messages in other keys. And some Enigma messages, like those used by the Luftwaffe, were relatively easily and almost constantly solved, while others, like those used by the U-boats, sometimes were solved and sometimes were not.

As a consequence, even a question that can be put simply—What if the Allies had not cracked Axis codes?—is complex. It hides many parts. The answer depends upon the cryptosystem under consideration. The matter may be simplified somewhat by eliminating the Japanese. This is fair because Japan's codes were not modern mechanical marvels but old-fashioned book codes. Such codes and their ancestors had been solved since the Renaissance. Thus, though Japan changed its codes at intervals, the new ones were constantly being solved on the basis of widely known principles of cryptanalysis. There was little chance that the Allies would entirely lose that source of information. This situation differs from that of the Enigma. Though the Enigma was employed with different keys and in slightly different ways in the several services and their various communication nets, it remained a single machine cloaking a great many medium- and high-level operations in all theaters of war. And its solution rested in the end upon a few ingenious ideas that applied to all its uses. If Marian Rejewski in Poland in 1931 and Alan Turing and Gordon Welchman in England in 1939 had not had those ideas, the Enigma might well not have been solved. So the suggestion that the Allies may not have cracked Enigma is not a blue-yonder possibility but one that enjoys substantial probability.

Again, the question—What if the Allies had not cracked the Enigma?—hides many parts. Which Enigma is being talked about? When and where was it used? Managing the question means reducing it to a single case. And that case must be relatively simple. To ask what would have happened if the Allies had not cracked the U-boat Enigma engages so many other factors as to make it all but unanswerable. Were there so many U-boats in the North Atlantic that convoys could not divert around all of them? Conversely, was air cover so complete that even if the Allies steered right

THE PERFECT MACHINE

*This photograph of a German Enigma cipher machine shows the typewriter-sized device with the interchangeable rotors. The Nazis, who used it to send top-secret military orders, believed that its codes were all but unbreakable. But the British, employing thousands of code-breakers and primitive computers, managed to crack the codes.*

(Hulton/Archive)

through wolf packs the U-boats would not attack? And it must not be forgotten that the enormous successes of the U-boats off the eastern coast of the United States in the first half of 1942 owed nothing to the temporary inability of the Allies then to read Enigma. Rather that so-called "killing time," just after the United States had entered the war, came before convoys had been introduced and while the seaboard cities still blazed with lights, silhouetting tankers and making them easy targets for submarines, who often sank their targets in sight of watchers on the beach.

Still, though numbers cannot easily be attached to the question of what effect the Allies' reading of the U-boat Enigma had, a vague answer can be: It helped. It reduced the number of U-boat sinkings of Allied cargo vessels and so raised the quantity of supplies that crossed the Atlantic from America to Britain. This meant that the buildup of ammunition, guns, fuel, food, and the other necessities of war proceeded more rapidly than it otherwise might have. As a consequence, the invasions of North Africa, Sicily and Italy, and Europe itself were not delayed and had a greater chance of success than if ULTRA had not worked its wonders on the Enigma messages.

One case, however, permits a relatively straightforward response. What if the Enigma messages that told the Allies where and when ships would carry fuel to Rommel's forces in Africa had not been solved? For those solutions enabled the Allies to sink many of those vessels and choke off the fuel that was critical to his motorized campaign.

Rommel's panzer army used 300 tons of gasoline on quiet days for supply deliveries and other routine activities. In battle, it needed 600. This came to him by tanker across the Mediterranean from Italy. It had fueled his race hundreds of miles across the desert by the end of October 1942, ending near a railroad stop called El Alamein. A glorious prize glittered ahead: Cairo, the Suez Canal, and the gates to the Middle East. He wanted to leap forward. But the advance had exhausted his gasoline stock. As the enemy fortified the ridge of Alam el Halfa, Rommel felt that he had enough fuel only to advance thirty miles. On October 24, he was informed that he had only enough for three days' battle. One reason was the sinking of the tanker *Panuco*, which had been carrying 1,650 tons of gasoline. One of his staff officers demanded another tanker immediately and insisted on being told when it would arrive. Headquarters in Italy enciphered a reply in Enigma and radioed it to Africa: "Tanker *Proserpina* sailing evening 21st with 2,500 tons army gasoline, arriving Tobruk early 26th. Tanker *Luisiana* ready to sail with 1,500 tons army gasoline on 25th; if tanker *Proserpina* arrives, tanker

*Luisiana* will sail with tanker *Portofino* from Taranto evening of 27th, put into Tobruk approximately 31st. *Portofino* has 2,200 tons army gasoline."

But the British code-breaking establishment at Bletchley Park, sixty miles northwest of London, had solved a message of Rommel's reporting that his fuel consumption had exceeded his resupply and that he had enough fuel to last only until August 26. Based on this information, the British chiefs of staff instructed the forces in the Mediterranean to do all they could to interrupt Rommel's fuel supply. And they did. Ship after ship was sunk—either by Royal Air Force bombers or by submarines based in Malta. Rommel's fuel situation grew tighter and tighter, limiting his ability to maneuver and to fight. Thus, when General Bernard Law Montgomery fell upon him at El Alamein, Rommel could do little more than put up an ineffectual defense—and retreat. It was, as Churchill said, "the end of the beginning."

But imagine that Britain cannot learn of Rommel's precarious supply situation and that Enigma solutions do not let her partially choke off his fuel supply? Of course, some of the tankers are sunk even without that information, but the panzer army is now not thirsting for gasoline. Rommel, no longer restrained by fuel problems, has the freedom to continue the advance that had taken him so many miles along the coastline of North Africa.

He is aided in this advance by a useful bit of German codebreaking. They had broken the U.S. military attaché code, named the black code for the color of its binding, and were reading the messages of the American observer in Cairo, Colonel Bonner Fellers.

Fellers was an intelligent, energetic officer. He sought to send home information that would enable his army to learn the lessons of desert warfare. And the British, who desperately wanted American help, gave him access to almost everything. Visiting the British front, he discussed the capabilities of their forces, analyzed tactics, revealed their strengths, weaknesses, and expected reinforcements, even foretold plans. He dutifully encoded his messages in the black code and sent them through the Egyptian Telegraph Company by radio to the War Department.

So rich, so full of information were these messages that the Germans assigned two radio intercept posts, one at Treuenbrietzen and one at Lauf-an-der-Pegnitz, to pick them up to make sure that they missed not a precious word. The solutions were then radioed to Rommel, encrypted in Enigma. He called them his "good source," for, coming from an observer who had unparalleled access in the enemy camp, they gave him fabulous insight into his foe's intentions. Hitler himself commented that he hoped "that the American minister [attaché] in Cairo continues to inform us so well over the English military planning through his badly enciphered cables." Rommel probably had the broadest and clearest picture of enemy forces and intentions of any Axis commander during the war.

Early in 1942, for example, he was getting information like this from the Fellers intercepts:

Jan. 23: 270 aircraft being withdrawn to reinforce Far East

Jan. 29: List of all British armor, including number in working order, number damaged, number available and their locations

Feb. 6: Iteration of British plans to dig in along the Acroma–Bir Hacheim line

This helped him rebound in the seesaw desert warfare starting January 21, 1942, with such vigor that in seventeen days he threw the British back 300 miles.

Momentum hurls him along. His new adversary, General Bernard Law Montgomery, does not have time to build up his defenses at El Alamein, much less prepare an offensive. Rommel sweeps the few score miles into Cairo. Fellers flees but his intercepts are no longer needed. The British destruction of bridges across the Nile does not slow Rommel; he throws pontoons across and sends his tanks rumbling across their shaky spans. The populace cheers its relief from the hated British colonizers, who run south, to Ethiopia, which they had liberated in 1941 from its Italian conquerers. Rommel, with greater visions in mind, ignores the remnants of Montgomery's army. Wearing his goggles atop the visor of his cap as he rides a scout car, he waves back at the Arabs. Mussolini sits atop the white charger he has had flown in for his entry into the capital of a country that was bounded south (until recently) and east by Italian territory and that, he believes, naturally belongs to the ruler of the Mediterranean. He thinks himself a successor of the emperors who 2,000 years ago rode in golden chariots through the triumphal arches of ancient Rome, captive kings and lions crouching before them.

He and Rommel then drive the eighty miles to the Suez Canal. They watch amazed as vessels, behind the levees that hold the water higher than the desert, seem to sail through the sand. No Royal Navy warships, no freighters flying the red ensign of the British merchant marine will henceforth take that shortcut from India and the dominions beyond the seas. They will have to steam around the Cape of Good Hope, adding weeks to their voyage and subtracting effective men and supplies from the Allies' armory. The Mediterranean is again for Italy, as it was in Roman times, a *mare nostrum*.

The world is as shaken by the fall of Cairo as it had been by that of Paris two years earlier, and armchair strategists and pundits foretell dire results. But they do not know of all plans. Some things happen that they never foresaw; some that they predicted do not happen at all, and some not when they said. Gabriel Heatter, a newscaster with a lugubrious voice on New York's radio station WOR, forecasts that Spain will soon join the Axis. It doesn't happen. Franco sees no loot to grab, any more than he did when France fell in 1940. He was cooperating with Hitler anyhow, and while Britain was still standing, as was the United States, he sees no reason to stop hedging that bet. Like Switzerland, Spain remains neutral.

Everyone realizes that Malta, though it had bravely withstood Luftwaffe air attacks, is now utterly isolated, with support possible only from Gibraltar through a hostile sea. Emotionally, Britain would have liked to sustain its faithful colony, and militarily it would have liked to retain its powerful naval base there. But to what end? What could its ships do from there? Harass the Italian fleet, perhaps, only to be sunk by overwhelming Axis naval and aerial forces. Could help be sent? Churchill would dispatch neither ships nor men on a suicide mission that could bring no hope of positive results. He abandons the island. Hitler, who had promised Mussolini to invade Malta and then postponed doing it, recognizes that he can redeem that promise the easy way. He will let the isolated island wither. Il Duce is happy to get a coveted new possession so easily.

Momentous as is the fall of Cairo, it cannot stop other events that have been set in motion. The United States and Britain have been planning for months finally to shift to the offensive. Convoys had sailed even as Rommel and Mussolini were marching through Cairo. And on the night of November 7 and 8, American and British troops come ashore at Oran and Algiers and western Morocco. The areas are poorly or not defended at all and the Allies are soon lodged on the continent of Africa—their first holding beyond the island of Great Britain.

It worries the Axis not at all. To them, it is a mere pinprick, and in their rear at that. It cannot stop their march of conquest. Rommel dispatches a corps—infantry, not panzer—to stop the silly, inexperienced Americans. And for a few months, at Kasserine Pass in Tunisia and elsewhere, he does so. Meanwhile, true to the German tradition of aggressive action, he focuses on his next advance. Where will it be?

The decision, of course, is not his alone. It will be made in Berlin. And Hitler must choose between two axes of advance. One is east. It would strike through Arabia and its oil toward Iran; it would sever the Allied supply lines across Iran to Russia and across India to China. The Germans would shake hands with the Japanese advancing from Burma and outdo Alexander the Great. The other axis drives north. Rommel would roll through Palestine and Iraq to bite the underbelly of the Soviet Union and shake neutral Turkey into the Axis camp. Oil does not figure into this scenario because Hitler is confident that Army Group B, driving southeast through the Ukraine, though temporarily slowed at Stalingrad, will soon capture the fields around Baku on the Caspian Sea. Moreover, the Axis control of Egypt means that Allied bombers will no longer fly from there to strike the oil fields of Ploiesti in Romania. In the end, Hitler decides on the northern advance. It will speed the defeat of the Soviet Union, both through the German invasion from the south and Turkey's attack on its old enemy Russia. The Mideast oil is far away and not immediately available. Moreover, with the Soviet Union gone, Iran, which cannot defend itself, even with British help via the Persian Gulf, will submit to Hitler's demands.

With the British neutralized in the Mediterranean, Hitler can send major reinforcements to Egypt.

After a short rest and refitting, Rommel's panzers mount up, and, gas tanks full, thunder into the desert east of Cairo in December. They cross the canal and traverse the top of the Sinai Peninsula, then turn north through Palestine and northern Transjordan, across Iraq to Kirkuk, and then north again through the outliers of the Caucasus to enter the Soviet Union through Armenia. As the armored columns pass threateningly close to Turkey, that country, bordered by Axis partners or conquests, seeing no option other than cooperation, and hoping for the destruction of Russia, jumps onto the Axis bandwagon. It doesn't gain the advantages it hoped. Armenian troops, remembering the massacres of their fathers by the Turks during World War I and resisting the invasion by Turkey's new allies, fight hard for their homeland. They cannot turn back Rommel's armor and battle-hardened troops. But they delay them. And while they do so, Army Group B gets stopped at a city of rubble and doom and glory named Stalingrad. Rommel indeed reaches Baku at the end of the winter of 1943. The German troops that reached the western Caucasus the previous summer have already been forced to retire. Soviet troops keep Rommel from driving the 600 miles to link up with Army Group B. And then what? He is stuck. He can't get the oil out. Hitler's grand plan has failed. To save himself, Rommel turns tail and returns home to Africa—a wornout corps, with no mission, no heroes, and no future.

In western North Africa, meanwhile, the Americans have learned to fight better, and their greater material strength—more men, more airplanes, more tanks, more ammunition—is gradually telling. They are advancing more and more against the battle-tested but now battle-weary Germans. In the months that Rommel has been away, the Allies have pressed eastward. The British forces in Ethiopia are reinforced from India, Australia, and New Zealand and move northward to squeeze the Germans out of Africa. This takes time, of course, and Rommel and his troops escape to Greece and Italy. By 1944, the Allies hold all of North Africa. They consolidate and consider invading Italy.

The Russians slog forward in the bitter, ideological, racist war that Hitler forced upon them. They are helped by their code breakers, who frequently resolve German tactical cryptosystems. It is often noted that Russians are good in music, mathematics, and chess—three characteristics that seem to predict ability in cryptanalysis. But no more than the Western Allies can they achieve a general solution of the Enigma. At best, they occasionally capture a machine with its associated key lists and read messages during the key's validity. Throughout 1943 and 1944 and into 1945 they bleed as they advance against the Wehrmacht. And they scream for a second front.

They are not alone. The American and British publics call for the same thing. Why haven't we invaded northern Europe, they cry? That is the only way to drive a stake through Hitler's Reich. But the buildup for that operation lags, as the U-boats take their toll on the growing number of Liberty ships and sometimes troopships that lumber into packs of submarines. Direction-finding is not precise enough to locate these underwater fleets. The Allies indeed intercept the reports from the U-boats and the directions for their attacks from Germany. The code breakers count the letters in the messages, seek repetitions, analyze them, hypothesize, but hammer futilely upon the impregnable walls of the Enigma. Occasionally they read a cryptogram or two, when a code clerk errs and resends one plaintext twice, each at a different machine setting, giving them an isomorphism that they use to pry open the pair. But most messages remain unreadable. The U-boats roam at will. The Allies seem unable to get enough men and supplies to Britain to mount a successful invasion.

Then suddenly it is all over. A new weapon, in which something too small to see makes the biggest explosion men have ever seen, obliterates Berlin. That nuclear flash makes code breaking unnecessary. World War II in Europe ends.

ROBERT KATZ

# PIUS XII PROTESTS THE HOLOCAUST

*Could the wartime pope*
*have prevented the Final Solution?*

*The one person other than Hitler who might have had the power to stop the Holo-*
*caust was the wartime pope, Pius XII. That he chose not to use it and to remain*
*silent has become part of the ongoing debate both worldwide and within the*
*Catholic Church itself over the movement to elevate him to sainthood. There are*
*some who would argue that the compromising of the future pope began with the*
*Concordat of July 1933, which the then papal nuncio, Eugenio Pacelli, negotiated*
*with the just-installed Nazi government of Adolf Hitler. The Concordat guaran-*
*teed the freedom of the Catholic religion in Germany and the right of the church*
*"to regulate her own affairs." But there was a price: a tacit admission that the*
*Church would not resist the power of the Nazi state. Indeed, many historians*
*regard the Concordat as a major building block of the Holocaust. Once war*
*came, Pacelli, now Pope Pius XII, took the position that his greatest strength lay*
*in the neutrality of silence: How else could he maintain a role as a genuine*
*peacemaker? "An attitude of protest and condemnation," a later pope, Paul VI,*
*put it, ". . . would have been not only futile but harmful." Such is the broad out-*
*line of the case for Pius XII—though, as the scholar Susan Zuccotti has written in*
*Under His Very Windows, "the Church has not yet completed the process of*
*dealing honestly with its history during the Holocaust." Pius XII himself would*
*openly denounce Nazism as "the arrogant apostasy from Jesus Christ, the denial*
*of His doctrine and of His work of redemption, the cult of violence, the idolatry*
*of race and blood, the overthrow of human liberty and dignity." But these strong*

*words were uttered in 1945, after Nazism had been crushed, too late for several million souls.*

*In the view of Robert Katz, who has frequently written about Rome in this period, Pius XII had two golden opportunities, about a year apart, to speak out against the deportation and murder of Europe's Jews, and indeed came close to doing so. If he had, would Hitler have scaled back the Final Solution, saving countless lives in the process? What would have happened if the pope had put his own life at risk? Would his action have ended the war in the West sooner, the very thing Pius XII most devoutly hoped for?*

ROBERT KATZ is the author of twelve books, including *Death in Rome*, a study of the World War II Ardeatine Caves massacre; *Black Sabbath*, the story of the roundup and deportation of the Jews of Rome; and *Days of Wrath*, a report on the terrorist kidnapping and murder of the Italian statesman Aldo Moro. Katz divides his time between New York and Tuscany.

WHAT IF, in the darkest days of World War II, the Vicar of Christ had raised his voice against the perpetrators of the horror of horrors of this or any other age?

The great debate that has accompanied Pope Pius XII throughout the second half of the twentieth century—and seems destined to intensify rather than recede as he continues to be moved by the Vatican along the road to sainthood—concerns the position he took when faced with the unspeakable evil of Hitler's systematic extermination of Europe's Jews. There is no dispute, however, about what choice he made. He would remain publicly silent, never once uttering the word "Jew" in his many lamentations over the death and destruction caused by the global war. "There where the Pope would like to cry out loud and strong," he confided to the Catholic bishops in Germany early in 1943, "it is rather restraint and silence that are often imposed on him."

This policy of silence had not been lightly assumed and it went beyond the Holocaust. He was among the first to learn that reports of Nazi genocide were not Allied propaganda, as many believed. Maintaining silence, however, was thought to be an imperative of his strategy: to be seen by both the Western Allies and Germany as an impeccable neutral and so play a decisive role as peacemaker. Pius's view that Stalin's Russia was a greater menace than Hitler's Germany and that he sought a general rapprochement in the West to contain if not roll back godless Communism are elements of the controversy also not in dispute. Nor does anyone deny that the Church worked behind the scenes to provide sanctuary to persecuted Jews in religious institutions, including the Vatican itself. The number of lives saved remains hotly contested, ranging from a documentable few thousand to much higher figures still lacking substantiation.

But the question to ask, and herein lies the rub, is not about the thou-

THE FATAL CHOICE

*One man—Eugenio Pacelli, Pope Pius XII (shown in a 1945 photograph)—had the moral authority to check the Holocaust. Why didn't he exert it? The great debate about Pius's role in World War II, Robert Katz writes, "concerns the position he took when faced with the unspeakable evil of Hitler's extermination of the Jews."*

(Hulton/Archive)

sands who to their great fortune found a rare hiding place in a Vatican en-clave but about the millions who were sucked into the machinery of death and came out corpses at the other end. What did papal silence mean for them? One cogent answer—"the long and the short of the matter," its au-thor called it—was provided in 1963 by Pope Paul VI at the time of his ac-cession to the Chair of St. Peter and it set the tone for all subsequent defenders of Pius XII. "An attitude of protest and condemnation," he said, ". . . would have been not only futile but harmful"; the wartime pope would have been guilty of unleashing "still greater calamities involving innumer-able innocent victims, let alone himself." Of equal pithiness, but never on so high an authority, has been the irremovable reply of Pius's detractors, who have argued that in the historical context of how the Holocaust un-folded it is all but impossible to conceive of anything worse than what ac-tually happened.

Both of these positions had solidified by the mid-1960s. They had arisen in a storm of polemics let loose by the 1963 appearance of a play, *The Deputy*, a dramatization of the papal silence written by a young German playwright named Rolf Hochhuth, whose raw outrage caught the world's attention. Before long, however, one of the subtlest of the pope's critics, the historian Leon Poliakov, declared that one could go on forever debating whether Pius's policy caused more harm than good or vice versa. He noted that the only thing certain was the silence itself "at the most tragic moment of modern history." The pope, he suggested—later to be joined by some Catholic writers—should have lifted his voice simply because it was morally the right thing to do whatever the consequences; he left it to his-torians of the future to make better-informed judgments once the archives of the Vatican were opened. That meant waiting out the Vatican's fifty-year rule for unsealing its documents, but so intense was the clash of indignation that Pope Paul announced in 1965 that *all* of the archives concerning World War II would be made public, and a period of watchful expectation brought a measure of calm to the fray.

Over the next twenty years thousands of wartime papers were indeed published in a collection of eleven volumes that completed the project, though even the Vatican admits that the work was selective, "edited," one spokesman assured us, "according to exact scientific standards." Meanwhile, independent researchers produced a concurrent and far more voluminous outpouring of scholarly works and analyses of more or less exactitude on both sides of the issue. In any event, those future historians, now filling the empty chairs of the old debaters, came brimming with new information, but were still a long way from ready when the matter flared up again in the '90s. In a major policy departure, Pope John Paul II, in 1996, acknowledged and later apologized for a failure in which the number of Catholics who opposed the Nazis was "too few," but he went on to formulate the strongest defense of Pius XII yet by advancing the case not only for his earthly ministrations but for his canonization as well. He had in fact planned Pius's beatification—the penultimate step to sainthood—as a central event of the Holy Year 2000, but because of the new uproar concluded that it would be more prudent to postpone the event for a lower-profile moment after the Jubilee.

As for Poliakov's future historians, they were left in limbo. At this late date the issue of whether the papal silence was more harmful or less, when based on the thrust and parry of mere documents, seems thoroughly exhausted no matter how many secrets are still to be unlocked from the Vatican's archives. The reason is clear. The fine-tooth comb had already been applied for more than three decades: the strongest documents in support of Pius surely have already seen the light of day and if there had been anything irreparably damning, it would have long ago sapped the powerful forces within the Church seeking Pius's sainthood. John Paul II is nobody's fool and he has staked his legacy on his predecessor's elevation. On the other hand, today's information-loaded historians, and for that matter, playwrights and ponderers in general, are in a more advantageous position than ever to wonder in the sublime arena of "what if?"

Rather more information is extant, for example, about the two known crisis moments in which it appeared that Pius XII, taking pen in hand, would in fact speak out, only to revert to silence in the end. If ever public protest would have made a significant difference in the outcome of events, its greatest impact would have probably been felt in either of those two situations.

Testimony before the Vatican secret tribunal examining the case for Pius's sainthood provides a vivid account of the first of these two crises. It was given by Mother Pasquilina, the German nun who was Pius's longtime housekeeper and confidante both before and during his papacy.

It is the summer of 1942. There has already been a series of Nazi atrocities in Eastern Europe, the work of the Einsatzgruppen mobile killing units. Indeed, well over a million Jews are already dead, and though the events, not to speak of the figures, are imprecisely known to the outside world, the Western media have been reporting eyewitness accounts of hundreds of thousands slain (*The Boston Globe*, June 26: "Mass Murders of Jews in Poland Pass 700,000 Mark"). Nevertheless, the "Final Solution," the actual decision to exterminate all of Europe's eleven million Jews, is only months old. The vast bureaucratic matrix as well as the state-of-the art technology of cost-efficient genocide, though in prototype stages for years, has taken all this time to gear up. The newly built killing centers—the six camps designed as assembly-line, death-only facilities—have just begun to run at capacity, feeding on the July-August deportations from France and the Netherlands. An assembly-line machine has been invented and is running: You get off a train in the morning and by nighttime the ashes of your existence are dumped in a river and your clothes are packed for shipment to Germany, not to mention your hair and gold fillings. In short, the world is on the cusp of what in the coming months will become the bloodiest time in all of history. In the outside world by now, the size of the deportations can no longer be kept secret and the fate that awaits the victims is becoming less and less blurred—to all but the victims. Inside the Vatican, that fate is known.

The pope, according to Mother Pasquilina, has just received word that in response to a fiery protest by the Dutch bishops against the deportations, the Nazis have retaliated by rounding up 40,000 Catholics of Jewish origin. "The Holy Father," she stated, "came into the kitchen at lunchtime carrying two sheets of paper covered with minute handwriting. 'They contain,' he said, 'my protest [to appear] in *L'Osservatore Romano* this evening. But I now think that if the letter of the bishops has cost the lives of 40,000 persons, my own protest, that carries an even stronger tone, could cost the lives of perhaps 200,000 Jews. I cannot take such a great responsibility. It is better to remain silent before the public and to do in private all that is possible.' . . . I remember that he stayed in the kitchen until the entire document had been destroyed."

I suspect that many historians when reading this testimony, released in 1999, felt a bit of a cringe, uncomfortable with the improbable touches of domestic color and the overly formal kitchen-talk attributed to the pope. Some who looked back at the record found both figures cited wildly wrong: the 40,000 Catholic-convert deportees of Mother Pasquilina's recall, for one, were at that time actually 92 and never more than 600. Nevertheless, the incident of the bishops' protest has long been known and there is no reason to doubt Pius's most informed advocate, Peter Gumpel, the Jesuit historian constructing the case for beatification for the Vatican's Congregation of the Causes of Saints, when he tells us that the pope, on that occasion, was indeed on the verge of issuing a public protest against the persecution of Jews. At the last moment, says Gumpel, when news reached him of the Nazi response to the Dutch bishops' initiative, he concluded that public protests only aggravated the plight of the Jews and he burned the only copy of his text, four pages long, he says, not two.

Before rescuing that text from the flames of reality and sending it on to the Vatican newspaper, *L'Osservatore Romano*, for publication to see what might have happened next, let us review Pius's second chance. Now it is a year and a season later, October 1943. The overall peace-seeking strategy, including the policy of silence, has not gone well for the pope, and he has seen or heard unimpeachable reports that Jews are being put to death at the rate of 6,000 a day. The Allies, with the war turning in their favor, are all but ignoring Vatican diplomacy, toughening not softening their stance on Nazi Germany. There can be no separate peace in the West, they have repeatedly proclaimed, only unconditional surrender. Worse, in terms of the papal strategy, Mussolini has fallen, arrested by the king; the new Italian government has switched to the Allied side, and Hitler, enraged as never before, has sent twelve divisions down the peninsula, blasting his way into Rome to occupy the city. Although the Holy See has received assurances from Berlin that its extraterritoriality will be respected, the periphery of the Vatican city-state is ringed with German troops. Still worse, Rome's Jews have been targeted for deportation to Auschwitz and the pope, though not the target, knows it. The policy of silence is about to be put to its severest strain.

On October 16, Adolf Eichmann's raiders strike at dawn in the very heart of Rome. In a house-to-house sweep of the ghetto and twenty-five other Nazi-designated "action-precincts," 365 SS police, over the next several hours, seize more than a thousand Jews, many carted off in the line of sight from the pope's own windows. Never before has a Supreme Pontiff been so affronted. In an unprecedented diplomatic maneuver, hastily arranged that very morning, Pius authorizes a resident German bishop to threaten Berlin with a papal protest. A letter is drafted for transmission to the Nazi Foreign Office, in which the prelate appeals with "great urgency" for an immediate suspension of the roundup. "Otherwise," he warns, "I fear that the Pope will take a position in public as being against this action." The explicit threat, again unprecedented, is delivered that afternoon by the pope's personal liaison to the occupation High Command. Although at this hour, the raid is in fact over, a follow-up dispatch—solicited by Pius's secretary of state—is sent by the German ambassador to the Holy See. He confirms that the bishop is speaking for the Vatican and recommends soothing the papal displeasure by using the Roman Jews for labor service inside Italy. The confrontation between pope and führer has never been more sharply drawn and all that is left is the question of who will blink first.

One week later, the same German ambassador, assessing the postroundup mood in the Vatican, reports again to the Foreign Office. "The Pope," he writes, "although under pressure from all sides, has not permitted himself to be pushed into a demonstrative censure of the deportation of the Jews of Rome." Pius, he concludes, "although he must know that such an attitude will be used against him . . . has nonetheless done everything possible even in this delicate matter in order not to strain relations with the German government and the German authorities in Rome." As for the thousand Jews snared in the net, not only have they already detrained at Auschwitz, they are, with few exceptions, already incinerated. Their fate will be shared by another thousand Roman Jews, seized catch-as-catch-can before the occupiers withdraw, but as the ambassador's second dispatch predicted, "this matter, so unpleasant as it regards German–Vatican relations, has been liquidated."

Securely buckled up in our what-if machine, we now travel back first to that awful summer of '42, touching down on the marble floor of the Vatican kitchen. It should not be too hard—knowing all that we do in our time—to respectfully persuade the Holy Father not to set his protest aflame but to let it roar. Having an "even stronger tone" than the Dutch censure, it is addressed to all of the world's Catholics (then a half billion), including of course 35 million Germans. It is a clear denunciation of the deportations and genocidal fulfillment of Hitler's pledge to annihilate the Jews of Europe. Apart from appearing in the *L' Osservatore Romano*, it is broadcast worldwide by Vatican radio and, wherever possible, read by bishops to their congregations, revealing to the world's Christians and Jews—and most importantly, Europe's Jews—that what has been cast by the executioners and their defenders as Allied propaganda is indeed true: A whole people is marked for extinction. Providing credible confirmation of the Holocaust in the making, Pius has thus done what he was being urged to do, particularly throughout 1942, on both sides of the Atlantic.

Moreover, he has transcended the skittishness of the Western powers to take concrete steps to alleviate the effects of the persecutions. With the one-way deportation railroad to the killing camps operating at its peak, movements are under way in the Allied countries to devise means of rescuing the intended victims. They are making little headway, but now that Pius has launched his protest, the escalation of public outrage is manifold, tearing down the wall of apathy. In the United States, for example, the July rally in Madison Square Garden, the December "Day of Mourning and Prayer" and the April 1943 bilateral U.S.–U.K. rescue conference in Bermuda end not in hortatory appeals or, as in the Bermuda event, utter failure, but with specific plans, ranging from relaxing immigration restrictions to bombing the railways to the death camps—and later the camps themselves.

Hitler, to be sure, is incensed. Privately he rages (as he would in fact rage a year later) that he has no qualms about breaking into the Vatican "to clear out that gang of swine." For now, however, the papal enclave, though under the protection of his fellow dictator Mussolini—who will remain in power until July 1943—is well beyond the führer's reach. Any notion of an Italian government, Fascist or not, marching on the Vatican is inconceivable. The führer cannot vent enough of his anger by killing many more Jews than his daily 6,000 (the five-fold increase in the slaughter envisaged by Mother Pasqualina's Pius in the kitchen, or anything like it, is simply organizationally impossible at this or any other stage in the war); nor does the idea of persecuting Catholics solely on the basis of their religion appear very attractive. Roman Catholics, woven in every fold of German society, comprise one-third of the Reich's population, including Hitler himself. He is therefore faced with two choices: either scaling back the Final Solution or ignoring the pope and the mounting cries for rescue. The scaling-back option is not as unlikely as it might seem. In August 1941, after resounding protests by the German clergy, Hitler halted the Nazi euthanasia program—the "mercy" killing of the incurably sick—and since then (and throughout the war), every time high Church officials strongly intervened in specific cases, he took a backward step from the carnage. These precedents, however, fall short of the magnitude of the present provocation, so we must assume that his fury is such that he chooses the second alternative and, while surely increasing his enemies list, he stonewalls.

Whatever additional censorship and psychological browbeating are undertaken by his propaganda minister, Joseph Goebbels, to deepen the benighted isolation of the German people, if possible, the tsunami unleashed by the evaporation of the credibility question cannot be stemmed. Planned Allied airdrops of millions of leaflets over Germany informing the people of the extermination of the Jews now go operational with the substitution of Pius's protest, and any lingering doubts of its authenticity in the minds of Catholics inside the Reich are stilled by the nation's priests. Internal resistance grows. The admonition printed in the paybook of every German soldier to disobey an illegal order begins to take on meaning. The highly placed and unbelievably patient circle of anti-Nazi conspirators, whose various schemes to assassinate the führer are finally being activated, broadens, and is emboldened.

But the greatest service that the pope has performed, earning him everlasting gratitude, is to have sounded the alarm to those Jews most in jeopardy, significantly altering the character of their response. Until now, wherever Jewish communities are threatened, they have almost invariably sent their leaders forward to petition the Nazi juggernaut with feckless strategies aimed at negotiating a less-than-final solution. These often ad hoc Jewish Councils, as they came to be called in many languages, would establish an abysmal record of failure and, in spite of usually irreproachable intentions, bequeath a dark side to the Holocaust, scarred with compliance, assistance, and abject collaboration. One of their most fatal miscalculations is the suppression wherever possible of Jewish armed resistance, but Pope Pius's revelation of what lies in store for all Jews, ranking or otherwise, has not only removed the very rationale of the Jewish Councils but has given life to what our hindsight has shown as the only sensible response to the implacable foe, fight-and-flight resistance.

Thus attempts to crush the 1943 Warsaw Ghetto rebellion and uprisings in the death camps (notably Treblinka, Sobibor, and Auschwitz) are carried out against greater odds and with less resolve, some of the uprisings succeed. Contemporaneously, the Allies, yielding to public opinion, bomb Hitler's death-camp railways and finally the gas chambers themselves. Eichmann's deportation organization bogs down. Warned, Jews wherever possible scatter, taken in by the Allies and neutrals, like Switzerland—all of whom have eased their immigration policies, again, under the pressure of the moral chain reaction begun in Vatican City. Future projects such as the roundup of the Jews of Rome in the presence of this protesting pope are as unthinkable as is the late-in-the-war deportation of 430,000 Hungarian Jews.

In the end, one must speak of *a* holocaust, but the Final Solution has failed. We will not be too far from truth if we adopt an estimate that of the six million Jews it would have claimed and the five million non-Jews—

Gypsies, Jehovah's Witnesses, Russian prisoners of war, and political, homo-sexual, and other declared pariahs—who would die with them, as many as 90 percent have survived.

Say, however, that before setting out for the Vatican kitchen, much to our dismay we discover a glitch in our time-traveling device and we can only go as far back as the scene of our second destination, Rome, October 16, 1943. We are, as already glimpsed, in a very different set of circumstances now. In the first place, this being more than a year later, the number of Holocaust victims is dreadfully higher, perhaps more than three million, and the Eter-nal City, feeling a lot less so, is securely in the hands of the German occu-pation forces. The Hitler who railed about the Vatican "gang of swine" in July believed that the Church stood behind the king's men who arrested Mussolini and he quickly hatched a scheme to drop a parachute division on the capital, arrest the king and his new government, and, to use Goebbels's phrase, "seize the Vatican." Goebbels recorded that he and others emphat-ically opposed breaking into the Vatican because of its effect "on the whole of world opinion," and later that very day the führer agreed. The coup proved to be logistically unfeasible (though he did manage a daredevil res-cue of Mussolini from captivity). But now, three months later, Hitler is in an unopposable military position to act against the Vatican at will and he is exceedingly more infuriated than he was in July—"betrayed" not only by Italy's September unconditional surrender to the Allies but also by its Oc-tober 13 declaration of war against the Reich.

If we hone in precisely on that standoff moment when Berlin has been threatened with a papal protest over the roundup of the Roman Jews, inside the Vatican—where the pope, again persuaded by what is known in our day, is already drafting his condemnation—the situation is as follows. At least 1,060 of those captured in the morning's raid—one-third of whom are men and two-thirds women and children—are being held less than a kilo-meter from the pope's study, awaiting the train of boxcars that will trans-port them to Auschwitz. For some days now, because of a blunder on the part of a high Nazi diplomat in Rome, the pope has known the exact lan-guage of what lies in store on disembarking. On October 6, the acting head of the German embassy, young Consul Eitel Moellhausen, in a noteworthy attempt to forestall the coming roundup, sent a message to the foreign minister and used the term "liquidate" when speaking of the Jews in question. This was the first time someone in the Foreign Office had used so naked a word in an official document, and news of the consul's misstep has been leaked to the Vatican. The pope is also aware that the train that will carry off the Roman Jews is already in the nearby Tiburtina rail yards being assembled for imminent departure. Seeking maximum effect, he therefore issues his protest now, publishing it in the *L'Osservatore Romano* and all other media at his command.

The impact of a papal protest in the fall of 1943, though obviously not as lifesaving as in mid-1942, has many of the same general features already depicted, thus giving Jews wherever they may be in the remaining danger zones, particularly Hungary, greater chances for survival. Even if it is too late to prevent the departure of those Roman Jews, every one of whom believing that he or she is headed for a labor camp, with the truth out, the several opportunities for escape that arose during their historical five-day journey to Auschwitz are not now completely ignored. The essential difference between the 1942 and 1943 predicaments is the führer's dilemma, the outcome of which will determine the fate of the hero-pope himself.

When Pius's defender, Pope Paul VI, as quoted above, spoke of a papal protest victimizing additional innocents, he included Pius as well ("let alone himself"). He was undoubtedly referring to Hitler's long-known, though weakly documented plan to arrest the pope, some versions of which add a provision for his being "shot while trying to escape." The most recent rendering to come to light lies among the sainthood documents, in an affidavit taken from the former head of the SS in Italy, General Karl Wolff. During the occupation of Rome, he says, he was asked by Hitler to draw up a detailed operation for the pope's arrest and transfer to the Reich, a captivity for which there are in fact two historical precedents (in the fourteenth and eighteenth centuries). Wolff, like Goebbels in July 1943, takes the lion's share of credit for dissuading his führer from implementing such a plan, but neither effort required extensive argument beyond pointing to the inevitable backlash. The present public-protest situation, with the stakes immeasurably higher, is barely comparable to the real event but manifests much greater difficulties in imagining *any* benefit Hitler might derive: only a silent pope can be blackmailed into continued silence. If Hitler manages to douse his fury, he is left in the same position as he was in the 1942 scenario (scale back or ignore), facing more or less the same consequences. If, however, he loses it, so to speak, and kidnaps (not to speak of martyring) this Vicar of Christ, who has lifted his voice and shaken the skies, well, we can feel safe in concluding that the ensuing backlash will make the Ten Plagues that rained down on the pharaoh of Jewish slavery in Egypt look like confetti.

The further out one moves from the single event, historian Stephen Ambrose wrote in his essay in the first volume of the *What If* series, "things get extremely murky, as they always do in what-if history." But that shouldn't keep us, as it did not keep Professor Ambrose, from taking one last look in our clouding crystal ball.

In many ways, anti-Semitism was the glue that held Nazism together. It delivered up the external enemy, "international-finance Jewry," by which the führer succeeded in galvanizing and mesmerizing a Germany feeling itself victimized by otherwise less-definable outside forces. In 1939, Hitler prophesied in the Reichstag that in spite of the "hyenous laughter" of the Jews at his earlier prophecies, now fulfilled, if they were to cause another world war, it would bring on their annihilation as a people. Nobody was laughing at Hitler then or at any time afterward but he was still hearing it in the background of his mind when he repeated the same prophecy during the war. But with the Final Solution laid bare and shattered by a papal protest as early as 1942, or even in 1943, what effect would that have had on the prosecution of the military side of that war? Certainly the internal anti-Nazi resistance, which compromised most of its moral advantage and the cover of secrecy in trying endlessly to negotiate a privileged settlement with the West, would have taken a more aggressive turn, extending its reach through the hierarchy. Could the General Staff have been far behind?

History records that the extermination of the Jews was stopped six months before the war was over, when Reichsführer Himmler, realizing all was lost and contemplating his own survival, ordered the killing machines dismantled. In our conceit of what might have been, not only the Holocaust but perhaps the war itself would have ended sooner. Such an outcome would undoubtedly have rippled through the rest of history, changing it day by day, we dare not ask to what—the murkiness of history's outer space being the price of admission to our game.

CALEB CARR

# VE DAY–NOVEMBER 11, 1944

## The unleashing of Patton
## and Montgomery

*The summer of 1944 was the most violent season in human history. In Europe alone, anywhere from a million to one and a half million German troops were killed, wounded, or captured between June and the middle of September. Russian losses in the same period ran into the hundreds of thousands. The combined losses of the Western Allies in all the European theaters was well over 200,000. And we should not forget those who perished in the Nazi death camps, which were working overtime. Germany, which could least afford such losses, had suffered the most. Its cities lay in ruins, its once vaunted air force had practically ceased to exist—and to this was added the turmoil that followed the July 20 attempt on Hitler's life. As Allied armies surged across France and into Belgium that August and German resistance disintegrated, there seemed a very real possibility that the war in Europe would end that autumn.*

*It didn't, as we know. The Germans would turn and fight west of the Rhine, and there would be savage battles at Arnhem, the Bulge, and the Hurtgen Forest; the war in Europe would go on for another half a year, and the death toll would mount by the hundreds of thousands. Had the prospect of an autumn ending, instead of the May 7, 1945, surrender in a French technical school in Rheims, been a cruel mirage? Of all the questions surrounding the final year of war in Europe, none is greater or more surrounded by controversy.*

*In the essay that follows, Caleb Carr argues that the failure to destroy Germany that fall was not just a great military blunder but "one of the most serious moral lapses in Western history." The Allies, he believes, unwittingly contributed to the German military renaissance with the "broad front" strategy that took shape in the Supreme Headquarters that August, even as George S. Patton Jr.'s Third Army was racing for the German frontier. What if Patton's gas had not been "turned off" (as the British military historian B. H. Liddell Hart put it)? What if Patton and the British commander, Bernard Law Montgomery, had been allowed to plunge deep into Germany, as they pleaded to do? As Carr writes, "The chance to sow strategic confusion, panic, and despair behind enemy lines— the very essence of blitzkrieg—was present in September 1944, as at no other time during the entire European campaign, and had it been seized, a decisive victory could well have resulted." If the Western Allies had reached Berlin first, Carr asks, how different would the Cold War have been? Would there even have been a Cold War?*

CALEB CARR is the author of three bestselling novels, *The Alienist, The Angel of Darkness,* and *Killing Time.* He has also earned a considerable reputation as a military historian, notably through his books *The Devil Soldier* and *America Invulnerable* (with James Chace).

CERTAIN SPECULATIVE HISTORICAL questions defy academic detachment. In the case of the whether or not the Western Allies could have defeated Nazi Germany in the fall of 1944 rather than some eight and a half months later, the specter of what took place during that additional time period—the Allied firebombing of German civilians, the vicious combat of the Bulge and Ruhr campaigns, the various and infamous German executions of Allied prisoners of war and, above all, the drastically increased rate of genocide in the Nazi death camps—adds a terrible human dimension to the debate, making dispassionate discussion seem merely callous. If any chance to avoid the ensuing nightmare in fact existed during that autumn, then failure to seize it represents not only one of the great military blunders of all time, but one of the most serious moral lapses in Western history.

Was it possible? Could the Allies have chosen a different strategic course and brought the conflict to a much earlier end, thereby making at least some of the horrors of the late winter of 1944 and early 1945 either unnecessary (on the Allied side) or (on the German side) impossible?

In August 1944, the military forces of the Third Reich on Europe's Western front were in a state of nearly complete disarray and collapse. Having first failed to throw the invading forces of the Allied powers off the beaches of Normandy and back into the sea on June 6 (as Field Marshal Erwin Rommel had repeatedly declared that they must do), and then proved unable to stop those same forces from breaking out of their beachheads on July 25, the German army had stood by almost helplessly as the Allies, particularly the Americans on their left flank, had raced across France toward the German border with breathtaking speed. Outmaneuvering and encircling huge numbers of enemy troops, the Allies gained ground with a speed unseen since German armor, moving in the opposite direction, had originally conquered France in 1940. On August 25, Paris was liberated; yet American tanks were already in action far to the east of that city, and by the close of the month they had reached and crossed the River Meuse. Try as they might, the overwhelmed Germans could not cobble together an effective defense: the situation was so bad that it had already caused Germany's highly respected Field Marshal Gerd von Rundstedt, German commander in the west, to answer a desperate query from Hitler's headquarters as to what course to take with the famous remark: "Make peace, you fools! What else can you do?"

Yet mere days after reaching the Meuse, the Allied advance slowed and then came to a virtual halt. The high command had voluntarily applied the brakes to its own troops' progress, giving the Germans a desperately needed respite and ensuring that the European campaign would become a protracted affair. The decision was controversial at the time and has been closely and repeatedly examined ever since; indeed, because of the despicable carnage that followed, as mentioned above, the slowdown of the Allied advance at the German frontier has remained one of the most loaded and passionately argued moves of the entire war. And out of the heat of those passions a set of assumptions have emerged to become something very close to conventional wisdom. They run to this effect:

The very success of the Allied spearheads during August caused their supply lines to become so long that their rapid pace could no longer be supported. And even if it could have been, the political necessity of assuaging both American and British egos by not letting either Field Marshal Bernard Montgomery's British and Canadian 21st Army Group in the north or American General Omar Bradley's 12th Army Group in the south gain a disproportionate amount of ground and glory made it imperative that no individual, decisive stroke into the German heartland be made. Taking these logistical and diplomatic considerations into account, the supreme commander in Europe, General Dwight Eisenhower, formulated the "broad front" strategy, according to which all armies would advance along a linear front and at a roughly equal pace toward Berlin.

This interpretation of events has been supported most vigorously (as might be expected) by the popular and scholarly cult of personality that

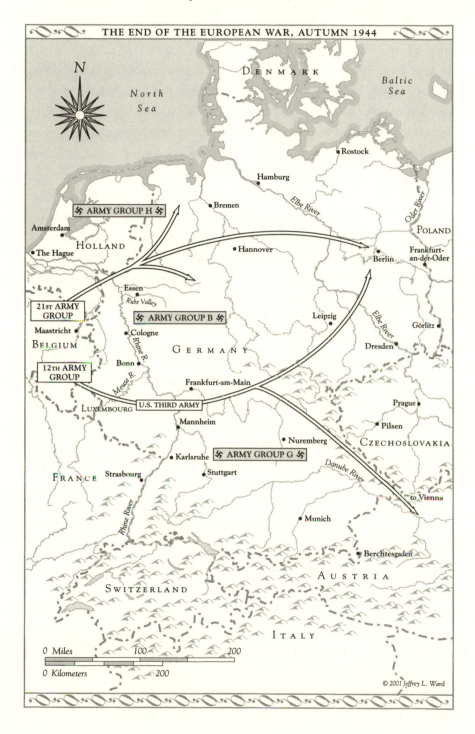

THE END OF THE EUROPEAN WAR, AUTUMN 1944

N

*North Sea*

*Baltic Sea*

DENMARK

• Rostock

Hamburg •

• Bremen

*Elbe River*

*Oder River*

ARMY GROUP H

• Amsterdam

HOLLAND

• Hannover

• Berlin

POLAND

Frankfurt-an-der-Oder •

• The Hague

• Essen

*Ruhr Valley*

21ST ARMY GROUP

ARMY GROUP B

• Leipzig

*Elbe River*

Görlitz •

Maastricht •

• Cologne

*Rhine R.*

GERMANY

Dresden •

BELGIUM

• Bonn

12TH ARMY GROUP

*Meuse R.*

• Frankfurt-am-Main

LUXEMBOURG

U.S. THIRD ARMY

Prague •

• Mannheim

Pilsen •

CZECHOSLOVAKIA

• Nuremberg

ARMY GROUP G

• Karlsruhe

FRANCE

Strasbourg •

Stuttgart •

*Danube River*

to Vienna •

*Rhine River*

• Munich

• Berchtesgaden

SWITZERLAND

AUSTRIA

ITALY

0 Miles          100          200

0 Kilometers          200

© 2001 Jeffrey L. Ward

formed around Eisenhower following the Allied victory; and Eisenhower's subsequent election to two terms as American president made it almost certain that criticisms of the broad front strategy would never be given widespread credence. Finally, of course, there is the fact that the strategy did deliver eventual victory. Because of all this, over time Eisenhower's (and it was above all Eisenhower's) broad front approach became generally viewed as not only the best solution to the problems facing the Allies in the late summer of 1944, but indeed the only realistic one.

But was it? Was there really no other workable option available to Eisenhower, one that might have allowed the Allies to operate in Germany with the same speed and decisiveness that they had displayed in France? Was the adoption of the broad front strategy really an example of military pragmatism? Or did it in fact represent the reassertion of traditional thinking over a campaign that had, for a few brief, remarkable weeks, defied nearly all of American and British military tradition?

Long before July's Operation Cobra (the plan that called for Montgomery's forces to draw German fire on the Allied left flank in Normandy while the Americans broke through on the right to disrupt the German rear), before even the June 6 Overlord undertaking, Eisenhower and his senior subordinates had expressed severe gloom about the prospects for a rapid and dramatic prosecution of the liberation of Europe. Even should the Normandy invasion prove successful, nearly all senior commanders believed that a return to First World War conditions (in other words, a static battle of attrition fought along a linear front) was inevitable. And although they did not relish the prospect, such was the sort of situation for which those same American and British officers were by training and experience most prepared. The high command did not anticipate approaching the German frontier for roughly a year following the Normandy landings: Their operational and supply schedules were all geared to this estimate, and when their men proved able to cover the distance in a small fraction of that time, none of them was fully prepared—or able to comprehend the opportunity.

The fantastic possibilities inherent in the European situation that summer could only be appreciated by soldiers instinctively appreciative of what the Germans had long ago dubbed *Blitzkrieg*, or lightning war. Operations and lines were utterly fluid; and armored commanders as daring as their German counterparts had long since proved that the opportunities were almost unlimited, as the dash across France made plain. Indeed, some have argued that Eisenhower's orders following the July 25 breakout show that in fact he was, at crucial moments, capable of being immensely progressive, and of giving mobile armored columns their head without worrying excessively about either flank protection or supply (two anxieties that, when excessive, were anathema to the concept of blitzkrieg). But in fact the days immediately following the Cobra breakout only further demonstrated Eisenhower's limited understanding of what was happening. For instead of applying blitzkrieg's most basic rule—that armor should move in force toward one key strategic objective—Eisenhower and his lieutenants (even George Patton, the supposed Allied master of mobile operations) allowed their armored units to attack simultaneously in all directions, including, most egregiously, west toward the ports of Brittany.

Those ports had been labeled indispensable for purposes of supply in the Overlord plan; yet by the time they fell to the Allies the armored spearheads were so far east, and other, more ad hoc methods of keeping the tanks moving had been so effectively deployed, that they were irrelevant. What the Brittany move actually revealed was that Eisenhower was deeply uncomfortable with blitzkrieg as a strategic, rather than merely a tactical, notion. Striking deep into the enemy heartland without having completely secured all flanking territory was truly unbearable to him, and though he tried to give a brave show by letting U.S. armor race forward for as long as he did, he did not devote enough strength to the eastward thrust to make it truly decisive. As even Stephen Ambrose, no Eisenhower detractor, has written of Eisenhower's failure to either secure the Brittany ports right away or support a strategically crushing blow toward Germany, "In effect, he failed everywhere."

Yet he still had an opportunity to redeem that failure in September. In fact, he had two, one offered by Montgomery's 21st Army Group, which might have stormed into the weakly defended and industrially vital Ruhr district, and one by Bradley's 12th Army Group, which could have taken the "indirect approach" into Germany, through the virtually abandoned Saar district and then turning northeast. Both commanders were anxious to make the attempt, especially Montgomery—but what would either of these bold moves have had as its objective? Annihilation of the entire German army in the West was certainly, in September 1944, out of the question; but it was also unnecessary. One goal was paramount, and it was a goal for which the strategy of blitzkrieg was uniquely suited: the severing of all road, rail, air, and radio links between Hitler's headquarters and the German armies in the field.

There was and remains every reason to believe that, whether a deep Allied strike was made along the northern or southern route, Germany's senior commanders would have ordered their men to surrender once they were safely cut off from Hitler's suicidal orders to stand and fight, as well as from the possibility of retributions ordered by the Nazi high command. Isolate Hitler in Berlin, in other words (taking the city would likely not even have been necessary), and German commanders could have been induced to do what Grand Admiral Karl Dönitz in fact did once the führer was safely dead: surrender and spare the German people and fighting forces further suffering. The added incentive of avoiding occupation by the vengeful Soviets, a nightmare to German soldiers high and low, could only have been more pointed in the late summer or fall of 1944, when Russian troops had still not made the dramatic advances that the following winter and spring would see, and more of the Fatherland was available for the saving. But all such scenarios depended first and foremost on Hitler and his high command being cut off from their troops—and only a bold strike into the heart of Germany could have brought this about. In short, the chance to sow strategic confusion, panic, and despair behind enemy lines—the very essence of blitzkrieg—was present in September 1944, as at no time during the entire European campaign, and had it been seized a decisive victory could well have resulted.

Thus the question of whether the strike should have been made from the north or from the south, also much discussed over the years, is almost a secondary point. It is probably true that Field Marshal Montgomery did not possess the daring or the offensive acumen for such an operation; whereas

Bradley's divisional commanders were all quickly learning how to conduct just such a campaign from their colleague, Fourth Armored Division's Major General John S. Wood, the man who had led the way across France and been labeled "the Rommel of the American forces" by Basil Liddell Hart, one of the theoretical godfathers of blitzkrieg during the interwar years. Liddell Hart himself believed that Bradley's army group should have been given the nod in September, and that the war could have ended in a matter of months if it had; and taking into account the statements of German generals on the "other side of the hill"—all of whom confirmed, after the war, the mortal weakness of Germany's defensive forces during late August and early September, and few of whom could believe that the Allies paused at their frontier before even attempting a coup de grâce—this assessment is to difficult to argue.

Except if one fails, as Eisenhower and his staff so thoroughly failed, to understand the principles of, and opportunities offered by, modern, mobile, mechanized warfare. Such critics have continued to argue that the supplies for a deep strike were simply not available, failing to appreciate that Eisenhower's worries over supply had proved destructively excessive throughout the French campaign, during which units such as the Fourth Armored Division had stripped down, improvised, and scrounged to such an extent that they were able to move quickly without either major ports behind them or the rather luxurious amounts of supplies that the supreme commander's staff said an American armored division required. The Eisenhower camp has gone on to complain that even if supplies could have been delivered and a Berlin strike effected, much of the German army would have been left undestroyed; and it is here that they betray their most fundamental misunderstanding of blitzkrieg, and unintentionally highlight Eisenhower's own.

The supreme commander often stated his belief that "freedom of action" could only be gained "through destruction of a considerable portion of the enemy forces facing us"; it was this that led him to focus Allied attention, in July and early August, on slaughtering German troops in the area around Falaise—what became known as the "Falaise pocket"—rather than much more vigorously pressing the eastward advance. But the principal tenet of blitzkrieg was that freedom of action, by creating confusion and panic, would in itself bring about the defeat of enemy forces, and this defeat did not necessarily imply their destruction: surrender was quite sufficient. Certainly this result was available to the Allies in September 1944, and on an enormous, indeed a vital, scale. But the high command lacked the ability to understand either the method or the moment. Like his countryman, Ulysses S. Grant, Eisenhower identified annihilation with victory; the fact that an enemy could be defeated in the field and still left alive was lost on him. And so he collected his forces for the final push along a linear front, giving the incredulous but grateful Germans enough time to recover and mount a coherent defense. Certainly, victory over the Nazi Reich was eventually attained—but at an additional cost that must finally be deemed unforgivable.

As to the political rationalization of the broad front strategy, it can be more easily dispensed with. Certainly, if Eisenhower had elected to let Bradley's 12th Army Group strike toward Berlin while the Canadians and British were again assigned the task of pinning the Germans down along the pivot point of the American swing, both Prime Minister Winston Churchill and Field Marshal Montgomery would have been outraged. But Eisenhower's supporters rarely go on to ask: So what? Exactly what would Churchill and Montgomery have done when they were finished bellowing? Ordered their men to lay down their arms? Withdrawn from the Allied cause? That Eisenhower was keenly sensitive to keeping his allies contented in order to prevent their straying into the Soviet orbit after the war had already been demonstrated by his extreme attempts to placate Charles de Gaulle during the liberation of Paris—but does anyone really think that Winston Churchill was prepared to become a postwar Soviet stooge simply because the Americans were given the more glamorous role in ending the war early? Such questions seem too ludicrous to warrant asking; yet they are no more than the logical extensions of the arguments made by those who support the broad-front strategy.

In short, neither military nor political necessity was behind the Allies' decision to slow and then halt their forces at the end of August: it was sheer timidity and ineptitude. As for what would have happened if the war had ended eight and a half months before it did, the list is almost endless. Certainly, the Allied air forces would not have had to commit mass murder, and the German SS would have seen their own efforts to do so severely curtailed—to say nothing of the soldiers whose lives would have been spared. Politically, many of the European countries that ended up under Soviet domination might not have suffered that unfortunate fate; indeed, the Cold War itself might arguably have been averted, or at least mitigated. As in the case of the Persian Gulf War half a century later, the Allied, and especially American, failure to understand how and why one must strike at the head of a snake rather than along its body if one hopes for swift and complete success ensured that suffering and conflict went on far longer than was necessary. The tools and techniques to avert such a result were readily available, just as they would be in Iraq; the supreme commanders simply lacked the will or the perception to properly use them.

ROGER SPILLER

# THE FÜHRER IN THE DOCK

*A speculation on the banality of evil*

The *"what ifs?"* of the Second World War in Europe go beyond the possibility, less dim than most would imagine, that Hitler might have won. The Western war was, in fact, very much in the balance until the autumn of 1942, when the British broke through at El Alamein and Hitler squandered his legions at Stalingrad. After that only an Allied miscalculation of Stalingrad-like proportions could have tipped the war in his favor. If the Allies had attempted to invade the Continent in 1943, which the Americans originally pressed for, the result might have been a disaster that saved Hitler and his brief empire. Thereafter the question becomes: What, for the Allies, was the most expeditious way to win the war? As Caleb Carr has argued, the war could have come to an end in the autumn of 1944, with the saving of hundreds of thousand of lives and the prevention of the Cold War. It didn't, and by the dreary winter of 1945, after Arnhem, the Battle of the Bulge, and Hurtgen Forest, setbacks that should never have happened, the question turned to what should be done with Germany and its Nazi leadership in the thirteenth and final year of the Thousand-Year Reich?

Roger Spiller reminds us here that powerful Allied voices spoke in favor of a Carthaginian solution: the complete dismemberment of German industry and the reduction of the country to a permanently impoverished agricultural republic. There would be summary field executions of the Nazi leaders, military and civil. Hitler, the man who had started and led the National Socialist revolution, would be at the top of the list. The assumption was that he would be taken alive (though

744

*Hitler had already announced to his intimates in the Berlin bunker that he was prepared to commit suicide if worst came: unlike Lenin, he was not a physical coward). Curiously, it was Stalin, the greatest killer of the twentieth century, who took the most legalistic line: No executions without public trials first. And unlike the Moscow purge trials of 1937, they should not be rigged. That brings us to the most intriguing question of all: What if Hitler had lived? "Hitler," Spiller writes, "could have just as easily decided not to kill himself after all. Change nothing else but this and one changes everything."*

ROGER SPILLER is the George C. Marshall Professor of Military History at the U.S. Army Command and General Staff College, Fort Leavenworth, Kansas. He has written and lectured widely on contemporary military affairs and military history in governmental, academic, and public venues. Spiller was the editor of the three-volume *Dictionary of American Military Biography* and *Combined Arms in Action Since 1939*. His most recent published work is *Sharp Corners: Urban Operations at Century's End*.

A PRIL 20, 1945: Fifty feet under the ruined city of Berlin, Adolf Hitler marks his birthday, his fifty-sixth. It will be his last.

Allied air raids have hit Berlin more than eighty times in the last three months. Miraculously, some Berliners still live in the wreckage. Hitler's glittering chancellery, the Reichskanzlerei, has been pounded into a smoldering hulk. No birthday parties there. So a small affair has been arranged below ground, in the claustrophobic warren of bombproof rooms and hallways that serves as the Führerbunker.

Naturally, many well-wishers who would have been happily present for such an important occasion now find it difficult to attend. Most of Hitler's intimates are still within reach, however. Reichsmarschall Hermann Göring can be coaxed from his country estate this one last time. Foreign Minister Joachim von Ribbentropp and Propaganda Minister Joseph Goebbels are only a bunker away. The minister for armament and war production, Albert Speer, has a dangerous commute, but he will go to some trouble to attend this meeting. He feels he must tell his führer personally that he will disobey his orders: the so-called Nero Directives—to deny the enemy any fruits of victory by laying the entire Reich to waste. Reichsführer Heinrich Himmler is plotting a separate peace with the Western Allies at the moment, but he will come into the city too. A few more, some of the lesser lights of the fading Reich, contribute their presence to the grimy air below: Martin Bormann, who in the ever-more confined atmosphere of the bunker, is fast becoming Hitler's indispensable man; Artur Axmann, the head of the Hitler Youth, who sees in the coming battle for Berlin a great opportunity for his armed children. Admiral Karl Dönitz and Generals Wilhelm Keitel and Alfred Jodl are in attendance, along with several Berlin area commanders thrown in for good measure. A few days earlier, Eva Braun, Hitler's mistress, arrived without notice to take up residence in the bunker. She seemed an omen. But of what?

As the air raids continued, as the Allied armies fought their way toward the heart of the Reich from virtually every direction, those who remained with Hitler anxiously wondered when he would finally see that it was time to quit the city. He had been heard to say that he would leave Berlin on his birthday, transfer his headquarters to his Alpine redoubt at Obersalzberg, and carry on the war from its mountain fastness. Eva Braun's dramatic arrival cast a new and dreadful light on everyone's speculations. Could it be that Hitler meant to stay to the bitter end? And what would happen then?

Perhaps Hitler knows by now. He is sliding in and out of reality. On occasion he is brutally realistic. The war is lost, so everything is lost. His poisonous worldview tolerates no half measures: success or oblivion, total victory or utter destruction of his nation, its cultural and material wealth, its people, of himself. Then he imagines that the war itself has defeated him, or that the German people have failed him. He wonders whether the German people are worthy of his great ideals. Perhaps he has not been sufficiently demanding. "Afterward," he muses, "you rue the fact that you've been so kind." Then he decides, no. All will go down in ruin, and deservedly so. Even abandoned cities are to be burned.

But in these final days Hitler lives in several worlds. He was a man of whom Lord Tedder would write later that "by ordinary standards would be judged insane." Hitler occasionally dreams that victory may not be lost after all. Burning the cities is not a tacit admission of defeat, but a clever tactical ploy to deny the enemy any possible advantage. Shattered armies can be reconstituted for the final apocalyptic battles on the approaches to Berlin. Seized by imaginings of a rejuvenated Wehrmacht, Hitler visits the front lines for the last time in March 1945, venturing as far east as the Ninth Army's headquarters, then in the castle at Freienwalde. There, the generals and staff officers saw a stooped old man with gray hair and sunken face who occasionally, with an effort, ventured a confident smile. Hitler's old headquarters in East Prussia, at Rastenburg, was the site of the most promising assassination attempt against him, one attempt of forty-two in

LAST HURRAH

*In April 1945, Adolf Hitler emerged from his Berlin bunker to award medals to members of the Hitler Youth. It was his last photograph. On the final day of the month, as Soviet armies prepared to swallow the Nazi capital, he would commit suicide.*

(Hulton/Archive)

all, by Richard Overy's count. Since the bomb exploded on July 20, 1944, historians have been tempted to see the explosion as the cause of Hitler's mental and physical decline. But neither the danger of assassination nor the bomb were catalysts of his deterioration. One would expect a certain correspondence between wartime stresses and a leader's mental and physical health, but humans do not react so literally to dramatic events. One of Hitler's physicians thought that until 1940 Hitler looked younger than he was, thriving on the stresses and strains of his megalomania. Between 1940 and 1943, he began to catch up with his age. Even his most admiring followers began to see signs of physical and mental decline. Joseph Goebbels rhapsodized that Hitler's face was that "of an Atlas, bearing the whole world on his shoulders."

By 1943, the quack who served as one of Hitler's attending physicians, Theodore Morell, was administering injections of a brew made up of twenty-eight different drugs. Well before the bomb exploded at Rastenberg, his downward slide had begun. His extremities trembled. His left arm and leg occasionally shook so much as to be useless to him. He began to stoop and shuffle as he walked. Some of those who saw him most often thought he might have Parkinson's disease, but these symptoms as commonly described could just as easily have been hysterical paralysis of a type all too common among soldiers in the Great War. What is quite clear, however, is that Hitler's physicians were of no help to him. Quite the opposite. They contributed importantly to their patient's miseries. By the spring of 1944, Dr. Morell had developed the practice of simply giving Hitler's aides and servants bulk supplies of pills—Dr. Koester's Antigas Pills—containing a mixture of strychnine and belladonna, to be taken whenever the patient demanded. How one might gauge the effect of these minor poisonings upon Hitler is a nice question. Too many other factors must be allowed their influence upon his behavior at the time. One cannot imagine that any of these actually contributed to his command of self or state during the final days of the war.

After the commencement of Operation Barbarossa—the invasion of the Soviet Union—Hitler spent less time in Berlin and more time in his headquarters at Rastenburg. By the end of November 1944, Russian advances forced him to abandon East Prussia once and for all and return to Berlin. Toward the middle of December, he ventured to his Western Headquarters at Ziegenberg near Bad Neuheim to lend his strategic genius to the direction of the Christmas offensive in the Ardennes that collapsed into the Battle of the Bulge. By mid-January, he was back in Berlin, and with the exception of his visit to the Ninth Army's headquarters, there he would remain.

The führer's bunker at Rastenberg had been no palace; it was dark, airless, dank, certainly cheerless. Even Hitler's doctors advised him not to return after the bomb of July 20. But the bunker in Berlin was even more confining than the one in Rastenberg. It was hardly a place designed for recuperation. By February 1945, Hitler's doctors were adding to the list of his symptoms an inability to concentrate and a certain forgetfulness—or was this merely indifference? By then, time had turned itself inside out in the bunker. Daily military conferences began very late in the evening and usually were not finished before six in the morning. Afterward, Hitler "with shaking legs and quivering hand," stood to dictate instructions to his secretaries and aides. That done, he would collapse on a sofa and engorge himself with his favorite foods, chocolate and cake. During these gastronomic performances, one of his secretaries remembered, "He virtually did not talk at all." Axmann professed to being shocked by his leader's appearance and manner. Hitler seemed to be in his dotage, yet Axmann thought he exuded "will power and determination" all the same. A much less worshipful description of Hitler at the time comes to us from an "elderly General Staff Officer," who saw a Hitler who "dragged himself about painfully and clumsily, throwing his torso forward and dragging his legs after him from his living room to the conference room of the bunker . . . saliva dripped from the corners of his mouth."

That day's military conference—Hitler's birthday conference—offered no hope at all that Berlin could escape destruction by the Red Army. General Hans Krebs, who delivered the briefing, told Hitler that the capital would be completely surrounded within a few days at most, or at worst, within a few hours. Only a few Wehrmacht and SS formations survived. Military units depicted on Hitler's situation maps were little more than ghosts of their originals. Hitler imagined them as up to full strength and combat power. He began directing movements and concentrations of these phantom units, creating a gossamer defense against the Red invaders. All these units he placed under the command of SS Obergruppenführer Felix Steiner, and in Hitler's mind, if nowhere else, the so-called Steiner Offensive was born, another phantom flitting through a mind that was fast losing its intellectual cohesion.

Swinging back and forth between lucidity and near-stupor, Hitler announced that he would remain in Berlin after all, that he would not remove himself and his entourage to the Obersalzberg. He told one of his adjutants that the coming battle for Berlin "presented the only chance to prevent total defeat," although precisely how, Hitler could not then say. With General Alfred Jodl, Hitler was more forthright: "I shall fight as long as the faithful fight next to me and then I shall shoot myself."

Word of the führer's intentions was not long in spreading beyond the bunker, throughout the city. On that day, all Reich administrative agencies in Berlin and elsewhere closed for good. Shops, streetcars, subways, police, garbage, mail deliveries all quit even the pretense of operating. The Berlin Zoo closed its gates. On April 20, the office of the commandant of Berlin issued 2,000 permits to leave the city. Himmler found reasons not to visit the Führerbunker again. Reichsmarschall Göring discovered "extremely urgent tasks in South Germany," and decamped hurriedly from his estate with a truck convoy full of loot.

Those who stayed behind with Hitler for the cataclysmic battle will watch a man falling inexorably into a self-dug grave. The military situation outside formed the perfect accompaniment to the atmosphere of Hitlerian *Götterdämmerung* in the Führerbunker. "There is only one thing I still want," Hitler cried out: "the end, the end!" He was, in Hugh Trevor-Roper's memorable phrase, like "some cannibal god, rejoicing in the ruin of his own temples." He would not have to wait long: On the morning of April 21, Soviet artillery began bombarding the outskirts of the city.

Of course it was the Red Army that had aimed itself most deliberately at the Nazi capital. Stalin had feigned indifference to the fate of Berlin, going so far as to tell General Eisenhower that the city had "lost its former strategic importance." In truth, Stalin believed no such thing: Berlin was to be where the Red Army's war would end. Eisenhower had agreed with Stalin that Berlin was "nothing but a geographical location" of little remaining military significance. Characteristically, Stalin assumed Eisenhower was as duplicitous as he himself was, and on the following day Stalin told his defense committee, "the little allies intend to get to Berlin ahead of the Red Army."

A race for Berlin had thus begun, but only the Red Army would be running it. Stalin set his two most experienced generals, Georgy Zhukov and Ivan Konev, against one another to see who could whip his soldiers faster through the crumbling resistance put up by the Wehrmacht and the SS. By early April, Zhukov is slightly closer than Konev. Zhukov has amassed four field armies and two tank armies at the Kustrin bridgehead on the Oder River. For each kilometer of his front lines, Zhukov has placed 250 artillery pieces virtually wheel to wheel. Eleven thousand of these wait to be fired at Berlin. Konev's forces were equally strong and lay alongside Zhukov's, just to the south. Combined, the Soviet armies driving for Berlin numbered more than a million soldiers, happily anticipating revenge. "Berlin for us was an object of such ardent desire," wrote Konev, "that everyone, from soldiers to general, wanted to see [it with his] own eyes, to capture it by force of arms."

The question of which of the Allied armies was going to take Berlin having been more or less settled in the Soviets' favor, there naturally arose the question of what to do with the city and its inhabitants once captured. Inevitably, high-ranking Nazis would be swept up in the last great battle of the European war—perhaps even Hitler himself. On this latter question, Allied policy had yet to take shape. In the meantime, Allied opinions differed wonderfully.

Churchill had considered what eventually was to be done with Axis leaders as early as the summer of 1941, when he was heard to wonder if Hitler and his cronies might be exiled to some remote island. St. Helena, Napoleon's old prison after Waterloo, would not do, however; Churchill "would not so desecrate" the place by putting Nazis on it. The most extreme punishment, he thought, should be meted out to Mussolini: that "bogus mimic of Ancient Rome" should be "strangled like Vercingetorix in old Roman fashion." Naturally, such opinions would grow even less forgiving over the course of the war. Axis leaders were storing up credits for beastliness at a pace that quickly outran any impulse of Allied mercy. After D day, Eisenhower startled Lord Halifax one day by arguing that all members of the German General Staff, the Gestapo, and any Nazi above the rank of major should be executed. By the spring of 1945, Churchill and the Foreign Office were of one mind: summary field executions for the highest-ranking Axis leaders.

Although Churchill distinguished between the Hitlerites and the rest of Germany, most of his countrymen did not. Nor did the Americans. Roosevelt most certainly did not absolve the German people of responsibility for Nazism. More than once, FDR suggested mass castration of the Germans once the war was safely over, so as to forestall a resurgence of militarism. The president also agreed, at least at first, with his treasury secretary, Henry Morgenthau, who had a plan to de-industrialize Germany and transform it into a permanently impoverished agricultural republic. These were the provisions that seemed to attract the most attention, but Morgenthau also made recommendations for dealing with war criminals that followed Churchill's line. Once a list of Axis "archcriminals" was drawn up and identities confirmed, Morgenthau's plan called for their field execution by military firing squads. One estimate at the time held that many thousands of war criminals all across Europe would be rounded up by war's end.

The American secretary of war, Henry Stimson, was horrified by Morgenthau's plan. At first, President Roosevelt was attracted to the severity of the plan, but Stimson would not hear of it. The Morgenthau Plan was unbecoming of a truly great nation, Stimson argued. The Allies had sacrificed their lives and treasure in defense of the highest moral purposes. Those sacrifices must not be disgraced by the imposition of a Carthaginian peace. Crude vengeance should make way for higher principles of international law and justice. Only a trial by an international tribunal could be acceptable under these circumstances, Stimson insisted. And in this opinion Secretary Stimson could count on the support of none other than Joseph Stalin himself, as Churchill would discover. On a trip to Moscow in October 1944, Churchill had broached this subject with Stalin, and to his surprise found the Soviet leader taking "an unexpectedly ultrarespectable line." Stalin would not budge on the question, Churchill later told Roosevelt. Stalin said "there must be no executions without trial, otherwise the world would say they were afraid to try them." Confronted by an immovable Stalin and a wavering Roosevelt, Churchill gave in to the idea of a trial for the leading Nazis.

Hitler could not have known of Churchill's concession. He almost certainly did know of the Declaration of St. James, an official pronouncement made three years earlier in London by representatives from the nine European governments-in-exile. Constituting themselves as the "Inter-Allied Commission on the Punishment of War Crimes," the conferees foreswore summary retributions against enemy war criminals, and instead demanded "the punishment, through the channel of organized justice, of those guilty of or responsible for these crimes." The leading Allies would eventually come around to this position as the European War bled to a close. The St. James's declaration of high-minded legal purpose could hardly have made any impression on a dictator who had so thoroughly subverted his own nation's legal system. Anyway, Hitler had long thought himself and his party beyond the pale of any law. On the eve of Germany's invasion of Russia in the summer of 1941, Hitler confessed his feeling that they had all passed a moral point of no return. "We have so much to answer for already that we must win," he told Goebbels. Four years later, an international trial was the most humane fate Hitler might have hoped for, but he was in fact contemptuous of any such prospect. He refused, he said, to become "an exhibit in the Moscow Zoo" for the edification of the enemy's "hysterical masses."

By the afternoon and evening of April 22, such prospects as were left to Hitler were disappearing one by one. At the daily military conference in the bunker, it was clear to all present that the Steiner Offensive would never materialize. By then, every Wehrmacht formation in the path of the Red Army was either disintegrating on the spot or falling back in confusion along the roads to Berlin. Virtually all of Berlin itself was now within range of Zhukov's artillery. The city was being drenched in artillery fire, its muffled thumps now discernible in the Führerbunker. Every notion of retrieving the disastrous military situation, of fending off the enemy's advance into the capital, of somehow wresting the initiative from the Russians, of heroic resistance, all these possibilities were rendered impossible by the few reports still being transmitted from the wreckage of the once-proud, seemingly irresistible Wehrmacht.

Hitler listened sullenly as the reports were briefed to him. All of a sudden, casting off any pretense of composure, he unleashed a storm of hysterical ravings. No one was worthy of his regard. All about him were incompetent, corrupt, traitorous weaklings. And so his fit of denunciations went on for who knows how long, draining all those present of self-regard, energy, any reserve of hope. The historian Joachim Fest depicts a scene worthy of a Wagnerian opera: "He shook his fists furiously while he spoke, tears ran down his cheeks; and as always in the disastrous disenchantments of his life, everything collapsed along with the one hysterically magnified expectation. This was the end, he said. He could no longer go on. Death alone remains. He would meet death here in the city." His outburst was so violent, some present thought Hitler had completely lost his senses. On the day after this near-psychotic episode, a corps commander had been ordered to report to the bunker to receive the hopeless command of Berlin's defenses. General Karl Weidling, was dismayed to see his führer sitting behind a table strewn with maps, his face puffy "with feverish eyes. When he tried to stand up, I noticed to my horror that his hands and legs were constantly trembling. . . . With a distorted smile he shook hands with me and asked in a hardly audible voice whether we had not met before." Weidling noticed that when Hitler sat down again, "his left leg kept moving, the knee swinging like a pendulum, only faster."

If Hitler was frenzied by the state of affairs as he knew them, what he did not then know would have rendered him completely insensible. Two reports in particular, tumbling down the stairs on top of one another, cast an even darker shadow over the denizens of the bunker, if that was possible. Unknown to Hitler, Himmler had entered into secret negotiations with Sweden's Count Bernadotte for a separate peace with the Western Allies. If anything, Himmler was even less in touch with reality than his leader. Presenting himself to Bernadotte as "the only sane man left in Europe," Himmler was at the same time considering how to colonize the Ukraine with a religious sect that had been brought to his attention by his masseur. Of course, the Allies were in no mood to entertain any alternative to unconditional surrender, and Himmler's negotiations went nowhere, except, late in the evening of April 28, to be announced by Reuters news service. Hitler happened to be in a discussion with Ritter von Greim when a valet appeared with the report. Von Greim reported that his führer turned purple.

This news was followed the next day by reports that Mussolini and his mistress had been taken prisoner by Italian partisans and summarily executed in the small town of Mezzagra. Their bodies had been taken to Milan and hanged by the heels in a garage on the Piazzale Loreto, where a mob wreaked its vengeance on the corpses. Hearing this news, Hitler began preparing for his suicide, a final contribution to the Armageddon he had shrieked out for the German nation that had so disappointed him. He would show them, those "petty bourgeois reactionaries" who thought they had defeated him. Without him, Germany would be leaderless, carrion to be picked over by the wretched Allies.

Most accounts given by those present who survived this final day in the bunker agree that, having spent most of the evening of April 29 writing his "Political Testament," Hitler retired to his rooms with Eva Braun, there to receive occasional visitors from among the dwindling population of the bunker. Sometime in the middle of the afternoon of April 30, Hitler and Braun took their own lives. Braun used poison. Hitler used a pistol. Following his last wishes, several of Hitler's underlings carried the two bodies to the surface, where they were incinerated in the ruins of the chancellery garden, and where the Russians discovered the remains several days later.

So did Hitler take his own life, by his own hand and of his own volition? No doubt he was hysterical, but he was not deranged. Neither madness, nor the approach of the enemy then less than half a mile away in the Tiergarten, nor entreaties from Goebbels or his other courtiers, compelled Hitler to take this course of action. Nor did the deeper impulses of culture drive him toward self-destruction. This was not an act of seppuku. He did not aim to retrieve his honor or ennoble his death in any way. His suicide was an act of spite. He killed himself in the same spirit in which he had issued orders to kill Germany itself. He meant to punish history by absenting himself from it.

Goebbels followed his master not long after. "There must be someone at least who will stay with him unconditionally until death," Goebbels wrote in a codicil to the political testament Hitler had left behind. After a half-hearted attempt to negotiate with the Russians, Goebbels destroyed himself, his wife, and their five children. Heinrich Himmler's dalliance with the role of peacemaker came to a similar end, and he killed himself within days of Hitler and Goebbels. Göring, of course, was still alive, soon to be taken prisoner and stand trial at Nuremberg. The whereabouts of Martin Bormann, after Hitler the most powerful politician in Germany, were unknown. He was believed to have been killed while trying to escape the Führerbunker at the last minute, but no body was found there.

Uncertainties about Hitler's fate were not assuaged entirely. When his death was announced over the radio by Admiral Canaris, Marshal Zhukov thought, "So that's the end of the bastard. Too bad it was impossible to take him alive." Stalin did not believe Hitler was dead. The Soviet historian Dmitri Volkogonov depicts a Stalin intensely interested in the fate of his mortal enemy. "Stalin's triumph would be complete if he could take the Nazi leader alive and have him tried by an international tribunal," Volkogonov writes. Even though Hitler's remains had been discovered by Russian troops, Stalin seems to have been unwilling to trust his own forensic specialists. When Stalin arrived at Potsdam in July for the Allied conference, he startled the American secretary of state James Byrnes by suggesting that Hitler was still alive, hiding somewhere beyond Germany. And Stalin was by no means alone in his suspicion. Rumors of escape continued to fly about, not only about Hitler, but about Bormann too. The Nuremberg prosecutors then preparing charges against the Nazi elite, not at all confident that Hitler was dead, just in case added Hitler's name to the list of defendants.

All of which brings us to an uncomfortable, even unwelcome question. If Hitler had chosen to live, what then? Historians usually find these questions tiresome. Some speculation might be in order, they say, but one ought to be cautious. One may go too far too quickly, slide into fantasy. Besides, simply finding out what did happen is hard enough, sometimes just impossible. Why add to the confusions history already throws in our way? Protests of this sort, against the variant that has come to be called "alternative" or "counterfactual" history, might best be seen as reactions to intellectual shock—reactions that cannot bear the weight of much argument.

For, in one sense, alternative history is history. The confluence of human action creates contingencies and uncertainties that often do not yield an authoritative version of process, event, or person. More often than any historian would prefer to think, one is reduced to educated guessing about which of several versions of the story one ought to accept as credible. In the end one must decide even if there is a chance of deciding badly. History—not only the living of it but the writing of it too—is a chancy business in which a certain tolerance for the calculation of probabilities comes in handy.

In practice, historians exercise restraint bordering on abstinence when they encounter an opportunity to calculate alternatives. Their calculations show up, quarklike, as the merest shadow of a regret that events in a certain case did not turn out differently. Others are a bit bolder, registering disapproval or rendering judgments. Thucydides cast his *History of the Peloponnesian War* as a tragedy because he grieved over the death of Periclean Athens. And he leaves no doubt about what he thought of the second-rate demagogues who succeeded Pericles and led Athens to ruin. A kind of standard is set up, against which successors are made to struggle—this is just one of any number of puzzles the historian may pose for the reader. Indeed, the practice of hypothetical, or alternative calculation is so common one might even argue that the doing of history without it is well nigh impossible. As the editor of the present volume has written, "'What if' is the historian's favorite secret question.'"

The obverse of history in Hitler's particular case, therefore, is not at all hard to imagine credibly. Reacting to precisely the same circumstances, acting upon the very same stew of perception and delusion, Hitler could have just as easily decided not to kill himself after all. Change nothing else but this and one changes everything. One might impose a measure of control over any alternative scenario by asking no more of inventiveness than one might ask of a prediction. How far ahead might one justifiably attempt to see in April 1945? Whatever one answers, one should go no farther than that.

In April 1945, some very real and very important questions about the future awaited answers. Statesmen, policy makers, and soldiers the world over had to guess about what would happen in a most uncertain world. But they did guess. We know, for instance, that there was no agreement between the Allies over how to treat the leaders of the defeated Reich, save that they would not be shot out of hand. What that meant was that for the contingent moment the leading Nazis who were within reach were to be scooped up and interned. Once the Allies agreed on questions of international law and jurisprudence, there remained the business of setting the actual machinery in place, and all of this required some time. Göring spent this interregnum with his wife and daughter in the safety and relatively comfortable custody of the Western Allies. Those taken by the Russians were neither so safe nor comfortable.

So if we may imagine a living Hitler, one who survived the battle of Berlin, we can see now that a good deal of this canvas has already been painted for us. We know that at 12:50 in the afternoon of May 2, General Karl Weidling's chief of staff and several other official representatives flew a white flag at the Potsdam Bridge, that they were escorted promptly to General Chuikov's headquarters, and that an armistice was arranged forthwith. We also know that at about the same time Russian troops took the Reichskanzlerei and, after some confusion, finally discovered the Führerbunker itself. We can easily envision a resigned, even an indifferent Hitler, still alive, having ordered General Weidling to seek a ceasefire. Perhaps Hitler might still have harbored a fantasy of a negotiated peace, but of course he had nothing left with which to strike any sort of bargain. We can also see without fear of contradiction that the Russians would not have been in a mood especially conducive to negotiation, having lost nearly 100,000 casualties in the Berlin campaign alone. No, Hitler would have been hustled off to see one of the Russian commanders, Zhukov or Chuikov. Immediately, a signal confirming his capture would have gone out to Stalin, and then, to the rest of the world. In all likelihood, the prisoner Hitler would have been on his way to Moscow before the day was out.

But, we have now reached the outer limits of a reasonably safe scenario. Before going further, we are forced to consider a less plausible, certainly a less attractive, alternative. How likely was it that Hitler chose escape over suicide—precisely what many suspected at the time? Here, our answers need not be so speculative; we have testimony of just what was required to make good such an escape at this point in time. Escape was possible, but only just. In the chaotic final hours of the war, several small groups took their chances outside, in a wrecked city engulfed by artillery and small arms fire. The chances of success were minuscule. In the aftermath of Hitler's and Goebbels's suicides, an ill-assorted bunch of soldiers, secretaries, and party officials, including Hitler's own secretary Martin Bormann, tried to get out through the New Chancellery exits and into the city with the aim of working their way northwest of the city. All were killed or captured. Bormann's body was not found.

But the fortunes of battle favored others. Major Willi Johannmeier, Hitler's army adjutant, was chosen to carry a copy of Hitler's final testament to Field Marshal Schoerner, the newly appointed commander in chief of the Wehrmacht. Two other petty functionaries, Wilhelm Zander and Heinz Lorenz, drew similar missions. This party was rounded out by the addition of a fortunate corporal named Hummerich, presumably assigned to assist Major Johannmeier. Johannmeier, an experienced and resourceful soldier, was detailed to lead the group to the safety of German lines. His skills were about to be tested. The Russians had established three battle lines in a ring around the city center, at the Victory column, at the Zoo station, and at Pichelsdorf. The Pichelsdorf sector was where Johannmeier and his party had to go. At noon on April 29, the four men left the chancellery through the garage exits on Hermann Göring Strasse and struck westward, through the Tiergarten toward Pichelsdorf, at the northernmost reach of the large city lake, the Havel. By four or five in the afternoon, having spent the last several hours evading Russians, the party arrived in this sector. The sector was in German hands for the moment, defended by a battalion of Hitler Youth awaiting reinforcements.

Johannmeier and company rested until dark and then took small boats out onto the lake, making southward for another pocket of defense on the western shore, at Wannsee. There, Johannmeier managed to get a radio signal off to Admiral Dönitz, asking for evacuation by seaplane. After resting in a bunker for most of the day, the small group set off for a small island, the Pfaueninsel, where they would await their rescue by Dönitz's seaplane.

In the meantime, another group of bunker refugees arrived. On the morning of April 29, just as Johannmeier and his party were preparing to leave, Major Baron Freytag von Loringhoven, Rittmeister Gerhardt Boldt, and a lieutenant colonel named Weiss asked and received permission to attempt an escape and join General Wenck's imaginary army of relief. The next day, April 30, they would follow the same but even more dangerous route west as Johannmeier's group. The Russians were as close as a few blocks now, already at the Air Ministry. And they had nearly closed the ring on the Pichelsdorf sector at the Havel. Freytag and his group had set out already when they were joined by Colonel Nicolaus von Below, Hitler's Luftwaffe adjutant. Below seems to have been the last one to leave the bunker before Hitler killed himself.

All of these fugitives collected for a time on the lake, awaiting the salvation of the seaplane. A seaplane did materialize eventually, but owing to the heavy enemy fire, its pilot chose between discretion and valor and flew away before taking on his passengers. Now all were left to their own devices. By ones and twos most of the escapees managed to get away, if only to be taken prisoner later. Johannmeier and his group worked their way down past Potsdam and Brandenburg and crossed the Elbe near Magdeburg. Posing as foreign workers, they passed through enemy lines a few days later. Johannmeier simply continued his journey all the way back to his family home in Westphalia. There in the garden he buried Hitler's last testament in a glass jar. Zander made his escape good all the way to Bavaria, as did Axmann, the chief of the Hitler Youth. Nicolaus von Below enrolled in law school at Bonn University. His studies were to be interrupted by the Allied authorities.

All of these men were considerably younger, healthier, and more physically resourceful than Hitler. The vision of Hitler negotiating all these difficulties is an alternative that is defeated by Hitler's psychological and physical states, neither of which, singly or in combination, conduced to the demands of such a choice. By this time, Hitler simply did not have the physical or mental vigor necessary even to attempt an escape, much less actually succeed in one.

But, as the eminent British historian Hugh Trevor-Roper has reason to know, "Myths are not like truths; they are the triumph of credulity over evidence." Immediately upon the conclusion of the war, Trevor-Roper was given access to Allied intelligence and prisoner interrogation reports for the purpose of disentangling the confusions of Hitler's last days, and, by implication, his ultimate fate. Behind Trevor-Roper's assignment were the rumors that swept Europe in the summer of 1945: Hitler had escaped after all, the rumors said. He had gone to ground in Bavaria. Or he was in the Middle East. Or perhaps he had made for the Baltic coast, there to be rescued by submarine and deposited among sympathizers somewhere in South America. These rumors did not merely enthuse the gullible. Stalin startled the American secretary of state at the Potsdam Conference in July by arguing that Hitler was, in fact, alive and in hiding. Allied prosecutors drawing up charges against the leading Nazis took due care to see that Adolf Hitler was indicted, if only in absentia.

But no, given even the unlikely event of survival, it must be to Moscow that he goes. However, this most plausible of alternatives leads us to an important question straightaway. Does he stay there to stand trial, or is he shipped off to Nuremberg for the main proceedings? The Allies had agreed to locate their war crimes trials there because most of the principal defendants had been captured by the Anglo-Americans. The Russians held only a few for the very good reason that the leading Nazis did their best to flee westward, the least immediately dangerous direction, they thought. But if one adds Hitler to Russia's haul of Nazi leaders, the advantage is not quite so certain. The Russians were not particularly difficult on the question of where the trial would be, so long as there was one. Would the Russians have been so obliging if they had held Hitler in the Lubyanka Prison? Would they have insisted upon a grand show trial in Moscow?

There is no way to know for certain. So, one sees, even the most conservative speculation takes one into the shadows of uncertainty quite soon. From this point on, history will insist that we grant more and more "for the sake of the argument," knowing very well that while history is usually explicable it is often irrational. When dealing with the past, the test of common sense is no test at all.

However, we can be sure enough that a living Hitler would have posed considerable problems for the Allies, assuming he would have been moved to Nuremberg. Most immediately, the question was whether he would have been in a condition to stand trial? Wherever he was imprisoned he would have been treated correctly but certainly not lavishly. Stalin had hoped to put Hitler and fascism on trial, and when the Anglo-Americans finally agreed on the principle of an international tribunal, so did they. A damaged or deranged Hitler would have been less suitable for the event. In prison, no longer in command of his own time, his own diet, or his own medicines, and well beyond the clutches of the malign Dr. Morell, Hitler's physical health might well have improved. Most of the Nuremberg defendants fared well enough. The prison regime even improved the dissolute and rotund Göring. He had been weaned from his addiction to drugs and lost eighty pounds. Had Göring not committed suicide on the day of his execution, he would have gone to the gallows a healthier man.

Imagining Hitler's mental state, once he was captured, is less problematic than one might think. Confinement, in and of itself, could not hold terrors for one who seemed so predisposed to bury himself even when he was at large. As we have seen, first at Rastenburg, and then back in Berlin toward the end, Hitler was downright troglodytic. Of course, Hitler was already familiar with prison life, having served a few months in 1923 for his part in the unsuccessful Munich Beer Hall putsch. This earlier sentence, served no doubt in the presence of admiring wardens, afforded him the opportunity to work on *Mein Kampf*. But even criminals know that every sentence is different. In the event he might have forgotten how to behave in prison, the American Army commandant, Colonel Burton C. Andrus, would have been present to reacquaint him. Andrus imposed very strict rules of confinement upon his charges: only one letter per week, one walk per day, no conversations with fellow prisoners except at lunch, and rations in precisely the same amounts provided to the German refugee population during that severe winter of defeat. What had Hitler done for the past twenty years but write and talk. Denied a freedom of movement, of association, Colonel Andrus would have cast his severe eye over a man who had done little else but talk and write for the past twenty-five years and now was allowed neither. The chances for another *Mein Kampf* would have been very small indeed.

If this strictly regimented environment did not improve Hitler's state of mind, it would not have mattered in the end. Rudolf Hess, whose celebrated flight to Britain in 1941 had shaken Hitler like few other events, arrived in Nuremberg from his wartime confinement as a barely functional amnesiac. He had moments of lucidity punctuated by long spells in which he was detached from reality and barely responsive to social interaction. At first, suspecting him of an elaborate malingering, the Allies subjected Hess to extensive psychiatric examinations and were satisfied that even though he was barely competent he was sufficiently so to stand trial. Hess would spend the rest of his life in Berlin's Spandau Prison. Another defendant, the virulent anti-Semitic propagandist Julius Streicher, scored so low on his IQ tests that he was examined further by psychiatrists. A third defendant, Robert Ley, leader of the German Labor Front, managed to commit suicide after he heard the charges against him. If we require further evidence that the Allies were disinclined to forgive, postpone, or otherwise soften their prosecution of enemy leaders on any grounds whatsoever, we need only recall that Japan's wartime leader, Hideki Tōjō, shot himself in the chest in a botched suicide attempt. He ended up in Tokyo's Sugamo Prison all the same, and at the end of the gallows. Hitler could have expected no less, were he to have stood trial.

Allied officials charged with conducting the International Military Tribunal's business at Nuremberg had any number of worries to disturb their nights. One of them was whether one or more of the defendants would somehow turn the trial to his advantage. More than merely convincing the tribunal that they were not guilty, but by some means of guile or rhetoric, was it within the power of these once mighty and feared defendants to emerge from the ordeal as heroes or national martyrs? In the event, this fear was groundless. The justices on the tribunal exercised strict control over courtroom behavior. Göring was able to mug and scowl and rustle in his chair to indicate his reaction to testimony, but no more. The white-helmeted military policemen just behind the defendant's box would have removed any unruly defendant from the court's presence, had the court's decorum been violated. The behavior of all the defendants, Göring's included, was, like their persons, rather more confined than in ordinary circumstances. Even the most extravagant personality, like the nail that came out too far, would be hammered down. Doubtless, Hitler himself, the most extravagant of these personalities, would have responded along the same lines.

We must return, then, to Hitler himself. Exposed, yet confined in the dock day after day, Hitler, Göring, and the other defendants personified the banality of evil. "There had been quite a metamorphosis," William L. Shirer remembered. "Attired in rather shabby clothes, slumped in their seats fidgeting nervously, they no longer resembled the arrogant leaders of old. They seemed to be a drab assortment of mediocrities." Hitler's mana would have faded to blandness, as if scrubbed by each of the prosecution's witnesses, until he was made finally to disappear. In the early morning hours of October 16, 1946, the death sentences for ten of the twenty-one convicted defendants at the Nuremberg Trials were carried out. Göring, who was to have gone to the gallows first, had killed himself the night before, perhaps with the aid of a sympathetic guard. Hitler might have managed to do the same to avoid what he had cried out for, *das Ende, das Ende!*

In the end, our alternative scenario would have given Hitler a year and a half more of life. If a history would not give him the life he no doubt preferred, it was a great deal more than he had allowed the pathetic millions who died because he lived. One would think humankind would be all too ready to consign Hitler to his well-deserved fate, but as Trevor-Roper has reminded us, "The form of a myth is indeed externally conditioned by facts; there is a minimum of evidence with which it must comply, if it is to live; but once lip-service has been paid to that undeniable minimum, the human mind is free to indulge its infinite capacity for self-deception. . . . When we consider upon what ludicrous evidence the most preposterous beliefs have been easily, and by millions, entertained, we may well hesitate before pronouncing anything incredible."

The scenarios imagined here, though barely plausible, are more than enough to disturb one's quiet moments with a glimmer of anxiety. At any one moment an infinitude of contingencies await History's choice. When History finally chooses we say, yes, that must be fitting or right or appropriate to the case. But humankind has seen History make bad choices too. What if Hitler had lived, what if History had been wrong once more?

RICHARD B. FRANK

# NO BOMB: NO END

## The Operation Olympic
## disaster, Japan 1945

*Nearly six decades have passed since the United States dropped two atomic bombs on Japan, but the debate over the morality of Harry S Truman's decision has hardly dimmed. Did ending the war in the Pacific justify the obliteration of between 100,000 and 200,000 lives at Hiroshima and Nagasaki? The horror of what did happen—and those who were wiped out in the first instants were the lucky ones—may blind us to a question that has been too seldom asked: What if the United States had chosen not to drop the bombs? Richard B. Frank is one military historian who has examined in detail the plausible scenarios that would have resulted from not pursuing an atomic conclusion. In this case, as he makes clear, "what ifs?" may give us a better understanding of the unpleasant choices facing American military planners in the summer of 1945. As J. Robert Oppenheimer, the scientific director of the Manhattan Project, later put it, "We didn't know beans about the military situation in Japan."*

*If the bombs had not been dropped, how much longer would Japan have held out? Could Operation Olympic, the projected November 1 invasion of the southernmost home island, Kyushu, have succeeded? Or would the greatest invasion fleet ever assembled have run into disaster costly beyond the wildest estimates of its planners—or the recent revisionist historians? What about alternatives to the bomb, such as a naval blockade or the destruction of Japan's transportation system? Then there was the true, if unrecognized, wild card in the counterfactual deck, the Soviet Union. What would have been the effect of a Soviet invasion of*

*Japan? Would, ironically, postwar Japan have been in worse shape if the bombs had not been dropped but hostilities had continued? Would just as many, indeed more, lives have been lost?*

*In Frank's view, speed was of the essence. The war had to end when it did.*

RICHARD B. FRANK is the author of two notable works of military history, *Guadalcanal: The Definitive Account of the Landmark Campaign* and *Downfall: The End of the Japanese Empire.*

T HE DECISION TO lash Japan with nuclear weapons stands as the greatest and most enduring controversy of the Pacific War. Its defenders view it, in the words of Secretary of War Henry Stimson, as the "least abhorrent choice." Its impassioned critics argue that history would have taken a more humane and wiser path if nuclear weapons were not available or were not used. Which of these views is correct requires a careful examination of the facts, not the fantasies, about the forces steering events in the summer of 1945.

There can be no meaningful expeditions down the channels history did not follow without first comprehending the realities of power in Japan. Militarists held the destiny of Imperial Japan in a rigid grip. They possessed a legal veto over the formation, or continuation, of governments. Bolstering this formality was the implicit threat of their arms, and a history of terror. Between 1921 and 1944, some sixty-four spasms of right-wing political violence, including the murder of two prime ministers, thoroughly cowed those few individuals franchised to participate in any fashion in shaping the nation's fate.

In Japan's misshapen political structure, only eight individuals exercised any meaningful power of decision. An inner cabinet called the Supreme Council for the Direction of the War constituted ultimate governmental authority, but only if its members achieved unanimity. The contemporary shorthand for this body was the "Big Six": Prime Minister Suzuki Kantaro, Foreign Minister Togo Shigenori, War Minister Anami Korechika, Navy Minister Yonai Mitsumasa, Chief of the Army General Staff Umezu Yoshijiro, and Chief of the Navy General Staff Toyoda Soemu. Only Togo was a civilian. Suzuki was a retired fleet admiral and the rest were serving flag officers. The remaining two men who wielded real authority were the emperor and his intimate adviser, Keeper of the Privy Seal Kido Koichi. Kido's power lay in his ability to sway the emperor, and the emperor's power depended upon the compliance of the government and the armed forces to his orders.

To this day, no pre-Hiroshima document has been produced from Japan demonstrating that any one of these eight men ever contemplated a termination of the war on any terms that could, or should, have been acceptable to the United States and her allies. What history does document about their thinking illustrates just how intransigent they remained as late as August 9. On the day the second atomic bomb struck Nagasaki—and following three years of almost unrelenting defeats, the destruction of Japan's shipping lifelines, the incineration of sixty cities, and Soviet intervention—the Big Six for the first time seriously discussed, and agreed on, a set of terms for ending the war. Three members were prepared to surrender if Japan received a guarantee that she could retain the Imperial system. But the other three insisted on a trio of additional terms: Japan's right to repatriate her servicemen; Japan's authority to conduct "so called war crimes trials" only in Japanese forums; and, finally, no Allied occupation of Japan. Since the Big Six could only act in unanimity, these conditions denominated Japan's position.

And what of the emperor? The Japanese—with American complicity—took pains postwar to depict an image of Hirohito as a "symbol emperor" who reigned but did not rule. He was projected as a man who desired peace, but was barred from imposing his will until an extraordinary impasse in Japanese political structure—the deadlock of the Big Six over the terms for surrender—permitted him to intervene in the "Sacred Decision" to halt the war.

The emperor himself confessed that he actually shared the core convictions of the Big Six at least until June 1945, and he never moved decisively away from that stance. This explains why these men failed to move to end the war and points to what their response would have been in the absence of Hiroshima and Nagasaki. Plainly stated, they believed, and with good reason, that Japan still possessed an excellent chance to obtain a negotiated peace that would maintain the old order in Japan—in which they would be dominant.

In the first three months of 1945, Japan's military leaders forged a strategy they called *Ketsu Go* (Operation Decisive) to obtain the political bargaining chips to terminate the war in a manner they could abide. They were confident that no amount of blockade and bombardment, even if it cost the lives of millions of their countrymen, could compel them to yield. Moreover, they believed an impatient American populace would propel their antagonist to avoid a protracted siege and attempt to end the war swiftly. That dictated an invasion of the Japanese homeland.

Japanese strategists next examined the map in light of American operational habits. The United States could be expected to bring its huge preponderance of air strength to bear in support of an invasion. Land-based aircraft constituted the majority of U.S. air assets and thus dictated that the invasion must fall on an area within range of land-based fighter aircraft. From the positions the Japanese expected their opponent to hold by the summer of 1945, the nearest bases would be Okinawa and Iwo Jima. Okinawa, but not Iwo Jima, could support thousands of tactical aircraft, smaller than the B-29s that were already bombing the home islands. From Okinawa, American flyers could reach Kyushu and parts of Shikoku. Of these two, Kyushu offered the better set of potential air and sea bases from which to mount an attack on the obvious supreme objective—Tokyo, the political and industrial hub of Japan. A simple scan of the topographical map of Kyushu easily revealed to Japanese commanders three of the four chosen American invasion sites. Thus, the Japanese anticipated not only an invasion, but the two most probable invasion areas, the sequence of the two probable invasions, and the exact landing sites on Kyushu.

With a firm grasp of the strategic essentials, Japan embarked on a massive mobilization program. By midsummer there would be sixty divisions and thirty-four brigades mustering 2.9 million men in the homeland. A strict conservation program, plus the conversion of the aviation training establishment into kamikaze units, yielded the Japanese over 10,000 aircraft, half suicide planes, to confront the invasion. These forces were arrayed with primary emphasis on defending southern Kyushu and Tokyo.

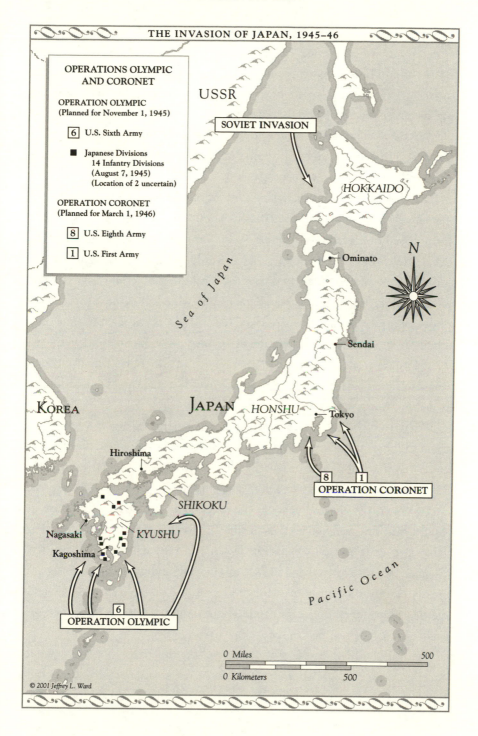

THE INVASION OF JAPAN, 1945–46

OPERATIONS OLYMPIC
AND CORONET

OPERATION OLYMPIC
(Planned for November 1, 1945)

6   U.S. Sixth Army

■   Japanese Divisions
14 Infantry Divisions
(August 7, 1945)
(Location of 2 uncertain)

OPERATION CORONET
(Planned for March 1, 1946)

8   U.S. Eighth Army

1   U.S. First Army

USSR

SOVIET INVASION

HOKKAIDO

N

Ominato

Sea of Japan

Sendai

KOREA

JAPAN

HONSHU

Tokyo

Hiroshima

8   1

OPERATION CORONET

SHIKOKU

Nagasaki

KYUSHU

Kagoshima

Pacific Ocean

6

OPERATION OLYMPIC

0 Miles      500

0 Kilometers      500

© 2001 Jeffrey L. Ward

By comparison to the tortured, military-dominated Japanese political structure, its well-designed American counterpart placed ultimate authority in civilian hands. But those hands changed on April 12, 1945, with the death of Franklin D. Roosevelt, which thrust Harry S Truman into the presidency. Roosevelt signally failed to ready Truman for his responsibilities, so the new president turned to his senior advisers for guidance on political and military strategy. Truman's military advisers, however, were not in accord on the strategy to end the war.

The United States Navy, led by Fleet Admiral Ernest King, had reached a number of fundamental conclusions about the conduct of a war with Japan based on decades of intense study. None of these precepts was more deeply held than the principle that it would be absolute folly to invade Japan. Naval officers calculated that the United States could never mount expeditionary forces across the Pacific that would even equal the manpower Japan would mobilize to defend the homeland and the terrain would wholly negate American advantages in heavy equipment and vehicles. Therefore, entrenched Navy doctrine held that the sound way to bring a war with Japan to a close was by a campaign of blockade and bombardment, including intense aerial bombing.

When the United States Army, led by General George C. Marshall, came to focus attention belatedly on how to bring a war with Japan to a close, it swiftly adopted the view that only an invasion could bring the conflict to an acceptable conclusion. After extended debate over these competing views, the Joint Chiefs of Staff reached an unstable compromise in April 1945. The army secured ostensible approval for a two-phase invasion campaign, code-named Operation Downfall. The first phase, Operation Olympic, set for November 1, 1945, involved a landing designed to secure approximately the southern third of Kyushu. This would provide air and naval bases to support a second amphibious assault, Operation Coronet, set for March 1, 1946, aimed to secure the Tokyo region.

The Joint Chiefs justified this strategy on the basis that the overall American war aim was an unconditional surrender that would assure that Japan never again posed a threat to peace. But history raised formidable doubts about the practicality of that goal. No Japanese government had capitulated in 2,600 years; no Japanese detachment had surrendered in the entire course of the Pacific War. Accordingly, there was no guarantee either that a Japanese government would ever capitulate, or that Japan's armed forces would bow to such a command. Thus, the American nightmare was not the initial invasion of the homeland, but the prospect that there would be no organized capitulation of Japan's armed forces, over four million strong. Indeed, the official rationale for the invasion plan declared that it would be more likely than blockade and bombardment to produce the capitulation of Japan's government, and it would best position the United States to deal with the situation if Japan's armed forces did not surrender.

The navy obtained agreement that the campaign of blockade and bombardment would continue at an accelerating rate for six months prior to Olympic. Admiral King, however, explicitly warned his colleagues on the Joint Chiefs in April that he only concurred that orders for an invasion must be issued promptly so that all the preparations for such a gigantic enterprise could be mounted. He warned that the Joint Chiefs would revisit the necessity for an invasion in August or September.

Radio intelligence proved King prescient. During July and August, ULTRA unmasked for American leaders the ambush awaiting Olympic. The 680,000 Americans, including fourteen divisions, slated for the invasion of Kyushu had been expected to confront no more than 350,000 Japanese, including eight to ten divisions. But decrypted communications identified fourteen Imperial Army divisions as well as a number of tank and infantry brigades—also *at least* 680,000 strong—most positioned on southern Kyushu. Moreover, rather than only 2,500 to 3,000 aircraft to support their ground troops against 10,000 American planes, the ULTRA sources and photographic evidence revealed the Japanese had at least 5,900 to more than 10,000 aircraft, half of them kamikazes, waiting to pummel the invasion convoys.

Only reasonable estimates can be offered of likely casualties in a collision between *Ketsu Go* and Olympic. If the Japanese committed at least a half-million men to southern Kyushu for the customary fight to the death, it is hard to imagine that fewer than a minimum of 200,000 to 250,000 of the emperor's loyal soldiers and sailors would have fallen by the end of the campaign. Moreover, Japan had thoroughly mobilized its adult population, regardless of gender, and organized them into a gigantic militia. Japanese commanders intended to use this sea of erstwhile civilians in a combat support and then combat role, similar to what occurred on Okinawa. According to the 1944 census, the three prefectures over which fighting on Kyushu would have raged contained a population of 3,804,570. If only one in ten of this populace died, a much lower rate of loss than on Okinawa, another 380,000 Japanese would have perished, bringing total Japanese fatalities to the 580,000 to 630,000 range.

When the Joint Chiefs authorized the invasion strategy in April 1945, they formally adopted a planning paper that addressed expected casualties. Rather than a raw number, however, this paper effectively provided a range of possible casualties based upon a pair of ratios derived from European and Pacific combat experience, both in rates per thousands of men committed per day.

|  | PACIFIC AMPHIBIOUS CAMPAIGNS | EUROPEAN PROTRACTED CAMPAIGNS |
|---|---|---|
| *Killed in action* | 1.78 | .36 |
| *Wounded in action* | 5.50 | 1.74 |
| *Missing in action* | .17 | .06 |
| *Total* | 7.45 | 2.16 |

A troop list designating the expected number of men committed for the campaign and an estimate of the duration of the campaign permit the application of these ratios. By August 1945, there were two troop lists of 766,700 and 681,000 (apparently differing mainly on the count of support units for base construction). Washington also was projecting a ninety-day campaign (a low estimate before the intelligence revelations). Applying these numbers to the ratios generates in the following range of potential losses:

| PROJECTED CASUALTIES FOR OLYMPIC | | | | |
|---|---|---|---|---|
| *for 90-day campaign* | | | | |
| | PACIFIC EXPERIENCE | | EUROPEAN EXPERIENCE | |
| | Troop list case 1 | Troop list case 2 | Troop list case 1 | Troop list case 2 |
| *Total Troops* | 766,700 | 681,000 | 766,700 | 681,000 |
| *Killed and Missing* | 134,556 | 109,515 | 28,981 | 25,471 |
| *Total casualties* | 514,072 | 456,610 | 149,046 | 132,385 |

Even these terrible numbers are not comprehensive, for they represent only casualties ashore on Kyushu. Kamikaze attacks would produce most naval casualties, supplemented by mines, shore batteries, air crew losses, and losses among naval personnel ashore. Using Okinawa as a reference point, the number of sailors likely to die in suicide plane attacks ranges between about 5,700 to 11,400. If other losses were merely equal to non-kamikaze losses on Okinawa, the additional 1,500 bluejacket deaths would push the range of naval fatalities up to around 7,200 to 12,900. Thus, the overall range of American losses *just to seize one-third of Kyushu* would probably rest between 140,000 to 527,000, including between 32,700 and 147,500 deaths.

But in 1945 American leaders ignored speculation on casualties and focused on the fundamental question of whether Olympic was still rational. A ratio of only one American for every Japanese defender "is not the recipe for victory," warned one intelligence officer. On August 7, General Marshall asked General Douglas MacArthur, the designated army commander for the invasion of Japan, whether he still regarded Olympic as feasible. MacArthur replied that he did not believe the intelligence and therefore he was prepared to forge ahead. After this exchange, however, Admiral King sent copies of both messages to Admiral Nimitz and demanded his views. King knew the answer to the question before he asked it. On May 25, after two months of grueling fighting on Okinawa that generated an

American casualty list exceeding any prior campaign of the Pacific War, Admiral Nimitz privately informed King that he could no longer support an invasion of Japan. King's message of August 9 was clearly intended to bring on a full-scale confrontation over the viability of not only Olympic, but also the whole invasion strategy.

Thus, the first crucial issue confronting American leaders without nuclear weapons would be the prospects for Olympic. While Truman had initially approved Olympic in June, this was before the shocking intelligence revelations on Japanese preparations. Moreover, he singled out the fact that the Joint Chiefs had unanimously supported the operation as a key reason for his sanction. Even with MacArthur and Marshall's obdurate support, if the navy withdrew its endorsement, and the radio intelligence picture appeared so bleak, Olympic could not have survived a second review by Truman. Moreover, the ULTRA portrait of Japanese ground deployments to greet Coronet was equally appalling. Chances are zero that either of these operations would have been executed in 1945.

The two obvious alternatives to invasion were diplomacy and the blockade and bombardment strategy. With the possible exception of Joseph Grew, the assistant secretary of state, however, no senior American policy maker was likely to press for negotiation since the minimum Japanese position involved the preservation of not just the imperial system, but of the old order that produced the war. Intelligence analysts had expressly warned policy makers on July 27 that so long as the Imperial Army remained convinced of its success in *Ketsu Go*, there was no prospect that Japan would yield to terms America could abide. It is vastly more likely that policy makers would have switched their attention to blockade and bombardment and just at that moment they would have learned the prospects for that strategy were waxing dramatically.

In May 1945, a survey team from the United States Strategic Bombing Survey (USSBS) mounted a whirlwind investigation of Germany to derive lessons that could be applied against Japan. The USSBS party concluded that attacks on oil production and the Reich's transportation system had "contributed in decisive measure to the early and complete victory." Added to the very dim American understanding of Japan's war economy, this information triggered a fundamental change in the direction of the strategic bombardment program in the Pacific.

On August 11, 1945, Major General Curtis LeMay, who was then the chief of staff for General Carl Spaatz, the commander of United States Strategic Air Forces, Pacific, promulgated a new targeting directive. Under Spaatz's command were the Twentieth Air Force, based in the Mariana Islands, and the Eighth Air Force, redeploying from Europe to Okinawa. For the over 1,200 B-29s these two air forces would field by October 1, 1945, the directive listed a total of 219 targets. The new blueprint drastically curtailed the program of systematic incineration of Japan's cities begun in March and instead gave top priority to fifty-six railway yards and facilities and thirteen bridges that formed the core of Japan's land transportation system. Then came targets in the aircraft industry, munitions storage, and thirty-five urban industrial centers.

On cursory inspection, this new directive appears far more satisfactory as a means of reducing noncombatant casualties than city burning. But its actual effect would have been to inflict a catastrophic mass famine. In 1945, three of four Japanese resided on Honshu, the largest of the four main home islands. Nearly half the total population clustered in the southwestern half of that island. Japan harvested the great bulk of her food on Hokkaido, northern Honshu, and parts of Kyushu. The annual rice harvest in September and October marked the crucial event in the food supply. A host of factors tumbled the rice production from over 10 million tons in 1942 to only 6.3 million tons in 1945.

Japan customarily bridged the gap between domestic food production and need with imports, but the destruction of her merchant fleet virtually extinguished that source by August 1945. The collapse of the water transportation system threatened even more dire peril. Unlike any other major industrialized nation, Japan relied upon seagoing transportation for domestic as well as international trade. If Japan lacked ships to haul food from surplus to deficit areas, her only alternative was her railway system. That system, however, was limited and extraordinarily vulnerable to air attack. Postwar study by USSBS calculated that a mere half-dozen cuts of the major net along the Pacific coast of Honshu would have incapacitated the whole system. The B-29 force, not to mention carrier-based aircraft, would have inflicted many times this damage in a few days.

Destruction of the railroads would have been cataclysmic. After the surrender in August 1945, as it was, Japan tottered through the 1945–1946 Rice Year in desperate shape. The food ration officially dropped to 1,042 calories per day in Tokyo by May 1946. This was with functioning railroads and a civil administration in place. The effects of the new air-targeting directive would have first struck Japan's heavily industrialized and populated region along the southwestern rim of Honshu. These cities filled the rice needs of their populations with shipments. Tokyo, the worst case, met only 3 percent of requirements from local growers. Without water or rail transportation, these teeming centers would have swiftly depopulated, sending millions of hungry refugees swarming into the countryside. Not only would this have brought the collapse of industrial production, it also would have unhinged the civil government, essential to ration and distribute the available food. By late spring of 1946, all food supplies in the southwestern half of Honshu would have been consumed. This would have compelled the weakened survivors of what was originally half the nation's population to migrate in search of food, or perish.

Within days after the first systematic attacks on Japan's internal rail transportation system, her leaders would have recognized their implications. Moreover, those implications would rip open the key fault line separating the great majority of the leaders of Japan's armed forces from the emperor and a small minority of officers. The former fervently cherished the dogma that the only threat to the old order in Japan was from without. The latter, however, recognized and deeply feared that mass famine and civil disruption would spark revolution from within. To forestall that nightmare, the emperor and those of like insight realized a capitulation might at least maintain some possibility of retaining internal bulwarks to sustain the imperial institution.

But the almost simultaneous Soviet intervention may have obliterated the ability of the emperor to secure a capitulation. Even without the impetus of Hiroshima, the Far Eastern offensive by Soviet forces on August 9 probably would have been set back one or two weeks. Once launched, however, the Red Army juggernaut would have overrun Manchuria, seized all of Korea, and annihilated Japanese units on Sakhalin and in the Kuril Islands.

This was not all. Stalin was poised to launch an invasion of Japan proper in August 1945. Only the delay exacted by the fierce fighting by Japanese troops on Sakhalin that denied the Soviets a key staging area, and Truman's insistence that the Soviets not cross the occupation boundaries fixed at Yalta, halted the thrust into Hokkaido, the northernmost of the four main home islands.

Soviet intervention imposed a horrific cost in human life. Approximately 2.7 million Japanese nationals, about one-third military personnel, fell into Soviet hands. The dead and permanently missing numbered as many as 376,000. If Japanese civilians on Hokkaido fared the same as their compatriots on the continent, at least another 400,000 would have perished.

The more critical effect of Soviet intervention, however, would be in Tokyo. While critics have asserted that the Soviets, not the atomic bombs, triggered Japan's surrender, that view rests upon the thesis that the Japanese recognized the hopelessness of their situation when the Red Army smashed the Japanese Kwantung Army in Manchuria, and thus proved that Japan could not defeat an invasion. But the Imperial Army and other leaders in Tokyo were clueless for several days as to the size and success of Soviet attacks. The Imperial Army—having already written off Manchuria and stripped the Kwantung Army of its first-class units—reacted not with resignation but defiance. Staff officers in Tokyo whipped up plans to declare martial law and to prepare to eliminate all vestiges of authority outside Imperial General Headquarters. This would have eradicated the governmental structure, whose deadlock permitted the meeting before the emperor in which he rendered the "Sacred Decision" to end the war. This alone may have destroyed the chance for the emperor's intervention.

There is, however, a still more fundamental point about why Japan's organized surrender stemmed from the atomic bombs, not Soviet intervention. Halting the war required both the decision of a legitimate Japanese authority that the war must end, and the compliance of Japan's armed forces with that decision. In explaining Japan's surrender shortly after the war, Prime Minister Suzuki testified that Japanese leaders remained devoted to continuing the war so long as they believed that Imperial Army and Navy could ultimately conduct the "decisive battle" against the U.S. invasion. Suzuki confessed that Japan's leaders agreed to surrender only after the advent of nuclear weapons: They recognized that the United States would no longer need to invade Japan. If there was no invasion, Japan had no military and political strategy short of national suicide. The atomic bombs also worked to save face for military leaders since they could claim they only submitted to supernatural forces of the atom, not due to errors of strategy or lack of spiritual stamina.

Therefore, if the emperor and those of like mind had contemplated ending the war even a few days or weeks later, they would have faced two hurdles. First, by that time there likely would have been no remaining governmental apparatus to permit the emperor's intervention in the form it actually took in mid-August 1945. Second, if the armed forces still believed they could execute *Ketsu Go*, they possessed a rational military-political strategy to continue the war—and a reason to refuse to comply with an Imperial order to halt the war. Even as it was, for several days it was not clear to Japanese or American leaders that field commanders would accede to the surrender order. The result could have been that either the emperor would lack the opportunity or the will to attempt to order a halt to the war, or even if he did make such an attempt, that the armed forces would refuse to comply.

The resulting tragedy would have engulfed the Japanese and other peoples in a catastrophe. Millions would have perished in Japan from starvation or disease due to the famine during the 1945–1946 Rice Year. The vastly diminished population of Japan would have been reduced for years to a crude rural subsistence-level existence stalked by the continual ravages of a food shortage. Moreover, all of the Allied prisoners of war and civilian internees in Japan would have perished—as would millions of others. Most, if not all of the two million Japanese under arms outside the homeland would have held out until annihilated by battle, disease, or starvation. With them would have died millions of noncombatants throughout Asia. The Allied prisoners of war and civilian internees would have shared the fate of their peers in Japan, bringing the total deaths in this category to over 300,000.

Soviet intervention would have reshaped the burgeoning American debate over strategy to end the war in August 1945. The most likely result would have been to discard Olympic for a draft plan to invade northern Honshu in an attempt to prevent the Soviets from overrunning more of Japan. Once this operation was complete, however, American leaders would have balked at the prospect of conquering the remainder of the home islands, hole by hole, rock by rock. The devastating results of the blockade and bombardment strategy, as revealed from radio intelligence and other sources, would have argued for the navy strategy of starving Japan into submission. Only the possibility of liberating some POWs and internees would have roused interest in further land campaigns in Japan, so long as they remained limited with acceptable losses. Rising American frustration and fury would likely have sparked the decision to unleash chemical warfare against the 1946 rice crops, as well as succeeding ones—a project under consideration in 1945. The use of poison gas against Japan in support of the invasion had also been under consideration in 1945. The prospect of an endless continuation of the war to annihilate Japanese detachments in the home islands may have lifted that taboo as well. American air power and logistics, but not ground forces, would have aided the Allies in defeating Japanese units on the Asian continent.

The Pacific War would have dragged on for probably two to five more years—perhaps longer. The overall cost would have easily exceeded five million deaths in Japan alone by conservative estimates, and equal or double that number among all the nations and peoples caught in this protracted agony. While there would have been no division of Korea and hence no Korean War, there would have been a sharply divisive Soviet-American rivalry in the home islands to match the one along the uneasy borders of Europe. The surviving Japanese people would have languished in poverty and bitterness for decades. Thus the atomic bomb, for all its horror, was the "least abhorrent choice."

# THE PRESIDENCY OF HENRY WALLACE

*If FDR had not dumped his*
*vice president in 1944*

Henry Wallace is chiefly remembered today as the vice president who, at the Democratic convention of 1944, was dumped in favor of Harry S Truman. Like another accidental president, Theodore Roosevelt, Truman would go on to become one of the signal figures of the century just passed. His decision to drop two atomic bombs on Japan as well as policies that he initiated, such as the Truman Doctrine, the Marshall Plan, and the formation of NATO, would, by containing the spread of Communism, go far to alter the historical direction of our times. But for the behind-the-scenes machinations of a few big-city bosses at the convention, "Give-'em-hell Harry" would hardly have rated a niche in the American imagination. The investigations by the senator from Missouri of contract fraud and mismanagement in the war effort would have remained the fodder of Ph.D. theses.

Instead it is Wallace who became the forgotten man, something few would have wagered on at the time. Throughout the New Deal era and into the war years, he was a major player in government and politics. As James Chace writes: "Henry Agard Wallace—geneticist, agronomist, editor, economist, and businessman—was the best secretary of agriculture that the United States has ever had." Even with his shock of graying hair, he remained boyishly handsome; his ebullience and competence made him the ideal person to replace the dead star of John Nance Garner on FDR's national ticket in 1940. But Wallace's outspoken views, in particular his continuing courtship of the Soviet Union, earned him powerful enemies in the Democratic Party—the very people who were determined to deny him a place on the ticket in 1944, and who succeeded in doing so.

The replacement of Wallace by Truman, Chace reminds us, was by no means a forgone conclusion. FDR waffled. Wallace was enormously popular, and there was a moment at the convention when he seemed about to prevail in spite of his powerful opposition. What if—and it is one of the true might-have-beens of American political history—Wallace had gone on to be renominated? What if, when FDR died of a stroke the following April, he had found himself the thirty-third president of the United States? Would he have ordered the dropping of the bombs? Would his often expressed fears of an arms race that would lead to World War III and his efforts to placate the Soviet Union have prevented the Cold War? Or would they, in the end, only have made it more dangerous? And what about that other ticking time bomb—men marked for prominence in a Wallace administration who had been supplying confidential information to the Soviet Union? Would America have gone through a time even more bitter and tumultuous than the McCarthy era?

JAMES CHACE is the author of Acheson: The Secretary of State Who Created the American World, as well as five previous books on international affairs, including Solvency, America Invulnerable (with Caleb Carr), and The Consequences of the Peace. The former editor of World Policy Journal, he is the Paul W. Williams Professor of Government and Public Law at Bard College.

O N Saturday, April 14, 1945, President Harry Truman was driven to Union Station, Washington, along with former vice president Henry Wallace and James F. Byrnes, former supreme court justice and FDR's "assistant president," to meet the train bearing Franklin Delano Roosevelt's body from Warm Springs, Georgia. Either Wallace or Byrnes might well have been in Truman's place; these had been the two main contenders for the vice presidential nomination at the 1944 Democratic convention. Both were better qualified to be president than Truman, a little known senator from Missouri who had gained office there through the support of the Kansas City Pendergast machine.

Eleanor Roosevelt, who had flown to Warm Springs in order to accompany her husband's body, seemed particularly pleased that Wallace was there. As the funeral procession made its way back to the White House, some 350,000 people lined Pennsylvania Avenue to watch FDR's flag-draped coffin pass on a caisson drawn by six white horses. At the White House itself, a simple Episcopal funeral service was held at four P.M. Six hours later the casket was reloaded onto the train for the final trip to the Roosevelt home at Hyde Park, accompanied now by Roosevelt's personal and official families, including Wallace, Treasury Secretary Henry Morgenthau, Labor Secretary Frances Perkins, and Secretary of the Interior Harold Ickes—those who had been with FDR at the creation of the New Deal.

That it was Harry Truman rather than Henry Wallace who had the political savvy and generosity to ask his two former opponents to join him in saluting the martyred president was not inevitable. But if, as the Greek philosopher Heraclitus suggests, character is fate, then Henry Wallace's presence as FDR's secretary of commerce rather than his vice president was due in no small part to Wallace's inability to embrace the role of politician;

on the other hand, Harry Truman's vocation in life was as a politician, and he reaped the rewards, often unsought, by his willingness to play politics.

No more Byzantine game was played than the one that Roosevelt engaged in prior to the 1944 convention. Tired as he was after twelve years as president, his face hollowed out by the wartime cares of office, he might well have retired to his beloved Hudson Valley. But even had FDR been a less ambitious man, he was almost honor-bound to run again unless World War II ended abruptly. Wallace himself believed that Roosevelt would seek a fourth term; FDR's son Elliot said, "Pop has tried for twenty-five years to become president and he is going to keep on being president as long as he can." That supposition struck Vice President Henry Wallace as true.

But beyond winning the war, Roosevelt needed to maintain his influence with Congress and the Democratic Party, and, above all, to ensure that the coalition of Southern Conservatives and urban bosses remained intact. Neither of these groups were particularly friendly to the vice president. But Wallace held a large following among progressive forces—farmers, professionals, and labor—who were the core of his constituency. Moreover, Wallace believed he still had Roosevelt's personal confidence, as he wrote in his diary: "Roosevelt is really very fond of me except when stimulated by the 'palace guard' to move in other directions." As a candidate to be once again FDR's vice president he would simply have to appeal to the people, and he was more than comfortable with this approach. A Chicago politician sympathetic to Wallace offered him the practical advice on how to secure the vice presidential nomination: "Set up an organization with a name like United Nations for Peace to work on his behalf and then line up Democratic National committeemen and potential convention delegates." No, Wallace retorted: "practical politics of this kind simply did not appeal to him."

How did such a man—an American Dreamer, as his biographers have labeled him—become FDR's vice president in 1940? And why did he defy the Democratic Party to run against Harry Truman on a third (or, as it turned out, a fourth) party ticket as the standard bearer of the Progressive

WALLACE TAKES A BACK SEAT

*In one of his rare campaign appearances in the fall of 1944, a visibly aging FDR (left) rides with his newly appointed vice-presidential candidate, Senator Harry S Truman of Missouri (center) and the vice president he dumped, Henry A. Wallace. In six months, Roosevelt would be dead; Wallace, who narrowly lost out at the Chicago convention, could have been president.*
(CORBIS)

Party in the presidential election of 1948? Had he won that election—an impossible task, as he himself realized—or had he secured the vice-presidential nomination in 1944 and thus inherited the mantle from FDR on the very eve of the Cold War, the conflict with the Soviet Union would have almost surely taken a different course. Could the Cold War, in fact, have actually been avoided? And if not, what would have happened to Wallace, who was so eager to preserve the wartime alliance? To try to answer these questions goes to the very heart of Cold War history.

# The Presidency of Henry Wallace

...

Henry Agard Wallace—geneticist, agronomist, editor, economist, and businessman—was the best secretary of agriculture that the United States has ever had. Wallace came from a family of editors from the Farm Belt; his grandfather, the first Henry Wallace, founded *Wallace's Farmer*, a journal dedicated to the propagation of scientific agriculture, which involved not only science but planning and good management. His father, who took over the journal, was appointed secretary of agriculture in Warren G. Harding's administration and turned over the editorship to his son, Henry. When Wallace became editor he was not only committed to the modernization of agriculture, but also to the belief that farmers, who had not shared in the halcyon prosperity of the jazz age, needed federal support to achieve stable incomes. Brought into Franklin Roosevelt's first Cabinet as secretary of agriculture, Wallace became a fervent New Dealer, and, above all, a scientist whose own research allowed him to develop and spread the process of hybrid corn, a process that revolutionized the yield of corn and led to a global agricultural revolution.

In FDR's Cabinet, he concerned himself not only with commercial farming but also with subsistence farming and rural poverty. And he instituted programs for land-use planning, soil conservation, and erosion control. In the twenty-first century, largely as a result of Wallace's reforms and proselytizing, Americans employed in agricultural occupations make up fewer than 2 percent of the population yet produce more than their grandfathers did seventy years ago.

With these successes, it was hardly surprising that FDR picked him as his running mate in 1940. By then Wallace had become, in historian Arthur Schlesinger Jr.'s words, "the unofficial philosopher of the New Deal."

But Wallace was also a man who was privately a mystic, more often than not naive politically, a kind of hero out of Dostoyevsky, an Alyosha or Prince Myshkin, whose work constituted for him a spiritual quest for an enlightenment that went far beyond anything the New Deal could provide. During the 1920s and '30s, he explored Roman Catholicism, theosophy, astrology, and American Indian religions. During his early years as secretary of agriculture, he corresponded with the Russian mystic Nicholas Roerich.

These letters fell into the hands of his political foes and almost became public during the 1940 campaign; portions of them were finally published in 1948, by which time his hidden spirituality seemed a further indication of his political liability.

No vice president has ever enjoyed more power than did Henry Wallace. Roosevelt appointed him head of the wartime Economic Defense Board. By 1942 he was at the zenith of his influence and authority as head of three wartime bodies: chairman of the Supply Priorities and Allocations Board, chairman of the Board of Economic Warfare, and a member of the Top Policy Group that worked on the report to FDR on the feasibility of constructing an atomic weapon.

As James Reston, Washington bureau chief of *The New York Times*, wrote, he was "the administration's head man of Capitol Hill, its defense chief, economic boss and No. 1 postwar planner. He is not only Vice President, but 'Assistant President.'" Yet Roosevelt knew Wallace had his limitations, and so it came as somewhat of a shock to the vice president when FDR appointed Donald Nelson, not Wallace, as chief of the revamped War Production Board. Both Nelson and James F. Byrnes came to play a more central role in the civilian conduct of the war than Wallace—Nelson as a hard-driving former vice president of Sears, Roebuck; and Supreme Court Justice Byrnes, who as a former senator provided Roosevelt with invaluable political assistance.

In wartime, Wallace therefore became the spokesman for a kind of international New Deal: he preached international economic cooperation, an end to imperialism, the abolition of poverty and illiteracy, and a global federation of nations with sufficient power to maintain world peace. All of these aims were shared by Franklin Roosevelt, but FDR was far too much of a realist to expect that all these goals were achievable.

Wallace's vision was most salient in his commitment to progressive idealism as he spelled it out in his speech in 1942 that became identified around the world by its most famous phrase, "The Century of the Common Man." "Everywhere the people are on the march," Wallace said, "The peace must mean a better standard of living for the common man, not merely in the United States and England, but also in India, Russia, China, and Latin America—not merely in the United Nations, but also in Germany, Italy and Japan."

The 1942 congressional elections cut deeply into the Democratic majority in both houses, and FDR had to deal with a coalition of Southern conservative Democrats and conservative Republicans. Wallace, the standard bearer of liberalism, came under criticism from the new conservatives for his unabashed New Dealism. For much of the war, stripped of the power to direct the wartime economy, Wallace concentrated on foreign policy. In particular, he told Roosevelt that "the conservatives in both England and the United States are working together and that their objective will be to create a situation which will eventually lead to war with Russia." He believed that the president seemed to agree with him.

By March 1943, Wallace was even more convinced that a preventive war might be waged by the United States against Russia. Speaking at a conference on world order at Ohio Wesleyan University, he warned: "We shall decide sometime in 1943 or 1944 whether to plant the seeds for World War III. That will be certain if we allow Prussia to rearm either materially or psychologically. The war will be probable in case we double-cross Russia. . . . Unless the Western democracies and Russia come to a satisfactory understanding before the war ends, I very much fear that World War III is inevitable." Although Wallace was severely attacked in the press for asserting that the United States would ever "double-cross" Russia, he continued to believe that he had Roosevelt's confidence.

Roosevelt's chief concern outside of winning the war was to maintain his influence with the city bosses and the Southern conservatives, and while he allowed Wallace to exercise his interest in foreign policy, he kept him out of the domestic war effort. Wallace was very much aware of FDR's political needs, and he therefore concluded that his future rested with his popularity with the people. He had good reason to believe that public opinion was on his side: a Gallup poll in March 1944 showed that Wallace had a "commanding lead" among Democrats over his most likely opponents for the vice presidential nomination. Nationwide, Wallace's approval rating of 46 percent equaled the next three candidates combined.

As the Democratic convention approached, however, Roosevelt granted Wallace's wish to go on a fact-finding, goodwill mission to Soviet Asia and China in May of that year; the trip lasted almost two months. Spending almost four weeks in Siberia, Wallace came back with glowing reports of life in a "collective society." In his report, Wallace described the Siberian port city of Magadan as a "combination of TVA and Hudson's Bay Company." In fact, Magadan was a slave labor camp, which Soviet officials had transformed into a Potemkin village prior to his visit. Watchtowers were dismantled, wire fences removed, and prisoners kept out of sight. (Years later Wallace admitted that "after reading accounts by former slave laborers who had escaped from Siberia [I can see] that I was altogether too much impressed by the show put on by high Russian officials."

By the time Wallace got back, a campaign by Roosevelt's advisers was fully underway to deny him a place on the Democratic ticket in 1944. At the heart of the conspiracy was Ed Pauley, the party's treasurer and chief fundraiser; he was joined by General Edwin "Pa" Watson, presidential appointments secretary, and Robert Hannegan, chairman of the Democratic National Committee, a Missouri man whose career had been promoted by Senator Harry Truman. Big-city political bosses such as Chicago's Mayor Edward Kelly, the Bronx boss Ed Flynn, Frank Hague of Jersey City, and Postmaster General Frank Walker, a former party national chairman, completed the cabal. For these men, Wallace was too radical and too much of a dreamer. And there were others who coveted Wallace's job: Senate Majority Leader Alben Barkley, Supreme Court Justice William O. Douglas, "Assistant President" James F. Byrnes, and House Speaker Sam Rayburn.

In a two-hour meeting with Roosevelt on July 10, 1944, the day of his return to Washington after his Asia trip, Wallace met with two Roosevelt confidants, Interior Secretary Harold Ickes and Sam Rosenman, FDR's speechwriter. Both men urged Wallace not to run. Although they said that FDR preferred Wallace, they implied that the president did not think Wallace could win at Chicago. Wallace discounted their advice, preferring to hear what FDR himself would say. Later that day, he did see the president, who told him that if he were a delegate to the convention, he would vote for Wallace; he also agreed to make a statement to this effect. Nonetheless, he told Wallace that many people had told him that Wallace could not be nominated. Once again, the vice president asked for his support, and FDR gave it to him.

The next day Roosevelt met with the anti-Wallace cabal. None of the bosses wanted Wallace. Nor did they like Jimmy Byrnes, a Southern conservative and a lapsed Catholic, who had converted to Episcopalianism; he surely would be unacceptable to blacks and labor, and could easily alienate both Catholics and Protestants. Despite FDR's preference for him (in 1943, he told Harry Hopkins that if something happened to him, the best man for the job would be "Jimmy Byrnes"), Roosevelt then put forth the name of Justice Douglas. But the bosses saw him, like Wallace, as no party regular. At this point Bob Hannegan floated the name of Senator Harry Truman from his home state, a strong supporter of the president. Roosevelt gave no commitment, but he did say that both Douglas and Truman were good candidates. At the close of the session, Hannegan got FDR to scribble on an envelope a brief message saying that he would be happy to run with either Douglas or Truman. But he did not say he would not run with Wallace.

Neither Wallace nor Byrnes was willing to drop out, even after being told by Hannegan and Walker that the president would prefer others. Moreover, Byrnes persuaded Truman to place his name in nomination, and Wallace flatly declared that he would not withdraw "as long as the president prefers me."

On the eve of the convention, Sidney Hillman, head of the CIO labor union's Political Action Committee, said that labor fully backed Wallace. Philip Murray, president of the United Steel Workers and the CIO, gave a press conference on July 13, at which time he gave an unqualified endorsement of Wallace. A poll among Democratic voters showed Wallace with a 65 percent preference leading in all regions of the country, including the south.

When Wallace took leave of Roosevelt just before the convention, FDR said, "While I cannot put it that way in public, I hope it will be the same old team." Finally, in a letter to Senator Samuel D. Jackson, the convention chairman, to be released on July 17, the president wrote, "I personally would vote for his [Wallace's] renomination if I were a delegate to the Convention. At the same time, I do not wish to appear in any way as dictating to the convention. Obviously the convention must do the deciding. And it should—and I am sure it will—give great consideration to the pros and cons of its choice." This was hardly a ringing endorsement, but it may well have reflected the president's inclination: he was willing to run with Wallace if the vice president could garner the strength needed to put him over the top; otherwise, he would accept another man.

For Hannegan this was not what he wanted, and in a meeting with Roosevelt in Chicago's Rock Island Railroad yards, where the president's private railroad car was sidetracked en route from Hyde Park to San Diego, and where FDR intended to remain throughout the convention, Hannegan pressed FDR to name others who would be acceptable to him. Roosevelt therefore wrote a longhand letter, postdated July 19, the day that the convention was to open, that stated: "You have written me about Harry Truman and Bill Douglas. I should, of course, be very glad to run with either of them, and believe that either one of them would bring real strength to the ticket."

It was not easy to get Byrnes to drop out and Truman to accept the nomination. But Roosevelt did say to both Hannegan and Boss Ed Kelly that the nomination must have the approval of Sidney Hillman—"Clear it with Sidney," he ordered. As Hannegan and his aides conceived it, their strategy was to make Byrnes the front-runner, and then persuade Hillman to back someone other than Wallace to stop Byrnes. Arriving in Chicago, Byrnes was convinced he had the votes for the nomination wrapped up. Moreover, the duplicitous Hannegan had told him that the vice presidency was his, that the "president has given us the green light" to support you.

Once Byrnes learned that the nomination had to be cleared with Sidney, he desperately sought support from Hillman and Philip Murray; he got nowhere. On July 17, according to Frank Walker, when the bosses called Roosevelt on his train somewhere near El Paso, the president told them that Byrnes would be a "political liability" and that Truman was the man.

The next day Hannegan told Byrnes of FDR's wishes and it was over for the "assistant president." That evening Byrnes wrote a letter withdrawing his candidacy.

What was probably decisive in Wallace's inability to secure the nomination was less FDR's refusal to back him from the outset than his own unwillingness to do anything about it. He hated backroom deals, and while he was the nominal chairman of the Iowa delegation he had not even planned to go to the convention. When the CIO bosses set up shop in Chicago, Wallace remained silent in Washington. The so-called Wallace organization was hardly organized: when headquarters in Chicago opened there were neither placards nor floor managers. When his backers finally persuaded him to come to Chicago on July 18, he was surprised at the crowds that greeted him. And when reporters asked him if he would withdraw, he asserted, "I am in this fight to the finish."

On Thursday, July 20, Truman was still balking at accepting the nomination. Hannegan decided he needed Roosevelt's help once again. With Truman present in a hotel room, the party bosses placed a call to FDR in San Diego. Hannegan held the phone out from his ear so that everyone could hear the president's deafening telephone voice. "Bob," Roosevelt boomed, "have you got that fellow lined up yet?" "No, Mr. President," said Hannegan, "he is the contrariest goddamn mule from Missouri I ever dealt with."

"Well, you tell the senator that if he wants to break up the Democratic Party in the middle of the war, that's his responsibility." With that Roosevelt slammed down the phone.

Hannegan looked at Truman. "Now, what do you say?"

"Oh, shit," Truman replied. "Well, if that's the situation I'll have to say yes, but why the hell didn't he tell me in the first place?"

Wallace, unaware of these machinations, gave an electrifying speech at the convention. The bosses were startled. It now appeared Wallace could win, and Roosevelt would do no more to stop it from happening. Hannegan's letter from FDR saying that he would be willing to run with Truman or Douglas was no endorsement of either of them. When Hannegan finally released the letter to reporters, the letter was seen as only a confirmation of Harry Truman as the bosses' candidate.

At the convention that night, cries of "We Want Wallace" were deafening. Senator Claude Pepper of Florida, Wallace's strategist, tried to get the chairman's attention in order to have the vote taken that night, in which case it was certain that Wallace would be nominated. Hannegan saw that the convention was getting out of his control. Chairman Jackson was unwilling to adjourn the session until Hannegan, desperate to stop Pepper, shouted at Jackson to cut things off: "You're taking orders from me, and I'm taking orders from the president." At this, the chairman gave in, and it was over.

Overnight the bosses worked to defeat Wallace. According to John C. Culver and John Hyde in *American Dreamer*, their biography of Wallace, "Ambassadorships were offered. Postmaster positions were handed out. Cold cash changed hands. Frank Walker was said to have called every state chairman that night, assuring each one that Roosevelt wanted the Missouri senator as his running mate."

In the voting that day, Wallace peaked on the second ballot at 489 votes, 100 short of the goal—and then the dam broke. Truman started gaining, and in the gallery box where Truman and his family sat, Boss Ed Kelly held the senator's hands aloft in a prizefighter's sign of victory. Bob Hannegan later said he would like to have inscribed on his tombstone: "Here lies the man who stopped Henry Wallace from becoming president of the United States."

Roosevelt still needed Wallace as the hard-core standard-bearer of liberalism to campaign hard for him in the upcoming election. He offered to make him secretary of commerce in the next administration, and Wallace accepted. He knew that Roosevelt could have insisted on his nomination as vice president at Chicago, and that Roosevelt had capitulated to the bosses in the name of party unity. But Wallace believed he had to support Roosevelt, who now stood as the symbol of liberalism to both the nation and the world. Crowds loved Wallace, and he did not stint in his calls for a further expansion of New Dealism: for civil rights for blacks and minorities, a peacetime economy of 60 million jobs, decent health care and housing. It was no surprise to him that the president would win a resounding victory, but in less than six months FDR was dead of a cerebral hemorrhage. A shaken Harry Truman, unprepared for the vast responsibilities that Roosevelt had borne, begged Wallace to stay on. The understanding that Wallace and Truman reached was to continue Franklin Roosevelt's policies, but how they interpreted that legacy was manifestly different. Truman's respect for other professional liberals, as he called them, was dim: he rapidly purged his administration of New Dealers. Within six months only two men who had been part of Roosevelt's team from the outset remained—Harold Ickes and Henry Wallace. And by September 1946, there was only Wallace.

For Wallace, fears of a clash between America and Russia were paramount. But while Wallace remained untouchable politically, he had little effect on actual policy. In the year following FDR's death, the Truman administration had not yet found its course; its foreign policy fluctuated like a compass needle seeking the right azimuth, as it zigzagged between trying to find an accommodation with an increasingly truculent Soviet Union and fashioning tough responses to what it perceived as Soviet attempts at expansion. The reluctance of the Russians to pull their troops out of Iran where they had been stationed during the Second World War met with a sharp American diplomatic note in March 1946, protesting Soviet policy in that region; but Washington also allowed the Russians to have "a graceful way out," in Undersecretary of State Dean Acheson's words. After a tough negotiation with the Iranians, the Russians did withdraw.

But that same spring, when the Soviets began menacing Turkey with hostile troop movements on the Turkish border and demands for basing rights in the Straits of the Dardanelles, no graceful way out was offered them. In August 1946, an American naval task force was sent to the straits. Washington was prepared to risk war if the Soviets did not pull back and abandon any ideas of having a naval or military presence in the straits. Once again, the Russians pulled back. By now Dean Acheson, who had sought cooperation with the Russians—and was seen as a dovish Cabinet member second only to Wallace himself—assumed that the Soviets, like their czarist predecessors, were seeking expansion wherever and whenever the opportunity presented itself.

There was now less and less room for the excessively sympathetic interpretation of Soviet behavior that Wallace espoused. Fearful of an arms race, Wallace was quite prepared to accord the Russians a sphere of influence in Eastern Europe, where, he said, a "complete absence of direct conflicts in national interest" existed between Moscow and Washington. In July 1946, he sent a 5,000-word letter to Truman, stressing his view that Soviet behavior was in no small part a response to American policy. Truman was apparently disturbed at the tenor of the letter but also worried that Wallace might resign from the cabinet, which could hurt the Democrats in the forthcoming congressional elections. He therefore wrote a perfunctory reply, hoping that Wallace would calm down. Wallace, however, was determined to change the direction of American foreign policy by appealing to the larger public.

It was in this atmosphere of growing anti-Sovietism that Wallace came to Truman with a speech he intended to give at a rally on September 12 at Madison Square Garden, New York. He and Truman went over the proposed foreign policy address together, and Truman expressed emphatic agreement with the substance of what Wallace would say. When copies of the speech were handed to the press hours before Wallace was to deliver it, one reporter asked Truman at his press conference that day if Wallace's words "represented the policy of this Administration." Truman responded crisply: "That is correct." He then added, "I approved the whole speech."

The speech, however, was hardly critical of the Soviet Union. On the contrary, it was Britain that Wallace attacked: "Make no mistake about it— the British imperialistic policy in the Near East alone, combined with Russian retaliation, would lead the United States straight to war unless we have a clearly defined and realistic policy of our own."

If this was not enough to undermine the thrust of U.S. foreign policy, what he added was intolerable to Washington's view of the world and American security. "The tougher we get, the tougher the Russians will get,"

Wallace warned. "We have no more business in the political affairs of Eastern Europe than Russia has in the political affairs of Latin America, Western Europe, and the United States." To Wallace, this was an even-handed description of geographical reality. To James Byrnes, now secretary of state and negotiating with the Russians in Paris, this was a direct attack on U.S. policy—which aimed to get Moscow to allow free elections in Poland and democratic norms throughout the rest of Eastern Europe.

When Truman read the newspapers the next morning he realized he had made a grave blunder. Then, when he tried to explain away his error by asserting that he had approved only "the right of the secretary of commerce to deliver the speech," *Time* magazine rightly branded his explanation as "a clumsy lie." Meanwhile, in Paris, Byrnes was threatening to resign in protest, until Truman reassured him that Wallace would never again be allowed to speak out on U.S. policy.

In a meeting on September 18, Truman complained to Wallace that "Jimmie Byrnes says I am pulling the rug out from under him." He told Wallace he could make no more speeches on foreign policy. Then, in a remarkable turnabout, Truman declared that he did not have a get-tough policy toward Russia. He said he liked Stalin personally and thought he could do business face to face with him." He even promised that he would ask for a loan for Russia as soon as the peace treaties were signed. Wallace was stunned and was surprised that Truman insisted he make no more speeches on foreign policy. Reluctantly he agreed and told reporters he expected to stay in the Cabinet.

But two days later, Wallace was in his office when an aide brought in an intemperate letter from Truman asking for his resignation. Wallace promptly picked up the phone and called the president directly. You don't want this letter out, he told him. Truman agreed. After the White House sent a man over to pick it up, Truman destroyed the letter and recognized that Wallace had made a courtly gesture. "He was so nice about it I almost backed out," Truman wrote his mother and sister. But he did not; and Wallace hung up the phone and wrote out his letter of resignation. The break was final, and both Truman and Wallace would pay dearly for it.

. . .

Soon after leaving the government, Wallace accepted the editorship of the left-leaning *New Republic*, but he did little editing. His interest was in writing, and he became a regular contributor to the magazine. But by the end of 1946, he was deeply involved in politics: two political action organizations, the National Citizens Political Action Committee, an offshoot of the labor-affiliated CIO's political action committee, and the independent Citizens Committee of the Arts, Sciences, and Professions, joined together to form the Progressive Citizens of America (PCA). For Wallace, the new organization was a mechanism to push Truman to the left; to others, such as C. B. "Beanie" Baldwin, who was charged with the day-to-day operations of the PCA, it was to become a political party. In the spring of 1947, labor leaders like Philip Murray withdrew support from the organization, which had welcomed American Communists to its ranks.

That year saw the enunciation of the Truman Doctrine of the containment of the Soviet Union. Specifically, Truman asked Congress to appropriate $400 million in military and economic aid to Greece and Turkey. Wallace's response to Truman's speech before Congress, in which the president said that "the policy of the United States [must be] to support free peoples who are resisting attempted subjugation by armed minorities or by outside pressures," came the next day in a radio address over NBC. Wallace asserted that the president had proposed "that America police Russia's every border. There is no regime too reactionary for us provided it stands in Russia's expansionist path. There is no country too remote to serve as the scene of a contest which may widen until it becomes a world war."

Wallace was not far off the mark in predicting the eventual trend toward the *global* containment of Communism, even though the Truman administration intended to send military and economic assistance only to the eastern Mediterranean. The Progressive Citizens of America opposed the Truman Doctrine, as well as Truman's "loyalty" program, which gave government loyalty boards the power to try and dismiss any worker who belonged to an organization deemed subversive by the attorney general.

By summer, Wallace was threatening to run on a third-party ticket; even Truman's support for the Marshall Plan to rebuild Europe, while initially greeted with cautious praise by Wallace, was later repudiated by him and the Progressives after Moscow refused to participate in the plan. Wallace now came to see the Marshall Plan as an instrument in the Cold War that aimed "to revive Germany for the purpose of waging a struggle against Russia." As for the number of Communists who had joined the Progressives, Wallace dismissed their participation by telling Michael Straight, the publisher of *The New Republic,* that the Communists were useful in getting out the crowds.

The near-inevitable clash between Truman and Wallace that led to Wallace's third-party campaign for the presidency took shape in the spring of 1948. Wallace spoke repeatedly in favor of showing understanding for Russian policy. The Czech coup of February 1948, when the Communists took over the government, led Wallace to say, "The Czech crisis is evidence that a 'get tough' policy only provokes a 'get tougher' policy." He even suggested that the Communist coup was in response to a right-wing plot to take over the government.

The Progressive Party mobilized for a presidential campaign in which Truman ran against the Republican standard-bearer, former New York governor Thomas Dewey; "Dixiecrat" candidate Strom Thurmond further split the ranks of the Democratic Party. Of the 3,240 delegates to the Progressive Party convention in Philadelphia, almost half of them were trade unionists; more than a quarter were military veterans. Not surprisingly, Wallace's speech labeled the Truman administration's foreign policy as warlike: Even the 1948 Berlin Blockade, which the Soviets set up to prevent Allied troops from land access to Berlin, was described by Wallace as caused by Truman's "get tough" policy.

Wallace, like most everyone else, believed Truman would be handily defeated by the Republicans. But Truman surprised Wallace by espousing a liberal platform—calling for a higher minimum wage and lower inflation, and for decent housing and universal health care. According to the pollster George Gallup, "as many as one-third of the people who said in late October that they were going to vote for Mr. Wallace shifted to Mr. Truman" during the final ten days of the campaign.

The rout of the Progressives was absolute. Truman received 303 electoral votes to Dewey's 189; Strom Thurmond ran third, with 39 electoral votes. Although Wallace garnered 1,157,063 popular votes, he received no electoral votes. In the entire country, he carried only thirty precincts. Nonetheless, if Wallace had taken just 29,294 votes in Illinois, California, and Ohio, the shift in electoral votes would have given the presidency to Dewey.

In the years to come, Wallace opposed the creation of the NATO alliance and continued to believe that the Soviet Union did not have any greater moral superiority than did the United States; both countries, he believed, should put their faith in the United Nations. As for the Progressive Party, its membership shrank, while its control by Communists and hard-line leftist ideologues grew. Once Wallace clearly saw the direction in which the party was headed, he set forth in its 1950 convention the terms on which he would support the Progressives. The party must demonstrate concretely its independence from Communist control and pledge its support for "progressive capitalism" in the United States.

The outbreak of the Korean War in June 1950 was the turning point for Wallace. The fact that the United Nations endorsed the actions of the Truman administration in opposing the North Korean military attack on the south persuaded Wallace to support the UN response. In a public statement issued in July 1950, Wallace said: "Undoubtedly the Russians could have prevented the attack by the North Koreans and undoubtedly they could stop the attack any time they wish . . . when my country is at war and the United Nations sanctions that war, I am on the side of my country and the United Nations."

On August 8, 1950, Wallace resigned from the Progressive Party. He was sixty-one years old, and for the rest of his life he played no significant role in politics. Living at his farm in New York state, he worked to develop the perfect chicken, which would lay the perfect egg in less time and at lower cost than other varieties. And he remained in constant touch with other scientific farming experts in their efforts to develop new types of high-yielding, disease-resistant corn.

He remained a liberal to the end of his life; in 1952, he came to see the

Progressive Party as little more than a Communist sect and voted for the Democratic candidate, Adlai Stevenson. In 1956, he voted for Dwight Eisenhower, believing that Eisenhower was better able to control the military than Stevenson. On November 18, 1965, he died, and on this occasion his old opponents spoke kindly of him. Harry Truman called him "an asset to the country." But perhaps the most just evaluation came from Lyndon Johnson's secretary of agriculture, Orville Freeman: "No single individual has contributed more to the abundance we enjoy today than Henry Wallace."

If Henry Wallace had indeed become FDR's running mate in 1944—and, as we have seen, this was not beyond the realm of the possible—would the Cold War have broken out? Would the United States and the Soviet Union have composed their differences? Would the United Nations have played the power role Wallace desired of it?

In the light of history, I think that in broad terms the Cold War could not have been avoided. Two superpowers vying for power and influence, espousing radically different ideologies, would surely have become mortal rivals. That said, it seems most likely that Wallace would have made greater efforts than Truman to find ways of accommodation with Russia. Wallace would certainly have pressed Moscow harder to see if Stalin's desire to work with the Allies to set up a neutralized and demilitarized Germany was in earnest.

Like Undersecretary of State Dean Acheson in 1945 and '46, he would have supported the Acheson-Lilienthal plan to put control of the whole field of atomic energy under international authority—from mining through manufacturing. Truman, while voicing support for this approach, nonetheless allowed a hard-line anti-Communist, Bernard Baruch, to shepherd it through the United Nations, which led to a Soviet veto and its ultimate demise. Although as a member of the Top Policy Group Wallace gave his blessing to the project to build the atomic bomb, but by mid-1942, his official involvement in the project came to an end, when FDR put the program under the control of Brigadier General Leslie Groves of the Army's Corp of Engineers. Nonetheless, informally Wallace met with Vannevar Bush, the scientist who headed what came to be called the Manhattan Project, and he was also briefed from time to time by Groves. Although Wallace gave much thought to the need for postwar control of the bomb by some form of international regulation, there is no evidence that he opposed the dropping of the A-bomb on Japan. Indeed, as a strong anti-fascist he might well have endorsed it as a way of saving the lives of American soldiers. But in the aftermath of Hiroshima, aware that there were no scientific secrets as such that could be kept much longer from the Russians, he would surely have pushed far harder than Truman did in enlisting the Soviet Union in a shared arrangement to control the resources needed to build atomic weaponry. Such a stance would surely have confirmed suspicions in Congress that he was dangerously soft on the Soviets: his only alternative at that point would have been to take a far tougher line than he had initially hoped to do, or risk further criticism and the likelihood that his political career would end in shambles, if not threatened with impeachment, as he tried to complete Roosevelt's unfinished term.

Nevertheless, laudable as Wallace's efforts might have proved, it is unlikely that the Soviets would have loosened their grip on the East European satellites; had there been no Truman Doctrine, the Russian's military movements on the border of eastern Turkey might have led to war; the Greek Communists, supported by Yugoslavia's Tito, might well have triumphed, even though Stalin was wary of Yugoslavia's growing influence. Could Wallace have continued his somewhat benign interpretation of Soviet behavior? And could he have rejected the fears of the Allies, in particular Britain and France, that the Soviet Union was bent on establishing a sphere of influence in Western Europe if not actual military occupation? I think not. Wallace may have been a dreamer who shunned power politics, but he was not a fool. Nor did he sympathize with Communist ideology. An emotional man who was often blinded by his own idealism, he was embittered when he perceived that his would-be allies were dangerous to his own hopes and beliefs.

Try as he might to avoid militarizing U.S. foreign policy, he would have almost surely been pushed in this direction, not least by Congress. To do otherwise might have brought about impeachment proceedings, as anti-Communist sentiment—indeed hysteria—swept the nation in 1947 and '48.

Wallace could hardly have avoided being singled out by the House Un-American Activities Committee (HUAC) as a dupe for Soviet agents and sympathizers. According to Christopher Andrew and Vasili Mitrokhin's *The Sword and the Shield*, the secret history of the KGB, Wallace had said that if FDR had died and he had become president, he would have named Lawrence Duggan as secretary of state and Harry Dexter White as Treasury secretary. Duggan, a State Department official who had served as chief of the Latin American division, was almost surely a Soviet agent. Harry Dexter White, a Treasury official who was a key figure in drafting the International Monetary Fund at Bretton Woods, apparently did provide information on U.S. economic policy to the Russians. In 1948, both were publicly named in testimony before the HUAC in 1948 as Soviet agents. White died of a heart attack before he could answer these charges, as he intended to do; Duggan fell to his death from a window in New York City.

There is some dispute over whether Wallace actually declared his intention to appoint Duggan and White to his "Cabinet," but he was known to admire both men, and Wallace would have come under severe fire had he indeed become president and appointed them to his administration. Even if he had been renominated in 1948, Dewey would have had a searing issue with which to destroy him. Such revelations would have surely made the Cold War even more frigid than it was—and perhaps more dangerous.

But even the most naive of men can be stripped of their illusions, and, given Wallace's temperament, the apologist can easily turn into the avenger. Despite his tendency to shoot from the hip, Harry Truman at bottom sought to avoid war; his principal foreign policy advisers, General Marshall and Dean Acheson, promoted a policy of containment, not rollback, and above all, no preventive war against the Soviet Union. With Wallace as president, the militarization of American foreign policy might have well been retarded. But in the end, America and Russia, inheritors of a broken world, would have engaged in the age-old struggle for power, and Wallace, if he were to survive politically, would have had to embrace it.

LANCE MORROW

# A TALE OF THREE CONGRESSMEN, 1948

## America without Nixon, Johnson,
## and Kennedy

Any time in which great changes take place is ripe for counterfactual scenarios. Nineteen forty-eight was one of those crossroads, a year (to use that tautology so beloved by politicians) of "new beginnings." Americans had begun to enjoy the kind of prosperity they had not known since the late 1920s, only spread wider and deeper. There was another difference. The intervention of oceans no longer guaranteed the kind of isolation that had once been almost a birthright. The world was very much with Americans in 1948, and it was not always a friendly or a peaceful place. The end of World War II had only produced fresh upheavals, and like it or not, many had become their responsibility. Meanwhile, old bulwarks like the British Empire were crumbling: England had just pulled out of its largest and richest colony, India, leaving Hindus and Muslims to tear each other apart. It had washed its hands of fractious Palestine, handing the mandate to a U.N. still in its infancy. A new world war, the Cold War this time, was taking shape, and with the threat of subversion at home and Communist power grabs abroad, Americans could no longer feel their familiar insular security. What if there had been no Marshall Plan to rescue Western Europe—or if the Americans and British had flinched when Stalin blockaded Berlin? Would more Communist coups have followed, like the one that drew Czechoslovakia within "the Iron Curtain"— Churchill's phrase, which was barely a year old? Would Greece survive as a Western partner? What if an improvised Israeli army had been unable to relieve a besieged Jerusalem? Would the new Jewish state have been stillborn, a bleak foot-

*note to the bleaker text of the Holocaust? And what of China? Did Chiang Kai-shek's Nationalists still have a chance of reversing the red tide of Mao's Communist armies?*

*That, of course, was the big picture of 1948. But as Lance Morrow reminds us, there were personal crossroads as well. Three would involve the political fortunes of young congressmen whose names would shortly become familiar. Still, in the drama that was 1948, each could easily have traveled different ways to obscurity. But as it would turn out, those would be roads not taken.*

LANCE MORROW is University Professor at Boston University and a longtime essayist for *Time* magazine. He won the National Magazine Award for Essay and Criticism in 1981 and was a finalist for the same award in 1991. He is the author of five books.

NINETEEN FORTY-EIGHT was a year of crowded historical convergence—a postwar *annus mirabilis*.

It witnessed the murder of Gandhi, the birth of Israel, the onset of the Cold War (Communist coup in Czechoslovakia, Berlin blockade and airlift, start of the Marshall Plan, Mao's incipient takeover of China), the liftoff of American television as a mass medium, and Truman's astonishing victory over Thomas E. Dewey.

And at almost exactly the same moment in August 1948, two young congressmen, Richard Nixon and Lyndon Johnson, were caught up in dramas that lifted them out of the House of Representatives and propelled them toward their vexed places in American presidential history. A third, John F. Kennedy, had just survived one.

If these dramas had not occurred at all, or had come to different outcomes, then Kennedy, Johnson, and Nixon arguably would not have become president. American history in the sixties and seventies (the years of Vietnam and Watergate) might have taken a different road.

The distinctive, flawed, somewhat mysterious personalities of the three men shadowed those passages of American history, in the ways we know—from the aftermath of the assassination in Dallas, on through the Great Society and Vietnam, to Watergate. If presidents other than Kennedy, Johnson, and Nixon had occupied the White House between November 1963 and August 1974—eventful years—how would history have been different?

In August of 1948, Richard Nixon of Whittier, California—a smart, young, ambitious freshman working among the comparative dinosaurs of the House Un-American Activities Committee—was introduced to a senior editor from *Time* magazine named Whittaker Chambers, a disheveled, evasive, apostate undercover Communist who seemed to brim with dark knowledge about Un-American Activities.

Chambers led Nixon—and HUAC and America—to Alger Hiss, the urbane head of the Carnegie Endowment for International Peace and former high State Department official whom Chambers accused of having been a Soviet agent operating in Washington during the thirties.

Controversy. Headlines. Day after day on the front page. Political liftoff. Nixon became, in a matter of weeks, a familiar national figure—jowly, shrewd, earnest in that darkling way that would become famous later. On the strength of his role in the Hiss case—which until the onset of Joseph McCarthy's anti-Communist career two years later was the focus of American anxieties about the Soviet Union and the deepening Cold War— Nixon ran for the Senate in 1950 in California against the actress Helen Gahagan Douglas and won. In 1952, at age thirty-nine, only four years after the obscure freshman Representative Nixon had met Chambers, Dwight Eisenhower chose the young Californian to balance the Republican ticket (by age, geography, ideology) as his vice presidential running mate.

Eight years as vice president led to the near-miss 1960 presidential race against John Kennedy and, after another eight years of misadventures and Republican missionary work in the political wilderness, to January 1969, when Nixon was inaugurated to succeed the ruined Lyndon Johnson.

It is difficult now to recapture the absorption, fascination, and divisiveness that the Hiss case produced in America when it erupted in August 1948. It was the O. J. Simpson trial of the forties, except that its implications were not only sensational but historic. As with Watergate a generation later, the cast of characters was riveting, the stakes high, and the issues elemental. The details of the story—the Woodstock typewriter, the microfilm hidden in a pumpkin, the prothonotary warbler that Chambers recalled Hiss having seen on the C&O Canal in Washington—were indelible, novelistic. America chose sides.

Chambers seemed at first a squalid, unsympathetic figure—a heavy, dumpy, secretive man with rotting teeth and a melodramatic air, a transplant from Dostoyevsky. Alger Hiss, by contrast, appeared lithe, elegant, patrician, with something of the look of Fred Astaire. To most Americans, he was by far the more credible of the two—at first anyway.

What to make of Chambers? He seemed so melodramatic. Chambers told the committee: "I do not hate Mr. Hiss. We are close friends, but we are caught in a tragedy of history. Mr. Hiss represents the concealed enemy we are all fighting and I am fighting."

Chambers's accusations had been made before. He would say later that his account of Communist activities was "an open secret among government officials and newsmen" before he ever answered the HUAC subpoena.

Chambers told Nixon and the HUAC staff the same story he had given nine years earlier to Assistant Secretary of State Adolph Berle, a member of Franklin Roosevelt's original "Brain Trust" and then the president's ranking adviser on internal security. Chambers described a Communist network, of which he himself had been an important member, that operated in various federal government agencies in the late thirties and that engaged in espionage. As Chambers talked in 1939, Berle made notes about "aerial bomb sight detectors" and "plans for two superbattleships—secured in 1937." In Roger Morris's *Richard Milhous Nixon: The Rise of an American Politician*, Berle is said to have reported Chambers's accusations to Roosevelt over a White House croquet game. "But FDR insouciantly waved aside the whole tale as one more witchhunt to discredit the New Deal, and between croquet shots he snapped angrily at his security adviser. Berle could tell his informer, said the president with unusual vulgarity, 'to go fuck himself.'"

But between 1939 and 1948, much had changed. The Soviet Union, a wartime ally, had become a Cold War adversary. The Soviets, as we know now from the decoded Venona traffic between Moscow spymasters and their agents, maintained an enormous espionage network in America.

Nixon studied Chambers and was, at first, skeptical of the strange man, but gradually was persuaded that he was telling the truth. Nixon, with a sharp lawyer's mind, listened to Hiss, who seemed at first confident in his denials of the Chambers story, and noticed odd notes of prevarication, a tendency to weasel about whether he had known Chambers in the thirties. Fairly soon, Nixon decided Hiss was lying. Nixon's pursuit—of Hiss, and of what he came to recognize as his own future—became relentless and obsessive.

At almost exactly the same moment that Nixon was interrogating Chambers for the first time, Lyndon Johnson was gambling his entire political future down in Texas in a too-close-to-call—in fact, too-close-to-count—race for the Democratic senatorial nomination against a former governor named Coke Stevenson.

The popular Stevenson—a deeply conservative, self-made goat rancher with a spread down on the Llano River, a laconic man in the Gary Cooper or John Wayne style—was running a low-key, traditional campaign. He drove from small town to small town in an old Plymouth, talking quietly to the old boys on the courthouse squares. Stevenson conducted himself with traditional West Texas reserve. He gave an impression of competence and silent strength. If someone asked him a question, he would light up his pipe and squint through the smoke for a minute or two before answering. Bragging was bad form and unnecessary. The voters knew where he stood. It was enough that he showed himself and offered himself for senator, in a manly, understated way.

Johnson's biographer Robert Caro made Coke Stevenson out to be a hero out of the old West, bulldozed by an unscrupulous LBJ. Other historians have portrayed Stevenson as a racist and isolationist reactionary—a "mountebank," in Sam Rayburn's word.

Johnson knew that he was losing the race and knew that his political path ahead, out of the House of Representatives where he had served for fourteen years, was blocked. The Texas governorship was tied up for the foreseeable future, and no other Senate seat would become available until 1954. Now or never. He told a backer: "I am either in the Senate or I'm out [of politics] completely."

In 1948, Johnson invented a frantically efficient, ingenious new way to campaign. Working twenty-hour days, he leapfrogged across Texas in a helicopter—something that had never been done before in a campaign. He covered 118 cities and towns in seventeen days. Johnson's three-passenger Sikorsky S51 would clatter down in remote farming communities—Lyndon ex machina!—the candidate emerging from the chopper to tell astonishing but effective lies about Stevenson (claiming that the arch-Conservative was somehow in bed with big labor, for example, implying that he had made a deal with labor to oppose the Taft-Hartley Act). Sometimes, when he did not have time to land, Johnson would get on the helicopter's loud-speaker and shout down to an amazed farmer: "Hello! This is your friend, Lyndon Johnson . . ."

In the end, George Parr, the "Duke of Duval" and political boss of south Texas, apparently stuffed the ballot boxes with enough illegal Mexican votes to give Johnson the election by eighty-seven votes. Historians and political witnesses seem to agree that Stevenson's people were also stealing votes, especially in East Texas; the trail of evidence has gone cold, and it has become impossible to say which of the men, Stevenson or Johnson, would have won if the race had been honest.

"Landslide Lyndon" shrewdly fought off Stevenson's dogged legal challenges. Once installed in the Senate, LBJ rose with astonishing rapidity to the job of minority, then majority leader, where he eventually became legislative boss to a man to whom he condescended as a feckless puppy dog and playboy, the frequently absent junior senator from Massachusetts, John F. Kennedy.

It was, of course, a surprise to everyone—certainly to Bobby Kennedy and, some say, to John Kennedy himself—when Lyndon Johnson wound up on the presidential ticket in 1960.

None of that would have happened if Johnson had not won the 1948 Senate race. Without that victory over Coke Stevenson, Johnson's political career would almost certainly have ended. He would surely have become a Texas businessman, running the radio stations, or a corporate lobbyist in Washington.

When you embark on fantasies of "what ifs?," you enter into abstract forests of luck and chance, of contingency and probability. Each speculative path opens onto a thousand new possibilities. After venturing down the path of nonfact for a moment, you tend to retrace your steps to the solidity of what actually happened.

Nixon might, of course, have come to the presidency by another route. So might Lyndon Johnson. While drifting in counterfactual speculations around that moment in 1948, one might add a third presidential "what if?"—regarding John Kennedy.

How might history have been changed if Kennedy—another of that generation who had come back from World War II and gone to Congress and later became president—had died the summer before, in 1947, when he was stricken by Addison's disease while traveling in Ireland. A priest gave Kennedy the last rites. A British doctor told Pamela Churchill: "That young American friend of yours hasn't got a year to live."

For the rest of his life, Kennedy lied about his health. He told an interviewer in 1959: "From 1946 through 1949, I underwent treatment for . . . malaria—the fevers ceased—there was complete rehabilitation . . ." After the 1960 election, he declared flatly: "I have never had Addison's disease."

But he did. Addison's—an insufficiency of the adrenal glands, a problem that is often fatal—prompted Kennedy's father to stash supplies of cortisone, the best known treatment, in safe deposit boxes around the United States, in case of emergency while Jack was traveling.

It was in 1948 that JFK adopted his father's patterns of living concealed lives. John Kennedy projected a vigorously glamorous and idealized image of himself in public, in politics, while dangerous truths (his grave illnesses; his reckless, active sex life) remained hidden.

What if Johnson had become a private citizen in 1948? What if Nixon had not met Chambers? What if Kennedy had died?

With Jack Kennedy gone, presumably old Joe Kennedy would have transferred the tribe's presidential ambitions to Bobby—with what result, far down the road, it is impossible to guess. One thinks mordantly, for a second, that RFK might thus have arrived at the same destination, the Ambassador Hotel in 1968, by taking a somewhat different route.

It would be hard to imagine Lyndon Johnson out of politics entirely. If he had become a corporate lobbyist or radio station executive, presumably he would have evolved into a Texas kingmaker, a wheeler-dealer, the political boss of Texas. But he would not have become president. He would not have fused his personality with the power of the White House—and would not have produced the great work he did, especially in civil rights. On the other hand, he would not have been brought to the terrible dilemma of Vietnam, which destroyed him. It is possible that the nation would not have been brought to that dilemma either.

As for Nixon and Chambers: Suppose they had not met. Would Chambers have repeated his story about Hiss to someone else in power? Would that someone else have used the case as the foundation of a political career? Would the Hiss case have arisen in any event, forced to light by the hardening of the Cold War? Without the Hiss case, would Joseph McCarthy have been so important? Would the quality of American anti-Communism have been different, less bitter and divisive?

The decoded Venona papers, released in the 1990s, make clear the extent of Soviet Communist activities in the United States before, during, and after World War II. The 1948 coup in Czechoslovakia, the Communist takeover of China a year later, the Soviet acquisition of nuclear weapons (by way of spies Klaus Fuchs, Julius and Ethel Rosenberg, and others), the invasion of South Korea by the North Korean Communists in June 1950—all these make it likely that the anti-Communist movement in America would have proceeded even without the Hiss case.

If Nixon had not been propelled to national prominence by the Hiss case so early in his career, he would have advanced by other opportunities. He might well have made it to the White House.

On the other hand, suppose that Dwight Eisenhower, surprised by the news in 1952 that his young running mate Richard Nixon had accepted $18,000 in secret donations from wealthy California businessmen, had indulged his famous temper and said, "I will not be fooled by maudlin nonsense about a dog named Checkers. There is something in his character I do not like. I want him off the ticket!"

WILLIAM H. McNEILL

# WHAT IF PIZARRO HAD NOT FOUND POTATOES IN PERU?

## The humble roots of history

*A world without potatoes? William H. McNeill asks us to consider some of the historical landmarks that the starchy tuber, high in calorie yield but low in prestige, has created in the past five centuries. It is as much despised by dieters today as it was by the soldiers of the Spanish conquistador Pizarro as they brought down the Inca empire of the Andes in 1531–32. Potatoes are native to the Peruvian altiplano (they did not originate in Virginia, as early Anglophilic historians would have us believe) and the indigenous peoples of the region depended on the shriveled globules that looked like small rocks and could be stored for years. Pizarro and his handful of martial thugs had ridden in on a wave of smallpox that had decimated the Inca population and its leadership: they had brazenly manipulated their disease-borne advantage, which they saw as a token of God's favor. That, and their greed, is a familiar story. The potatoes the Spaniards called* chuno *"must have seemed a mere nothing compared with the wealth of booty they seized," McNeill writes. "Yet I propose to argue that the humble potato played a larger part in shaping the subsequent history of the world than did all the gold and silver that so delighted Pizarro and his successors."*

*But for the potato, what different roads history might have taken? Would Spain have become such a vast imperial power, presiding over the first empire in history on which the sun never set? (Its wealth would be rooted in a mound of silver mined by potato-fed conscript laborers.) Would Frederick the Great's Prussia have survived without the potato in the Seven Years' War (1756–63), paving the way, ultimately, for the ascension of Germany? How different would the social landscapes of the United States, Canada, and Australia have been without an Irish potato famine? Would Europe's imperial and industrial expansion in the nineteenth century have been possible without the potato? How many crises of the Cold War, one wonders, were fueled by potato-based vodka? And would we now, in a rare interval of relative peace, be appreciating van Gogh's first major, and truly memorable, painting,* The Potato Eaters?

*This final chapter is one that spans centuries, continents, and natural boundaries—what we might call a counterfactual by subtraction.*

WILLIAM H. McNEILL, professor emeritus at the University of Chicago, won the National Book Award for his *Rise of the West*. Among his twenty-six other books are a survey of military history, *The Pursuit of Power*, *Plagues and Peoples*, and most recently *Keeping Together in Time: An Essay on Dance and Drill in Human History*. In 1997, he received one of the most prestigious international prizes for a lifetime of distinguished scholarship, the Erasmus Award.

THIS QUESTION IS likely to sound strange to most readers and to most historians as well, while Pizarro himself, and the ruffians he led, would have thought such a question absurd. Yet without cheap and abundant food, provided mainly by potatoes, the severe climate of the Peruvian altiplano could not have supported the Inca civilization that so amazed the Spaniards when they climbed into the Andes to conquer it (1531–32). For Pizarro and his followers, the fact that the peoples of Peru did not raise wheat or cattle was a trivial inconvenience, since it meant they had to eat unfamiliar, distasteful substitutes for the bread and meat they preferred. To them that must have seemed a mere nothing compared with the wealth of booty they seized. Yet I propose to argue that the humble potato played a larger part in shaping the subsequent history of the world than did all the gold and silver that so delighted Pizarro and his successors.

In particular, the Spanish hegemony in Europe (1559–1640) could not have been achieved without that humble tuber, for it fed the miners of Potosí, and it was they who produced the unparalleled quantities of silver that allowed the Spanish government to pay its soldiers (at least most of the time) and sustain all the other imperial expenses incurred by Phillip II and his immediate heirs. Nor did world-shaking side effects of potato cultivation come to an end after 1650, when the principal silver lodes at Potosí ran out. Instead, the potato, transferred to Europe, allowed the native Irish to survive efforts of the English government to settle Cromwell's disbanded soldiers on confiscated land after 1652. The same plant rescued Prussian peasants from the ravages of invading armies during the Seven Years' War (1756–63) and their resilience made the survival of Frederick the Great's army and government possible. Then, in the nineteenth century, an expanded supply of calories from potato fields sustained Europe's demographic and imperial expansion by assuring ample labor for factories and other urban occupations, while sustaining massive emigration overseas, as well as overland into Siberia. In short, ever since 1545, when Spanish prospectors discovered the "silver mountain" at Potosí, the military and political history of the world has been profoundly affected by the availabilty of potatoes to fuel human effort, first on the South American altiplano, then in Ireland and across the north European plain, and, with less conspicuous results, throughout other well-watered and relatively cool regions of the earth, most notably in China.

Understanding why requires a bit of explanation. Potatoes, known to botanists as *Solanum tuberosum*, were native to the Andes. They do best in sandy soils with a relatively cool growing season, but adapt readily to diverse latitudes so long as there is enough water in the ground to allow them to form their moist, starchy tubers. Potatoes had several advantages over grain as a food for humans. First and most importantly, in suitably moist soils, the calorie yield from potato fields is usually much larger than what grain produces. This was not true of irrigated rice paddies in East Asia, but in northern Europe, calorie yields per acre from potatoes are between two and four times greater than from grain. Moreover, the tubers have enough vitamin and mineral content to constitute a complete and well-balanced diet when supplemented by the fat, protein, and calcium of whole milk from cows.

On the other hand, potatoes cannot be stored nearly as long as grain. Ripe grain is too dry to sprout without exposure to water. Storage therefore only requires protecting the seeds from water, and from animal and insect would-be consumers. Potatoes, on the contrary, are moist enough to sprout in response to a built-in biological clock that is usually triggered by slight changes in temperature, and do so whether they lie in cellars and storage bins or remain underground where they grow. Stored tubers are also vulnerable to airborne fungi that feed on them as readily as people do; and once fungi start to grow they rot the tubers quickly. Storing potatoes for more than a few months is therefore impractical even today.

Without satisfactory methods of long-term storage, potatoes could not support civilized forms of society as grain did, for it was by taking possession of stored grain and using it to feed urban dwellers that priests and rulers

### HARVESTING HISTORY

*What would the world be like without the potato? The question is hardly a whimsical one: for the past five centuries, the humble tuber has played a considerable role in history. In the drawing above, made by a Spanish colonial artist around 1565, native farmers of the Andes, where the potato originated, harvest the calorie-rich foodstuff that the Spanish called* chuno.

(Felipe Guaman Poma, Inca harvesting potatoes, from *El Primer Nueva Corónica y Buen Gobierno,* ca. 1565. Royal Library, Copenhagen, Denmark. Nick Saunders/Barbara Heller Photo Library, London/Art Resource, NY) constructed the earliest civilizations. Rents and taxes, whether in money or in kind, continued to effect the same transfer of grain from farmers to rulers and managers and their urban dependents throughout subsequent millennia of civilized history, and did so until quite recently, when market exchanges between urban and rural dwellers began to dominate the same process.

In their raw form, urban folk could not depend on collecting perishable potatoes from their producers, largely because, since they do not need to be dug from the ground until it is time to eat them, potato gardeners escaped the problem of having to protect stores of valuable food. Grain farmers, on the contrary, were radically vulnerable to armed marauders since ripe grain had to be harvested and stored, and stocks of harvested grain were easy to find and carry away. Civilized rent and tax collectors, who took only part of the harvest, might or might not be able to protect rural dwellers from raids. But it was clearly better for grain farmers to share the harvest with powerful rulers and landlords who had a clear and direct interest in doing all they could to protect those who produced the grain upon which everyone depended. Hence grain farming and civilization went together from the time civilizations arose.

Nonetheless, in their original Andean habitat, potatoes did become the principal food of the Inca empire and its predecessors. That was because the peculiar climate of the South American altiplano made it possible to preserve potatoes by exposing them to the dry night air when, despite Peru's tropical location, temperatures sometimes went below freezing. Shriveled, freeze-dried potatoes, called *chuno* by the Spaniards, were fully equivalent to grain since *chuno* could be stored for years without loss of nutritional value. Hence Inca tax collectors could and did require potato gardeners to supply *chuno* to official storehouses just as they required maize-growers at lower altitudes to hand over corn; and officials could then issue food from such warehouses to maintain the soldiers, public works laborers, and all the household servants, administrators, and priests who combined to make Inca government and civilization what it was.

In 1532 the Spaniards took over this administrative system and after 1545 used it to supply *chuno* to scores of thousands of conscripted silver miners at Potosí. Their efforts, in turn, produced a freshet of silver that sustained Spanish imperial power in Europe and the Americas and, in the course of the following century, inflated prices around the world. Rapidly rising prices, in turn, upset older economic and social relationships in civilized societies everywhere. Thus it was that between 1545 and about 1650, potatoes, processed into *chuno*, fueled an unprecedented scale of silver mining in Peru, provoking worldwide economic and social upheaval, while lifting Spanish military power to new heights in Western Europe. No one understood what was happening at the time; still less did anyone credit *chuno*—a nasty, unpalatable food in Europeans' eyes—with making it possible. Yet so, surely, it was.

But this initial impact on the world's history was only a prelude to what the same plant did when transferred to European soil. How it got there is unrecorded; but plain enough since Spanish ships that entered the Pacific had to stock up on food for their return voyages. Familiar European cereals were not available, so sailors on the way home had to rely on maize and potatoes for most of their calories, which was all that the Pacific coast of South America could supply. We also know for sure that on returning to Spain, sailors carried specimens ashore, and some apparently thought enough of the new foods to try planting them. Most parts of Spain were too dry for potatoes; but Atlantic winds brought enough moisture to the Basque country along Spain's northwest coast for them to thrive there.

Accordingly, within a few decades of Pizarro's conquest, potatoes took root in Basque country, and Basque fishermen soon began to stock their fishing boats with potatoes when setting out for the Grand Banks off Newfoundland. It was they who introduced the crop to the west coast of Ireland, where they habitually came ashore for rest and recuperation on their return voyages. Exactly when potatoes began to flourish on Irish soil remains unknown, but by 1650 the crop was sufficiently widespread in the westernmost province of Connaught to become a lifesaver for the Irish people after their defeat by Cromwell's soldiers (1649–52).

As a result, when the English government undertook to solve its Irish problem by distributing confiscated lands in Leinster and Munster among disbanded veterans while crowding the surviving natives of these provinces into Connaught, the defeated Irish found it possible to survive by planting potatoes on small patches of land, and supplementing this new food with milk from cattle that had long been the principal basis of the Irish economy. Irish soil and climate were such that a single acre of potatoes and enough grass for a cow sufficed to feed an entire family, with enough left over to raise a pig. However monotonous it may seem to us, this diet sustained rapid population growth among a conspicuously healthy Irish population from the time Cromwell's soldiers compelled them to accept it.

English settlers, by contrast, ate bread and cheese and were entirely unwilling to change their habits, even though wheat often failed to ripen in the Irish climate and rye and oats yielded far less per acre and cost more to harvest and process into bread than did potatoes, which had only to be dug from the ground and thrown into a pot of boiling water to be ready for the table. This meant that the Irish could live far more cheaply than the English, and when Cromwell's veterans found that the style of grain farming with which they were familiar in England did not produce satisfactory results in the moister, cooler Irish climate, they sold out to land-jobbers, who soon found that raising beef cattle was the only feasible way to wring cash income from the land.

These upstart landowners needed hired hands to tend their herds and quickly discovered that Irish laborers were experienced herdsmen—and dirt cheap, only needing access to an acre for potatoes and enough grass for a cow. As a result, and despite the intentions of the English government, Catholic Irish laborers and their novel subsistence style of potato cultivation displaced far more expensive bread-eating English laborers from almost all of rural Ireland. Thanks to the potato, therefore, the majority of the population of Ireland remained Irish, except in Ulster, where an earlier rebellion against the English had led to the settlement of Protestant Scots on conflated lands after 1607. Scottish farming, featuring oats rather than wheat, was readily transferable to Irish soil; and since the potato was unknown in Ulster until early in the eighteenth century, the Scots-Irish successfully displaced the Irish in most of that province, with political and social results that still command headlines today.

Then, in the nineteenth century, when faster and larger steamships began to traverse the seas, they inadvertently introduced a South American fungus into Europe that, under wet, cool conditions, proved lethal to the potatoes that by then had established themselves throughout Ireland and across most of the north European plain. The summers of 1845 and 1846 were unusually cool and wet in Western Europe, and the resultant failure of potato harvests brought stark famine to Ireland and serious food shortages elsewhere in northern Europe. In Ireland, more than a million people died of starvation and of infections induced by hunger; while millions of others emigrated during and in the aftermath of the famine. The resulting Irish diaspora altered the social landscapes of the United States, Great Britain, Canada, Australia, and elsewhere. This, perhaps, counts as a second world-changing consequence of potato cultivation, and of an Irish way of life that was dangerously dependent on that single crop.

Nonetheless, the principal impact of potatoes on modern European history was felt on the Continent rather than in Ireland. This story requires backpedaling to the time when Spanish sailors first carried the tubers across the ocean. As we saw, most of Spain itself was inhospitable, but potatoes did well in the Po valley of Italy, which became part of the Spanish empire in 1535. Anonymous sailors must have carried them there, and hard-pressed Italian peasants found them valuable—not least because they escaped taxation since city folk had no use for the new food at first. Potato gardens then spread northward very rapidly, from Italy across the Alps into Franche-Comté, the Rhinelands, and the Low Countries before the end of the sixteenth century.

Potatoes followed this path to the north European plain because it was here that local peasants were regularly exposed to military requisitioning by detachments of Spanish soldiers marching along the so-called "Spanish Road." That, in turn, was because, when Dutch rebels inaugurated eighty years of on-again, off-again warfare against Philip II of Spain and his heirs (1568–1648), their naval superiority made the sea unsafe for Spanish shipping. The Spanish government was therefore compelled to reinforce its armies in the Low Countries by shipping troops to northern Italy, whence they marched northward to the theater of war. From time immemorial, European armies had lived off the land when on the march, since limitations on transport made it impossible for them to do otherwise. Accordingly, Spanish soldiers en route to the Low Countries requisitioned grain from villages along the way, and did so year after year. Under these circumstances, peasants quickly discovered that potatoes were a lifesaver. Simply by leaving them in the ground until wanted for food, they could be sure of having something left to eat even after military foraging parties had carried off all available stores of grain. We can only assume that word of mouth and harsh experience combined to spread news of the lifesaving capabilities of the new crop from village to village, for the spread of potatoes northward from Italy left no trace in contemporary records as far as anyone knows.

Eventually, the existence of potatoes along the "Spanish Road" did come to learned attention, when, in 1588, a botanist who Latinized his name into Carolus Clusius painted a watercolor of a potato plant he had discovered growing in a garden near Mons, Belgium. Clusius subsequently published the watercolor in his book *Rariorum plantarum historia* (Antwerp, 1601) along with a description of what he called "Papas Peruanorum," together with a brief account of what he had discovered about the plant. He correctly reported that it had come from Peru and was "common" in northern Italy, where it was valued both as animal fodder and as human food. This is the first written record of the existence of potatoes on the continent of Europe yet discovered, and a thoroughly believable, but incomplete, description of where the plant initially flourished. To be sure, Clusius quite failed to understand why grain farmers along the Spanish Road were so ready to adopt the new crop, and he knew nothing about Basque fishermens' potato gardens. Their existence can safely be surmised, however, from the provable fact that Irish potatoes derived from Spain and not from Francis Drake's subsequent introduction of a different strain of potatoes into England in 1580. An English botanist promptly took note of the potatoes Drake brought back from his famous circumnavigation of the globe, but though John Gerard chose to make a large woodcut of the new plant into the frontispiece of his *Herball, or General Historie of Plantes* (London, 1597), thereby antedating Clusius's published notice of potatoes by four years, Gerard erroneously named the new plant "potatoes of Virginia," thereby introducing an error into English learning that lingered through most of the nineteenth century.

Until the eighteenth century, potatoes remained only a garden crop, whether in Basque country, Ireland, northern Italy, the Rhinelands, or adjacent areas. Most European grain farmers cultivated strips in open fields, and custom required everyone to plant the same crop in adjacent strips so that subsequent routines of harvesting, gleaning, and plowing could proceed on schedule. This meant that new crops could not ordinarily enter the open fields. Nonetheless, as we just saw, between 1560 and 1700 the spread of comparatively small potato gardens cushioned the customary demographic destructiveness of military requisitioning in some of Europe's most fought-over regions. This was significant, for as the size of European armies increased, rural death by starvation in the wake of marching soldiers became more and more widespread and reached a devastating climax in Germany during the Thirty Years' War (1618–48). Its horrors were long remembered because this was the last time a prolonged war was fought in northern Europe before potatoes became generally available to forestall rural starvation even after grain stocks had all been carried away by foraging soldiers.

That, in turn, became possible because, after 1750, the spread of potatoes across European landscapes ceased to depend on the initiative of illiterate peasants, relying solely on word of mouth. Instead, government officials intervened and set out, first only in Prussia, to propagate potatoes with the deliberate purpose of safeguarding rural taxpayers from wartime famine. This got started when the youthful Prussian king, Frederick the Great, campaigning in the Rhinelands during the War of the Austrian Succession (1740–48), noticed how potatoes permitted peasants to survive military requisitioning. Accordingly, in 1744 he decided to introduce the crop to Prussia, ordering local administrators to distribute free seed potatoes with instructions on how to raise them.

Frederick's initiative paid off handsomely during the Seven Years' War (1756–63) when Prussian peasants endured repeated invasions by Austrian, Russian, and French armies without suffering serious famine. Survival of the Prussian state and army against apparently overwhelming odds depended on the new and surprising resilience of the Prussian peasantry as much as it did on Frederick's famous victories, British subsidies, and Russia's sudden change of sides. It follows that the subsequent history of Germany would certainly have been very different without the presence of potatoes in Prussian fields and gardens during the Seven Years' War. But there is no point in speculating about how the victorious forces of France, Austria, and Russia might have redirected German affairs, forestalling Bismarck's unification of Germany under Prussian leadership in 1870 almost for sure.

Instead, during the Seven Years' War the secret of Prussia's ability to withstand repeated invasions became obvious to the attacking armies, and when peace returned the French, Austrian, and Russian governments all set out to imitate the Prussians by propagating potatoes among their own peasants as a matter of official policy. The French led the way, due partly to the efforts of an army doctor, Antoine Parmentier, who, having encountered potatoes in Prussia, spent the rest of his life investigating their nutritional value and how best to grow them. He published his results in a book entitled *Examen chymique des pommes des terres* (Paris 1774). And on one occasion, official efforts to make potatoes acceptable in France induced Marie Antoinette to advertise the plant's virtues by appearing at a court ball wearing a coiffeur of potato flowers. Austrian and Russian official efforts to catch up with Prussia also produced relatively rapid results, though inertia and the restraints of open field cultivation meant that potatoes remained mostly a garden crop in that part of Europe until the 1820s and 1830s.

By then, in France, the Low Countries, and Germany, potatoes had broken through garden fences and become a field crop, thereby enormously expanding the quantity of calories available to fuel the efforts of rapidly growing populations. To understand the magnitude of this effect one must remember that traditional grain farming in Europe required leaving fields fallow every second or third year. This was needed to clear fields of weeds by plowing the fallow in summer before weed seeds had formed. In potato gardens hoeing by hand was the only way to remove weeds, so from a human point of view potato fields required far more summer labor than did grain, which was too thickly sown for hoeing to be possible. Potatoes could not therefore become a major field crop unless enough labor to hoe the ground they occupied could be found.

But, for reasons still disputed among demographers, Europe along with the rest of the civilized world began to experience sustained population growth after about 1750. Where agricultural land was already fully occupied, the resulting spurt of human numbers meant smaller family holdings and lowered standards of living. Peasant revolts, which began to trouble the Chinese imperial government in the 1770s, registered this unhappy circumstance in China. But across northern Europe, potatoes were available to invade the fallow grain fields, and official governmental policy stood ready to forward the process. Food supplies multiplied accordingly, so that growing numbers of well-fed northern Europeans became available to intensify agricultural, industrial, military, and other forms of organized effort. The rapid surge of northern European nations to world dominion in the nineteenth century depended on this serendipity.

It is easy to understand how the availability of extensive fallow fields allowed a very powerful feedback loop to establish itself in northern Europe after 1750. Simply by planting potatoes on the fallow, a new and enormous supply of food could be produced without the slightest reduction of traditional grain harvests! What a bonanza! Instead of the customary fallowing, a third to a half of Europe's cultivated fields could be planted with potatoes (or other row crops, such as turnips and sugar beets), and as long as the growing plants were hoed by hand once or twice in early summer, weeds were very effectually controlled. Hence potato fields could be planted with grain next year, entirely as usual, while new row crops took over another, no-longer fallow, field. Extra labor was essential for this intensification of European farming; but potatoes, yielding as they did two to four times the number of calories per acre that grain fields did, were instantly available to feed the growing numbers needed for their cultivation. On top of that, leftover potatoes remained for animal fodder and for conversion into vodka, which, in fact, became a very important source of revenue for the Russian government.

Under these circumstances, once potatoes became a field crop, population could and did rise far above older ceilings, and potatoes, being cheap, became the principal food of the poorer classes throughout the north European plain, all the way from northern France and the Low Countries through Germany and Poland into Russia. Bread was never displaced entirely as happened among the Irish, so the impact of the famine years (1845–47), when potatoes failed almost everywhere, was correspondingly diminished on the European Continent (and in England), though the "hungry forties" were long remembered by those who suffered through them.

The potato blight required damp, cool conditions to prosper; and when dryer summers returned to Europe after 1847, the blight diminished or even disappeared. But every so often, cool, wet summer weather, when sufficiently prolonged, allowed the fungus to resume its ravages until the 1880s, when protective chemical sprays were introduced. Shortly before chemical sprays (and artificial fertilizers) began to alter European agriculture, the invention of horse-drawn shufflers reduced or eliminated the need for hoeing potatoes and other row crops, thus releasing a host of rural laborers for industrial employment in the mines and factories that began to sprout near Europe's coal fields while also provoking massive emigration overseas and eastward into Siberia as well.

The effect, therefore, of deliberate official patronage of potato cultivation, pioneered by Frederick the Great in 1744, turned out to be very considerable. First of all, potatoes quickly became a field crop and an increasingly important source of human food throughout northern Europe. Consequently, the intensified warfare attendant on the French Revolution and Napoleon's subsequent career (1793–1815) became bearable for Europe's rural populations thanks largely to the food reserves their potato gardens and fields provided for them. Otherwise European governments could not possibly have mobilized millions of soldiers while continuing to feed their armies in the field in traditional fashion by ruthlessly requisitioning grain and animals from local villagers. But instead of provoking death and disaster on an even greater scale than that of the Thirty Years' War, intensified warfare between 1793 and 1815 wrought only minimal damage to European rural populations.

Then as potatoes continued their expansion into once-fallowed grain fields, and as hand hoeing ceased to be necessary, the European countryside began to empty out. Millions of migrants began to labor in new factories and mines and provided other services in rapidly expanding urban centers, while still others emigrated overseas and eastward into Siberia. The swarming of European peoples in the nineteenth century was indeed remarkable; not least because of the extraordinary fact that first within Europe itself and then overseas and in Siberia, Europeans found empty land to provide their swarming population with adequate, indeed abundant, food.

Elimination of fallowing did the trick across northern Europe itself, and here potatoes played the lead role, as we have just seen. Overseas and in Siberia, it was destruction of indigenous populations by exposure to civilized diseases and the disruption of older ecological balances by civilized demand for furs and a few other commodities that disrupted indigenous societies in Siberian, American, Australian, and other overseas landscapes, opening the way for European settlement. Military conquest merely sealed European emigrants' success in supplanting older inhabitants wherever familiar European crops and agricultural methods proved viable. The resulting cultural and political transformations of the Americas, Australia, and parts of Siberia were drastic indeed, and citizens of the United States and of Russia are today the most conspicuous heirs of this process.

Without the extra food potato fields provided, the swarming of north European populations could not have occurred. Maize also played a similar but less prominent part in southern Europe; but that is another story. Of course much else entered into Europe's rise and recent withdrawal from world dominion; but it is surely safe to say that potatoes from Peru were essential for fueling the swarming human biomass that sustained Europe's imperial ventures. Potatoes thus powerfully affected the general course of world history since 1750. Silver and gold glittered, all right, but potatoes, inconspicuous and unnoticed at first, nevertheless were more important, since they altered the course of human history in far-reaching ways, and did so repeatedly, from the time Pizarro first encountered and disdained them.

So what if Pizarro had not found potatoes in Peru? Our world would be radically different for sure, even though no one can say exactly how very different it would be.